Windows® 2000
Professional
On Site

D1369308

Erik Eckel

Brian Alderman

President, CEO
Roland Elgey

Publisher
Steve Sayre

Acquisitions Editor
Charlotte Carpentier

Product Marketing Manager
Tracy Rooney

Project Editors
Toni Zuccarini Ackley
Julie McLaughlin

Technical Reviewer
J. Peter Bruzzese

Production Coordinator
Carla J. Schuder

Cover Designer
Laura Wellander

Layout Designer
April E. Nielsen

CD-ROM Developer
Chris Nusbaum

Windows® 2000 Professional On Site

Limits of Liability and Disclaimer of Warranty

The author and publisher of this book have used their best efforts in preparing the book and the programs contained in it. These efforts include the development, research, and testing of the theories and programs to determine their effectiveness. The author and publisher make no warranty of any kind, expressed or implied, with regard to these programs or the documentation contained in this book.

The author and publisher shall not be liable in the event of incidental or consequential damages in connection with, or arising out of, the furnishing, performance, or use of the programs, associated instructions, and/or claims of productivity gains.

Trademarks

Trademarked names appear throughout this book. Rather than list the names and entities that own the trademarks or insert a trademark symbol with each mention of the trademarked name, the publisher states that it is using the names for editorial purposes only and to the benefit of the trademark owner, with no intention of infringing upon that trademark.

The Coriolis Group, LLC
14455 N. Hayden Road
Suite 220
Scottsdale, Arizona 85260

(480) 483-0192
FAX (480) 483-0193
www.coriolis.com

Library of Congress Cataloging-in-Publication Data
Eckel, Erik.
   Windows 2000 professional on site/by Erik Eckel and Brian Alderman.
      p. cm.
   Includes index.
   ISBN 1-57610-967-4
    1. Microsoft Windows (Computer file)   2. Operating systems (Computers) I. Alderman,
Brian. II. Title.
QA76.76.O63 E2345   2001
005.4'4769--dc21

2001032384

Printed in the United States of America
10 9 8 7 6 5 4 3 2 1

The Coriolis Group, LLC • 14455 North Hayden Road, Suite 220 • Scottsdale, Arizona 85260

A Note from Coriolis

Coriolis Technology Press was founded to create a very elite group of books: the ones you keep closest to your machine. In the real world, you have to choose the books you rely on every day *very* carefully, and we understand that.

To win a place for our books on that coveted shelf beside your PC, we guarantee several important qualities in every book we publish. These qualities are:

- *Technical accuracy*—It's no good if it doesn't work. Every Coriolis Technology Press book is reviewed by technical experts in the topic field, and is sent through several editing and proofreading passes in order to create the piece of work you now hold in your hands.

- *Innovative editorial design*—We've put years of research and refinement into the ways we present information in our books. Our books' editorial approach is uniquely designed to reflect the way people learn new technologies and search for solutions to technology problems.

- *Practical focus*—We put only pertinent information into our books and avoid any fluff. Every fact included between these two covers must serve the mission of the book as a whole.

- *Accessibility*—The information in a book is worthless unless you can find it quickly when you need it. We put a lot of effort into our indexes, and heavily cross-reference our chapters, to make it easy for you to move right to the information you need.

Here at The Coriolis Group we have been publishing and packaging books, technical journals, and training materials since 1989. We have put a lot of thought into our books; please write to us at **ctp@coriolis.com** and let us know what you think. We hope that you're happy with the book in your hands, and that in the future, when you reach for software development and networking information, you'll turn to one of our books first.

Coriolis Technology Press
The Coriolis Group
14455 N. Hayden Road, Suite 220
Scottsdale, Arizona
85260

Email: ctp@coriolis.com
Phone: (480) 483-0192
Toll free: (800) 410-0192

Look for these related books from The Coriolis Group:

Windows 2000 Professional Upgrade Little Black Book
By Nathan Wallace

Windows 2000 Professional Advanced Configuration and Implementation
By Morten Strunge Nielsen

MCSE Windows 2000 Professional Exam Cram
By Dan Holme, Dan Balter, Todd Logan, and Laurie Salmon

MCSE Windows 2000 Professional Exam Prep
By James Bloomingdale, Neall Alcott, and Michael Stewart

Also published by Coriolis Technology Press:

Microsoft Project 2000 Black Book
By Tracey J. Rosenblath

Windows 2000 Server On Site
By Joli Ballew

Exchange 2000 Server On Site
By Göran Husman

IIS 5 On Site
By Scott Reeves and Kalinda Reeves

Active Directory On Site
By Mark Wilkins

SQL Server 2000 On Site
By Anthony Sequeira

To my entire family and all of my friends who made this an enjoyable experience.
—Brian Alderman

&

To Lauren and Hannah, for whom my unending love is but a small measure of appreciation for their unwavering support and wondrous inspiration.
—Erik Eckel

&

About the Authors

Brian Alderman is a senior technical instructor with KnowledgeNet, the world's leading e-learning training company. He presents Microsoft Windows 2000 operating system and SQL Server 2000 training over the Internet. He has provided worldwide remote technical support for Windows NT 3.51 and NT 4 while employed with Digital Equipment Corporation as a Systems Support Specialist. He also holds his MCSE 2000, MCSE+I, MCDBA, and MCT certifications. He enjoys playing golf, running, and traveling.

Erik Eckel serves as editor in chief for TechProGuild, a subscription IT news and information Web site owned by TechRepublic. He received a B.A. in English from the University of Louisville (1990) and a Microsoft Network Engineer diploma from Sullivan College (1999). He earned MCP+I and MCSE certifications from Microsoft in 1999, and possesses a Certificate of Achievement for successfully completing Microsoft 2000 Accelerated Training classes. He's a voracious reader who enjoys jazz, cycling, mountain biking, and relaxing with his wife, daughter, two dogs, and cat.

Acknowledgments

There are many people who made this a successful project by assisting and supporting me throughout the project. I want to thank the entire Coriolis staff—including Charlotte Carpentier, Acquisitions Editor; Carla Schuder, Production Coordinator; and Laura Wellander, Cover Designer—for their outstanding support and coordination of the project, with a special thanks to Toni Zuccarini Ackley for managing the frequent interaction between the authors and The Coriolis Group. Thanks to Mike Vasquez (MCSE 2000, MCSE+I) and Mike Foster (MCSE 2000, MCSE 4) for their contribution to the success of this book. Thanks to my entire family, particularly my parents and my brother Jeff, for their unsurpassed support and inspiration throughout this project. Finally, thanks to my friends for their kind and encouraging words.
—*Brian Alderman*

Projects of this magnitude are seldom completed due to the efforts of just a few individuals. Many thanks to The Coriolis Group's qualified and talented staff, including Charlotte Carpentier, whose timely support will always be appreciated. The authors wish to thank Toni Zuccarini Ackley for keeping everything focused and on track, Paul LoPresto for ensuring we could move large amounts of files quickly and securely, and Peter Bruzzese and Chuck Hutchinson for their editing assistance.
—*Erik Eckel*

Contents at a Glance

Table of Contents

Chapter 11
Administering Resources Using Windows 2000 Professional 401

Chapter 16
Security 655

Introduction

Thanks for buying *Windows 2000 Professional On Site*. Everyone, from small offices to large corporations, is quickly realizing the numerous benefits and features of Windows 2000 Professional. It is the most powerful desktop operating system ever released by Microsoft and has received rave reviews for its stability, security, and performance.

The extremely powerful new features and functionality included in Windows 2000 Professional warrant a discussion of the numerous options available to you. We have provided an in-depth explanation of the major topics in an easy-to-read yet thorough format. This book includes all of the information you will need to successfully plan, install, configure, and maintain your Windows 2000 Professional operating system while lowering your total cost of ownership.

Many IT professionals believe Windows 2000 Professional is not just an upgrade from Windows NT 4 Workstation, but an entirely new operating system. In order to achieve the full potential of Windows 2000 Professional, it is imperative that you obtain a thorough understanding of its capabilities. Microsoft took some giant steps to implement industry-wide technology standards and to reduce Microsoft proprietary technology. The standardization in Windows 2000 makes it much easier to communicate with other operating systems in a heterogeneous networking configuration.

Is This Book for You?

Windows 2000 Professional On Site was written with the intermediate or advanced user in mind. Among the topics covered are the following:

- Installing Windows 2000 Professional

- Calculating deployment costs

- Configuring and troubleshooting your network

- Managing Registry settings

- Monitoring and optimizing performance

How to Use This Book

This book was written to provide you with the information required to perform intermediate to advanced tasks in Windows 2000 Professional. Although we recommend that you
read the entire book, you can go directly to a chapter that contains a specific topic. Each
chapter contains enough information to provide you with the flexibility of reviewing the
chapters in any order.

The *On Site* Philosophy

Written by experienced professionals, books in The Coriolis Group's *On Site* series guide
you through typical, day-to-day needs assessment, planning, deployment, configuration,
and troubleshooting challenges. The *On Site* series uses real-world scenarios and indis-
pensable illustrations to help you move flawlessly through system setup and any problems
you may encounter along the way. The illustrations, including concise flowcharts with
clear and logical steps, help professionals diagnose problems and assess needs to reduce
total cost of ownership.

We welcome your feedback on this book. You can email The Coriolis Group at
ctp@coriolis.com. Errata, updates, and more are available at **www.coriolis.com**.

Chapter 1

The Windows 2000 Family

First, a Little History

How far have computers come? I remember sitting on the floor one Saturday in 1972 or so with a massive "portable" my father brought home. As a manager for Bowling Green State University's data processing department, he was charged with testing the machine's remote access capabilities.

Although it was portable, this computer was no laptop. It weighed close to 20 pounds, and it was a little bigger than a good-sized hard-shell suitcase. Flip the latches open, raise the lid, and three things greeted you: a large roll of paper (that was the then-equivalent of a 15-inch, high-resolution SXGA+ screen), two rubber doughnuts into which you sank your Ma Bell-provided telephone, and a keyboard.

My brother and I couldn't believe it, of course. Here was a real, live computer, and it was portable. It even included an outrageous game. My dad would boot it up and load Toro, a bull-fighting game.

To play, you selected one of the following: <, >, a, or z (I think it was). You would enter your key, wait 30 seconds or so for the transmission to be sped at maybe 1,200 baud to the massive mainframe, which would calculate your move, and then return the wildly anticipated result. You would receive something similar to one of these messages:

```
The bull missed! (1) Try again...
The bull gored you! (0)
```

That was it. The more you evaded the bull, the higher your score. I would remember more about the game, but in the Eckel household, my older brother Ted usually wrestled the machine away when my parents weren't looking (a scene probably replayed in your home if you own a PlayStation 2).

Computers have experienced incredible evolution since then, and so have the operating systems (OSs) that run them. Windows 2000 Professional continues the trend begun with the earliest programming languages.

In fact, Windows 2000 Professional introduces several important new features and capabilities, all of which are covered in this text. Some IT professionals will even tell you that Microsoft's Windows 2000 family finally delivers the complete set of computing features the enterprise has sought since my dad brought that oversized Samsonite home from the office when Richard M. Nixon was commander in chief.

A Quick Timeline

Depending on whom you ask, the first modern computer was the ABC, built in 1939 by physicist John Atanasoff and Clifford Berry, a graduate student, at Iowa State College. By *modern*, historians mean it used electricity. Some will tell you the abacus was the first computer, whereas others credit Blaise Pascal with building the first digital computer in 1642.

Probably the most famous of the first computers, the ENIAC, came in 1946. Ultimately, it was classified as a calculator. In 1951, the UNIVAC became what's believed to be the first commercially marketed computer.

In 1952, IBM added computing devices to its product line. FORTRAN was created in 1957, followed by COBOL in 1959. The year 1964 brought Basic, which was also the year giving rise to the first local area network (LAN). In 1966, the first wide area network (WAN) experiment was run with ARPAnet.

Intel manufactured the 4001 chip in 1970, a year before Pong rose to prominence. In 1973, Ethernet hit the scene. Two years later, Microsoft and Microsoft Basic arrived. The year 1975 also saw the debut of the Altair 8800, widely considered to be the first personal computer.

While the United States was celebrating its bicentennial, a small computer company named Apple formed. The next year, 1977, may have found you playing chess on a black-and-white-screened TRS-80 at a nearby Radio Shack.

Two years later, in 1979, the Usenet collection of online bulletin boards arrived. The next year, IBM selected Intel's 8008 chip for its first microcomputer.

Then, things really began heating up. In 1981, Microsoft purchased the rights to 86-DOS from a small company in Washington. Just a month later, Bill Gates released the first version of MS-DOS.

IBM's PC-XT shipped in 1982, the same year Compaq was born and the 8-bit Commodore 64 stormed the scene. A year later saw the birth of NetWare and the second version of MS-DOS, as well as TCP/IP becoming an Internet standard. In 1983, the world received the two-button mouse and CD-ROM drive.

In 1984, IBM's PC-AT shipped. It blazed a new trail at 6MHz and featured DOS 3. In 1985, Windows 1.0 debuted. A year later, America Online was born. Here's hoping you made a note to buy stock when the company went public. In 1987, Microsoft released Windows 2.01. The next year, Microsoft began developing its New Technology platform, which would become known as NT.

The year 1990 saw Windows 3.0, followed a year later by Windows 3.11. Meanwhile, a student named Linus Torvalds began writing a Unix derivative now known as Linux.

Windows began consuming market share, and by 1992, it earned almost a third of the market for personal computer operating systems. Microsoft looked to build on its momentum with the release of its NT software the following year. At the same time, the Mosaic Internet browser was being written.

The next year gave new meaning to the word *Chicago*, as computer enthusiasts eagerly awaited the release of what would become known as Windows 95. The Pentium was introduced, and Microsoft Windows' market share climbed to almost 75 percent.

In 1996, the U.S. Justice Department began rattling its sabers in Redmond's direction. Also that year, Windows NT 4 was released. Windows 98 arrived a little later, followed by Windows 98 Second Edition.

In February 2000, the family of Windows 2000 operating systems began appearing on store shelves, as Windows 2000 Professional, Windows 2000 Server, and Windows 2000 Advanced Server were released. In late summer 2000, Windows 2000 Datacenter Server became available.

Windows 2000: "The Next Generation of PC Computing"

Marketed as "the next generation of PC computing," Windows 2000 was released to the traditional fanfare associated with a new operating system from Microsoft. Only this time, things were different.

In news releases, trade show speeches, and media appearances, Microsoft officials worked diligently to position Windows 2000 as delivering superior reliability, enhanced manageability, improved uptime, a decreased total cost of ownership, and the ideal platform for conducting business on the Internet. However, that had been done before.

Designed for worldwide deployment and implementation, Windows 2000 was built to power everything from laptops to desktops to powerful workstations and servers to massive data center servers. The difference became readily apparent after IT manager after IT manager and system administrator after system administrator began deploying Windows 2000 on test networks.

What have they found? They've discovered a powerful, robust, scalable operating system that runs well. Many claim that Windows 2000 manages errant processes efficiently and simplifies administration once installed.

Let's meet the players earning such high accolades.

The Windows 2000 Family

Each of the Windows 2000 operating systems boasts unique features and applications. The following operating systems comprise the Windows 2000 family:

- Windows 2000 Professional

- Windows 2000 Server

- Windows 2000 Advanced Server

- Windows 2000 Datacenter Server

Microsoft's Windows 2000 family of operating systems introduces several new features. Strengthened security, enhanced reliability, improved capacities, increased capabilities, and simplified ease of use are just the beginning.

Systems engineers have new tools for administration and deployment. Support personnel enjoy improved configuration and troubleshooting tools. End users benefit from increased reliability and bolstered security, as well as enhanced remote access capabilities. The result is improved efficiencies that are felt throughout an entire organization.

Picking up where Windows NT left off, Windows 2000 aims to reduce an organization's total cost of ownership; provide a powerful, reliable, and scalable enterprise-computing platform; and offer an adaptive infrastructure for information-technology–based solutions deployment.

All these benefits are the result of numerous refinements, enhancements, and improvements in Microsoft's past NT operating systems. All the Windows 2000 operating systems utilize Microsoft's NT kernel, which in the past was stable but didn't offer widespread compatibility.

That's all changed with Windows 2000, which combines the compatibility and ease of use of Microsoft's consumer operating systems with the power, scalability, and performance of its business-class systems. We'll take a look shortly at the most important new features and enhancements available in Windows 2000. But first, let's look at the differences between the Windows 2000 platforms. We'll start with Windows 2000 Professional.

Windows 2000 Professional at a Glance

Windows 2000 Professional combines the ease of use and widespread compatibility associated with Windows 9x systems with the power, scalability, and security of the Windows NT platform. Further, Windows 2000 Professional supports upgrading from all the operating systems it replaces:

- Windows 95

- Windows 98

- Windows 98 Second Edition

- Windows NT Workstation 3.51

- Windows NT Workstation 4

Should you have older Windows 3.1 or Windows 3.11 systems on your network, you'll want to take note. Windows 2000 does not support upgrading from Windows 3.x platforms. You probably wouldn't want to do that anyway because your legacy systems likely wouldn't meet Windows 2000's heightened hardware requirements.

You should note a few other upgrade considerations. One item of importance is whether you've implemented beta Windows 2000 software in your enterprise. We often hear of organizations that have loaded beta or release candidate software for testing and then moved those servers and workstations into production. Before you know it, you're dependent on these systems. It's usually at an inopportune time that you realize a trial TechNet or evaluation version of the software has been deployed. Apparently, it occurs frequently enough that Redmond has chosen to address the issue. If you're in that situation, you'll be happy to hear release candidates can be upgraded.

If you're using a beta version, however, you're out in the cold. Windows 2000 Professional Beta 3 cannot be upgraded directly to Windows 2000 final code. However, you can upgrade Beta 3 to Release Candidate 2. After you've done that, you can upgrade Release Candidate 2 to the final Windows 2000 code, should you need to do so.

The following trial Windows 2000 versions can be upgraded to the final Windows 2000 code:

- Release Candidate 1 (RC1)

- Release Candidate 2 (RC2)

- Release Candidate 3 (RC3)

Microsoft doesn't recommend upgrading directly to the final code from RC1. Again, you would want to upgrade RC1 machines to RC2 and then upgrade the RC2 software to the final code.

What's New in Windows 2000 Professional?

Windows 2000 Professional boasts many new enhancements over previous Windows platforms, including Windows 95, Windows 98, and Windows NT Workstation 4. You'll find the following in Windows 2000 Professional:

- Improved installation and setup routines

- Improved configuration features

- New configuration and administration wizards

- An enhanced user interface

- Bolstered Internet services

- Strengthened security

- Better file management capabilities

- Enhanced printing support and services

- Improved mobile computing and power conservation platform

- New troubleshooting utilities

- Faster performance

- Simplified networking

- Accessibility features

- Bolstered fax services

- New multimedia features

- NetMeeting (Version 3.01)

- New rescue and recovery features

Let's take a closer look at each of the new features and enhancements included in Windows 2000.

Improved Installation and Setup

New setup utilities simplify the Windows 2000 installation. Working together, the setup utilities permit a smoother installation.

Here's one quick example. An error during Windows NT Workstation's installation process might bring the installation to a quick halt; however, the Windows 2000 installation process plows on. It stops only if it encounters what it considers a critical error. Further, Windows 2000 makes assumptions of how a system should be configured based on information it learns during its own setup process.

One of many new Windows 2000 wizards that greatly simplifies complicated configuration tasks, the Setup Manager Wizard helps customize the Windows 2000 installation. It lets you select configuration parameters and store them in a script file, which can be used later to automate installations on other systems.

One new feature quickly winning system administrators' hearts is the System Preparation tool. The system preparation utility (SYSPREP.EXE) simplifies the hard disk imaging process, which is an important step in preparing clones for the efficient deployment of

1

Microsoft's Top 10 Reasons to Upgrade to Windows 2000 Professional

Not to be outdone by David Letterman, Microsoft has published its own top 10 list it says warrants deploying the Windows 2000 Professional platform. The 10 reasons are as follows:

1. *Value*—Windows 2000 offers enhanced management features and improved performance, which decrease the total cost of ownership. Administrators no longer need to restore critical files users deleted when they chose to "help" the IT department and free up some space on a hard disk. Administrators also can troubleshoot more errors remotely due to included enhancements. This alone can save on travel costs.

2. *Reliability*—Fundamental improvements to the Windows 2000 operating system contribute to dramatic improvements in uptime.

3. *Mobility*—Windows 2000 Professional includes key productivity and time-saving features.

4. *Manageability*—Centralized management utilities, troubleshooting tools, and support for self-healing applications all make it simpler for administrators and users to deploy and manage desktop and laptop computers.

5. *Performance*—Microsoft claims Windows 2000 Professional provides a 32 percent performance improvement over Windows 95 and 27 percent over Windows 98, when using 64MB of RAM. Versus Windows NT and 32MB of RAM, Windows 2000 boasts a performance increase of 19 percent.

6. *Security*—Security has been strengthened considerably in the new Windows platform and includes such enhancements as use of the Encrypting File System, IP Security, Layer 2 Tunneling Protocol, virtual private networking, and more.

7. *Internet*—Internet features and applications have been tightly integrated into the operating system.

8. *Usability*—Windows 2000 possesses the approachability of Microsoft's consumer operating systems and the capabilities of its business platforms.

9. *Data access*—All aspects of data access and control have been improved, from file and share permissions to the use of IntelliMirror profiles and security policies and more.

10. *Hardware*—Windows 2000 Professional is compatible with a wide and ever-growing range of hardware devices and includes support for DVD drives, universal serial bus- and FireWire-connected devices.

multiple, similarly configured systems. With the use of third-party tools, such as PowerQuest's Drive Image and Norton's Ghost, hard disk images can more easily be duplicated and deployed to other systems.

Configuring hardware devices and peripherals is much easier in Windows 2000 Professional than it was with Windows NT Workstation. Although it was labeled in the past as "plug-and-pray" by some, you'll be pleasantly surprised to find that Windows 2000 plugs-and-plays well. Windows 2000 supports a wide range of hardware out-of-the-box.

When installing, Windows 2000 automatically detects hardware. When booting Windows 2000 machines, the operating system checks for changes in a system's hardware configuration. When necessary, it launches another new wizard, the Windows 2000 Hardware Wizard. This addition of automatically configured support for thousands of hardware devices (including DVD drives and USB and FireWire peripherals) saves valuable time and countless headaches.

Improved Configuration Features

Also improved are the tools and utilities used to configure Windows 2000. The new configuration features make it easier to create a consistent and simplified computing experience both in the home and in the enterprise.

An Improved Control Panel

The Windows Control Panel offers several new applets. It also includes new functionality, including the ability to sort programs by name, frequency of use, size, and last date used. Applications can be installed simply by pointing to them from within the applet. For more information on all the Control Panel's new applets, see Chapter 7.

The Windows Installer

Another important new service is the Windows Installer. The Windows Installer service monitors application and program installations, modifications that are made to those applications and programs, any repairs that are made, and the uninstallation of those programs. As a result, the days of bits and pieces of old, no-longer-installed programs hanging out all over your and your users' hard drives, taking up valuable and needed space, are gone.

The process is simple. The Windows Installer service builds a database to track software installations and any modifications that are made to those programs. Should a file become corrupted, the service will catch the error and notify the user of any needed repairs. The database also tracks any changes that are made to applications as a result of being updated or patched. The removal of software programs is much more complete, because the database knows where all the bits and pieces of a program are parked.

Computer Management

Configuration and administration of physical machines are easier, thanks to several new computer management utilities. Windows 2000's Computer Management program includes the following:

- *System Tools*—Includes diagnostic and service management tools, including the Event Viewer, System Information, Performance Logs and Alerts, Device Manager, and Services applets.

- *Storage*—Collects common disk management utilities, including Disk Defragmenter.

- *Services and Applications*—Permits configuration of Windows 2000's various services and applications.

Several critical applications and programs are housed in the Computer Management applet, as shown in Figure 1.1. In addition to disk management tools, this console serves as a repository for important system and diagnostic information.

The Microsoft Management Console

In the past, administrators and support personnel often needed to open numerous windows to solve desktop computer issues. No more.

The Microsoft Management Console (MMC) is one of the most powerful new features you'll find in the new operating system. Its capabilities are the result of its tremendous elasticity.

The MMC can easily be customized to provide access to a variety of powerful tools and utilities using a single console, as shown in Figure 1.2. The following list shows some of the tools or applets, known as *snap-ins*, that can be folded into a single MMC interface:

- Certificates

- Component Services

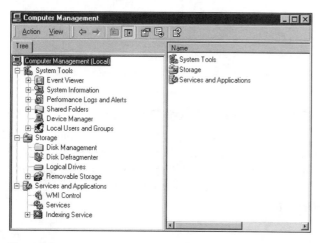

Figure 1.1
The Windows 2000 Computer Management applet collects multiple utilities conveniently in a single console.

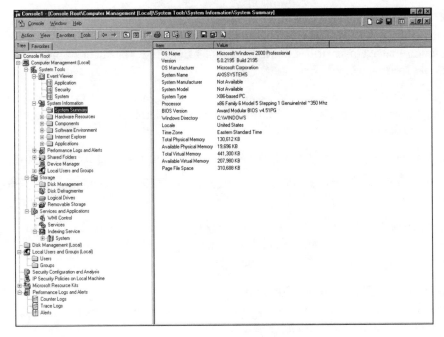

Figure 1.2
The Microsoft Management Console can easily be customized to include numerous applets. Here, several snap-ins have been saved in a single console, and the System Summary, available from the System Information snap-in, is displayed.

- Computer Management

- Disk Management

- Fax Service Management

- Local Users and Groups

- Performance Logs and Alerts

- Resource Kits

- System Information

New Configuration and Administration Wizards

As enterprise networks and operating systems become increasingly complex, it stands to reason that the installation, configuration, and maintenance tasks of software would become increasingly difficult. Although Windows 2000 packs more punch than previous operating systems that Redmond has produced, its programmers have done an excellent job of simplifying administration.

You'll find numerous new configuration and administration wizards in Windows 2000. From device installation to network connection creation to security settings, you'll find easy-to-use wizards waiting to guide you through processes step-by-step. Some wizards are mercifully short, whereas others require more menus be navigated, depending on the task being performed.

Before any changes are made to your system, the wizards present you with a summary screen. It lists all the changes you've requested the system make, but until you select Finish, none of the changes will be applied.

For more information on troubleshooting wizards, read the section titled "New Trouble-shooting Utilities" later in this chapter.

Enhanced User Interface

Can an operating system be made both more powerful and simple to use? The first time you fire up Windows 2000, you'll find the answer is yes.

Personalized Menus and Toolbar Customization

Menus and applets have been updated to consolidate functions and applications that sometimes confused less sophisticated users. Network administrators and other IT personnel, however, can still find the powerful and dynamic tools they require to exploit the full functionality provided by Windows 2000.

Less frequently used applications are hidden in regular menu views as part of a new feature known as *Personalized Menus*. Should you wish to execute a seldom-accessed application, you only need to click on the double-arrow icon at the bottom of the menu (see Figure 1.3). Alternatively, you can hover the mouse pointer on the menu, and after a few moments, the rest of the menu will be displayed.

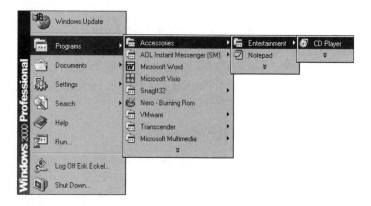

Figure 1.3
Applications that are not used frequently are hidden from view, as indicated by the double-arrow icons that appear on the bottom of these menus.

Figure 1.4
From the Advanced tab of the Taskbar And Start Menu Properties dialog box, administrators can specify and set Start Menu Settings they wish for a system to use.

Tip: Should you find Personalized Menus annoying, it's easy to turn the feature off. Just right-click on the taskbar and select Properties. From the Taskbar And Start Menu Properties screen, uncheck the Use Personalized Menus checkbox.

The Start menu can be customized easily (see Figure 1.4). Again, limiting the number of applications and program options that appear helps ensure that a system's operators don't become confused or operate utilities with which they are not familiar or shouldn't be using.

Programs and applications can be easily added or removed. Other options administrators can configure here include the following:

- Display Administrative Tools
- Display Favorites
- Display Logoff
- Expand Control Panel
- Expand My Documents
- Expand Network and Dial-Up Connections
- Expand Printers
- Scroll the Programs Menu

New IntelliMirror Profiles

Many of Windows 2000's benefits can be realized simply by installing the OS on a compatible system. When some features are installed in a native environment, or one in which all the systems are running Windows 2000 (including a server), additional benefits are realized.

IntelliMirror is one of those features. With assistance provided by a Windows 2000 server, you can configure the same desktop settings to follow users around an enterprise network or small LAN, regardless of which machine they log on to.

Similar to Windows NT 4 roaming profiles, IntelliMirror enables users to access their data, software, and preferences anywhere on a network. The technology works by using policy definitions to deploy, recover, restore, or replace users' data, software, and personal settings when they move from one computer to another on the same network.

Improved Dialog Boxes

Dialog boxes for Logon and Shutdown options are smaller and easier to use in Windows 2000 than they were in Windows NT Workstation. Not only have they been simplified, but users' options are explained in greater detail than in the past.

Enhanced Scheduled Tasks

Scheduling unattended tasks is easier, too. Scripts and programs can be run at specified times using the Scheduled Tasks applet. It can be configured to run applications at startup or to schedule other tasks. The Scheduled Task Wizard is another wizard included to help make complex processes error-free.

As shown in Figure 1.5, the Scheduled Task Wizard makes it easy to schedule programs to run regularly. Several applications can be run by default, and other programs are added as they're installed on your system.

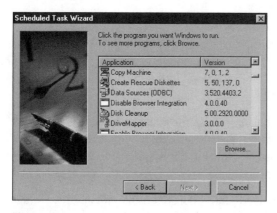

Figure 1.5
The Scheduled Task Wizard simplifies the running of regularly scheduled programs.

Bolstered Internet Services

Windows 2000 Professional includes, whether the Justice Department wants it to or not, integrated Internet browser and communications functionality. Both Internet Explorer 5 (IE5) and Outlook Express are included with the OS.

Internet Explorer 5

IE5 includes many new features aimed at simplifying Internet usage. IE5's Search Assistant simplifies searching by offering categories and enabling users to access multiple search engines without retyping queries. IE5's AutoComplete feature activates a drop-down list of previously visited sites in the browser's Address bar, which can shorten the number of keystrokes needed to reach a location or enter information.

The Windows 2000 desktop expands AutoComplete functionality by providing assistance when entering network addresses, URLs, folder names, and more. IE5 can also be set to remember frequently used passwords.

Automatic configuration is another benefit of IE5. The browser can locate and configure Internet connections automatically through the use of the Internet Connection Wizard. Further simplifying its use, you can request that proxy settings be automatically discovered.

Outlook Express 5

Outlook Express offers Windows 2000 users a scaled-down version of Microsoft Outlook. Although it doesn't boast all the full-blown Outlook version's features, you'll still find a powerful client utility for managing email, contacts, and newsgroup subscriptions.

Using Outlook Express, users can send and receive Hypertext Markup Language (HTML) or Rich Text Format (RTF) messages. Multiple Outlook Express accounts can be hosted on the same machine, too, enabling users to switch identities.

Better File Management Capabilities

Compared to earlier Windows operating systems, Windows 2000 Professional expands file storage and management capabilities. In addition to supporting a refined version of NT File System (NTFS), Windows 2000 Professional offers many new file management features, including the following:

- Support for the File Allocation Table 32 (FAT32) file system, introduced with Windows 95 Operating System Release 2 (OSR2). Past versions of NT-powered Windows systems didn't support FAT32, which is used by Windows 95, Windows 98, Windows 98 Second Edition, and Windows Me operating systems.

- NTFS partitions no longer require third-party tools to ensure efficient file storage. Defragmentation software originally produced by Executive Software has been incorporated as a native application. Out-of-the-box, Windows 2000 Professional can defragment any file system it supports.

- Windows 2000's backup utility is more powerful and robust than its predecessor, making command-line backup scheduling a thing of the past.

- Native support is now included for removable storage devices such as Zip drives, CD-RW devices, logical tape drives, and external hard drives (including those attached by USB and FireWire connections).

- Windows 2000 introduces dynamic volumes to Windows. After a volume is adjusted, a system doesn't require rebooting for the changes to take effect.

- Volume administration can be performed remotely over a LAN or WAN connection.

- Local drives and partitions can be mounted at any empty folder, as long as the target folder exists on an NTFS volume. In the past, volumes had to be mounted at the root of a drive letter.

A Disk Cleanup feature is also available. It can be used to help users clean numerous unneeded files from their hard drives.

You can start the Disk Cleanup application from the Start|Programs|Accessories|Systems Tools menu. You'll be greeted with a dialog box asking which drive you wish to clean up. Windows then performs a check to determine how much space can be freed.

As you can see in Figure 1.6, you can select to remove temporary Internet files, temporary offline files, files from the Recycle Bin, and more.

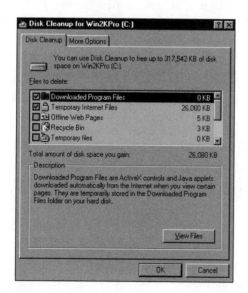

Figure 1.6
Disk Cleanup can help less sophisticated users remove files that are no longer needed from their hard drives.

Disk Cleanup also offers, under its More Options tab, additional methods for freeing up hard disk space. For example, Disk Cleanup can be used to delete unused Windows components.

Strengthened Security

Ask administrators their top three IT concerns, and you're sure to hear security listed. Windows 2000 Professional addresses these concerns by including support for many new security standards. Several new features aimed at protecting data and network communications from prying eyes have been included, too.

Enhanced Public Key Infrastructure

The foundation of many Windows 2000 Professional security features is the extensive public key infrastructure found in the new OS. Developers can leverage security mechanisms using encrypted keys.

A collection of complex cryptographic algorithms incorporated into public keys and bolstered by the use of certificates of authority to help prove the issuer's identity helps Windows 2000 Professional protect against intrusion and the unauthorized access of resources. Applications that benefit from the enhanced public key infrastructure include network authentication, email, and resource access.

Introducing the Encrypting File System

Files and information stored on NTFS-formatted partitions can now be encrypted. The Encrypting File System (EFS) provides an added security measure by requiring users who log on locally to a machine to also possess the appropriate public key for unlocking the files they access.

Files can be encrypted easily. Users need only click the Advanced button on a document's Properties and select a checkbox, as shown in Figure 1.7. Windows 2000 Professional does the rest.

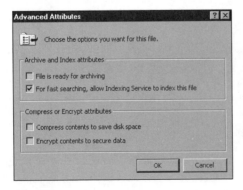

Figure 1.7
Encrypting resources is easy. Users need only select the Encrypt Contents To Secure Data box.

Note: *If you want to use the Windows 2000 Encrypting File System, documents must reside on an NTFS partition.*

Through the use of public-key–based cryptography, EFS technology prevents thieves from accessing data on stolen hard drives, even if they reload Windows 2000 Professional. Merely accessing an NTFS partition via a third-party tool or reinstallation isn't sufficient for accessing encrypted data. And, because EFS runs as an integrated system service, it's easy to manage, difficult to defeat, and virtually transparent to users.

Support for Internet Protocol Security

An Internet standard established by Request For Comment (RFC) 1825, Internet Protocol Security (IPSec) encrypts Transmission Control Protocol/Internet Protocol (TCP/IP) traffic that traverses the public Internet. As a result of this support, Windows 2000 Professional enjoys the benefit of secure communications when packets traverse intranets and Internet virtual private networks (VPNs).

Tip: *You can find a Request For Comments archive at **www.ietf.org/rfc.html**. RFCs are used to set Internet standards.*

IP security can be implemented for users in both domain and workgroup environments. Windows 2000's IP Security Policy Management MMC interface is used to configure IPSec settings, as shown in Figure 1.8.

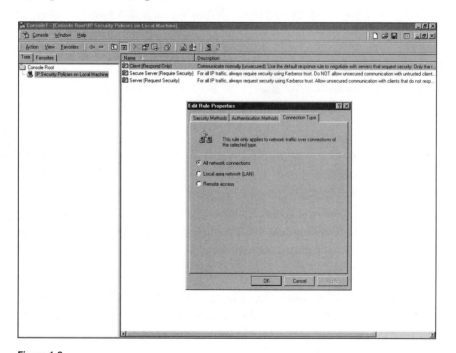

Figure 1.8
The IP Security Policy Management MMC snap-in can be used to configure IPSec settings for local area networks, remote access connections, or all network connections.

Introducing Layer 2 Tunneling Protocol

You're probably familiar with the Point-to-Point Tunneling Protocol (PPTP), which helps create VPNs for secure communications using the Internet. The Layer 2 Tunneling Protocol (L2TP) provides a more secure version of PPTP. Thanks to the use of public key infrastructure, Windows 2000 Professional can make use of L2TP.

Because Windows 2000 incorporates Kerberos version 5 in its distributed security model, users benefit from a single network logon for access to network resources, including files, printers, and other resources. Windows 2000 relies on the industry-standard Kerberos protocol for user authentication. Advantages include strengthened security and improved authentication and network response times.

Introducing Smart Card Support

In the past, sensitive authentication information and private keys had to be sent over the public switched telephone network or other unsecured infrastructure. Clever thieves could intercept them. Now, the risk is eliminated with the introduction of support for smart cards.

Smart cards, which resemble credit cards, hold public key certificates, digital signatures, and private key information. They're tamper-resistant and enable portability of personal information.

The sensitive information on a smart card is further protected through the use of passwords. Should thieves try to use a lost or stolen smart card, they'll find it useless unless they know the password.

Enhanced Printing Support and Services

Printing is a critical function that wasn't overlooked by the development team that built Windows 2000 Professional. Several important new innovations target enhanced printing.

Support for Browser-Enabled Printing

The addition of browser-enabled printing support simplifies printing significantly in the enterprise. Users can now use their Internet browsers to print documents, spreadsheets, Web pages, presentations, and more.

The Internet Printing Protocol (IPP) enables browser-based printing via intranet and Internet connections. Users can now print to URLs, download and install printer drivers, and view printer-related information easily using their browsers.

A New Printing Wizard

The Add Printer Wizard simplifies printer installation, whether the printer is a local or networked device. Users no longer need to specify printer types, select ports, or choose print languages.

Improved Printing Service

1

High-quality files, including color printouts, can be created faster due to improvements in the way Windows 2000 Professional processes print requests. The introduction of Image Color Management 2 works to ensure images are reproduced on scanners and printers with the same colors shown on a user's monitor.

Windows 2000 Professional also serves up an improved Print dialog box. As a result, it's easier to learn which printers possess the shortest queues, which printers are installed, where the printer is located, and more.

If one or more Windows 2000 servers support your Windows 2000 Professional system, you can also search the network for printers possessing the qualities you need. For example, if you need a color printer located in a nearby office, you could search for a printer based on type and location. This feature is particularly valuable in large organizations and companies in which folks travel often between corporate locations with laptop computers.

Improved Mobile Computing and Power Conservation Platform

Windows 2000 includes numerous features aimed at improving mobile computing experiences. These benefits aren't limited to software configuration enhancements and synchronization tools, either.

Power consumption has been significantly improved. The main mobile computing platform features and improvements are as follows:

- Multiple network connections can be configured through a single utility, the Network Connection Wizard. Dial-up connections, VPNs, direct connections to other computers, and incoming calls can all be configured with the Network Connection Wizard.

- New support is included for securing virtual private networks that connect via the public switched telephone network. As laptops are often used to connect from remote locations, this is a particularly valuable feature.

- Users can store network-based documents in offline folders on their hard drives, enabling use of the documents when the network is unavailable, such as when cruising at 32,000 feet in coach class.

- The Synchronization Manager can be configured to automatically update files and folders when a user logs back on to the network (such as when he reconnects in an airport's lounge or back at the office). Changes made to files and folders, including Web pages and email messages, can be kept current using this utility.

- Windows 2000 Professional supports the Advanced Configuration and Power Interface with the goal of extending battery life.

- New power management and suspend and resume capabilities contribute to improved battery performance, including Hibernate mode, which shuts off power but maintains programs' open states and hardware connections.

- Hot-swapping capabilities are enhanced. Portable computers no longer require rebooting when connecting to or disconnecting from docking stations.

- Improvements to plug-and-play are particularly important for notebook computers, which were notorious for raising issues with the Windows NT Workstation 4 platform. In addition, more PC cards and laptop peripherals are supported by the operating system.

- Six preset Power Schemes are provided to help maximize battery life. Each scheme is tailored to a particular computing environment.

Windows 2000 Professional also includes support for the Infrared Data Association (IrDA) protocol. The protocol is often used by laptops and other systems to transfer data without wires using infrared signals.

Should things go wrong with network connections, or should other issues arise, you'll find excellent help in Windows 2000.

New Troubleshooting Utilities

Troubleshooting is greatly improved in Windows 2000 Professional. In addition to expanded plug-and-play support, troubleshooting wizards help solve common problems. Several new troubleshooting wizards are available, including:

- *Client Service for NetWare (CSNW)*—Assists with accessing NetWare servers and Novell Directory Service objects, printing on Novell networks, using NetWare login scripts, and logging on to an NDS tree.

- *Display*—Assists with the configuration of video cards, drivers, and display adapters.

- *Hardware*—Helps troubleshoot issues with peripherals, such as CD-ROM drives, hard drives, input devices, and more.

- *Internet connections*—Helps users connect to Internet service providers (ISPs).

- *Modem*—Assists with modem setup and configuration.

- *MS-DOS programs*—Helps users run MS-DOS programs in Windows 2000.

- *Multimedia and games*—Supports installation and configuration assistance for DirectX drivers and computer games.

- *Networking*—Troubleshoots Internet and intranet connections that use TCP/IP.

- *Print*—Assists in troubleshooting network and local printer setup and configuration.

- *Remote access*—Helps users link to remote computers using telephone connections.

- *Sound*—Provides sound card and speaker assistance.

- *System setup*—Helps users with problems related to Windows 2000 installation and setup.

- *Windows 3.x programs*—Provides assistance to users running 16-bit Windows applications.

In addition to the preceding Troubleshooting Wizards, other troubleshooting utilities include the following:

- *Add/Remove Hardware applet*—Control Panel's Add/Remove Hardware applet includes the Add/Remove Hardware Wizard. The wizard offers troubleshooting assistance for error-ridden hardware devices. It can also be used to permanently or temporarily unplug or eject a locked-up device.

- *Windows 2000 Compatibility Tool*—When a Windows 95, Windows 98, or Windows NT Workstation 4 installation is upgraded, the Windows 2000 Compatibility Tool warns users of any application and component incompatibilities. It's an incredibly helpful tool that can forecast, and help eliminate, most problems before they occur.

- *Energy conservation features*—A variety of features, including selectable power schemes, user-configurable settings, and Advanced Power Management support, contribute to improved conservation of energy resources.

- *MMC*—MMC support in the client operating system provides powerful administration capabilities from client machines. MMC integration simplifies remote administration on enterprise networks because multiple tools can be wrapped into a single window. Multiple MMC configurations can be stored and shared, further extending MMC's power.

- *Plug-and-play*—The improved functionality and reliability of plug-and-play support eliminates many troubleshooting situations common in older Windows operating systems.

- *Power Options applet*—As mentioned earlier, new options aimed at preserving mobile computer battery life are available via Control Panel's Power Options applet.

- *Secondary Logon Service*—Taking a hint from Unix and Linux systems, developers have included a secondary logon service in Windows 2000. Network administrators no longer need to log users off a network to make system changes when sitting at a client machine. Windows 2000 includes a Secondary Logon Service for launching administrative programs and applications via a trusted administrator account.

Further assistance with troubleshooting comes from improved dialog boxes. When errors occur, you'll find the dialog boxes present more detailed information. Help files have also gotten much better.

When any problems that arise are fixed, you'll enjoy faster performance, too. Depending on the operating system users are moving from to Windows 2000 Professional, many of the performance improvements will be quite noticeable.

Faster Performance

Windows 2000 Professional also benefits from an improved architecture. The operating system better handles multitasking as a result. It also runs applications requiring large amounts of memory and processor power better.

Performance improvements are realized with the inclusion of support for NTFS version 5. Disk defragmentation utilities are shipped with the OS, which help to greatly improve access times to data. Networking enhancements contribute to improved performance, too.

Simplified Networking

In addition to increasing Windows 2000's networking capabilities, Microsoft's developers also simplified everyday networking functions. Network Neighborhood, which proved confusing for many users, has been replaced by My Network Places.

What's different other than the name? First, the new interface removes from view those servers the user uses infrequently. Second, users can customize their new network interface by creating shortcuts to resources they use frequently. These resources can be servers, file shares, documents, printers, and the like.

Windows 2000 Professional can be used as a standalone system. Windows 2000 Professional systems can also be used in workgroup environments, in which each system fulfills client and server roles by sharing files and other resources, as shown in Figure 1.9.

Windows 2000 Professional machines can also be configured as client systems. They function well in Windows NT Server domains.

The fullest use of Windows 2000's features is realized, though, in native domains in which the servers run a Windows 2000 server operating system, as shown in Figure 1.10.

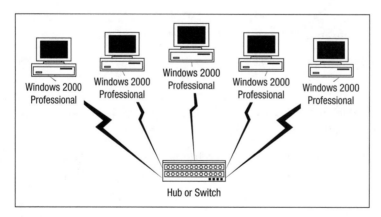

Figure 1.9
Windows 2000 Professional systems can be networked easily to create a workgroup environment.

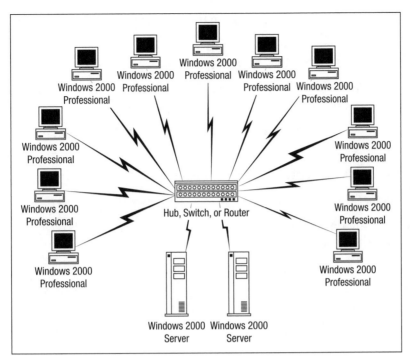

Figure 1.10
Windows 2000 Professional systems can be configured easily to join domains.

As mentioned earlier, users will also find simple wizards to help with the creation of network connections. Connecting to ISPs and VPNs is much easier.

Thanks to the introduction of indexing services, users can also search the network more easily. They enjoy easier access to documents, spreadsheets, presentations, printers, and other resources as a result.

Along with all the new applications, utilities, programs, and tools you'll find in Windows 2000 Professional are some old standbys. You'll find continued support for faxing, multimedia, and collaboration. You'll also find typical rescue and recovery options, such as the use of Emergency Repair Disks, along with a new Rescue Console. Accessibility features many users depend on can also be found in Windows 2000 Professional.

Accessibility Features

A wide range of accessibility features is included in Windows 2000 Professional. These features help users with special needs operate Windows 2000. Many of Windows 2000 Professional's accessibility features come in handy even if a user doesn't suffer from poor vision, poor hearing, or another physical problem.

Most of these features can be configured from the Accessibility Options applet in Control Panel. For example, the following keyboard options can be set:

- *Sticky Keys*—Permits use of the Shift, Ctrl, or Alt key by pressing one key at a time.

- *FilterKeys*—Ignores brief or repeated keystrokes. This feature can also be used to slow the keyboard input repeat rate.

- *ToggleKeys*—Sounds special tones whenever the Caps Lock, Num Lock, and Scroll Lock keys are pressed.

The following sound options can be configured as well:

- *SoundSentry*—Creates visual warnings when system sounds are triggered.

- *ShowSounds*—Informs applications to display captions for the sounds they make, including speech.

The screen display can also be changed, using a High Contrast setting. Several accessibility options can be set for use of the mouse, as well. Further, the numeric keypad located on most keyboards can be set to control the mouse pointer.

Another general accessibility option that can be set is the use of SerialKey devices as alternatives to traditional keyboards and mice. All these options help ensure that all employees can make the most of the new operating system.

Bolstered Fax Services

Has email killed the fax? In many organizations, certainly. Others, depending on their lines of business and other needs, still require the use of fax services. Windows 2000 Professional won't disappoint them.

If Windows 2000 Professional finds a fax device, such as an internal fax modem, it installs fax services by default. Don't look for Fax Services as an applet in Control Panel, though. Instead, you'll find it in the Printers folder, which you can reach by clicking on Start|Settings|Printer.

Faxing a document is easy. Instead of "printing" it to a print device, you simply select the Fax option instead of the printer as your output device.

Along with the fax service and driver, Windows 2000 Professional also installs an editor you can use to create cover pages. You'll find four predesigned templates, too.

You can enable reception of incoming faxes, too. A Fax Service Management Console is provided for managing both outgoing and incoming faxes.

Windows 2000 Professional also packs enhanced multimedia features.

New Multimedia Features

Although you probably aren't purchasing and deploying Windows 2000 Professional to play games, it's nice to know you can. The new OS includes native support for DirectX 7, a collection of application programming interfaces (APIs) designed to enable speedy communication between software programs and hardware devices, such as video and sound cards.

You'll find an improved audio CD player, DVD movie playback support, and an updated Windows Media Player. Windows 2000 Professional also includes a range of sound recording and playback features for those multimedia sources.

NetMeeting (Version 3.01)

NetMeeting encourages office collaboration, even if everyone's not present in the same location. You can use NetMeeting, depending on your needs, to help eliminate traveling required by meetings.

In close to realtime, NetMeeting uses an Internet connection to conference together users in different locations. They can exchange sound, video, files, and even "chat." When a NetMeeting concludes, the information generated during the conference can be saved for later use, further adding to its functionality.

New Rescue and Recovery Features

Despite the best of efforts, things sometimes go wrong. Users try to assist the IT department and begin deleting files they believe are no longer needed from their hard drives. Programs become corrupted. Viruses invade. The list of things that can go wrong is ever increasing.

Fortunately, Windows 2000 Professional includes support for Emergency Repair Disks. It also introduces a new Recovery Console. The Recovery Console works from a command line; thus, it's not for beginners. However, it can rescue a system and return it to operation even when a Safe Mode Boot cannot.

The following actions can be taken from the Recovery Console:

- The Master Boot Record (MBR) can be repaired.

- Data on local drives (including NTFS partitions) can be read and written.

- File attributes can be changed.

- Batch files can be executed.

- Files can be copied (but not from floppy disks).

- Windows 2000 services can be started and stopped.

- Device drivers, often the primary cause of a catastrophic crash, can be enabled and disabled.

- Partitions can be created and deleted.

- Drives can be formatted.

And, Windows 2000 Professional is smart enough to recognize when critical files have been deleted. It simply checks the database kept by the Windows Installer Service and corrects the deletion.

As you can see, Windows 2000 Professional possesses many advantages over other operating systems. Before most of the new innovations and features can be used to their maximum potential, though, one or more Windows 2000 servers need to be implemented. Let's take a look at differences between Windows 2000 Professional and the Windows 2000 server platforms.

Windows 2000 Server Platforms

To make the fullest use of Windows 2000 Professional applications, features, programs, services, and advantages, you need to understand how it integrates into an enterprise network. In an environment in which more than a dozen or so workstations are being networked, it's probably best that a Windows 2000 server power the client machines. Ultimately, which environment is best (workgroup versus domain) depends on the tasks and applications being executed and the demands placed on the network.

Three different Windows 2000 server platforms exist:

- Windows 2000 Server

- Windows 2000 Advanced Server

- Windows 2000 Datacenter Server

Each platform possesses different capacities and purposes. Decision Tree 1.1 provides a decision tree for selecting the server platform that's best for specific needs.

Let's begin our look at the differences and characteristics of each of the server platforms with a look at Windows 2000 Server.

Windows 2000 Server at a Glance

Windows 2000 Server includes Windows 2000 Professional's features and further extends the strengths developed in the Windows NT Server 4 operating system. The new OS performs functions faster, offers a more reliable system architecture, boasts significantly increased scalability, and offers several new tools and utilities that simplify administration and lower costs.

Windows 2000 Server is designed to provide small to medium-sized businesses with robust workgroup and department server functionality. The platform is ideal for powering file-and-print sharing services, running applications, accessing Web services,

1

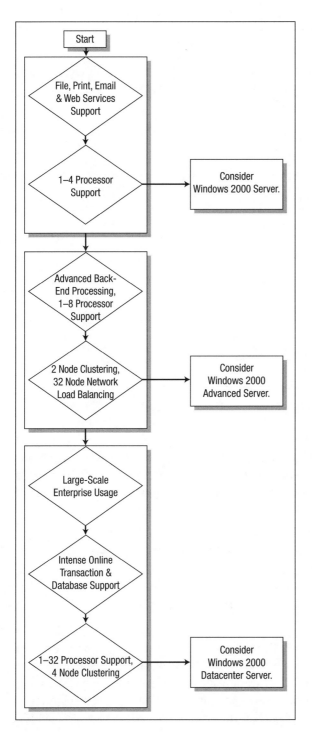

Decision Tree 1.1
The three Windows 2000 server platforms cover environments with a range of demands.

enabling remote communications, linking remote branches, and more in small to medium-sized enterprises.

Windows 2000 Server supports up to two processors on fresh installations. However, it can support four processors if you're upgrading from a Windows NT 4 platform. Windows 2000 Server also supports up to 4GB of RAM.

In addition to reliable performance and ease of administration, Windows 2000 Server offers new and enhanced features in several areas, namely:

- Active Directory changes the manner in which enterprise networks are administered.

- Management functions are simplified.

- Networking services and communications are improved.

- Web services are enhanced.

- Remote access services are improved.

- Security is strengthened.

- File storage is enhanced.

- Configuration management is improved.

- Integration with Microsoft Exchange Server 2000 is optimized.

- Printing functions are expanded and simplified.

Introducing Active Directory Services

Possibly the most important new feature in Windows 2000 is Active Directory. The Active Directory service greatly simplifies administration and maintenance of file, print, and Web services; users; security; site management; email messaging; printing; and numerous other critical functions.

Group policies, user accounts, computers, site management, and resources can all be administered from a single directory tree within Active Directory. Having access to several frequently used tools within a single interface saves IT professionals time and simplifies administration. Further, Active Directory helps eliminate the need for administrators to travel across a corporate campus or to a different site for the purposes of configuring client machines.

Because Active Directory consolidates information about users, sites, and resources in a single directory tree, multiple menus, consoles, and applications are no longer required. Users benefit, too. Simplified administration and management make it easier for users to locate files, printers, and other resources on a network. Control of such objects can be extended to users, which further reduces the demands placed on an organization's support and help desk.

In Windows NT 4, domains have practical limitations of 40,000 objects. If you're an IT administrator or manager for a small to medium-sized company, this limitation poses no issues. If you're responsible for IT management or systems administration at a large company, though, it can impose a prohibitive ceiling. In large-scale enterprise networks, this limitation results in the creation of multiple domains and numerous additional administrative headaches. These issues are nonexistent in Windows 2000 because millions of objects are now supported.

Active Directory's support of standards-based protocols, such as the Lightweight Directory Access Protocol (LDAP), and synchronization permit seamless integration with other vendors' systems, applications, directories, and services. Such integration enables control and management of multiple applications and programs from a single console.

NetWare engineers have enjoyed such simplicity for years. Unfortunately for them, NetWare share has fallen consistently as more and more NT networks are deployed.

You'll find many other services and utilities in Windows 2000 Server, too. Let's take a look at some of the new system management tools next.

New System Management Tools

Several new services contribute to simplified systems management in Windows 2000 Server. These services, combined with other capabilities such as remote installation and device-reporting features, assist administrators in improving their own operational efficiencies.

As an administrator, you'll enjoy the benefit of freeing up time previously spent on other tasks. As an IT manager or director, you'll appreciate the efficiency these tools bring to your department.

Introducing Dynamic Domain Name Service

The Domain Name Service (DNS) has been a staple service powering Internet communications for a long time. Now, get ready for the Dynamic Domain Name Service (DDNS), which eliminates the need for manually editing DNS databases when client configurations change or new machines are added to a network. Windows 2000 Server's support for DDNS means administrators can free even more time that was previously spent managing DNS databases.

The larger your organization, the more time you'll save. Better yet, the benefits don't stop there.

Introducing Remote Installation Services

Windows 2000 Professional, using a Windows 2000 Server's Remote Installation Services (RIS), can be installed on client machines over the network from one location. This capability saves valuable time by enabling administrators to install multiple client machines simultaneously from a central location.

Again, the larger your organization, the more time you'll save. Even if you're administering systems for a small to medium-sized company that's growing quickly, you'll enjoy the benefits of remotely installing systems. This is particularly true if your organization has many small satellite offices.

Enhanced Performance Monitoring and Optimization

Performance monitoring and optimization of both client machines and servers are enhanced. Windows Management Instrumentation (WMI) supports the collection of data based on the Desktop Management Task Force's Web-Based Enterprise Management (WBEM) standard.

Why is that important? WMI helps keep administrators knowledgeable regarding the performance of vendors' peripheral devices and applications. Information, including performance data and failure notifications, can be automatically collected from device drivers and peripherals and fed directly to an application for reporting.

Bolstered Terminal Services

Get ready for bolstered Terminal Services, too. Multiple client sessions are supported on the server, which can be configured to easily power many client applications.

For at least a while, there, thin was in. Everywhere you looked, you likely read about the rise of thin-client computing and the coming death of the PC. Don't be fooled so easily. PC power continues to march along according to Moore's Law (which stated—in 1965—that the processing power of computer chips would double every 18 months), and prices don't seem to be increasing much.

However, should thin clients become popular, or you find yourself having to support legacy hardware with not as much horsepower as you would like, Terminal Services might be able to save you. Although Terminal Services will require more resources on the server side, you can usually get by with far fewer resources on the client side.

Before you can do any networking, though, you must have protocols in place. Windows 2000 has made significant strides there, too.

Improved Networking Services and Support

Almost all of Windows 2000's enhancements and improvements mean nothing if you haven't networked systems in an enterprise. Windows 2000 Server now supports the following network protocols to help maximize networking efforts:

- *Multiple protocol routing*—Supported protocols include IP, IPX, AppleTalk, Open Shortest Path First (OSPF), and Routing Information Protocol (RIP).

- *High-speed Asynchronous Transfer Mode (ATM)*—The primary benefit of ATM's exceptional bandwidth is its capacity for transmitting voice, data, and video signals simultaneously. It's superfast.

1

- *Network Address Translation (NAT)*—Windows 2000 provides support for NAT, which can be used to translate, or share, IP addresses.

Enhanced Web Services

The Internet is computing's future. Microsoft embraced this fact by creating the .NET initiative. Thus, you should not be surprised that Web services in Windows 2000 include the widespread extension of Indexing Services, which originally appeared with Internet Information Server (IIS) 4. In Windows 2000 Server, server data is indexed automatically, providing enhanced search capabilities for users seeking resources on a network.

Further, Windows 2000 updates IIS to version 5. Internet Information Server 5 enables easy sharing of data over Internet and intranet networks. Among the most important new features is IIS's ability to plug into the Active Directory architecture. IIS 5 also offers Kerberos version 5, clustering capabilities, and improved administration.

The improvements in IIS help your network share information with others. But, what happens when remote users want to share information with your network? Those issues are addressed with refinements made to Windows' remote access services.

Remote Access Refinements and Improvements

Hang around most offices for a day or two, and you're liable to hear someone say he's got to head home to meet the cable guy or wait for a delivery, but he can send the file after he makes corrections there.

Remote access to local and wide area networks is becoming increasingly important. As greater demands are placed on employees' time, the ability to work from home or when traveling can be a lifesaver.

One of the most pressing challenges systems engineers face is the growing demand for providing secure access to these remote users. Not only do they require offsite access to email services, but file and resource access, too. Windows 2000 Server introduces several new features to help meet remote access requirements in enterprise environments and make the most use of the Windows 2000 Professional platform.

New remote access policies and profiles let administrators control connection properties with a high level of granularity. Remote access policies can be associated with profiles and preconfigured conditions, thereby enabling more secure use of network resources.

You'll also find support for the Remote Authentication Dial-In User Service, known as RADIUS. Should you need to log users' network sessions for billing purposes, such as you might wish to do in a law firm, public relations agency, or other professional firm, RADIUS permits the tracking of network usage. It can also authenticate users. ISPs have long used the service to calculate how much time subscribers spend online.

The actual configuration of network connections is simplified as a result of the new Connection Manager, which assists in creating and configuring dial-up connections. The Configuration Manager can be set using predefined settings, which can help reduce support calls.

Strengthened Security

Security is, quite simply, a huge consideration. Firewalls, share permissions, user accounts, passwords, and other tools and utilities are all deployed for the sole purpose of keeping people from seeing and using resources they shouldn't.

Windows 2000 Server includes many new protocols and changes to strengthen the data it's charged with protecting. These improvements also help Windows 2000 Server protect the integrity of data on Windows 2000 Professional machines when transmitted over local and wide area networks.

Windows 2000 Server security is bolstered in many ways, including the following:

- Active Directory can be used to restrict resource access.

- Policy usage has been enhanced.

- Security templates collect security attributes into a single location.

- Security templates can be used in their default states or customized.

- Support exists for important new security protocols, including Kerberos, IPSec, and L2TP.

- Windows 2000 Server permits the creation of computer-specific security databases.

Enhanced File Management Features

File services can be considered a server's bread-and-butter operation. Day in and day out, servers help control network file access. The goal, of course, is to have servers secure these resources so well that you don't even realize the servers are there.

In moving toward this goal, you'll find several new file management features have been improved. New file management features in Windows 2000 Server include the Distributed File System (Dfs), disk quotas to help ensure users don't exceed their share of network storage, and remote storage monitoring.

In Windows 2000 Server, a single directory tree consolidates files housed on multiple servers, even if the files are located in different physical locations. Dfs greatly simplifies users' access to files and resources. The benefit is particularly noticeable on large enterprise networks.

Possibly one of the peskiest issues IT departments have faced is users' hunger for file storage space. First, there were large graphics files for presentations, then audio and video clips. Then, to many IT departments' dismay, came the likes of Napster and Web sites offering bootleg movies. Now, users can download everything from Abba to Led Zeppelin to each reel of the newest *Star Wars* movie.

Disk quotas, which administrators have been seeking for quite a while, can be used to police and even limit the amount of disk space and network storage users are permitted to

1

consume. No longer must network administrators fear the release of a new George Lucas film, even if the cost/MB ratio of data storage is decreasing fast.

Windows 2000 Server grants administrators the ability to manage local disk space automatically, even if they're not seated at a user's machine. In addition, remote storage can be configured to kick in when preset limits are surpassed, so file management in Windows 2000 works both ways. You can set it to provide more disk space, should it be needed. On the other hand, you can use disk quotas to restrict additional storage, should you wish.

How all these new features are administered is another matter. That's where Windows 2000's improved configuration controls come into play.

Improved Configuration Management

Windows 2000 Server possesses many powerful new configuration utilities. They include the MMC, enhanced group policies, use of the Windows Scripting Host (WSH), and other specialized services.

Once an add-on for Windows NT 4, the MMC is a native administration tool in Windows 2000. Although the MMC serves as a powerful management utility within Windows 2000 Professional, its use is exponentially extended within Windows 2000 Server.

Because the console can include Active Directory objects within it, network functions, resources, management, security, and other tools can be consolidated within a single MMC. Add the fact that MMC is highly customizable, and it becomes one of the most powerful management tools ever extended to network administrators.

Enhanced group policies provide administrators with increased control and granularity of user settings. Administrators can now control specific workstations, data, and applications via group policies and from a single location.

WSH extends the functionality of clunky batch files left over from the days of MS-DOS. WSH helps administrators and users save time by automating common processes and tasks. The use of scripts on the server side can bring added functionality and automation to the client side, as well.

In addition to the management capabilities found in Windows 2000 Professional, Windows 2000 Server adds extras. It receives support for Microsoft Systems Management Server (SMS) version 2 and other server management services, including Indexing Services, WMI Control, Telephony settings, and more.

Tight Integration with Exchange 2000

Microsoft Exchange 2000 Server integrates extremely well with Windows 2000 Server. The Back Office platform is a natural for powering Windows 2000 Professional's messaging and collaboration services.

Working together, Windows 2000 server platforms and Exchange 2000 Server offer numerous integration benefits, including the following:

- Integration with Active Directory, which simplifies account administration.

- Use of the Active Directory Connector, which simplifies migration from Windows NT 4 and Exchange Server 5.5.

- Tight integration with IIS, resulting in faster performance for Internet-based applications.

- Support for multiple message databases, which decreases costs and increases application availability.

- Use of fault tolerant message routing, which helps ensure email messages are delivered quickly.

- Implementation of a single security model for both Windows 2000 and Exchange 2000.

- Deployment of policy-based administration, which enables configuring changes across servers, folders, and mailboxes via a single operation.

- Enhanced Outlook Web access for traveling employees and offsite staff.

Bolstered Printing Support

As with Windows 2000 Professional, printing receives several improvements in Windows 2000 Server. In addition to Windows 2000 Professional's printing, the server platform enjoys a few improvements of its own.

For example, printers and print permissions for multiple sites and domains can be administered from a single Active Directory console. Printers can also be published in Active Directory, making it easier for users to find the closest printer.

Another advantage is support for a wider range of printing devices. Windows 2000 Server supports printing on more than 2,500 printers from a wide variety of manufacturers, and that number is sure to grow.

Depending on the size of your organization, you may need to support e-commerce and enterprise-scale business applications. In that case, Windows 2000 Advanced Server may be for you.

Windows 2000 Advanced Server at a Glance

Windows 2000 Advanced Server contains all the features of Windows 2000 Server. As its name implies, it also possesses advanced capabilities. These additional services make Windows 2000 Advanced Server ideal for line-of-business and e-commerce applications.

Windows 2000 Advanced Server is targeted at large enterprises. It excels at powering database-intensive work, clustering, and load balancing. Instead of supporting two to four processors, Windows 2000 Advanced Server scales up to eight processors and supports up to 8GB of physical memory for Intel-based systems.

Windows 2000 Advanced Server provides the ability to link server clusters and have them work as a single system, while also providing very high levels of availability. Cluster services include support for MMC and Active Directory, rolling upgrades, Windows Internet Naming Service (WINS), Dfs, and Dynamic Host Configuration Protocol (DHCP). It also boasts a cross-platform API for the development and support of large-scale enterprise applications. Clustering, meanwhile, is supported for up to two nodes.

Windows 2000 Advanced Server can network load balance (NLB) up to 32 clustered servers. Software scaling enables administrators to add NLB-configured servers to preexisting server farms as required to increase a system's capacity. The benefits of NLB include highly scalable performance and high availability for the applications and data it powers.

Finally, commercial sorting of large data sets is optimized in Windows 2000 Advanced Server. This makes the Advanced Server ideal for data warehousing applications and large sort operations.

But, maybe your organization is looking for the serious computing capacity typically associated with Unix-powered servers. Microsoft has taken Unix in its sights and built an incredibly powerful, stable, and reliable platform with its Datacenter Server offering.

Windows 2000 Datacenter Server at-a-Glance

Microsoft released Windows 2000 Datacenter Server just a few months after Windows 2000 Professional, Windows 2000 Server, and Windows 2000 Advanced Server. Some observers will tell you Microsoft saved the best for last.

The Windows 2000 Datacenter Server scales higher than Windows 2000 Advanced Server. It's the most powerful server operating system Microsoft has ever produced, and it was designed to meet the most demanding levels of availability and scalability. We're talking about IT departments where uptime is measured using four or five nines, as in 99.99 percent uptime.

Fortune 500 companies, large academic institutions, application service providers, ISPs, and other large enterprises will want to consider Windows 2000 Datacenter Server for data warehousing, intensive online transaction processing, and applications service provisioning. Whereas other Windows platforms might not have been able to take the heat in the Unix kitchen, the Datacenter Server platform "Kicks it up a notch," as famous New Orleans chef and Food Network celebrity Emeril Lagasse says.

How much horsepower will it hold? A lot. Windows 2000 Datacenter Server provides support for up to 32 processors. It supports up to 64GB of physical memory. Clustering is supported for up to four nodes.

Windows 2000 Datacenter Server also enhances the scalability of its clustering and load balancing services. As a result, the Datacenter Server is optimized for large, enterprise projects. Applications include data warehousing, econometric analyses, science and engineering simulations, online transaction processing, server consolidations, and hosting of Web sites with heavy traffic.

Table 1.1   The Windows 2000 family.

Platform	Intended Market	Max Processors	Max RAM	Clustering
Windows 2000 Professional	Single installations to large organizations	2	4GB	N/A
Windows 2000 Server	Small to medium businesses	4	4GB	N/A
Windows 2000 Advanced Server	Medium to large businesses	8	8GB	2 nodes
Windows 2000 Datacenter Server	Large-scale enterprises	32	64GB	4 nodes

In fact, the OS is so powerful that it's available only through the Windows Datacenter Program. The program, according to Microsoft, provides customers with an integrated hardware, software, and service offering.

Do you need a scorecard yet to keep track of the different OSs' characteristics? Never fear. We've built one for you in the form of Table 1.1.

Summary

Windows 2000 has been promoted as "the next generation of PC computing." Will it enjoy the same success other Windows NT operating systems did? Will it pick up where Windows NT left off?

One thing's for sure. Some 10 million copies of Windows 2000 sold within its first year. By the end of 2001, an IBM representative has estimated that Windows 2000 Professional will be deployed in 85 percent of enterprise organizations. As a result, network administrators, support technicians, and IT executives will have to change the way they design, deploy, configure, and maintain corporate enterprise networks. New features will change the way users operate. New hardware will be needed. And most important, IT professionals will have to upgrade their skills to maintain pace with all of the changes.

For this reason, it's important that IT professionals understand all of the new enhancements and capabilities the new operating system offers. It's important that all IS staff understand the differences and capabilities of each Windows 2000 platform. This chapter aimed to keep you abreast of all the new features and utilities you'll find in Windows 2000.

Moving forward, we'll begin an in-depth, comprehensive look at Windows 2000 Professional. We'll start by taking a look at methods you can use to help calculate your total costs of ownership. We'll also take a look at what other companies' experiences have been and examine case studies of others' enterprise deployments.

Chapter 2

Ownership and Deployment Costs

Calculating Costs

In the movie *Mr. Mom,* Michael Keaton plays a stay-at-home dad who has just left corporate life. As can be expected, he struggles to learn and complete even simple household chores after his wife returns to the workforce. Soon, he feels threatened by the male manager who picks up his wife on the way to a business meeting. In an effort to demonstrate his manliness, Keaton's character discusses his latest home improvement project with the manager. When the manager asks what type of wiring he will use, Keaton's character replies "220, 222, whatever it takes." Keaton merely pulls a figure out of the air. It is often tempting to calculate the costs of a Windows 2000 Professional deployment in the same manner.

Some IT departments try to calculate the costs of a new client deployment by adding the dollar amount that must be spent on the new software. Other IT professionals estimate their costs by including in their figure the number of client access licenses that will be required. Unfortunately, both methods leave out considerable costs, making their total cost of ownership calculations as inaccurate as Keaton's 222-volt-wiring statement.

Although every organization has different needs, and no two organizations are alike, each and every institution that plans to deploy a new operating system should take several steps to ensure it prepares as accurate an estimate as possible.

Over the next several pages, and on the CD-ROM included with this text, we provide worksheets and spreadsheets you can use to help determine the costs your organization will incur as a result of a Windows 2000 Professional deployment. Among the factors to consider are the following:

- Analyst comments

- Required hardware upgrades

- Software costs

- Licensing expenses

- Deployment costs

- Network administration and support savings

As with any large purchase, time spent researching a software product's benefits, liabilities, competition, and enterprise impact is time well spent. Although some companies may skip calculating purchase, deployment, and administration costs altogether, those that do not skip this step will have a better idea not only of what they can expect from the new software, but also how long it will last and how the software will benefit them most.

Determining the cost savings is difficult. Although some costs are easy to calculate, such as the fees an organization must pay for software, licenses, and hardware upgrades, other costs prove more challenging to identify. For example, how can you estimate the human resource costs? Network administrators and others will require training. In addition, IT staffers will have to dedicate considerable hours preparing for and completing a migration or installation.

When Windows 2000 is deployed, calculating the savings realized due to operational efficiency improvements is doubly difficult. Calculating the value of employee productivity improvements is always a slippery proposition. Thus, we'll focus on providing you with hard and fast calculations you can use to determine your actual software, licensing, and hardware costs. Meanwhile, we'll point you in the right direction regarding strategies you can use to determine the costs your organization will incur as a result of deploying the new operating system, while also examining the savings your organization will realize as the result of productivity improvements. In the end, you'll want to be sure to review all cost calculations with your accounting, finance, human resources, IT, and legal departments.

Let's start the cost determination process by reviewing analyst comments. Are trusted industry analysts praising a new product for its ease of migration and improved reliability, or are pundits warning against incompatibilities and administrative nightmares? Their comments will give you an idea of what lies ahead.

In the case of Windows 2000 Professional, the news is mixed. Although almost everyone agrees that you'll enjoy enhanced features and improved reliability, the migration will take a toll. When you're preparing your Windows 2000 Professional deployment or expansion, consider what the analysts have to say.

Analyst Comments

Industry analysts and consultants make a living studying IT industry developments and identifying trends. Their careers live and die based on the advice they provide. They also publish forecasts and results of painstaking research.

Analysts' predictions, although sometimes slightly off target, often prove insightful. Although we are not suggesting you perform each and every action an analyst or consultant recommends, we feel their comments, reports, and research bear credence.

What do the industry's most-respected analysts have to say about Windows 2000? Quite a bit, actually.

Many analysts have made bold statements. Many state that Windows 2000 deployments decrease a company's expenses, offer attractive costs of ownership over the operating system's life span, and improve an organization's efficiencies.

According to a report audited by Gartner Group that Microsoft published on its Web site, a study undertaken by Eastman Chemical Co. predicted that deploying Windows 2000 Professional "can help Eastman achieve an 8 percent annual reduction in Desktop Operations Costs, and pay for itself, and the cost of the desktop lease refresh, within one year." Further, the study predicted that Eastman could reduce the costs of software deployments and help desk operations. (For more details on this study, refer to **www.microsoft.com/ windows2000/guide/professional/profiles/eastman.asp**.)

All those benefits don't come without a price, however. Consider Gartner analyst Thomas Bittman's comments, published in February 2001 by C|NET.com (see **http://news.cnet.com/ news/0-1003-201-4761583-0.html?tag=st.ne.ni.gartnerbox.gartnercomm**): "Windows 2000 Server delivered on many of Microsoft's promises for improvements in scalability, uptime, and directory services." However, he warned that organizations are not rushing to deploy Windows 2000's full functionality immediately. Instead, he noted that most companies are introducing the new operating system "gradually and pragmatically."

IDC analyst Roger Kay's statements support Bittman's comments. In a C|NET.com article published in December 2000 (see **http://news.cnet.com/news/0-1003-200-4165668.html**), Kay said "Switching to Windows 2000 turned out to be more difficult than many people thought it would be."

Although some companies struggle with enterprise-wide deployments, Windows 2000 Professional acceptance has proven to be better. In a Bloomberg News item published by C|NET.com in December 2000 (see **http://news.cnet.com/news/0-1003-200-3990384.html**), IDC reported that Windows 2000 client sales were "going faster than the version of the software designed for servers."

Although Windows 2000 deployments and migrations won't be easy, the benefits are clear. Improved reliability, simplified administration, and enhanced security are only a few of the advantages.

An article published by *Computerworld* in February 2000 (see **www.computerworld.com/ cwi/story/0,1199,NAV47_STO43017,00.html**), when Windows 2000 was released, included total cost of ownership (TCO) savings companies could expect to experience as a result of Windows 2000 deployments. The article noted that savings of 10 to 26 percent were possible in the case of sample companies whose TCO figures were researched and confirmed by independent third parties, including Gartner Group Inc. and Giga Information Group Inc.

Microsoft released the TCO figures the *Computerworld* article references in a conference call. Obviously, Microsoft worked to place the best spin on the numbers, whether they were posted on its Web site as with Eastman, or released in a conference call when Windows 2000 debuted. Nevertheless, it should be clear that Windows 2000 can result in significant cost savings as a result of the improved efficiencies and reliability it provides an enterprise.

Of course, it's important to calculate the costs of a Windows 2000 Professional deployment. The first factor to consider is the expense your organization will incur as a result of having to upgrade system hardware.

Required Hardware Upgrades

Many IT professionals forget to consider the impact that necessary hardware upgrades will have on their budgets. You will do nothing for your career if you purchase a new operating system, exhausting all your funds in the process, and then determine the systems in place do not possess sufficient hardware resources to run the software.

You can avoid such surprises by conducting a physical audit of the hardware on systems to ensure that each and every machine possesses appropriate components. When you're calculating a deployment budget, be sure to include the costs of all new replacement systems and hardware upgrades.

If you'll be migrating to a native Windows 2000 environment, in which Windows 2000 will power all clients and servers, don't forget to consider the costs of server upgrades, too.

The worksheet in the following section is a sample of a spreadsheet that you can use to calculate which hardware upgrades will be necessary and how much they'll cost.

Note: The CD-ROM bundled with this book includes each worksheet published in this text. Further, it combines all the cost configuration worksheets into a single worksheet, titled TCOCALC.XLS.

The Windows 2000 Professional Hardware Cost Forecasting Worksheet

Use the following worksheet (a blank version of which can be found on the CD-ROM included with this book) after you use the Windows 2000 Professional Deployment Worksheet in Chapter 3 to learn which systems will require hardware upgrades or replacement before Windows 2000 can be deployed. Although sample entries are provided here, you will have to factor your own costs based on the purchasing relationships you have established with your respective vendors.

After you've determined which systems require upgrading or replacing, as well as the costs that will be incurred, you're ready to calculate the software costs associated with a Windows 2000 deployment.

Systems receiving Windows 2000.					
Location	Computer Name	First Component Needed	Second Component Needed	Third Component Needed	Total Price
Bowling Green/ Alumni Office	Sales1SRVR	128MB RAM	10GB Hard Disk	NA	$325
Bowling Green/ Finance	Accounting4	64MB RAM	NA	NA	$75
Bowling Green/ Finance	Accounting 5	64MB RAM	2GB Hard disk	NA	$175
Bowling Green/ Hockey Arena	Tickets1	2GB Hard Disk	NA	NA	$100
Bowling Green/ Administration Office	Admissions2	32MB RAM	2GB Hard Disk	NIC	$175
Bowling Green/ Administration Office	Admissions5	64MB RAM	NA	NA	$75
Bowling Green/ Operations	Sales1	P-350 Processor	NA	NA	$200
Bowling Green/ Operations	Sales2	P-350 Processor	NA	NA	$200
Bowling Green/ Operations	Sales14	New Machine	NA	NA	$1,300
Perrysburg/ Residence	Sales 3	64MB RAM	NA	NA	$75
Perrysburg/ Residence	Sales 4	64MB RAM	NA	NA	$75
Total					$2,775

Software Costs

Some costs are easier to predict than others. Certainly, the actual cost of a software purchase can be calculated with confidence. Microsoft publishes the cost of various Windows 2000 platforms on its Web site.

Keep in mind that we're working with street prices here. You could expect to pay these amounts if you walk into a computer superstore or office center near your business and pluck a copy off the shelf. Of course, most companies do not purchase software in that fashion. Odds are your IT department negotiates multiple purchase discounts directly with Microsoft, so your pricing is likely to be different than those shown in Table 2.1.

For the purposes of demonstrating software cost calculation, we will assume your organization is paying the street price. Remember, though, that your organization will probably

Table 2.1 Street prices for Windows 2000 software.

Windows 2000 Product	Description	Price
Windows 2000 Professional Version Upgrade	Windows NT Workstation 3.51 or 4.0 Upgrade	$149 (includes $70 rebate)
Windows 2000 Professional Product Upgrade	Windows 9x Upgrade	$219
Windows 2000 Professional	Standard Windows 2000 Professional OS	$319
Windows 2000 Server Version Upgrade	Windows NT Server 3.51 or 4.0 Upgrade	$599 (includes 10 upgrade Client Access Licenses, or CALs)
Windows 2000 Server	Standard Windows 2000 Server OS	$1,199 (includes 10 CALs)
Windows 2000 Advanced Server	Standard Windows 2000 Advanced Server OS	$3,999 (includes 25 CALs)
Windows 2000 Datacenter Server	Standard Windows 2000 Datacenter Server OS	Set by server vendor

negotiate improved prices depending on its size and the type of relationship it has with Microsoft. In the worksheet that follows (which can be found on the accompanying CD-ROM), replace the stock street prices with the amount your firm negotiates.

The Windows 2000 Professional Software Cost Forecasting Worksheet

Use the following worksheet to conduct an audit and determine how many systems will be receiving Windows 2000 Professional. When you're conducting the audit, pay close attention to the current operating system a machine is using. Don't forget that, in many cases, you will not have to purchase a standard version of Microsoft Windows 2000 Professional. Instead, upgrades are supported by several operating systems, as noted in Chapters 1 and 3.

After you've determined which systems support upgrading, which machines will require an upgrade purchase, and which will necessitate a standard purchase, all that's left is for you to plug in the Windows 2000 Professional purchase price you negotiated with your vendor or directly from Microsoft. For this explanation, we'll use the scenario from the last worksheet.

After you've determined which software programs you must purchase, as well as the costs that will be incurred, you're ready to calculate the licensing expenses associated with a Windows 2000 deployment.

Licensing Expenses

Software licenses must be purchased for each Windows 2000 system that connects to a Windows 2000 Server. Just purchasing Windows 2000 Professional or Windows 2000 Server doesn't give you that license. When you purchase the Windows 2000 Professional operating system, you receive the operating system software and the accompanying user license permitting the software's use (within the confines of the End User Licensing

Systems receiving Windows 2000.				
Location	**Computer Name**	**Current OS Version**	**Type of Purchase Required**	**Price**
Bowling Green/ Alumni Office	Sales1SRVR	Windows NT Server 4.0	Windows 2000 Server Version Upgrade	$325
Bowling Green/ Finance	Accounting4	Windows NT Workstation 4.0	Windows 2000 Professional Version Upgrade	$149
Bowling Green/ Finance	Accounting 5	Windows NT Workstation 4.0	Windows 2000 Professional Version Upgrade	$149
Bowling Green/ Hockey Arena	Tickets1	Windows 95	Windows 2000 Professional Product Upgrade	$219
Bowling Green/ Administration Office	Admissions2	Windows 95	Windows 2000 Professional Product Upgrade	$219
Bowling Green/ Administration Office	Admissions5	Windows 95	Windows 2000 Professional Product Upgrade	$219
Bowling Green/ Operations	Sales1	Windows 95	Windows 2000 Professional Product Upgrade	$219
Bowling Green/ Operations	Sales2	Windows 95	Windows 2000 Professional Product Upgrade	$219
Bowling Green/ Operations	Sales14	New Machine	Windows 2000 Professional Standard Version Upgrade	$319
Perrysburg/ Residence	Sales 3	Windows NT Workstation 4.0	Windows 2000 Professional	$149
Perrysburg/ Residence	Sales 4	Windows 95	Windows 2000 Professional Product Upgrade	$219
Total				$2,405

Agreement, or EULA). You do not receive a required license for connecting to other Windows 2000 servers.

Note: When you purchase a Windows 2000 server platform, typically a set number of licenses are included (usually 5 or 10). You must purchase extra CALs should you have additional machines that will be connecting to the Windows 2000 server.

Do not forget to budget properly for Terminal Services licensing. If your organization is using or will deploy Terminal Services, you must purchase the appropriate number of Terminal Services CALs. CALs are required for each system that accesses a Windows 2000 server. Clients accessing Terminal Services require additional CALs.

Table 2.2 lists the typical street prices for Windows 2000 CALs. Terminal Services licensing fees are also included.

Table 2.2 Typical street prices and Terminal Services licensing fees for Windows 2000 CALs.

CAL	Price
5 Windows 2000 Upgrade CALs	$100
20 Windows 2000 Upgrade CALs	$399
5 Windows 2000 Terminal Services Upgrade CALs	$359
20 Windows 2000 Terminal Services Upgrade CALs	$1,289
5 Windows 2000 CALs	$199
20 Windows 2000 CALs	$799
5 Windows 2000 Terminal Services CALs	$749
20 Windows 2000 Terminal Services CALs	$2,669
Unlimited Windows 2000 Server Internet Connector licenses	$1,199
200 concurrent anonymous Windows 2000 Terminal Services Internet Connector licenses	$9,999

Tip: Microsoft offers volume license pricing, which can reduce many enterprise's costs. Organizations that subscribe to Microsoft's Upgrade Advantage/Maintenance program or have an Enterprise Agreement in force are eligible for free Windows 2000 upgrades from Windows NT products.

The following worksheet calculates the license costs that would result using the scenario from the previous worksheets in this chapter.

The Windows 2000 Professional Licensing Cost Forecasting Worksheet

You can use the following worksheet (which can be found blank on the accompanying CD-ROM) to calculate the number of server CALs and Terminal Services CALs your organization will require. When you're budgeting licensing costs for Windows 2000 enterprise deployments, be sure to consider the following three factors:

- Some licenses, usually 5 to 10, come with Windows 2000 Server.

- Additional CALs may be purchased as upgrades, depending on the current Windows NT CALs an organization possesses.

- Organizations using Microsoft BackOffice software must also purchase the appropriate number of BackOffice CALs because Windows 2000 licenses and CALs do not cover BackOffice licensing.

For the purpose of this sample, we are omitting the preceding considerations.

After you've determined the number of licenses and CALs needed to complete a migration, you can assign dollar costs. For large license purchases, calculate costs by factoring roughly for the following:

- $20 for each Windows 2000 Upgrade CAL required

- $40 for each Windows 2000 CAL required

- $142 for each Windows 2000 Terminal Services CAL required

- $67 for each Windows 2000 Terminal Services Upgrade CAL required

Again, understand that the prices shown here are street prices reflected at the time this text went to press. The pricing you find could well vary widely. Microsoft could change its pricing structure, or your organization may negotiate a better pricing model.

When you have a handle on actual hardware, software, and licensing costs, you should turn your attention to calculating the costs of deployment.

Calculating Windows 2000 license and CAL fees.

Location	Computer Name	Current OS Version	Windows 2000 CALs	Windows 2000 Upgrade CALs	Windows 2000 Terminal Services CAL	Windows 2000 Terminal Services Upgrade CALs	Price
Bowling Green/ Alumni Office	Sales1SRVR	Windows NT Server 4.0	0	1	0	0	$20
Bowling Green/ Finance	Accounting4	Windows NT Workstation 4.0	0	1	0	0	$20
Bowling Green/ Finance	Accounting 5	Windows NT Workstation 4.0	0	1	0	0	$20
Bowling Green/ Hockey Arena	Tickets1	Windows 95	0	1	0	0	$20
Bowling Green/ Administration Office	Admissions2	Windows 95	0	1	0	0	$20
Bowling Green/ Administration Office	Admissions5	Windows 95	0	1	0	0	$20
Bowling Green/ Operations	Sales1	Windows 95	0	1	0	0	$20
Bowling Green/ Operations	Sales2	Windows 95	0	1	0	0	$20
Bowling Green/ Operations	Sales14	New Machine	1	0	0	0	$40
Perrysburg/ Residence	Sales 3	Windows NT Workstation 4.0	0	1	1	0	$162
Perrysburg/ Residence	Sales 4	Windows 95	0	1	1	0	$162
Total			1	10	2	0	$524

Deployment Costs

Calculating deployment costs is more difficult than determining hardware, software, and licensing expenses. However, forecasting deployment costs is easier than trying to figure out network and support administration savings. Take this disclaimer seriously, because a myriad of factors can derail even the best-prepared forecasts.

Trained employees could leave a migration midstream, for example. You might need additional systems that weren't originally considered. Your organization could add an additional remote site or two between the time the purchase decision is made and the deployment occurs.

Although you can't plan for every contingency, you can plan for most deployment costs. Essentially, your organization will experience additional costs associated with a Windows 2000 deployment in these two core areas:

• Training

• Time (required to complete the deployment)

Keep in mind that different employees learn at different rates. Some perform better in classroom environments, whereas others excel in a small test lab with self-paced training texts.

Certainly, classroom instruction provides an uninterrupted environment and generally excellent training materials. Should you pursue classroom training, plan on spending $1,300 to $1,700 in training costs and study materials for each IT employee you wish to become certified as a Microsoft Certified Professional (MCP). Add another $1,300 to $1,700 for each additional exam you wish an IT staff member to pass using a formal training provider. Be prepared to invest $9,000 to $10,000 (or more) in classroom training and instruction for each employee you wish to achieve Microsoft Certified Systems Engineer (MCSE) status.

Self-paced training is a much less expensive endeavor. Typically, you can purchase an entire line of MCSE materials (including study aids) for less than $2,500. An MCP, meanwhile, can be earned for as little as a $200 to $350 investment. Those funds can be invested in exam study guides, books, and even CD-ROM tutorials.

The best training method for your organization depends on several factors, not the least of which is employees' preference. Even if you elect self-paced training, be prepared to devote considerable in-house time to setting up a test lab.

The second additional deployment cost comes into play here. Windows 2000 deployments require a tremendous amount of time to plan, organize, coordinate, research, design, prepare, implement, and administer. The actual number of IT manager, network adminis-trator, and support hours required to complete a deployment depends on several factors, including the size of your organization, the current technology platforms in use, the skill sets the IT department possesses, how much training is required, how many locations the organization supports, and the hardware in place, among other items.

The Windows 2000 Professional Training Cost Forecast Worksheet

Although there are no hard-and-fast rules, you can use the following worksheet (which can be found blank on the accompanying CD-ROM) to estimate the training dollars that will be required to achieve the requisite knowledge among the IT staff members in a department. Use these results only as a baseline, because the myriad factors mentioned in the preceding sections could sway your forecasts dramatically.

The time, measured in hours, that it takes an organization to prepare is even more difficult to calculate. Regardless, you can try to create a reasonable baseline. Use the worksheet in the following section to calculate the amount of time that must be devoted to preparing and deploying Windows 2000.

Although the estimates will be different for each organization, we have attempted to create a baseline you can customize to meet the specific needs of your enterprise. Although some organizations will use Norton Ghost to create preconfigured disk images and deploy Windows 2000 Professional, others might try installing the client OS over a network or using sophisticated answer files and unattended installations. Therefore, you should use the figures from Table 2.3 only as a foundation from which to begin your forecasts.

Using the values in Table 2.3, the entire planning and deployment time for a single client is 1.35 hours. The entire planning and deployment time for a single server is 6.35 hours.

Calculating Windows 2000 training costs.			
IT Staff Member	**Expertise Needed**	**Training Needed**	**Cost**
NetAdmin 1	MCSE	Self-paced training	$2,500
NetAdmin 2	MCSE	Classroom instruction	$10,000
NetAdmin 3	MCSE	Self-paced training	$2,500
Help Desk 1	MCP	Self-paced training	$350
Help Desk 2	MCP	Classroom instruction	$1,500
Senior Help Desk	MCP	Self-paced training	$350
Total			$17,200

The Windows 2000 Professional Time Investment Forecast

Use the following worksheet (which can be found blank on the accompanying CD-ROM) to create a baseline estimation of the time an IT department will have to invest in preparing and deploying Windows 2000.

Table 2.3   Baseline estimates of the time required to install and configure basic systems and services.

Task	Average Completion Time
Check system to determine Windows 2000 compatibility	0.20 hour
Design network infrastructure/per client	0.20 hour
Design network infrastructure/per server	0.75 hour
Install and configure Windows 2000 Professional	0.75 hour
Install and configure Windows 2000 Server	5.0 hours
Prepare Active Directory entry/per computer and user	0.20 hour
Prepare Active Directory entry/per server	0.40 hour

The total number of training and support hours is 1,539.6. For the preceding worksheet calculations, it is assumed that the network administrators participated equally in designing the network infrastructure for each client and server. The network administrators also assumed responsibility for installing the server operating systems and configuring server information in Active Directory.

The Help Desk and Support staff members, meanwhile, created user accounts in Active Directory for client systems, as well as installed Windows 2000 Professional on client machines. Support personnel also checked client systems for migration compatibility, and network administrators confirmed that the server hardware was Windows 2000–compatible. When you're making your calculations, be sure to budget time for any needed hardware repairs or upgrades, too.

Considering the total hours the Windows 2000 Professional Time Investment Forecast worksheet produced, and considering the times allotted are only baselines (because many companies may have proprietary software and systems that add time to each deployment),

Calculating time required to deploy Windows 2000.

IT Staff Member	Expertise Needed	Training Time Required	Number of Client Systems Supported	Number of Server Systems Supported	Total Support Time
NetAdmin 1	MCSE	400 hours	30	2	18.7 hours
NetAdmin 2	MCSE	400 hours	30	2	18.7 hours
NetAdmin 3	MCSE	400 hours	30	2	18.7 hours
Help Desk 1	MCP	60 hours	30	0	34.5 hours
Help Desk 2	MCP	60 hours	30	0	34.5 hours
Help Desk 3	MCP	60 hours	30	0	34.5 hours
Total		1,380	180	6	159.60

you can easily see why analysts state Windows 2000 deployment is more difficult than many IT professionals anticipated. This is especially true considering that the worksheet was calculated using a sample enterprise with just 6 servers and 90 users.

But, we do have good news. Organizations deploying Windows 2000 often claim significant improvements in reliability and operational efficiencies, as noted earlier in this chapter. Although measuring these improvements is difficult, you can take an educated stab at it beforehand.

Network Administration and Support Savings

Almost everyone agrees that network administration and support tasks are greatly simplified *after* Windows 2000 is deployed. Whether you're talking to Gartner, Giga, or another authority, Windows 2000 delivers on Microsoft's many promises of improvements. Following the introduction of Windows 2000, Microsoft undertook a heavy advertising campaign aimed at communicating Windows 2000 Server's "five-nines" potential to help spread the word.

What was Redmond trying to say with its five-nines campaign? Windows 2000 Server can achieve 99.999 percent uptime. Microsoft claims that, configured and administered properly, Windows 2000 servers providing five-nines reliability will experience only five minutes of downtime per year. As a result, the time your network administrators and other IT staff spent putting out fires in the past by rescuing failed servers can be devoted to new tasks. Support personnel that used to field calls related to server and client outages will benefit from the enhanced reliability, too.

Quantifying those improvements is difficult, though. Calculating the time and cost savings an IT department will experience as a result of a Windows 2000 deployment is an academic exercise that truly requires involvement from a number of participants. Thus, creating a spreadsheet or chart permitting you to specify explicitly the savings your firm will enjoy as a result of its Windows 2000 deployment would be a disservice. You will simply have too many variables related to your organization to list.

Should executives or finance personnel be pressuring you for data, point them to the research conducted by Gartner, Giga, and other analysts. You could also point them to the article "From Investment Boom to Bust" in the March 3, 2001, issue of *The Economist*. The respected UK financial publication explored the link between the United States' investment in information technology and an associated increase in productivity. The article states that "several studies suggest that increases in the amount of IT capital per worker . . . have accounted for two-fifths of the total increase in labour productivity growth since 1995."

Thus, it won't be hard to establish a link between IT spending and improved corporate efficiencies. Other employees in an enterprise benefit when new technologies are deployed, too; the benefits aren't limited to IT staff. However, you'll need to dig deeper with the help of your organization's accounting, finance, and IT executives to ensure you present relevant data that they can use to make informed purchase decisions.

Calculations related to cost, reliability, security, operational, and administrative savings will depend on the same variables discussed in the preceding sections. If your organization is currently running on Microsoft Windows 95 and experiencing troublesome client failures daily, most of those problems may go away when Windows 2000 Professional is deployed.

As any seasoned IT professional in the trenches will tell you, though, replacing an OS to fix old problems often creates new issues. Thus, you're always going to be trying to hit a moving target. You may eliminate the typical "My screen froze" help desk calls, but you'll have to begin fielding "My old applications won't work" calls. You may make it easier to expand a corporate network using Windows 2000, but you could run into issues trying to configure Active Directory. You may eliminate data storage issues, but run into unanticipated hardware incompatibilities.

Either way, rest assured. The stresses and issues you dealt with in the Windows 9x and Windows NT platforms of the past may go away, but new ones are certain to arise. Don't let these problems worry you too much, though. That's called job security.

We hope that you'll find the answers to the new problems that arise in the rest of this book. We begin discussing technical aspects of the new operating system in the next chapter.

Summary

Accurately forecasting your organization's Windows 2000 deployment costs is a difficult proposition. Many factors influence costs, including the size of your organization, the number of sites it operates, the hardware in place, the software being used, and more.

To create an accurate estimate of the expenses you will incur moving to Windows 2000, be sure to consider these six key areas:

- Analyst comments

- Required hardware upgrades

- Software costs

- Licensing expenses

- Deployment costs

- Network administration and support savings

After you've reviewed these core expenses and savings, you and your organization will understand better the enhancement and improvements you stand to realize from a Windows 2000 deployment. Although Windows 2000—and Windows 2000 Professional in particular—have been praised for enhanced reliability, efficiency, and administration, don't expect your deployment to be trouble-free.

In fact, you could encounter difficulty from the start, when you install your first Windows 2000 Professional client system. In the next chapter, you will examine the ins and outs associated with installing Windows 2000 Professional.

Chapter 3

Windows 2000 Professional Installation and Deployment

First Things First

You've heard and read all about Windows 2000 Professional's benefits. Faster performance, strengthened security, improved network communications, simplified administration, and a more approachable interface for users are just a few of the advantages Windows 2000 offers IT professionals.

However, none of these improvements and enhancements will be realized until the operating system is installed. Although the Windows 2000 client system is easy to install, installation is no longer as simple as dropping in a few floppy disks or a CD-ROM and answering a few simple questions as the installation program executes.

In some cases, you'll be able to install Windows 2000 Professional with that little effort. In medium- to large-sized enterprises, though, Windows 2000 Professional's cost benefits come into play as soon as you prepare to install the operating system. Even if you're administering systems for a small business, you'll find the new installation and deployment features of Windows 2000 Professional assist with its deployment, no matter how large the setting. It's just that the benefits resulting from support for disk imaging, remote installation, and network-based installations become exponentially more valuable in larger organizations.

Consider the facts. If you're rolling out 15 systems, and Windows 2000 Professional's new disk-imaging feature saves you 40 minutes per client deployment, you've just saved 600 minutes, which translates to 10 hours.

However, suppose you're the administrator for a medium-sized business with 325 systems that require upgrading. If you save the same 40 minutes per machine, you've just won an extra 216 hours to devote to other IT issues. That's more than a week!

As you can see, it's with the deployment of Windows 2000 Professional that the rubber meets the road. Before you can start, though, be sure the target client systems possess sufficient resources to power the new operating system.

In this chapter, we'll examine the importance of creating a preinstallation checklist. In addition, we'll examine Windows 2000's minimum, as well as recommended, hardware requirements. Although the operating system will run using Microsoft's minimum hardware requirements, you should consider using the minimum *recommended* resource configuration. Systems with the minimum required hardware configuration take longer to boot, complete processes, open applications, complete tasks, and finish other operations. You and your users will be much more satisfied using systems that meet minimum recommended requirements.

In addition, in this chapter we'll examine the different Windows 2000 Professional licensing options that are available. We'll take exhaustive looks at CD-ROM–based installations, network-based installations, deployments using Remote Installation Services (RIS), and cloning-based deployments.

You'll find Windows 2000's installation and setup routines similar to those of the Windows 9x and Windows NT platforms. They do have important differences, however, that we'll cover in detail. For example, Windows 2000's new configuration tools and services make Windows 2000 easier to install, whether you're deploying it with the CD-ROM, over a network, via disk duplication, or using Remote Installation Services. To maximize Windows 2000 Professional's new installation and deployment features, and to ensure your organization enjoys the best return on investment it can, you absolutely must plan deployments in advance.

Take a little extra time on the front-side, and you'll be rewarded handsomely. Remember, an ounce of prevention is worth a pound of cure, and that holds true for Windows 2000 Professional deployments. By carefully planning your deployment, and ensuring you have all the necessary hardware and software information beforehand, you will avoid common problems.

Should you encounter difficulty, this chapter will also target troubleshooting strategies. Let's get started by taking a look at your preflight checklist.

The Preflight Checklist

Before any important National Football League contest, head coaches invest a significant amount of time preparing a game plan. Doing so ensures their teams are prepared for all the different defensive schemes they'll see from their opponent, tactics are in place for scoring touchdowns, and accommodations have been set for overcoming obstacles that arise. You'll need a similar game plan for deploying Windows 2000 Professional.

Although developing such a game plan might sound like a daunting task, it could be worse. You won't have 300-pound linebackers pummeling you into a hard concrete slab padded only by a thin strip of green plastic grass. Instead, you're likely to have 300 users (not to mention your director or CIO) complaining bitterly that they can't access the Internet, retrieve files, or print.

Although Windows 2000 Professional's setup and installation routines are similar to those you're most likely familiar with from past Windows NT platforms, important differences exist, including the following:

- New installation options, such as the use of Remote Installation Services and support for disk duplication

- Plug-and-play support

- Windows 2000 Professional's requirement for additional system resources

In addition to knowledge of these differences and others, IT departments should properly design and plan their deployments. Although network architecture and infrastructure design are beyond the scope of this text (in fact, entire doctoral dissertations will be written on the subject), we will examine the following preflight checklist planning and deployment steps:

- Hardware compatibility issues and requirements

- Software application compatibility and requirements

- Installation partitions

- File system selection

- Licensing options

- Namespace determination

- Installation method options

Because everything begins with the hardware, let's begin our look at Windows 2000 Professional installation and deployment there.

Hardware Compatibility Issues and Requirements

Power, or system resources, and compatibility problems are the two biggest hardware issues you'll face. With proper preparation, though, you can eliminate most issues.

Because Windows 2000 Professional uses the NT kernel, and because it uses several new critical services, compatibility and outright system horsepower requirements are increased. You'll want to be sure you've prepared for the increased demands.

Your first step should be to conduct a review of the current systems already in use that will be migrated to Windows 2000. If you're purchasing new equipment for those new machines, or if you're purchasing new systems, you'll want to ensure all the components you buy are compatible. Thus, you'll want to get to know the Windows 2000 Hardware Compatibility List (HCL). Whereas the NT 4 HCL used to exist only as a long text file, Redmond has made significant improvements. You can still find the old-style text file (HCL.TXT). It's on the Windows 2000 CD-ROM, under the Support folder.

However, we recommend you visit Microsoft's Web site for the latest in compatibility information. The CD-ROM's text file is already out-of-date. Just think, how many new hardware peripherals have been introduced in the last six months, the last year, or the last year and a half? They won't be included in the HCL text file because they didn't exist when the CD was burned. Or, if they had already been introduced, there may not have been sufficient time to test the devices for compatibility, so even though they might work and work well, they won't be listed.

You can find Microsoft's up-to-date HCL on its Web site. Just surf to the following Internet address: **www.microsoft.com/hwtest/hcl**. At the time this book was sent to press, you could also find complete hardware compatibility information for Windows 2000 here: **www.microsoft.com/windows2000/upgrade/compat/search/devices.asp**.

What's nice about the latter URL is that it permits searching on the following criteria:

- The name of the company that made the device

- The device's model number

- The device type

You'll want to confirm that all your systems' devices and peripherals, such as the following, are listed on the HCL:

- CD-ROM and CD-R/RW drives

- Controller cards

- Digital cameras

- DVD drives

- Input devices

- Modems

- Monitors and video displays

- Motherboards and chipsets

- Networking devices, including network interface cards (NICs)

- PC Cards

- Printing devices

- Scanners

- Smart card readers

- Sound cards

- Storage devices

- TV tuners

- Uninterrupted power supplies

- Universal Serial Bus (USB) devices

- Video and graphics cards

If you can't find a device listed on the HCL, don't panic. Try the vendor's Web site next. You're likely to find the manufacturer provides its own driver.

If you find a driver provided by the manufacturer, feel free to give it a go. Keep in mind, though, that Microsoft may not have certified it for use with Windows 2000 Professional. Third-party drivers can prove unreliable, so a little suspicion and skepticism are warranted.

Microsoft will tell you that you should use only hardware that's included on the HCL. Hardware has to meet numerous requirements to receive a compatible rating, so keep that in mind. It doesn't mean you can't use a device that hasn't been proven compatible. It just means you should be very careful.

Even if the device in question isn't critical, such as an inexpensive sound card, don't assume it's OK to just roll it out. It's possible that the sound card driver could overwhelm a system's CPU requesting data it's never going to receive. Or, it could interfere with other properly configured peripherals.

Remember, too, how Microsoft usually approaches incompatible hardware. Its technical support staff generally (and understandably) won't support incompatible devices.

After you've ensured you have compatible devices, you're ready to focus on the second hardware issue: power. Along with all of Windows 2000's new features and services come increased system requirements.

Odds are many of your older systems will require hardware upgrades. CPU cycles, RAM, and hard disk space all play critical roles in contributing to smooth operations when you're running Windows 2000 Professional.

You should examine all your systems to ensure they meet minimum requirements announced by Microsoft. Again, we feel it's best that your systems meet minimum *recommended* requirements. You should take this step, of course, before the Windows 2000 installation and deployment process begins. It really should be part of the planning process. Otherwise, you run the risk of delaying deployments later.

Windows 2000 Professional operates slowly on systems possessing the minimum hardware requirements, as shown in Table 3.1. We've run it on a common Toshiba Satellite Pro with the following configuration:

- Pentium I 120MHz CPU (see note)

- 32MB RAM (Microsoft recommends 64MB RAM)

- 1.2GB hard disk (see note)

Table 3.1   Microsoft's minimum hardware requirements for Windows 2000 Professional.

Component	Requirement
CPU	Pentium-compatible 133MHz or higher (up to two processors are supported)
Input devices	Keyboard and mouse or other input device
Disk space	650MB free space on a 2GB or larger hard disk
RAM	32MB minimum
Secondary drives	12X or better CD-ROM, 3.5" disk drive, or 10/100MB NIC
Display	VGA or better

Note: Microsoft previously published 650MB as the minimum hard disk size. The Setup program doesn't enforce minimum hard disk size or the Pentium 133MHz requirement, other than requiring sufficient disk space for the Windows 2000 Professional files and a Pentium (or faster) CPU.

With a clean installation, Windows 2000 Professional requires almost five minutes for the hard drive to quit chewing data and complete the boot cycle (past the logon screen) and arrive at a functional desktop. Some of the chewing occurs because the processor is short some 13MHz versus what Microsoft lists as the stated minimum. Nevertheless, it provides a decent indication of how quickly the OS will operate on the minimum-required hardware.

You'll find performance improves markedly on machines possessing beefier processors and additional RAM. At a minimum, you'll probably want more disk space because 2GB doesn't leave much room for office applications, email messages, documents, and spreadsheets.

Table 3.2 lists our recommended hardware requirements for Windows 2000 Professional. Although they are just that, a recommendation, we believe you'll find much improved performance as a result.

Note: Microsoft no longer creates software builds for the 32-bit or 64-bit Alpha platforms. However, future 64-bit software products are being developed for Intel-based systems. When this book went to press, the next Windows release (code named Whistler) was on track for a 2001 release.

Table 3.2   Recommended hardware requirements for Windows 2000 Professional.

Component	Requirement
CPU	Pentium II-compatible 266MHz or higher
Input devices	Keyboard and mouse or other input device
Disk space	650MB free space on a 4GB or larger hard disk
RAM	128MB minimum (Microsoft recommends 64MB)
Secondary drives	36X or better CD-ROM, 3.5" disk drive, or 100MB NIC
Display	VGA or better

The Windows 2000 Professional Deployment Worksheet

Use the following worksheet to learn which machines will require hardware upgrades or replacement before you can install Windows 2000 Professional on them. The completed worksheet shown here is provided as an example. For instance, the system named Hinault in Toledo will require upgrading, as it doesn't possess a processor that meets minimum hardware requirements or a NIC or CD-ROM. A blank worksheet can be found on the accompanying CD-ROM. Print as many copies as are needed to determine necessary upgrades and replacements before beginning your Windows 2000 Professional deployment.

Systems that will be receiving Windows 2000 Professional.					
Location	**Computer Name**	**Processor**	**Hard Disk**	**RAM**	**CD-ROM or NIC**
Toledo	Bartali	P-133	2GB	64MB	Y
Toledo	Coppi	P-266	2GB	64MB	Y
Toledo	Hinault	P-100	2GB	32MB	N
Louisville	LeMond	P-350	6GB	128MB	Y
Louisville	Armstrong	P-350	6GB	128MB	Y
Louisville	Merckx	P-500	6GB	128MB	Y
Scottsdale/East Side	Indurain	P-500	6GB	128MB	Y
Scottsdale/Central	Anquetil	P-350	4GB	64MB	Y
San Francisco/North Beach	Gaul	P-350	4GB	64MB	Y
San Francisco/Twin Peaks	Garin	P-500	10GB	128MB	Y

After you've determined that a system possesses the appropriate hardware requirements, you're ready to move on to installation. The next step is often overlooked. It involves making a quick check to ensure the software applications you have in use are compatible.

Software Application Compatibility and Requirements

When you upgrade an older Windows operating system to Windows 2000 Professional, the Setup program checks for software compatibility issues. You can also execute that program by running the following command from a command prompt:

```
D:\i386\winnt32 /checkupgradeonly
```

Be sure to substitute the appropriate drive letter, represented by *D*, for your system's CD-ROM drive.

The results of the compatibility test will be displayed on screen. They're also saved in a text file, labeled either UPGRADE.TXT on systems running versions of Windows 95 or

Windows 98 or WINNT32.LOG on systems running Windows NT Workstation 3.51 or Windows NT Workstation 4.

This upgrade-only switch presents you with a summary. It can help you identify any potential issues arising from an upgrade. Read it carefully.

If you're preparing a fresh installation or planning a deployment, plan ahead. Try to anticipate the software applications and programs Windows 2000 Professional will be required to run. Then, check them for compatibility *before* you load the other programs.

Again, you'll want to surf out to Microsoft's site. Enter this URL in your browser: **www.microsoft.com/windows2000/upgrade/compat/search/software.asp**. You'll find the following search parameters:

- Name of the company producing the software

- The name of the software product

- A software product category

- Language

In addition, you can check for compatibility with Windows 2000 Server and Windows 2000 Advanced Server.

You can search several categories of software products. They include, but aren't limited to, the following:

- Commerce

- Connectivity and communications

- Cross-platform tools and integration

- Data processing

- Data warehousing

- Network infrastructure

- Systems management

- Utilities and servers

If all the software programs you intend to use are listed, you're in good shape. If you cannot find an application listed, you should ask the vendor whether it has submitted its code to the MSDN Business Connection for certification. You can find an overview of that program at this Internet address: **http://msdnisv.microsoft.com/overview.asp**.

The software manufacturer may, indeed, inform you that the application has been tested. Or, it may not. You may hear that it is believed to work, but the program hasn't been certified. Just as with hardware, you have a decision to make. Either you can try your luck, or you can migrate to another application. As the latter isn't always possible, you might need to update an application to work with Windows 2000 Professional. Should this

3

be the case, you'll want to ensure your organization's developers work with Microsoft to avoid unpleasant surprises when the software is deployed.

Always be suspicious, too, of software applications that aren't certified. Whether you download programs from the Internet, purchase them from a retailer, or write them yourself, if the operating system begins behaving strangely, that's the first thing we recommend you check.

As always, when trouble arises, ask yourself "What changed last?" Or, check the physical connections. Those are often the two best pieces of advice any IT professional can give another. But, if your physical connections aren't causing a problem, and you've just deployed an uncertified software program, odds are that it's the source of your problem.

After you've checked and determined that your systems possess the necessary horsepower and you have compatible devices and software, it's time to select a file system.

Installation Partitions

In the planning phase, you should select the partition your Windows 2000 Professional machine will use. The time to determine the partition you will use isn't when the installation program prompts you for the answer to just that question. Decide in advance.

When you load the Windows 2000 Setup program, it examines a system's hard drive. It then asks whether it should install the operating system on an existing partition. Or, you'll be given the option of creating a new partition for installation.

If you're using a brand-new hard drive, you'll have to create and size the installation partition, or the section of the hard drive on which you'd like to install Windows 2000. If a previously used hard drive possesses sufficient nonpartitioned space, you can create a partition and use that space.

Maybe you've got a hard disk that holds an existing partition that's already formatted. You can use it, if it's large enough, but you'll lose all the data it holds (unless you back it up to another hard disk or drive).

You may have an existing hard disk partition that contains data or another operating system. If you no longer need that data or OS, you can reformat it and install Windows 2000 on it.

Of course, a hard drive can have up to four primary partitions, or three primary partitions and an extended partition. Microsoft says a Windows 2000 installation requires a minimum of 650MB on a 2GB or larger hard disk (although we've installed it on smaller hard drives). Never mind all that, anyway, as you'll want a larger hard disk to support using additional applications, for storing documents, spreadsheets, presentations, email messages, and more.

Tip: This isn't Linux. Don't try creating additional storage partitions during Windows 2000 setup. You should use the Setup program to create the partition only where you intend to install the new operating system. Use a third-party program, such as PowerQuest's PartitionMagic, to create additional partitions after the operating system has been installed.

If you're planning to dual-boot Windows 2000 with another operating system, partition management becomes exponentially more complex. See Chapter 4 for more information on dual-booting and partition selection when using multiple operating systems.

The next item on your preflight checklist is the file system. You need to know, at a low level, how all your data will be formatted.

Selecting a File System

After you've selected your partition, you need to determine the file system your organization will use. It's probably best, for systems administration simplicity, to standardize on a single format.

Get ready for a déjà vu: In the planning phase, you should select the file system your Windows 2000 Professional machine will use. The time to determine the file system you will use isn't when the installation program prompts you for the answer to just that question. You should determine the file system in advance.

All Windows 2000 platforms support the File Allocation Table (FAT), FAT32, and NT File System (NTFS) file systems. Microsoft recommends that you use NTFS for your entire system. We recommend that you use NTFS, at a minimum, for your system partition holding the Windows 2000 operating system.

Warning! *You may not wish to use NTFS if your system will support other operating systems or dual-booting. Only Windows NT Server, Windows NT Workstation, and the Windows 2000 family of operating systems support the use of NTFS. Windows 9x and other platforms cannot read files stored on an NTFS partition.*

There are several benefits of using NTFS. We'll examine all of them in just a moment, but trust that they include security enhancements. In fact, Windows 2000 domain controllers require that NTFS partitions be available on server platforms upon installation of Active Directory for specific folder structures that are put in place. The use of new encryption features also requires NTFS on Windows 2000 Professional platforms.

In case you need a quick lesson or refresher on the characteristics and differences between the different file systems, Table 3.3 charts them for you.

You should note that VFAT (originally introduced with Windows for Workgroups 3.11) is not natively supported in Windows 2000. This file system may still be in use on older systems, so you should keep an eye out for it.

Note: *VFAT was supported by the original releases of Windows for Workgroups 3.11, Windows 95, Windows NT 3.51, and Windows NT 4. Although VFAT boasts the same basic file system features as FAT, it provides long file-name support and carries no restriction on the number of files contained in nonroot directories. FAT nonroot directories are limited to 65,535 files.*

Table 3.3   FAT, FAT32, and NTFS capabilities and characteristics.

Feature	FAT	FAT32	NTFS
Maximum volume size	2GB	4TB	16EB
Maximum file size	2GB	4TB	16EB
Maximum files in root directory	512	No limit	No limit
Maximum files in nonroot directory	65,535	No limit	No limit
Maximum file name length	11	256	256
File-level security	No	No	Yes
File compression	Requires third-party utilities	Requires third-party utilities	Natively supported
Transaction logging	No	No	Yes
POSIX support	No	No	POSIX1
Dual-boot support	Yes	Yes	No
Self-repairing	No	Limited	Yes

Each of the different file systems supported by Windows 2000 boasts strengths and weaknesses. The FAT and FAT32 file systems support dual-booting, or the use of multiple operating systems on the same machine. However, they don't offer compression. NTFS, meanwhile, boasts file- and folder-level security, encryption, compression, and disk quotas.

Which file system is best for you depends largely on your needs and the environment in which Windows 2000 is being installed. If dual-booting is an important feature and file- and folder-level security is not, FAT32 will do the trick. Should you need file- and folder-level security and the use of compression or encryption, you'll want NTFS.

FAT and FAT32 Strengths

Although the use of FAT and FAT32 restricts Windows 2000 Professional's capabilities, they do offer time-tested functionality. These file systems have been proven time and time again in the trenches.

One benefit of FAT is its propensity to support dual-booting. Whether you wish to use Windows 9x, Windows Me, or Windows NT 4 on the same system, using FAT ensures you can share files between the two operating systems.

Warning! *In the past, many administrators loaded Windows NT Server on a FAT partition and stored their data on an NTFS partition. The goal was to help emergency recovery operations. However, you shouldn't do this. The practice leaves critical system data, including security and account information, less secure than possible. That's why we recommend using an NTFS partition for Windows system data.*

NTFS Advantages

Still not convinced NTFS is best? Although some argue its performance is a little slower than FAT, NTFS drastically improves security. It also adds compression, repair, and reliability benefits. The following list provides a quick look at NTFS's advantages:

- Provides superior compression versus FAT and FAT32
- Offers folder- and file-level security
- Supports encryption
- Enforces disk quotas
- Provides an unlimited number of files in the root and nonroot directories
- Supports long file names
- Possesses self-repairing characteristics

Rescue and Recovery

Have you ever wished you could use some of the rescue and recovery features from the Windows 9x family on an NT machine? Now you can. One of the new "rescue" features is Windows 2000's Recovery Console, which enables the use of a command line for troubleshooting a nonbooting system. Using the Recovery Console, you should be able to access data on secured NTFS partitions, assuming you possess the proper administrative permissions.

It's also important to note that Windows 2000 includes a Safe Boot option, similar to that in Windows 9x, that was previously unavailable in Windows NT operating systems. You should be aware that this option now exists, should worries about data access be your sole reason for selecting FAT or FAT32 as the operating file system.

Although the use of the Recovery Console can quickly repair a failed system, if you're operating machines in an environment in which data recovery is critical, you may wish to dual-boot. At a minimum, you should back up your data often. At a maximum, such as for an environment in which high availability is paramount, you should mirror your system. However, doing so requires redundant resources, which can be costly.

We accidentally discovered what some have known all along. Having an old OS, left resident on another partition while the new Windows 2000 system is tested, can come in handy. You can use it to boot the system and access files and folders. You can also use the older OS, whether it's Windows 9x or Windows NT Workstation 4, to troubleshoot corrupted data.

Many new data protection and recovery features are available in Windows 2000. You can read more details about all of them in Chapter 17.

After you have reviewed and weighed all the advantages and disadvantages, you can select the file system that best meets your needs. Next, you must choose a licensing mode.

Licensing Options

Every Windows 2000 Professional system that's installed must possess a license. Licenses cannot be used multiple times. Be sure to read the entire Licensing Agreement during setup before agreeing to it.

If a Windows 2000 Professional machine is accessing a Windows 2000 server, a Client Access License (CAL) is required, too. You must possess CALs for each client that accesses a Windows server.

Warning! You should be aware that Windows 2000 licenses cover their respective use of the desktop and server operating systems, and CALs cover access to Windows 2000 servers only. Windows 2000 licenses do not cover access to BackOffice products, such as Site Server Commerce Edition, Exchange Server, Proxy Server, BackOffice Server, SQL Server, Systems Management Server, SNA Server, and others. Terminal Services also requires separate licensing.

Just as in Windows NT, you can select from two licensing options in the Windows 2000 OS. Both Per Seat and Per Server licensing are offered. Let's take a look at the difference between the two options:

- *Per Seat licensing*—Requires each client accessing the server to have its own CAL. Clients with a CAL can access as many servers as they want. This is the most commonly used licensing mode.

- *Per Server licensing*—Requires the server to possess a CAL for each concurrent connection it hosts. If Per Server licensing is selected, and 25 concurrent licenses are purchased, 25 users can access the server at any time. This licensing mode works best when an organization uses a single server or a server for Internet or remote access services.

Organizations with more than one server generally select Per Seat licensing because that mode enables connection to as many different servers as required without the burden of additional licenses for each server that's contacted. Instead, just a single CAL is required per client. Small organizations with just a single server often opt for Per Server licensing. In Windows NT, you could select Per Server mode but upgrade (just once) to Per Seat licensing, should it become necessary.

In Windows 2000, you can change from Per Server to Per Seat if you discover that the number of CALs required to support the Per Server mode is greater than your number of client PCs. This change is made on the server side. However, you should know the conversion can be performed only once, and you can do so only for the following products:

- Windows 2000 Server

- Microsoft Exchange Server

- SQL Server

- SNA Server

Note: Per Seat licensing is commonly selected when using Windows 2000 Terminal Services. Per Server mode, however, must be selected when using Windows 2000 Terminal Services Internet Connector Licenses.

Several services don't require licenses. Connections that do not require CALs include anonymous or authenticated access to a Windows 2000 server running Internet Information Services and Web servers providing HTML files via HTTP. CALs also are not required with Telnet and FTP connections.

Another question exists with Windows 2000 licensing: Should you purchase new licenses, or should you upgrade existing licenses? If you're considering upgrading, the first action you should take is to confirm you own a product that's eligible for upgrading. Remember, as discussed in Chapter 1, the following operating system licenses can be upgraded:

• Windows 95

• Windows 98

• Windows 98 Second Edition

• Windows NT Workstation 3.51

• Windows NT Workstation 4

Real-World Licensing Examples

How does licensing really work? Here are two examples.

Elliot is an administrator for Good Jazz Records. He supports three departments (accounting, marketing, and sales) that must interact and share strategic documents, sales spreadsheets, publication schedules, and album artwork. These departments have a total of 56 client machines, served by three servers. Each of the servers contains resources all three departments access.

If Elliot selected Per Server licensing, he would have to purchase 56 Windows 2000 Professional licenses and 168 CALs (to ensure all users could access all servers).

If Elliot chose Per Seat licensing, he would need to purchase only 56 Windows 2000 Professional licenses and 56 CALs (thereby ensuring all users can access all servers). Thus, Per Seat licensing would be the most appropriate license option for Good Jazz Records.

Allison is an administrator for ACME Scientific Supply. She supports 19 users and has a single server. She would want 19 Windows 2000 Professional licenses and probably 20 CALs for the server. The extra CAL ensures that, if a new or temporary employee is hired, a license is available. Purchasing Per Seat licensing wouldn't make much sense for her because she's not supporting a large number of clients and she operates only a single server.

Should a 21st user try to log on, and the server has only 20 CALs, the 21st connection would be denied. Thus, it's important to plan well for licensing issues.

Windows 2000 Professional licensing prices are listed in Table 3.4. Remember that these prices were set by Microsoft at the time this book went to press. They may change, so be sure to check Microsoft's Web site for the latest pricing information. You can search for licensing on Microsoft's Web site, or enter this URL in your browser: **www.microsoft.com/ windows2000/guide/professional/pricing/default.asp**.

Other licensing options exist, too. If you or your organization enrolled in an enterprise licensing agreement, you could be eligible to receive upgrades for no additional charge. Table 3.5 lists the upgrade paths for such licenses.

Warning! The Microsoft Windows 95 and Windows 98 Upgrade Advantage/Maintenance program doesn't qualify for free upgrades to Windows 2000 Professional. If your organization participated in this enterprise licensing program, you must purchase new Windows 2000 Professional licenses.

After selecting your licensing mode, you're ready to determine a namespace. Before you can proceed, you must choose whether the Windows 2000 Professional machine will be part of a workgroup or a member of a domain.

Table 3.4   Windows 2000 Professional pricing.

Product	Price	Description
Windows 2000 Professional	$319	Standard edition
Windows 2000 Professional Product Upgrade	$219	Supports upgrading from Windows 95, Windows 98, or Windows 98 Second Edition
Windows 2000 Professional Version Upgrade	$149 (after a $70 rebate)	Supports upgrading from Windows NT Workstation 3.51 or Windows NT Workstation 4

Table 3.5   Upgrade paths for enterprise licensing agreements.

Product	Eligible Upgrade
Windows NT Workstation 3.51	Windows 2000 Professional
Windows NT Workstation 4	Windows 2000 Professional
Windows NT Server 3.51	Windows 2000 Server
Windows NT Server 4	Windows 2000 Server
Windows NT Server 4 Enterprise Edition	Windows 2000 Advanced Server
Windows NT Server 3.51 CAL	Windows 2000 CAL
Windows NT Server 4 CAL	Windows 2000 CAL
Back Office Server 4.5	Windows 2000 Server
Windows NT Server 4 Terminal Server Edition CAL	Windows 2000 Terminal Services CAL

Namespace Determination

You must specify the network security group that the new Windows 2000 Professional system will join. It will be either a workgroup or a domain.

Workgroups link a series of Windows 2000 Professional and other client systems together. In a workgroup, client machines serve both client and server functions. In a domain, a series of clients are members of a group, or domain, managed by one or more servers.

Workgroup Membership

Joining a workgroup is simple. If you've worked with other Windows platforms, you're probably already familiar with the process. You must know simply the name of the workgroup. A DNS server and the existence of a computer account aren't required.

Rather than requiring a Fully Qualified Domain Name (FQDN), such as *computer. domain.suffix* or client1.coriolis.com, you'll merely use the NetBIOS name when adding a system to a workgroup. This 15-character name identifies your new client machine to existing computers in the workgroup.

It's that easy to add a workgroup. You enter it by selecting the No, This Computer Is Not On A Network, Or Is On A Network Without A Domain entry during setup. Adding a system to an existing domain is another matter.

Domain Membership

Before you can join a system to a domain, you must do the following:

- Know the DNS name for the domain you want the new computer to join (such as coriolis.com)

- Have a computer account created in the existing domain or administrative privileges to create a computer account in the existing domain

- Ensure that the domain controller and DNS server are online and available

Note: Joining an existing domain requires that you know the Domain Name System (DNS) name for the domain. For example, the DNS name for Coriolis is coriolis.com. If you were to add a machine named Axis in the Coriolis Editorial domain, the FQDN would be axis.editorial.coriolis.com.

First, you'll need to know the DNS name for the domain you're joining. Second, you'll need to create a computer account for your new computer on the existing domain. If you possess administrative rights, you can create the necessary computer account during installation. Otherwise, you'll need to contact the network administrator and request the computer account be created. The computer account must exist, though, before the new computer can join the domain.

Third, a domain controller must be available. And, DNS service must be running in the domain and you must have access to it. Although DNS can run on the domain controller, both must be available, or your new computer won't be able to join the domain.

When you have your necessary workgroup or domain information on hand, you're ready to begin installing the operating system. Before you jump to the installation option, be sure to review your preflight checklist, as shown in Decision Tree 3.1, and ensure you haven't forgotten anything.

After you've checked your systems' hardware for compatibility, selected a file system, reviewed Microsoft's licensing options, and acquired the information you need for joining a workgroup or domain, you should review the preinstallation checklist. Pay close attention to any systems or domain naming changes that could have occurred between the time you began the checklist and the time you approach a system for the actual installation of Windows 2000.

After you have reviewed hardware and software compatibility issues, partition and file system options, the licensing format that's appropriate for you, and whether the new system will be joining a workgroup or domain, you're ready to select the installation method.

Windows 2000 offers the following five installation options:

- Installation using a compact disc (CD)

- Installation over a network

- Automated installation using the Windows 2000 Setup Manager Wizard

- Automated installation using Disk Duplication

- Installation via Remote Installation Services

Let's begin in-depth looks at each of these methods by examining what's likely to be the most often used: We'll start with installation using a CD.

Installing Using a Compact Disc

As with most operating systems, Windows 2000 can be installed using a compact disc. You can start the CD-based installation using floppy disks, or if your system's BIOS supports booting from the CD-ROM drive, you can boot directly from the installation CD.

If you're upgrading a previous Windows installation, you may wish to use the Windows 2000 Professional CD-ROM's auto-run feature. Whichever method you select, you'll find the Windows 2000 Setup program guides you through the setup and configuration processes.

The Windows 2000 Setup program consists of four stages. Figure 3.1 presents the four stages the Windows 2000 Setup program follows.

The Setup program stage consists of six steps, as shown in Figure 3.2. The first step is the Setup program being loaded into memory. The process ends with Setup files being copied to the hard disk and the computer restarting. However, a lot happens in between. For example, the text-based version of startup begins, you're prompted to specify partition information, and a partition must be created for the files being copied.

Decision Tree 3.1
You should review your complete preflight checklist to ensure you have answers for all the options the Windows 2000 installation will offer.

3

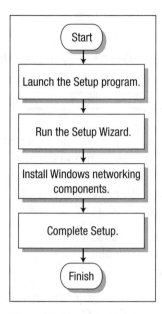

Figure 3.1
The Windows 2000 Setup process involves four stages.

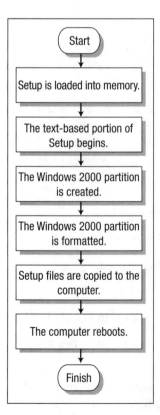

Figure 3.2
The first stage of the Windows 2000 Setup process includes six steps.

Speeding Up Mass Installations

The Smartdrive utility can be used with boot floppies or the bootable Windows 2000 Professional CD-ROM. This utility provides quicker installs than a DOS install using the WINNT.EXE switch. Consider installing Smartdrive on DOS systems first and then executing WINNT.EXE if you're rolling out multiple machines.

The second stage begins with the Setup Wizard prompting you, in graphical user interface (GUI) mode, for regional settings, naming and password information, and the product key. The networking stage detects and identifies installed NICs and installs network components such as Transmission Control Protocol/Internet Protocol (TCP/IP). It's also at this stage that workgroup and domain-naming information is provided.

The last stage occurs when the Windows 2000 Professional installation program writes final information to a system's hard drive and cleans temporary files from the hard disk. The complete Setup stage consists of five steps, as shown in Figure 3.3.

Although the entire process generally includes a couple of dozen steps, as shown in Figure 3.4, it's not as daunting as it may appear. We've performed numerous CD-ROM–based Windows 2000 Professional installations on a variety of hardware platforms. All have run smoothly and efficiently.

You can trigger installation in a few ways. You can open a command prompt and enter commands. You can also use the menu the CD-ROM's auto-run file will display, should you be using a previous version of Windows that Windows 2000 Professional supports upgrading from.

Should your system not support booting from a CD-ROM drive, never fear. Using the CD-ROM, you can make floppy boot disks to jump-start the installation. Be sure to use blank, formatted floppy disks. Just follow these steps to create the four boot disks Windows 2000 Professional requires when a system doesn't support booting from a CD-ROM drive:

1. Obtain four 1.44MB floppy disks.

2. Label the first one Windows 2000 Professional Setup Boot Disk.

3. Label the second one Windows 2000 Professional Setup Disk #2.

4. Label the third one Windows 2000 Professional Setup Disk #3.

5. Label the fourth one Windows 2000 Professional Setup Disk #4.

6. Insert the Windows 2000 Professional CD-ROM into your system's CD-ROM drive.

7. Click on No if you receive a dialog box asking whether you would like to upgrade to Windows 2000.

8. Open a command prompt by clicking on Start|Run and entering "command" (if you're using Windows 9x) or "cmd" (if you're using Windows NT Workstation 3.51 or Windows NT Workstation 4).

3

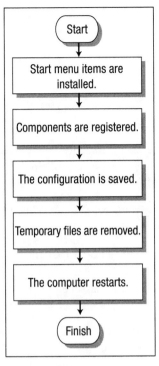

Figure 3.3
The fourth stage of Windows 2000 Setup includes five steps.

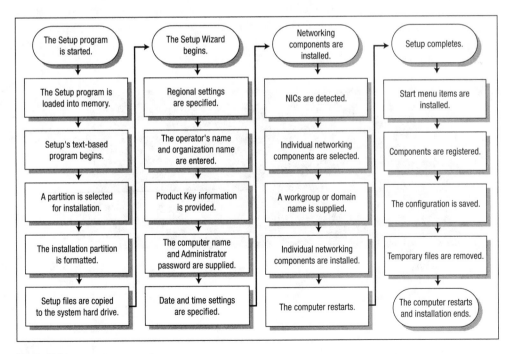

Figure 3.4
The stages and steps required to complete the entire Windows 2000 Professional CD-ROM–based installation.

9. Type "*D:*", with *D:* representing the drive letter reserved for your system's CD-ROM drive, and press Enter.

10. Move to the Bootdisk folder on the CD-ROM by typing "cd bootdisk" and pressing Enter.

11. Confirm you see the following command prompt:

```
D:\Bootdisk\>
```

12. Type "makeboot *a:*", where *a:* represents the drive letter reserved for your system's floppy drive, and press Enter. The program will display a message confirming that it will create the four boot disks, as shown in Figure 3.5.

13. Press any key to continue. The program prompts you to insert Disk #1. This is the disk you labeled Windows 2000 Professional Setup Boot Disk.

14. Insert the disk you labeled Windows 2000 Professional Setup Boot Disk into your system's floppy disk drive and press any key to continue. Windows 2000 Professional will write data to the disk. When it finishes, it will display a message requesting that you remove the disk and insert Disk #2, as shown in Figure 3.6.

15. Insert the disk you labeled Windows 2000 Professional Setup Disk #2. Press any key to continue. Windows 2000 Professional will write data to the disk. When it finishes, it will display a message requesting that you remove the disk and insert Disk #3 in the series.

16. Insert the disk you labeled Windows 2000 Professional Setup Disk #3. Press any key to continue. Windows 2000 Professional will write data to the disk. The program will track its progress, as shown in Figure 3.7. When it finishes, it will display a message requesting that you remove the disk and insert Disk #4.

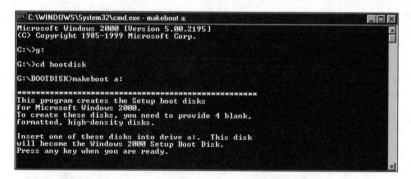

Figure 3.5
The makeboot program will confirm it will create four boot disks. In this example, the CD-ROM drive is represented by the drive letter G.

Figure 3.6
You'll be prompted to insert Disk #2 and press any key to continue.

Figure 3.7
The makeboot program tracks its progress as it writes information to each disk.

17. Insert the disk you labeled Windows 2000 Professional Setup Disk #4. Press any key to continue. Windows 2000 Professional will write data to the disk. When it finishes, it will display a message stating the process has completed, as shown in Figure 3.8.

18. Type "exit" in the command prompt window and remove Disk #4 and the Windows 2000 Professional CD-ROM from the machine.

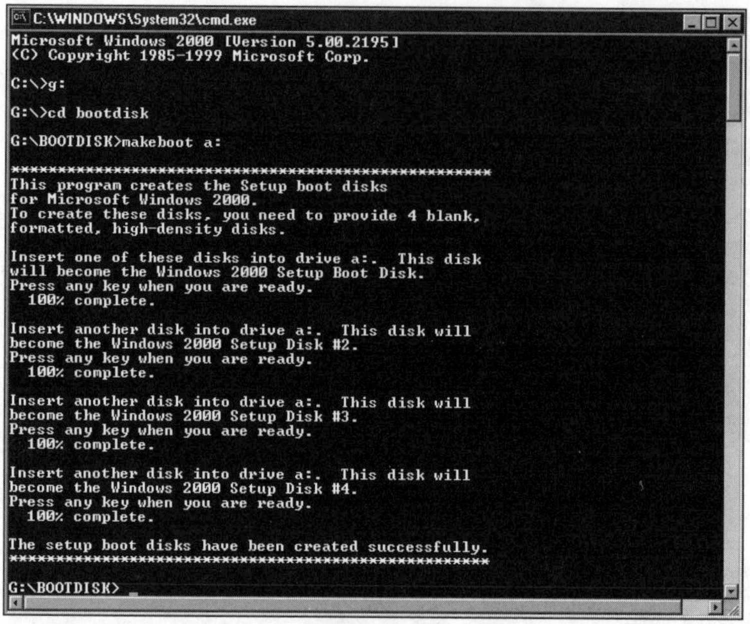

Figure 3.8
The makeboot program will announce the program has completed successfully.

Let's take a closer look at each of Setup's stages. As in Windows NT, the WINNT.EXE command starts a new installation.

WINNT.EXE Installation

When WINNT.EXE is executed, a miniature version of Windows 2000 is loaded. After the text-mode portion of the Windows Setup program begins, you should press F6 to load third-party SCSI and RAID drivers.

Next, you must specify which partition will receive the new installation and the file system you'll be using. You'll also have an opportunity to format the partition.

After copying files, the Setup program reboots the computer. The Windows 2000 Setup Wizard then takes over. It will prompt you for the following information:

- *Regional settings*—These determine how numbers, currencies, and dates are presented. Your keyboard layout is also specified as a regional setting.

- *Name and organization*—This information is used by the operating system to personalize your software.

- *Licensing mode*—The Setup program asks you to enter your 25-character Product Key. You can find the key on a yellow sticker on the back of the Windows 2000 Professional CD-ROM.

- *Computer name and administrator account password*—After you've entered the Product Key information, you must specify the computer name and administrator password.

- *Date and time settings*—These ensure that the date and time settings are accurate because many processes, including file date and time stamps, rely on this information to perform properly. You can also elect to have Windows 2000 Professional automatically adjust its clock for daylight savings changes by filling in the checkbox.

Next, the Setup Wizard installs networking components. You'll be presented with two options: Typical Settings and Custom Settings. Choosing a typical installation instructs the Windows 2000 Setup Wizard to install the following:

- Client for Microsoft Networks

- File and Printer Sharing for Microsoft Networks

- TCP/IP

Selecting a custom installation enables you to specify network settings. Your needs, and your network's configuration, will dictate which method works best for you.

Tip: *For more information on networking in Windows 2000 Professional, see Chapter 14. You can find comprehensive step-by-step directions for configuring network connections there.*

The Setup Wizard then prompts you to indicate whether the new system will belong to a workgroup or a domain. You'll need to specify whether the computer is a member of a domain.

If the system is to be a standalone machine, or a computer that connects only to other clients (a network without a domain), you'll probably want to select the following radio button: No, This Computer Is Not On A Network, Or Is On A Network Without A Domain. Type A Workgroup Name In The Following Box.

If the system is to join a domain, you'll want to select the second radio button: Yes, Make This Computer A Member Of The Following Domain.

Next, you'll need to supply the workgroup or computer domain name. If you don't know it, consult with your IT department or system administrator. If you're an IT professional creating a workgroup, enter the name of the new workgroup in the box.

After you provide the workgroup or domain information, Windows 2000 Setup continues by copying additional files, applying the configuration settings you supplied, saving the configuration settings, and removing temporary files created during the Setup process.

You should remove the installation media (any floppies and the Windows 2000 Professional CD-ROM). Then, the system reboots, and you're done with the installation.

Let's take a look at an actual CD-ROM–based installation.

A Sample CD-ROM–Based Installation

Sometimes, it's best to have a real-world example. In this section, you'll see all the screens you can expect to encounter during a typical Windows 2000 Professional CD-ROM–based installation.

When WINNT.EXE executes, the Setup program loads in memory, and the text-based portion of Setup begins. It immediately begins loading files. Windows 2000 Setup then asks whether you wish to set up or repair Windows 2000. You can also quit Setup, as shown in Figure 3.9. Press Enter to continue or press R to repair an installation. For this example, press Enter to install Windows 2000.

Setup displays a message stating the hard disk is new or erased. You are prompted to press C to continue, as shown in Figure 3.10. The licensing agreement appears (see Figure 3.11). Although most people don't read it (be honest), you should do so by pressing Page Down. After the agreement is read, demonstrate acceptance of the terms by pressing F8. Pressing Esc causes Setup to end.

Next, you must select the partition where Windows 2000 Professional should be installed. Your options are to select the highlighted partition by pressing Enter, creating a partition in the highlighted space by pressing C, or deleting a partition by pressing D.

Because the partition shown in Figure 3.12 is where we wish to install Windows 2000 Professional, press Enter. Note that, because this is only an example, the 879MB partition is of ample size. Normally, you would want a much larger partition capable of holding applications, files, and other programs.

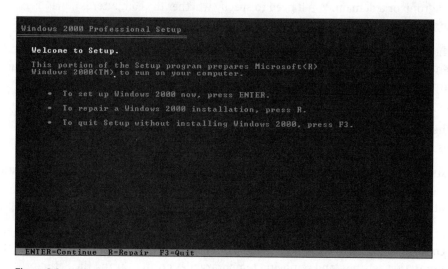

Figure 3.9
You can install Windows 2000 or repair a previous installation. Or, you can cancel Setup without installing Windows 2000 by pressing F3.

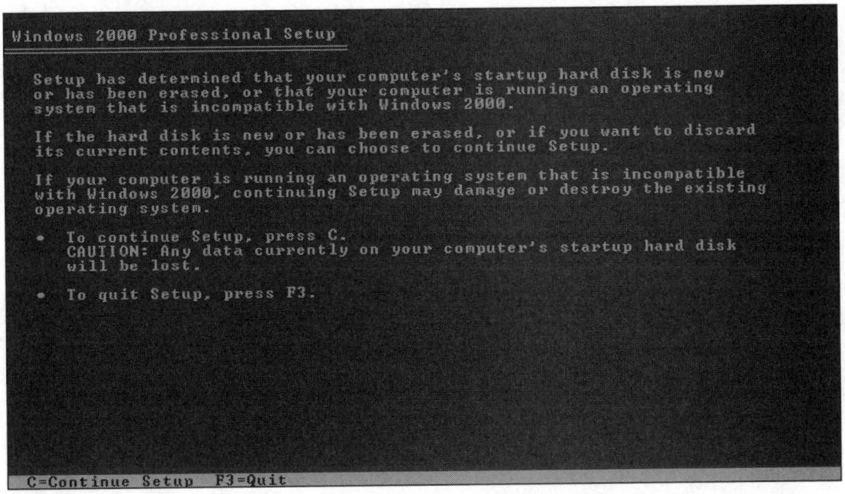

3

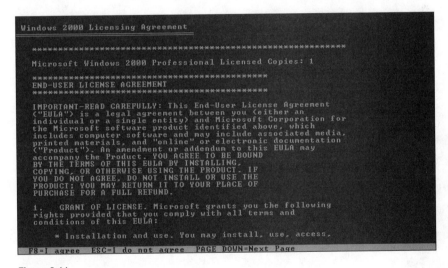

Figure 3.10
Setup confirms the hard disk is new or erased. Pressing C continues the Windows 2000 installation.

Figure 3.11
You must agree to the terms of the Windows 2000 Professional End User Licensing Agreement (EULA) for Setup to continue.

Next, you must specify the file system Windows 2000 should use. The options, as shown in Figure 3.13, are NTFS and FAT. In this example, we'll choose NTFS. After you've highlighted the file system you wish to use and pressed Enter, Setup begins copying files to the system's hard disk. The progress is tracked on screen.

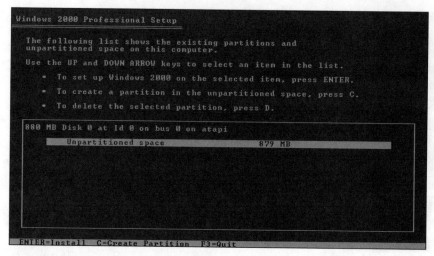

Figure 3.12
You must select the partition where you would like Windows 2000 Professional installed.

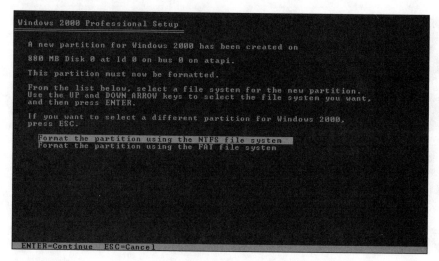

Figure 3.13
Select the file system you would like Windows 2000 to use and press Enter to continue.

Setup then begins initializing configuration. It will display a message, as shown in Figure 3.14, confirming it has reached that stage. When the initialization is complete, the system reboots. A message is displayed showing the system will reboot. You can press Enter to speed up the process, as shown in Figure 3.15.

You'll know you're on the right track when the Windows 2000 Professional image appears on your screen, as shown in Figure 3.16. It's a sign the Setup process is progressing properly.

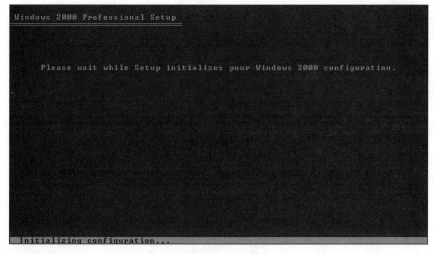

Figure 3.14
Setup begins initializing the Windows 2000 configuration.

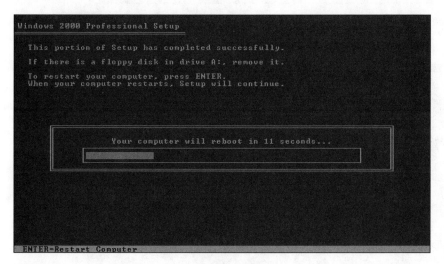

Figure 3.15
The system must reboot before continuing with the installation.

The splash screen then hands off the Setup process to the friendlier GUI. Here, the Setup Wizard begins to take over, as shown in Figure 3.17. This begins the second of Windows 2000 Professional's four Setup stages.

Plug-and-play kicks in next. Figure 3.18 shows Windows 2000 detecting and installing hardware devices and peripherals. After the keyboard, mouse, and other important devices are in place, regional settings must be defined, as shown in Figure 3.19. Regional settings can be customized easily. All you need to do is select the appropriate Customize button.

Figure 3.16
The Windows 2000 Professional splash screen should appear.

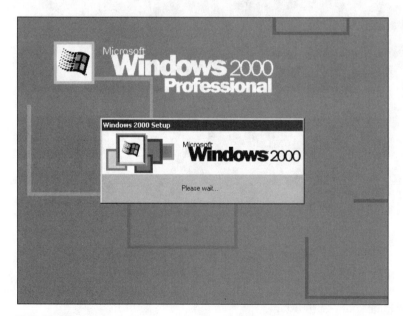

Figure 3.17
Users are instructed to wait while the Setup Wizard prepares to take over the Setup process.

3

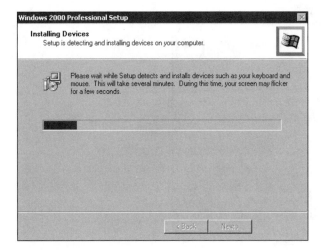

Figure 3.18
The keyboard, mouse, and other critical hardware devices are found and configured.

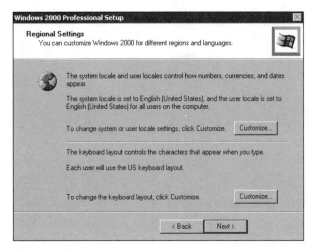

Figure 3.19
You must define regional settings.

Next, you must enter your name and organization, as shown in Figure 3.20. This information is used to personalize Windows 2000 software. The name entered should be the name of the individual owning the software license, incidentally.

After you've supplied the name and organization information and clicked on Next, the Setup program requires that you enter your Product Key, as shown in Figure 3.21. It is a unique 25-character code that you can find on the back of the Windows 2000 Professional CD-ROM.

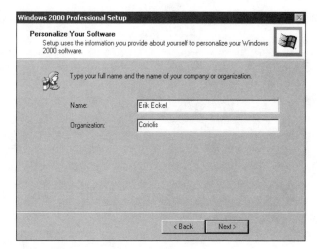

Figure 3.20
Windows 2000 Professional asks for your name and organization.

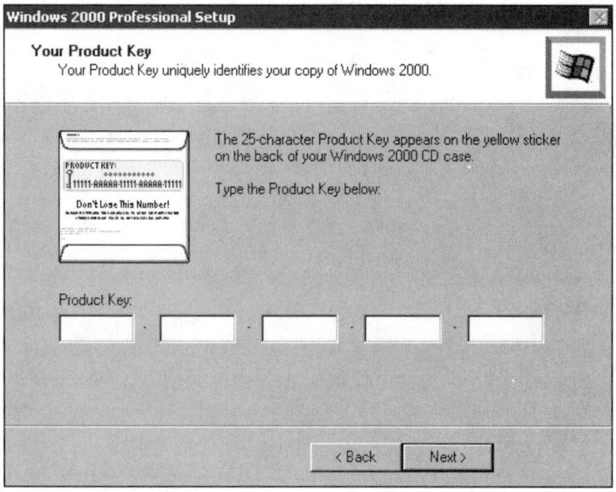

Figure 3.21
You must enter a unique Product Key supplied by Microsoft.

Next, you must provide a computer name and a password to be used by the Administrator account, as shown in Figure 3.22. Windows 2000 automatically creates the Administrator account, which is similar to the root, or superuser, account on Unix and Linux systems. This account is used to administer resources on the system.

The Setup program, as Figure 3.23 demonstrates, requests the correct date and time information next. Windows 2000 Professional then begins installing networking components, as shown in Figure 3.24. This step begins the third stage of the Windows 2000 Setup process.

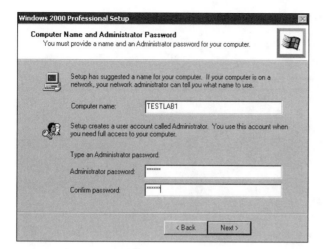

Figure 3.22
The computer name and Administrator account password must be provided.

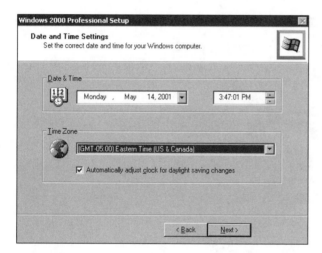

Figure 3.23
Supply the correct date and time for Windows 2000 Professional.

You must select whether you want to use a Typical or Custom Networking Settings installation, as Figure 3.25 demonstrates. Because we wish to use a typical installation (Client for Microsoft Networks, File and Print Sharing for Microsoft Networks, and TCP/IP), select the Typical Settings radio button and select Next to continue.

Pay attention when specifying whether the computer will be a member of a workgroup or a domain. Changing it later requires extra time, so it's best to get it right the first time. After selecting whether the computer will be joining a workgroup or a domain, you must specify the workgroup or domain name, as shown in Figure 3.26.

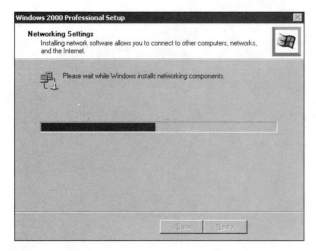

Figure 3.24
You are asked to wait while Windows 2000 Professional installs networking components.

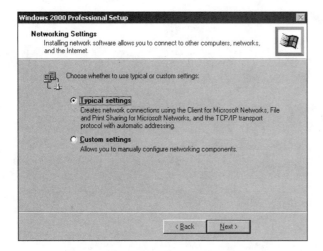

Figure 3.25
You must choose between a Typical or Custom Networking Settings installation.

Clicking on Next prompts Windows 2000 to begin installing the networking components. The Setup program then finishes the third stage of the Setup process and enters the fourth stage. Start menu items are installed, components are registered, settings are saved, and temporary files created by the Setup program are removed. Progress is tracked with another dialog box, as shown in Figure 3.27. You'll be rewarded with a screen stating Windows 2000 Setup has completed successfully, as shown in Figure 3.28. You should remove the Windows 2000 CD-ROM and click on Finish. Doing so prompts the system to reboot and Setup to complete.

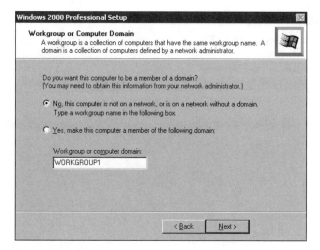

Figure 3.26
You must specify whether the computer is a member of a workgroup or a domain, and you must provide the name of the workgroup or domain.

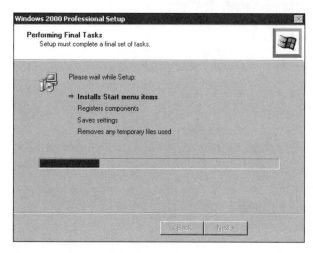

Figure 3.27
The Setup process tracks its progress as it begins the fourth and final stage of installation.

Upon rebooting, you'll be greeted by the Network Identification Wizard, as shown in Figure 3.29. It configures the computer's actual network connection, which is discussed in more detail in Chapter 14.

When the wizard finishes, or if you select Cancel, you'll be taken directly into Windows 2000, as shown in Figure 3.30.

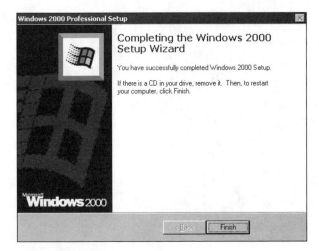

Figure 3.28
Windows 2000 Professional's Setup program confirms Setup has completed properly.

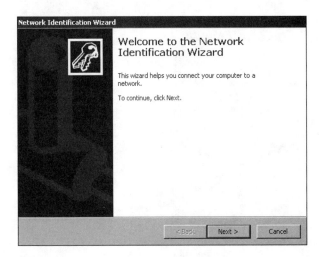

Figure 3.29
The Network Identification Wizard connects to a network.

A Getting Started guide appears on the desktop by default. You can use it to help familiarize yourself with Windows 2000, or you can close it. Don't forget to clear the Show This Screen At Startup checkbox, or you'll be greeted with the Getting Started screen every time you log on.

That's how you install Windows 2000 Professional. But, what if you want to convert an older version of Windows? Then, you'll want to perform an upgrade installation or use the WINNT32.EXE command. Let's take a look at that procedure next.

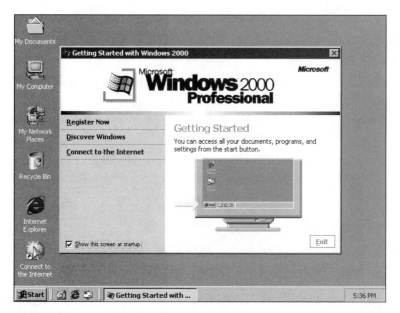

Figure 3.30
The Windows 2000 desktop resembles other Windows platforms. However, you'll find updated icons and some new names for familiar applications and utilities.

Is an Upgrade Right for You?

If you're planning to upgrade a previous Windows platform, you should consider a few facts. It's easy to think you receive the same functionality and performance Windows 2000 offers regardless of whether you upgrade a previous Windows installation or install Windows 2000 Professional fresh. After all, that sounds logical, right?

We're sorry to say that's not quite the way it works. At least not in the real world.

We've installed systems both ways. And, although we haven't tested our theory using a double-blind study in a hermetically sealed, constant-humidity environment, we feel it's safe to say you're likely to experience improved performance with a clean installation.

Too many old system files, configuration files, and Registry entries are left behind when you upgrade. They may be left over from the old operating system, or third-party programs may have added them. They consume hard disk space, they can steal RAM, and they may rob valuable processor cycles. Further, some old and unnecessary programs might still be installed, and legacy Registry entries are likely still in place. All these legacy items contribute to less-than-ideal performance.

If you upgrade from Windows 95 or Windows 98 to Windows 2000 Professional, don't be surprised if you run into a little trouble. CD-RW drives, graphics cards, printers, sound cards, USB devices, and other peripherals can all fail to function properly. Windows 2000's plug-and-play may not find these devices.

Don't fret, yet. You may be able to install the devices independently, after the upgrade finishes. This is yet another reason you should check both your system's hardware and software for compatibility before launching the upgrade.

We don't need to tell you, too, to ensure you have a working backup copy of all your data before you attempt an upgrade. Just in case, try your backup on another machine. A backup does no good if the disk is corrupt or another issue prevents you from accessing the data you thought you backed up adequately.

Microsoft has provided several guidelines for helping determine whether you should install Windows 2000 Professional fresh or select the upgrade option. Microsoft recommends upgrading if *all* of the following apply to you:

• You're already using a previous version of Windows that supports upgrading.

• You want to replace your previous Windows operating system with Windows 2000.

• You want to maintain your existing user settings and files.

It should come as no surprise that Microsoft recommends you perform a clean installation if *any* of the following apply:

• Your hard drive has no operating system installed.

• Your current operating system does not support an upgrade to Windows 2000.

• You have two partitions and want to create a dual-boot configuration with Windows 2000 and your current operating system.

Should you decide you're a candidate for upgrading, then have at it. Just make sure you back up your data first and check it to ensure the backup operates properly.

WINNT32.EXE Installation

The WINNT32.EXE command triggers a Windows 2000 upgrade. Alternatively, you can insert the Windows 2000 Professional CD-ROM, and if auto-run is enabled on the system, you can begin the upgrade by selecting Yes from the dialog box that appears.

Selecting Yes triggers the upgrade. You must read and accept the EULA. You must also specify any upgrade packs your software programs require to work with Windows 2000.

Next, you'll be required to select your installation partition. The upgrade process will then examine your system's configuration.

Just as the standard Setup program used a dialog box to monitor progress of the installation, so too does the upgrade process. The system will prepare a report, as shown in Figure 3.31, outlining potential software and hardware conflicts.

If the report finds incompatibilities, you should replace the offending devices or obtain updated drivers. In many cases, Windows 2000 Professional will operate properly, despite incompatibilities. Some software programs and hardware devices might provide only

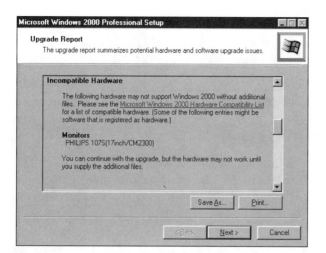

Figure 3.31
Windows 2000 prepares a compatibility report, which is also saved to the hard drive, for review.

limited functionality, though. And, the potential exists for a wayward device or program to lock up other components and services. Thus, it's best to ensure everything is compatible.

Should you need to remove offending hardware, you can do so without physically removing it from the machine. Windows 2000 will let you disable troublesome devices. Just click on Start|Settings|Control Panel. From there, double-click on Add/Remove Hardware.

After you resolve incompatibility issues, the next step is to begin installing Windows 2000 Professional files. One last dialog box will appear. It will warn you that the operation will require a specified range of time to complete the upgrade and that the machine will restart several times.

If you must deploy Windows 2000 Professional on several systems, a CD-ROM–based installation may not be your best bet. Instead, you may wish to deploy the new operating system over your organization's network.

Installing Windows 2000 over a Network

Imagine being as cool as Officer Frank Poncherello on *CHiPs* and as potent as the Incredible Hulk. That's what installing Windows 2000 Professional over a network can do for your image. You can make frequent use of powerful network-based installations, and you won't have to walk around the office carrying installation CDs.

If you need to deploy Windows 2000 Professional on multiple clients, you should consider installing the operating system over your organization's network. Worried that you have too great an assortment of hardware deployed throughout your firm? Don't sweat it. There's no requirement that all the machines receiving Windows 2000 share identical configurations when using a network-based installation.

The Windows 2000 network installation is much like a CD-ROM installation. The process starts when you execute the Setup program from a shared folder. As long as you can configure limited network access on a machine and get to a shared folder on your network, you're good to go.

The Setup program copies necessary installation files to the client system over your network, hence the name. Although it's good to have a 100Mbps network, we've conducted network-based installations on networks running at 10Mbps.

Ultimately, the demand your organization places on network bandwidth will determine the best time of day for installing Windows 2000 Professional over the network. If network traffic is particularly heavy in the morning and afternoon, which is typical, you'll want to get in extra early or stay late. Another alternative is to deploy the software on a weekend. However, if you're running a network that boasts decent network utilization rates, you probably won't have any trouble installing Windows 2000 Professional over the network in the middle of the day. Just keep an eye on the situation by tracking network utilization with Windows' Performance Monitor.

Note: For more information on monitoring network traffic, see Chapter 15.

You must ensure the following items are in place before proceeding with a network installation:

- An i386 directory from the Windows 2000 Professional CD-ROM must be present and shared.

- Target machines must have a partition with 685MB of free space.

- Target systems must have loaded network client software that enables them to connect to the shared folder.

The network client software can be a little tricky. Older NICs don't tend to support such functionality. Your best bet is to go with 3Com NICs because they tend to support all of Windows 2000 Professional's remote boot and network installation capabilities. They cost extra—in some cases twice as much. But, the added functionality can be well worth the cost, especially if you're planning to deploy the OS remotely.

After you've ensured the preceding criteria have been met, you're ready to proceed. You can follow these steps to install Windows 2000 Professional over a network:

1. Start the target machine using its client network software.

2. Establish a connection between the client machine and the network share housing the i386 files. The machine holding the network share is known as the *distribution server*.

3. Run WINNT.EXE to begin the Windows 2000 Setup program.

4. Windows 2000 Professional's Setup program will restart the client machine and installation begins.

3

When WINNT.EXE or WINNT32.EXE are run from the shared folder on the distribution server, two things happen. First, the Win_nt.~ temporary folder is created on the client machine. Second, the Windows 2000 installation files are copied from the shared folder on the distribution server to the Win_nt.~ folder on the client machine.

Of course, you're probably going to need to modify the default Setup program at one time or another. You'll find full-blown support for just that in Windows 2000.

Modifying the Windows 2000 Setup Program

The Windows 2000 Professional Setup program is highly customizable. The Setup program can be customized for all forms of installation the new OS supports.

Whether you're preparing for a clean installation or readying an upgrade, modification of the Setup program becomes complicated quickly, so you'll want to have a solid understanding of the different commands, or switches, that exist. That said, let's take a look at the options. Several switches are available for modifying WINNT.EXE, or standard, installations. They are listed in Table 3.6.

Note: The /u: switch requires use of the /s: parameter to specify the answer file location.

Keep in mind that the switches you may have used for creating boot disks in the past on older Windows NT platforms are no longer used. They've been replaced by MAKEBOOT.EXE.

Upgrades, or those Windows 2000 Professional installations triggered with the WINNT32.EXE command, possess their own set of switches. Table 3.7 lists WINNT32.EXE switches and their functions.

Table 3.6   WINNT.EXE switches and their functions.

WINNT.EXE Switch	Function
/a	Turns on accessibility options.
/e:[*command*]	Executes the supplied command before Setup's final phase.
/i:[*inf file name*]	Specifies the information file name Setup is to use. DOSNET.INF is the default. Only the file name is required, not the path.
/r:[*folder name*]	Specifies an additional folder to be created during Setup.
/rx:[*folder name*]	Specifies an additional folder to be copied during Setup.
/s:[*source path*]	Specifies the location of Windows 2000 Setup files; requires a full path.
/t:[*temp drive*]	Specifies the drive where temporary files are to be copied. The default is the drive offering the most free space.
/u:[*answer file name*]	Specifies the use of an answer file for unattended installation. ***answer file name*** indicates the name of the answer file to be used.
/udf:[*identifier, UDF*]	Specifies a uniqueness database file, indicated by **UDF**, to be used during installation. ***identifier*** specifies which parameter in the answer file should be replaced with information from the UDF file.

Table 3.7   WINNT32.EXE switches and their functions.

WINNT32.EXE Switches	Function
/checkupgradeonly	Checks a computer for incompatibilities; saves a WINNT32.LOG report for NT upgrades and UPGRADE.TXT report for Windows 9x upgrades.
/copydir:[*folder*]	Creates an additional systemroot folder each time **/copydir** is used.
/copysource:[*folder*]	Creates an additional folder in the systemroot folder to be deleted after the installation is finished.
/cmd:[*command*]	Executes the supplied command before Setup's final phase.
/cmdcons	Installs files necessary for loading the file repair and recovery console.
/debug [*level:file*]	Creates a debug log at the level specified.
/s:[*source path*]	Specifies the location of Windows 2000 installation files. Multiple /s: switches can sometimes shorten transfer times.
/syspart:[*drive letter*]	Copies Setup files to the specified hard disk and marks the drive active.
/tempdrive:[*drive letter*]	Copies temporary Setup files to the specified drive for installation there and marks it active.
/unattend [*number:answer file name*]	Triggers an unattended installation. ***number*** specifies the number of seconds between the time Setup finishes copying the files and when it restarts. ***answer file name*** specifies the name of the answer file to be used during Setup.
/udf:[*identifier, UDF*]	Specifies a uniqueness database file, indicated by ***UDF***, to be used during installation. ***identifier*** specifies which parameter in the answer file should be replaced with information from the UDF file, which overrides the value supplied by the answer file.

Tip: The /syspart switch requires use of the /tempdrive parameter. Syspart starts Windows 2000 on one drive but then pauses after startup files are copied and the drive is marked active. Why? Having the hard drive loaded with the startup files and marked active while it's paused lets you remove it from the system it's in and place it in another machine. Then, you can complete the Setup process on a different machine.

Another available Windows 2000 installation method is an automated installation using the Windows 2000 Setup Manager Wizard. This method can further modify Windows 2000 Professional installations.

Installing Windows 2000 Using the Setup Manager Wizard

Before Windows 2000, you had to create elaborate scripts to automate multiple client installations. If you fear scripts, take heart. You still need elaborate scripts, but Windows 2000 Professional includes a powerful new Setup Manager Wizard to quickly create customized scripts.

The use of the wizard helps eliminate many of the errors, including simple typographical errors, that brought past installations to a standstill. It works by providing a graphical interface you use to create answer files the Setup program needs to automate a customized installation.

Tip: You can still manually edit the UNATTEND.TXT file used to supply hardware configuration variables during unattended installations. You don't really want to do that, though, do you? Using the Windows 2000 Setup Wizard helps eliminate common syntax and keystroke errors.

3

To use the Windows 2000 Setup Manager, you have to install support tools from the Windows 2000 Professional CD-ROM. Follow these steps to transfer the Setup Manager and its related files from the Windows 2000 Professional CD-ROM to your system's hard drive:

1. Log in as Administrator and insert the Windows 2000 Professional CD-ROM in the system's CD-ROM drive.

2. Open Windows Explorer.

3. Create a folder—named Support Tools, for example—on your hard disk to house the files you'll be transferring from the CD-ROM.

4. Navigate to the Support\Tools folder on the CD-ROM in Windows Explorer and right-click on the DEPLOY.CAB file.

5. Select Open from the pop-up menu, and Windows 2000 will display seven files (unless you've loaded a WinZip utility, in which case you'll follow its directions to unzip the files to the Support Tools folder you created on the system's hard disk).

6. Select all seven files by holding the Ctrl key and right-clicking on any one of them. Then, select Extract from the pop-up menu.

7. Select the Support Tools folder you created from the Browse For Folder dialog box and click on OK.

8. Wait while the files are copied. When the copying finishes, click on the Support Tools folder to view the seven files on your hard drive.

9. Double-click on the SETUPMGR.EXE file to launch the Setup Manager Wizard.

The Windows 2000 Setup Manager can specify computer- and user-specific rights during setup. The wizard lets you specify the distribution server folder that will house the Windows 2000 Professional installation files, applications to be run, and much more.

A number of different options can be configured using the Setup Manager, including the following:

- The operating system to be installed (Windows 2000 Professional or Windows 2000 Server)

- The interaction level to be extended to the user during installation

- Computer names

- Administrator password

- Display settings

- Workgroup and domain names

- Network settings

- Browser and shell settings

- Additional commands

When the Windows 2000 Setup Manager begins, you must select from one of three options:

- Create A New Answer File

- Create An Answer File That Duplicates The Current System's Configuration

- Modify An Existing Answer File

If you choose Create A New Answer File, you must specify which one of the following the answer file is for:

- An unattended Windows 2000 installation

- A Sysprep installation

- Remote Installation Services

For example, say you wish to create an unattended answer file for a Windows 2000 Professional installation. Further, say you need to specify typical network settings, a default interaction level, and a share named Win2KPro to house the installation files.

You would need to make several changes to default settings. You would follow these steps after opening the Setup Manager Wizard:

1. Click on Next on the Welcome To The Windows 2000 Setup Manager Wizard screen.

2. Select Create A New Answer File and select Next, as shown in Figure 3.32.

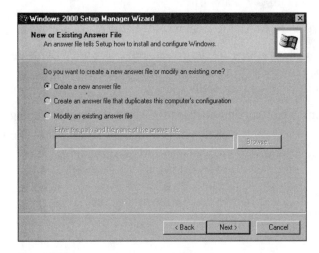

Figure 3.32
You must specify whether you're creating a new answer file or modifying an existing answer file.

3. Select Windows 2000 Unattended Installation and click on Next.

4. Select Windows 2000 Professional. Your other option is Windows 2000 Server.

5. Enter the user interaction level as Provide Defaults and click on Next, as shown in Figure 3.33.

6. Enter the default name and organization you want the Setup program to use. If these fields are left blank, the answer file won't specify these values when installing Windows 2000 Professional, and the individual performing the installation will have to enter them.

7. Supply the computer name and click on Next. You can also import computer names from a text file or automatically generate computer names based on the organization name.

8. Specify whether the user should be prompted to supply the Administrator password or one should be supplied. You can also specify whether the system should automatically log on as Administrator when it starts, as well as the number of times to auto log on. Click on Next.

9. Specify display settings, including colors, screen area, and refresh frequency. You can choose to use Windows default settings or use customized display settings. Click on Next.

10. Select Typical Settings for Network Settings and click on Next. (Your other option is Custom Settings.)

11. Specify the workgroup or domain name. You can also create a computer account in the domain. If you do, you'll have to provide a username and password that have permission to do so. Click on Next.

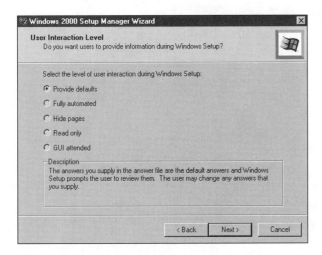

Figure 3.33
You can select from five different levels of user interaction.

12. Enter the time zone and click on Next.

13. Specify whether to edit or review additional settings and click on Next.

14. Provide telephony settings, such as the country/region and whether a number must be dialed to access an outside line and if so, what it is. Click on Next. You can also choose not to specify this setting.

15. Provide regional settings or elect to have the user provide them during Setup. Click on Next.

16. Select the language to use (most likely Western Europe and United States, which you'll find at the bottom of the dialog box after scrolling down) and click on Next.

17. Specify Internet browser and shell settings for Windows 2000. You can choose default Internet Explorer settings, use an autoconfiguration script created by the Internet Explorer Administration Kit, or individually specify proxy and default home page settings. Click on Next.

18. Specify the folder into which Windows 2000 Professional should be installed. You can select Winnt, a uniquely named folder generated by the Setup program, or a folder you specify, as shown in Figure 3.34. Click on Next.

19. Specify the name of network printers you wish the computer to be configured to use. Click on Next.

20. Specify any run-once commands you wish to use. Click on Next.

21. Specify whether you wish to create or modify a distribution folder or the answer file will be used to install from a CD. In this case, we'll create the distribution folder by selecting the Yes radio button and clicking on Next.

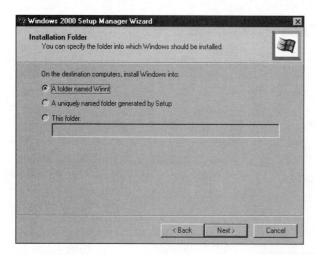

Figure 3.34
You must specify the name of the folder into which you install Windows 2000 Professional.

22. Specify whether a new distribution folder is being created or an existing distribution folder is being created. For this example, we'll specify the Win2KPro folder on a server with a drive letter of F:, as shown in Figure 3.35. Click on Next.

23. Provide new or additional mass storage drivers for installation and click on Next.

24. Specify a replacement Hardware Abstraction Layer (HAL), or select the default by clicking on Next.

25. Specify any additional commands to be run that don't require logging on and select Next.

26. Specify any Original Equipment Manufacturer (OEM), or custom, branding you wish Windows Setup to use. Your choices are for the logo to be displayed during Windows Setup and the background to be used during Windows Setup. Click on Next.

27. Specify any additional files or folders you want copied to the destination machines. Click on Next.

28. Provide the answer file name, as well as the location where you want it stored. For this example, we'll label it UNATTEND.TXT and park it in the F:\Win2KPro folder, as shown in Figure 3.36. Click on Next.

29. Specify where the Windows Setup files should be copied from to the distribution folder. Click on Next.

30. Wait while the Setup Manager Wizard copies the Setup files. This step could take a while, depending on the speed of your network and CD-ROM and hard drives.

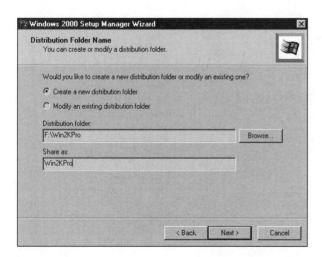

Figure 3.35
You must specify whether to create a new distribution folder or modify an existing one. In addition, you must provide the name of the distribution folder.

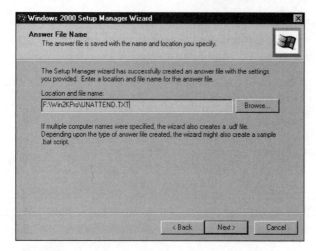

Figure 3.36
You must provide a name and location for storing the answer file you're creating.

31. When the process finishes, the Setup Manager will present you with a confirmation screen. It verifies that the UNATTEND.TXT and UNATTEND.BAT files were completed and indicates where they're located. The batch file provides information about using the unattended file you just created. Click on Finish, and you're done. You're ready to use your unattended file.

The resulting UNATTEND.TXT file contains the following text:

```
;SetupMgrTag
[Data]
    AutoPartition=1
    MsDosInitiated="0"
    UnattendedInstall="Yes"

[Unattended]
    UnattendMode=ProvideDefault
    OemPreinstall=Yes
    TargetPath=\WINNT

[GuiUnattended]
    AdminPassword=toledo
    OEMSkipRegional=1

[UserData]
    FullName="Erik Eckel"
    OrgName=Test
    ComputerName=*
```

```
[RegionalSettings]
    LanguageGroup=1

[SetupMgr]
    DistFolder=F:\Win2KPro
    DistShare=Win2KPro

[Identification]
    JoinWorkgroup=WORKGROUP

[Networking]
    InstallDefaultComponents=Yes
```

Note that this file is rather short because mostly default settings were chosen. Note also how the default values that were changed during Setup are reflected in the text file. For example, under **[SetupMgr]**, the distribution folder now reads **F:\Win2KPro** and the distribution share reads **Win2KPro**.

Tip: You can find real copies of the UNATTEND.TXT and UNATTEND.BAT files on the CD-ROM included with this book.

Remember that you also can use answer files when booting from a CD-ROM, as Step 21 demonstrates. Using the Setup Manager, specify the installation folder, select the No, This Answer File Will Be Used To Install From A CD option, and save the newly created file to a floppy with the name WINNT.SIF. The WINNT.EXE program searches for the WINNT.SIF file when you're booting from a CD-ROM drive. It can be used to specify the answer file the Setup program uses to customize installation.

The Setup Wizard also prompts you to specify the interaction level between users and the Setup program, as Step 5 demonstrates. Your selection determines how much expertise a user requires to complete installation. Table 3.8 describes the five user interaction levels available in Windows 2000.

If you need to install Windows 2000 Professional on multiple systems that share identical configurations, there may be a quicker, easier way. The key is having similar hardware configurations. Let's take a look.

Installing Windows 2000 Using Disk Duplication

The popularity of Norton Ghost, PowerQuest Drive Image, and other disk duplication programs attests to the value IT professionals place on such utilities. Using cloning or disk-imaging software can save tremendous time when you're deploying Windows 2000 Professional. Although the use of a third-party software program is required, Windows 2000 Professional includes support for disk duplication.

Table 3.8   User interaction levels that can be selected using the Setup Manager.

Level	Description	Intended Use
Fully Automated	Uses the values provided in the answer file to completely automate the remaining steps of the Windows 2000 installation.	Best used when deploying multiple systems with the same configurations.
Provide Defaults	Requests that users confirm the values provided by the answer file when completing the Windows 2000 installation.	Best used for situations in which just a few changes might be made to the configuration values supplied by the answer file.
Hide Pages	Automates the portions of the Setup process for which values are provided in the answer file but requires users to supply necessary information not provided in the answer file.	Best for preparing a system with a particular configuration when a user might also need the ability to configure a limited number of settings.
Read Only	Automates the sections of the Setup process for which values are provided in the answer file but requires users to supply information not provided in the answer file. With Read Only, only the portions of the dialog boxes requiring more information are shown.	Best used when you want users to provide only the information not supplied by the answer file.
GUI Attended	Completely automates the text-based portion of the Setup process. A user completing the Setup program must then provide the remaining information needed by the Setup program to complete installation.	Best used when you want to completely automate the text-based portion of Setup but provide users with the ability to completely customize the GUI portion of the Setup process.

The SYSPREP.EXE program plays a critical role in cloning Windows 2000 Professional systems. SYSPREP.EXE, which is often used with the Windows 2000 Setup Manager Wizard, prepares a disk for the imaging process. After the SYSPREP.EXE program is run, the third-party tool can be used to capture an image and copy it to other hard disks.

Problems used to arise due to the need for unique security identifiers (SIDs). Older Windows NT operating systems didn't feature Sysprep, so they couldn't easily overcome the problem posed by SIDs, which contain unique and sensitive user- and computer-specific information. That's all changed now. Sysprep can strip SIDs and other unit-specific information from an image before it's captured and duplicated.

Note: Systems installed using disk cloning generate unique SIDs on their own following the disk duplication process.

Several switches, described in Table 3.9, can be used with Sysprep. They customize use of the System Preparation utility.

Several steps are involved when you're cloning other systems for deployment. You can follow these steps when cloning a Windows 2000 Professional system:

1. Install and configure Windows 2000 Professional.

2. Install and configure the applications, programs, and proprietary software you want to include in the automated deployment.

Table 3.9   Switches for customizing the SYSPREP.EXE utility.

Switches	Function
-quiet	Instructs the SYSPREP.EXE utility to run with no user interaction
-pnp	Specifies that plug-and-play detection is forced at the next startup
-reboot	Specifies the system should restart instead of shut down when SYSPREP.EXE completes
-nosidgen	Indicates that a security identifier should not be generated when the reference system reboots

3

3. Run the System Preparation tool (SYSPREP.EXE) on the master computer featuring the image you want to clone and copy to other machines. Alternatively, you can run the Windows 2000 Setup Manager Wizard to create a SYSPREP.INF file. This file, which the Setup Manager's Mini-Setup program seeks, is stored in the SYSPREP folder created by the Setup Manager at the root of the drive image. It can also be stored on a floppy, which must be inserted into the destination computer's floppy drive (usually designated by drive letter A) prior to the Mini-Setup program launching in Step 6.

Note: The SYSPREP.INF file can be used to specify that customized drivers should be loaded during the installation process.

4. Restart the master computer and run a third-party disk-cloning program to create a master image, which should be stored on a shared folder (or burnt to a CD-ROM). Use a floppy disk created by the third-party disk-imaging utility to boot the system on which you intend to install the image, and then connect to the network share containing the drive image.

5. Use the third-party disk-imaging program to copy the image file onto the destination machine. Alternatively, you can load the destination machine using the CD-ROM if you chose to burn a copy.

6. Reboot the destination system. The Windows 2000 Mini-Setup program runs, and you'll be prompted for computer-specific information, such as an administrator password for the new computer, the computer name, and so on. The Mini-Setup program generates a new SID, and the system becomes operational.

Tip: When you're using disk duplication, remember that systems do not need to possess the same configurations. However, the mass storage controllers (SCSI controllers or IDE chipsets) and hardware abstraction layers (Advanced Configuration and Power Interface [ACPI] systems can't be mixed with non-ACPI systems) used on both the test and destination systems must be identical.

Disk cloning may not be for you if you have machines distributed throughout several physical locations. If that's the case, you may wish to consider deploying Windows 2000 Professional using Remote Installation Services.

Installing Windows 2000 Professional Using Remote Installation Services

If you thought you were cool installing Windows 2000 Professional over a network, imagine installing Windows 2000 Professional over a network to a *remote location*. Using Windows 2000 Professional's Remote Installation Services (RIS), you can do just that, if specific criteria are met, making you as cool as, well, Arthur Fonzarelli from *Happy Days*.

Seriously, RIS packs a lot of punch. However, the wallop RIS packs carries a price. You'll need a variety of resources available. For starters, a Windows 2000 server must exist as part of your RIS deployment recipe.

RIS enables Windows 2000 servers to remotely install Windows 2000 Professional on other networked machines. Windows 2000 Professional cannot deploy Windows 2000 Professional using RIS. A machine running the Windows 2000 server platform must be used.

RIS also can be used to configure Windows 2000 Professional machines, when they're installed, throughout an entire network. Both the installation and configuration of client machines can be completed from a single location, which is where RIS's value really comes into play. No longer must administrators travel to remote locations to install and configure Windows 2000 Professional.

Other benefits of Windows 2000 Professional deployment using RIS include the following:

- The requirement for maintaining hardware-specific images is eliminated because RIS supports Setup's use of plug-and-play hardware detection.

- RIS provides another option for fixing networked computers that have failed because of corrupted operating systems.

- RIS contributes to improved total costs of ownership because other technical staff can be entrusted to install Windows 2000.

- Fully configured systems can be easily deployed using RIPREP.EXE.

Before IT professionals can realize the benefits resulting from deployment of Windows 2000 Professional systems using RIS, the following requirements must be met:

- Windows 2000 servers must be present on the network and running Remote Installation Services. RIS servers can be domain controllers or member servers.

- A Windows 2000 server must be running the DNS service.

- A Windows 2000 server must be running the Dynamic Host Configuration Protocol (DHCP) service.

- A Windows 2000 server must be running Active Directory.

- Sufficient (2GB) NTFS-formatted hard disk or partition space must be available for holding the operating system images you plan to transfer to destination systems. Group policies are used to control access to the different images housed here. This partition or drive cannot be housed on the drive running the Windows 2000 server operating system.

- The destination machines should support remote boot or Preboot Execution Environment (PXE) network interface cards.

- The client machines should be Network PC compatible.

The Network PC specification has the following requirements of its own:

- The NIC must be set as the primary boot device within the system BIOS.

- The user account performing the installation must be able to log on as a batch job user.

- Users must be granted permission to create computer accounts in the domain they are joining, unless the computer account has already been created using Active Directory.

All these required items need not be available on a single server. However, they must all be available on the network.

RIS works by booting a destination or target system without requiring that Windows be installed. It requests an IP address from the DHCP server that it requires. This DHCP server also supplies the IP address of the closest RIS server.

If a remote system doesn't support remote boot, don't fear. All hope is not lost. You can create a RIS boot disk that can be used. However, someone must physically place it in the destination machine. You create the RIS boot disk by running the RBFG.EXE command. It is located in the RemoteInstall\Admin\i386 folder of the Windows 2000 Server CD-ROM.

If a computer account is configured in Active Directory for the target system, the client system then contacts the RIS server. The RIS server checks Active Directory for the globally unique identifier (GUID) for the target machine. This is one of the reasons the computer account must exist for it. Then, the RIS server transmits the images that the destination machine has privileges to receive and install automatically.

What happens if a computer account isn't configured in Active Directory for the target client system? If no computer account is found, the Client Installation Wizard is triggered, enabling selection of an operating system image.

Using RIS, of course, requires that it be installed on a server. The Remote Installation Services Startup Wizard assists with installation. Before you can run the wizard, you must add the RIS component using the Windows Components Wizard located in Control Panel's Add/Remove Programs applet on a machine running a Windows 2000 platform. Remote Installation Services must be selected.

The server must be restarted after the Windows Components Wizard finishes. Running RISETUP.EXE from a command prompt or the Start|Run command line triggers the Remote Installation Services Setup Wizard. The first item the wizard requests is the path to the Remote Installation Folder location.

Next, two options are provided regarding initial RIS settings. You can enable the server to support client computers requesting service immediately, before the server has been configured to do so. You can also configure the server to respond to unknown client computers. Neither option is supported by default.

The RIS wizard then requires that you specify the path for the installation files. The path directs RIS either to a shared folder or a CD-ROM drive.

Tip: *Personal experience has proven that a standard edition Windows 2000 Professional CD-ROM must be used. RIS doesn't support installing Windows 2000 Professional using an Upgrade version of Windows 2000 Professional.*

You'll be asked next to provide a friendly description and help text language for the Windows 2000 Professional installation image. The wizard will then present the installation settings for review and confirmation, as shown in Figure 3.37.

If the information is accurate, click on Finish. As you'll see many times in Windows 2000, a dialog box will track the installation progress. When the installation finishes, click on Done, and you're ready to begin imaging Windows 2000 Professional client machines for deployment.

Follow these steps to create a RIS image:

1. Open Active Directory Users And Computers.

2. Right-click on the server that's running the RIS service. Select Properties and click on the Remote Install tab.

3. Select Advanced Settings and then click on the Images tab.

4. Select Add to trigger the Add Wizard.

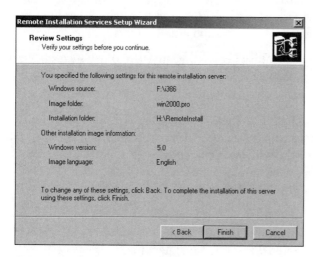

Figure 3.37
RIS will present you with a summary dialog box before completing.

5. Skip over the Associate A New Answer File To An Existing Image option because no images exist yet and select Next.

6. Select the Add A New Installation Image option and click on Next.

7. Using the Add Installation Image Wizard, create the new Windows 2000 Professional image and select the option to associate it with an answer file. Then, click on Finish to complete the wizard.

8. Specify the location of the answer file and click on Next.

9. Select the Windows 2000 Professional image you just created to apply the answer file (also just created) to it and click on Next.

10. Provide the name of the answer file.

11. Enter a user-friendly name and a more detailed description of the image in the Help Text box and click on Finish to complete the RIS image-creation process.

You might have to complete one more process before you can proceed with the Windows 2000 Professional installation. You may need to make a RIS boot disk for target systems that aren't Network PC compliant.

You must complete these steps to create a RIS boot disk:

1. Place a formatted 1.44MB disk in the destination machine's floppy drive.

2. Connect to the RIS server and execute the RBFG.EXE command from the RemoteInstall\Admin\i386 folder.

3. Select the appropriate drive letter designation (A: is usually the floppy drive) as the floppy drive you wish to use in the Remote Boot Disk Generator dialog box.

4. Click on the Adapter List button to quickly ensure the NIC the destination machine possesses is supported. Here again is another reason to use 3Com NICs because they are largely supported by Windows 2000.

5. Click on Create Disk to build the remote RIS boot disk.

When you're ready to transfer the Windows 2000 Professional image from a server to a destination client, you should follow these steps:

1. Place a boot disk, created using the RBFG.EXE command in the RemoteInstall\ Admin\i386 folder of the Windows 2000 server CD-ROM, in the floppy drive of the units not featuring the remote boot capability. Press F12 when prompted to boot from the network.

2. Press Enter from the first screen to trigger the Client Installation Wizard.

3. Supply the name of the domain the system should join and then Tab to the password box.

4. Enter the password for the Administrator account and press Enter.

5. Provide the IP address for the network's DNS server.

6. Select Custom Setup and press Enter.

7. Provide the appropriate computer name for the system. Then, specify the path to the share you created on the server that houses the Windows 2000 Professional image the destination system is to use and press Enter.

8. Select the image you intended to transfer to the destination system.

9. Confirm the settings were correct and press Enter, triggering the Windows 2000 Professional installation.

Certainly, many steps are involved in completing a RIS-based installation. However, if you're troubleshooting remotely located machines or deploying Windows 2000 Professional to systems located in branch offices or other locations, you'll find it can save a lot of time.

Now that we've covered all the different methods available for installing Windows 2000 Professional, it's time to discuss another subject. What should you do when the Setup program throws a few curveballs your way?

Troubleshooting Windows 2000 Professional Setup

Despite your best planning and preparation, Windows 2000 Professional's Setup program will sometimes encounter errors it can't fix itself. That's where you come in. As an IT professional, you need to understand common installation issues and how to solve them.

There are several common Setup errors, and each has a quick fix available. If you encounter any of these issues, try the provided solution:

- *Windows 2000 Professional fails to install or start.* Check the HCL to ensure you don't have an incompatible device that's foiling the Setup program.

- *Windows 2000 Professional Setup locks up midway through the installation process.* Attempt to reboot the system using the infamous three-finger salute (pressing Ctrl+Alt+Delete all at the same time). If you don't get a response, try the same command again. If you still get no response, try pressing your computer's reset button. If a boot menu appears, select Windows 2000 Setup. If you don't see a boot menu, try executing Setup again.

- *Setup fails or freezes while copying files.* Check your BIOS and ensure IDE controllers are configured properly. Also, check to ensure another peripheral isn't interfering with your hard disk controller. Although taking these steps is inconvenient, it can simplify troubleshooting exponentially. Simply remove all unneeded peripherals in an attempt to eliminate the offending device.

- *Multiple faults are experienced.* Forcibly reboot the machine as many times as faults are encountered. The Windows 2000 Setup program can learn from previous faults it experiences, and this technique might get you past the stumbling block.

3

- *You experience installation trouble due to scratched or faulty CD-ROMs.* Contact Microsoft or your vendor. Using another CD-ROM or a replacement CD-ROM can often eliminate the problem.

- *Windows 2000 Professional doesn't support your CD-ROM drive.* Reach for the purchase orders because you need a new CD-ROM drive. In a pinch, you can try a network-based installation to circumvent the error.

- *The Setup program finds insufficient disk space for the Windows 2000 Professional installation.* We've seen this one often in testing environments. You'll have to find room. Specify another drive or partition. Should no other drives or spaces be available, purchase new drives or delete data you no longer need. You must free up disk space, or Setup won't be able to complete.

- *A dependent service fails to start.* Check the Network Settings page and ensure the correct protocol and adapter are installed. Also, check that the NIC is properly configured and has the correct transceiver type specified. Verify, too, that the local computer name is unique.

- *After installing Windows 2000 Professional, you can't connect to a domain controller.* Perform the following procedures:

  - Ensure you've entered the correct domain name.

  - Verify you've entered the correct DNS and DHCP server addresses and that both services are online.

  - Verify that the network card and protocol settings are configured correctly.

  - If Windows 2000 Professional is being reinstalled and is using the same computer name, delete and then re-create the computer account on the server.

- *No domain controller is available, or the DNS or DHCP services are unavailable.* You can complete the installation by joining a workgroup. Later, when the failed services come online or a domain controller becomes available, you can join the domain.

Don't be afraid to try reading the Setup logs, too. They can provide valuable troubleshooting information.

Using the Windows 2000 Professional Setup Logs

Several Setup logs gather valuable information. It's important you know which logs can help and what information each provides. You'll probably want to focus on two principal Setup logs:

- *The Action Log*—Lists actions that Setup performs. These actions are listed in chronological order. It is stored as SETUPACT.LOG in the *systemroot* folder.

- *The Error Log*—Collects descriptions of errors that occur during Setup. It also includes severity values for each error that it lists. Stored as SETUPERR.LOG in the *systemroot* folder.

You might also find help from the multimedia log, saved as MMDET.LOG in the *systemroot* folder. It details port ranges for each device.

The SETUPAPI.LOG logs an entry each time an error from an INF file is triggered. The NETSETUP.LOG, located in the *systemroot*\debug folder, logs activity associated with joining workgroups and domains.

If you can't find relief using the log files or the troubleshooting steps we've listed, your best bet is to visit Microsoft's Web site. Check the Knowledge Base and TechNet and tighten your searches as much as possible. Be on the lookout for patches and drivers that you can use to fix common Setup problems.

Summary

Installing Windows 2000 Professional no longer means just grabbing the CD-ROM and a tall cup of java, and heading out into the office to begin loading desktops. There are many new options now, including image-based installations, remote installations, and un-attended installations.

Before you determine which deployment method is best for you, make sure you've answered all the basic questions up front. We have supplied Decision Tree 3.1 to help you with that process.

Sometimes it will be necessary to dual-boot with other operating systems. You may need to maintain a Windows NT 4 Workstation or Windows 9x install. You may even wish to run Linux. In the next chapter, we'll examine the tricks, tips, and issues involved when dual-booting a system using Windows 2000 Professional. We've even triple-booted systems running Windows 2000 Professional with no trouble. Although you may not wish to do so every day, it's nice to know you can.

Chapter 4

Dual-Booting with Windows 2000

Understanding Dual-Booting

Dual-booting with Windows 2000 Professional enables you to have multiple operating systems running on one machine. This capability can be beneficial if you have legacy business applications that require a specific operating system, prompting you to maintain multiple operating systems. Dual-booting is also referred to as a *multiple-boot configuration* because you are not limited to having just two operating systems on a machine. For instance, Windows 98, Windows NT 4, and Windows 2000 Professional can all be installed on the same machine. Furthermore, you can have multiple versions of the same operating system on the same machine.

It is important to understand that you can boot to only one of these operating systems at a time. You define a default operating system to boot into, but during the boot process, you have a choice of booting into any other operating system you have installed on that machine.

You must take many precautions and facts into consideration if you choose to configure a multiple-boot system. They include what operating systems you are considering installing, the number of logical volumes, possibly the number of hard drives required, and what, as well as where, current applications are installed on the machine. Probably one of the biggest considerations is what file system you choose when you format your volumes. This choice will directly affect where you choose to install each operating system.

Disks and Volumes

It is important to understand the terminology and concepts of data storage in order to create the most efficient and flexible environment in Windows 2000 Professional. In this section we'll discuss the various disks, and the volumes that can be created on those disks.

Disks

Disks are physical data storage devices attached to the computer. They come in a variety of sizes, and you can have multiple disks in one computer. For instance, you can purchase a 20GB disk and a 30GB disk and attach them to your computer.

Fault tolerance, performance, and disaster recovery are all critical considerations when you're determining the number and size of disks required in your configuration. Table 4.1 lists the terminology and defines the sizes you will see and hear about when referring to your computer's disks, and in some instances your computer's memory as well.

Windows 2000 supports two types of disks: basic and dynamic. Basic disks, which are the ones you are probably most familiar with, are the disk type you have been using in all your Windows environments. They are the default disk type when you add a disk in any Windows configuration. Windows 2000 introduces dynamic disks, eliminating some of the restrictions, such as the maximum of four partitions per disk, that a basic disk imposes on your configuration of disks. You can mix and match the two types of disks in one configuration, as shown in Decision Tree 4.1.

Volumes

You can break down or segment your disk into smaller, more manageable areas of storage by creating partitions or volumes, which function as if they were their own physical disks. The term *partition* is used to name these sections of your disks in the earlier versions of the Windows environments. Furthermore, basic disks in the Windows 2000 environment are still referred to by the term *partition*. However, when you're referring to these sections on dynamic disks, which are available only in Windows 2000, they are referred to as *volumes* (see Table 4.2 for an explanation of the terminology used when referring to basic and dynamic disks in Windows 2000). For the most part, up until Windows 2000, everyone used the terms *partitions* and *volumes* interchangeably. These terms are not specific to the Windows operating systems environments; they are generic terms used when dividing the areas of storage on disks in any environment.

You need to be familiar with two critical volumes when installing an operating system and choosing your file systems: the boot volume and the system volume. The boot volume contains the operating system files and the files required to support the operating system.

Table 4.1 Size terminology and definitions.

Size	Full Word	Definition
1B	Byte	8 bits (characters)
1KB	Kilobyte	1,024 bytes
1MB	Megabyte	1,024KB
1GB	Gigabyte	1,024MB
1TB	Terabyte	1,024GB
1PB	Petabyte	1,024TB
1XB	Exabyte	1,024PB
1ZB	Zettabyte	1,024XB
1YB	Yottabyte	1,024ZB

4

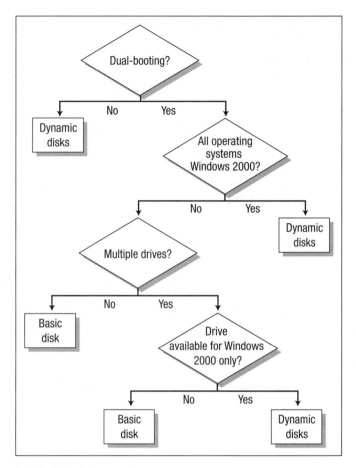

Decision Tree 4.1
Choosing your disk type.

Table 4.2   Basic and dynamic disk terminology.

Basic Disk	Dynamic Disk
Primary partition	Simple volume
System and boot partition	System and boot volumes
Active partition	Active volume
Extended partition	Volume and unallocated space
Logical drive	Simple volume
Volume set	Spanned volume
Stripe set	Striped volume
Stripe set with parity	RAID-5 volume
Mirror set	Mirrored volume

The system volume contains the hardware-specific files required to load the appropriate operating system and boot to the chosen operating system. In other words, the boot volume contains the operating system files, and the system volume contains the required boot files. They appear to have been named the opposite of what they should have been named based on what actions they perform, but it is important that you understand the difference between the two volumes. The boot and system volumes can be the same volume. Figure 4.1 shows a basic disk with three partitions and specifies the boot and system volumes.

The utility used to manage your disks, disk types, file systems, partitions, and other disk functions is called Disk Management. This utility is available from the Computer Management snap-in via the Microsoft Management Console (MMC), which is located inside your Administrative Tools. Figure 4.1 shows the Disk Management utility provided by Windows 2000. This utility provides a graphical user interface (GUI) to manage your hard drives, floppy drive, CD-ROM, and removable storage devices.

Figure 4.2 shows the properties of one of the partitions located on a Windows 2000 installation. On the General tab within the Properties dialog box, you see a graphical display of the size of this partition and the amount of free space available. Also, using the Disk Cleanup button, you can compress the drive and run a cleanup program that will allow you to delete

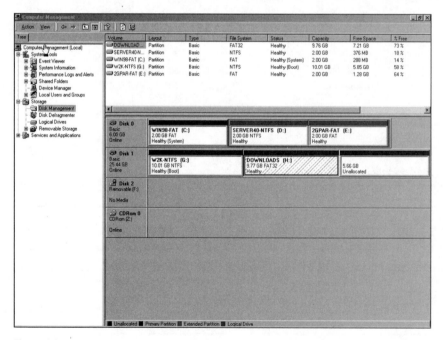

Figure 4.1
Disk Management utility.

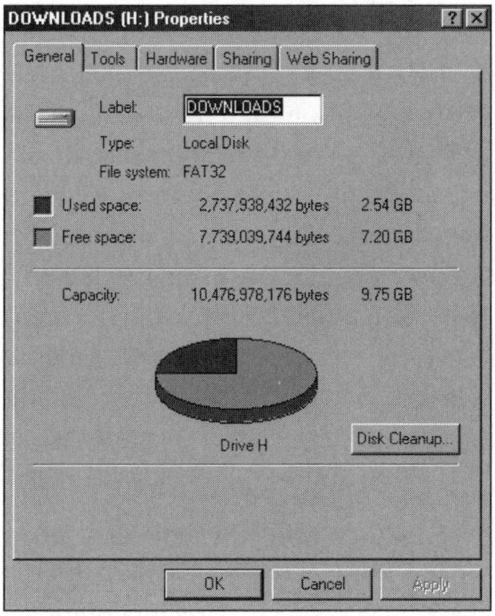

Figure 4.2
Properties dialog box of a disk volume.

temporary files. Other tabs available include the Tools tab, which provides tools you can use to manage your disks to handle problems such as fragmentation. The Hardware tab enables you to view the device properties of all available storage devices. The Security (only available on NTFS partitions), Sharing, and Web Sharing tabs provide interfaces for setting permissions for both local and remote access. Other tabs may be present if the partition uses that functionality. For example, a Remote Storage tab will be available on a partition configured for remote storage management. The Quota tab enables you to turn on disk quotas for the volume. These disk quotas can limit the amount of space a user consumes on the drive. This consumption is based on the files the user owns.

Now that you are familiar with basic and dynamic disks, as well as partitions and volumes, you must format them with the correct file system before you can store data on them. Windows 2000 supports three primary file systems: FAT, FAT32, and NTFS. Each of these file systems has strengths and weaknesses, determines accessibility between operating systems, and provides unique functionality.

Supported File Systems

When you format a volume, it applies the file system and is prepared to receive data. The file system defines the overall structure in which files are named, stored, and organized. The file system also determines which files can be accessed from which operating systems and may also provide a built-in level of security between volumes and operating systems.

FAT

The file allocation table (FAT) is the de facto standard for hard disks installed on many PCs. The FAT is one of the main logical structures the file system uses, so it isn't exactly the best way to refer to the entire file system. This file allocation table serves two primary purposes: It holds the allocation information for each file on the volume in the form of linked lists of allocation units (which are also called *clusters*), and it indicates which allocation units are available for assignment to a new file that is being created or an existing file that is being extended. The file allocation tables are stored in the area of the disk immediately following the volume boot sector. Each volume actually contains two identical copies of the file allocation table. The second one is meant to be a backup in case of any damage to the first copy. Damage to the file allocation table can result in data loss because the information about which parts of the disk contain which files is stored here.

The FAT file system is simple and reliable. It is less likely to lose data because of a computer crashing in the middle of an update, and the file allocation table does not consume a lot of memory. However, it does add a lot of extra administrative I/O to different areas of the volume. You can choose from two command-line utilities to maintain the file allocation table: The CHKDSK utility examines the file allocation table, and the SCANDISK utility fixes the file allocation table if it becomes corrupt.

The original FAT file system is sometimes called FAT16 because of its use of 16-bit binary numbers to represent cluster numbers. The size of your FAT volume determines the size of your allocation units. An allocation unit is the minimum amount of space used by each file; each file occupies one or more allocation units. For instance, if you have a volume that is less than 32MB, the allocation unit size is 512 bytes. However, if you have volume that is greater than 128MB but less than 256MB, the allocation unit size is 4KB. When your allocation units are larger and you create a large number of small files, you are wasting disk space. These allocation units also prevent you from creating a FAT volume greater than 2GB. FAT16 is used for hard disk volumes ranging in size from 16MB to 2,048MB.

File names are limited to eight characters with a three-character file extension (as in the name AUTOEXEC.BAT). You can control different aspects of the files by setting four attributes: whether it is a System file; should it be Hidden in the DIR display; should it be Archived the next time you perform a disk backup; and is it Read-only, preventing changes from being saved to the file. Information regarding when the file was last modified is also provided.

Even though FAT16 is the primary operating system for most PCs, it does have some limitations. It allows only 8.3 file names, has a maximum volume size of 2GB, uses 16-bit architecture, and provides only a handful of file attributes.

FAT32

The limitations of FAT16 prompted the need for an enhanced version of the FAT16 file system. Microsoft introduced FAT32 in its release of Windows 95 Operating System Release 2 (OSR2). This file system is called FAT32 because it introduced the use of a 28-bit **4** binary cluster number (not 32 because 4 of the 32 bits are "reserved").

FAT32 was primarily created to eliminate the 2GB volume size limitation on a disk. FAT32 has extended the maximum size of a volume to 8GB in its original implementation but can use larger volumes with the same basic structure. The maximum size of a FAT32 volume that provides improved performance appears to be 32GB. Although you'll hear claims you can theoretically have volumes up to 2TB in size because of the allocation units, you begin to encounter degradation of performance on a volume that is larger than 32GB.

FAT32 also reduces wasted space by reducing the cluster size. Because FAT32 reduces the cluster size, you can gain additional free space on a volume that is converted from a FAT16 file system to a FAT32 file system. However, a FAT32 volume experiences a small performance hit due to the extra amount of overhead required scanning the additional clusters (in addition to the extra memory required to hold the larger file allocation table).

VFAT (Virtual FAT)

Microsoft released a file system called VFAT that introduced several enhancements into the disk management capabilities of Windows 95. These enhancements include high-speed, protected-mode, 32-bit driver access to the file system, as well as compatibility for the older DOS 16-bit routines, support for disk locking, and support for long file names.

However, the long file names had to meet the following goals defined by Microsoft:

- They must support access from existing pre–Windows 95 applications.

- They could be stored on existing DOS volumes for compatibility.

- Windows 95 and Windows 95 applications must be able to access file names that exceeded 11 characters.

For the most part, the VFAT file system accomplishes these goals as follows: Long file names of up to 255 characters per file can be assigned to any file under Windows 95 or by any program written for Windows 95. The long file name is limited to the same characters as standard file names, except that the following additional characters are also allowed: + , ; = [ ].

To provide access by older software, each file that uses a long file name also has a standard file name alias that is automatically generated and assigned to it. This alias is achieved by truncating and then modifying the file name as follows:

- The long file name's extension (up to three characters after a ".") are transferred to the extension of the alias file name assigned to it.

Note: You can use the extension to identify a particular type of file. The extension tells you, and your computer, at a glance the type of file it is. For example, a file with the extension .exe is normally an executable program file and one with .bat is usually a DOS batch file.

- The first six non-space characters of the long file name are analyzed. Any special characters that are valid in long file names but not in standard file names are replaced by underscores. All lowercase letters are automatically converted to uppercase. These six characters are stored as the first six characters of the file name.

- The last two characters of the file name are assigned as "~1". If a conflict occurs because a file already has this alias in the directory, VFAT tries "~2", and so on until it finds a unique alias name for the file.

As an example, let's take a file called Windows 2000 Professional.doc. The alias created for this file is WINDOW~1.DOC. If you create a second file called Windows 2000 Server.doc in the same directory, the alias WINDOW~2.DOC is generated because the alias WINDOW~1.DOC already exists in the directory.

NTFS (NT File System)

The NT File System (NTFS) used by Windows NT is completely different from the FAT file system used by DOS and the other Windows operating systems. An NTFS volume can be accessed only from Windows NT and Windows 2000 operating systems. The primary reason for not formatting a volume with NTFS is the lack of interoperability between operating systems in a multiple-boot configuration.

NTFS, which is extremely robust, provides numerous benefits over both the FAT16 and FAT32 file systems. NTFS is a full-featured system that includes file-by-file compression, complete file and folder permissions control and attribute settings, transaction-based operations, long file names, and many more features. It also does not have the problems with cluster sizes and hard disk size limitations that the FAT16 and FAT32 file systems do, and it includes other performance-enhancing features such as Redundant Arrays of Inexpensive Disks (RAID) support.

Note: The NTFS 4 file system of Windows NT 4 and the NTFS 5 file system of Windows 2000 have some major differences. NTFS 5, available only in Windows 2000, provides additional functionality such as file encryption, disk quotas, and the capability to create mounted drives.

NTFS provides built-in fault tolerance by recording changes made to data into a log file. If you encounter a power failure, NTFS will automatically check the log file and attempt to correct any data that may have been corrupted during the disturbance. Furthermore, it will attempt to fix disk errors automatically without displaying an error message. When a file is written to an NTFS volume, it keeps a copy of that file in memory and after completing the

4

write, it will read the file back to be sure it matches the copy in memory. If the two do not match, NTFS will mark that area of the disk as being bad and will write the data to another location. Figure 4.3 shows a disk that is partitioned and formatted with the appropriate file systems.

File System Conversion

What if you format a volume with one file system and decide later you want to change to a different file system? Well, the answer to that question depends on which file system you originally formatted your volume with. The good news is that you can easily convert a FAT16 or FAT32 volume to an NTFS volume without losing any data. You can do so by using the **CONVERT** command from the command line. Be aware that because the conversion requires exclusive access to the volume, you cannot convert the current drive without restarting the computer. Figure 4.4 shows the command used to convert a partition from FAT16 or FAT32 to NTFS.

The conversion from a FAT volume to an NTFS volume is a one-way operation. You cannot use the **CONVERT** command to convert from an NTFS volume to a FAT volume. The only way you can change an NTFS volume to a FAT volume is to back up all the data on the NTFS volume you want to change, format the volume with the new file system, and then restore the backed-up data onto the newly formatted volume. As you can see, this process is not nearly as easy as converting from a FAT volume to an NTFS volume, so be very careful when choosing file systems for your volumes.

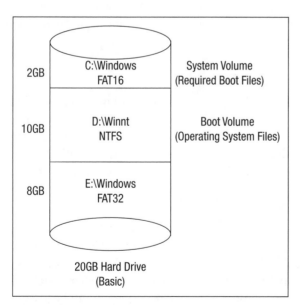

Figure 4.3
A formatted, partitioned disk.

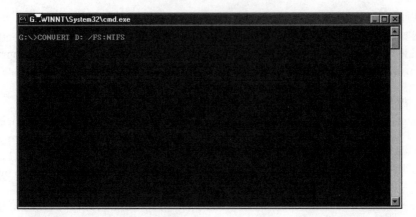

Figure 4.4
CONVERT syntax from the command line.

Your file systems directly reflect what operating systems you can install and what volumes will be accessible from each operating system installed on a machine. Certain operating systems require a specific file system, whereas other operating systems can access multiple file systems.

Now that we have discussed the file systems that are recognized by Windows 2000 Professional, we need to look at the many different operating systems that can be installed in a multiple-boot configuration. Your choice of file system in conjunction with your choice of operating system clearly define what volumes, files, and applications can be accessed after you have booted up.

Supported Operating Systems

Windows 2000 Professional supports dual-booting with many operating systems. Each operating system you choose to install may have a required file system, or you can choose from multiple file systems depending on the interoperability between operating systems and your security requirements. Dual-booting is supported with the following operating systems: DOS, Windows 3.1, Windows 95, Windows 98, Windows NT 3.51, and Windows NT 4.

DOS

The DOS operating system recognizes only the FAT file system, which is sometimes referred to as FAT16 to help differentiate it from FAT32. This operating system is available for legacy DOS-based applications and is often the first operating system installed in a multiple-boot environment. DOS may also be the first operating system installed on a blank computer, along with the drivers for the CD-ROM to allow an installation of another operating system from a CD.

Windows 3.1

Windows 3.1 recognizes only the FAT file system. This operating system is available for legacy Windows-based applications. The Windows 3.x operating system runs 16-bit applications using a cooperative multitasking environment, meaning the operating system required an application to check the message queue periodically and relinquish control of the system to other running applications. Poorly designed applications that did not check the message queue frequently prevented users from switching to another application.

Windows 3.1 uses initialization files (INI) to store system-specific or application-specific information on the configuration or state of the system. For example, the WIN.INI file stores information about the appearance of the Windows environment, and the SYSTEM.INI file stores system-specific information on the hardware and device driver configuration of the system. These INI files have several limitations and cause some difficulties.

Windows 95

The initial release of the Windows 95 operating system recognizes only the FAT file system. However, Windows 95 OSR2 also recognizes the FAT32 file system. This operating system first introduced the new Windows look and feel. Windows 95 introduced support for Win32-based applications using preemptive multitasking. This means the operating system takes control away from or gives control to another running task, depending on everyone's needs. Win32-based applications also take advantage of multithreading. This mechanism allows applications to run concurrently. These Win32-based applications run as a process in regards to the operating system. Each process consists of at least a single thread of execution that identifies the code path flow as it is being run by the operating system. A *thread* is a single unit of code that can get a time slice from the operating system to run concurrently with other units of code. The great thing about Win32-based applications is that they can be defined to have multiple threads, improving throughput and responsiveness.

Windows 95 also introduced the central information database called the *Registry*. This hierarchical database provides two primary benefits: adaptability and simplification of the operating system. The simplification of the database is achieved by eliminating the need for AUTOEXEC.BAT, CONFIG.SYS, and INI files (unless a legacy application requires them). The Registry provides adaptability by storing both configuration-specific and user-specific information so that you can share a single computer with multiple users but allow more than one configuration on that computer. Furthermore, the Registry acts as a central repository for hardware-specific information used by the hardware detection and plug-and-play components.

Windows 98

The Windows 98 operating system recognizes both the FAT and FAT32 file systems. Windows 98 is an enhanced version of Windows 95 and provides much more stability and reliability than Windows 95. It was released to improve the home users' environment by providing improvements in five essential areas:

- Ease of use

- Optimization

- Web integration

- Reliability

- Entertainment

Ease of Use

Windows 98 provides ease of use with its user interface enhancements, including a customizable Start menu, which allows you to limit what options you have available to you and eliminates or hides the options you don't use. Windows 98 also introduced support for Universal Serial Bus (USB), which is an external bus that supports plug-and-play, and allows you to connect devices without shutting down and restarting the machine. One USB port can support up to 127 peripheral devices, including speakers, modems, joysticks, telephones, CD-ROMS, tape drives, cameras, scanners, and keyboards.

Windows 98 also provides multiple-monitor support for up to eight monitors, providing tons of desktop space. Each configured monitor can have its own resolution settings. Windows 98 also supports Advanced Configuration and Power Interface (ACPI) for easier device management on new PCs and improved battery performance on new mobile PCs.

Optimization

The FAT32 file system was enhanced to store files more efficiently, requiring less disk space for storage. It even provides an in-place converter to convert existing FAT16 volumes to FAT32. The Windows 98 system startup, shutdown, and loading of applications were all improved, providing quicker access to the desktop environment. Microsoft also provided a Tune-Up Wizard to assist you in getting faster system performance.

Web Integration

Windows 98 includes Internet Explorer 4 (IE4), which includes Outlook Express as an email client, NetMeeting for Internet conferencing and application sharing, and NetShow for networking multimedia software for on-demand video and audio capabilities.

The Active Desktop environment puts Internet and intranet information directly on the desktop. Furthermore, you can configure channels to subscribe to Web sites for up-to-the-minute information.

Dial-Up Networking was modified to include the ability to link and synchronize multiple modems. Microsoft also provides the Internet Connection Wizard to assist you in configuring hardware for your ISDN connection.

Reliability

Microsoft integrated the Windows Update option, enabling you to update your operating system and drivers on an ongoing basis. This option is a Web-based resource for which you register, and you are automatically notified when updates are available for download.

Windows 98 can be configured to regularly test your hard disk, configuration information (increasing system reliability), and system files. In some cases, it can automatically fix detected problems. Numerous refinements and improvements were made to keep your systems running smoothly.

An improved Dr. Watson 32 is provided to generate detailed information when an application causes a General Protection Fault (GPF). This additional detail is extremely helpful when you're troubleshooting the application, reducing the time required to resolve a problem.

Entertainment

Support for enhanced television, which combines television and HTML content, delivers many new entertainment possibilities. You can watch TV on your PC and review and search for your favorite TV programs with the built-in program guide. The support provided for the IEEE 1394 bus provides an industry-standard interface to control stereos, VCRs, and other electronic devices.

If you are a movie buff, you'll find support for DVD and digital audio, providing high-quality digital movies and audio directly to your TV or PC monitor. If movies aren't your thing, you can take advantage of the DirectX APIs provided to improve video and graphics to your games.

Windows NT 3.51

Windows NT 3.51 Server and Workstation are both supported in a multiple-boot configuration with Windows 2000 Professional. Windows NT 3.51 can access volumes formatted with FAT16 and pre–Windows 2000 NTFS. Windows NT 3.51 provides a more secure, robust, and efficient operating system than all the ones discussed so far.

Windows NT 3.51 is a 32-bit, preemptive multitasking operating system. Its interface is similar to the Windows 3.1 interface but was designed with five key goals in mind:

- Extensibility

- Portability

- Reliability and robustness

- Compatibility

- Performance

Extensibility

NT 3.51 was designed with change in mind. When designing NT 3.51, the developers wanted to be sure they built in the capability for expansion. As with all operating systems and applications, they knew change was inevitable, so they designed NT to allow for easy growth. They provided this extensibility by creating two modes in the NT environment: kernel mode and user mode.

The kernel mode utilizes the privileged processor mode of the processor. This portion of the processor allows all machine instructions and provides access to the system memory. Usually, the operating system executes only in this mode.

The user mode utilizes the nonprivileged processor mode of the processor. This portion of the processor prevents certain instructions from executing, and the system memory is inaccessible. User applications execute in the user mode except when calling operating system services.

The developers also broke down NT 3.51 even further by creating a modular environment called *subsystems*. This modular environment allows for easier modifications and enhancements. The Microsoft developers also introduced objects to represent system resources, again providing ease of modifications. Furthermore, they introduced the Remote Procedure Call (RPC), allowing an application to call remote services without concern for their location on the network.

Portability

Closely related to extensibility is portability, which allows an entire operating system to move to another machine containing a different processor or configuration. This move should require very little recoding for the operating system to function on the new hardware.

One reason this portability is possible is that NT is primarily written in the standardized C language, in which compilers and software development tools are widely available on most hardware. Some of the graphics portion of NT is written in C++. Only the sections of NT that need direct access to the hardware are written in assembly language.

Windows NT 3.51 encapsulates platform-dependent code inside the dynamic link library (DLL) known as the Hardware Abstraction Layer (HAL). This DLL abstracts hardware, such as caches and I/O interrupt controllers, with a layer of low-level software, eliminating the need to change the higher level layers when moving from one platform to another.

Reliability

Reliability actually focuses on two different but related ideas. First, the operating system should be robust enough to respond predictably to both hardware and software errors. Second, the operating system should proactively protect itself and its users from damage.

Structured exception handling is the method used for capturing error conditions and responding to them in a consistent manner. This includes a safe way to handle unexpected errors, whether they are hardware or software. These errors must be handled cleanly and safely to reduce the risk of damaging the system or a user application.

4

Another feature included in NT is the new NTFS file system. NTFS can recover from most types of disk errors, including those errors that occur in critical disk sectors. Furthermore, it takes advantage of redundant storage and a transaction-based scheme for storing data to help assist in the recovery of data.

NT implemented a U.S. government-certifiable security architecture. This architecture provides a variety of security mechanisms, such as user logon, object protection, and resource quotas. This government-certifiable security (Class C2 level), as defined by the U.S. Department of Defense, is required for use of government applications. Also, virtual memory controls the placement of every program in memory, preventing one user from reading or writing memory occupied by another user.

Compatibility

The fourth design goal is to be able to allow applications written for one operating system to run in another operating system environment. Two types of applications are supported in Windows NT 3.51: binary and source.

A binary application is an executable that will run on multiple operating systems without compiling the source code to create a new executable. A source application requires you to compile the source into an executable before it will run on a different operating system.

Intel processors allow binary-compatible applications written for MS-DOS, 16-bit Windows, OS/2, and LAN Manager. Intel processors also support POSIX source-level applications that comply to IEEE Standard 1003.1.

Reduced Instruction Set Computer (RISC) processors support binary-compatible applications for MS-DOS, 16-bit Windows, and LAN Manager. They also support POSIX source-level applications that comply to IEEE Standard 1003.1.

Performance

The final design goal was to achieve optimal performance. Processor-intensive applications such as simulations, financial analyses, and graphics require rapid processing in order to provide good response time to users. Fast hardware and an efficient and fast operating system provides this response time.

This goal was achieved by taking advantage of the modularity and being sure each module was operating at its best. The modularity prompted the need for an efficient way for the modules to communicate with each other. The communication between modules was implemented by a high-speed message-passing mechanism called the Local Procedure Call (LPC). Also, each module was designed to maximize access to frequently called system services. Finally, the critical components of the networking software were built into the privileged portion of the operating system to achieve the best possible performance.

These design goals are the primary reason NT greatly exceeds the operating systems we have introduced to this point. The goals, along with the need for a reliable and secure operating system, greatly increased the presence of Windows NT.

Generally, the NT 3.51 operating system is used in business environments. An administrator will find many features beneficial when managing a network—for instance, the consolidation of startup files. These files have been replaced by the Registry, which stores system and user information in a centralized, hierarchical format. Fault tolerance and system recovery are implemented using the RAID options, the Emergency Repair Disk (ERD), and the NT Backup utility. Windows NT 3.51 offers many networking capabilities and interoperability with other systems, including Novell, Unix, and Macintosh. It offers remote access capabilities to provide access to your environment from remote offices or employees who work from home. Finally, it offers networking services such as Windows Internet Name Service (WINS) and Dynamic Host Configuration Protocol (DHCP) to help reduce the workload when you're managing your TCP/IP network.

Windows NT 4

Windows NT 4 supports everything we discussed in the previous section from both the design aspect and the administrator's perspective. Enhancements have been made to many areas of the features we discussed, however. Probably the biggest change is the look and feel of the NT environment.

Windows NT 4 Server and Workstation are both supported in a multiple-boot configuration with Windows 2000 Professional. Windows NT 4 will recognize FAT16 and Windows NT 4 NTFS volumes. Notice that we didn't mention FAT32 or Windows 2000 NTFS volumes. Windows NT 4 does not support FAT32, which causes some havoc if you try to dual-boot between NT 4 and Windows 98.

NTFS for Windows NT 4 is different from NTFS in Windows 2000. The primary concern about these file system differences is that they can prevent you from accessing a Windows 2000 NTFS volume. If you want access to the NTFS 5 volumes, your Windows NT 4 operating system must have at least Service Pack 4 installed. A Windows NT 4 installation will not be able to access any folders, files, or applications on a Windows 2000 NTFS volume without Service Pack 4 installed.

With Windows NT 4, the importance of the available networking services is stressed. NT 4 introduced the Domain Name Service (DNS) and the requirement of host name resolution within organizations that have an Internet presence. NT 4 introduced the need to provide the capability to recognize FAT32 partitions with the strong presence of Windows 98. It also provides a way to share information with other computers using the directory replication service. This capability is extremely helpful for replicating the system policies that allow an administrator to customize users' desktops and the functionality available to them. Finally, NT 4 provides Point-to-Point Tunneling Protocol (PPTP) for secure access to remote sites over the Internet, and a DHCP Relay Agent to provide DHCP functionality on subnets that do not have a DHCP server running on them.

4

Windows 2000 Professional

The latest operating system, Windows 2000 Professional, supports all three file systems: FAT16, FAT32, and NTFS. In a multiple-boot configuration between Windows NT 4 and Windows 2000, remember that the Windows NT 4 installation requires at least Service Pack 4 to be able to recognize a Windows 2000 NTFS volume. The good news is that the Windows 2000 installation can access Windows NT 4 volumes because the installation will automatically locate and upgrade any existing Windows NT 4 NTFS volumes for you. As a result, you can access these volumes after completing your Windows 2000 installation without taking any additional steps.

Windows 2000 Professional provides numerous new features. The first is the Synchronization Manager, which is a turbocharged Briefcase (a feature present in previous versions of Windows). It also now supports the Internet Printing Protocol (IPP), allowing you to print over the Internet to a printer configured to use IPP. True plug-and-play is also available for locating new hardware added to your system. Windows 2000 also includes a Device Manager to manage all your hardware settings and drivers. It includes both the Setup Manager and the Windows Installer for installing and managing applications.

Security has been greatly improved with the introduction of Kerberos version 5, which is an Internet standard security protocol for handling authentication of users and systems. Kerberos also provides the encryption used when transmitting user authentication information across the network. Encrypting File System (EFS) provides security for individual folders and files by providing the capability to encrypt them using public and private keys. This capability can be beneficial for laptop users or shared desktop computers. There is also smart card support for Windows 2000 logon. You can use a smart card and a personal identification number (PIN) to log on instead of providing a username and password. Finally, the **runas** command can be used to execute applications on behalf of someone else. By executing this command, an administrator can use her unprivileged account to execute normal applications but then execute an administrative application without logging off from the unprivileged account.

You now have an understanding of the available disk types, volumes, file systems, and operating systems in a multiple-boot configuration. Now, let's look at different possible multiple-boot configurations with Windows 2000 Professional.

Deployment

Now that you have an understanding of all the available operating systems, as well as the file systems that work with each other, it's time to decide which operating systems are required in this multiple-boot configuration. Along with the decision of which operating systems are available, you need to consider the type of interoperability between the operating systems and whether you would like to secure any resources. These considerations and determinations will greatly affect the file system you choose when formatting your volumes. Decision Tree 4.2 will assist you in determining which file system must be on the critical system partition.

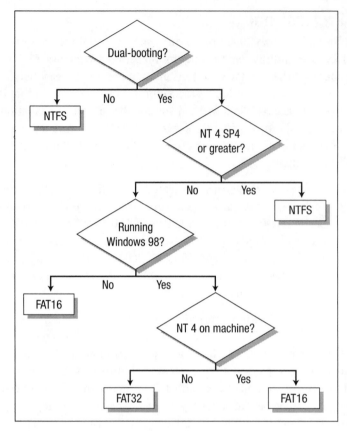

Decision Tree 4.2
Choosing a system partition file system.

The first question is this: What is prompting you to configure a multiple-boot system? Are you configuring it because you have legacy applications on your system that require specific operating systems and no upgrades are available for the software to run under more current operating systems? Or, maybe you're configuring it because you want to take advantage of a peripheral device and no drivers are available for it under Windows 2000 Professional. Whatever the reason may be, it is imperative that you understand the steps necessary to configure a multiple-boot environment while still preserving any software, settings, and devices currently installed. Let's look at the different dual-boot configurations available and the benefits and risks associated with each of them.

Warning! *Each operating system must be installed on a separate volume on your computer for it to retain its own file and configuration information.*

Dual-Booting with DOS

Dual-booting with DOS can provide a couple of benefits but can potentially pose a security risk. Why would you want to dual-boot with DOS? The primary reason would be to use legacy DOS-based line-of-business applications that directly access your hardware (a huge no-no in the later operating systems) and are instrumental in supporting your business. These applications have not been rewritten to run in a Windows environment and can be run only from the DOS environment.

If you have configured a DOS dual-boot configuration and have other volumes formatted with FAT16, you can boot to DOS and access any other volume formatted with the FAT16 file system. This capability can be extremely helpful in troubleshooting other operating systems in your multiple-boot configuration. For instance, you have a dual-boot configuration between Windows 2000 Professional and DOS. You discover that a change you recently made in the Windows 2000 Professional environment is preventing you from booting up under Windows 2000 Professional. If this file resides on a FAT16 volume, you can access the file on the Windows 2000 Professional volume and modify it, potentially allowing you to resolve the boot-up error from the command line.

At the same time, this dual-boot configuration can pose a security risk. If the computer is not stored in a secure area, an unauthorized individual can boot up to DOS. After he has booted to DOS, he now has access to all FAT16 volumes on that machine. This means he can access any files located on any FAT16 volume, including where Windows 2000 Professional is installed. Yes, you're right: this individual can now delete operating system directories and files because no file permissions are available on a FAT16 volume. Deleting files that reside on the Windows 2000 installation partition can cause problems and may even prevent you from booting up to Windows 2000.

Order of Installation

The required order of installation is to install DOS and then install Windows 2000 Professional. This order is required whenever DOS is involved in any multiple-boot configuration. For instance, if you're creating a multiple-boot environment with DOS, Windows 95, and Windows 2000 Professional, DOS is always the first operating system installed, regardless of how many and what other operating systems you are going to install. Suggested file systems include FAT16 for the DOS volume and NTFS 5 for the Windows 2000 Professional volume.

Dual-Booting with Windows 3.1

Dual-booting with Windows 3.1 provides the same features as dual-booting with DOS. It provides support for legacy applications written specifically for Windows 3.1 that will not run under any other operating system. Similar to the DOS operating system, Windows 3.1 also supports only the FAT16 file system, enabling you to boot to it and use it to assist in troubleshooting the Windows 2000 Professional installation that resides on a FAT16 volume. This dual-boot configuration can also pose the same security risk discussed in the previous section regarding the ability to access Windows 2000 Professional operating system files and exposing the system to corruption.

Order of Installation

The required order of installation when you're dual-booting between Windows 3.1 and Windows 2000 Professional is to install Windows 3.1 first and then install Windows 2000 Professional. Unless you have a specific reason to access the partition on which Windows 2000 is installed from the Windows 3.1 installation, be sure to use an NTFS volume for the Windows 2000 Professional installation. Suggested file systems include FAT16 for Windows 3.1 and NTFS 5 for Windows 2000 Professional.

Dual-Booting with Windows 95

Dual-booting with earlier versions of Windows 95 (pre-OSR2) provides the same benefits and risks as dual-booting with Windows 3.1. This operating system supports only the FAT16 file system. However, remember this is the operating system that introduced multithreading capabilities and the Registry to reduce the numerous startup and configuration files.

Windows 95 OSR2 introduced the FAT32 file system. This new file system is recognized only by Windows 95 OSR2, Windows 98, and Windows 2000 operating systems. This configuration supports applications written for Windows 95 that will not run under the Windows 2000 operating system. This version of Windows 95 recognizes both FAT16 and FAT32 file systems.

A dual-boot configuration between pre–Windows 95 OSR2 and Windows 2000 Professional introduces a new level of security. The file system itself prevents access to a Windows 2000 Professional operating system installed on a FAT32 file system. Remember that while you're booted up under DOS, Windows 3.1, or pre–Windows 95 OSR2, these alternate operating systems recognize only FAT16 and will be unable to access the Windows 2000 Professional operating system files.

Order of Installation

In this dual-boot configuration, you should begin with Windows 95 and then install Windows 2000 Professional. If you are configuring a multiple-boot configuration with DOS as well, you should install DOS, Windows 95, and then Windows 2000 Professional. Suggested file systems include FAT16 for the DOS volume, FAT16 for pre–Windows 95 OSR2, FAT32 for Windows 95 OSR2, and NTFS 5 for Windows 2000 Professional.

Dual-Booting with Windows 98

Dual-booting between Windows 98 and Windows 2000 Professional provides an environment in which you can dual-boot to Windows 98 to take advantage of the awesome graphic capabilities for your graphic-intensive games. But, you still have the opportunity to boot to Windows 2000 Professional to take advantage of all the new features provided in the more secure environment.

Remember that Windows 98 supports both FAT16 and FAT32 file systems, but not NTFS. When you boot up to Windows 98 and you have formatted your Windows 2000 installation volume with FAT16 or FAT32, you will be able to easily access any folders, files, and applications on that Windows 2000 installation volume.

4

Order of Installation

The order of installation for Windows 98 is the same as for Windows 95. You install Windows 98 and then Windows 2000. Remember that you cannot have both Windows 95 and Windows 98 in the same multiple-boot configuration. If you have Windows 95 and need Windows 98, you can upgrade Windows 95 to Windows 98 and then install Windows 2000 Professional. Suggested file systems include FAT32 for the Windows 98 volume and NTFS 5 for Windows 2000 Professional.

Dual-Booting with Windows NT

You can dual-boot between Windows 2000 and Windows NT 3.51 operating systems. You can also dual-boot between Windows 2000 and Windows NT 4 operating systems. However, you'll discover some huge differences between the two configurations in regards to accessibility between the two operating systems. Furthermore, you'll find some differences on what NTFS volume-specific options are available.

Dual-Booting with Windows NT 3.51

A dual-boot environment between NT 3.51 and Windows 2000 has some critical accessibility and configuration problems. Windows NT 3.51 does not recognize a Windows 2000 NTFS volume. These volumes remain as NTFS volumes from the NT 3.51 environment.

Dual-Booting with Windows NT 4

A dual-boot configuration between Windows 2000 and Windows NT 4 can provide complete compatibility between the two installations using the latest and greatest NTFS version (NTFS 5) from the Windows 2000 installation. Or, you can configure the installations to be completely inaccessible to each other, even though they are both using NTFS with your choice of disk type.

Using NTFS on a Dual-Boot System

Notice that every scenario discussed up to this point included the Windows 2000 installation on a FAT16 or FAT32 volume. If you install Windows 2000 on an NTFS partition, you are implementing a level of security by preventing access to that volume from some of the earlier operating systems. In fact, these earlier operating systems will not even recognize that the volume exists. Having Windows 2000 Professional on an NTFS volume provides a huge layer of security in a DOS, Windows 3.1, Windows 95, or Windows 98 dual-boot configuration. If you boot to any of these earlier operating systems and your Windows 2000 installation is on an NTFS partition, they are unable to detect the volume, thereby preventing access to any of the files on that NTFS volume.

During the installation of Windows 2000, NTFS 4 volumes automatically convert to NTFS 5 volumes. This conversion process allows you to access Windows NT 4 volumes from your Windows 2000 installation. However, if you want to be able to access Windows 2000 volumes from a Windows NT 4 installation, the NT 4 installation must be running at least NT 4 Service Pack 4. This configuration allows both NTFS partitions to be accessed from both operating systems.

What if you have a Windows NT 4 installation and Windows 2000 installation on the same machine, and you would like to completely prevent access to the Windows 2000 volumes from the NT 4 installation? Of course, you have your NTFS permissions, but an administrator can still use her permissions to modify existing permissions and gain access to the volumes. Remember the earlier discussion of basic disks and dynamic disks and that dynamic disks are new to Windows 2000 and can be recognized only by a Windows 2000 installation? If you choose to install Windows 2000 on a dynamic disk, no pre–Windows 2000 operating system will be able to access that installation partition.

If you dual-boot between Windows NT 4 Workstation and Windows 2000 Professional and they are both part of the same NT 4 or Windows 2000 domain, the two configurations must have a different computer name.

Order of Installation

When you're configuring a multiple-boot configuration with Windows NT, be sure the Windows NT 4 installation has Service Pack 4 applied. Install Windows 2000 Professional on a separate volume. If you want an additional layer of security, install Windows 2000 Professional on a dynamic disk. Doing so will prevent the NT 4 installation from accessing the Windows 2000 Professional installation hard drive. Suggested file systems are NTFS 5 on both volumes.

Table 4.3 lists the compatibility between the file systems and operating systems in a multiple-boot configuration. Review this table prior to creating your multiple-boot configuration.

Table 4.3   The compatibility between the file systems and operating systems in a multiple-boot configuration.

File System	DOS	Win 3.1	Win 95	Win 98	NT 4	Win 2K
FAT16	Y	Y	Y	Y	Y	Y
FAT32	N	N	Y(OSR2)	Y	N	Y
NTFS 4	N	N	N	N	Y	Y
NTFS 5	N	N	N	N	Y(SP 4)	Y

Configuring the Default Operating System

The default operating system is the operating system booted to if you do not choose an alternate operating system. By default, you have 30 seconds to choose an alternate operating system, although this amount of time can be modified. If you do not choose an alternate operating system, the system will boot up to the operating system you have defined as the default. The last operating system installed is the default operating system. For all the multiple-boot configurations we discussed, we suggested that you install Windows 2000 Professional last, so Windows 2000 Professional would always be your default operating system.

You can modify the default operating system as well as the time allotted to choose the operating system you want to boot to. You can modify this information through the System properties. After you open the System properties, go to the Advanced tab and then choose the Startup And Recovery option (see Figure 4.5). Within this option, you will notice you have a drop-down menu to choose which operating system you want to be your default.

You can also modify the amount of time that is available to choose an alternate operating system. This time can be between 0 and 999 seconds, with the default of 30 seconds. However, if you choose 0, the system will automatically go to the default operating system on bootup, and you will not have the opportunity to choose an alternate operating system.

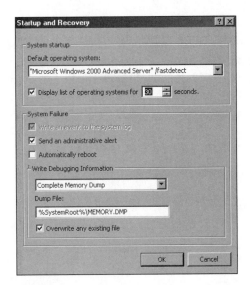

Figure 4.5
Startup And Recovery options.

Summary

As you can see, configuring a multiple-boot configuration requires careful planning from the very beginning. This planning includes deciding whether it is really necessary to create a multiple-boot configuration. During this decision process, you will be contemplating which operating systems are required in this multiple-boot configuration.

The operating system may directly affect which file system you choose when creating volumes on your hard drive. It also includes deciding how many partitions will be required. Remember, each operating system should have its own volume. Choosing the correct file system for each of these operating systems will greatly affect compatibility and, in some cases, security between the operating systems installed on your system. You can create security risks when creating a multiple-boot configuration with the incorrect file systems.

The order of installation is critical when you're configuring a multiple-boot configuration. Installing the operating systems in an incorrect order may result in a reinstallation of one or more of your operating systems.

Your default operating system is the operating system you will boot to if you do not choose any other operating system during the boot process. This default operating system and the time designated to choose an alternate operating system can be configured through the Startup And Recovery option of the System properties dialog box.

Planning for the configuration of either a single-boot or multiple-boot environment is driven by your needs as an administrator. Once the environment is installed, you need to understand how you can modify specific portions of Windows 2000 Professional through the Registry. Modifications made to Windows 2000 directly through the Registry, using one of the Registry editors, are performed when there isn't a way to make the modification through one of the desktop tools provided by Windows 2000 Professional. The Registry is a critical component of Windows 2000, and you should have a thorough understanding of it before attempting to make direct modifications to it.

Chapter 5

The Windows 2000 Registry

What Is the Registry?

Windows 2000 Professional leaves nothing to accident. It uses a highly sophisticated central nervous system, called the *Registry*, to track all the installed hardware devices and software programs. The Registry also tracks information about every user who logs on at a machine, as well as all hardware configurations for the user who is currently logged on.

An operating system (OS) has a tough job. It must serve as a liaison between hardware and software. It must set priorities and determine which applications get use of the almighty processor and when. And, it must manage incredible amounts of data in memory and push the overflow out to a swap file on a hard disk.

An operating system also must coordinate the use of various software programs, from word processors to email clients to spreadsheets to video presentations and streaming media. An OS is charged with overseeing the use of an unlimited number of peripheral devices, including printers, monitors, audio systems, hubs, switches, hard disks, CD-ROM and DVD drives, scanners, cameras, keyboards, mice, floppy drives, removable drives, and smart card readers, just to mention a few.

The operating system must also translate communications between every one of these software programs and all installed hardware peripherals. As you can see, the job quickly becomes exponentially more complicated.

An operating system, such as Windows 2000 Professional, manages and coordinates these communications, often so smoothly that it's easy for the average user to forget the OS is even there fulfilling this role.

Remember the scene from National Lampoon's *Christmas Vacation* in which Clark "Sparky" Griswald climbed all over his house installing 25,000 imported Italian twinkle lights and then threw the switch with his entire family (including his skeptical in-laws) watching on the front lawn? Nothing happened. His thankless in-laws commented on what a silly waste of resources the effort was. At that point, Clark's daughter said her dad had worked really hard, and the father-in-law said, "So do washing machines."

Sparky could have used a method for tracking which of his lights were plugged into which circuit. He would have benefited from a central repository storing information about which circuits depend on which breaker. Instead, he had to rely on his wife to discover that he had plugged all the lights into an outlet powered by a wall switch. And, just like washing machines, that central repository—the Registry—doesn't always receive the credit it deserves.

The Registry: Windows 2000's Nerve Center

Think of the Registry as Windows 2000's spinal column. It's the nerve center from which all Windows 2000 functions emanate.

If you've worked before with older versions of Windows, you're familiar with initialization, system, and component files bearing .ini, .sys, and .com file-name extensions. The Windows 2000 Registry replaces most of the functionality such files provided. Don't be surprised if you still find stray INI files and the like on your hard drive. Some applications and components rely on them for backward compatibility.

When you install a hardware device, such as a floppy drive, several entries are added to the Windows 2000 Registry database. The Registry tracks such information as the interrupt request line (IRQ) that the device receives, the memory location that will be used to process information received from the floppy drive, and more. For example, information regarding the exact manufacturer and model of the drive is written. Should a communication port be necessary, the Registry tracks that information, too.

In fact, the Registry tracks information for all the following installed components:

- Hardware peripherals
- Hardware drivers
- Software programs
- Protocols

The information stored in the Registry's hierarchical database is used by many Windows 2000 components. For example, the following rely on information located in the Registry to function properly:

- NTOSKRNL.EXE, the Windows NT kernel powering Windows 2000
- NTDETECT.COM, the system startup process
- Hardware device drivers
- Hardware profiles
- User profiles
- Setup and installation programs

Think of the OS as the brain and the Registry as the spinal column. Just like you wouldn't want to go fiddling around with your central nervous system, you don't want to tinker with the Windows 2000 Registry—that is, unless you're absolutely sure of what you're doing. One false move and paralysis can result.

The Registry is a powerful collection of values a system uses to operate. Make one slight mistake, one tiny typographical error in an entry, and you may lose the entire system. Your only option might be to reformat a hard drive and reinstall the operating system, losing every piece of data that wasn't already backed up to another location.

For this reason, Microsoft has included numerous applets that provide users and even the most advanced administrators with simple graphical interfaces that can be used to manipulate the Registry values.

Consider Control Panel, for example. Each applet (such as Display or Network Dial-up Connections) you see in Control Panel is just a graphical interface that simplifies the manipulation of Registry values. When you adjust the repeat delay for a character in the Keyboard applet, for instance, you're really making a change to a Registry key.

However, the graphical front end is provided to help ensure you don't enter an invalid entry or incorrect value. The graphical interface presents the options Windows recognizes as valid, thereby drastically reducing the odds that the Registry will become corrupted.

Sometimes, though, you need to manually edit the Registry. We'll take a look at which different Registry keys exist, what they do, how they can be adjusted, what happens when they're changed, utilities you can use to edit the Registry, and best practices you should follow when working with the Registry. Let's begin our look at the Windows 2000 nerve center with a discussion of the different keys that make up the Registry.

The Registry Structure

The Windows 2000 Registry is organized much like a collection of folders and files on a hard disk. Instead of drives, folders, and files, though, each component has a different name. Let's look now at the structure used to organize the Registry.

The Difference between Subtrees and Keys

The Windows 2000 Professional Registry is composed of *subtrees* (you can think of them as folders) that collect specific information about a system. These subtrees contain *keys*. Often, the subtrees are referred to as *subtree keys*. You can tell the subtrees apart from keys because the subtrees begin with the HKEY label. (HKEY stands for Handle Key.)

Keys contain other subkeys. Keys can also contain data or Registry values. Subkeys can hold additional subkeys or data.

Many people will tell you there are five unique predefined subtrees, but that's not really true. Registry editing tools will present you with five predefined subtree keys, but three of them are really just subsets of two higher-level subtrees. The two real predefined subtrees are HKEY_LOCAL_MACHINE and HKEY_USERS.

HKEY_LOCAL_MACHINE

The HKEY_LOCAL_MACHINE subtree key, as shown in Figure 5.1, collects a wide range of information about a machine, regardless of the user who is currently logged on to the system. Many of this key's Registry entries are rewritten each time the system boots. The HKEY_LOCAL_MACHINE Registry settings cannot be directly edited using either of Windows 2000's default Registry Editors.

The HKEY_LOCAL_MACHINE subtree key contains information specific to the system being used. It includes the following configuration data:

- Installed hardware device information

- Port assignments

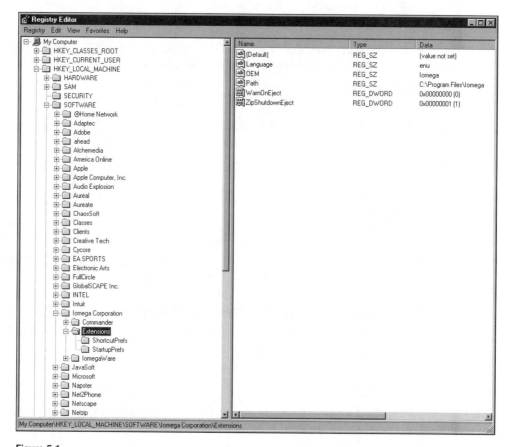

Figure 5.1
The HKEY_LOCAL_MACHINE subtree houses system-specific information, such as information about the computer's operating system and installed hardware.

- Hardware profiles (configuration information)

- Security accounts management data

- Information on installed software programs

- Security settings

The HKEY_LOCAL_MACHINE subtree holds the following five subkeys:

- Hardware

- SAM

- Security

- Software

- System

Each of these subkeys holds specific information. Data in the Hardware subkey is regenerated each time the system is booted. Windows 2000 builds this data during startup. The Hardware subkey records hardware peripheral information, such as which CPU is present, what type of keyboard is attached, the mouse in use, and other component data. It also collects pointer and video data. Applications communicate with the Hardware subkey to learn about a system's different hardware components.

The SAM subkey can be contacted by applications only if they use the proper application programming interfaces (APIs). The SAM hive stores information related to the Windows 2000 machine's Security Accounts Manager. This subkey serves as the system's Directory database. It maps to the SAM and SAM.LOG files located in the *Systemroot*\System32\ Config folder. The SAM subkey works with the Security subkey to store important security account information.

The Security subkey houses the local computer's security information. As with the SAM subkey, applications must modify data in the Security subkey using the proper APIs. The Security hive maps to the SECURITY and SECURITY.LOG files located in the *Systemroot*\ System32\Config folder.

The Software subkey contains information about software applications installed on the system. The Software subkey maps to the following files in the *Systemroot*\System32\ Config folder: SOFTWARE, SOFTWARE.LOG, and SOFTWARE.SAV. The file association and object linking and embedding (OLE) data are entered in the Software subkey.

The last HKEY_LOCAL_MACHINE subkey, System, contains data related to system hardware peripherals and services. The System hive maps to the following files located in the *Systemroot*\System32\Config folder: SYSTEM, SYSTEM.LOG, and SYSTEM.SAV.

The System subkey is particularly important because it contains critical information related to startup. Under this key, you'll find boot information kept in separate Control

Sets. They're labeled ControlSet001 and ControlSet002. A CurrentControlSet is also housed in this subkey. These subkeys trigger the default startup process, revert to the Last Known Good configuration, or track (in the Failed key) the last time the Last Known Good configuration was used.

Note: *The Last Known Good configuration loads the last set of configuration settings known to have booted the system properly. For more information on Windows 2000 Professional rescue and recovery operations, please see Chapter 17.*

The System key also houses information related to the current system launch. The information kept in this key is so important that the Registry takes further measures to safeguard the System hive data by automatically creating a backup file, titled SYSTEM.ALT. It is stored in the *Systemroot*\System32\Config folder.

HKEY_USERS

The HKEY_USERS subtree key holds system default information. This data is used to customize the desktop environment and track identity information for each user. The HKEY_USERS subtree key, as shown in Figure 5.2, also collects the profiles for a system's users.

The HKEY_USERS subtree key collects a wide range of information related to each user. For example, the HKEY_USERS subtree key stores the following, among other values:

- File type information and associated program data

- Control Panel settings (including desktop and interface configuration)

- User profile information

- Custom software settings

- Remote access settings

Typically, the HKEY_USERS subtree will house two user profiles. The first profile listed is for the active user. The second profile is the default user profile. It is used when a user isn't logged on to the system. The information contained in the second profile determines what is shown when the Login prompt is displayed by Windows 2000.

The profile listings exist as long text strings. A profile Registry key security ID appears similar to this: HKEY_USERS\S-1-5-21-527236240-1201670629-1060284248-1000.

Other Predefined Registry Subtree Keys

The other three predefined subtree keys are provided for convenience. These additional subkeys make it easier to find and sort Registry entries.

The Registry editing tools display the following additional predefined keys:

- *HKEY_CURRENT_CONFIG*—This subtree key collects information on the system's active hardware profile (the profile currently in use).

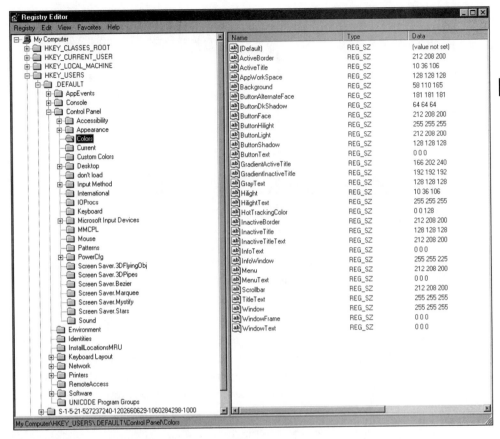

Figure 5.2
The HKEY_USERS subtree key holds data on the system's users.

- *HKEY_CURRENT_USER*—This subtree key holds profile information for the user currently logged on to the system.

- *HKEY_CLASSES_ROOT*—This subtree key gathers information about the applications and the different file types that exist on the system, including OLE data.

The Registry editing tools provide these additional subtrees for your convenience. They do not hold unique information. Instead, HKEY_CURRENT_CONFIG, shown in Figure 5.3, is a subkey of HKEY_LOCAL_MACHINE. You also can find information from the HKEY_CLASSES_ROOT and HKEY_CURRENT_USER subtree keys in the HKEY_USERS subtree key.

Let's look at some of these subtrees' more important subkeys. The predefined HKEY_CURRENT_CONFIG subtree contains these two subkeys by default:

- Software

- System

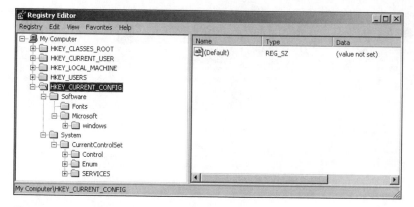

Figure 5.3
HKEY_CURRENT_CONFIG contains active system hardware profile information.

You're likely to see the following pair of additional subkeys if you've upgraded to Windows 2000 from a Windows 9x installation:

• Display

• Enum

HKEY_CURRENT_CONFIG is used only to maintain compatibility with Windows 9x systems. Data stored in this key is also kept in the HKEY_LOCAL_MACHINE\System\ CurrentControlSet\Hardware Profiles\Current subkey. Data regarding the active hardware profile is kept there.

The predefined HKEY_CURRENT_USER subtree, shown in Figure 5.4, holds the active user's profile. Customized sounds, various Control Panel settings, Outlook Express identity information, and more are stored here.

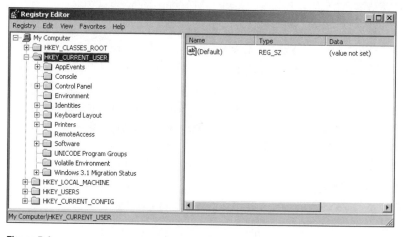

Figure 5.4
HKEY_CURRENT_USER stores the active user's profile settings.

Under HKEY_CURRENT_USER, you'll find the following subkeys by default:

- *AppEvents*—This subkey stores application event information, such as a new mail sound notification configured to sound when a new email message arrives.

- *Console*—This subkey contains information on the Windows 2000 console behavior, such as the default window size to be used when a command prompt is opened.

- *Control Panel*—When users modify settings in Control Panel for items such as screensavers, accessibility options, and desktop colors, those values are stored here.

- *Environment*—This subkey stores values set in Control Panel's System applet.

- *Identities*—If Outlook Express has been installed, user identities are stored in this subkey. User identity subkey names are about as user unfriendly as a user profile subkey name. The following is an example of a user identity key name: HKEY_CURRENT_USER\ Identities\{94856CD1-D421-10D3-8427-00A0D216J49F}. However, if you wade deeper into the key, you'll find the friendly name listed as Username. It's easily read. The Username for the identity key name listed here is shown as ErikE.

- *Keyboard Layout*—Input Locales information configured from Control Panel's Regional Options applet is kept here.

- *Printers*—Information regarding each installed print device is stored in this subkey.

- *Software*—Software program configuration settings are stored in this subkey.

- *Unicode Program Group*—Unicode information required for backward compatibility with older Windows NT 4 systems is housed in this subkey.

You're also likely to see other Registry subkeys present in the HKEY_CURRENT_USER subtree key. They include the following:

- *Remote Access*—Configuration settings for remote system connections are housed in this Registry subkey.

- *Volatile Environment*—This subkey contains directions identifying where the user's application data should be stored by default and logon server or workgroup membership information.

The HKEY_CLASSES_ROOT subkey, shown in Figure 5.5, keeps track of which file extensions are associated with which software applications. For example, information stored here instructs Windows 2000 to open DOC files with Microsoft Word and XLS files using Microsoft Excel. The file association listing grows as additional software is installed on a machine.

Tip: You're tempting fate by editing file associations within the Registry. We don't recommend that you perform this action from within the Registry. The best practice is to specify file associations using Windows Explorer. Click on Start|Programs|Accessories|Windows Explorer. Next, click on the Tools menu and select Folder Options. Then, select the File Types tab and modify file associations by selecting the file type you wish to change and clicking on Change. Specify the program you wish to use and click on OK.

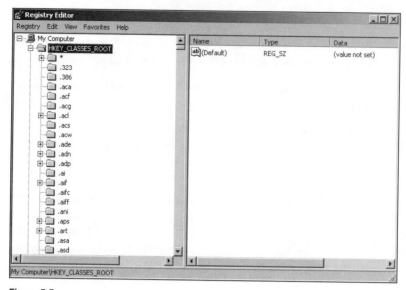

Figure 5.5
HKEY_CLASSES_ROOT stores file association, data types, and COM settings.

Information regarding COM objects and data types is also collected in the HKEY_CLASSES_ROOT subkey. Windows 2000 uses the data type and COM information it finds in these keys to understand how it should execute associated data requests.

Table 5.1 lists the five different Registry subtree keys. It also describes the different information each Registry subtree contains.

Understanding Hives

If you're going to work with the Windows 2000 Professional Registry, you also need to be familiar with *hives*. Similar to subtree keys, hives collect information about significant installed components. Hives are different from subkeys because they collect information from other keys, subkeys, and Registry entries.

Table 5.1   Each Registry subtree collects specific system data.

Registry Key	Hierarchy	Description
HKEY_LOCAL_MACHINE	Top-level subtree key	Contains information specific to the system being used
HKEY_USERS	Top-level subtree key	Collects information related to a system's users
HKEY_CLASSES_ROOT	Subkey of HKEY_USERS	Stores application and file type data
HKEY_CURRENT_CONFIG	Subkey of HKEY_LOCAL_MACHINE	Collects information on a system's hardware currently in use
HKEY_CURRENT_USER	Subkey of HKEY_USERS	Stores profile information for the user who is currently logged on to the system

Table 5.2   Several hives exist by default in Windows 2000 Professional.

Registry Subtree Location	Associated Files
HKEY_CURRENT_CONFIG	SYSTEM, SYSTEM.ALT, SYSTEM.LOG, SYSTEM.SAV
HKEY_LOCAL_MACHINE\SAM	SAM, SAM.LOG, SAM.SAV
HKEY_LOCAL_MACHINE\Security	SECURITY, SECURITY.LOG, SECURITY.SAV
HKEY_LOCAL_MACHINE\Software	SOFTWARE, SOFTWARE.LOG, SOFTWARE.SAV
HKEY_LOCAL_MACHINE\System	SYSTEM, SYSTEM.ALT, SYSTEM.LOG, SYSTEM.SAV
HKEY_USERS\Default	DEFAULT, DEFAULT.LOG, DEFAULT.SAV
HKEY_CURRENT_USER	NTUSER.DAT, NTUSER.LOG

One way to identify hives is to look for their telltale Registry files located in the *Systemroot*System32\Config folder. These ALT, LOG, and SAV files track changes made to the Windows 2000 Registry. Table 5.2 describes the different Windows 2000 Professional hives.

Other files associated with Registry values are stored in the *Systemroot*System32\Config folder, too. For example, you'll find USERDIFF and USERDIFF.LOG files if you've updated to Windows 2000 Professional from another Windows operating system.

Note: Registry information stored in hives is not dynamic, meaning it does not change each time the system boots. Instead, hives track systems' more permanent information.

Registry Values

We've discussed the Registry keys, subtree keys, and hives that collect information about installed hardware and software components. But what about the actual entries housed in each key? Although you might have five keys, you can have hundreds and hundreds of Registry entries. You might have so many entries because Registry keys hold multiple entries, as previously shown in Figures 5.1 and 5.2.

As mentioned earlier, Registry keys and subkeys can contain other subkeys or data. Subkeys help organize the Registry. It's the Registry entry data that Windows 2000 uses to configure hardware and software settings.

You can keep Registry value entries straight in your mind by remembering that Registry entries are composed of three components:

• The subkey entry name

• The subkey data type

• The subkey data value

Let's look at a real-world example. The Windows 2000 Registry must store information about the input, or pointing, device your system has installed. Using a system with a Microsoft IntelliMouse generates the Registry entries shown in Figure 5.6.

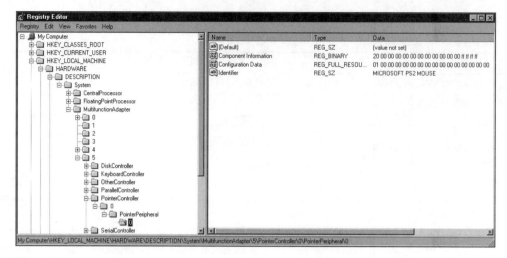

Figure 5.6
An example of the common, real-world Registry entry for a Microsoft IntelliMouse.

The subkey name is 0. The full key name is HKEY_LOCAL_MACHINE\Hardware\
Description\System\MultifunctionAdapter\5\PointerController\0\PointerPeripheral\0. It
contains the four entries shown in the right pane in Figure 5.6.

For the data entry named Identifier, the subkey data type is REG_SZ. The subkey data
value is MICROSOFT PS2 MOUSE.

Each of the several Registry data types is treated differently by Windows 2000. Table 5.3
describes the different Registry data types.

Table 5.3   The Registry possesses several data types.

Data Type	Description
REG_BINARY	A single value that must be provided as raw binary data in hexadecimal string form not readily read by most humans. Windows 2000 interprets each pair of REG_BINARY hexadecimal digits as a byte value. An example of a REG_BINARY hexadecimal string is 69 2f 31 01 69 2f 31 01 7a 56 31 01 69 2f 31 01 e2 35 ef 05.
REG_DWORD	A single value that must be provided as a hexadecimal string four bytes long, such as 394bf53a.
REG_EXPAND_SZ	A single value that Windows 2000 interprets as a string to be restored, like REG_SZ data types, with the ability to expand text strings by replacing specific variables, such as %systemroot%. This data type is easily read by humans.
REG_FULL_RESOURCE_DESCRIPTOR	A data type used by Windows 2000 to store resource lists for hardware components and drivers that can't be added or modified by the user.
REG_MULTI_SZ	Multiple values that Windows 2000 interprets as separate entries. REG_MULTI_SZ entries can be binary, hexadecimal, or text strings.
REG_SZ	A single value text string (readily readable by humans) that Windows 2000 interprets as a string to be stored.

Using Windows 2000's Registry Editors

As you can see, Microsoft's developers have given careful thought to the development, use, and placement of Registry entries and values. So many settings, configuration parameters, and execution instructions are collected in the Registry that just a single keystroke error could cause catastrophic consequences.

Get the wrong character in the wrong place, and Windows 2000 might refuse to boot. Worse, unrecoverable errors could occur. It's for this reason that you won't find preexisting shortcuts to the Registry.

However, you will find Registry editing tools lurking beneath the surface of Windows 2000. You can create shortcuts for both of these editors, but we recommend running the editors' associated executable files from a command prompt. Leave a Registry shortcut on your desktop, and a stray child in the office or a few inadvertent clicks could spell disaster. Don't chance it!

You can choose from two Registry Editors: REGEDIT.EXE and REGEDT32.EXE. You can use both of these Registry editing utilities to review Registry configurations, troubleshoot errors, identify problematic entries, fix errant settings, or modify current Registry data values.

Warning! You should not make any changes to your Registry using either REGEDIT.EXE or REGEDT32.EXE unless you have backed up system information and important data and verified that your backup copy works. Don't make any changes to any Windows Registry values unless you're certain your changes are warranted and correct.

Both Registry editing utilities are named Registry Editor. However, each offers slightly different functionality. You can tell them apart immediately by looking for three telltale signs. First, each boasts a different icon. Second, REGEDIT.EXE displays a twin-pane view by default. Third, and most important, REGEDT32.EXE presents the Registry by breaking each predefined subtree key into a separate menu.

You'll notice one other important difference between the two Registry Editors. If you wish to view only Registry information, and you want to ensure you don't accidentally make any changes, REGEDT32.EXE offers a read-only mode. Selecting Read Only Mode from the Options menu triggers this protected view.

REGEDT32.EXE is best if you wish to secure the Registry. REGEDIT.EXE makes it easy to search keys, subkeys, and values. If you're seeking specific Registry values, but you're not sure where they're located, you'll probably want to use REGEDIT.EXE. Decision Tree 5.1 examines which Registry editing tool is best depending upon your needs.

Which Registry Editor you open depends on which executable file you select. Let's examine REGEDIT.EXE first.

Decision Tree 5.1
Both REGEDIT.EXE and REGEDT32.EXE possess advantages and disadvantages. Select the editor that works best, depending upon the task you must perform.

Using REGEDIT.EXE

REGEDIT.EXE is immediately recognizable by its default dual-paned view. On the left, you'll see the predefined subtree keys and subkeys, as shown in Figure 5.7. In the right pane, you'll see the corresponding values for the Registry key highlighted in the left pane.

Open REGEDIT.EXE by following these steps:

1. Click on Start|Run.

2. Type "REGEDIT".

3. Click on OK, and the Registry Editor will open.

After you highlight a key, you can expand it like you would a folder by clicking on the plus (+) sign next to the key or by pressing Alt and the keypad's asterisk (*) key simultaneously. Be careful when testing this feature because it can take a while to complete. In addition to expanding each key underneath it, it expands each subkey it finds.

Tip: *If you wish to expand every single Registry key using REGEDIT.EXE, highlight My Computer in the left pane and press Alt and the keypad's * key simultaneously. If you discover the process takes too long to complete, you can stop the expansion underway by pressing Esc.*

Of course, just like clicking on the minus (-) sign collapses folders, so too does it collapse Registry keys. If you're still in a Registry Editor session, and you've expanded many keys or all of them, collapsed them, and you wish again to expand them but only one level at a time, you can do so. Pressing F5 restores the default one level of key expansion per click behavior.

Making Registry changes using REGEDIT.EXE is fairly straightforward. Let's examine an example of a simple, safe Registry edit. We'll show you how to change the name of Windows 2000's registered owner. You can find the subkey holding this Registry entry in HKEY_LOCAL_MACHINE\Software\Microsoft\Windows NT\CurrentVersion. Clicking on it reveals the values shown in Figure 5.8.

Next, right-click on the RegisteredOwner entry displayed in the right pane and click on Modify. Doing so reveals an Edit String dialog box, from which you can change the entry

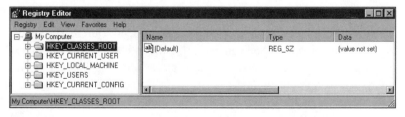

Figure 5.7
REGEDIT.EXE offers a twin-pane view of the Windows 2000 Registry.

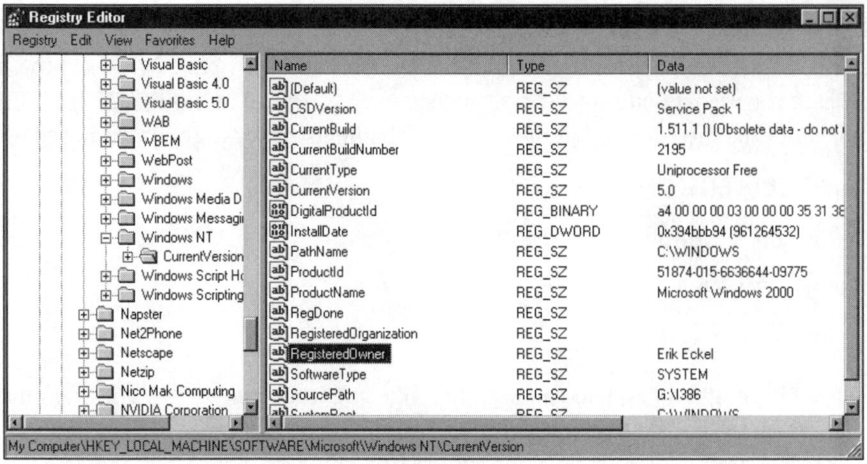

Figure 5.8
HKEY_LOCAL_MACHINE contains the Registry information for the operating system's registered owner.

value (in this case, Erik Eckel). You can type your name ("Erik J. Eckel" in this case), then click on OK, and it appears as updated in the right pane.

You also can perform the following operations using REGEDIT.EXE:

- Import a Registry file

- Export a Registry file

- Connect to a remote Registry via a network connection

- Print Registry information

- Add a new Registry entry

- Delete a Registry key or entry

- Rename a Registry key or entry

- Copy a key name (place it on the clipboard)

- Find a Registry key

Some of these operations are straightforward. For example, you can find a Registry key just like you would search for a file using Windows Explorer, and you delete Registry entries in much the same manner. You can print the highlighted Registry key by selecting Print from the Registry menu. Copying a key name places it on the clipboard much like copying text does when you're using Microsoft Word or Notepad. Further, renaming a key works much like renaming a file using Windows Explorer. Other operations are more difficult. They, along with others requiring the use of REGEDT32.EXE, are covered later in this chapter.

5

Using REGEDT32.EXE

Because REGEDT32.EXE presents each predefined Registry subtree key as a separate menu, you can more easily compare Registry entries from different keys side by side. Figure 5.9 shows each of the predefined keys in a cascaded view.

You can select the following view- and display-related commands when using the REGEDT32.EXE Registry Editor:

- Expand Branch

- Expand All

- Collapse Branch

- View Tree Only

- View Tree and Data

- View Data Only

- Split the display

- Change the font

- Cascade the subtree key menus or tile them

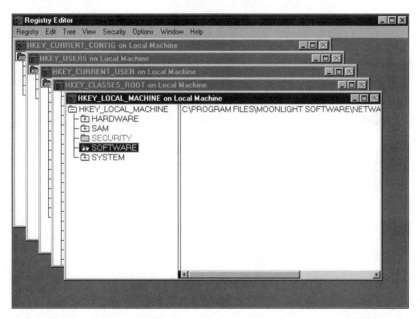

Figure 5.9
REGEDT32.EXE presents each predefined Registry subkey in its own menu.

REGEDT32.EXE is triggered much like REGEDIT.EXE. Follow these steps to open REGEDT32.EXE:

1. Click on Start|Run.

2. Type "REGEDT32.EXE".

3. Click on OK, and the Registry Editor will open.

You can cascade the menu view using REGEDT32.EXE by selecting the Cascade command from the Window menu. Alternatively, you can press Shift and F5 simultaneously. You can tile the menu view using REGEDT32.EXE by selecting the Tile command from the Window menu. Alternatively, you can press Shift and F4 simultaneously.

You'll notice a few differences between REGEDT32.EXE and REGEDIT.EXE when it comes to expanding and collapsing keys. For example, you'll drive yourself crazy trying to expand REGEDT32.EXE keys by clicking on the + signs that indicate further values are entered beneath the key. Clicking only selects the key; it doesn't expand the key. You need to double-click on the + sign to expand the key. Alternatively, when a key is highlighted using the REGEDT32.EXE Registry Editor, you can expand the key by pressing the keypad's or keyboard's + key. If you wish to collapse a key, press the keypad's or keyboard's - key.

Expanding entire keys works differently when you're using REGEDT32.EXE, too. Instead of pressing Alt and the keypad's * key, you should press the Ctrl key and the * key.

Modifying Registry values works differently in REGEDT32.EXE than it does when you're using the REGEDIT.EXE Registry Editor. After you've selected a subkey in the left pane, you can't right-click on it in the right pane and select Modify because Modify isn't available in the pop-up menu using REGEDT32.EXE. Instead, double-click on the value in the right pane. Then, you can view and edit the Registry entry value.

Among the Registry operations you can perform using REGEDT32.EXE are the following:

• Opening the local Registry

• Loading a hive

• Restoring a key

• Saving a key

• Printing a key

• Adding and deleting Registry values

Similar to REGEDIT.EXE, many of REGEDT32.EXE's operations are straightforward. Selecting Print from the Registry menu lets you print the highlighted key, and selecting Open Local from the Registry menu opens a copy of the local machine's Registry. Deleting keys is as simple as highlighting the key to be discarded and selecting Delete from the Edit menu. Alternatively, you can press the Delete key to delete the highlighted key.

Just like with REGEDIT.EXE, REGEDT32.EXE boasts other operations that are more complicated. Let's examine the more complicated Registry operations that both Registry Editors offer.

Performing Registry Operations

Here's where the rubber meets the infamous road. The more complex actions that we'll look at here can make or break attempts at fixing Registry errors. We'll look at each of the following:

- Connecting to remote Registries via a network connection

- Importing and exporting Registry files using REGEDIT.EXE

- Loading hives using REGEDT32.EXE

- Creating new Registry entries

- Saving and restoring Registry keys using REGEDT32.EXE

- Saving a subtree as a file using REGEDT32.EXE

Let's begin by looking at how to connect to remote Registries.

Connecting to Remote System Registries

Remotely administering System Registries can be convenient. Using remote connections, Windows 2000 IT professionals don't have to leave their offices or help desks to troubleshoot or fix errors on a user's machine located down the hall, in another building, across town, or in another city.

You can just do the following:

1. Click on Start|Run.

2. Type "REGEDIT" and click on OK.

3. Click on Registry and select Connect Network Registry.

4. When the Connect Network Registry dialog box appears, you can enter the computer name manually, or you can click on the Browse button. Clicking on Browse opens the Browse For Computer dialog box. Use it to navigate to the system whose Registry you wish to view or modify. When you locate the system you wish to connect to, highlight it and click on OK. The computer name box will be completed for you. Next, click on OK.

5. The remote system's Registry will appear in the left pane, as shown in Figure 5.10.

You can also connect to remote System Registries by using REGEDT32.EXE. The process is the same, with the exception that you must click on Select Computer from the Registry menu rather than Connect Network Registry. And, instead of adding the Apollo Registry in the left pane, the remote system's keys appear as separate menus.

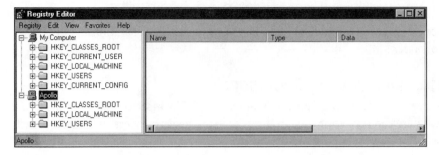

Figure 5.10
A special icon in the left pane denotes that the Apollo system is a remote machine.

How does this procedure work in the real world? Let's run through a quick example. Suppose you have a workgroup named Coriolis. The Coriolis workgroup, for test purposes, includes three machines: Apollo, Gemini, and Mercury. Say you need to connect to the Apollo system from Mercury. Follow these steps on the Mercury machine to permit remote administration of the Apollo system:

1. Click on Start|Run.

2. Type "REGEDIT" and click on OK.

3. Click on Registry and select Connect Network Registry.

4. When the Connect Network Registry dialog box appears, you can enter the computer name manually, or you can click on the Browse button. Clicking on Browse opens the Browse For Computer dialog box. Use it to navigate to the system whose Registry you wish to view or modify. In this case, you need the Apollo system, shown in Figure 5.11. Highlight it and click on OK. The computer name box autofills the Apollo name. Click on OK.

5. The Apollo machine appears in the Registry Editor, and you can now modify its values.

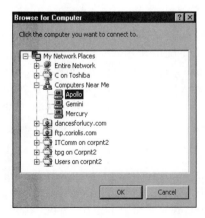

Figure 5.11
You must navigate to the system you wish to modify using the Browse For Computer dialog box.

5

Note: *Not all five predefined subkeys are displayed when you access remote System Registries. Instead, to help the Registry information load quickly over a network connection, duplicate key information isn't displayed. It's for this reason that only a few subkeys appear when you connect to the Apollo machine.*

Disconnecting from the remote system is simple. Follow these short steps:

1. From within the Registry Editor, select Disconnect Network Registry from the Registry menu.

2. When the Disconnect Network Registry dialog box appears, select the remote system you wish to disconnect by highlighting it.

3. Click on OK, and the remote system is disconnected.

Disconnecting from a remote system using REGEDT32.EXE requires that you highlight the remote system key, select the Registry menu, and click on Close.

Now that you know how to connect to and disconnect from remote Registries, let's examine how to import and export Registry files using REGEDIT.EXE.

Importing and Exporting Registry Files Using REGEDIT.EXE

Often, you might need to import or export Registry files. You may have identically configured machines, and a user may have corrupted a Registry key, for example. In such a case, you could export Registry files from a properly functioning system and then import these files on the offending machine. You might also wish to test a Registry configuration from one machine on another. You also might want to study Registry entries in a text editor. The Windows 2000 Registry offers such functionality.

Follow these steps to export a Registry file:

1. Click on Start|Run.

2. Type "REGEDIT" and click on OK.

3. In the left pane, select the key you wish to export by highlighting it.

4. Select the Registry menu and click on Export Registry File.

5. When the Export Registry File dialog box appears, as shown in Figure 5.12, navigate to the location where you want to export the file. Browse to the location, provide a name for the file, and select Save. The key is then exported and saved as an REG file.

You can open the Registry file you just created in a text editor by right-clicking on the file and selecting Open With from the pop-up menu. Select Notepad. You'll see such Registry information as displayed in Figure 5.13.

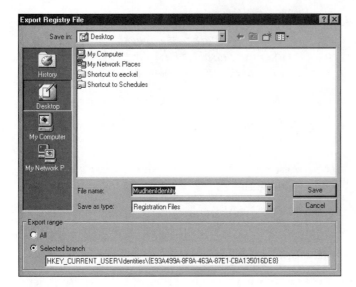

Figure 5.12
Use the Export Registry File dialog box to provide the name and location where you want to export your Registry key.

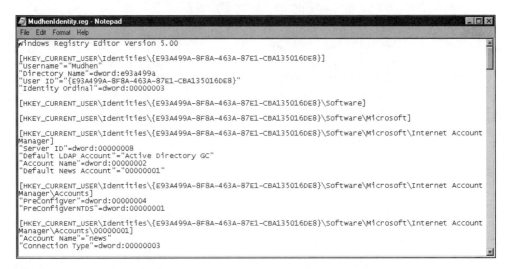

Figure 5.13
Registry key information can be read using a text editor, such as Notepad.

You may wish to import the Registry file to another Registry. You can do so by following these steps:

1. Open the Registry Editor by clicking on Start|Run, typing "REGEDIT", and clicking on OK.

2. Select the Registry menu and click on Import Registry File.

3. When the Import Registry File dialog box, which looks just like the Export Registry File dialog box, appears, navigate to the file you wish to import and highlight it.

4. Select Open. A confirmation message will appear, stating that the information has been successfully loaded into the System Registry.

Sometimes, you might want to load or unload Registry hives. REGEDT32.EXE should be your tool of choice for that operation.

Loading and Unloading Registry Hives Using REGEDT32.EXE

Depending on the predefined key you've highlighted in REGEDT32.EXE, the option of loading and unloading hives will be present in the Registry menu. For example, you could unload a hive from the HKEY_CURRENT_USER key, should you wish to remove a hive that was previously loaded.

According to Microsoft's included Help file for the REGEDT32.EXE utility, "Load Hive and Unload Hive allow a part of your system to be temporarily downloaded onto another computer for maintenance." The Help file continues, noting that before the hives can be unloaded, they must be saved as a key.

Tip: Both REGEDIT.EXE and REGEDT32.EXE include excellent Help files. These Help files provide searchable tips, as well as an index you can use to troubleshoot Registry repairs.

Follow these steps to unload a hive:

1. Open the Registry Editor by clicking on Start|Run, typing "REGEDT32", and clicking on OK.

2. Highlight the desired key in the left pane and select Registry.

3. From the Registry menu, select Unload Hive.

4. You'll receive a warning dialog box stating that the "Registry Editor will unload the currently selected key and all of its subkeys." You will be asked to confirm that you wish to continue the operation. Click on Yes to remove the hive.

Loading a hive works the same way, only in reverse. Follow these steps to load a hive:

1. Open the Registry Editor by clicking on Start|Run, typing "REGEDT32", and clicking on OK.

2. Highlight the desired key in the left pane and select Registry.

3. From the Registry menu, select Load Hive.

4. When the Load Hive dialog box appears, navigate to the location of the stored hive and click on Open.

5. A confirmation box will appear, confirming that the hive loaded properly.

Next, let's examine the manner in which Registry entries are created.

Creating New Registry Entries

Occasionally, network administrators and others will need to create new Registry entries. The process is simple. Follow these steps to add new Registry entries:

1. Open a Registry Editor by typing "REGEDIT" in the Run dialog box or from a command prompt.

2. Navigate to the location in the predefined key where you wish to add the new Registry entry.

3. Select New from the Edit menu. The new key will be created.

4. Provide a name for the new key.

5. Create new string, binary, or DWORD values by clicking on the respective value command from the menu that appears when you click Edit|New.

6. Provide a name for the new string, binary, or DWORD value you created.

7. Provide entry values by highlighting each value you create in the right pane, right-clicking on it, and selecting Modify from the pop-up menu.

It's no secret that system administrators and other IT professionals are increasingly relying on cable modems and DSL circuits for remote access to corporate networks. Such Internet services are being used in greater numbers not only by IT professionals to access their own networks remotely, but for their users' remote services as well.

Here's a real-world Registry modification, originally noted by *PC Magazine* author Linden deCarmo, that can be made to enhance the performance of Windows 2000 Professional machines using such broadband connections.

Out-of-the-box, Windows 2000 Professional has been tuned to perform best in local area networks and for use with dial-up connections of typically 56Kbps. Broadband connections offer significantly enhanced bandwidth. Making the Registry change can result in download performance improving by 30 to 50 percent. As always, your mileage may vary.

Warning! Again, you should not attempt Registry modifications until you have created a verified backup. Registry modifications could result in the loss of system data, making the backup necessary to prevent data loss.

1. Open the Registry Editor by clicking on Start|Run, typing "REGEDIT", and clicking on OK.

2. Navigate to the HKEY_LOCAL_MACHINE\System\CurrentControlSet\Services\Tcpip\Parameters key.

3. With the Parameters key highlighted, select New from the Edit menu and then select DWORD Value.

4. Enter the following DWORD entry name: "TcpWindowSize".

5. Right-click on TcpWindowSize in the right pane and select Modify.

6. Change the Value Data box to read "00007fff", ensure the Hexadecimal radio button is selected, and click on OK.

7. The key is added to the right pane with a Data value of 0x00007fff (32767).

8. Close the Registry Editor.

9. Reboot the PC, and the new TCP/IP receive window setting will be implemented.

You can also use REGEDT32.EXE to create new Registry keys and values. The process is basically the same, although you will need to select Add Key or Add Value from the Registry Editor's Edit menu.

You may not always need to create new Registry keys. You may have had occasion to save a Registry key. Or, you may wish to restore a Registry key after you've modified a value only to find that your modification didn't correct an error.

Saving and Restoring Registry Keys Using REGEDT32.EXE

REGEDT32.EXE's save and restore commands work differently than REGEDIT.EXE's. Instead of saving Registry keys as REG files that can be read by text editors, files are saved, by default, without extensions.

Tip: Because REGEDT32.EXE doesn't save keys by default in a format permitting them to be read by text editors, you should use REGEDIT.EXE when you plan to use a text editor to search Registry values. Alternatively, you can save files using REGEDT32.EXE with .txt file extensions. However, this approach will not make all Registry entries readable. For example, Identities entries housed under HKEY_CURRENT_USER can be read using Notepad if saved in REGEDIT.EXE, but they cannot be read if saved as TXT files using REGEDT32.EXE.

Several steps are required to save a Registry key. Specifically, this example will demonstrate how to save the HKEY_CLASSES_ROOT subkey. Follow these steps:

1. Click on Start|Run, type "REGEDT32", and click on OK.

2. Navigate to the key you wish to save (in this case, HKEY_CLASSES_ROOT). Select Save Key from the Registry menu.

3. When the Save Key dialog box appears, provide the location to store the key as a file and the file name. Click on Save. Depending on the size of the key, the process can take a few moments. For this example, the HKEY_CLASSES_ROOT file is larger than 4MB, so it is saved to the system's hard drive. It could also be saved to a network share, should you choose.

As you might guess, restoring a Registry key is essentially the same process in reverse. However, you should note that, when you're restoring a key, the entire key will be restored. Any changes made to the system conducting the restore since the key was saved as a file will be lost.

For this example, let's restore the HKEY_CLASSES_ROOT key we just saved. Just follow these steps:

1. Open REGEDT32.EXE on the system you wish to restore the key to by clicking on Start|Run, typing "REGEDT32.EXE", and clicking on OK.

2. In the left pane, navigate to the key you wish to restore.

3. Select Restore from the Registry menu.

4. Navigate to the location of the file you saved, highlight it, and click on Open. Alternatively, you can double-click on the file.

5. A dialog box will appear, warning that the key will be restored on top of the currently selected key. The box also warns that all value entries and subkeys of the current key will be deleted. Click on Yes to continue the operation, and the key will be restored.

You may wish to save an entire subtree as a file. REGEDT32.EXE includes a command permitting you to do just that.

Saving a Subtree as a File Using REGEDT32.EXE

Using REGEDT32.EXE, you can easily save a Registry subtree as a file. Just follow these steps:

1. Open the Registry Editor by clicking on Start|Run, typing "REGEDT32", and clicking on OK.

2. Navigate to the subtree you wish to save as a file and highlight it.

3. Select Save Subtree As from the Registry menu.

4. In the Save As box, provide a location and name for the file. Click on Save.

You can restore the subtree you saved as a file by following the directions described earlier for restoring a key.

Tip: When attempting to restore keys, you may encounter dialog boxes stating that the operation failed. You may get these messages for two common reasons. First, the key may be in use, in which case, you'll have to stop the respective services or utilities before the associated Registry entry can be added. Second, you may not have the appropriate permissions.

Setting Registry Security and Permissions

Changes to the Registry are protected with security permissions. These security permissions operate similarly to file permissions.

You can check a Registry's security permissions by selecting Security from the REGEDT32.EXE Registry Editor's menu. You can set different permissions for different Registry keys.

For example, highlighting the HKEY_USERS subtree key and selecting Permissions from the Security menu displays the Permissions For HKEY_USERS dialog box, as shown in

Figure 5.14. From here, you specify which users and groups should have which permissions to modify the Registry key.

You can add administrators and other users to the Name box by clicking on the Add button. Doing so calls up the Select Users, Computers, Or Groups dialog box, shown in Figure 5.15. Click on the Look In drop-down box to add remote users and administrators.

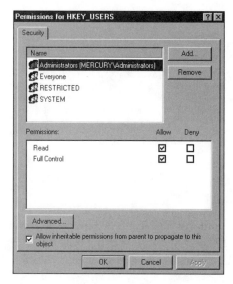

Figure 5.14
Appropriate permissions must be set before Registry changes can be executed.

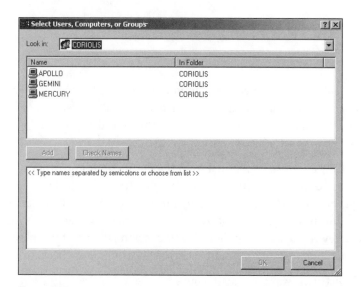

Figure 5.15
In the Select Users, Computers, Or Groups dialog box, you can select other users to be given Registry-editing permissions.

You can set Allow or Deny rights for two permissions: Read and Full Control. You also can assign additional rights by clicking on the Advanced button. Among the advanced rights that you can assign using the View/Edit button are the following:

- Query Value

- Set Value

- Create Subkey

- Enumerate Subkeys

- Notify

- Create Link

- Delete

- Write DAC

- Write Owner

- Read Control

Setting Allow Full Control from the Permissions For HKEY_USERS dialog box provides allow permissions to all the permissions in the preceding list. Setting only the Allow Read permission in the Permissions For HKEY_USERS dialog box, meanwhile, provides allow permissions only for the following:

- Query Value

- Enumerate Subkeys

- Notify

- Read Control

By default, if Full Control is selected, Read permissions are selected. The Deny permissions work in the same way. Should you select Deny Read in the Permissions For HKEY_USERS dialog box, the same four permissions in the preceding list would be denied. If Deny Full Control is set, all the permissions are denied.

Auditing and owner settings are also configured from the Permissions For HKEY_USERS dialog box. Just click the Advanced button. You can also state that inheritable permissions from parent keys be permitted to propagate (or apply to) the object you're configuring the rights for. By the same token, you can also override other permissions that have been set for child objects of the key you're assigning rights to by checking the Reset Permissions On All Child Objects And Enable Propagation Of Inheritable Permissions checkbox.

When you have the Registry the way you like it, you would be well served to back it up. Fortunately, Windows 2000 Professional provides a tool for performing such a backup.

Backing Up the Registry

You can back up the Registry by using Windows 2000 Professional's Backup and Recovery Tools program, which is located in the System Tools folder.

Before you start, you should be aware that the utility backs up more than just the Registry. All the following are backed up as well:

- Registry files

- Boot files

- COM+ database

Tip: *You can use two additional programs to back up the Windows 2000 Professional Registry. They are included as part of the Windows 2000 Professional Resource Kit. Unlike the native Backup utility, REGBACK and REGREST back up only Registry files. For more information on using REGBACK and REGREST, see the documentation included in the Windows 2000 Professional Resource Kit.*

Follow these steps to use the Windows 2000 Professional Backup utility:

1. Click on Start|Programs|Accessories|System Tools|Backup.

2. When the Backup utility opens, select the Backup tab.

3. Search for the System State entry in the left pane and check it, as shown in Figure 5.16.

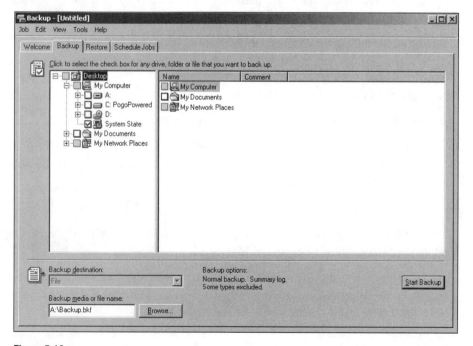

Figure 5.16
Select System State to back up Registry files.

4. Select the location for your backup and enter a file name for the backup file to be created in the Backup Media Or File Name box. Because the Registry can be fairly large, you'll want to specify another hard drive, network share, or Zip drive.

5. Click on the Start Backup button.

6. The Backup Job Information dialog box will appear. It will display a description of the backup to be performed, ask whether any preexisting backups should be overwritten, and provide a label to be used if old backup data is to be overwritten. Click on Start Backup to create the backup file. Selection Information and Backup Progress dialog boxes will appear and track the creation of the backup file.

When the backup is complete, the dialog box will provide you the opportunity to read a report chronicling such important information as the following:

- Backup name

- Backup set

- Backup description

- Backup type

- Number of files backed up

- The time the backup took to complete

The Registry is restored in the same manner. Using the same Backup utility, you select the Restore tab instead of the Backup tab. Follow these steps to restore a backup:

1. Click on Start|Programs|Accessories|System Tools|Backup.

2. When the Backup utility opens, select the Restore tab.

3. Expand the File folder in the left pane.

4. Select the System State backup file you wish to restore.

5. Specify where you would like to restore the files to by providing the correct location in the Restore Files To box. Most likely, you will want to specify that the backup files be restored to their original location.

6. Click on the Start Restore button on the bottom right of the menu.

7. A dialog box will appear, warning that restoring the System State will overwrite the current System State. Click on OK to proceed.

8. A Confirm Restore dialog box will appear. You can set advanced restore options here. Click on the Advanced button to specify that security, removable storage databases, junction points, and other settings be restored. Click on OK.

9. The Enter Backup File Name dialog box appears, providing the name of the backup file that will be used. Ensure the correct file is listed, or edit the file name or browse to specify the correct file. Click on OK to execute the restore operation.

10. The Restore Progress dialog box will track the completion of the restore operation. When the process finishes, the Restore Progress dialog box will list the total elapsed time and confirm that the restore has finished.

11. After you click on OK, a dialog box will appear, stating that the machine must be rebooted for the new System State to take effect. After the machine has rebooted, the entire restore process is complete.

Should you have any questions regarding the restore action, the restore process also generates a report. Click on the Report button in the Restore Progress dialog box to read the details of the backup restoration.

Tip: *The Backup utility also offers Backup and Restore Wizards. Should you wish to be guided through the previous processes step-by-step, you can select the wizards from the Backup utility's Welcome tab.*

If you're worried about the size of your Registry, you can easily check it. You may wish to perform this action before creating a backup to ensure you possess sufficient empty disk space. Fortunately, it's also easy to limit the amount of hard disk space the Registry can be permitted to consume.

Controlling Registry Size

As additional peripherals are added to a system, and as various software applications are installed, the amount of space Registry values consume can blossom. The Windows 2000 Registry includes the five predefined (but not unique) subtree keys. That's the same number of subtree keys that Windows NT Workstation 4 systems have and less than the number of subtrees in Windows 9x systems (which boast six subtree keys). However, more subtree keys exist in Windows 2000 than in Windows NT Server 4, which has only four subtrees.

As discussed previously, Windows 2000 collects and maintains a great deal of data about a system. Information on every user, any hardware peripheral that's attached and configured, and all software that's been installed is filed away for safekeeping. Thus, the more a system is used, the larger the Registry grows.

How big can it get? Quite big. Bigger than you can fit on a floppy disk, that's for sure. We're talking Zip disks, folks.

On a fresh system running Windows 2000, a machine might have a Registry as small as 9MB. Use a system for a while, though, and it can grow exponentially. We've seen Windows 2000 Professional machines with Registries growing larger than 20MB. We've heard stories of Registries growing three times that size, but such sizes are usually encountered with server platforms.

You can check the size of your system's Registry easily by using a Control Panel applet. Using the same applet, you can specify a maximum size for the Registry, too, as shown in Figure 5.17.

To specify a Registry's maximum size using Windows 2000 Professional (or to view the Registry's size), follow these steps:

1. Click on Start|Settings|Control Panel.

2. Select the System applet.

3. Select the Advanced tab.

4. Click on the Performance Options button.

5. Click on the Change button.

6. In the Registry Size section, specify the maximum size for the Registry in the Maximum Registry Size (MB) box.

Tip: If you just want to view the size of your Registry, that information is located above this box.

7. Click on OK three times to close the dialog boxes and accept the changes.

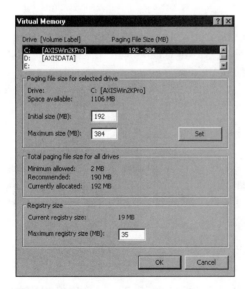

Figure 5.17
You can check and limit the Windows 2000 Registry size by using the System applet.

Summary

As you can see, the Registry tracks an incredible amount of information. Much of the information is critical to maintaining a steady system state and ensuring the proper performance of installed hardware devices, software programs, and network connections. Make even one small keystroke error, and the entire contents of a system could be lost. It's for that reason that IT professionals should always maintain verified backups when working with the Registry and making modifications.

Numerous actions and operations can be performed using the two Registry Editors that Windows 2000 Professional provides by default. Subtree values and entries can be modified, subtrees and keys can be saved and restored, and the entire Registry can be backed up. The Registry can also be modified remotely, should sufficient permissions be in place.

Ensuring a working backup copy of the Windows 2000 Registry is safely stored away can prevent disaster. Predicting the amount of hard disk space that will be required to store the Registry is simple, thanks to a slightly hidden feature that displays the Registry's size.

Often, many Windows 2000 Professional features and settings are also configured using the powerful Microsoft Management Console. The MMC, as it is known, is also highly customizable, making it the favorite administration tool of many IT professionals. We'll look at it in the next chapter.

5

Chapter 6

Using the Windows 2000 Microsoft Management Console

Introduction to the Microsoft Management Console

The Microsoft Management Console, often referred to as the MMC, is the administrative interface you use to manage your Windows 2000 Professional and Server environments. The interface is not new to all Microsoft Windows 2000 users, however. The first version of the MMC was introduced in some of the Microsoft BackOffice products, such as SQL Server 7 and Internet Information Server (IIS) 4.

The MMC is a robust interface used to create, save, and open administrative tools (called *MMC consoles*) that manage software, network, and hardware components of your Windows 2000 operating system and BackOffice applications. Although the MMC is a new feature of Windows 2000, you can run it on the Windows 95, 98, and NT operating systems.

The MMC itself does not perform administrative functions but is customized to provide the primary tools, called *snap-ins*, which are a type of tool you can add to a console supported by the MMC. You use snap-ins to perform both local and remote administration of your Windows 2000 operating system and BackOffice environments. Furthermore, you can add other tools such as ActiveX controls, links to Web pages, tasks, taskpad views, and folders. You can save this customized interface to a file and then share it with other users in your organization, eliminating the need for creating redundant configurations of the customized consoles.

Becoming Familiar with the MMC

The MMC contains two panes. The left pane contains the console tree, and the right pane, called the *details pane*, displays information about, and the associated functions pertaining to, the items selected in the console tree. The details pane can also display other types of information, such as Web pages, charts, tables, graphics, and columns.

The left pane contains two tabs: Tree and Favorites. The Tree tab shows the items that are available for use in the specified console. The console tree can contain *nodes*, which are locations on the tree that can have links to one or more items, or subcomponents, below them. You use the Favorites tab to create shortcuts to items in the console tree. You can also use it to organize taskpad views and to make it easier for novice users to complete tasks by simplifying their views.

The MMC operates in two modes: Author and User. The Author mode grants full access to all MMC functionality, including the ability to add or remove snap-ins, create taskpad views and tasks, create new windows, add items to the Favorites list, and view all portions of the console tree. The three User mode levels restrict the available options within the MMC. The three User modes are explained in more detail in the section "Securing Your Customized MMC."

By default, when you open a new MMC, it does not contain any objects. You can create a blank, or empty, MMC by going to the Start menu, clicking on the Run command, and then typing "MMC". Figure 6.1 shows the output from this command. You can also go to the command prompt, type "MMC", and press Enter to open a blank MMC.

Looking for Assistance?

The MMC contains a dynamic built-in help utility to help you become familiar with the MMC options and their capabilities. The Help drop-down menu has three options. The first option, called Help Topics, is a dynamic help menu that starts out with help that pertains only to the MMC. This type of help is called *context-sensitive help* because it pertains to the context of the MMC environment only. For instance, when you first open a blank MMC, only MMC help is available to you. Figure 6.2 shows the help available in a blank MMC. However, as you add items to the customized console tree, the help associated

Figure 6.1
A blank Microsoft Management Console.

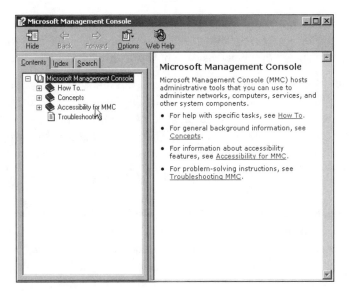

Figure 6.2
Context-sensitive help in a blank MMC.

with those items is also added. So, the more options added to your customized MMC, the more help options available to you within the MMC.

The second option provides Web-based help. The Microsoft On The Web option located on the same drop-down menu as Help Topics locates help on the Web. Some of the options available here include Product News, Frequently Asked Questions, and the Microsoft Home Page. This information is *dynamic*, meaning that it constantly changes. Because this information is not built into the help installed on the machine, you can access it on the Web to receive more current information.

The third option, About Microsoft Management Console, contains information about the MMC itself and the operating system. Like most Microsoft Windows software, it provides version information about the utility running—which, in this case, is the MMC—and the operating system build number, as well as the latest service pack applied to the operating system.

Tip: Using this third help option is a great way to quickly check three primary components of your Windows 2000 environment: the build number, the latest service pack, and the amount of memory installed on the machine.

Customizing the MMC

You customize your MMC using the Add/Remove Snap-in option located within the Console toolbar of the MMC to add both local and remote snap-ins to your console tree. You can also add snap-ins that are published in the Active Directory. In addition, you can customize your MMC to include taskpad views and tasks. You can add items to your Favorites list, thus streamlining access to your console items. You can also customize how the rows and columns appear in the details pane of your console.

When you select the Add/Remove Snap-in option, the dialog box shown in Figure 6.3 will appear. The Add/Remove Snap-in dialog box contains two tabs: Standalone and Extensions. With these two tabs, you can add snap-ins and further customize individual components within the chosen snap-ins, respectively. When this dialog box is initially displayed, it will contain any previously configured snap-ins. You can add new snap-ins by clicking on the Add button. The Add button will display the snap-ins you have available to you to add to your MMC.

Figure 6.4 shows some of the snap-ins available on a Windows 2000 Professional machine. (The options available depend on what services and applications you have installed on your machine.) You select each object one at a time that you want to install and click on the Add button at the bottom of the dialog box. By doing so, you will add each component you have chosen to install. After you finish installing each component, you click on the Close button.

When you choose the Extensions tab, you can select specific components of the snap-in you want to add to the MMC. By default, all extensions are added; however, you can deselect the Add All Extensions checkbox and choose specific extensions you wish to add. Figure 6.5 shows the Extensions tab with the Add All Extensions checkbox deselected. Deselecting this option will allow you to choose exactly which components of the Computer Management snap-in to install.

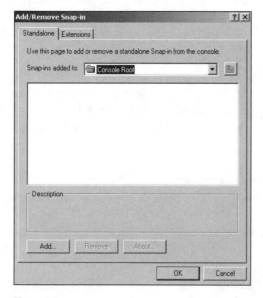

Figure 6.3
Preparing to add snap-ins.

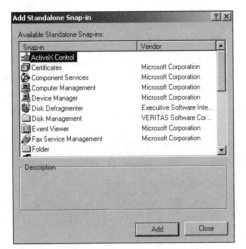

Figure 6.4
Choosing the snap-ins to add.

As you select each option, a brief description is provided in the Description area. Some of the extensions have additional information about them. If you want to view additional information on a specific extension, you can select the extension option and click on the About button. When you do, you will receive a detailed description of the selected extension. Some extensions you add to your MMC themselves contain extensions, providing you the opportunity to further customize the extensions as well as the snap-in.

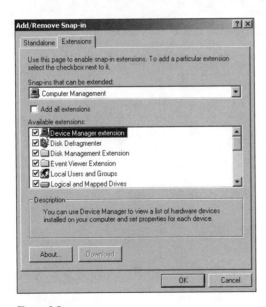

Figure 6.5
Selecting the extensions of your snap-in.

Local Snap-ins

Local snap-ins added to the MMC provide administrative tools for the local machine, or the machine the MMC actually resides on. When you add a local snap-in to the MMC, the console tree will contain the new entry, which will end with **(Local)**, identifying that the snap-in is used to manage the local machine. Figure 6.6 shows an example of an MMC that contains the Computer Management snap-in for the local machine. Notice that the details pane lists the tools available within the selected System Tools of the console tree located in the Computer Management snap-in for the local machine.

Remote Snap-ins

Some snap-ins include the capability to perform administration of remote computers. Computer Management, Disk Management, and Removable Storage Management are examples of snap-ins that you can use to remotely administer computers on your network. When you're creating your customized MMC and adding those types of tools to your console, it presents a dialog box asking whether this snap-in is for the local computer or a remote computer. If it is for a remote computer, you can specify the name of the remote computer, or you can browse the network for the computer. In addition, there is a checkbox (shown in Figure 6.7) that allows you to dynamically select the computer you want to manage when you launch the snap-in from the command line. If this choice is checked, you have the option of using this snap-in for a different remote machine when you open the MMC from the command prompt.

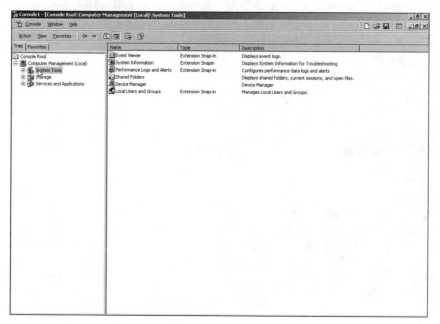

Figure 6.6
MMC with a local Computer Management snap-in.

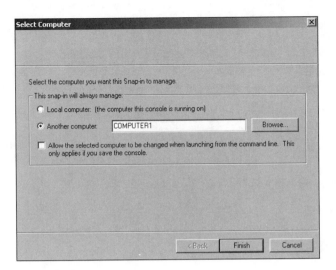

Figure 6.7
Selecting the computer to manage.

After you add your local and remote administrative tools, the MMC allows you to easily identify which computers the snap-ins are configured for. Each tool added to the console tree has an extension that identifies whether it is for the local machine or a remote machine. For instance, if you add the Computer Management snap-in for the local machine and also add the Computer Management snap-in for a computer called COMPUTER1, both of them will show up in the console tree with the identity of the computer they are associated with. Figure 6.8 shows an example of a customized MMC with two instances of Computer Management, one for the local computer and one for the computer named COMPUTER1.

Adding Published Snap-ins

Published snap-ins are published in the Windows 2000 Active Directory. You add these snap-ins the same way you add the local and remote snap-ins; however, you will see "not installed" under the Vendor column of the Add Standalone Snap-in dialog box, shown earlier in Figure 6.4. To access the published snap-ins, you must be running Windows 2000 in a Windows 2000 domain. The same is true of extensions published in a Windows 2000 Active Directory environment. Examples of published snap-ins include Active Directory Users and Computers, Distributed File System, and other snap-ins not available on Windows 2000 Professional.

Adding Taskpad Views and Tasks

Taskpad views are pages that you can use to add customized views of the details pane of a console. Taskpad views can also contain shortcuts to functions within a specific console or outside that console. Those shortcuts run tasks such as starting wizards, running command lines, opening Web pages, and performing menu commands. You can configure a

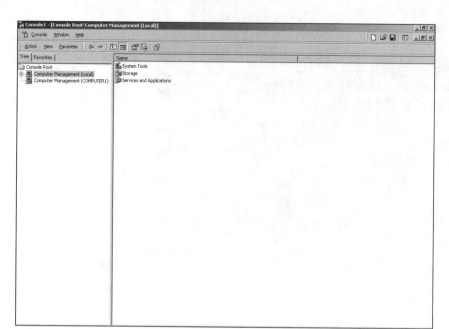

Figure 6.8
Identifying local and remote snap-ins.

taskpad view to contain all tasks a given user might require. A console can contain multiple taskpad views, providing the capability to group tasks by user or function.

The taskpad views make it easier for users to perform their jobs. For instance, you can create a taskpad view that contains specific tasks and then hide the console tree from the user, reducing the time required to locate particular items within the console tree or operating system. Taskpad views can also be used for simplifying complex tasks. For instance, in a single location, you can combine multiple snap-ins and other tools that open or run all the necessary dialog boxes, command lines, property pages, and scripts associated with a frequently executed task.

Before you create a taskpad view or add a task to a console, you should determine how many taskpad views you need. If you need multiple taskpad views, you also need to determine how each task is going to be divided among the different taskpad views. Furthermore, you need to decide what kind of taskpad view you want to use—one that displays a list and tasks or one that displays tasks only.

If you want to create a taskpad view for a console, the existing console must already contain at least one snap-in. You can create the titles, headings, and lists that appear in the taskpad view by using the New Taskpad View Wizard. You also can use the wizard to associate a taskpad view with multiple items or a single item within the console tree.

After you create the new taskpad view, you can use the New Task Wizard to add tasks to it. The tasks can include menu commands for the items in the console, as well as commands that run from the command prompt. These commands can act on part of the console tree or the details pane, or they can open another component on your computer.

To create a taskpad view in your MMC, open the MMC console and select a snap-in item from the console tree. From the Action drop-down menu, click on New Taskpad View to initiate the New Taskpad View Wizard, which will walk you through the steps required to create the taskpad view within the console. The final screen of the New Taskpad View Wizard asks whether you want to create a task via the New Task Wizard. Figure 6.9 shows a taskpad view of the MMC Help icon created in the details pane of the MMC.

After you create a taskpad view, you can modify it by selecting the component within the Console Root and then choosing Edit Taskpad View from the Action drop-down menu. To delete the taskpad view, you can take the same steps, but this time, choose Delete Taskpad View.

Adding Web Site Links

You can also use a snap-in to create a link to a Web site. The Link to Web Address snap-in provides you the capability to add links to Web addresses in the console tree section of your customized MMC. When defining the link, you provide the URL and a name to identify the Web site. This is extremely helpful for users who visit specific Web sites frequently. After the snap-in is added to the console tree, the user clicks on the name of the Web site you provided, and the Web page is displayed in the details pane of the MMC.

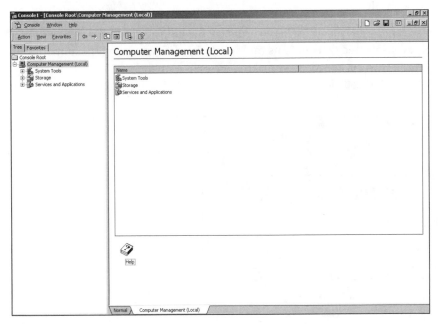

Figure 6.9
Adding a taskpad view to your console.

Managing the MMC Favorites List

The Favorites list is located in the console tree area of the MMC console. The tab will appear automatically if you open the MMC in Author mode or if you already added an item to the Favorites list in the MMC.

You use the Favorites menu to create shortcuts to items that reside in the console tree. You can then access these items from both the Tree and Favorites tabs. You can use this list to shorten the time required to locate tools you use often or to access tools located several levels down in the console tree. The Favorites list also makes it easier for novice users to complete tasks. For instance, you can create a Favorites list that includes shortcuts to only the items in the console tree that a specific user needs to perform his or her job. Figure 6.10 shows the dialog box you use to add entries to your Favorites list.

You add items to your Favorites list via the Favorites menu option by using the following steps:

1. Highlight the option you want to add.

2. Click on the Favorites menu.

3. Click on Add To Favorites.

4. Click on the folder that will contain the new item, or click on the New Folder button to create a new folder in the Favorites list and specify a folder name.

5. Click on OK.

You also can use the Favorites list to organize the taskpad views. This way, you can take a complex console tree that contains multiple taskpad views among the numerous items in the console tree and add all these taskpad views to a single Favorites list, simplifying access to the taskpad views.

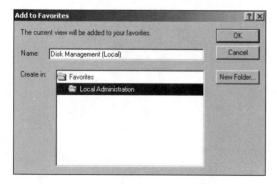

Figure 6.10
Adding an entry to your Favorites list.

Organizing Your Favorites List

The Favorites option can be used to create folders to organize your Favorites. You can move items between folders, create new folders, rename existing folders or items, or delete existing folders or items. To organize your Favorites list, access the Favorites menu and then click on Organize Favorites.

You can modify the folders and their contents after you create them by using the Organize Favorites dialog box, shown in Figure 6.11.

You move an existing item to a folder by following these steps:

1. Click on the item you want to move.

2. Click on the Move To Folder button.

3. Click on the folder you want to move the item to.

4. Click on OK.

You can rename these folders by following these steps:

1. Click on the existing folder name.

2. Click on the Rename button.

3. Type the new folder name.

4. Press Enter.

To remove an item or folder from the Favorites list, simply click on the item and then click on Delete.

Figure 6.12 shows the result of adding a new folder called Local Administration into the Favorites list and then adding two local administrative tools, Computer Management and Disk Management, to the Local Administration folder.

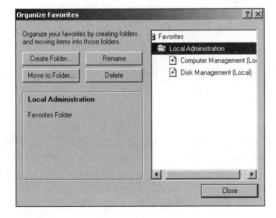

Figure 6.11
The Organize Favorites dialog box.

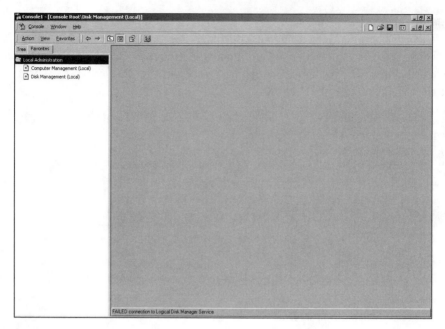

Figure 6.12
Viewing an MMC Favorites list.

Customizing the View for Saved Consoles

Using the Customize View dialog box, you can hide or display items of a console. You access this dialog box by choosing the Customize command from the View menu in the console. It provides complete customization of which items are displayed or hidden and the capability to define what order the displayed items appear in the console. In fact, you can even hide the View menu itself.

To hide or save features of a saved MMC, choose the Customize command from the View menu. Under MMC, perform the following:

- To display or hide the console tree, select or deselect the Console Tree checkbox. If you hide the console tree, the Favorites tab, if applicable, is still displayed.

- To display or hide the View and Action menus, select or deselect the Standard Menus (Action And View) checkbox. If you hide the Action and View menus, the Favorites menu, if applicable, is still displayed.

Warning! *If you clear the Standard Menus (Action And View) checkbox and close the Customize View dialog box, you can no longer access commands on the Action and View menus, including the Customize command. To access the Customize View dialog box, you have to click on the system menu (the icon in the upper-left corner of the console) and then click on Customize View.*

- To display or hide the status bar at the bottom of the console window, select or deselect the Status Bar checkbox.

- To display or hide the console toolbar, select or deselect the Standard Toolbar checkbox.

- To display or hide the tabs along the bottom of the details pane, select or deselect the Taskpad Navigation Tabs checkbox.

- To display or hide the description bar along the top of the details pane, select or deselect Description bar.

To hide or display menus and toolbars for all snap-ins, follow these steps:

1. Open a saved MMC.

2. Choose Customize from the View menu.

3. Under Snap-in, perform one or both of the following:

    - To display or hide menus specific to snap-ins, select or deselect the Menus checkbox.

    - To display or hide toolbars specific to snap-ins, select or deselect the Toolbars checkbox.

Warning! When you select or deselect the Menus and Toolbars checkboxes, the menus and toolbars are displayed or hidden for all snap-ins in the console, not just the snap-in currently selected. If you seem to be having a problem because the view is not changing, the currently selected snap-in does not have custom menus or toolbars.

Managing Columns in Saved Consoles

The columns and rows saved in the details pane of a saved console can be customized to appear how you choose. For instance, you can hide or reorder columns. You can also reorder rows chronologically or alphabetically by clicking on the appropriate column heading. Furthermore, you can filter columns based on additional attributes within specific snap-ins of your console. If this feature is enabled, you will be presented with a row of drop-down list boxes that contain options for filtering beneath the specific column headings. Figure 6.13 shows the Modify Columns dialog box you use to manage your columns in a customized MMC.

Reordering Columns

To reorder columns in an MMC console, follow these three steps:

1. Click on an item in the console tree that displays columns in the details pane.

2. Click on Choose Columns in the View menu.

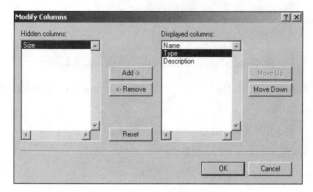

Figure 6.13
Modify Columns dialog box.

3. In the Displayed Columns box of the Modify Columns dialog box, click on a column name and then click on Move Up or Move Down to change the position in the desired direction.

You can also reorder columns in the details pane by using your mouse to drag a column heading to the right or left of its current position. You will notice highlighting between the column headings as you are dragging the column. However, you cannot change the position of the leftmost column in the details pane. You can also use your mouse to resize columns by dragging column headings.

Note: *This reorder feature is not enabled for all items. If the Choose Columns option on the View menu is not visible, this feature is unavailable for the currently selected item.*

Hiding or Displaying Columns

You can also hide or display columns in an MMC console by following these three steps:

1. Click on an item in the console tree that displays columns in the details pane.

2. Click on Choose Columns in the View menu.

3. In the Modify Columns dialog box, perform the following:

   • To display a column, select the column that you want to display from the Hidden columns and then click on Add.

   • To hide a column, select the column that you want to hide from the Displayed columns and then click on Remove. You cannot hide the leftmost column in the details pane.

Note: *This hide and display feature is not enabled for all items. If the Choose Columns option on the View menu is not visible, this feature is unavailable for the currently selected item.*

Exporting Columns

You may want to save the configuration of the details pane to a text file for use on another machine or to have a backup of the configuration. You can do so by using the Export List option located on the Action menu.

This text file can be formatted in one of the following four ways:

- Text (tab delimited) with a file extension of .txt

- Text (comma delimited) with a file extension of .csv

- Unicode Text (tab delimited) with a file extension of .txt

- Unicode Text (comma delimited) with a file extension of .csv

Note: Unicode file formats are available only on a system running Windows NT or Windows 2000. Unicode text-based data allows for 65,536 possible unique characters. With this large number, almost all the written languages of the world can be represented using a single character set, eliminating the need for multiple character sets in an environment using multiple native languages.

Take the following steps to export your MMC information out to a text file:

1. Click on an item in the console tree that displays columns in the details pane.

2. To export specific rows from the details pane, select those rows. Skip this step if you want to export all rows in the details pane.

3. Choose Export List from the Action menu.

4. In the Save As dialog box, enter the following information:

   - To export only specified rows, select the Save Only Selected Rows checkbox.

   - Click on a directory location in the Save In section to specify where to save the file.

   - Provide a file name for the file in the File Name section.

   - Choose the file format from the drop-down menu in the Save As Type section.

5. Click on the Save button.

Note: In some snap-ins, you cannot choose specific rows from the details pane. You will have to export all rows in the details pane for these snap-ins.

Filtering Rows

You can filter the rows located in a customized MMC by following these steps:

1. Click on an item in the console tree that displays columns in the details pane.

2. Choose Filtered from the View menu. (Filters appear below the column headings in the details pane.)

Note: This filtering feature is not enabled for all console items. If the Filtered option on the View menu is not visible, this feature is unavailable for the currently selected item.

Saving and Sharing Your Customized MMC

After you create your customized MMC, you will want to save it, and you may even want to share the console with other individuals so that they can perform the administrative tasks you defined inside the MMC. Saving a customized MMC to a file preserves the list of snap-ins, the arrangement and contents of console windows in the main MMC windows, the default mode, and information regarding permissions. All these settings are saved and then restored when the console is reopened.

Saving Your Customized MMC

You save the customized consoles to a file name with an .msc (Management Saved Console) file extension. To save changes made to a console, simply click on the Console option on the menu bar in the MMC, and choose Save or Save As from the drop-down menu. The operating system you are using may already have some saved and preconfigured consoles in the default folder called Administrative Tools of your Windows 2000 operating system environment. The entire path will include the drive where you installed the Windows 2000 operating system, along with the following directory path: *%systemroot%*\Profiles\ All Users\Start Menu\Programs\Administrative Tools. Storing the MSC file in this directory will allow all users who directly log on to the machine to access the file.

If you want only specific users to have access to the saved MSC file, you can place it in their specific directories. Say you have a user whose user name is John Doe. You want him, but not everyone else on that machine, to access the MSC file. You can save the MSC file to the default directory path %systemroot%\Profiles\John Doe\Start Menu\Programs\ Administrative Tools. Remember this is the default directory pathname. You can save the file to another directory on the user's machine, but you must notify him where you placed it.

Sharing Your Customized MMC

Now that you have saved a customized console out to the MSC file, you have the option of sharing it with other users on other machines in your environment. You can do so by placing the file on a shared network location or on the Web and assigning the correct permissions for only those users you want to access this file. This can be an efficient way to share an MSC file that changes constantly. The Read permission is the only permission required for users to download the MSC file to their machines. When you place it in the default directory path, they can access it by going to the Start menu and then choosing Programs|Administrative Tools and finally selecting the saved name of the MSC file as a menu option.

Another way to share a customized MSC file is to email it to the users you want to share it with. This approach is a little more secure because the file is not stored on a shared

6

network; by emailing the file, you reduce the risk of an unauthorized individual obtaining a copy of it. When you email the MSC file, only the users you want to receive it will receive it.

Another way to share the customized MSC file is to save it to a floppy disk, or if you are running Windows 2000, you can use Active Directory to publish or assign consoles to users. All these sharing options require the users to be aware of how and where to store the file for easy access from their desktops.

Now that you have created and saved a customized console, you will see additional help available under the help options. Remember that each item you add to your console also updates the help available in the MMC.

Securing Your Customized MMC

After you create your MMC and save it to a file for future use and maybe share it with other individuals in your environment, you need to be concerned with protecting the interface. As you learned previously, a Windows 2000 MMC has two general modes that define what users can do in the console when they open it. The two general modes in which you can save a customized MMC are Author and User. There is one Author mode and three types of User modes. Each User mode defines what tasks users can perform while working in the console. Each User mode also has three options that can further restrict users. Other ways to restrict users' capabilities are to implement group policies on your customized MMC and to implement NTFS permissions.

Author Mode

The Author mode provides complete flexibility in what you can do within the MMC environment. This mode, which is the most powerful, is used to create customized consoles. You have the option of adding new snap-ins, adding shortcuts to the Favorites list, adding taskpad views and tasks, and then saving the changes you made to either an existing or a new MSC file. As you learned previously, you can then share this file with other users, providing them with the tools within the MMC interface you created. How you save the console determines whether the users can also modify the interface or are restricted to just performing the tasks set up within the interface.

Author mode is the default mode when you're using an MMC as an administrator, although this can be changed while creating the console. This mode is normally permitted only to administrators. Nonadministrative users will generally be assigned one of the three User modes.

The tasks discussed up to this point in the chapter have all been performed using the Author mode of the MMC. The Options dialog box shown in Figure 6.14 presents the current mode being used. Here, you can change the mode from Author to one of the User modes. You access this dialog box from the Console drop-down menu located on the menu bar in an open MMC. This dialog box also provides a description of the mode

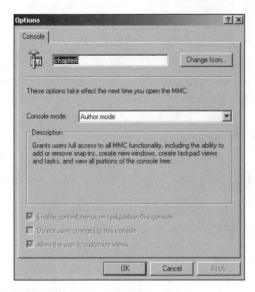

Figure 6.14
Locating and configuring the console mode.

selected. You can also modify the icon associated with the console by clicking on the Change Icon button and specifying the pathname for an icon or browsing your computer for available icons. Some users may want to change icons because not all default icons are very intuitive and some can be misleading.

Tip: Notice the three checkboxes at the bottom are dimmed while you're in Author mode. These options are not available until you choose one of the User mode options.

User Mode

User mode is used to work with existing MMC consoles to administer either a local or remote system or systems. One console can contain items in the console tree to administer both local and remote systems. This mode provides a level of security by limiting the actions available when someone is using a customized console. Three User modes are available, each providing a different level of access and functionality:

- *User Mode - Full Access*—The Full Access mode provides users with full access to all available window management commands and full access to the console tree. However, they cannot add or remove snap-ins or change any console properties. This level is the most powerful of the three available User modes in a customized console.

- *User Mode - Limited Access, Multiple Window*—The Limited Access, Multiple Window mode provides access only to the areas of the console tree that were visible when the console was last saved. Users can create new windows but cannot close existing windows while in a console that was saved in this mode.

- *User Mode - Limited Access, Single Window*—The Limited Access, Single Window mode is similar to the previous mode regarding access to the available areas of the console. This mode provides access only to the areas of the console tree that were visible when the console was last saved. However, unlike in the previous mode, users cannot open new windows while in a console that was saved in this mode.

Figure 6.15 shows three checkboxes and their default settings if you choose one of the three User modes. You can turn on or off each option by clicking in the appropriate checkbox.

To provide a secure environment when creating a customized console for your users, you must understand what each checkbox provides. The first checkbox, Enable Context Menus On Taskpads In This Console, determines whether the users can right-click and view commands that are available for objects on the taskpads. If this checkbox is deselected, right-clicking on an object on the taskpad does not display the shortcut menu for the taskpad object.

The second checkbox, Do Not Save Changes To This Console, is fairly intuitive. If this checkbox is selected, the users cannot save changes they have made to the console. This option can be powerful if you are trying to maintain a consistent console for all users across all machines. Notice that it is deselected by default.

The third checkbox, Allow The User To Customize Views, determines whether users can add windows based on items available in the console.

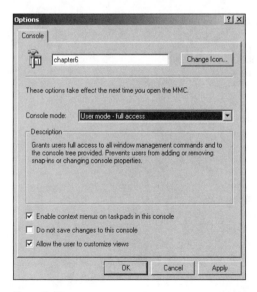

Figure 6.15
User mode configuration.

Group Policies

Group policies are an administrator's primary tool for defining and controlling how programs, network resources, and the operating system behave for users and computers in a Windows 2000 operating system environment. The group policies can be used to decide whether a user accesses a console in Author mode and what snap-in or snap-ins a user has permissions to access.

You configure the group policies by adding either the local or remote group policy snap-in, or both, to the MMC as part of the customization. After you add this snap-in, you traverse down to the area of the group policies called Microsoft Management Console, as shown in Figure 6.16. You must be using Windows 2000 to configure group policies for MMC. Group policies are specific to Windows 2000 and cannot be applied on an MMC running on any other operating system.

As with all group policies, you decide which options you want to enable, disable, or set as not configured. You can use these policies to control exactly what tasks MMC users will be able to perform when they open a customized MMC. The group policies allow you to create a more generic MMC and then restrict what the users can do with the MMC without your having to create multiple MMCs to accommodate each user.

NTFS Permissions

As with all Microsoft Windows NT and Windows 2000 operating systems, users or groups have to obtain the correct permissions to be able to access resources or perform tasks.

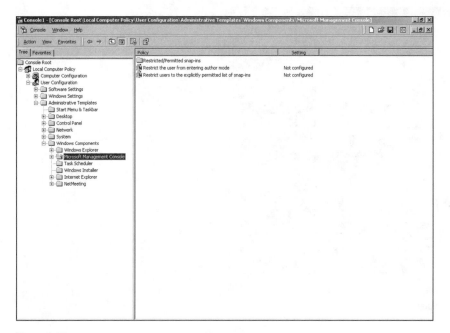

Figure 6.16
Locating the MMC group policies.

Providing the customized MMC is just one step in delegating administrative tasks. The appropriate permissions must also be assigned to the group or user who is attempting to perform the assigned tasks.

After you provide someone with a customized MMC, you need to ensure that he or she has the correct permissions or rights to perform that task. For instance, a nonadministrative user who is given a customized MMC containing the published snap-in for Active Directory Users and Computers must be in a group that allows him or her to access the resources associated with managing users, computers, and groups.

6

Opening Your MMC

Now that you understand how to create the consoles, customize them, save them, and secure them, it's time to look at the different ways to use the consoles in a Windows 2000 environment. You can start the consoles from Start|Run, the command prompt, a short-cut, by using the **Runas** command, or by double-clicking on an MSC file.

You can invoke all MSC files in their default mode by locating them on your system and double-clicking on them. Or, if you wish to open them in Author mode, you can right-click on the MSC file and click on Author. After opening the MMC, you can perform the tasks within the MMC that you have been given permissions and rights to perform.

Remember, when you are customizing your MMC and adding snap-ins for the utilities that can be used for both local and remote administration, you are presented with an additional dialog box in which you can choose whether a snap-in is for local or remote administration. If you are going to use it to remotely administer a machine, you type the name of the remote machine you will be administering to configure the instance of that utility for that machine.

Using the MMC Command-Line Utility

You open a customized MMC by opening the Start menu and choosing the Run option. Another way to open a customized MMC is to enter "MMC" at the DOS command prompt. You can open the DOS command prompt by choosing the Run option and then typing "CMD" or by going to the Start menu and choosing Programs|Accessories|Command Prompt. After you open the dialog box for the Run command (or have a command prompt), you enter the MMC command, along with any of the optional information or switches used to access an MMC.

*Note: You also can use the command prompt to create shortcuts for opening MMC and saved consoles. You can use the **mmc** command from Start|Run, in any command prompt window, in shortcuts you create, or in any batch file or application that calls the command.*

Switches customize how a command-line program is executed. Most command-line utilities have switches associated with them to allow you to modify how the commands operate. The syntax for opening a console from the command prompt is "mmc *path\ filename*.msc". Optionally, you can use the **/a** switch to open the specified console in Author mode. For instance, to open the Computer Management snap-in in Author mode, use the following command:

```
mmc c:\winnt\system32\compmgmt.msc /a
```

When you specify the **/a** switch with the **mmc** command, it will open the console in Author mode, regardless of its default mode. This switch will not permanently change the default mode for the console. It opens it in Author mode only for that particular session. This capability can be useful if you want to go in and make a change to a console file that was previously saved.

Warning! After a user opens an MMC or a console file in Author mode, that user can access any existing console by choosing Open from the Console menu.

Using the **Runas** Command-Line Utility

Runas is a Windows 2000 command that allows you to execute programs or commands under an account name other than the one you are logged in to. **Runas** allows an administrator to be logged on to a system in a nonprivileged account yet perform tasks requiring administrative permissions.

You can use the **Runas** command to open an MMC interface containing snap-ins requiring administrative permissions. For instance, you could use the **Runas** command from the command line to execute the Computer Management MSC file using the administrators' account. The syntax for this command would be as follows:

```
Runas /user:companydomain\administrator "mmc c:\winnt\system32\compmgmt.msc"
```

An alternative to using the **Runas** command from the command line is to locate and right-click on an MSC file. Then, click on Run to open a dialog box in which you can run the MSC file as the user you are currently logged in as, or as another user. If you choose to open the MSC file as a different user, you supply the username, password, and domain name of the user's logon credentials to open the MSC file with his or her permissions.

Creating Shortcuts to Open an MMC

You can create shortcuts to provide quick access to your MMC consoles without having to try to locate them on your Start menu or on your system. As an administrator, you spend lots of time in the MMC environment, so creating shortcuts to your MMC is an efficient way to access the MMCs you access frequently.

Desktop Shortcuts

You create desktop shortcuts on your Windows desktop. These shortcuts provide fast access to frequently used MSC files.

To create a desktop shortcut to an MSC file, follow these steps:

1. Right-click on an open area on your Windows desktop, point to New, and then click on Shortcut.

2. The Create Shortcut Wizard will prompt you for the location of the MSC file you want to access. You can either type the directory path of the MSC file or browse for it on your system.

3. Provide a name for the shortcut that will be placed on your desktop after you click on Finish.

Folder Shortcuts

Another way to create a shortcut to an MMC is to use Windows Explorer. You can do so by opening the Start menu and then choosing Programs|Accessories|Windows Explorer. Locate and click on the folder where you want to create the shortcut. After you select the folder, choose File|New|Shortcut and follow the same instructions in the Create Shortcut Wizard that were discussed in the preceding section.

Runas Command-Line Shortcuts

You can also create shortcuts for an MMC opened from a command prompt by using the **Runas** command. To do so, you open the Create Shortcut Wizard and, when prompted for the location, enter the **Runas** syntax. For instance, to create a desktop shortcut for the Computer Management utility on the local machine that will be accessed using the local administrator's account, type the following command:

```
Runas /user:machinename\administrator "mmc c:\winnt\system32\compmgmt.msc"
```

If you wish to create a **Runas** shortcut for a domain administrator account to access the Active Directory Users and Computers snap-in, the syntax would be as follows:

```
Runas /user:domain name\administrator "mmc c:\winnt\system32\dsa.msc"
```

To create a **Runas** shortcut to an Active Directory Users and Computers snap-in that resides on a computer in another forest, type the following command:

```
Runas /netonly /user:domain name\username "mmc.exe dsa.msc"
```

Using Preconfigured MMCs

Most of the primary administrative tools used in the Windows 2000 environment are implemented as MSC files. Table 6.1 lists some of the default MSC files created during the installation of Windows 2000 Professional.

It is important to understand what some of these tools provide for you in the Windows 2000 operating system. The next section discusses the functionality available in the Computer Management console.

Table 6.1 Windows 2000 preconfigured MSC files.

File Name	Location	Description
Compmgmt.msc	C:\WINNT\system32	Computer Management
Devmgmt.msc	C:\WINNT\system32	Device Manager
Fsmgmt.msc	C:\WINNT\system32	Shared Folders
Ddfrg.msc	C:\WINNT\system32	Disk Defragmenter
Diskmgmt.msc	C:\WINNT\system32	Disk Management
Eventvwr.msc	C:\WINNT\system32	Event Viewer
Faxserv.msc	C:\WINNT\system32	Fax Service Management
Gpedit.msc	C:\WINNT\system32	Group Policy Editor
Lusrmgr.msc	C:\WINNT\system32	Local Users and Groups
Perfmon.msc	C:\WINNT\system32	Performance
Secpol.msc	C:\WINNT\system32	Local Security Settings
Services.msc	C:\WINNT\system32	Local Services

Computer Management

The Computer Management utility manages either local or remote computer configurations from within one consolidated desktop tool. Computer Management combines several Windows 2000 administration utilities into a single console tree, providing easy access to the computer's tools and efficient management of the administrative properties. You use Computer Management to perform the following tasks:

- Start and stop system services such as the **Runas** service, Windows Installer, and Messenger

- Create and manage network shares

- Monitor system events such as application errors and logon times

- Set properties for storage devices

- Manage server applications and services such as the Windows Internet Name Service (WINS) or the Domain Name System (DNS) service

- View a list of users currently connected to a local or remote computer

- Add new device drivers and view device configurations

The console tree of Computer Management contains three nodes. The nodes and their default order of loading are System Tools, Storage, and Services and Applications. Figure 6.17 displays the Computer Management MMC with all three nodes collapsed. You can click on any of the plus signs and expand those utilities to show subcomponents, or click on a minus sign to collapse the utilities, reducing the number of subcomponents being displayed.

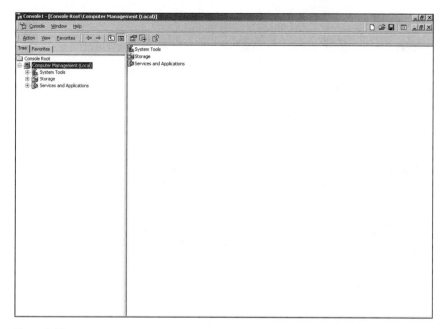

Figure 6.17
The Computer Management interface.

To perform administrative tasks, you select the appropriate tool in the console tree and use menus and toolbars to perform an action on that tool in the details pane. The details pane will display the tool's data and attributes, as well as any available subtools. The details pane will display different types of results, depending on what you choose in the console tree. For example, if you choose Event Viewer, it will display the Application, Security, and System logs in the details pane. If you then expand Event Viewer in the console tree and click on one of the available logs, the details pane will display the contents of that log.

Note: You must be a member of the Administrators group to perform all tasks available in Computer Management. If you are not a member of the Administrators group, you won't have rights to access the administrative properties, and you won't have the required permissions to perform administrative duties.

System Tools

System Tools is the first of the three nodes in the Computer Management console tree. By default, the following six system tools are provided in the System Tools node:

• Event Viewer

• System Information

• Performance Logs and Alerts

• Shared Folders

- Device Manager

- Local Users and Groups

You can use these tools to administer your local computer environment. However, if the snap-in is for a remote computer, you can use the six system tools to manage the remote computer.

Event Viewer monitors various software and hardware activities. It performs this task by examining the different event logs. These logs record system, security, and application events that you may have defined and when they occured. The system log holds events logged by Windows 2000 system components—for instance, the failure of a system service to start or a driver to load during startup.

The security log records security events, which are events that you want logged in a secure environment. These events could be successful or failed attempts to access resources, including attempts to create, open, or delete files. A successful or failed user logon attempt is another example of a security event you might log in the security log.

The application log records events logged by programs or applications installed on your operating system. Events of this nature are written to this log by an installed application. The developer of the application decides which events to record to the log. Examples of applications that would write to the application log include Microsoft SQL Server and Exchange Server.

Five types of events can be written to the Event Viewer logs:

- *Error*—Describes significant problems, such as a loss of functionality or data

- *Warning*—Indicates that an event is not significant now, but it may be an indication of a problem

- *Information*—Describes successful operation of a driver or service

- *Success Audit*—Indicates successful access to an audited security access event

- *Failure Audit*—Indicates failed access to an audited security access event

The *System Information* utility quickly gathers and displays system configuration information. This information can be useful for your help-desk support people when they are trying to troubleshoot an individual's computer problems. System Information contains detailed information regarding your hardware, software, and system components. By default, the information is organized into a system summary and three top-level categories that directly correspond to Resources, Components, and Software Environment nodes located on the console tree. Additional categories may appear as they are installed on your system:

- The System Summary node of the System Information utility displays basic information about your computer configuration, along with the current version of the Windows 2000 operating system. This information, shown in Figure 6.18, includes the name and

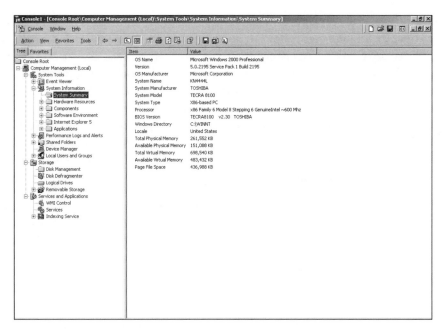

Figure 6.18
System Summary information.

type of system, the location of your Windows system directory, physical and virtual memory statistics, and your computer's processor information.

- The Hardware Resources node of the System Information utility provides hardware-specific settings, including DMA, IRQs, I/O addresses, and memory addresses. The Conflicts/Sharing node assists in identifying devices that are in conflict or are sharing resources. This information can be very helpful in troubleshooting device problems.

- The Components node of the System Information utility provides information regarding the status of device drivers, multimedia software, and networking components in your Windows 2000 configuration. It can also provide driver history information, displaying the changes made to the various components of your system.

- The Software Environment node provides information regarding the software loaded into your computer's memory. This information can be helpful in determining the version of the software running, as well as checking for processes currently running.

As you add software to your system, you can add more nodes to the System Information utility, providing information specific to that application. These additional nodes can be used to assist in troubleshooting those applications.

Tip: You can use the View menu to switch between Basic and Advanced information. The Advanced view shows the same information as the Basic view as well as additional information that may be helpful when advanced users are troubleshooting your system.

Performance Logs and Alerts is the system tool used to configure the log files that record performance data. It also sets system alerts to notify you when a specified counter's value has exceeded or fallen below a defined threshold. This tool can also gather data about the activity of the system and about its hardware usage. This logging can occur automatically based on predefined schedules, or it can occur manually when you decide you want to log. Say you have noticed performance degradation over the past week during the early morning hours. You decide you want to turn on logging for a couple of hours during this time frame to gather data. You then can view this data by using System Monitor or by exporting it to either a spreadsheet or database where you can generate reports to assist you in determining what is causing the poor performance.

Shared Folders lists resource usage and a summary of connections to local and remote computers. This system tool replaces the different resource-related components located in the Control Panel of Windows NT 4. The information provided by this system tool is arranged in the following three columns:

- *Shares*—Provides information about shared resources, including pathname, number of sessions, type of system connected to the resource, and comments

- *Sessions*—Provides information about the users connected, including user and computer name of the connection, number of open files, and length of connection

- *Open Files*—Provides information about all open files on the computer, including the name of the open resource, the name of the user accessing the resource, and what permission was used to access the resource

Device Manager is the system tool used to verify the status of any device installed on the computer. You also use Device Manager to install current drivers of devices installed on your computer. This utility provides a graphical view of the hardware installed on your computer. You can also use Device Manager to make hardware configuration changes. The following are a few tasks you can perform using this utility:

- Check status of hardware to determine whether it is performing properly

- Change hardware configuration settings

- Identify and update device drivers

- Enable, disable, and uninstall device drivers

- Print a summary of devices installed on your computer

Warning! *Making an incorrect change to your hardware settings can disable your hardware and may render your computer inoperable. Hardware settings should be modified only by users with expert knowledge of hardware and hardware configurations.*

Local Users and Groups is a system tool used to manage local users and groups. This tool is available only on computers running Windows 2000 Professional and Windows 2000 servers participating in a domain but not acting as a domain controller. This utility is not available on Windows 2000 domain controllers. Domain controllers use Active Directory Users and Computers to manage domain users and groups.

Local users or groups are accounts that can be granted rights and permissions from your computer. This is in contrast to domain users and groups, which are managed by your network administrator. These local groups can contain local users, domain users, and domain groups. Rights allow a user to perform certain actions on a computer, such as setting the system time or shutting down the computer. Permissions define rules associated with objects (files, folders, printers) and control what objects each user or group has access to and what they can do with those objects.

Figure 6.19 shows the Computer Management console tree with all six options in the System Tools expanded to their first level. To see all subcomponents available in the System Tools node, you would click on all visible plus signs to display all the system tools available.

Storage

The second node in the Computer Management console is Storage. By default, this node displays all storage devices currently installed on the computer. You can manage and view the properties of all detected storage devices through this node. Tasks you can perform from this node include managing your drive labels, controlling disk space usage, administering remote storage devices, and managing disk fragmentation.

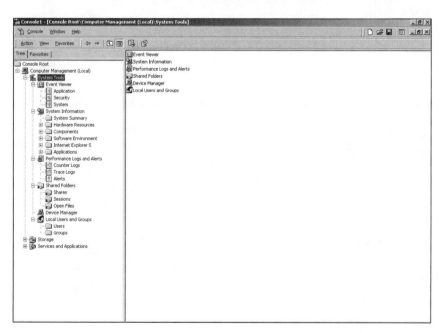

Figure 6.19
Computer Management System Tools.

The *Disk Management* snap-in, which is located in the Storage node, provides a useful graphical tool for managing your disks and volumes. You can open this utility outside the Computer Management MMC by locating the diskmgmt.msc file and either double-clicking on it, or right-clicking on it and choosing Open or Author (to open it in Author mode). Figure 6.20 displays the Disk Management utility opened outside the Computer Management console. Notice that it does not have the MMC console tree on the left side.

Disk Management is the primary administrative tool located under the Storage node. This utility manages storage on the local computer it was installed on or for a remote computer that was configured during the installation of the snap-in. Disk Management replaces the Disk Administrator used in the Windows NT operating systems and provides many new features, including the following:

- Support for partitions, volumes, and new dynamic disks.

- Online disk management. You can perform most tasks without having to restart the computer. Most changes take effect almost immediately.

- Easy-to-use interface, simplifying your disk management tasks.

Note: *You must be a member of the Administrators group to run Disk Management. Also, you must be a member of the Administrators or Server Operators group on a computer you are remotely administering.*

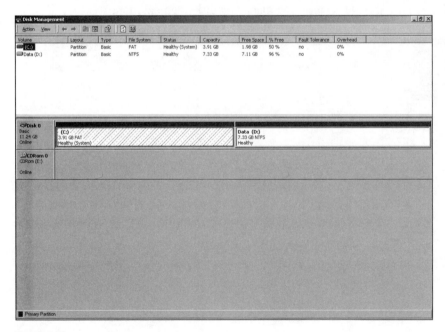

Figure 6.20
Accessing the Disk Management snap-in outside Computer Management.

Windows 2000 Disk Terminology

Let's take a quick refresher course on the terms used in Windows 2000 regarding disks. You are familiar with *basic disks* from previous Windows operating systems; *dynamic disks* are new in Windows 2000. Only the Windows 2000 operating system recognizes dynamic disks. Basic disks allow a maximum of four partitions, whereas dynamic disks allow an unlimited number of volumes. *Volumes* are similar to partitions in that they are sections of a hard drive formatted with one of the file systems (FAT16, FAT32, NTFS). You use volumes to divide a large drive into smaller, more manageable sections acting as independent disks.

6

Warning! *Dynamic disks and volumes are not supported on portable computers.*

Regardless of how you open Disk Management, it allows you to manage various aspects of your hard drives in a Windows 2000 Professional operating system environment. Managing your hard drives includes creating and formatting your volumes, maintaining adequate free disk space, maintaining drive letters, and implementing disk quotas. All these tasks are achieved through the Disk Management interface.

If you can add a new drive while the system is running, you can go to the Action menu and click on Rescan Disk to see whether Windows 2000 Professional detects the new disk. If it doesn't, you may have to restart the machine before it is recognized by Windows 2000. A new disk is always installed as a basic disk, requiring you to upgrade the new disk to dynamic if you want a dynamic disk. To perform this upgrade to a dynamic disk, right-click on the basic disk you want to upgrade and then click on Upgrade To Dynamic Disk and follow the instructions on the screen.

Tip: *You cannot upgrade a portion of a disk; you have to upgrade the entire disk. If you do not see the Upgrade To Dynamic Disk option, you may have clicked on a volume instead of a disk. Furthermore, this Upgrade To Dynamic Disk option will not appear if it is already a dynamic disk or if the disk resides on a portable computer.*

You can move a disk to another computer by following these steps:

1. Verify the status of the disk is Healthy. If not, repair it before you move it.

2. Turn off the computer and remove the disk. Install the disk on the other computer and restart that computer.

3. Open Disk Management on the computer that contains the newly installed disk.

4. Click on Action and then Rescan Disks.

5. If any disk is marked Foreign, right-click on it and click on Import Foreign Disks. Then, follow the instructions on your screen.

You can also use Disk Management to assign, change, or remove a drive letter. For instance, to change the drive letter of your CD-ROM drive, do the following:

1. Right-click on the drive and click on Change Drive Letter And Path.

2. When the Change Drive Letter And Paths For (Existing Drive Letter) dialog box appears, click on the Edit button to see the Edit Drive Letter Or Path dialog box.

3. Using the Assign A Drive Letter option, as shown in Figure 6.21, type a new drive letter or use the drop-down menu to locate the new drive letter.

4. Click on OK and then click on Yes to confirm that you want to change the drive letter. The change will take place immediately, and you will see the new letter assigned to the volume or drive.

In Figure 6.21, notice that you can mount an NTFS folder using these same procedures. This capability is helpful if you want to create a connection to an empty NTFS folder but do not want to consume a drive letter. Only 24 drive letters, from *C* through *Z*, can be used for local volumes and connections to network shares. *A* and *B* are usually reserved for floppy disks. However, in Windows 2000, if you do not have a second floppy disk using drive B, you can use the letter *B* for a mapped network drive.

Warning! You cannot change the system volume or boot volume drive letter.

A new feature in Windows 2000 that is managed from Disk Management is the implementation of disk quotas on NTFS 5 partitions. Disk quotas enable you to track and limit how much space users are allowed to consume on a volume. The quotas are set for everyone storing files on that volume but can be overridden on a per-user basis. You access the Disk Quotas tab by right-clicking on any NTFS 5 volume and selecting the Properties option.

Tip: If you install Windows 2000 Professional on a computer that Windows NT 4 is currently installed on, the NTFS 4 partitions are automatically upgraded to NTFS 5 volumes. All NTFS features that are new in Windows 2000 Professional can be used on these upgraded volumes.

You can configure disk quotas by using the interface shown in Figure 6.22. Many options are available to you when configuring disk quotas for a volume. When you turn them on

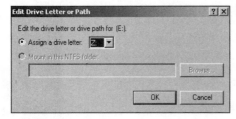

Figure 6.21
Assigning a new drive letter.

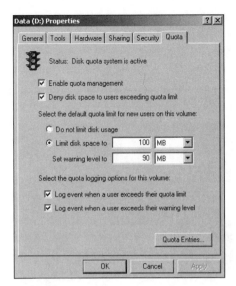

Figure 6.22
Configuring disk quotas.

and define the quota limit, you need to determine what actions occur if someone is nearing his or her quota limit and what happens when someone exceeds the quota limit. Quotas are based on the ownership of files.

You can set up a threshold warning that will notify you if someone is nearing his or her quota limit. The user does not receive the warning; it is written to the system log of the Event Viewer. You can configure it to log an event when the user actually exceeds the quota limit. You can also define whether you want to prevent the user from consuming more space after he or she has exceeded the quota or allow the user to continue creating files on the volume.

Disk Defragmenter, another utility available in the Storage node, allows you to check for file and folder fragmentation on local volumes and optionally perform defragmentation. Fragmentation of files and folders occurs when the files and folders are split up into numerous pieces and placed in different areas of the volume. Fragmentation can decrease performance on your system while it is trying to locate the scattered pieces of files and folders throughout the volume. It can also decrease performance when writing files to the volume because the system will have to write them to many different areas and keep track of each of those areas.

You can use Disk Defragmenter to relocate files, programs, and unused space on your volume and therefore increase both read and write performance. The Disk Defragmenter can be used on FAT16, FAT32, and NTFS partitions. It provides a graphical interface that allows you to check for fragmentation before running the defragmenter. This utility, shown in Figure 6.23, will present the results of the analysis and provide feedback on whether it would be beneficial to perform the defragmentation.

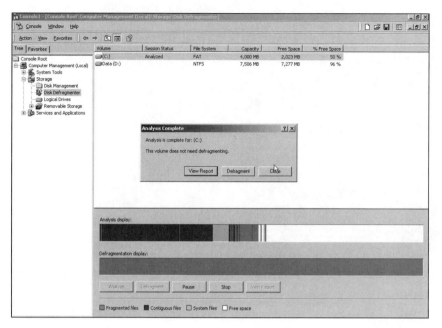

Figure 6.23
Disk Defragmenter.

If Disk Defragmenter suggests that you defragment your volume, you can choose to defragment when it completes the analysis, or you can manually run Disk Defragmenter later and choose the Defragment option instead of the Analysis option. No scheduler is available with the Disk Defragmenter, so you cannot schedule it for a later time. You will have to run it manually.

Warning! *Many factors are involved when estimating the time required to defragment a volume. These factors include the percentage of fragmentation, the size of the volume, the number of files on the volume, and available system resources. Running the Disk Defragmenter on a heavily fragmented volume will cause performance degradation. Consider running Disk Defragmenter during off-peak hours.*

The *Logical Drives* option of the Storage node is a Windows Management Instrumentation (WMI) used to maintain both local and mapped drives on a remote or local computer. WMI is the Microsoft implementation of Web-Based Enterprise Management (WBEM). WBEM is attempting to establish standards for accessing and sharing information over an enterprise network. The Logical Drives option allows you to perform the following three primary tasks, given the correct permissions and using the correct file systems:

- *View drive properties*—View properties, including driver letters, the file system, security settings, and free space available on the drive

- *Set drive labels*—Set up a unique label with up to 11 characters to help identify drives

- *Change security settings*—Modify access permissions, audit entries, and ownership of files on both local and mapped drives

The *Removable Storage* option included in the Storage node tracks your removable media (optical discs and tapes) and manages hardware libraries (jukeboxes and changers) that contain the removable media. Removable Storage allows you to perform numerous operations, including labeling and cataloging; tracking media; controlling library drives, doors, and slots; and cleaning drives.

Removable Storage works in conjunction with your data-management applications, such as Backup. The data-management applications manage the data that is actually stored on the media. Removable Storage allows multiple programs to share the same storage resources, which can reduce costs.

Figure 6.24 shows the Computer Management console tree with all four options in the Storage node and, where applicable, expanded to their first level. To see every subcomponent available in the Storage node, click on all visible plus signs to display all the storage tools available.

Services and Applications

The third node in the Computer Management console is Services and Applications. This node provides the interface used to view and manage properties of any server service or application that is installed. Examples of applications and services include the Indexing

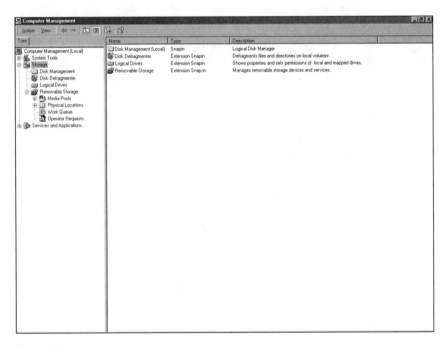

Figure 6.24
Computer Management storage components.

Service, WINS, DHCP, and DNS. The configuration of your computer will greatly affect what services and applications will be listed.

WMI Control configures WMI settings on both remote and local computers. It enables you to perform five primary tasks. These tasks, listed here, generate a consistent management environment throughout your enterprise:

- *Authorize users or groups and set permission levels*—Allows you to authorize access and perform WMI tasks and services. Then, you can set permission levels of tasks.

- *Configure error logging*—Allows you to turn error logging on or off and, if it's on, control the level of error logging. The default is errors only, but you can set it for all actions. This is used for troubleshooting WMI problems.

- *Back up the repository*—Allows you to schedule backups to occur automatically, or you can back up the repository manually. The repository is a database of objects that can be accessed through WMI.

- *Change the default namespace for scripting*—Allows you to modify the default namespace used in WMI scripts. The namespace is represented by the available resources in the MMC console tree.

- *Connect as a different user*—Allows you to log on under a different username so that you can change WMI control settings.

The Services option manages services on local and remote computers, including computers running Windows NT 4. Using Services, you can configure startup and recovery options, and you can start, pause, stop, or resume services. You also can set up recovery options in the event a service stops unexpectedly; for example, you can restart the service or restart the computer (on Windows 2000 computers only). You can also create custom names and descriptions for easier identification. Figure 6.25 shows the Fax Service with the default properties.

You configure services by clicking on a service in the details pane of the MMC and selecting Properties. Figure 6.26 shows a Properties dialog box for the Fax Service; you can see a modified Description, Display Name, and Startup Type on the General tab. On the Log On tab, you can identify the account used to start the service, as well as when to start the service based on the hardware profile used to boot. The Recovery tab defines the number of attempts to start the service and what to do if it does not start. The Dependencies tab lists the services that depend on this service in order for them to start, as well as other services that need to be running in order for this service to start.

After applying changes we made in the Properties dialog box shown in Figure 6.26, the Fax Service is now listed as Chapter 6 Fax Service, is disabled, and has a customized description, all shown in Figure 6.27.

Name	Description	Status	Startup Type
Alerter	Notifies selected users and computers of administrative alerts.		Manual
Application Management	Provides software installation services such as Assign, Publish, and R...		Manual
ClipBook	Supports ClipBook Viewer, which allows pages to be seen by remote ...		Manual
COM+ Event System	Provides automatic distribution of events to subscribing COM compon...	Started	Manual
Computer Browser	Maintains an up-to-date list of computers on your network and suppli...	Started	Automatic
DHCP Client	Manages network configuration by registering and updating IP addre...	Started	Automatic
Distributed Link Tracking Client	Sends notifications of files moving between NTFS volumes in a netwo...	Started	Automatic
Distributed Transaction Coordinator	Coordinates transactions that are distributed across two or more dat...		Manual
DNS Client	Resolves and caches Domain Name System (DNS) names.	Started	Automatic
Event Log	Logs event messages issued by programs and Windows. Event Log r...	Started	Automatic
Fax Service	Helps you send and receive faxes		Manual
Indexing Service			Manual
Infrared Monitor	Supports infrared devices installed on the computer and detects othe...		Disabled
Internet Connection Sharing	Provides network address translation, addressing, and name resoluti...		Manual
IPSEC Policy Agent	Manages IP security policy and starts the ISAKMP/Oakley (IKE) and t...	Started	Automatic
Logical Disk Manager	Logical Disk Manager Watchdog Service	Started	Automatic
Logical Disk Manager Administrative Service	Administrative service for disk management requests	Started	Automatic
Messenger	Sends and receives messages transmitted by administrators or by th...	Started	Automatic
NAV Alert	Norton AntiVirus alert service.	Started	Manual
NAV Auto-Protect	Norton AntiVirus Auto-Protect service.	Started	Automatic
Net Logon	Supports pass-through authentication of account logon events for co...	Started	Automatic
NetMeeting Remote Desktop Sharing	Allows authorized people to remotely access your Windows desktop u...		Manual
Network Connections	Manages objects in the Network and Dial-Up Connections folder, in w...	Started	Manual
Network DDE	Provides network transport and security for dynamic data exchange ...		Manual
Network DDE DSDM	Manages shared dynamic data exchange and is used by Network DDE		Manual
Norton Program Scheduler	Norton Program Scheduler service.	Started	Automatic
NT LM Security Support Provider	Provides security to remote procedure call (RPC) programs that use t...		Manual
Performance Logs and Alerts	Configures performance logs and alerts.		Manual
Plug and Play	Manages device installation and configuration and notifies programs ...	Started	Automatic
Print Spooler	Loads files to memory for later printing.	Started	Automatic
Protected Storage	Provides protected storage for sensitive data, such as private keys, ...	Started	Automatic
QoS RSVP	Provides network signaling and local traffic control setup functionality...		Manual
Remote Access Auto Connection Manager	Creates a connection to a remote network whenever a program refer...		Manual
Remote Access Connection Manager	Creates a network connection.	Started	Manual
Remote Procedure Call (RPC)	Provides the endpoint mapper and other miscellaneous RPC services.	Started	Automatic

Figure 6.25
Default Fax Service properties.

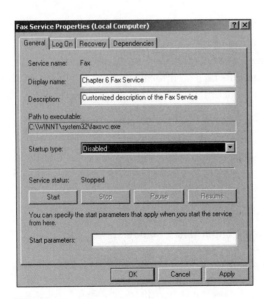

Figure 6.26
Fax Service Properties dialog box.

Name	Description	Status	Startup Type
Alerter	Notifies selected users and computers of administrative alerts.		Manual
Application Management	Provides software installation services such as Assign, Publish, and R...		Manual
Chapter 6 Fax Service	Customized description of the Fax Service		Disabled
ClipBook	Supports ClipBook Viewer, which allows pages to be seen by remote ...		Manual
COM+ Event System	Provides automatic distribution of events to subscribing COM compon...	Started	Manual
Computer Browser	Maintains an up-to-date list of computers on your network and suppli...	Started	Automatic
DHCP Client	Manages network configuration by registering and updating IP addre...	Started	Automatic
Distributed Link Tracking Client	Sends notifications of files moving between NTFS volumes in a netwo...	Started	Automatic
Distributed Transaction Coordinator	Coordinates transactions that are distributed across two or more dat...		Manual
DNS Client	Resolves and caches Domain Name System (DNS) names.	Started	Automatic
Event Log	Logs event messages issued by programs and Windows. Event Log r...	Started	Automatic
Indexing Service			Manual
Infrared Monitor	Supports infrared devices installed on the computer and detects othe...		Disabled
Internet Connection Sharing	Provides network address translation, addressing, and name resoluti...		Manual
IPSEC Policy Agent	Manages IP security policy and starts the ISAKMP/Oakley (IKE) and t...	Started	Automatic
Logical Disk Manager	Logical Disk Manager Watchdog Service	Started	Automatic
Logical Disk Manager Administrative Service	Administrative service for disk management requests	Started	Automatic
Messenger	Sends and receives messages transmitted by administrators or by th...	Started	Automatic
NAV Alert	Norton AntiVirus alert service.	Started	Manual
NAV Auto-Protect	Norton AntiVirus Auto-Protect service.	Started	Automatic
Net Logon	Supports pass-through authentication of account logon events for co...	Started	Automatic
NetMeeting Remote Desktop Sharing	Allows authorized people to remotely access your Windows desktop u...		Manual
Network Connections	Manages objects in the Network and Dial-Up Connections folder, in w...	Started	Manual
Network DDE	Provides network transport and security for dynamic data exchange ...		Manual
Network DDE DSDM	Manages shared dynamic data exchange and is used by Network DDE		Manual
Norton Program Scheduler	Norton Program Scheduler service.	Started	Automatic
NT LM Security Support Provider	Provides security to remote procedure call (RPC) programs that use t...		Manual
Performance Logs and Alerts	Configures performance logs and alerts.		Manual
Plug and Play	Manages device installation and configuration and notifies programs ...	Started	Automatic
Print Spooler	Loads files to memory for later printing.	Started	Automatic
Protected Storage	Provides protected storage for sensitive data, such as private keys, ...	Started	Automatic
QoS RSVP	Provides network signaling and local traffic control setup functionality...		Manual
Remote Access Auto Connection Manager	Creates a connection to a remote network whenever a program refer...		Manual
Remote Access Connection Manager	Creates a network connection.	Started	Manual
Remote Procedure Call (RPC)	Provides the endpoint mapper and other miscellaneous RPC services.	Started	Automatic

Figure 6.27
Customized Fax Service properties.

The *Indexing Service* extracts information from documents (any retrievable, unique file name that was created using an application program) and organizes it so that it can be retrieved when you perform a Windows 2000 Search function, search through a Web browser, or use an Indexing Service query form. The information can include text from inside the document or properties of the document, such as the author's name.

The Indexing Service uses a process called *indexing*, using a document filter to extract the text and properties of a document and pass this information to the indexer. The service automatically stores the necessary index information in the System or Web catalogs. These catalogs list all stored properties and index information for a specific group of directories that reside on the same file system.

Figure 6.28 shows the Computer Management console tree with all three options in the Services and Applications node and, where applicable, expanded to their first level. To see all subcomponents available in the Services and Applications node, click on all visible plus signs to display all support tools available.

The Computer Management utility is easily the most useful and powerful console in the Windows 2000 Professional environment. As you can see, it manages user access, resource protection, system optimization, and troubleshooting. You can access the Computer

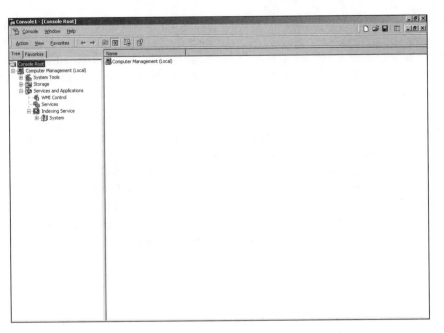

Figure 6.28
Computer Management Services and Applications.

Management console in numerous ways, providing tons of flexibility in a Windows 2000 Professional configuration.

Troubleshooting MMC

After you create a customized MMC, sometimes you might encounter problems, or you might want to customize it further to provide more options, but you have problems adding or removing tools. Three primary troubleshooting areas you should be familiar with will assist you in resolving any problems or complications.

If you are seeking help with a snap-in added to your MMC and cannot locate any Help on the snap-in, the problem is that the snap-in you added may not have been developed to customize the MMC Help. The Help made available through the MMC is supposed to be provided by the developers of the application. If they chose not to make it available, you will have to do some research to determine where they stored the Help and how to access it. Something you can try is to open the console in Author mode and click on the snap-in that you are trying to receive help on. Click on the Help command to see if a separate command for the snap-in is displayed on the Help menu above the Help Topics command. If not, check the options available to you on the toolbars and the details pane for a Help button, usually denoted by a page with a yellow question mark on it. If neither of these are available, the developers did not include MMC help for the snap-in.

If you are unable to add a snap-in on your computer that you have seen on other computers, there is a good chance you have not installed the software or service required to add the snap-in to the list of available components. Another possibility is that the administrators created a group policy on the computer or user account that prevents you from adding the snap-in.

Other problems you may experience while using the console include unexpected behavior, unfamiliar error messages, or the console timing out. Changes may have been made to the network, configuration changes may have been made to the console, or maybe the console has been corrupted. If any of these problems occurs, check to see whether the problems occur with all snap-ins or individual ones. Select each snap-in one at a time, right-click on an item, and then click on Properties. Hold down the Ctrl key and point to the appropriate tabs in the dialog box. If everything looks fine, add another instance of the snap-in to your console. If the new one works, remove the old one and continue using the new one.

Summary

Understanding the power of the MMC is imperative for both a network administrator and a local administrator. This interface can be customized to provide an efficient and effective management environment for everyone involved in maintaining your enterprise.

Your ability to create a customized MMC, save it, and then share will help reduce your administrative overhead. This new feature in Windows 2000 is something that was desperately needed to ease your administration as more applications become available and your networks become larger.

The Control Panel is still as popular and powerful as ever. It is still the primary utility used to configure your desktop, add hardware and software to your computer, customize your environment, and secure your Windows 2000 Professional operating system. The next chapter will give you plenty of details about benefits, strengths, and precautions when making modifications to your system through the Control Panel.

Chapter 7

The Windows 2000 Professional Control Panel

Not Just Another Pretty Face

Imagine trying to cook your favorite chili recipe without the benefit of your stove's temperature dial. You know, the one that reads Low, Medium, and High. It would be no easy task.

Instead of stirring your five-alarm dish over Medium heat, you would have to manually calculate how long 120 to 240 watts take to heat a metal coil 200 to 250 degrees. Then, you would have to perform multiple calculations to determine how long that 250-degree metal coil needs to adequately heat a two-pound concoction of meat, peppers, onions, cheeses, and other ingredients (some of them frozen, others not) while accounting for the heat absorption of the container in which the chili is being cooked. You would have to factor in heat loss due to cooler ambient air temperature, while also considering the impact of atmospheric pressure. Blow just one calculation and it's out to dinner you go!

That is what operating Windows 2000 Professional would be like without the benefit of Control Panel. You would have to make most of your hardware configurations and software setting adjustments manually through the Registry. The GUI would be gone, and that would be bad. You would be down to working with hexadecimal values and binary strings in many cases.

Consider this example. Which would your prefer when setting the mouse tracking speed? Here's your first option. Navigate to the HKEY_USERS\S-1-5-21-527237240-1202660629-1060284298-1000\Control Panel\Mouse key. (Keep in mind that the key beginning with the S-1 coding will be different on each machine.) You would have to memorize the identification strings for each user and commit thousands and thousands of other values to memory. Then, you would have to find and highlight the MouseSpeed entry, recall that it is a REG SZ value (again, you would have to commit that information to memory), create such an entry, and then assign it a value of 2 (which again, you would have to commit to memory while understanding fully and completely the velocity and spatial differences between a value of 1, a value of 2, and a value of 3).

Or, here's your second option. Double-click on the Mouse applet in Control Panel and move the sliding bar a single notch on the Motion tab.

Essentially, Control Panel is nothing more than a GUI for adjusting many of the most common values located in the Windows Registry. However, the most common values located in the Windows Registry play a tremendous role in the way both corporate and home users compute.

The Windows 2000 Professional Control Panel makes adjusting hardware and software settings much easier, as well as safer, than editing the Registry. Think of Control Panel as putting a pretty face on the Registry, while also helping to protect you from making changes that will cripple a system. That's not to say you can't; it's just that using Control Panel makes it much harder to inadvertently muck things up.

Just as when you're working with the Registry, you need to take care when making changes using Control Panel. Although it is unlikely you will render a system unbootable, the potential for data loss exists when you tinker with Control Panel settings. How's that possible? Many applications and programs are housed in Control Panel. One is even dedicated solely to adding and removing software programs. Other Control Panel applets manipulate display settings, change the desktop configuration, and more.

Before we examine each of these common applets, let's take a look at your options for accessing the Control Panel. Several methods are available. Which method you select will depend upon your needs and the task you wish to perform.

Control Panel Access

You can access Control Panel applets in many ways. The method you use depends on several factors, including how often you access the applets, your preference for viewing the applets, and more.

You've always been able to access Control Panel easily in Windows. The default access method requires only that you click on Start|Settings|Control Panel. Windows 2000, however, offers a new alternative in addition to that tried-and-true method.

Start Menu Configuration

New in Windows 2000 Professional is the capability to expand Control Panel applets from the Start menu. As a result, you can select individual Control Panel applets directly from the Start menu.

To enable Control Panel applet selection from the Start menu, follow these steps:

1. Right-click on an empty area of the Windows 2000 taskbar.

2. Select Properties from the pop-up menu to open the Taskbar And Start Menu Properties dialog box.

3. Click on the Advanced tab.

4. In the Start Menu Settings section of the dialog box, check the box next to Expand Control Panel.

5. Click on OK.

Shell Executable

Control Panel itself is a special shell program triggered whenever the CONTROL.EXE file, located in *systemroot*\system32, is executed. You can create a shortcut to Control Panel and place it on your desktop, in another area on your Start menu, or in a folder of your choice by following these steps:

1. Right-click on an empty area of the desktop.

2. Select New and click on Shortcut to open the Create Shortcut Wizard.

3. Type the location of the shell program (*systemroot*\system32\CONTROL.EXE). Alternatively, you can navigate to the file by using the Browse button.

4. Type "Control Panel" to serve as the name for your shortcut.

5. Click on Finish, and the shortcut will be created on your desktop.

Tip: Another method exists for creating a shortcut to the Control Panel. You can drag the Control Panel applet straight onto the desktop, where a new shortcut will appear.

What exactly can you expect when you double-click on the shortcut? The answer depends on the view you've chosen.

Control Panel Views

By default, each of the Windows 2000 Professional Control Panel applets is represented by an icon. You can also adjust the view so that the applets are displayed much the way folders are in Windows Explorer.

You access Control Panel, by default, by clicking on Start|Settings|Control Panel. Windows 2000 Professional's default view presents each Control Panel applet as a single icon (as shown in Figure 7.1).

Depending on your screen size preference, you may want to display Control Panel applets using smaller icons. To do so, just open the View menu and select Small Icons.

If you're like many hardened IT professionals, you're a fan of folder views. Select List from the View menu, and Windows 2000 will alphabetize the applets for you. Small icons will still be visible to help you quickly identify the applet you're seeking.

If you want to display Control Panel applets in a folder fashion, open the View menu and select Details. The Details view lists the applets by name, as if you were using Windows

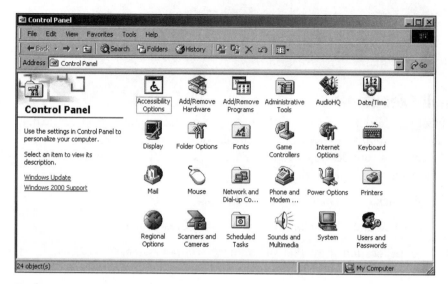

Figure 7.1
The Windows 2000 Professional Control Panel, showing the default view.

Explorer. Selecting the Details view also adds the Comment column, which provides brief explanations for each Control Panel applet.

If you use particular applets frequently, you'll probably want to create shortcuts.

Creating Control Panel Shortcuts

Two methods are readily available for creating shortcuts to commonly used applets. You can drag an applet from Control Panel (or the Start menu if you've chosen Expand Control Panel) to the place where you want to locate it. Alternatively, you can create a shortcut by right-clicking on the applet and then selecting Create Shortcut from the pop-up menu.

You can also create a shortcut from within Windows Explorer. Just look for telltale .cpl file extensions, which are the file types given to Control Panel applets. You can find them in the *systemroot*\system32 folder. When you find the target applet's CPL file, just follow the same steps as you would to create a shortcut from within Control Panel. The difference is that the shortcut will be created within the *systemroot*\system32 folder. After you create it, you should move it to the location where it serves you best.

Each applet, of course, offers a completely different set of configuration settings. The following sections describe the smorgasbord of applets you'll find housed in the Windows 2000 Professional Control Panel.

The Control Panel Collection

Depending on the Windows components, software programs, and hardware devices a system has installed, you might find two dozen or more applets living in Control Panel, as shown earlier in Figure 7.1.

7

The most common Control Panel applets are as follows:

- Accessibility Options

- Add/Remove Hardware

- Add/Remove Programs

- Administrative Tools

- Date/Time

- Display

- Folder Options

- Fonts

- Game Controllers

- Internet Options

- Keyboard

- Mail

- Mouse

- Network and Dial-up Connections

- Phone and Modem Options

- Power Options

- Printers

- Regional Options

- Scanners and Cameras

- Scheduled Tasks

- Sounds and Multimedia

- System

- Users and Passwords

- Wireless Link (found on many laptops)

All the applets are aptly named. The configuration options in each applet control those settings the applet's name implies.

Now, we can begin our examination of each applet located in the Windows 2000 Professional Control Panel by looking at Accessibility Options.

The Accessibility Options Applet

You use the Accessibility Options applet to customize system and display settings. Many of the features configured in this applet make computers easier to use for individuals with special needs. Even if a user doesn't require customized accessibility features, several of them can prove useful. For example, ToggleKeys can trigger a sound every time the Caps Lock, Num Lock, or Scroll Lock key is used.

When you open the Accessibility Options applet, as shown in Figure 7.2, you'll find the following five tabs:

- Keyboard

- Sound

- Display

- Mouse

- General

Accessibility Options—Keyboard Tab

You can set the following three options from the Keyboard tab:

- StickyKeys

- FilterKeys

- ToggleKeys

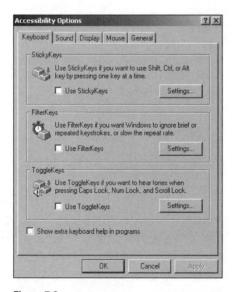

Figure 7.2
Accessibility Options are used to enable and configure special system settings that are required by some users and convenient for others.

From this tab, you also can specify that extra help be displayed within programs. Just check the Show Extra Keyboard Help In Programs checkbox.

StickyKeys

StickyKeys eliminates the need to simultaneously press the Shift, Ctrl, or Alt key with another key to perform a key combination. For example, to type a capital letter *A*, you press and hold the Shift key while pressing the A key. StickyKeys, if enabled, lets you press and release the Shift key and then press the A key to create the capital *A*.

You enable StickyKeys by checking the Use StickyKeys checkbox. Clicking on the Settings button opens the Settings For StickyKeys dialog box, from which you can enable a keyboard shortcut. The default shortcut for triggering StickyKeys is pressing any key five times quickly.

From the Settings For StickyKeys dialog box, you can also specify two options. The first is Press Modifier Key Twice To Lock. Checking this box permits the StickyKeys feature to stay locked if you press a modifier key (Shift, Ctrl, or Alt) twice. You can also specify that StickyKeys be disabled if two keys are pressed at the same time.

You can enable two Notification settings, too. The first specifies that a sound be triggered when a modifier key is pressed. The second specifies that the StickyKeys status be displayed on screen.

FilterKeys

You can specify that Windows disregard brief or repeated keystrokes by enabling the FilterKeys feature. You can also use FilterKeys to slow the rate at which keystrokes are repeated.

You enable FilterKeys by checking the Use FilterKeys checkbox. As with StickyKeys, you can also specify several additional FilterKeys settings by clicking on the Settings button. Check the Use Shortcut box from the Settings For FilterKeys dialog box to enable the FilterKeys shortcut. The default shortcut is pressing the right Shift key for eight seconds.

Filter options that you can set include ignoring repeated keystrokes or ignoring quick keystrokes and slowing the repeat rate. Each of the two filter options possesses additional settings that you can configure by clicking on the respective option's Settings button. These additional settings include configuring the values for how long Windows should wait before repeating and ignoring keystrokes.

You also can set two Notification features. The first specifies that FilterKeys generate a beep when pressed or accepted. The second Notification checkbox specifies that the FilterKeys status be displayed on screen.

ToggleKeys

You can instruct Windows 2000 to play tones when the Caps Lock, Num Lock, or Scroll Lock key is used. Just check the Use ToggleKeys checkbox to enable the feature.

You can specify that the ToggleKeys shortcut be used by clicking on the Settings button and checking the Use Shortcut box. The default ToggleKeys shortcut is pressing the Num Lock key for five seconds.

Accessibility Options—Sound Tab

You can set two sound accessibility options from the Sound tab: SoundSentry and ShowSounds. Check the Use SoundSentry checkbox to instruct Windows to display visual warnings when a system sound is triggered. You can also click on the Settings button to specify the type of visual warning generated for various programs. Check the ShowSounds checkbox when you want Windows 2000 to make applications display captions containing the speech and sounds the program generates.

Accessibility Options—Display Tab

From the Display tab, you can specify that Windows use high contrast colors and fonts. The high contrast configuration can make it easier for some people to read information presented on screen. Check the Use High Contrast box to use the special display feature.

Additional parameters that you can configure by clicking on the Settings button include enabling the shortcut and selecting the appearance scheme the high contrast feature should use. The high contrast feature shortcut is pressing the left Alt, left Shift, and Print Screen keys simultaneously. You can customize the appearance scheme the high contrast feature uses, or you can specify from two pre-existing schemes: white on black and black on white.

Accessibility Options—Mouse Tab

Although you might expect to find mouse accessibility options and settings on the Mouse tab, you will not. Instead, you can enable the use of MouseKeys. If you check the Use MouseKeys checkbox, the arrows on the keyboard's numeric keypad can be used to emulate mouse control of the pointer. The keyboard's numeric pad becomes the input device for the pointer.

Several advanced MouseKeys settings also can be configured. Click on the Settings button to access them. The first enables the use of the MouseKeys shortcut, which you trigger by pressing the left Alt, left Shift, and Num Lock keys all at once.

You can also adjust pointer speed and acceleration. Further, you can specify that the Ctrl key, when held down, speeds up the pointer and that the Shift key performs the opposite action. From the Settings For MouseKeys dialog box, you can also specify that MouseKeys be turned on or off when the Num Lock is on. The last advanced setting permits you to display the MouseKeys' status on screen.

Accessibility Options—General Tab

Other accessibility features are configured from the General tab. You can specify that accessibility features be turned off after the system has been idle for a specified period of time. You also can check boxes to ensure that warning messages are received and sounds are generated when accessibility features are enabled. Both sounds and visual warnings are set by default.

You enable SerialKey devices on the General tab. SerialKey components permit alternative keyboard and mouse functionality. For example, a system operator may require the use of a pointing peripheral other than a hand-operated mouse. Or, a user might use an augmented speech device. Windows 2000 Professional supports such needs. Check the Support SerialKey Devices checkbox to enable this feature and support for alternative keyboard and mouse devices. If you want to use the SerialKey feature, you may need to specify which serial port Windows should use and the appropriate baud rate. You can configure the port and baud rate by clicking on the Settings button.

The last two settings on the General tab specify administrative options. You can specify that accessibility features be applied to the logon desktop. By default, the accessibility features are not available to users until they log on to the system. If you want to make the accessibility features available to users before they log on, you should check the Apply All Settings To Logon Desktop box.

You can also specify that the settings you have configured be applied to new users automatically. Just check the Apply All Settings To Defaults For New Users box.

The Add/Remove Hardware Applet

Few system issues are more vexing than hardware devices that won't play nice with Windows. Or, is the problem that Windows 2000 won't play well with the hardware? Either way, one of the surest methods of raising IT professionals' blood pressure is to present them with a client machine possessing hardware devices that refuse to operate well or that won't install properly. The Add/Remove Hardware applet does more for such headaches than an industrial dose of ibuprofen.

Clicking on Add/Remove Hardware starts the Add/Remove Hardware Wizard. The wizard's purpose is to assist with the installation, removal, and troubleshooting of hardware components. It works like this: Double-click on the Add/Remove Hardware icon in Control Panel to open the wizard. Click on Next on the opening screen. The wizard then asks whether you want to add or troubleshoot a device or uninstall or unplug a device, as you can see in Figure 7.3. You should choose the Add/Troubleshoot option if you are installing a new component or experiencing difficulty with an existing device. Select Uninstall/Unplug if you want to remove or unplug a component.

If you select Add/Troubleshoot and click on Next, Windows will seek new plug-and-play–enabled hardware devices. If it finds such devices, the next screen will ask you to specify the location of any drivers Windows might need to make the component work properly. If Windows 2000 cannot find a new plug-and-play device, it will present a list of all known devices installed on the system. If you want to troubleshoot a component, select it from the list and click on Next. You'll go to a screen indicating the status of the device. If the device is working properly, a confirmation will appear.

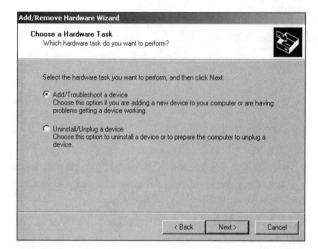

Figure 7.3
The Add/Remove Hardware Wizard assists with adding, troubleshooting, uninstalling, or unplugging hardware peripherals.

If, instead of selecting Add/Troubleshoot, you clicked on Uninstall/Unplug, the next screen will ask whether you want to uninstall a device or unplug or eject a component. If you elect to uninstall a device, you'll be asked to select the device you want to uninstall from a list. If you don't see the device you want to uninstall in the list that is presented, be sure you have checked Show Hidden Devices at the bottom of the device list. Click on Next, and the device will be permanently uninstalled.

If you elect instead to unplug a device, you'll see a list presenting devices that can be unplugged. Select the component you want to unplug and click on Next. Confirm that you want to unplug the listed device in the next screen and then click on Finish to temporarily disable the component. Depending on the device being unplugged, you might also be presented the option of displaying an Unplug/Eject icon on the system's taskbar. You should enable this option if you will be plugging and unplugging the device frequently, such as you might do with a network interface card (NIC) in a laptop computer.

The Add/Remove Programs Applet

Possibly the most dangerous applet in Control Panel's arsenal, Add/Remove Programs is also one of the most powerful applets at an IT professional's disposal. It houses three potent options:

- Change Or Remove Programs
- Add New Programs
- Add/Remove Windows Components

Change or Remove Programs

The Change Or Remove Programs feature performs the actions its name implies: It changes or removes software programs that have been installed on the system. Click on the Change Or Remove Programs icon, and Windows will generate a list of the system's installed software applications, as shown in Figure 7.4.

You can sort the list by name, size, frequency of use, or last date used. Windows tracks how often each program has been accessed, how much disk space each program occupies, and when a program was installed. Depending on the software program installed, you can make changes to applications that are installed or remove them from the hard disk. If Windows is unable to remove an application, it will generate a report listing the components that couldn't be uninstalled.

Add New Programs

The Add New Programs feature serves two purposes. You can use it to add programs from a CD-ROM or floppy disk, or you can use it to install new programs, drivers, updates, and more, directly from Microsoft.

If you want to add a program using Add New Programs, click on the CD Or Floppy button. When you do so, the Install Program From Floppy Disk Or CD-ROM Wizard appears. It instructs you to insert the program's first floppy disk or CD-ROM in the machine. Select Next, and the wizard searches for the installation program. If the wizard finds the installation file, the program path will be displayed, and you will be asked to confirm that the path is correct. If the wizard finds the wrong installation program, you can click on the Browse button and navigate to the file manually. If no installation program is found, the

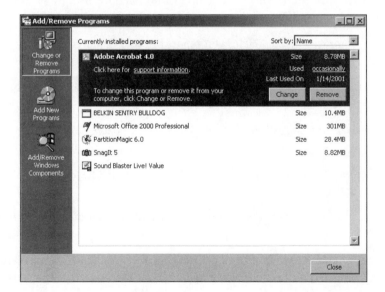

Figure 7.4
You use Change Or Remove Programs to make changes to, or uninstall, installed software applications.

wizard displays a message informing you so. Again, you are given the option to browse and find the file manually. If the correct installation file is found, just click on Finish. Installation will then proceed.

You can also add Windows components, device drivers, and system updates directly from Microsoft. Just click on the Windows Update button. You'll be taken to the Microsoft Windows Update Web page. From there, you can download device drivers, service packs, and other important updates, including security fixes.

At the time this book went to press, Product Updates appeared as one of the top options on the Microsoft Windows Update Web page. Clicking on the Product Updates option prompts Windows Update to conduct a customized search for product updates relevant to the system performing the update.

On a fresh Windows 2000 Professional installation, the following updates are available:

- *Critical Updates Package*—Contains security and other file updates

- *MSN Messenger Service 3.5*—Contains an instant message application

- *Windows Critical Update Notification 3.0*—Contains a notification program designed to alert you whenever critical updates are released

- *Internet Explorer 5.5 Service Pack 1 and Internet Tools*—Provides the newest version of Internet Explorer and accompanying Internet productivity tools

- *Windows Media Player 7*—Enables viewing of streaming media and other Internet multimedia files, including MP3s

- *DirectX 8.0*—Provides the multimedia system foundation Windows uses to maximize the use of hardware peripherals

- *Internet Explorer Error Reporting*—Helps you report Internet Explorer errors to Microsoft for debugging

- *Windows 2000 Service Pack 1*—Provides the latest setup, application compatibility, reliability, and security updates for Windows 2000

- *Internet Explorer 5.01 Service Pack 1*—Provides important updates for Internet Explorer 5.01

- *Recommended Update for Office 2000 SR-1*—Updates Microsoft Office 2000 with the latest patches and updates

- *High Encryption Pack for Windows 2000*—Enhances default Windows 2000 encryption settings

Select the boxes for each update you want to load and click on Download. A confirmation screen will appear. Confirm that the appropriate updates have been selected. The estimated length of time your updates will take to download will be provided.

You can view instructions for detailed information if you are not sure how each software update should be installed. The files will be transferred to your system when you click on the Start Download button.

Be aware that you may need to accept certain licensing agreements, depending on the software you choose to download. A final confirmation message should appear, stating that the download was successful. Depending on the updates you select, you may also see confirmation that installation occurred successfully, too.

7

Add/Remove Windows Components

The Add/Remove Windows Components icon also triggers a wizard. You use the Windows Components Wizard to add or remove those Windows 2000 components that shipped with the operating system when it was released.

The following components are listed in the Windows Components Wizard:

- Indexing Services

- Internet Information Services (IIS)

- Management and Monitoring Tools

- Message Queuing Services

- Networking Services

- Other Network File and Print Services

- Script Debugger

Note that most components also possess additional subcomponents. You can view them by selecting the Details button when the respective component is highlighted. Place checks next to all the components you want to install. Alternatively, you can clear checked boxes to remove Windows components. The wizard will also display the amount of disk space each component occupies or will require to be installed.

Confirm that you've selected or deselected components as you intended and then click on Next. The Windows Components Wizard will then configure the components you speci-fied. If you have chosen to add components, be prepared to insert the Microsoft Windows 2000 Professional CD-ROM in the system's CD-ROM drive. Click on OK after you have inserted the CD-ROM. Component configuration will continue. When it is complete, a confirmation screen will appear. Click on Finish to complete the installation process and close the wizard.

The Administrative Tools Applet

Eight important administrative utilities are stored in the Windows 2000 Professional Control Panel's Administrative Tools applet. The icons, or files, you see when viewing the Administrative Tools applet are actually shortcuts to powerful Windows 2000 administrative programs. These shortcuts provide another simple method for accessing the Windows 2000 Professional administrative tools that you can also find by clicking on Start| Programs|Administrative Tools.

The Administrative Tools included in Windows 2000 Professional are as follows:

- Component Services

- Computer Management

- Data Sources (ODBC)

- Event Viewer

- Local Security Policy

- Performance

- Services

- Telnet Server Administration

Warning! *The Windows 2000 Professional Administrative Tools are potent utilities. For this reason, Administrative Tools is hidden by default. Right-click on the taskbar, select Properties, click on the Advanced tab, and ensure the Display Administrative Tools checkbox is checked. Always make sure that you have verified backups of your data before performing administrative changes to a system.*

The Component Services Console

Double-clicking on the Component Services shortcut opens a Microsoft Management Console (MMC) screen configured to display Component Services. Also present in the MMC are the Event Viewer and Services snap-ins. You will examine them later in this chapter. First, we'll look more closely at Component Services.

You can configure Component Object Model (COM) component settings and COM+ applications by using the Component Services snap-in. Only those applications, components, and security settings you can administer will be displayed in the left pane, or console tree, of the snap-in. If you plan to make changes to default Component Services values, you should be familiar with how the Component Services administrative tool administers component values, including the following:

- *Applications*—You can change an installed application's properties by right-clicking on the application and selecting Properties.

- *Components*—You can change a COM+ application's component properties by right-clicking on the application and selecting Properties.

- *Interfaces*—You can change Interface Properties by right-clicking on the respective interface and selecting Properties.

- *Methods*—You can change an interface method by right-clicking on the method and selecting Properties.

- *Roles*—You can change the role assigned to a COM+ application by right-clicking on the role and selecting Properties.

- *Users*—You can add and remove users from roles by highlighting the Users folder, clicking on New, and selecting User. You can also delete users by clicking on Delete.

Under Component Services, you will also find the Distributed Transaction Coordinator. This tool tracks the transactions or processes in which a system participates. The Transaction List collects a system's active transactions, or the processes in which it is currently participating. You can access information on transaction performances, speeds, types, and response times by clicking on Transaction Statistics in the left pane of the MMC.

In most cases, IT professionals will have more than passing familiarity with COM and system transactions before opening the Component Services administrative tool. It's unlikely that most system administrators will use this tool often.

The Computer Management Console

Next, let's examine an administrative tool that's sure to be used regularly. Open the Computer Management administrative tool, and you will find that three MMC snap-ins have been configured in a single console, as shown in Figure 7.5:

- System Tools

- Storage

- Services and Applications

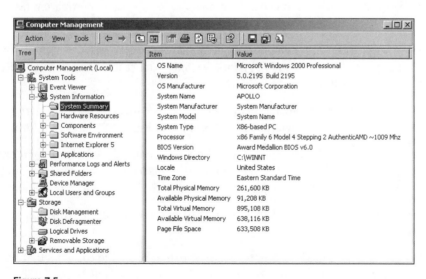

Figure 7.5
Computer Management collects some of the most useful and commonly used administrative utilities. Here, a System Summary is shown.

You can use these administrative tools to configure and administer user and access permissions, installed hardware devices, fixed and removable disk drives, a system's indexing service, Windows Management Instrumentation, and more. You can also view application, security, system, and performance logs.

System Tools

The System Tools tree is particularly valuable. Under System Tools, you will find the following administrative tools:

- Event Viewer

- System Information

- Performance Logs and Alerts

- Shared Folders

- Device Manager

- Local Users and Groups

You'll examine the Event Viewer a little later in this chapter because it also exists as its own utility in the Administrative Tools applet.

System Information is an important administrative tool. It has tremendous diagnostic value in that it collects information about a system, hardware components and devices, installed software applications, and more. This information comes in handy when you're troubleshooting errors.

All told, you can find information on the following using the System Information utility:

- *System Summary*—Provides a general summary of basic system information (as shown in Figure 7.5)

- *Hardware Resources*—Provides information on hardware conflicts, direct memory access (DMA), input and output (I/O) addresses, interrupt request assignments (IRQs), and memory information

- *Components*—Lists multimedia, display, infrared, input, modem, network, port, storage, printing, problem device, and Universal Serial Bus (USB) settings information

- *Software Environment*—Includes configuration data on installed drivers, environment variables, jobs, network connections, running tasks, loaded modules, services, program groups, startup programs, and Object Linking and Embedding (OLE) registration

- *Internet Explorer 5*—Stores information and settings associated with the Internet Explorer browser

The Performance Logs and Alerts tool tracks information related to counters that have been set using the Performance utility. Under Performance Logs and Alerts, you'll find the following three items:

- *Counter Logs*—Store hardware usage data and activity information from other system services, either local or remote

- *Trace Logs*—Record specific activities, such as page faults

- *Alerts*—Track the actions that are to occur when counter thresholds are surpassed

The Shared Folders section of the console tree provides a summary of shared folders, active sessions, and open files. For each share, the following information is recorded:

- The shared folder's name

- The share path

- Client redirection information

- The number of users connected to the share

- Comment information describing each share's type

If a share is active, the session can be tracked from the Sessions folder, as shown in Figure 7.6. For each active session, the following information is recorded:

- The share name

- The name of the user connected to the share

- The name of the user's computer

- The type of network connection the user is using

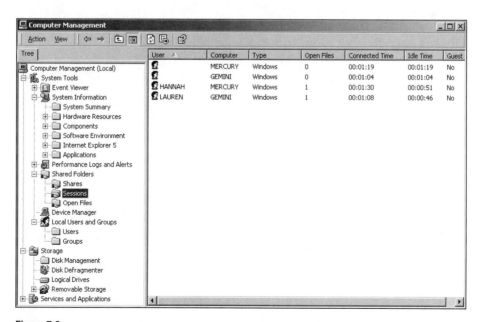

Figure 7.6
Windows 2000's Sessions folder records information about each active share.

- The total number of resources opened by the user

- How long the user has been connected

- The length of time that has elapsed since the user initiated an action

- The guest status of the user

You can configure share permissions, too, from within Computer Management's Shared Folders snap-in. Just right-click on the share you want to administer, select Properties, click on the Share Permissions tab, and configure permissions accordingly. You also can close sessions from the host machine, if you want. Just right-click on the session you want to close, select Properties, and click on Close Session.

The Open Files folder, meanwhile, permits you to view information about open files on a system. You can also find information on active print jobs from the Open Files folder in the console tree. For each open file, the following information is recorded:

- The files that have been accessed

- Which users have accessed the files

- The type of network connection the user used

- How many locks have been placed on the resource

- The permission granted to the users

Proceeding down the console tree, the next utility is the Device Manager. You should be familiar with it from past Windows platforms. The Device Manager collects, in a hierarchical format, the various hardware components that exist on a system. This administrative tool proves invaluable when you're troubleshooting wayward hardware devices. You'll take a closer look at the functionality it provides later, in the section on the System applet.

Local Users and Groups is the next utility you will cross when you continue the descent down the System Tools console tree. Here, you can review, configure, and administer user and group membership and permissions.

Note: For more information on administering users and groups, see Chapter 12.

Storage

The Storage folder houses the following four important snap-ins; they're of critical importance when you're working with hard disks and removable data storage devices:

- Disk Management

- Disk Defragmenter

- Logical Drives

- Removable Storage

You use the Disk Management utility to manage a system's disk drives. The snap-in provides a graphical representation of the system's hard disks and drives, and important drive information is displayed, as shown in Figure 7.7. For example, you can learn all the following about a disk by using the Disk Management snap-in:

- The number of installed disks

- The disk space each drive possesses

- Volume names

- The disk's status (whether it is online and what its partition types are)

- The file systems in use

- The free space available on each partition

You can perform the following critical administration tasks from within the Disk Management snap-in:

- Format partitions

- Make partitions active

- Change drive letters and paths

- Delete partitions

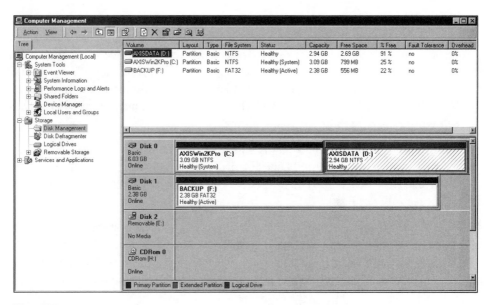

Figure 7.7
You use the Disk Management utility to configure and manage a system's drives.

Right-click on a disk and click on Properties from the pop-up menu to see an entire litany of options. From a disk's Properties dialog box, you can perform the following actions:

- Change disk labels

- Execute Disk Cleanup (a utility that removes unneeded files)

- Run error checking, backup, and defragmentation programs

- Update disk drivers

- Troubleshoot disk hardware

- Share folders

- Set security permissions

- Enable and configure disk quotas

Note: For more information on performing disk management functions, see Chapter 15.

Defragmentation can be a significant problem for hard disks, particularly as hard drives become increasingly larger. File data isn't always stored in adjacent clusters on a hard disk. The more files and programs are used, the more likely the hard drive head will have to hunt for various pieces of a single file spread across a disk. The hunt takes time. Files can become so fragmented that system performance is noticeably affected. By keeping files located in contiguous clusters, a system can recall files faster and the machine proves more efficient.

The Disk Defragmenter program provides a graphical representation of a disk's files. You can run the Analyze program for a report listing the state of stored files. Analyzing a disk provides information on volume size, cluster size, used space, free space, total fragmentation, file fragmentation, a list of the most fragmented files, and more. The report will also provide a recommendation as to whether a disk requires defragmentation. If files are too fragmented, you can click on the Defragment button. A display bar will track the defragment operation's progress in realtime.

Computer Management also contains a snap-in that you can use to administer both mapped and local drives. Using Logical Drives, you can view logical drive properties such as drive letters, drive types, and file system types. You also can configure drive labels and adjust security settings.

The Removable Storage snap-in manages a system's removable storage media, such as optical disks, tape drives, jukeboxes, and hardware libraries. Using the snap-in, you can name and organize a system's different removable storage devices. The snap-in works with native Windows 2000 Professional programs, such as the Backup program.

Services and Applications

The next major component you will find in Computer Management's console tree is the Services and Application snap-in. The following three important consoles live within this snap-in:

- WMI Control

- Services

- Indexing Service

The Windows Management Instrumentation (WMI) Control configures WMI settings on local and remote systems. You can use WMI to perform the following functions:

- Set permissions

- Enable and configure error logging

- Back up and restore the Repository (database of objects), which WMI monitors

- Change the default namespace that WMI scripts target

- Log on as a different user to configure WMI settings

The Services snap-in provides a list of a system's services, as shown in Figure 7.8. The following information is provided for each service:

- The service's name

- A description of the service

- The service's status

- Whether the service is set to start up automatically or manually

- The manner in which the service logs on

Right-click on any listed service and click on Properties to configure a service's settings and configuration. You can change a service's name, startup and logon behavior, status, recovery options, and dependencies from its Properties dialog box.

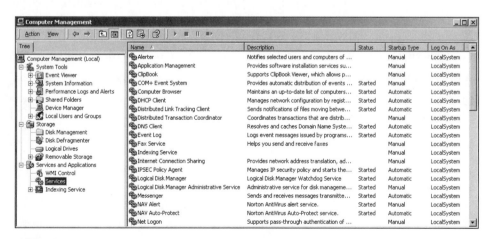

Figure 7.8
You can use the Services snap-in to manage Windows 2000 Professional services.

The Indexing Service, meanwhile, monitors the information stored in a system's files and enables searching for information in those files using the Windows native Search function. The Indexing Service, which runs automatically in the background, automatically stores information in special catalogs. A great deal of the information regarding the Indexing Service can be accessed from within the Computer Management console, including the following:

- The number of documents and directories included in the index's catalog

- The size of the catalog

- The catalog's status

- The catalog's physical location

The Data Sources (ODBC) Console

The next major snap-in in the Administrative Tools applet is the Data Sources (ODBC) snap-in. The odds are you won't use it often, but it's good to know what you will find in it. You can configure multiple Open Database Connectivity (ODBC) settings from the Data Sources shortcut. For example, from within the ODBC Data Source Administrator, you can configure user data sources, which store information instructing Windows 2000 Professional how to connect to specified programs and services and which software drivers should be used by those programs, services, and a system's users.

Using ODBC tracing, you can create log files that track all the calls made by programs and the operating system to ODBC drivers. You can use the ODBC Data Source Administrator dialog box to configure tracing, set the log file path, and specify the trace DLL files to use. Later, if problems arise and you suspect ODBC communications, you can review the trace log files to help determine the culprit.

From within the ODBC Data Source Administrator, shown in Figure 7.9, you can configure connection pooling. Connection pooling can save a system time by letting applications reuse open connection handles. Using existing connection handles eliminates the need for the system to establish new connection handles for ODBC communications.

You can obtain more information about ODBC components by clicking on the ODBC Data Source Administrator's About tab. There, you can find descriptions of ODBC core components, along with information regarding each component's version and the actual file name and physical location.

The Event Viewer Console

The Event Viewer is one of the most important diagnostic tools included in Windows 2000 Professional. Another MMC snap-in, the Event Viewer monitors faults, failures, and problems that arise with software applications, hardware components, and security

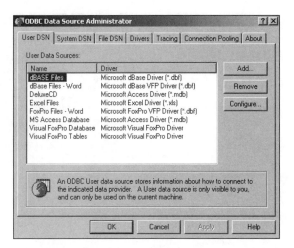

Figure 7.9
You use the ODBC Data Source Administrator to manage Windows 2000 Professional's ODBC connections.

events. The Event Viewer is composed of the following three log files, all of which provide valuable information:

- *Application Log*—Contains event information generated by software programs and applications, such as the completion of a successful third-party software installation

- *Security Log*—Records security events, such as resource access attempts and logons, if logging of such security events has been enabled

- *System Log*—Logs events generated by Windows 2000 system components, such as device drivers that fail to load properly upon system startup and services that fail to initialize

For application, security, and system events, the following information is tracked:

- The type of event

- The date of the event

- The time of the event

- The event's source

- The event's category

- An event number

- The user who triggered the event

You can learn more information about application events recorded in the Application Log by double-clicking on a specific event. Detailed descriptions of each application event appear in the resulting Event Properties box.

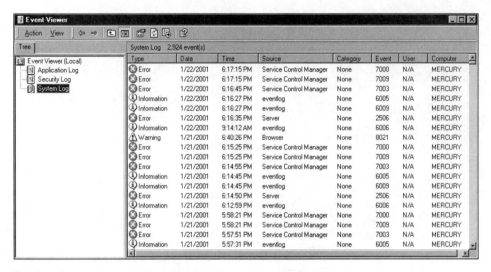

Figure 7.10
The System Log records information regarding various system events.

The Security Log and System Log, shown in Figure 7.10, record the same information as the Application Log. The Security Log records information generated from failed logon and resource access attempts. The System Log, meanwhile, records the starting and stopping of services, the failure of drivers to initialize, system updates, and more.

Table 7.1 describes the five types of events displayed in the log files.

Tip: Security is not enabled by default. Administrators must enable auditing of security settings using local and/or group policies.

The Local Security Policy Console

Security settings—determining which users receive access to which resources, which services they can and cannot administer, and which events are audited—are all configured from the Local Security Policy snap-in. But, they aren't the only items administered from within this snap-in. The Local Security Policy snap-in also houses administrative tools that configure public keys, encryption, and security settings for IP connections. All told, these four important components are housed within the snap-in:

• *Account Policies*—Set password and account lockout policies.

• *Local Policies*—Configure audit policies, user rights assignments, and other security options. For example, you can enable auditing for the use of backup and restore privileges, rename the administrator account, or prevent users from installing print drivers, among other actions.

Table 7.1   Events recorded in the Event Viewer's log files.

Type	Icon	Description
Error	Red circle with a white X	Represents a significant failure, such as a failed service
Warning	Yellow triangle with black exclamation point	Represents a problem that could result in future errors
Information	Lowercase blue i in a white balloon	Describes successful initialization of drivers or the starting of a service
Success Audit	Yellow key	Represents an audited security event that is completed successfully
Failure Audit	A lock	Represents an audited security event that fails to complete properly

7

- *Public Key Policies*—Configure encryption and public keys.

- *IP Security Policies on Local Machine*—Configure Internet Protocol Security (IPSec) settings.

IPSec, which is designed to secure data communications between computers as the data packets cross a network, uses encryption to protect the data. IP security rules must be set, instructing Windows 2000 how to process IPSec communications received from other systems. By default, settings are preconfigured for the client machine (respond only), a secure server (require security), and a server (request security). You adjust them by using the IP Security Policies on Local Machine console.

Note: *For more information on configuring Windows 2000 Professional security, see Chapter 16.*

The Performance Console

Often, you will need to track different counters in Windows 2000 Professional, either for security or performance reasons. To do so, you use the Performance console. The Windows 2000 Performance console is similar to the Performance Monitor, or Perfmon, utility many IT professionals are familiar with from the Windows NT 4 platform. One major difference is that the Windows 2000 version also incorporates a System Monitor, the SysMon utility, which administrators also used in Windows NT 4 systems.

Using System Monitor, you can track the performance for these objects:

- Browsers

- Memory

- Network interfaces

- Paging files

- Physical disks

- Protocols

After you have selected the objects you want to monitor, you have to specify which counters should be tracked. For example, if you choose to monitor a system's physical disks, you could monitor all the following:

- % Disk Read Time

- % Idle Time

- Avg. Disk Bytes Read

- Avg. Disk Bytes Transfer

- Avg. Disk Write Queue Length

- Current Disk Queue Length

- Disk Bytes/Second

Information gained from monitoring system performance often proves invaluable in identifying the need for an additional processor, a new disk drive, or a faulty network interface. But, before the information can be used, it usually needs to be logged. That's where performance logs come into play. They, too, are configured from the Performance console.

You use the Performance MMC snap-in, shown in Figure 7.11, to set counters, monitor system events, and log system performance data. From the Performance Logs and Alerts

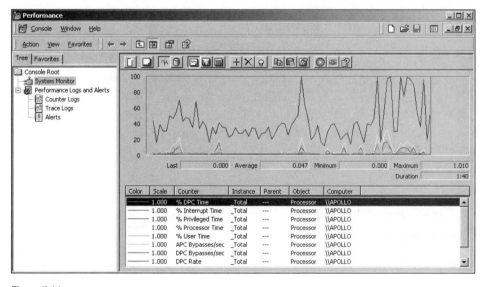

Figure 7.11
You use the Performance console to set and monitor system counters, log performance data, and trigger alerts. Here, it tracks a system's processor activity.

console, you can specify objects and counters to be tracked and the interval at which performance measurements should be taken. You can specify alerts to kick in when specific predefined thresholds are exceeded. You can also administer counter logs.

Additionally, you can administer trace logs. Unlike counter logs, which take snapshots of specific performance measurements at specific intervals that you define, trace logs log events only when they occur.

The Performance snap-in also collects counter logs, trace logs, and alerts within the console tree on the left side of the screen. After object monitors and alerts have been configured, you can view the results from within the same console. Just click on the specific log in the left pane, and detailed information on the log or alert will be displayed in the right pane.

Note: For more information on using the Performance console, see Chapter 15.

The Services Console

The next shortcut you'll find in the Administrative Tools applet is the Services console. This console, as explained earlier in this chapter, manages Windows 2000 Professional services.

Several services can be started, stopped, or configured from the Services console. They include the following:

• *Alerter*—Alerts selected users of administrative alarms

• *Computer Browser*—Updates and maintains a list of which systems are operating on a network

• *NT LM Security Support Provider*—Provides security to remote procedure call (RPC) programs using transports other than named pipes

• *System Event Notification*—Monitors a system for such events as network activity and logons and notifies COM+ Event System subscribers of such events

• *Windows Installer*—Installs, repairs, and removes software programs

The Telnet Server Administration Program

You can perform several actions using the Telnet Server Administration program located within the Administrative Tools Control Panel applet. Double-clicking on the shortcut executes the Telnet Server Administration console, which you use to operate Microsoft's Windows 2000 Telnet Server Administration program.

The following options are immediately available:

• Quit the application

• List the current users

• Terminate a user session

- Display/change Registry settings

- Start the Telnet service

- Stop the Telnet service

You can also configure a variety of settings for the Telnet service. To do so, right-click on the Telnet Server Administration shortcut in the Administrative Tools applet and select Properties from the pop-up menu. Among the configuration changes you can make for the Telnet service, which opens Telnet sessions, are the following:

- The location of the Telnet Server Administration utility

- Whether the Telnet Server Administration utility should be run as a different user

- The font and colors the command console should use

- The Telnet Server Administration utility's security settings

The Date/Time Applet

You configure a system's date and time settings from within the Date/Time applet located in the Windows 2000 Professional Control Panel. You can also open this applet by double-clicking on the time display that appears in the system tray.

Double-clicking on the Date/Time applet opens the Date/Time Properties dialog box. From the Date & Time tab, you can select the date and year from drop-down boxes. You set the time either by moving the hands of the analog clock or adjusting the spin boxes for the digital readout displayed beneath the analog clock.

The current time zone is displayed at the bottom of the Date & Time tab. If the incorrect time zone is configured, you can easily change it. The Time Zone tab enables you to configure a system's clock to automatically adjust for Daylight Savings Time. On this tab, you also can configure the time zone for the location in which the system resides. To set the time zone, simply select your location (or GMT zone) from the drop-down box. Click on OK after you complete all necessary adjustments.

The Display Applet

Double-clicking on the Display applet opens the Display Properties dialog box. You can also access this dialog box by right-clicking on an empty area of the Windows 2000 Professional desktop and selecting Properties from the pop-up menu.

Display—Background Tab

The Background tab is displayed by default. The scrollable menu lists the various backgrounds that can be displayed as the Windows 2000 background. Files with .bmp extensions located in the *systemroot*\Winnt folder and files with .jpg extensions located in the *systemroot*\Winnt\Web\Wallpaper folder appear as the options that you can set for the Windows desktop.

You can stretch, tile, or center the background image by specifying your preference from the drop-down box on the Background tab. If you choose the None option for a system's background image, you can click on the Pattern button and select from a number of predefined simple character patterns. You can also edit the default patterns by clicking on the Edit Pattern button. If you have another background image you want to use, you can click on the Browse button and navigate to the file you want to set as your background.

Display—Screen Saver Tab

You set screen savers and energy conservation settings on the Screen Saver tab. Advances in monitor displays have eliminated the need for screen savers, which used to prevent images from permanently burning themselves into a monitor screen. However, most users prefer to configure screen savers to kick in after a predetermined period of time. Several screen savers ship with Microsoft Windows 2000 Professional, and even more are available on the Internet and from third-party providers.

You specify the screen saver the system should use by selecting it from the Screen Saver drop-down box. You can also disable a system's screen saver by selecting the None option from the drop-down box.

You can configure screen savers possessing different features by clicking on the Settings button. Before committing a screen saver to use, you can test its configuration by clicking on the Preview button. You can also specify the length of inactivity that should pass before the screen saver executes.

You can enable password protection for screen savers, too. Just check the Password Protected checkbox. When the screen saver executes, if any key is pressed or the system's mouse is moved, a dialog box will appear, requesting the password that is provided for the screen saver. Unless the correct password is entered, the system's screen saver continues to lock the system's display.

Warning! *Password-protecting a screen saver is only a first step in securing data on an unattended machine. The screen saver password protection does not secure a system's data completely. However, password-protecting a system can prove convenient when you're stepping away for lunch. Just be sure that very sensitive data is not kept on the machine because an individual intent on obtaining system data could still do so easily. For starters, anyone could reboot the system, thereby eliminating any protection offered by the screen saver password.*

Clicking on the Power button opens the Power Options Properties dialog box. You'll see different tabs depending upon your system's hardware configuration and whether you're using a laptop or desktop machine. From there, you can configure preset Power Schemes to save energy if a system's hard disk and monitor aren't used for a specified period of time.

Tip: *You also can access the Power Options Properties dialog box by clicking on Control Panel's Power Options applet.*

Alarms Tab

The Alarms tab, found when a battery is present, can be configured to sound alerts if battery power falls below a preset threshold. You can set two alarms. One sounds to alert the user that the battery is running low. You can configure another critical battery alarm when a system is about to lose power as a result of a battery depleting its charge. Further, by clicking on the respective Alarm Action buttons, you can specify the actions the system should take for each alarm when the thresholds are reached.

Power Meter Tab

The Power Meter tab, often found on laptop systems, displays the charge status of installed batteries, as well as information on the current power source. Check the Show Details For Each Battery box if you want to view information on multiple batteries, which many laptops now carry.

Advanced Tab

On the Advanced tab, you can choose to display a Power icon on the taskbar, have the system prompt the user for a password when the system goes off standby, and specify the action to be taken when the system's power button is pressed.

Hibernate Tab

On the Hibernate tab, you can enable hibernate support. When the system is in hibernating mode, which you enable by checking the Enable Hibernate Support checkbox, it stores the contents of its memory on the system hard drive when powered down. Then, when you boot the system, the information is restored from the hard drive, returning the system to the state it held before being powered down.

Additional hibernation information is provided. Information on free disk space and the disk space required to enable hibernation also is displayed.

Display—Appearance Tab

On the Appearance tab, you can configure the color scheme Windows 2000 Professional should use. Several preset schemes are available. You can choose one by clicking on the drop-down box under the Scheme heading.

Individual colors and window and message text fonts can be specified for each Windows desktop component, too. For example, if you want to create a customized scheme using yellow as your desktop color, click the desktop in the preview pane or choose Desktop from the Item drop-down box. Then, select the shade of yellow you want to use from the Color drop-down box. You can find additional colors by clicking on the Other button.

After you have configured a color scheme you like, you can save it by clicking on the Save As button. Conversely, you can delete a scheme by highlighting it in the Scheme drop-down box and clicking on the Delete button.

Warning! After you click on the Delete button, whichever scheme is displayed in the Scheme drop-down box will be deleted immediately. The system does not present a confirmation box; it simply deletes the scheme.

Display—Web Tab

You can set Web content as a Windows background, too. Just check the Show Web Content On My Active Desktop checkbox on the Web tab. In the box that appears below, check the Web page you want to use. New Web pages can be added easily. Click on the New button, and a wizard will guide you through the process of selecting additional pages.

Additional settings can be configured for Web pages used as backgrounds, too. For example, imagine you specified that the My Current Home Page be used. Clicking on the Properties button will provide you with the additional options. You can specify that the Web page set as the Windows background be made available when the system is offline, or not connected to the Internet.

7

You can also specify a schedule the system should follow to update the Web page. The My Current Home Page Properties Download tab specifies how many pages should be downloaded, how much hard disk space can be used, and which actions should be taken when the page changes.

You can also specify which components are downloaded. Using the Advanced button, you can select images, sound and video, and ActiveX controls. From the Advanced Download Options dialog box, you can specify that links be followed only to HTML pages.

Display—Effects Tab

From the Effects tab, you can choose different icons to replace the default desktop selections. Just select Change Icon to replace the highlighted icon in the Desktop Icons box. If you want to switch back to the original icon, click on the Default Icon button.

Additional visual effects can be set, too. Checkboxes are provided for the following:

- Use Transition Effect For Menus And Tooltips
- Smooth Edges Of Screen Fonts
- Use Large Icons
- Show Icons Using All Possible Colors
- Show Windows Contents While Dragging
- Hide Keyboard Navigation Indicators Until I Use The Alt Key

Display—Settings Tab

Be careful when using the Settings tab within the Display applet. Configured incorrectly, options configured on the Settings tab can crash a system.

In addition to displaying the name of the monitor and video card used by the system, the Settings tab provides several other display options, as shown in Figure 7.12. You can select the number of colors you want the system to display from the Colors drop-down box. The higher the number, the better images should appear on screen.

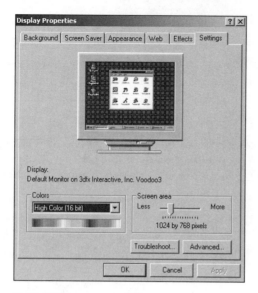

Figure 7.12
You use the Display applet's Settings tab to configure monitor settings.

The screen size is configured from the Settings tab, too. Move the slide in the Screen Area section to the right to make icons, images, and fonts smaller, thereby fitting more information on a screen at once. Move the bar to the left to make icons, images, and fonts larger.

If you are experiencing problems with your system's monitor configuration or video adapter, click on the Troubleshoot button. A Troubleshooting Wizard will help guide you to a solution. The wizard also provides help files.

If you are familiar with the monitor and know the video adapter that is installed, click on the Advanced button to trigger the monitor and video adapter Properties dialog box, which contains five tabs.

General Tab

On the General tab, you set the system's font size. Also, you can instruct the system to make display setting changes without rebooting. Alternatively, you can specify that the system ask you before applying new display settings. We prefer to apply the new display settings without restarting because this approach generally saves time.

Adapter Tab

On the Adapter tab, you can check and configure the driver and resources used by the video adapter. Click on the Properties button to review the driver and resources used by the video adapter and to troubleshoot or update the driver.

Monitor Tab

The Monitor Tab displays the Monitor Type in use. Click on the Properties button to review the driver and resources used by the system's monitor and to troubleshoot or update the driver.

You can also set the refresh frequency the monitor uses. If you have the specifications that came with the system's monitor, choose the refresh frequency that looks best to your eye. If you do not have the documentation that came with the monitor, you can try visiting the manufacturer's Web site and locating specification information there. Such information is often housed in a site's support section.

7

*Tip: Headaches are easy to come by if a system's refresh frequency is set improperly. The refresh rate specifies how frequently Windows 2000 Professional repaints the screen. If you notice flickering, you probably need to adjust the refresh rate higher. A good method of checking for flicker is to navigate to a Web site with a large white background (**www.cnn.com**, for example) and then avert your gaze to look above and beyond your monitor. If you see flickering out of the corner of your eye, you need to increase the refresh rate.*

Setting a refresh rate higher than a monitor was built to handle can ruin a monitor, though. Thus, it's important to check the monitor manufacturer's documentation. If you cannot find the documentation or information on the manufacturer's Web site, check the Hide Modes That This Monitor Cannot Display Safely box.

Troubleshooting Tab

If a system is experiencing problems with its graphics hardware, namely the video adapter, you can decrease the hardware acceleration rate. You do so by moving the sliding bar to the left on the Troubleshooting tab.

Color Management Tab

Default color profiles can be set on the Color Management tab. Color profiles change the default colors displayed on a monitor. You can add or remove color profiles by clicking on the Add Or Remove button. You can also specify that a color profile be set as a default. Just select it in the window and click on the Set As Default button.

The Folder Options Applet

The next applet you will find in the Windows 2000 Professional Control Panel is the Folder Options applet. This applet contains settings that dictate how content is displayed, how folders are presented, which applications are used to open specific file types, and the manner in which offline files are to be used.

Tip: The Folder Options applet is also accessible from Windows Explorer. From within Windows Explorer, select Tools/Folder Options.

Folder Options—General Tab

You can configure these four options from the Folder Options applet's General tab:

- Active Desktop
- Web View

- Browse Folders

- Click Items As Follows

Active Desktop

Two radio buttons are present in the Active Desktop section of the General tab. The first, Enable Web Content On My Desktop, determines whether the Active Desktop is enabled for the Windows 2000 Professional desktop. Select this button if you want to use the Windows 2000 Professional Active Desktop.

You may want to conserve system resources, or you may prefer the traditional Windows desktop environment. In such cases, select the Use Windows Classic Desktop radio button to enable the traditional Windows desktop on your system.

Tip: Active Desktop must be enabled to display Web pages as the Windows desktop background.

Web View

Depending on your preference, Windows folders can be displayed as Web content or in a traditional hierarchical format. If you want Windows folders displayed as Web content, select the Enable Web Content In Folders radio button from the Web View section.

The most notable difference between the two display formats is that displaying folders as Web content adds a Windows 2000 logo to the left column. In addition, information about the files or folders that are selected is provided in the left column, often along with information on related programs or files.

Selecting the Use Windows Classic Folders radio button prompts Windows to display folders in the traditional format. Instead of related information appearing in the left column, only the following data is provided for each file and folder listed:

- Name

- Size

- Type

- Modified Date

The Web content view offers more color but requires a few additional resources to power. Chances are, your users won't miss the additional resources but will prefer the added ease of use the Web content view adds. For this reason, you may wish to stick with the Web-enabled view as the default folder display.

Browse Folders

Settings configured in the Browse Folders section specify how folders are opened. You can configure Windows 2000 Professional to open a folder and its contents, including any subfolders, in a new window when you click on it. Select the Open Each Folder In The

Same Window radio button if you want to "drill down" into a series of folders on your way to locating a single folder or file in the same window.

However, depending on the task being completed, the preference might be that folders open in new windows. Setting such a configuration is easy. Just click on the Open Each Folder In Its Own Window radio button from the Browse Folders section.

Click Items As Follows

Some Windows 2000 Professional users may want to enable other Web behaviors (in addition to folder views) for their Windows 2000 desktops. For example, users may want to make all icons and options selectable using a single click. Select the Single-Click To Open An Item (Point To Select) radio button from the Click Items As Follows area to enable single-click selection. You can also choose, when using the single-click selection of items, to have icon titles appear as underlined. Underlining icons simplifies the user interface because it provides a standard computing environment for executing items, whether the items are icons to open Microsoft Word or Web sites using their browser. Another alternative is to specify that icon titles be underlined only when the pointer hovers over them. Select the Underline Icon Titles Only When I Point At Them radio button to ensure that icon names appear underlined when the pointer hovers over the icons.

The default Windows 2000 Professional setting requires a double click to open an icon (or other item). The first click typically highlights an icon (or selects an item). It's the second click that actually executes the program or shortcut that the icon or item represents.

If you like, you can easily reset system defaults. Just click on the Restore Defaults button.

After making any changes to the General tab, make sure that you click on the Apply (or OK) button. If the changes are not applied and the Cancel button is selected, none of the changes will be applied to the system.

Folder Options—View Tab

Many administrators, and power users for that matter, prefer to view hidden files and have known file extensions displayed. By default, Windows 2000 Professional does not display hidden files or known file extensions.

The Folder Options applet's View tab contains several settings that you can easily configure to adjust default file and folder views. For example, you can configure all the following from the Advanced Settings window of the View tab:

- Display Compressed Files And Folders With Alternate Color

- Display The Full Path In The Address And Title Bars (configured separately)

- Show Or Hide Hidden Files And Folders (configured separately)

- Hide File Extensions For Known File Types

- Hide Protected Operating System Files

- Launch Folder Windows In A Separate Process

- Remember Each Folder's View Settings

- Show My Documents On The Desktop

- Show Pop-Up Description For Folder And Desktop Items

If you want to have all folders emulate the configuration that is set for a currently open folder, click on the Like Current Folder button. All folder options will then mimic the configuration settings of the currently open folder.

All folders can also be reset to their defaults. Click on the Reset All Folders button to return all folders to their original settings. You also can return advanced settings to their defaults by clicking on the Restore Defaults button.

Folder Options—File Types Tab

When you double-click on a file, whether it's on the desktop, in a browser, or within a folder or menu, the file's extension tips off Windows 2000 Professional as to which program it should use to open the file. The file extension assignments are set on the File Types tab of the Folder Options applet.

By default, files are listed by extension in the first column of the Registered File Types window. A file type description follows, as shown in Figure 7.13.

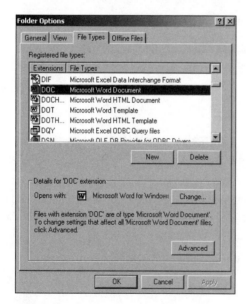

Figure 7.13
Windows 2000 Professional has been instructed to use Microsoft Word to open files possessing a .doc file extension.

File types are easily deleted. Highlight the extension assignment you want to remove by clicking on it in the Registered File Types window and clicking on the Delete button. Windows 2000 Professional will present a confirmation dialog box before deleting the file type.

You add new file types by clicking on the New button. Follow these steps to create a new file type assignment:

7

1. Open the Folder Options applet in Control Panel and click on the File Types tab.

2. Click on the New button.

3. Enter the file extension (.doc, .xls, .jpg, and so on).

4. To assign an associated file type to the file extension, click on Advanced and select the file type from the drop-down menu. For example, you can specify whether a file with the particular extension you are adding is an ActiveX control, font file, Windows NT command script, or other file type. Click on OK.

5. When the registered file type appears, highlight it and then click on the Change button. Specify the program Windows 2000 Professional should use when opening files with the specified extension. If you want to select a program that is not listed, click on the Other button and locate the program you want to use. Click on OK after you select the appropriate program.

You can configure further settings by highlighting the registered file type and clicking on the Advanced button. You also can change the program that is used to open a file. For example, you might want to use a third-party program to play CD audio files.

From the Edit File Type dialog box, which you open by clicking on the Advanced button from the File Types tab, you can change the icon associated with a file type. Just click on the Change Icon button.

You can also add actions by clicking on the New button. Existing actions can be adjusted by clicking on the Edit button. You delete configured actions by highlighting the respective action and clicking on the Remove button.

The three checkboxes in the Edit File Type dialog box permit administrators and users to have Windows 2000 confirm the open command after a download has completed, always display the file extension, and browse in the same window.

If default settings have been changed, you can return them to their original status by clicking on the Set Default button. As usual, be sure to click on the OK button after making changes.

Folder Options—Offline Files Tab

Windows 2000 Professional has made it easier to make files available when you are offline. You can use offline files to download a file from a network drive, disconnect your machine (likely a laptop) from the network, continue working on the file, and then update the network drive copy when the laptop is reconnected to the network.

Several offline file settings are configured from the Offline Files tab in the Folder Options applet. First and foremost, checking the Enable Offline Files box enables the use of offline files. Other options that you can set for offline files are as follows:

- Whether all offline files should be synchronized before logging off

- Whether reminders should be enabled

- How often reminders should be displayed, if enabled

- Whether a shortcut to offline files should be placed on the Windows desktop

- The amount of disk space to be used to store temporary offline files

Three buttons are present for administering offline files. Delete Files deletes temporary offline files stored on a hard disk. The View Files button displays the temporary offline files stored on a hard disk in the Offline Files folder. The Advanced button configures advanced settings, such as whether the user should be notified if a network connection is lost. You will also find an exception list, which is used to dictate the actions Windows 2000 Professional should take when a specified machine becomes unavailable.

Note: *For more information on running Windows 2000 Professional on laptop systems, please see Chapter 8.*

The Fonts Applet

You use the Windows 2000 Professional Control Panel's Fonts applet to manage the fonts installed on a system. Installed fonts can be used in both menu and application displays and printed in documents, presentations, spreadsheets, and other forms.

Right-click on font icons and select Properties from the pop-up menu for more information on each font. The Properties dialog box for each font usually includes three tabs:

- *General*—Provides information about the font, such as its size, creation and modification dates, file attributes, and type (whether it's a TrueType or other font)

- *Security*—Permits you to configure different permissions for each font

- *Summary*—Provides description and origin information about each installed font

For script fonts, an additional tab is provided. The Version tab, located between the General and Security tabs, provides information on the font version, copyright holder, and font's original file name. Other version information on the Version tab includes the name of the product with which the font shipped, the font's language, and the internal name given to the font by the system.

You install new fonts by selecting Install New Font from the File menu. Follow these steps to install a new font:

1. From Control Panel, open the Fonts applet. Select Install New Font from the File menu.

2. From the Add Fonts dialog box, specify the location of the font and click on OK. Fonts can be located on a floppy or removable disk, hard drive, or network share.

3. Highlight the font you want to install in the List Of Fonts window and click on OK.

4. A dialog box will appear and track the font installation's progress. When the installation is complete, the box will disappear. The font should now appear in the list of available fonts within applications.

Fonts can also be deleted. Just highlight the font, right-click on it, and select Delete. Alternatively, you can highlight the font and select Delete from the File menu.

From the View menu, you can choose to display fonts using large icons (as shown in Figure 7.14), a list format, a list format sorted by similarity, or a details format. You also can quickly change to any of those views by clicking one of the icons on the menu bar. If several fonts are installed, selecting Hide Variations from the View menu can hide variations of each font, such as the bold and italic versions.

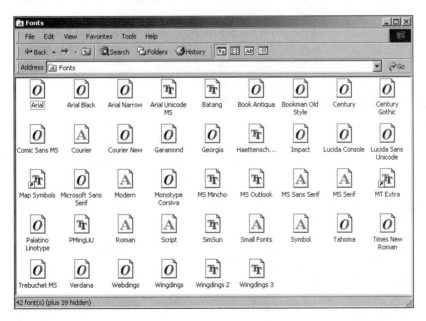

Figure 7.14
Fonts can be displayed in several formats. Here, fonts are displayed as large icons, with variations hidden.

Tip: Thousands of additional fonts are available for free on the Internet or from third-party providers. Many of these fonts work well. However, some third-party fonts have not been adequately tested and may not work as well as those that ship with Windows 2000 Professional. Be aware that you might experience display or printing issues with third-party fonts. Some fonts might display well but prove difficult to read when printed. In our experiences, the fonts shipped with Windows 2000 Professional and Microsoft Office consistently prove most reliable.

You will notice one additional nuance when using the Fonts applet. If you select Folder Options from the Tools menu, the Folder Options dialog box will open and feature a TrueType Fonts tab. If you want to view only TrueType fonts within applications, check the Show Only TrueType Fonts In The Programs On My Computer checkbox.

Tip: TrueType fonts originated with the Windows 95 operating system. They are scalable, meaning they can be used in different sizes without distortion. New in Windows 2000 is OpenType, a new font technology of which TrueType is a subset. OpenType uses a single Registry to manage TrueType and TrueType 1 fonts. As a result, TrueType and TrueType 1 (designed for use with PostScript printers) can be managed from a single Fonts applet.

The Game Controllers Applet

The next applet in the Windows 2000 Professional Control Panel—Game Controllers—is dedicated to installing, configuring, and troubleshooting game controllers. Unless you work for a company that produces computer games, you will probably have a hard time justifying the use of a game controller at work. If you work in an enterprise that encourages employees to play games, or if you are using Windows 2000 Professional at home, you will find game controllers relatively easy to install and configure.

Game Controllers—General Tab

If game controllers, such as joysticks, game pads, or steering wheels, are found during the system's boot cycle, Windows 2000 Professional will attempt to plug and play the devices. If a game controller is recognized, it will appear, along with its status in the Game Controllers window, on the General tab of the Game Controllers applet.

Click on the Refresh button to refresh the Game Controllers window. If any changes have been made, the window will update its display.

Click on Add to open the Add Game Controller dialog box. Various recognized game controllers are installed here. Check the Rudder/Pedals checkbox if Windows 2000 Professional should process rudder and pedal control information.

If a game controller is not listed in the Game Controllers window, you can click on Custom and specify the type of controller that has been added to the system. The four options are a joystick, game pad, flight or yoke stick, or race car controller. You will also need to specify the number of axes the controller uses and number of buttons the device possesses in the drop-down boxes. You must also give the device a name. A text box, where the custom name should be entered, is provided.

Clicking on the Add Other button opens the Select A Device Driver Wizard, which you use to select the manufacturer and model of the hardware device being installed. Select it from the list or click on Have Disk. You will need to have the Windows 2000 Professional CD-ROM or manufacturer's installation disks handy.

Clicking on the Remove button, near the bottom of the General tab, essentially uninstalls the controller from the system. Although the hardware component will still physically be connected to the system, the device's software drivers will be removed.

You use the Troubleshooting button to troubleshoot the game controller. The Properties button, meanwhile, houses information on the game controllers' drivers and configurations.

Game Controllers—Advanced Tab

The Advanced tab of the Game Controllers applet lists the Control ID assignments. The ID, name, game controller, and port information are listed. To adjust game controller settings, click on the Change button and edit the configurations accordingly.

The Internet Options Applet

When you're surfing the Internet, the Windows 2000 Professional Internet browser uses several defaults. For example, Internet Explorer must know which Web page should be used as the default home page, where Internet pages should be cached, what level of security should be used, which Internet connections should be used and how, and more.

All these settings are configured from within the Internet Options applet. Double-clicking on the Internet Options applet opens the Internet Properties dialog box, which contains six tabs that house various Internet options. (These options are also accessible from within Internet Explorer by choosing Tools|Internet Options.)

Note: *These settings only apply to Microsoft Internet Explorer. Netscape Navigator's controls are found within the program itself.*

Internet Options—General Tab

From the General tab, you can configure several settings. For example, this tab specifies the home page and location for storing temporary Internet files and the length of time pages should be kept in the history folder.

At the bottom of the General tab are four buttons:

* *Colors*—Used to specify text and link colors

* *Fonts*—Used to specify the fonts used on Web pages

- *Languages*—Used to specify Internet language preferences

- *Accessibility*—Used to specify color, font style, and font size options

Setting a Home Page

You can enter the default home page in the text box on the General tab. Or, if a Web browser is open to the current Internet page that should be made the home page, you can click on the Use Current button. The Use Default button resets the home page to the Microsoft Network Web page. Click on the Use Blank button if you prefer not to use a home page.

Temporary Internet Files

When you're surfing Internet sites, such as **www.coriolis.com**, images and other items are saved to the system hard drive. The next time you visit the page, the page will load more quickly because the stored images, such as the Coriolis logo, no longer have to be down-loaded from the Internet. Instead, the graphic file is recalled from the Temporary Internet Files folder on the local hard disk.

You can delete files kept in the Temporary Internet Files folder simply by clicking on the Delete Files button. Click on the Settings button to specify when Internet Explorer should check for newer versions of stored pages. The following options are presented:

- Every Visit

- Every Time Internet Explorer Is Started

- Automatically

- Never

From the Settings dialog box, you can configure the amount of disk space temporary Internet files can use. Both a sliding bar and a spin box are provided for configuring the amount of space, in megabytes, that the Temporary Internet Files folder is permitted to consume.

The Temporary Internet Files folder location is also listed. You can move it to a new location by clicking on the Move Folder button. The View Files button displays the files stored in this folder. The View Objects button, meanwhile, lists files that have been downloaded from the Internet.

Tip: *By default, the location of the Temporary Internet Files folder is* systemroot*Documents and Settings* username*Local Settings\Temporary Internet Files.*

The History Folder

The History file stores the Web addresses that you have visited using Internet Explorer. If you want to delete the list of Internet pages that have been visited, click on the Clear History button.

Using the spin box, you can specify the number of days that Internet pages should be stored in the History folder. When a Web page is not visited within the specified number of days, it is then deleted from the History folder.

Internet Options—Security Tab

The Security tab specifies security levels for the following four zones, by default:

- *Internet*—This zone includes all Internet sites and Web pages that have not been specifically placed in other zone categories.

- *Local Intranet*—This zone includes all Internet sites and Web pages that exist on the system's intranet.

- *Trusted Sites*—This zone includes all Internet sites and Web pages that are trusted by the user or yourself and not thought to possess any security threat to Windows 2000 Professional or system data.

- *Restricted Sites*—This zone includes all Internet sites and Web pages that are thought to possess the potential to damage Windows 2000 Professional or system data.

The Sites button has different purposes, depending on which zone is highlighted. If the Local Intranet zone is selected, the Sites button displays the following settings (all enabled by default):

- Include All Local (Intranet) Sites Not Listed In Other Zones

- Include All Sites That Bypass The Proxy Server

- Include All Network Paths (UNCs)

Clicking on the Sites button when the Trusted Sites or Restricted Sites zone is highlighted opens a dialog box in which you can add Web sites and Internet destinations to the respective zone. For the Trusted Sites zone, an additional option requires that the server use a secure HTTP connection to verify all the sites in the zone.

Sites are easily removed from their respective zones. Just highlight the site and click on the Remove button.

You cannot use the Sites button for the Internet zone. There is no need for it because the Internet zone is used for all Web pages and Internet destinations that have not otherwise been placed in a zone.

For each zone, you can set these four different security levels:

- Low

- Medium-low

- Medium

- High

Table 7.2   Multiple preconfigured Internet security levels exist in Windows 2000 Professional.

Zone	Default Security Level	Appropriate Site Usage	Default Actions	Feature Usage	Practicality
Restricted Sites	High	Sites that threaten malicious use or data loss	Cookies disabled	Less secure features are disabled	Safe, but threat exists that legitimate sites will be unreachable
Internet	Medium	Most Internet sites	Unsigned ActiveX controls are not enabled	Prompts are provided before potentially damaging actions are executed	Safe browsing, with little likelihood of locking out legitimate sites
Local Intranet	Medium-low	Local network and intranet sites	Unsigned ActiveX controls are disabled	Most content will run without prompting user for permission	Relatively safe browsing
Trusted Sites	Low	Trusted sites	Active content is enabled	Most content runs without prompts	Minimal safeguards, although warning prompts are provided

Table 7.2 lists the characteristics of each security level and the default security level for each zone.

Custom Internet security levels can be easily configured, too. Clicking on the Custom Level button opens the Security Settings dialog box for whichever zone is highlighted when the button is selected. Every security configuration is listed in the Settings window, as shown in Figure 7.15. You can make any necessary changes or adjustments and then click on OK.

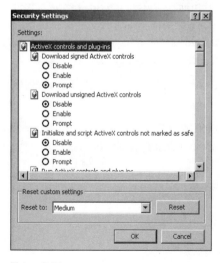

Figure 7.15
Custom Internet Explorer security levels can be set using the Internet Options applet.

You can also switch back to the original security level setting by selecting the desired security level in the Reset To drop-down box and clicking on the Reset button. If a zone's security level has been changed from the original setting, you can switch it back by highlighting the zone and clicking on the Default Level button and then the OK button.

Internet Options—Content Tab

Content ratings can be enabled to help ensure that only appropriate Internet content is viewed using a Windows 2000 Professional system. The Enable button under the Content Advisor area on the Content tab enables the Content Advisor feature, which you can set to prevent Internet pages from being viewed based on their language, nudity, sex, and violence ratings. Figure 7.16 depicts the Content Advisor's Ratings tab.

Tip: When the Content Advisor is enabled, the feature is enabled for all users who log on to the system. It cannot be configured for a single user.

A sliding bar sets the severity of each rating. A level of zero, or having the counter set all the way to the left, uses a less restrictive filter than a level of four, or having the counter set all the way to the right. Recreational Software Advisory Council Internet (RSACi) ratings determine access to individual Web pages based on the settings provided.

Should legitimate sites be locked out unintentionally, you can add Web addresses by entering them on the Content Advisor's Approved Sites tab. You can reach this tab by using the Settings button on the Content tab. Options that can be set from the Content

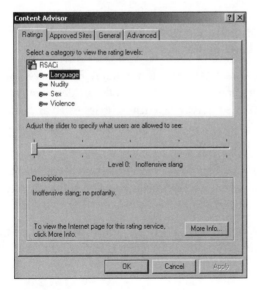

Figure 7.16
The Content Advisor helps prevent Internet Explorer from displaying inappropriate content.

Advisor's General tab include permitting users to see sites that have no rating and password-protecting sites known to have restricted content. Rating systems (other than RSACi) and supervisor passwords are both set from the General tab as well.

The Content Advisor's Advanced tab enables the use of a ratings bureau, which some ratings systems use. When using a bureau, be aware that it can significantly slow Internet response and page load times. You can choose which bureau to use in the Ratings Bureau drop-down box.

In addition, you can use the Content Advisor's Advanced tab to prioritize multiple Platform for Internet Content Selection (PICS) rules. The most restrictive rules should be placed first. Rules can be imported and removed. Highlight the appropriate rule and click on the Import or Remove button to perform the respective action.

Tip: PICS rules can be implemented in another attempt to prevent the viewing of restricted content. However, only Web sites that include PICS labels make use of such filtering.

Certificates are another item configured from the Content tab. Certificates are provided by a third party to confirm the identity of a Web site or system user. When you click on the Certificates button, you can review any personal certificates that have been installed on the Windows 2000 Professional system. The Certificates button displays information on whom the certificate was issued to, who issued the certificate, when the certificate expires, and more. Information is also provided on trusted authorities that can generate certificates.

Clicking on the Publishers button reveals certificate publishers trusted by Windows 2000 Professional. Trusted publishers are also easily removed. Highlight them in the Trusted Publishers window and click on the Remove button.

The last item on the Content tab is the Personal Information section. From here, you can enable AutoComplete, which remembers previous text entries and provides them for you. The end result is that you eliminate the need to type repetitive entries, such as mailing addresses, usernames, and passwords. If you use AutoComplete, you can configure it to be used for names and passwords, Web addresses, and forms.

From the AutoComplete Settings menu, you can also clear Web address entries by clicking on the Clear Forms button. If you want to remove passwords from the AutoComplete database, click on the Clear Passwords button.

Additionally, you can use the My Profile button in the Personal Information section to manage personal information. It gathers information located in Outlook Express Address Book entries to represent your profile.

Internet Options—Connections Tab

When executed, Internet Explorer must make several decisions. One of the most important decisions comes first: How should Internet Explorer connect to the Internet? The two methods are via a dial-up connection or using a LAN connection.

You can use the Internet Connection Wizard to specify how Internet Explorer should connect to the Internet. Just click on the Setup button to trigger the wizard. It will walk you through the process of creating a dial-up connection.

Existing dial-up and LAN settings can be configured by highlighting them in the Dial-up Settings window and clicking on the Settings button. You can configure and edit the following settings from the Settings dialog box:

- Whether the connection should automatically detect settings

- Whether an automatic configuration script should be used

- Whether a proxy server is in use and, if so, its address, port, and other configuration information

- The username the connection should use

- The password the connection should use

- The domain the connection should use

- Whether Internet programs should be permitted to use the connection

Advanced connection settings that you can configure include how many connection attempts should be made, how long a connection should stand idle before it is disconnected, and whether a connection should be disconnected if it is no longer needed. You also can view and edit a connection's properties from the dial-up connection's Settings dialog box.

Properties that you can view and edit include the following:

- The adapter or device (NIC or modem) the connection should use

- The phone number to be dialed

- Whether dialing rules are to be used

- Whether the connection progress should be displayed

- Whether the connection should prompt the user for name and password information, certificates, or other similar information

- Whether a Windows logon domain should be supplied

- The number of redial attempts that should be made

- The security validation to be used

You can also specify that Internet Explorer never dial a connection, dial a connection whenever a LAN connection is not present, or always dial the default connection.

If multiple dial-up connections are present, and you want to change the default, you should highlight the connection you want to use as the default and click on Set Default.

Dial-up settings and LAN settings can both be configured from the Connections tab.

Note: For more information on dial-up and LAN settings, see Chapter 14.

Internet Options—Programs Tab

Windows 2000 Professional makes use of several Internet services. For example, email is received and newsgroups are read via the Internet. You can configure the following six Internet service/program assignments from the Programs tab:

- HTML Editor

- E-mail

- Newsgroups

- Internet Call

- Calendar

- Contact List

Windows 2000 Professional uses specific programs for each Internet service. However, the default settings can be overridden, as shown in Figure 7.17. Changing the default Internet program is as easy as clicking on a drop-down box and selecting another option.

As usual, you can return settings to their original defaults, if they have been changed, by clicking on the Reset Web Settings button. Also, you can specify that Internet Explorer always check to learn whether it is the default by selecting the checkbox instructing Internet Explorer to perform just such a check. The checkbox is located at the bottom of the Programs tab.

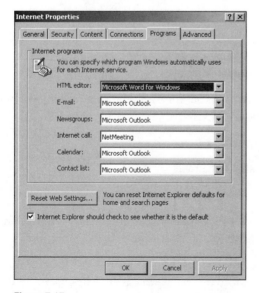

Figure 7.17
You configure Internet program and service assignments by using the Internet Options applet's Programs tab.

Internet Options—Advanced Tab

From the Internet Options applet's Advanced tab you can enable or disable several options. Accessibility, Browsing, and HTTP 1.1 settings are configured, as are Microsoft VM, Multimedia, Printing, and Security options.

For example, you can instruct Explorer to automatically check for updates, enable page hit counting, or use a personalized Favorites menu. Administrators can configure Windows 2000 Professional to check a publisher's certificate status to ensure that it has not been revoked, empty the Temporary Internet Files folder when the browser is closed, and much more.

All such options are configured using the checkboxes and radio buttons located on the Advanced tab. If you want to restore all the settings to the original defaults, the ubiquitous Restore Defaults button is present for just that task.

The Keyboard Applet

In the world of computers, things are not always as they seem. Don't skip this section saying "I know all there is to know about plugging the keyboard's PS/2 plug into a system; what more could there be to configuring a keyboard?" You will find many settings configured from the Keyboard applet that are not readily evident or intuitive.

Keyboard—Speed Tab

You set the cursor blink rate from the Keyboard applet's Speed tab. Other repeat rates are configured from the Speed tab, too. Sliding bars are provided not only for the cursor's blink rate, but also for the character repeat delay and character repeat rate, as shown in Figure 7.18.

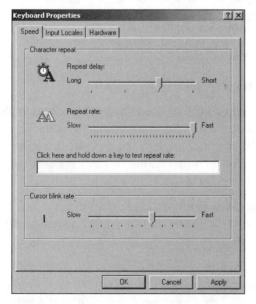

Figure 7.18
On the Keyboard applet's Speed tab, you can set character repeat rates.

Tip: The character repeat delay determines how long a key must be pressed before it begins repeating. The character repeat rate determines how quickly the character is repeated on screen.

Keyboard—Input Locales Tab

The Input Locales tab houses three important configuration settings. The first is the input language. The input locale is loaded into memory with the keyboard layout or Input Method Editor (IME) setting each time the system boots. This information is used by Windows 2000 Professional to process and interpret keystrokes.

The second important configuration setting involves the Caps Lock key. You can choose one of two radio buttons to have either the Caps Lock or Shift key turn off Caps Lock.

The third important item on the Input Locales tab is hotkey settings. Key sequences can be specified for switching between input locales and input language. You set the hotkey sequence by clicking on the Change Key Sequence button.

Keyboard—Hardware Tab

Along with advances in pointing devices, such as optical mice and trackballs, have come developments in keyboard technology. Windows 2000 Professional works with a wide variety of keyboards.

The Hardware tab provides information about the keyboard in use. The manufacturer, hardware revision, location, and device status are all displayed (if recognized by Windows 2000 Professional). The name of the keyboard and type are also displayed.

On this tab, you use the Troubleshoot button to correct driver or configuration errors that might exist with the installed keyboard. When clicked, the Troubleshoot button opens the Keyboard Troubleshooter Wizard.

The Properties button opens the hardware device's Properties dialog box, which houses three tabs:

- *General*—View additional device status information.

- *Driver*—View current driver information. Clicking on the Driver Details button displays additional driver information, including the location and name of the actual keyboard driver files Windows 2000 is using. You can easily update the keyboard driver by clicking on the Update Driver button. As with other hardware device driver updates, you will be prompted to specify the driver to be used and its location.

- *Resources*—Lists active memory input/output ranges and the IRQ the keyboard is occupying (typically 1). At the bottom of the Resources tab, conflicting device information is listed.

Depending on the configuration in use, you may have the option of selecting settings based on different configurations. When you're using different configurations, you can enable a checkbox that instructs Windows 2000 Professional to use automatic settings.

The Mail Applet

If you selected Outlook Express as an optional component to install when deploying Windows 2000 Professional, or if Microsoft Outlook has been installed, a Mail applet will be available in Control Panel. The Mail applet collects Outlook Express and Outlook account information.

New accounts can be added, accounts can be removed, and each account's properties can be reviewed and edited. For example, you can configure the following account properties by using the Properties dialog box:

- The address of the mail server (for both incoming and outgoing mail)
- User information, including name and organization
- Email and reply-to addresses
- Account names and passwords
- Server authentication information
- Connection instructions (such as through a modem or LAN)

Existing mail accounts from other machines can be imported and exported. Just click on the respective button to perform either action. You will be asked to provide the name and location of the account information you want to import or export.

The Mouse Applet

Different input devices feature different options. This is particularly true for a system's input device. Using a traditional Microsoft IntelliMouse with a scroll wheel or a similar Logitech mouse results in a Mouse applet stocked with four tabs. If a system is using a different mouse or different input device, such as a trackball, do not be surprised to find different options in the Mouse applet.

Double-clicking on the Mouse applet from within Control Panel opens the Mouse Properties dialog box. The four tabs available when using an IntelliMouse are as follows:

- Buttons
- Pointers
- Motion
- Hardware

Mouse—Buttons Tab

The first option set from the Buttons tab configures the mouse for right-handed or left-handed operation. Switching the setting reverses the effect of right-clicking and left-clicking. If you want to drive a coworker temporarily insane, switch the button configuration setting when the coworker is not looking. Improper settings can prove maddening, so button configuration should be one of the first items you check when a pointing device begins behaving erratically.

From the Buttons tab's Files And Folders section, you can direct Windows to use single clicks to open items. The default setting is the standard double click, in which the first click selects an item and the second click executes the item.

The last option configured from the Buttons tab is the double-click speed. When the speed is set slower, Windows 2000 allows a longer delay between two clicks before the operating system interprets the two clicks as two separate, single clicks. When it is set faster, Windows 2000 allows only a short time to pass before two clicks are considered a double click. A test area is provided to the right of the sliding bar to test the double-click setting that has just been configured.

Mouse—Pointers Tab

Individual pointers can be changed and customized using the Pointers tab. Current settings are shown for different pointer behaviors in the Customize window. In addition, you can select preconfigured schemes from the Scheme drop-down box.

After original pointer images have been changed, they can easily be returned to the default state. Just click on the Use Default button.

Changing a pointer image is straightforward; just follow these steps:

1. Select the pointer action you want to change from the Customize window, such as Working In Background, and either click on the Browse button or double-click on the action.

2. Locate the ANI or CUR file you want to use as the image and highlight it. Click on Open.

3. The image associated with the pointer behavior will be updated in the Customize window.

4. Click on Apply or OK to complete the change.

Tip: Typically, ANI and CUR files are stored in the sysdrive\systemroot\Cursors folder.

After you create a new scheme, you can save it by clicking on the Save As button. You will be prompted to supply a name for the scheme and the location where it should be stored.

Schemes are easily deleted as well. Highlight the scheme you want to delete in the Scheme drop-down box and click on the Delete button.

Mouse—Motion Tab

The pointing device's movement is configured from the Motion tab. The settings configured here are highly personal and often change from user to user.

Microsoft labels the two principal motion settings Speed and Acceleration, but these labels can be slightly misleading. Speed, while defined as the adjustment for how fast a pointer moves, might better be thought of as the distance a pointing device must travel relative to the distance the pointer moves on screen. For example, a slow speed setting might require the mouse to be moved four inches to direct the pointer completely across your monitor. A fast speed setting might require the same mouse to be moved only two inches to direct the pointer completely across your monitor. The speed is adjusted using a sliding bar. Adjust the bar to the left, and the speed slows. Move the bar to the right, and the speed increases.

The Acceleration setting determines how quickly the pointer gets moving. The acceleration speed is relative to how quickly the mouse gets up to speed. Set it high, move the mouse fast, and the pointer might travel a specified distance (say, two inches on the monitor screen) in a second. Set the acceleration low, move the mouse at the same speed, and the pointer might travel the same two inches across your monitor but take two seconds. The four Acceleration options, which you choose via radio buttons, are None, Low, Medium, and High.

The Snap To default setting configures the pointer to move to the default button in dialog boxes. Select the checkbox if you want to enable such pointer behavior.

Mouse—Hardware Tab

The Hardware tab lists the name and type of pointing device installed, as shown in Figure 7.19. Device property information also is displayed, including the pointing device's manufacturer, hardware revision, location, and device status (if recognized by Windows 2000 Professional).

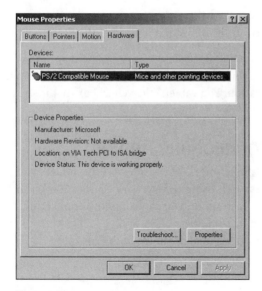

Figure 7.19
The Mouse applet's Hardware tab contains information on the system's pointing device.

On this tab, you use the Troubleshoot button to correct driver or configuration errors that might exist with the installed pointing device. When clicked, the Troubleshoot button opens the Mouse Troubleshooter Wizard.

The Properties button opens the pointing device's Properties dialog box, which houses four tabs: General, Advanced Settings, Driver, and Resources. Additional device status information is presented on the General tab. For example, the device's current status is noted.

The Advanced Settings tab permits configuration of the sample rate, or how often the input device checks for motion to process. A spin box sets the sample rate using a reports/second measurement (set at 60 for my mouse). The Wheel Detection drop-down box instructs Windows 2000 Professional whether to assume a wheel is present, disable wheel detection, or seek a wheel.

The pointing device's Input Buffer Length can be adjusted, too. The Input Buffer Length stores mouse location information. Microsoft recommends increasing the number of packets stored if the mouse begins behaving erratically.

Fast initialization can also be set from the Advanced Settings tab. If the Fast Initialization box is checked, Windows 2000 Professional generally boots more quickly. However, if the pointer begins behaving strangely, it is recommended that you clear the Fast Initialization checkbox. You can return all advanced settings to their original states by clicking on the Defaults button.

The Driver tab lists current driver information. On this tab, you also can update the mouse or pointing device driver. You should consider reinstalling the driver if the mouse is behaving erratically. As with other hardware device driver updates, you will be prompted to specify the driver to be used and its location.

The pointing device Properties' Resources tab lists active memory input/output ranges and the IRQ the mouse is occupying (typically 12). At the bottom of the Resources tab, conflicting device information is listed.

Depending on the configuration in use, you may have the option of selecting settings based on a different hardware configuration. You can enable a checkbox that instructs Windows 2000 Professional to use automatic settings.

The Network and Dial-up Connections Applet

The Network and Dial-up Connections applet is one of the most critical folders you will find anywhere in Windows 2000 Professional. Using the Network Connection Wizard, triggered from the Make New Connection shortcut, you can configure connections to the outside world and the Internet by using dial-up lines, LANs, and virtual private networks (VPNs). You can create incoming connections, too, as shown in Figure 7.20.

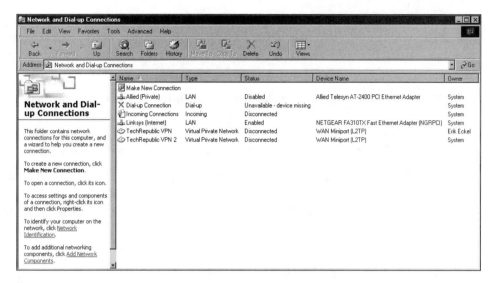

7

Figure 7.20
Several different connections can be configured on a single system. All are managed using the Network and Dial-up Connections applet.

You can view and edit existing connection settings by right-clicking on a connection and selecting Properties from the pop-up menu. From a connection's Properties dialog box, you can configure the following:

- The protocols in use, such as Internet Protocol (TCP/IP)

- The clients the connection uses, such as Client for Microsoft Networks

- The services in use, such as File and Printer Sharing for Microsoft Networks

- The network adapter or modem the connection should use

Additional protocols, services, and clients can be installed. They can also be uninstalled from the Properties dialog box. If you want a visual notification when the connection is active, check the Show Icon In Taskbar When Connected box located on the bottom of the connection Properties' General tab.

Note: For more information on creating, configuring, and troubleshooting network and dial-up connections, refer to Chapter 14.

The Phone and Modem Options Applet

Modems, dialing rules, and telephony providers are all configured from the Phone and Modem Options applet. Windows programs that use telephony services (such as an email client) use the Windows 2000 Professional telephony interface, which stores location information. The telephony interface works with a telephony application programming interface (TAPI) service provider, which you can configure from the Phone and Modem Options applet. Windows telephony applications obtain necessary dialing information from dialing rules, which you also can edit from this applet.

The Phone and Modem Options applet uses three tabs to configure telephony settings:

- *Dialing Rules*—Used to create, edit, and delete dialing locations

- *Modems*—Used to add, remove, and configure installed modems

- *Advanced*—Used to add, remove, and configure telephony providers

Tip: *If you have not tried connecting to another system or network using a telephony interface, you must enter some basic phone information before you will see these tabs.*

Phone and Modem Options—Dialing Rules Tab

Before you connect to another network using a telephone or modem connection, you must first create a dialing location. You can do so by clicking on the New button on the Dialing Rules tab.

Existing locations and the area code used by the location are listed in the Locations window. Click on the Edit button to configure existing locations. When you're editing a location, several configuration options exist. Among the items you can specify are the following:

- The location name

- The country or region from which you will be dialing

- The area code from which you will be dialing

- Whether an outside line must be accessed and, if so, how the line is accessed

- Whether call waiting should be disabled

- The type of dialing the connection should use (tone or pulse)

- Area code rules (such as whether prefixes are to be included)

- Calling card account and PIN information

Phone and Modem Options—Modems Tab

Modems are added, removed, and configured from the Modems tab. You won't find any surprises here.

You add a modem by clicking on the Add button. The Add/Remove Hardware Wizard will appear and walk you step-by-step through modem installation. If you don't want Windows to try to plug and play the device, be sure to check the Don't Detect My Modem, I Will

Select It From A List checkbox on the wizard's first screen. Be prepared to specify the modem driver the system should use and the driver's location.

Removing modems is simple. Highlight the modem you want to uninstall and click on Remove. A confirmation dialog box will appear, asking whether you are sure you want to remove the selected modem from your system. Click on Yes, and the modem will be removed.

Changing installed modem settings is straightforward, too. Highlight the modem from the Modems window that you want to configure. Then, click on the Properties button. The modem's Properties dialog box will appear. From its three tabs—General, Diagnostics, and Advanced—you can configure the following settings:

- Speaker volume

- Maximum port speed

- Dial control (whether a dial tone should be confirmed before dialing)

- Diagnostics and logging

- Initialization settings

Phone and Modem Options—Advanced Tab

As with dialing rules and modems, you add or remove telephony providers (which are used by applications that require telephone or modem connections) by clicking on the Add or Remove buttons. Existing telephony providers are easily edited, too. Highlight the appropriate telephony provider in the Providers window and click on the Configure button. The options that you can configure for telephony providers differ depending on which telephony providers are installed.

The Power Options Applet

The Power Options applet can prove to be of particular value if Windows 2000 Professional has been installed on a laptop machine. You can access this applet from several locations. For example, you can access it from the Display applet's Screen Saver tab. Alternatively, you can reach it directly by opening Control Panel's Power Options applet.

Most of the information and settings configured from this applet are similar to those described earlier in this chapter's "Display—Screen Saver Tab" section. However, different tabs might appear if a system is set up differently or possesses a different hardware configuration. For example, in addition to the Power Schemes, Alarm, Power Meter, Advanced, and Hibernate tabs, you might find others. Two common tabs on laptops are APM and UPS.

On the Advanced Power Management (APM) tab, you can reduce the power a system consumes. When battery power is present, APM will provide battery status information. If you want to enable APM, select the Enable Advanced Power Management Support checkbox.

You use the UPS tab to manage uninterruptible power supplies (UPS). If a UPS is detected, the UPS tab will display status and detailed information about the device in use. Many UPS devices can be selected and configured from within the UPS tab's Details dialog box.

Note: *It's not uncommon for UPS devices to include their own software, which often bypasses the functionality of the UPS tab. For this reason, don't be surprised if you have a UPS installed and this tab fails to appear. The UPS manufacturer's software will provide access to configuration settings instead of Control Panel.*

The Printers Applet

Using the Printers applet, you can manage and administer a system's installed fax services and printers. The Printers applet also houses the Add Printer Wizard.

Tip: *In addition to accessing the Printers applet from Control Panel, you also can reach it by clicking on Start/Settings/Printers.*

Follow these steps to install a printer:

1. Open the Printers applet in Control Panel. Double-click on the Add Printer icon.

2. When the Add Printer Wizard appears, click on Next.

3. Specify whether the printer being installed is local (attached directly to the system) or being accessed over a network. For this example, a network printer will be installed because that is the most common occurrence in corporate environments. Click on Network Printer and then click on Next.

4. Specify the printer's name (if you know it) or whether the printer is to be reached via the Internet. If the printer is being accessed via the Internet, provide the URL needed to access it. Click on Next after providing the URL or if you are connecting via a LAN and do not know the printer's name.

5. The Add Printer Wizard will browse for shared printers on the network. The results of its search will be displayed in the Shared Printers window, as shown in Figure 7.21. Select the printer you want to use and click on Next.

6. Specify whether you want Windows-based programs to use this printer as the default printer and click on Next.

7. The Add Printer Wizard will present a confirmation screen. Click on Finish to complete the printer's installation. The printer will then appear as installed within the Printers applet.

Configuring Installed Printers and Fax Services

You can manage printers and fax services by right-clicking on the respective item in the Printers applet and selecting from several options that appear on the resulting pop-up menu, including the following:

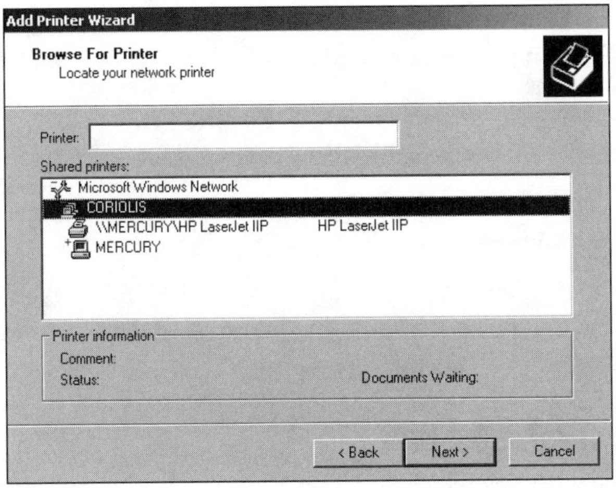

Figure 7.21
The Add Printer Wizard will search a LAN for shared printers.

- *Open*—Opens the printer's menu and checks the status of pending print jobs

- *Set As Default Printer*—Sets the highlighted printer as the default

- *Printing Preferences*—Configures layout and paper quality preferences

- *Pause Printing*—Pauses the printer

- *Cancel All Documents*—Deletes all print jobs currently in the print queue

- *Sharing*—Configures printer share permissions

- *Delete*—Deletes an installed printer

- *Properties*—Opens a printer's Properties dialog box, from which you can manage several options

A printer or fax service's Properties dialog box contains several important settings. Everything from security and permissions to ports and device setting information can be configured from a printer's Properties dialog box.

The number of tabs and actual configurable options in the Properties dialog box will depend on the print device and print drivers that have been installed. That said, you are likely to find a minimum of six tabs:

- *General*—Used to specify the print device name and location, list print device features, set printing preferences, and print a sample test page

- *Sharing*—Used to share a print device and add drivers for different Windows platforms that might access the print device

- *Ports*—Used to manage and configure port assignments for installed print devices

- *Advanced*—Used to configure the times when a print device is available, enter priorities, add new drivers, specify when print jobs should start, and configure spooling and other configuration options

- *Security*—Used to set printer access permissions

- *Device Settings*—Provides detailed information on printer trays, font cartridges, and other options specific to the print device

The items displayed in the Printers folder can be displayed using large icons, small icons, a list format, or a details format. You can select all these options from the View menu or by clicking icons on the toolbar.

Configuring Print Server Properties

You configure Print Server Properties by selecting Server Properties from the Printer applet's File menu. Print Server Properties are used to configure forms, ports, print drivers, and spool settings.

Note: *For more information on printer installation, configuration, administration, troubleshooting, and print server configuration, see Chapter 10.*

The Regional Options Applet

You set regional preferences in Windows 2000 Professional by using the Regional Options applet. You use this Control Panel applet to configure languages, input locales, time and date settings, monetary symbols, and the currency Windows applications use.

The Regional Options applet includes these six tabs:

- General

- Numbers

- Currency

- Time

- Date

- Input Locales

Regional Options—General Tab

On the Regional Options applet's General tab you can specify the locale, or region, in which the Windows 2000 Professional system is located. If you are located in the United States, you select the English (United States) locale from the Your Local (Location) drop-down box, as shown in Figure 7.22.

You also set the system language on the General tab. Seventeen languages are listed, by default. If you are using a Windows 2000 Professional system in Western Europe or the United States, that entry should be checked in the Language Settings For The System window.

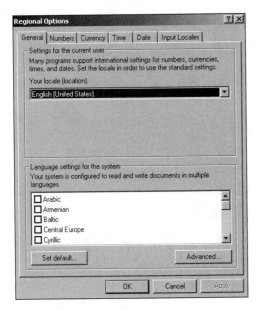

7

Figure 7.22
You set languages and locales on the Regional Options applet's General tab.

Advanced Regional Options that you can set from the General tab include code page conversion tables. If you are operating a system in the United States or Western Europe, the 10000 (MAC - Roman) selection should be enabled.

You configure the System Locale default by clicking on the Set Default button. It will open the Select System Locale dialog box, which includes a drop-down menu used to set the locale that should be used as the default.

Tip: The System Locale instructs applications to display menus and dialogs in a native language. Windows 2000 Professional uses the code pages and font for the respective language to generate application menus and dialog boxes. Note that Windows menus and dialog boxes are not affected.

Regional Options—Numbers Tab

On the Regional Options applet's Numbers tab, you can configure the manner in which numbers are displayed. From the Numbers tab, you can instruct Windows 2000 Professional to use different values for the following items, among others:

- The decimal symbol
- The number of digits to display after a decimal
- The symbol to be used to represent a negative value
- The negative number format
- The measurement system to be used

Regional Options—Currency Tab

On the Regional Options applet's Currency tab, you can configure the manner in which monetary numbers are displayed. From the Currency tab, you can instruct Windows 2000 Professional to use different values for the following items, among others:

- The currency symbol

- The number of digits to display after a decimal

- Positive currency format

- Negative currency format

Regional Options—Time Tab

You use the Regional Options applet's Time tab to configure how the time is displayed. From the Time tab, you can instruct Windows 2000 Professional to use different values for the following items, among others:

- The time format

- The symbol to be used for the time separator

- The AM and PM symbols

Regional Options—Date Tab

On the Regional Options applet's Date tab, you can configure date presentation. From the Date tab, you can instruct Windows 2000 Professional to use different values for the following items, among others:

- How two-digit years are to be interpreted

- Short date format

- Long date format

Regional Options—Input Locales

On the Regional Options applet's Input Locales tab, you can configure Input Locales, which were discussed earlier in the sections on the Keyboard and Mouse applets.

The Scanners and Cameras Applet

The Scanners and Cameras applet provides a shortcut to the Scanners And Cameras Properties dialog box. In this dialog box, you can add, remove, and configure Windows 2000 Professional for use with scanners and digital cameras. Installed scanners and cameras will appear in the Scanners And Cameras window on the Devices tab. Depending on the hardware devices installed, additional tabs might exist.

Adding a scanner or camera is straightforward and much like adding any other hardware device. Click on Add, and the Scanner And Camera Installation Wizard will appear. It will guide you step-by-step through the installation of scanners and cameras.

Removing a scanner or camera is even easier. Highlight the appropriate entry and click on Remove. You will be prompted to confirm the action. Just click on Yes to complete the removal.

The Troubleshoot button opens the Troubleshooting Wizard. The wizard will walk you step-by-step through solving configuration issues related to scanners and digital cameras.

A Wireless Device button is also located on the General tab. You use it to configure wireless connections to scanner and camera devices. You configure file and image transfer settings and hardware configuration settings from the Wireless Link dialog box, which you access from the Wireless Device button.

You can edit installed scanner and digital camera settings by highlighting the appropriate device on the Devices tab and clicking on the Properties button. Among the items that you can configure are the ports and applications the device uses. Other settings that you can configure will depend on the device that is installed.

The Scheduled Tasks Applet

The Scheduled Tasks applet provides a shortcut to the Scheduled Tasks folder, where you can automate regularly occurring tasks. Tasks that have already been scheduled appear in the folder along with the Add Scheduled Task icon, as shown in Figure 7.23.

Creating Scheduled Tasks

Follow these steps to create a regularly scheduled task:

1. Open the Scheduled Tasks applet in Control Panel.

2. Double-click on the Add Scheduled Task icon.

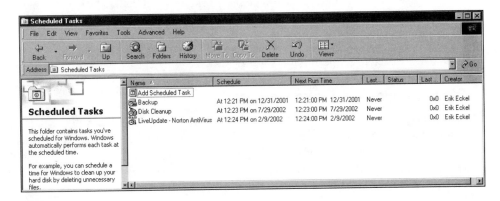

Figure 7.23
The Scheduled Tasks folder collects tasks Windows 2000 Professional has been configured to complete automatically.

3. When the Scheduled Task Wizard appears, click on Next.

4. A list of applications will appear. Select the application you want to schedule. If it is not listed, click on the Browse button and specify the location of the application. Then, click on Next.

5. Specify a name for the task. Then, specify the interval at which the task should be performed and click on Next.

6. Select the time, day, and month (if applicable) when the task should be performed and click on Next.

7. Provide a username and password that possesses sufficient rights to execute the task and click on Next.

8. The Scheduled Task Wizard will present a confirmation screen. You can elect to enable the checkbox that will open advanced properties when the Finish button is clicked. Click on Finish to complete the process.

9. If you checked the Open Advanced Properties For This Task When I Click Finish box, you will have to review and configure advanced settings. The advanced settings that can be configured will depend on the task that has been scheduled. The process then is completed.

Editing Scheduled Tasks

You can edit existing scheduled tasks by right-clicking on the task and selecting Properties from the pop-up menu. The following four Properties tabs collect the various options that can be configured for each scheduled task:

- *Task*—Used to specify the program to be run, comments regarding the program, and the user permission to be used to run the task

- *Schedule*—Used to configure when the task executes

- *Settings*—Used to specify actions to be taken when the scheduled task is completed, how long the system must be idle to perform the task, and whether to run the task if the system is running on battery power

- *Security*—Used to set permissions for the task

Other Scheduled Tasks Options

Scheduled tasks are easily deleted. Simply highlight the scheduled task in the Scheduled Tasks folder, right-click on it, and select Delete from the pop-up menu. An alternative is to highlight the task and press the Delete key. A dialog box will appear asking if you are certain you wish to delete the task; click Yes and the task will be deleted.

You also can access other options from the menu that appears when you right-click on a scheduled task. Scheduled tasks can be cut and pasted into other menus, renamed, and run. These same operations can be selected from the Scheduled Tasks applet's File menu.

As with other folders, scheduled tasks can be displayed in a number of formats. You can select large or small icons, a list view, or a details display.

From the Scheduled Tasks Advanced menu, you can specify that use of the Task Scheduler be suspended or paused. You can also configure notifications to be sent if a task is missed, set the AT Service Account to be used to run tasks, and view a log of past scheduled task activity.

The Sounds and Multimedia Applet

The next item you will find in Control Panel is the Sounds and Multimedia applet. It is used to configure a system's sounds, audio settings, and hardware configuration. Arguably, the Sounds and Multimedia applet is one of the most popular Control Panel applets that users access. It is second in popularity only to the Display applet, in which users configure different screen savers and backgrounds.

What do most users enjoy so much about the Sounds and Multimedia applet? The applet's fame probably has a great deal to do with the fact that configuring system sounds truly personalizes your system. We challenge you to locate a single office worker who has not delighted in assigning a custom sound clip alerting him or her to a new mail message.

The Sounds and Multimedia Properties applet boasts three tabs: Sounds, Audio, and Hardware.

Sounds and Multimedia—Sounds Tab

Easily the most popular tab in the applet, the Sounds tab is used to configure which files sound with which system events. From the Scheme drop-down box, you select preset sound schemes, which provide a set of similar sounds with associated system events. Individual sound events, meanwhile, are configured from the Sound Events window, as shown in Figure 7.24.

Choose Event Sounds Carefully!

Choose the sounds you associate with events carefully, at least at the office. Although many office workers might share your sense of humor, we could tell you the story of a telecommunications director who was hard-pressed to explain the *South Park* sound clip emanating from his system during a sensitive vendor meeting held in his office. As silly as it sounds, let's just say maintaining a tough negotiation face can be difficult when a *South Park* character speaks its uncensored mind. Avoid such unwanted surprises by selecting the sound files you use with care.

Figure 7.24
You use the Sounds and Multimedia applet's Sounds tab to configure which sound files Windows 2000 Professional will play when a specified system event occurs.

Sound schemes are easily deleted. Clicking on the Delete button deletes the scheme currently shown in the Scheme drop-down box.

If changes are made to an existing scheme, you can save those changes by clicking on the Save As button. The system will prompt you for the name to use for the scheme and the location where it should be stored.

If you want to test a system sound, click on the triangular Play button located next to the Browse button. You can use the Browse button to configure a system event to use a sound file other than those listed in the Sound Events window.

Tip: Typically, sound files are stored in the systemdrive\systemroot*Media folder.*

Sound volume is also configured from the Sounds tab. The sliding bar at the bottom of the menu increases the sound volume when moved to the right and decreases the volume when moved to the left.

Sounds and Multimedia—Audio Tab

Windows 2000 Professional possesses three different audio options. One is used for sound playback, another for sound recording, and the third for Musical Instrument Digital Interface (MIDI) music playback, which is often used by games.

On the Sound and Multimedia applet's Audio tab, you can specify which device processes which audio option. Select the devices you prefer Windows 2000 Professional to use for each option from the appropriate drop-down boxes. Each device also possesses separate

Volume and Advanced buttons, with the exception of the MIDI Music Playback option, which has Volume and About buttons.

The Volume buttons set left-right balances and volumes for the system's master volume control as well as line-in CD audio, MIDI, and WAV files. Different advanced properties are configured for Sound Playback and Sound Recording. The advanced properties options that are present and editable depend largely on the sound card the system has installed and drivers being used.

7

At the bottom of the Audio tab is a checkbox. Check it if you want Windows 2000 Professional to use only preferred audio devices.

Sounds and Multimedia—Hardware Tab

You use the Sounds and Multimedia applet's Hardware tab to troubleshoot and configure properties of installed multimedia devices. The Hardware tab lists all the installed multimedia hardware peripherals and provides a type label for each device.

You can troubleshoot a problematic multimedia device by selecting it from the Devices window and clicking on the Troubleshoot button. A Troubleshooting Wizard will guide you through solving configuration and connection issues.

You also can open the Properties dialog box for each multimedia device from the Hardware tab. Highlight the respective hardware component in the Devices window and click on the Properties button. The properties that are displayed will depend on the hardware devices attached to a system.

You can also use the Hardware tab to learn more information about each multimedia device that is installed. Highlight the respective multimedia component in the Devices window, and the manufacturer, hardware revision data, its location, and its status will be provided in the tab's Device Properties section.

The System Applet

One of the most important applets in the Windows 2000 Control Panel is the System applet, which you are likely to use regularly. It houses data and other information that can prove critical when you're troubleshooting system errors. The System applet controls everything from a system's hardware to its startup and recovery options.

You should always use care when making changes in the System applet because of the wide range of critical settings that you can configure from the System Properties dialog box. Put quite simply, used incorrectly, this applet can maim a system. Used properly, though, it can be a lifesaver.

System—General Tab

The System applet's General tab provides important information about the Windows 2000 Professional system. It lists the operating system that is installed, as well as the operating system's build number. The registered owner is listed, along with the Windows 2000 Professional registration number. Below the registration information is system data specific to the machine. The Computer section of the General tab lists the type of micro-processor that is installed, type of computer that is being run, and amount of memory the system possesses.

System—Network Identification Tab

From the Network Identification tab, you can learn the full computer name that has been given to the system. You can also determine whether the system is a member of a work-group or domain, and the name of that workgroup or domain.

Click on the Network ID button, and the Network Identification Wizard opens. The wizard helps you connect the system to a network.

Click on the Properties button to make changes to the computer name and domain or workgroup assignment. If you want to make changes to the DNS suffix and NetBIOS names, click on the More button. The DNS Suffix And NetBIOS Computer Name menu will open, providing the opportunity to change these settings.

System—Hardware Tab

The System applet's true power begins in the Hardware tab. From here, you can run the Hardware Wizard, which you use to install, uninstall, repair, unplug, eject, and configure a system's hardware.

Driver Signing

The Device Manager section of the Hardware tab houses two important buttons: Driver Signing and Device Manager. You use the Driver Signing button to set two important options to help a system ensure that the files being read from a Windows 2000 CD are, in fact, authentic Microsoft files.

The first option to be set from the Driver Signing Options dialog box is file signature verification. Three levels exist:

- *Ignore*—When this option is selected, all files are installed regardless of the file signature used.

- *Warn*—When this option is selected, users are prompted before an unsigned file is installed.

- *Block*—When this option is selected, unsigned files will not be installed.

The second option involves a single checkbox. Check the Apply Setting As System Default checkbox in the Driver Signing Options Administrator option section to apply the setting as the system default.

The Device Manager

The Device Manager button calls up the Device Manager console, which is easily the most important tool at an administrator's disposal when troubleshooting faulty hardware. The Device Manager lists all of a system's hardware components, from the disk drives to the display adapters to floppy disk controllers to network adapters to sound, video, and game controllers, as shown in Figure 7.25.

Right-clicking any hardware component listed in the Device Manager console calls up a pop-up menu featuring several options. Depending on the hardware component selected, your options will be to disable the device, uninstall the device, scan for hardware changes, or open a device's Properties dialog box.

Depending on the hardware device highlighted, the Properties dialog box offers a smorgasbord of options that can be reviewed and configured, including all the following:

- Device status

- Device usage

- The drive in use

- The connection type

- The resources the device uses

Using Hardware Profiles

The last button located on the Hardware tab is the Hardware Profiles button. You use it to create different hardware configurations. For example, say Sylvia is an accountant who travels often with a laptop to conduct audits. She may want to use one configuration

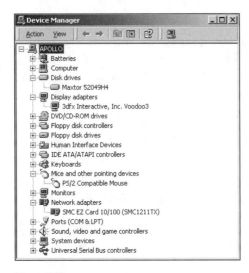

Figure 7.25
The Device Manager tracks all the hardware components installed on a system.

when she's working from her office, where she has a monitor, external mouse, a LAN connection, and an external keyboard all configured through a docking station. However, when she takes to the road on business, she leaves her docking station behind, along with all its peripherals. Therefore, she should elect to use hardware profiles. Doing so ensures that Windows 2000 Professional knows to use the integrated modem instead of the LAN connection, the laptop's LCD display instead of the monitor, and the laptop's pointing device and keyboard.

If different hardware configurations are enabled, Windows 2000 Professional provides a prompt at the beginning of the boot cycle. Available hardware profile configurations are presented.

Clicking on the Properties button on the Hardware Profiles dialog box presents hardware profile properties. Profile information specific to the machine and hardware installed will be provided. You can specify which hardware configurations are shown for selection during the Windows 2000 Professional boot cycle by checking the Always Include This Profile As An Option When Windows Starts box. You can find the checkbox at the bottom of the profile's Properties dialog box.

Hardware profiles are easily copied, renamed, and deleted. Highlight the respective profile in the Available Hardware Profiles window and select the appropriate button. You can reorder the profiles by using the arrows on the right side of the Available Hardware Profiles window. There's also an option to prompt Windows 2000 Professional to wait to start up until the user selects a hardware profile. Alternatively, you can specify that Windows 2000 Professional wait a specified period of time, set in seconds, before booting using the default configuration. Such preferences are set from the Hardware Profiles Selection section of the Hardware Profiles dialog box.

System—User Profiles Tab

User profiles are nothing new in Windows 2000 Professional. They contain a user's desktop setting configurations and logon information. A different profile can be created on each system a user logs on to, or a user can make use of roaming profiles, which are profiles that follow him or her around a network.

The System applet's User Profiles tab displays the profiles stored on a computer. In addition, the size of each profile, the type of profile, and the profile's last modification date are all displayed.

Profiles are deleted easily. Just highlight the profile you want to delete and click on the Delete button. Be aware, though, that you cannot delete the profile that is currently in use.

You can change a profile's type by highlighting the profile you want to change and clicking on the Change Type button. The two profile types are local and roaming.

Additionally, you can copy profiles from one system to another. To do so, ensure that the appropriate profile is highlighted in the Profiles Stored On This Computer window and click on the Copy To button. You will be prompted to provide the location for the copy of the profile being created.

If you possess appropriate permissions, you can also change which users are permitted to use the profile. Click on the Change button in the Copy To dialog box and select the appropriate user.

7

Note: For more information on configuring user profiles, see Chapter 13.

System—Advanced Tab

The following three important options are configured from the System applet's Advanced tab:

- *Performance Options*—In the Performance Options dialog box, you can specify whether performance should be optimized for applications or background services, as well as the paging file size to be used for virtual memory. This dialog box is shown in Figure 7.26.

- *Environment Variables*—Options on this dialog box specify temporary file locations and other system variables, such as the Windows directory and operating system in use. You can also create new user and system variables or edit or delete existing ones.

- *Startup And Recovery*—Options on this dialog box specify the default operating system and actions to be taken in the event of system failures, such as whether event logs should be created and the system should automatically reboot. The Startup And Recovery dialog box is shown in Figure 7.28.

The Users and Passwords Applet

From the Users tab of the Users and Passwords applet, you can specify that all users enter a username and password for access to the system. In addition, you can add, remove, and configure properties for each user.

Figure 7.26
The Performance Options dialog box optimizes memory for applications' use or background services.

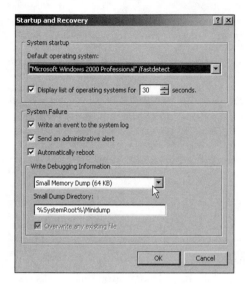

Figure 7.28
The Startup And Recovery dialog box specifies actions to be taken in the event of system failures and startup options.

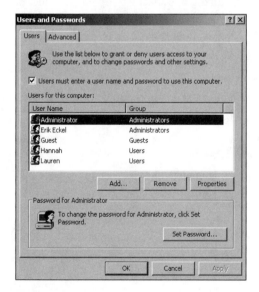

Figure 7.29
You use the Users tab to administer user accounts.

All the user accounts configured on a system will appear on the Users For This Computer window, as shown in Figure 7.29. Highlight the appropriate user and select Properties to edit the settings for that user. The following options can be set:

• Username

• Full name

- User description

- Group membership information

The Users tab also houses the Password For Administrator section, which you use to change the administrator password. Click on the Set Password button to update the Administrator account password. Before you can change the Administrator password, you will first have to enter the current Administrator password.

From the Users and Passwords applet's Advanced tab, you can maintain and administer certificate management (discussed in "The Internet Options Applet" section of this chapter), advanced user management, and secure boot settings.

The Advanced button in the Advanced User Management section opens the Local Users and Groups console. From there, you can use the console to perform advanced user actions, such as adding new users, changing user permissions, creating new groups, and moving user accounts between groups.

Note: *For more information on user and group management, see Chapter 12.*

We recommend that you enable the checkbox requiring users to press Ctrl+Alt+Delete simultaneously before they can log on. The Ctrl+Alt+Delete action ensures that password and account security are protected by canceling any malicious background programs that might have been loaded on a system.

The Wireless Link Applet

The Wireless Link applet is likely to be found only on laptop systems or on Windows 2000 Professional machines that have had wireless network adapters or other wireless devices installed. You use the applet to configure file transfer, image transfer, and hardware settings.

You may recall visiting the Wireless Link dialog box in the section on the Scanners and Cameras applet. A button within that applet opens the Wireless Link dialog box.

Wireless Link—File Transfer Tab

From the Wireless Link applet's File Transfer tab, you can configure the system to do the following:

- Display an icon on the taskbar indicating infrared activity

- Allow others to send files to your computer using infrared communications

- Display status while receiving files

From the File Transfer tab, you can also view the default location for receiving files. The location is easily changed. Click on the Browse button, navigate to another location, and click on the OK button.

Wireless Link—Image Transfer Tab

You can configure three options from the Image Transfer tab. In addition to changing the default transferred image subfolder location, you can instruct Windows 2000 Professional to use the Wireless Link to transfer images from a digital camera to your computer and to explore (or open) the location after pictures are received.

Wireless Link—Hardware Tab

You use the Wireless Link applet's Hardware tab, fittingly enough, to troubleshoot installed wireless devices. Clicking on the Troubleshoot button opens the Hardware Troubleshooter Wizard, which will walk you through the process of solving errors with the Wireless Link.

You can also configure wireless device properties by highlighting the appropriate wireless component from the Devices window and selecting the Properties button. The properties that can be configured will depend on the wireless device installed. Typical settings include Infrared Data Association (IrDA) settings, such as the maximum connect rate, the driver in use, and which resources (IRQs, memory addresses, and so on) the wireless link uses.

Other information provided on the Hardware tab includes the wireless link's manufacturer, hardware revision data, the location of the wireless link, and the device's status.

Summary

The Windows 2000 Control Panel collects a number of critical system tools, utilities, consoles, and dialog boxes used to configure and administer the Windows 2000 operating system. Although Control Panel includes many applets, its graphical user interface greatly simplifies its use. Rather than having to rely on complicated Registry entries to make changes, you can use Control Panel's easy-to-use dialog boxes.

Whether you are troubleshooting a system, editing hardware settings, configuring network connections, or adding or removing software or applications, Control Panel will often be your first stop. Become familiar with its many applets, consoles, and dialog boxes because, as an IT professional, you are likely to be clicking to Control Panel as often as accountants open Microsoft Excel or sales personnel fire up Microsoft PowerPoint.

The next chapter provides a close look at the features Microsoft has included in Windows 2000 Professional to make it more mobile-friendly.

Chapter 8

Mobility Features

Introduction to Mobile Computing

To handle today's rapidly growing need for increased productivity within organizations, many companies are realizing the necessity to acquire, configure, and maintain additional laptops. Initially, laptops were supplied to traveling executives, sales personnel, and other employees who did not spend a significant amount of time in a particular location.

As the price of laptops decreases, and their power, speed, and functionality increase, desktop computers are being used less, and laptops are becoming more widely used. Although laptops still have some unique requirements and limitations, their presence in today's computing environments is certainly becoming stronger. Laptops provide both the portability and flexibility that desktop computers don't.

As laptops become more popular, the demand to provide support for these machines increases as well. You need to address some areas of major concern when developing a support structure for your mobile computing environment. Windows 2000 Professional laptop support personnel require a thorough understanding of special hardware considerations, power management options, information sharing techniques, and document synchronization.

Mobile Hardware Considerations

Windows 2000 Professional laptop support personnel require a thorough understanding of four primary areas regarding the hardware involved: hardware compatibility with the operating system, unique laptop technology, desktop docking stations, and hardware profiles.

Hardware Compatibility

As with all hardware you want to install on a Windows NT or 2000 operating system, the computer system and all optional hardware components should be listed on the Microsoft Hardware Compatibility List (HCL). The HCL lists hardware that Microsoft has tested and approved for use with the Windows 2000 operating system. Along with the list of approved hardware, you need Windows 2000–specific drivers written for the hardware you are using. Checking the HCL for laptop hardware is especially important because of its unique requirements.

You can locate the HCL in two primary areas. The first location is on the Windows 2000 Professional operating system CD-ROM. This file, called HCL.TXT, is located in the Support folder of the root directory of the CD. The HCL.TXT file is broken into sections based on types of hardware.

Some of the hardware components listed on the HCL are as follows:

- Audio adapters
- Disk controllers
- Display adapters—single and multiple monitors
- Display monitors
- Imaging devices—cameras and scanners
- Keyboards
- Modems
- Network cards—Fiber Distributed Data Interface (FDDI), gigabit, token ring
- Pointing devices—mice
- Printers
- Processors—single processor and multiprocessor
- Storage devices—CD-ROM, DVD-ROM, hard drives, tape drives
- Universal Power Supply (UPS)
- Universal Serial Bus (USB) controllers
- Video adapters

This HCL was generated when the CD was generated, meaning it most likely does not contain the most recent list of hardware approved by Microsoft. A better way to check the HCL is to access the Microsoft Web site. This Web site contains the most current hardware components and their drivers that have been tested and approved by Microsoft. The URL for the Microsoft Web site containing the current HCL is **www.microsoft.com/hcl/**.

Tip: If the laptop hardware is not listed on the HCL, it does not mean you will not be able to use it with the Windows 2000 operating system. It means that Microsoft has not received, tested, and approved that hardware. We recommend that you contact the hardware's vendor and ask whether Windows 2000–compatible drivers are available to allow your hardware to function with the Windows 2000 operating system.

After you have verified that all components of your laptop are listed on the HCL, the next step is to be sure you have an understanding of the unique hardware differences between a desktop environment and a laptop environment, and how to manage this unique environment.

Laptop Technology

As mentioned earlier, laptops use some unique technologies that your support personnel must be familiar with in the event they are approached for assistance in installing, configuring, or troubleshooting Windows 2000 Professional.

Because of their size and flexibility, laptops cannot easily support the same bus technologies (Industry Standard Architecture [ISA], Peripheral Component Interconnect [PCI], and Integrated Drive Electronics [IDE]) as your desktop systems. Although some vendor-specific implementations of these desktop bus technologies are available on laptops, expansion is still limited because of the size of laptops. Because of this expansion limitation, a unique bus technology for laptops was needed. This need prompted the design of Personal Computer Memory Card International Association (PCMCIA) bus technology.

PCMCIA bus technology was designed specifically for laptop use to allow desktop hardware to function in a laptop environment using PCMCIA devices. For instance, the same Ethernet technology can be used on both a laptop using a PCMCIA network card and a desktop using a PCI network card. Devices that use the PCMCIA bus technology are referred to as *PCMCIA devices*. They may also be referred to as *PC Card devices* or *card devices*. These devices, which are about the size of a credit card, are inserted into PCMCIA slots on your laptop.

The Windows 2000 Professional operating system supports a few types of PC Cards that are replacements for devices that normally connect with PCI or ISA buses. These types of cards include network interface cards (NICs), modems, smart card readers, and hard disk drives. Hot swapping of PC Cards occurs if you are able to insert a PC Card into the computer or remove one without shutting down the laptop. If hot swapping is not supported, you have to shut down the laptop before inserting the new PC Card.

Tip: You must be a member of the Administrators group or logged on as an administrator to perform this task. However, if your system is connected to a network that contains a policy prohibiting you from performing this task, you cannot complete the procedure.

Although you can remove a card without shutting down the laptop, it is highly recommended that you follow these steps before removing a PC Card:

Warning! By following these steps, you can avoid serious problems with the device or computer and also avoid data loss.

1. Access the Add/Remove Hardware Wizard from Control Panel.

2. After you click on Next on the welcome screen, click on Uninstall/Unplug A Device on the second screen, as shown in Figure 8.1. Then, click on Next.

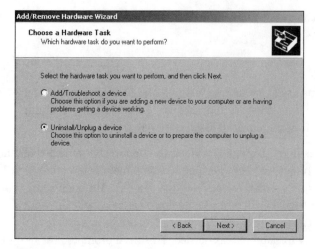

Figure 8.1
The Choose A Hardware Task screen.

3. Click on Unplug/Eject A Device on the third screen, as shown in Figure 8.2. Then, click on Next.

4. Select the PC Card that you want to remove from the Select Device To Unplug screen, as shown in Figure 8.3. If the checkbox labeled Show Related Devices is selected, all devices or subcomponents directly associated with the primary device are listed. These additional components will also be removed when you remove the selected primary device. To continue, click on Next.

   You can also select a listed device and get detailed information, as shown in Figure 8.4, by clicking on the Properties button. You can use this interface to view information about the device, troubleshoot the device, and update the device drivers.

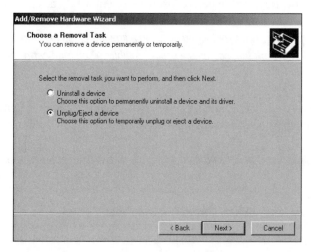

Figure 8.2
The Choose A Removal Task screen.

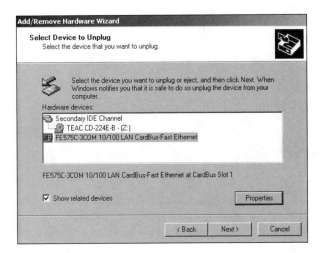

Figure 8.3
The Select Device To Unplug screen.

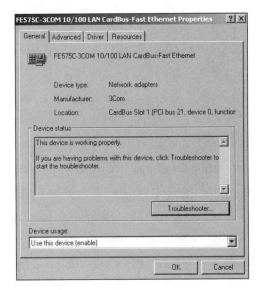

Figure 8.4
PCMCIA device properties information.

5. The next wizard screen asks you to confirm that the device selected is, in fact, the device you want to remove. If it is not the correct device, you can choose the Back button to go to the previous screen and select the correct device. If the correct device is selected, click on Next to stop the device and present the final wizard screen.

Warning! At this point, the device becomes inoperable and will no longer be recognized by the system.

Figure 8.5
Completing the Add/Remove Hardware Wizard.

6. The final screen of the Add/Remove Hardware Wizard, shown in Figure 8.5, informs you that it is now safe to remove the PCMCIA device from the machine. Click on Finish to complete the wizard, and you now can safely remove the card from the PCMCIA slot. You can select the Show Unplug/Eject Icon On The Taskbar checkbox to create an icon on the taskbar of your system. This feature is helpful if you frequently need to remove the device.

Warning! PC Cards can become very hot while in use. Wait a minute or so to allow your card to cool down before removing it from your laptop.

If a PC Card is plug-and-play and you want to add it into a laptop, you can insert the device into the PCMCIA slot. Windows 2000 will detect that new hardware has been added, and you will hear a beep. Windows 2000 will then automatically load the correct drivers for the newly detected PC Card. If a PC Card is not plug-and-play and you want to add it into a laptop, you can use the Add/Remove Hardware Wizard for the installation.

Laptops provide the flexibility to work pretty well anywhere. You can be traveling for business and have a laptop to perform work while flying or while you're stuck in an airport. Laptops can be just as beneficial for personal use. You can draft personal email messages while traveling or use the laptop to make plans, locate addresses, and even print out maps to your destination. However, whenever possible, it is nice to have the flexibility of a laptop and the functionality of a desktop computer. This can be achieved with the use of docking stations.

Docking Stations

Docking stations create a desktop environment using your portable laptop, providing the flexibility of a laptop and the convenience of a desktop computer. Docking stations contain expansion slots, power connections, and connections to peripherals such as a mouse, monitor, full-sized keyboard, and printer. *Docking bays* and *port replicators* are other terms used when referring to docking stations.

Some docking stations support *hot docking*. Hot docking is the ability to dock or undock your laptop with the docking station without shutting down and restarting your system. Similar to hot swapping the PC Cards, when you undock, you should run the Add/Remove Hardware Wizard to notify the Windows 2000 operating system that you are going to undock. This way, you will avoid data loss and any serious problems with the laptop or docking station.

8

Docking

You dock your laptop by sliding the laptop into the docking bay. Windows 2000 will recognize the docking bay peripherals, power connections, and available expansion slots so that your laptop can now be used like a desktop computer.

Undocking

You can undock your laptop in a few ways, depending on the laptop and docking station type. The first and easiest way is to go to the Start menu and click on the Eject PC option. You will see a message saying it is safe to undock your laptop. You can then undock the laptop, or if you have a motorized docking station, your laptop will automatically undock for you.

If the Eject PC option does not appear on the Start menu, using the Add/Remove Hardware Wizard from Control Panel to remove the laptop the first time should add the Eject PC option to the Start menu for future use. If this option still does not appear on the Start menu, your laptop may not support undocking, or you may not have security permissions to undock the laptop. If you still cannot undock the laptop using one of the Start menu options just discussed, review your docking station documentation to determine the location of the eject button on the docking station.

While your computer is docked, it may require a different hardware configuration and need other services running that are not needed when it is not docked. Hardware profiles allow you to easily make this adjustment.

Hardware Profiles

Hardware profiles control the hardware configuration and services available on a computer. When you're using a laptop with a docking station, you will want a certain hardware configuration when docked and another hardware configuration when undocked. You define these different hardware configurations by using hardware profiles.

You create, save, and name the hardware profiles to easily identify which profile to use when booting your system. You will have one profile for times when the laptop is docked and one for times when the laptop is undocked. The hardware profile chosen determines which device drivers to load. The hardware profile configuration information is stored in the computer's Registry, allowing Windows 2000 to attempt to choose the correct hardware profile based on the computer's current configuration.

Similar to a multiple-boot configuration when you have multiple hardware profiles and Windows 2000 cannot determine the correct profile, you will have an opportunity to choose one from those you have created. To access the hardware profiles, you open Control Panel, choose System, and then click on the Hardware tab. This tab contains three areas of configuration, including Hardware Profiles. In Figure 8.6, you can see where the Hardware Profiles option is located on the Hardware tab of the System Properties dialog box. You click on the Hardware Profiles button to open the Hardware Profiles dialog box that contains the existing hardware profiles and allows you to create new ones.

Note: *The creation and management of hardware profiles is discussed in greater detail in Chapter 15.*

When configuring the docked and undocked hardware profiles, highlight the hardware profile you want to configure for docking and select the docking properties. Figure 8.7 shows the Properties dialog box for the docked configuration of a laptop. Notice that the radio button is selected, indicating the laptop is currently in a docking station.

One use of docking stations is to provide power connectivity. When a laptop is connected to the docking station, the battery in the laptop is not used. However, it is important to save battery power when you do not have the laptop docked or plugged into an AC power source.

Advanced Power Management

Managing the use of a laptop's battery power is one of the most critical concerns a laptop owner has when the laptop is undocked or unplugged. You want to be able to reserve as much power as possible for use when you are unable to plug it into an AC power source or access a docking station.

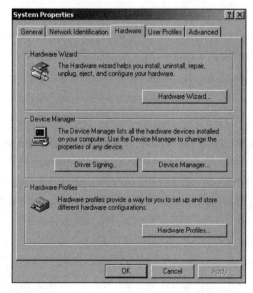

Figure 8.6
The Hardware tab.

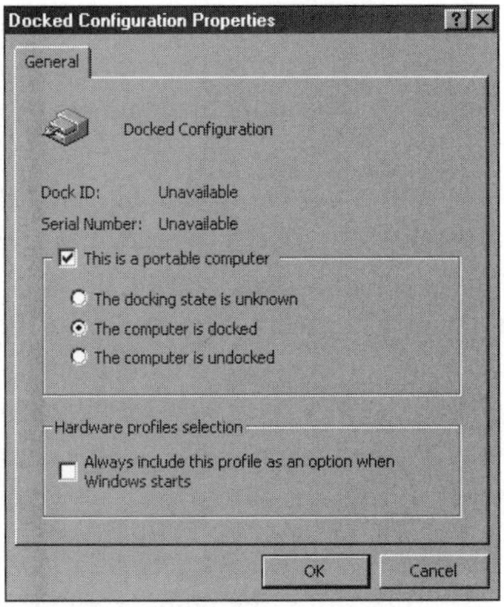

Figure 8.7
Docked laptop hardware profile properties.

Power Management Technologies

Advanced Power Management (APM) and Advanced Configuration and Power Interface (ACPI) are two power management techniques supported by the PC industry to help manage the power of your laptops. Windows operating systems use these technologies to manage the power used by the hardware.

Advanced Power Management

APM is the power management technology used in older operating systems, such as Windows 95, and older Basic Input/Output Systems (BIOS). The basic goal of APM is to enable the system to shut down or disable itself when inactive for a period of time. Unfortunately, the definition of inactivity is vague, and sometimes the system shuts down even though someone is performing a task on the system. For instance, downloading a large file over a slow connection is considered a long-running task. The system often detects this as user inactivity. APM defines inactivity as the lack of use of either the keyboard or mouse and therefore takes an action. The action may be to shut off the monitor, spin down the disk, or put the computer in low-power-use mode, known as Standby. To make matters worse, this alleged inactivity often discontinues the large file transfer. With these limitations of APM, it was deemed necessary to enhance the technology, hence, the introduction of ACPI.

Advanced Configuration and Power Interface

The enhanced power management technology called ACPI was a joint effort between many large corporations, including Toshiba, Microsoft, and Compaq (computer manufacturers), along with Phoenix (BIOS manufacturer) and Intel (processor manufacturer). The ACPI power management technology is integrated throughout the entire system, including software applications, hardware, and the operating system.

ACPI greatly improves the handling of detected inactivity, as well as redefining what the system detects as inactivity. With a fully compliant ACPI system, the shutting down of inactive components is cleaner, and it's possible to have the components power themselves back up when activity requiring those components occurs. Furthermore, you can configure clients to power down after hours (when the system is not being heavily used) or perform scheduled tasks such as running antivirus software after hours. The afterhours tasks are achieved by shutting down the system components during inactivity and then restarting the required components to perform the scheduled execution of the software. This functionality is quite different from APM, which doesn't allow scheduled tasks; it can reactivate components only by the movement of the mouse or keystrokes. ACPI implements the OnNow industry initiative, which allows system manufacturers to build systems that will start when a key is touched on the keyboard.

Remember that some of the support of ACPI and APM is specific to a computer's BIOS. The users cannot choose to implement one or the other. With that point in mind, you must ensure that some of the options in the computer's Complementary Metal Oxide Semiconductor (CMOS) setup program are configured to allow the operating system to control them. This will prevent any conflict between the BIOS settings and the Windows 2000 Professional operating system settings. Each computer's BIOS is different, so be sure to review your computer's documentation for information on whether it supports either ACPI or APM CMOS settings.

In Windows 2000 Professional, the APM/ACPI is automatically determined by the Windows 2000 Setup utility. This utility scans the computer's BIOS to determine whether the APM or ACPI power management scheme is supported. The operating system support for the detected scheme is installed. This scheme detection process occurs each time your system is booted during the execution of NTDETECT.COM. This information is then written in the HKEY_LOCAL_MACHINE\Hardware section of the Registry.

Tip: If you discover hardware-related problems with APM support, you can resolve them by booting into Safe mode and deleting the %Systemroot%\system32\drivers\ntapm.sys file. This step can resolve such problems as system instability when in reduced power mode, inability to shut down correctly, or problems after resuming.

Managing Power Options

Windows 2000 Professional manages both of these power management schemes through the Power Options applet, which you access through Control Panel. Up to five tabs are available for configuration in the Power Options Properties dialog box. Each of the five tabs will be discussed in detail over the next few pages. The settings available on these tabs directly affect the amount of power used, ways to preserve power, low battery notification configuration, and whether you want to use hibernation or standby modes.

Tip: You can also access this same interface by right-clicking on your desktop, choosing Properties, selecting the Screen Saver tab, and clicking on the Power button.

Power Schemes

On the Power Schemes tab, shown in Figure 8.8, you can set the power scheme used by the machine on which Windows 2000 Professional is installed. These settings define when the monitor and hard disks are turned off in an effort to preserve power on the machine when it is not in use. Each theme has two separate configuration settings: one for times when the machine is plugged into an AC power source and the other for times when the machine is running on a battery.

If your machine's manufacturer has designed it to support standby mode, you can also set system standby options to select the elapsed times for the monitor and disk drives before the machine goes into this mode. While on standby, your entire computer switches to a low-power state, therefore using less power. However, when you bring your computer out of standby mode, your desktop environment appears exactly as it was when it went into standby mode.

Warning! *Saving your work before putting your computer in standby mode is highly recommended. While the computer is in this mode, the information in memory is not saved on your hard disk. If you lose power to your system and you have not saved the data, the information in memory is lost.*

If your computer supports hibernation, you will have an additional System Hibernates option for setting the monitor's and hard disk's time options. Hibernation occurs when your computer shuts down to save power, but it first saves everything in memory out to your hard drive. Similar to the Standby option, when you restart your computer to bring it out of hibernation, your desktop environment appears exactly as it did when it went into hibernation.

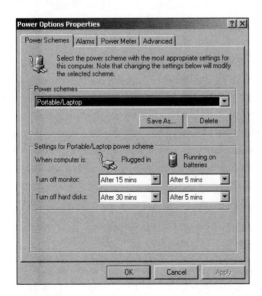

Figure 8.8
Power scheme options.

Table 8.1   Default power schemes.

Scheme Name	Monitor AC Time	Monitor DC Time	Disk AC Time	Disk DC Time
Home/Office Desk	After 20 minutes	After 5 minutes	Never	After 10 minutes
Portable/Laptop	After 15 minutes	After 5 minutes	After 30 minutes	After 5 minutes
Presentation	Never	Never	Never	After 5 minutes
Always On	After 20 minutes	After 15 minutes	Never	After 30 minutes
Minimal Power Management	After 15 minutes	After 5 minutes	Never	After 15 minutes
Max Battery	After 15 minutes	After 1 minute	Never	After 3 minutes

By default, six customizable schemes are created when you install the Windows 2000 Professional operating system. These six themes, listed in Table 8.1, are created with default settings. However, you can customize them from 1 minute to 5 hours using one of the 15 supplied time settings. A 16th setting called Never is the option that prevents the monitor or disks from ever shutting off.

Note: If your computer supports standby mode or hibernation, the six schemes will have additional default settings.

Along with the six default power schemes, you can create your own scheme by configuring the four time settings and clicking on Save As. You are then asked to supply a name for the newly defined scheme containing your configured time settings for your monitor and disks. If you want to delete a power scheme, simply select it and click on the Delete button. After you define your new settings, you can click on the Apply button, leaving you in the Power Options Properties dialog box, or click on OK, which will apply the settings and close the Properties dialog box.

Alarms

You use the Alarms tab, shown in Figure 8.9, to define two levels of battery alarms that notify you when the battery is getting low. The Low Battery Alarm defines when your battery reaches a configured level of available power. The Critical Battery Alarm notifies you that you are at a critical state of battery power and the machine will not be able to continue functioning unless you put in another battery or plug the machine into an AC power source. The Alarms tab of the Power Options Properties dialog box also provides a brief explanation of what actions are going to be taken when these battery power thresholds are reached.

Note: The default alarm settings for Low Battery and Critical Battery are 10 percent and 3 percent, respectively. You can adjust these settings by using the slide bar shown in Figure 8.9.

You define the actions you want to occur when these battery power settings are reached by using the Alarm Action button. The resulting dialog box, shown in Figure 8.10, provides four choices for you to configure when a battery level is reached. You can choose

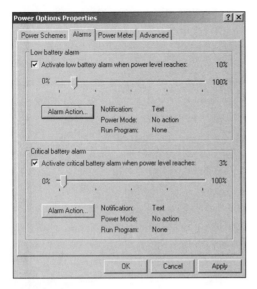

Figure 8.9
Battery alarm settings.

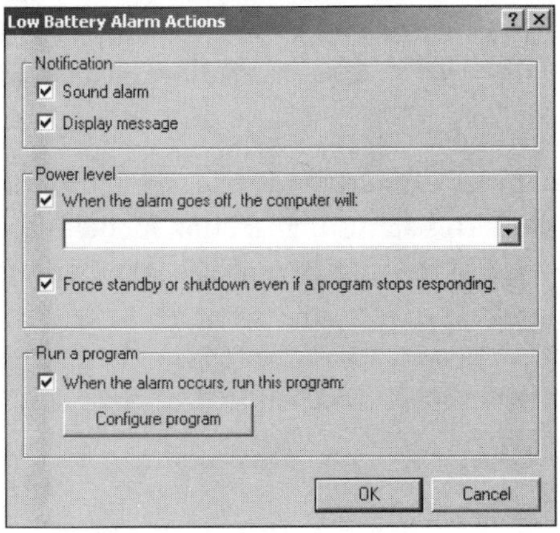

Figure 8.10
Low Battery Alarm Actions.

to be notified using an audio notification or by having a message displayed on your screen; you can have the machine perform a certain task, such as power off; or you can have the machine execute an application you have configured by using the Configure Program button. You can configure any or all of these events to occur when either the Low Battery or Critical Battery thresholds are reached.

Power Meter

You use the Power Meter tab of the Power Options Properties dialog box to review the current power source configuration. You also can use this tab, shown in Figure 8.11, to

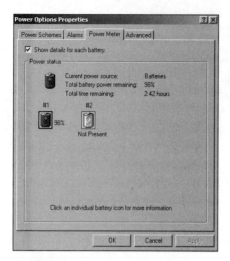

Figure 8.11
The Power Meter tab.

retrieve detailed information about the battery or batteries available in the system. This tab also displays which power source the machine is currently running under—AC power or batteries. If the machine is running on batteries, the Power Meter tab displays the percentage of remaining battery power and the length of time available for the machine to run on battery.

For more detailed information about the batteries installed on your system, you can click on a battery shown on this tab to see its status. This status information includes the name of the battery, its unique ID, the chemistry type of the battery, and also whether it is currently charging or discharging. If you are plugged into an AC power source, the Power Status area will display "On Line, Charging". However, if your laptop is not currently plugged into an AC power source, this area will display "Discharging" because you are using power from the battery.

Advanced

On the Advanced tab, you can configure your laptop's power management behavior. Figure 8.12 displays the options you manage through the Advanced tab. Here, you can define whether you want a power icon on your taskbar; you can use this icon to quickly identify whether you are operating on a battery or an AC power source.

Tip: If your computer supports either hibernation or standby mode, you can select a checkbox that will prompt for the user's password when the computer comes out of either of these modes.

You also define the actions you want the operating system to take when you perform certain operations. For instance, when you close the lid of the portable computer, you can have the computer go into a low-power state, power off the machine, or not perform any operation—simply remain as it was. You can also define what operation you want the

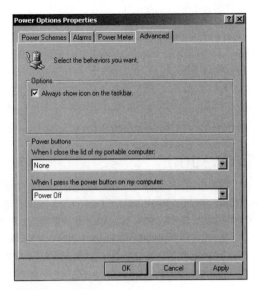

Figure 8.12
Advanced configuration options.

power button to perform when pressed. For instance, you can configure it to go into low-power state or shut off the power to the laptop.

Note: *If your system supports standby and hibernation, these options are available when you are configuring your desired actions.*

Hibernate

Systems that support hibernation will have a Hibernate tab on which you can configure its use of hibernation. On the Hibernate tab, you can choose whether you want the hibernation state enabled on your machine. You check the Enable Hibernate Support checkbox to turn on hibernation. When hibernation is enabled, another set of monitor and hard disk configuration options will be available on your Power Schemes tab.

Note: *You must be logged on as an administrator or a member of the Administrators group to configure your computer for hibernation. However, policy settings may be defined to prevent you from performing these tasks.*

The Hibernate tab also provides general information regarding the amount of hard disk space required to support the hibernation feature. You need to have sufficient disk space available on your boot partition to support the hibernation feature. The contents of memory will be dumped to a file that resides on the boot partition. Your system will require free disk space equal to the amount of RAM you have in your machine. For example, if you have 256MB of RAM, you need at least 256MB of free disk space on your boot partition.

Tip: *To manually put your computer into hibernation, you can select Hibernate when configuring what action you want to occur when you close the lid of your portable computer or when you press the power button.*

One of the great things about mobile computing is the ability to communicate with other computers or peripherals without using cables between the two devices. This wireless communication is accomplished in the Windows 2000 operating system using infrared, commonly called IR, communications. Infrared communications use a light that is beyond red in the color spectrum, preventing the human eye from seeing it. The infrared transmitters and receivers can send and receive these infrared signals. This is the same infrared light used almost universally by VCR and TV remote controls.

Configuring Infrared Communications

The implementation of infrared communications in Windows 2000 is designed according to the Infrared Data Association (IrDA) standards and protocols. The IrDA design standards allow low-cost components and low power requirements, and to enable connections by pointing infrared devices at each other. Nearly all the new laptop computers contain an IrDA port. IrDA transceivers can also be installed on other computers or easily connected to a serial COM port.

Note: *The infrared transceiver is the small red window on your laptop, camera, printer, or other device. Two transceivers must be pointed at each other and should be spaced less than a meter apart.*

The IrDA protocols define the procedures that support the link initialization, device address discovery, device address conflict resolution, connection startup and data rate negotiation, information exchange, disconnection, and link shutdown.

Tip: *For more information regarding IrDA standards and protocols, visit the IrDA Web site at **www.irda.org**.*

Infrared Device Support

The Windows 2000 operating system installs numerous components to support the broad range of wireless devices. Windows 2000 installs the Wireless Link file transfer program, infrared image transfer (IrTran-P), and infrared printing capability (IrLPT). Along with them, IrDA Winsock API support is available for programs created by other equipment and software manufacturers. These manufacturers sell applications that are developed using the Winsock API (or proprietary interfaces) to provide infrared connections to modems, digital pagers, electronic cameras, printers, cellular phones, and hand-held computers.

Windows 2000 Plug and Play architecture automatically detects and installs the component on computers containing the built-in IrDA hardware. For computers that do not contain built-in IrDA hardware, you can use the Add/Remove Hardware Wizard to install a serial IrDa transceiver attached to a serial COM port on your computer.

Tip: *To configure a serial port for infrared communication, enter setup mode for your computer. Under peripheral or serial port configuration, change the mode to IrDA or Infrared.*

Transmission Speeds

Most notebook and laptop computers now ship with IrDA transceiver ports that provide either 115,000 bits per second (bps) or 4Mbps transmission speeds, both of which are supported by Windows 2000.

Windows 2000 supports the Serial IrDA 115Kbps (called IrDA-SIR) standard requiring low-cost components that need no special or proprietary hardware. The most common implementation is a half-duplex system with a maximum data transfer speed of 115,200bps, but can easily adjust to devices using slower transfer speeds. This standard provides short-range infrared asynchronous serial transmission using one start bit, eight data bits, and one stop bit. The great benefit of this standard is that you can use existing serial hardware without incurring any additional costs. It also provides high immunity to "noise" in sunlight or illuminated offices, and it has low error rates.

Windows 2000 also supports Fast IrDA (IrDA-FIR), which is a faster standard that uses 4Mbps half-duplex transmissions. These fast transceivers are usually installed on the newer portable computers and laptops. The IrDA-FIR devices can communicate with the slower IrDA-SIR devices, providing compatibility between numerous infrared devices.

Image Transfer

The IrTran-P standard is also supported in Windows 2000. This standard defines the image exchange protocol used in digital cameras and other digital-imaging devices. You use this feature to transfer your images from a digital camera or any other device that supports IrTran-P to a Windows 2000 computer via an IrDA connection. The Windows 2000 implementation of IrTran-P is a listen-only service; therefore, it cannot initiate an IrTran-P connection.

Printer Support

Windows 2000 also supports the IrLPT standard that defines infrared printer support. The infrared device or infrared transceiver appears as a local port in the Add Printer dialog box. After you associate a printer with this port and print to that printer, Windows 2000 uses the IrLPT protocol to exchange data.

Transferring Files

You use Wireless Link, which is located in Control Panel, to send selected files or an entire folder to another computer running Windows 2000 or Windows 98. To send files to another computer or infrared device, you must first establish an infrared link between the two devices. To establish this link, simply reposition the infrared transceivers until the Wireless Link icon appears on the taskbar and the Wireless Link item appears on the desktop. When you see these items, the wireless devices are in range and are now ready to transfer files.

Tip: *You must use the Wireless Link dialog box, shown in Figure 8.13, to configure the icon to appear on the taskbar. In this dialog box, you also can control other File Transfer options, including images from digital cameras.*

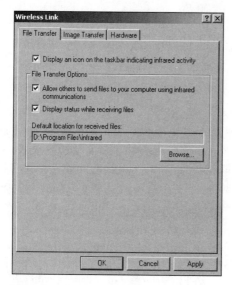

Figure 8.13
Wireless Link options.

Windows 2000 supports an unlimited number of simultaneous connections over an infrared link, allowing more than one program to use the same link. If you use a program other than Wireless Link to transfer files, refer to the program documentation for the procedures to transfer data.

The dialog box shown in Figure 8.14 appears on the computer initiating the link to send files. Use this dialog box to choose the correct files to be transmitted to the other device. After you select the files to be sent, click on Send to begin the transfer. Optionally, you can drag and drop the files to be sent onto the Wireless Link icon located on the desktop.

Figure 8.14
Wireless Link file transfer.

The user of the computer receiving the files will be asked to specify a location for the files being transferred and to verify that he or she accepts the transfer of files to his or her machine. Upon a successful transfer, the user will receive a message notifying him or her the files were transferred successfully.

Infrared Network and Dial-up Connections

The infrared technology provided with Windows 2000 also provides the capability to create a network connection to a remote access server without the use of modems, cables, or network hardware. You therefore can work with Windows Explorer and map to the shared drives on a host computer and the network.

Creating an Infrared Network Connection

Before you can establish a connection to a remote computer using an infrared connection, you have to create the network connection. You do so by using the Network And Dial-up Connection Wizard.

To create an infrared network connection, you must complete the following steps on both computers involved in the infrared network connection. One computer is configured as the host (containing the files you want to access); the other computer is configured as the guest (accessing the files on the host).

1. Open the Start menu, choose Settings, and select Network And Dial-up Connections.

2. Double-click on Make New Connection and then click on Next.

3. Click on Connect Directly To Another Computer and then click on Next.

4. Indicate whether the computer is receiving or sending files by choosing one of the following:

    • To receive dial-up connections, click on Host.

    • To dial out, click on Guest.

5. Click on Next.

6. Under Select A Device, click on Infrared Port and then click on Next.

7. To make the device available to all profiles, click on For All Users and then click on Next. Or, to make the device available only to the current profile, click on Only For Myself and then click on Next.

8. If you specified the computer as a host, select the users allowed to use the connection and then click on Next.

9. Supply a name for the newly created connection and click on Finish.

Tip: To view or modify properties for this connection, right-click on its icon in Network And Dial-up Connections to display the properties.

Using an Infrared Network Connection

After you establish the link for the infrared network connection, you must take the necessary steps to establish a connection to the remote computer. Six easy steps are required to connect to a remote computer using an infrared connection you previously created:

1. Open the Start menu, choose Settings, and select Network And Dial-up Connections.

2. Double-click on the connection you want to use to receive files.

3. In the Status dialog box, click on the Properties button.

4. Verify that the connection information is correct and then click on OK.

5. Click on Close.

6. On the File menu, click on Connect.

You now can remotely connect two computers using a wireless connection. As you can see, after you create the connections on the two computers, establishing the connection between the two computers is very efficient.

Printing Using Infrared Technology

Windows 2000 supports the IrLPT standard, enabling you to install and print to an infrared printer. Similar to the other infrared devices, infrared printers are easy to install, and you do not need to shut down or restart your computer for the printer to be recognized by Windows 2000.

Installing the Infrared Printer

To install the infrared printer, make sure that the infrared-enabled computer and infrared printing device are turned on. Position the two devices so that the infrared windows are in direct line with each other and are no more than 1 meter apart. Shortly after the alignment, the Plug and Play feature of Windows 2000 will recognize the printer, and the printer icon will appear in the status area of your taskbar. Next, the appropriate drivers will automatically be installed on your computer. The printer icon for the infrared printer will be added to your Printers folder and is now ready for use.

Printing to an Infrared Printer

Printing to an infrared printer is similar to printing to any other print device. The only difference between the two is how you establish the connection.

You must first position the IrDA transceivers on the printer and computer to create the infrared link between the two devices. You will know that the link has been achieved when the Wireless Link icon appears on the taskbar. After you establish the link between the two devices, you can print as you normally would.

No matter what technology you use to transfer files, connect to the network, or print a document, the requests to manage these documents while disconnected from the network are increasing constantly. You can manage this demand for file management quite easily in the Windows 2000 operating system by using two primary tools: Briefcase and Offline Files. Before you can choose which tool is best for you, it is important to understand the features and functionality available in both tools.

Briefcase

8

Sometimes you need to manage files or folders stored on your main computer or on a network share. However, you are not always connected to the network or to the main computer when you choose to manage these files. Windows 2000 offers tools for working with these files even while you're disconnected from the network.

Briefcase is not new to Windows 2000. It is available in the Windows 95, 98, and NT operating systems as well. It is the best tool for you to use if you often transfer files between computers using a direct cable connection or removable disk. Briefcase allows you to synchronize the files you modified on another computer with their counterparts on your main computer.

Briefcase Features

Briefcase is the tool of choice if you work on files outside your main computer (for example, on a portable computer). After you finish working on them, you can synchronize the files with their counterparts on your main computer. When you establish a connection from your portable computer to your main computer, or insert a removable disk containing the modified files, Briefcase automatically updates the files on your main computer using the revised files. You do not need to move the modified files out of Briefcase or delete the existing files on your main computer.

Briefcase also stores the files and displays status information regarding modifications made to the files. For instance, Briefcase can show you whether the file is linked to the original file located on your main computer, or whether it does not contain a link to a file on the main computer, often called an *orphan file*. This information assists you in keeping your files organized and also prevents you from accidentally copying over the most recent version of a file or accidentally deleting a file.

Note: When you are using Briefcase to copy files from your main computer to your portable computer, the two computers must be connected either by a direct cable connection or over a network.

In previous Windows operating systems, the tool that provided this file synchronization was called My Briefcase. In Windows 2000, My Briefcase is simply called Briefcase. Also, in Windows 2000, Briefcase is no longer located on the desktop as it was in previous versions.

Creating a Briefcase

To utilize the functionality Briefcase provides, you have to create an instance of Briefcase. You can organize your files by creating multiple Briefcases. You create a new Briefcase by following these steps:

1. Right-click on My Computer on your desktop and then click on Explore.

2. Click on the folder in which you want to create the new Briefcase.

3. On the File menu, click on New and then click on Briefcase.

Note: To create a new Briefcase on your desktop, right-click anywhere on the desktop, select New, and then click on Briefcase.

After you create a new Briefcase, you can drag and drop the files and folders you want to manage into the Briefcase. The files and folders contained inside Briefcase can be modified even when the computer is not connected to the network. However, as changes are made to either the files located on the server or the files located in Briefcase, you have to perform a manual synchronization to merge the changes.

Synchronizing Your Briefcase

In most situations, the logic used to merge changes made to files and folders is fairly simple. If a file is modified in one location but not in another, the entire modified file is copied to the other location. (Modifications are based on the file's timestamp and size.) A problem occurs if changes are made to both files since the last synchronization took place because Briefcase cannot determine which copy is most current. However, there are a few exceptions to this rule when you're using Microsoft Excel and Access files because they can merge cell and field-level changes made to both documents. As you can see, files that are shared with multiple users and that contain multiple changes cannot be easily resolved.

Figure 8.15 shows a Briefcase called Word Documents that contains two documents. New Microsoft Word Document.doc is up to date with the file on the server. However, Revised Microsoft Word Document.doc is currently not synchronized with the file on the server and needs updating. You perform this update by right-clicking on the document and then clicking on Update. Alternatively, you can select the document, open the File menu, and click on Update. You then see a dialog box providing the location, file name, timestamp, and status (modified or unmodified) of the two files. You can right-click on one of the files and choose which file should be replaced.

Tip: You can update all files on the server using the files located in the Briefcase by clicking on the Update All option on the Briefcase menu.

Briefcase synchronization can also occur with files stored on a removable disk. Follow these steps to synchronize removable media:

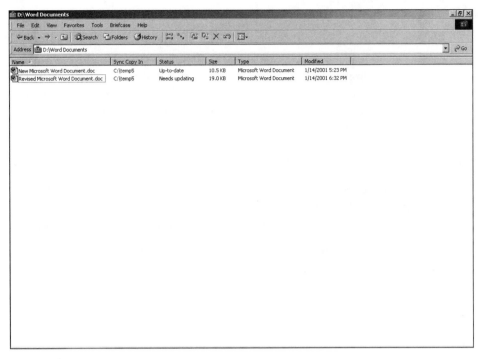

Figure 8.15
Briefcase status screen.

1. Insert the removable medium into a disk drive on your main computer.

2. Open Briefcase and copy the appropriate files to it.

3. Drag Briefcase to the disk drive of your main computer, located in Windows Explorer or My Computer, to copy the files in Briefcase to the disk.

4. Remove the disk from your main computer and insert it into a disk drive on your portable computer.

5. Open Briefcase from the disk and make any changes you want. When you are ready to synchronize the files, remove the disk from your portable computer and reinsert it into a disk drive on your main computer.

6. Open Briefcase from the disk and perform one of the following:

   • To update some of the files, select the files you want to update, open the Briefcase menu, and then click on Update Selection.

   • To update all the files, open the Briefcase menu and click on Update All.

After you synchronize files, they are maintained as one, and you control how often they are synchronized and which file replaces another. However, sometimes you might want to separate files stored in Briefcase from the copy located outside Briefcase. The separation of the two files is called a *split*.

To perform a split, open Briefcase and select the file you want to split. On the Briefcase menu, click on Split From Original to create an orphan file that can no longer be synchronized.

Briefcase is still available on Windows 2000 operating systems. However, as you can see, it does have a few limitations. You have to perform a manual synchronization, you may encounter problems if multiple users are modifying the files, and you have to keep track of the exact server location of the files. All these limitations are resolved in the Offline Files feature of Windows 2000.

Offline Files

Offline Files is the best tool for you to use if you want to work with shared files on a network. Using Offline Files, you can make changes to shared files while you are disconnected from the network and then synchronize them the next time you connect to the network.

Offline Files still allows users to maintain local copies of files stored on a central server, but it is designed to eliminate the need for the users to keep track of whether they are accessing the local or remote copy of the file. You are no longer limited to managing just files and folders. You can also manage mapped network drives and Web pages while working offline. Furthermore, you can synchronize the files manually or have synchronization occur automatically.

A great feature of Offline Files is that you maintain the same view of shared network items that have been made available offline, regardless of whether you are connected or disconnected from the network. When disconnected from the network, you can continue to work with these files just as though you are connected to the network. You also maintain the same access permissions to the files and folders as you do while connected to the network. This is helpful when you either knowingly disconnect or unexpectedly get disconnected from the network. The neat thing is that an Offline Files icon appears in the status area on the right side of your taskbar, along with an informational balloon, whenever your network connection changes.

When you reconnect to the network or dock your portable computer, any changes that you made while working offline are updated to the network. If multiple users make changes to the same file, you have the option of saving your version of the file, keeping the other version, or saving both versions.

You can configure synchronization to occur automatically using the Synchronization Manager, or you can initiate it manually. The Synchronization Manager also controls the type of synchronization that occurs: full or quick. The full synchronization ensures that you have the most current version of all network files that are available offline. The quick synchronization occurs much faster but may not provide the most current version of the available offline files. However, the quick version still ensures you have access to every offline file available, so you can continue working.

Many configuration options are available for Offline Files in Windows 2000, and you need a thorough understanding of these options so that you can create a stable and secure computing environment.

Implementing Offline Files

You frequently perform four tasks when implementing Offline Files. You do so to configure both the server and client machines involved in using Offline Files in Windows 2000. These four tasks include configuring your computer to use Offline Files, making the files and folders available for offline use, configuring how Offline Files respond to a network disconnection, and configuring Offline Files for mobile users.

Enabling Offline Files

The first step to implementing Offline Files requires that you configure your computer to allow files or folders to be made available offline. By default, Windows 2000 Professional machines are configured for Offline Files, but Windows 2000 Server machines are not. You can modify the configuration by following these steps:

1. Double-click on My Computer on your desktop to open it.

2. Click on Folder Options on the Tools menu.

3. Click on the Offline Files tab.

4. Enable Offline Files by selecting the Enable Offline Files checkbox.

5. Select Synchronize All Offline Files Before Logging Off.

After you complete these steps, Offline Files are enabled and a full synchronization occurs before you log off. For a quick synchronization to occur, deselect the checkbox in Step 5. The Offline Files tab shown in Figure 8.16 is from a computer configured to allow Offline Files and use full synchronization.

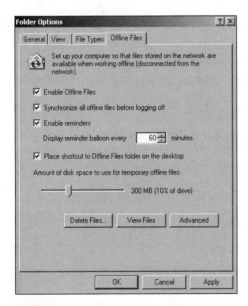

Figure 8.16
Enabling Offline Files.

Defining Offline Files and Folders

The second step is to choose which files and folders you want your users to be able to use while offline. You do so by clicking on the shared network file or folder that you want to make available offline. You then select the Make Available Offline option from the File menu in My Computer or Windows Explorer. To remove the file from offline use, you click on Make Available Offline again to remove the checkmark.

Tip: The Make Available Offline option will appear only if you have enabled Offline Files on your computer.

You can make an entire shared network folder or individual files available for use offline. If an entire folder is made available offline, any files placed in that shared folder will automatically be made available offline the next time your computers are synchronized.

Note: The first time you make an item available offline, the Offline Files Wizard guides you through the process. After the Synchronizing dialog box disappears, the item is available offline.

Responding to Network Disconnections

You have taken the two steps required to make Offline Files available for use when a user is disconnected from the network. Your third task is to configure how your computer responds to a network disconnection. By default, your computer is configured to notify you and begin working offline. You can modify this configuration by using the Advanced button on the Offline Files tab. You can choose Never Allow My Computer To Go Offline, which prevents network files from being available to you if you lose your connection to a specific computer or the entire network.

Warning! When the Never Allow My Computer To Go Offline option is selected, the behavior of your computer depends on the file type you are using when you are disconnected from the network. For instance, an application that accesses a temporary directory on the server will no longer be able to access that temporary directory to perform the tasks it was designed to perform. This will cause the application to stop responding on the local machine.

You can create different behavior for specific computers by using the Add button on the Advanced Settings dialog box. For instance, if you are disconnected from a particular server, you may want to continue working offline; however, for all other network disconnects, you don't want to access the offline files. Figure 8.17 shows the Advanced Settings dialog box configured to never allow a computer to go offline as the default, with the exception of SERVER1. If you lose the connection to SERVER1, you can continue working offline.

Configuring Offline Files for Mobile Users

The fourth task is configuring Offline Files for mobile users. Offline Files provides a way for mobile users to ensure they have the most current versions of the network files before they disconnect from the network. You can also ensure that any changes made while offline will be synchronized with the network when you reconnect.

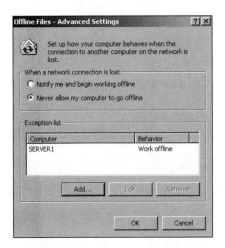

Figure 8.17
The Offline Files - Advanced Settings dialog box.

As a mobile computer user, you should use the following procedures, in this order, to ensure you work with the most current version of your network Offline Files:

1. Make the files and folders you want to work with offline available for use offline.

2. Use the Synchronization Manager to ensure you synchronize your Offline Files when you log on or off.

3. Undock your portable computer.

4. You will be able to browse network drives and shared folders in My Network Places or My Computer. However, you will see only the files made available offline and any files you have created since you were disconnected from the network.

Note: *A red X appears over the names of any disconnected network drives.*

5. When you are finished working offline and dock your portable computer again, you will be required to synchronize your files again. The changes you made to your files while you were offline will also be made to the network files.

When synchronizing your files with the network files, you may encounter file conflicts. These conflicts occur if someone else has made changes to the same network file that you updated while offline. When file conflicts arise, you are given a choice of keeping your version of the file, keeping the version on the network, or keeping both versions. To save both versions, you will have to supply a different file name for your version, and both files will appear in both locations.

If you delete the file on your machine while working offline but someone else modifies the network file, the file is deleted from your machine, but the network file will remain on the network. If you make changes to a file while offline and someone else deletes the network file, you can choose to save your version to the network or delete the file from your computer. If you are working offline and someone adds a new file to the shared network folder that you have made available offline, the new file will be added to your computer when you reconnect and synchronize.

After you perform the four common tasks when using Offline Files, the next step is to understand how the Offline Files are cached on the clients' computers, providing them the opportunity to manage the files. You configure the caching options through the Properties dialog box of the files and folders that are enabled for Offline Files management.

Offline Files Caching

When you make shared network files available offline, Offline Files stores a version of the files in a reserved portion of your disk space called the *cache*. The default cache size is 10 percent of your available drive space, although you can modify this setting using the Offline Files tab of Folder Options. Your computer accesses this cache regardless of whether it is connected to the network. You have three configuration options available when managing the caching of Offline Files in Windows 2000: manual caching for documents, automatic caching for documents, and automatic caching for programs.

Tip: By default, your cached Offline Files are stored in the root directory of your hard drive. However, you can modify this location by using the Offline Files Cache Mover (cachemov.exe) available in the Windows 2000 Professional Resource Kit.

Manual Caching For Documents

You use the Manual Caching For Documents option to cache only those files you specifically or manually identify for caching. You can use this option for shared network resources containing files that are accessed and modified by many people. This is the default caching option when you first configure a shared file for Offline Files use.

Automatic Caching For Documents

You use the Automatic Caching For Documents option to cache (for offline use) every file you open while connected to the shared folder. However, this does not make every file in the folder available for offline use—only the files you specifically opened are available. The unopened files in the folder are not available for use while you are disconnected from the shared folder.

Automatic Caching For Programs

You use the Automatic Caching For Programs option to provide offline access to shared folders containing files that are not to be modified. This caching option is great for making files available for referencing, executing, or reading while preventing modifications to the files. This option optimizes network performance by reducing network traffic that would normally be generated if the application were executed over the network. It also improves performance for the user because the application is stored locally.

Note: When you use Automatic Caching For Programs, ensure that the files contained in the shared folder have read-only access permissions.

Some of the Offline Files stored in the cache can be modified. The modified files need to be synchronized with the files located on the network share. Synchronization can occur manually or automatically using the Synchronization Manager.

Synchronization Manager

Synchronization ensures you have the latest information available on your network or from the Internet, while minimizing the disruption to your work on the system. The Synchronization Manager provides several configuration options when synchronization of **8** your files occurs:

- Every time you log on or off your computer or both.

- At scheduled times.

- At specific intervals while your computer is idle. By default, the computer has to be idle for 15 minutes if this option is chosen.

Note: You can use a combination of these options as well as specify different options for offline files from different shared resources.

The Synchronization Manager compares the items you opened or updated while working offline to those located on the network and makes the most current items available to both the network and your computer. Along with the capability to synchronize entire folders and individual files, you can also synchronize offline Web pages. Regardless of the type of file or program used to make the file available offline, the Synchronization Manager provides a single location where you can go to synchronize and share files that have been made available offline.

Follow these steps to manually synchronize individual files, folders, or Web pages in My Computer, Windows Explorer, or Internet Explorer:

1. Open the Synchronization Manager by choosing the Synchronize option on the Tools menu of your utility. The dialog box shown in Figure 8.18 then appears.

2. Select the checkboxes next to the offline items that you want to synchronize.

Tip: For detailed information about an item displayed, select the item and click on the Properties button.

3. Click on the Synchronize button to immediately begin synchronization.

Automatic Synchronization During Logon or Logoff

You configure the Synchronization Manager to synchronize offline items when you log on or off a computer through the Logon/Logoff tab of the Synchronization Settings dialog box, as shown in Figure 8.19, by following these steps:

1. Open the Synchronization Manager.

2. Click on the Setup button located on the bottom of the Items To Synchronize dialog box.

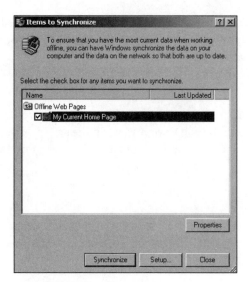

Figure 8.18
The Items To Synchronize dialog box.

3. Click on the Logon/Logoff tab, shown in Figure 8.19.

4. In the When I Am Using This Network Connection list, click on the network connection you want to configure.

5. In the Synchronize The Following Checked Items list, select the checkboxes of the items that you want to synchronize.

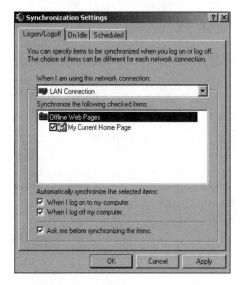

Figure 8.19
Configuring Logon/Logoff synchronization.

6. Under Automatically Synchronize The Selected Items, select either When I Log On To My Computer or When I Log Off My Computer, or you can select both.

7. If you want the Synchronization Manager to prompt you before automatically synchronizing, select the Ask Me Before Synchronizing The Items checkbox.

Automatic Synchronization During Idle Time

You configure the Synchronization Manager to synchronize offline items while your computer is idle through the On Idle tab of the Synchronization Settings dialog box, as shown in Figure 8.20, by following these steps:

1. Open the Synchronization Manager.

2. Click on the Setup button located on the bottom of the Items To Synchronize dialog box.

3. Click on the On Idle tab, shown in Figure 8.20.

4. In the When I Am Using This Network Connection list, click on the network connection you want to configure.

5. In the Synchronize The Following Checked Items list, select the checkboxes of the items that you want to synchronize.

6. Select the Synchronize The Selected Items While My Computer Is Idle checkbox.

You use the Advanced button on the On Idle tab to configure the idle settings shown in Figure 8.21. Here, you specify the number of minutes the computer is idle before an automatic synchronization occurs. The default for this setting is 15 minutes; however,

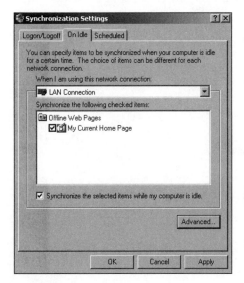

Figure 8.20
Configuring synchronization for an idle computer.

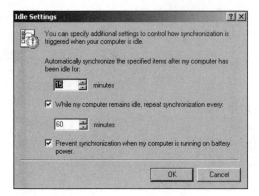

Figure 8.21
Configuring idle settings.

you can adjust it from 1 minute to 999 minutes. You also specify how often you want the synchronization to occur while your computer is idle. The default for this setting is 60 minutes, but you can set it from 1 to 999 minutes. You use the third option in the Idle Settings dialog box to prevent synchronization from occurring while the computer is running on battery power.

Scheduling Automatic Synchronization

You use the Scheduled tab of the Synchronization Settings dialog box, shown in Figure 8.22, to manage a customized schedule for synchronization. When you click on the Add button, the Scheduled Synchronization Wizard begins, allowing you to select the items you want to synchronize. It continues, providing the required dialog boxes to generate a customized schedule for automatically synchronizing the items you selected.

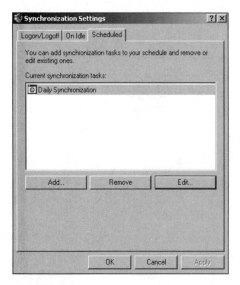

Figure 8.22
Modifying a scheduled task.

To modify a scheduled task, highlight the task and click on the Edit button. This presents a dialog box that allows you to modify the name, schedule, items, and other general settings associated with the task. You also have the option of configuring the computer to automatically connect to the network if it is not connected when the job is scheduled to start.

Summary

Mobile computing is quickly becoming more prevalent in organizations today. Being able to manage laptops in a dynamic environment requires that you understand the unique hardware requirements and technology used by mobile computers.

Windows 2000 provides numerous features to manage your mobile computing environment. Your ability to configure laptops to utilize infrared technology, defined in the IrDA standards and protocols, as well as being familiar with the power management options, provide you with the skills required to properly manage your mobile computing environment. Furthermore, the use of Briefcase and Offline Files provides flexibility for your users and increases their productivity.

You will need to be familiar with installing and troubleshooting the numerous peripheral devices in Windows 2000 Professional. Plug and Play certainly reduces the number of hardware conflicts in Windows 2000. However, many devices that are compatible with Windows 2000 Professional run on both desktop computers and laptops. It is imperative that you understand the peripherals and implement a strategy to assist you when resolving problems. Chapter 9 provides you the knowledge required to install, configure, and maintain peripherals in Windows 2000 Professional.

Chapter 9

Hardware Installation and Troubleshooting

Installing Hardware and Troubleshooting

In an ideal world, you might go down to the corner store, pick out a computer, set it up on a desk, and never need to open up the case. Reality dictates otherwise. Maintaining a network of computers often requires frequent upgrades, configuration changes, and troubleshooting. From installation and configuration to troubleshooting, it is vital to have an excellent grasp of the various peripherals and hardware you will encounter.

The variety of hardware we work with continues to grow. Although CD-ROM drives have been a standard PC peripheral for several years, DVD drives are also gaining popularity. Hard drive capacity is ever increasing, and Windows 2000 is right in step by providing support for the larger sizes. Windows 2000 provides better support for removable media drives and tape devices. If you use Windows 98 to take advantage of its support for multiple monitors, you'll be happy to know that Windows 2000 supports up to 10 monitors connected to one PC! If you're a gaming enthusiast, you will be delighted now that you can install high-end video cards and finally play the latest gaming software because Windows 2000 provides more support for these cards in addition to support for the latest DirectX versions. Of course, you'll still find support for devices such as printers and scanners, but you can now connect all types of USB devices to your Windows 2000 PC as well. Wireless devices, IrDA devices, network adapters, and multiple processors—a wide variety of hardware is out there, and Windows 2000 has finally caught up with the industry by vastly improving its hardware support.

Let's begin by looking at how Windows 2000 handles hardware. This chapter provides you with an overview of the resource management tools provided with Windows 2000: Device Manager and System Information. We will complete our look at hardware in Windows 2000 by discussing the installation and configuration of various devices.

Managing Hardware in Windows 2000

Managing your hardware in Windows 2000 is a vital task. Your computer and your business rely on dependable and consistent performance from the various components of the computer. It is wise to upgrade hardware components when your computer's performance no longer meets your requirements or as new technology evolves and becomes more economically feasible.

Win32 Driver Model

It is difficult to talk about hardware without including a discussion of drivers. A large part of keeping your hardware working properly includes using the latest drivers. These drivers often add new features or enhance the performance of your equipment. Microsoft drastically changed its driver design in Windows 98 and Windows 2000, using the Win32 Driver Model (WDM). WDM drivers handle installation and device detection differently. Older Windows NT 4 drivers did not support Plug and Play, for instance, whereas WDM drivers do. You can use older Windows NT 4 drivers on Windows 2000 in most instances; however, you will miss out on the new features and capabilities delivered in the WDM format.

The architecture of WDM drivers includes a layered approach to device drivers. Just as the Hardware Abstraction Layer (HAL) of Windows NT 4 helps stabilize the operating system by preventing direct hardware access, WDM drivers also provide an extra measure of stability. Hardware developers can now write a smaller piece of code, called a *minidriver*. Many of the functions previously provided by drivers are now a part of Windows 2000 itself. This change has greatly simplified driver writing and allowed for the creation of the minidriver.

Microsoft provides *device class drivers*, which work with the device minidriver. The minidriver is written for a specific piece of hardware, most often by the hardware manufacturer. Along with the device class driver is the *bus class driver*, which works with the bus minidriver to communicate with the HAL. The following class and bus drivers are built into Windows 2000:

• Power Management

• USB

• Digital audio

• Imaging

• Human Interface Device

• IEEE 1394 (also known as FireWire or i.LINK)

• DVD

A Windows 2000 driver for a USB mouse would include a device minidriver for interaction with the Human Interface Device class and also a bus class minidriver for the USB class. Although writing two drivers might seem more difficult, the device driver writer no longer needs to write cumbersome code for resource management and communication.

Hardware

WDM technology directly supports a wide variety of hardware. The supported hardware can be divided into these broad categories:

- AGP (Accelerated Graphics Port)
- Digital audio
- DVD
- Human Interface Device
- Still image capture
- Multiple display support
- Video capture

AGP technology has been a great boon for video card manufacturers. It provides improved performance beyond the limitations of Peripheral Component Interconnect (PCI). By using AGP video cards, the end user has greater bandwidth for communication—up to four times that of a PCI card. Less PCI bus congestion occurs, which improves the performance of other peripherals on the PCI bus, as well as boosting the performance of the video card.

The digital audio initiative in Windows 2000 is designed to improve overall performance of sound. A system with digital audio can use an external digital bus to transfer audio; this allows a simple design for high-fidelity solutions and the possibility of Plug-and-Play audio modules. USB speakers, for instance, can theoretically give the PC much more information regarding their status. If the speakers are not on, preventing sound from being heard, your PC can be aware of the cause. It could also synchronize movements of the speakers' volume dial with your PC's Volume Control slidebar.

The Human Interface Device encompasses all methods for entering information into the computer. This includes everything from mice and keyboards to game controllers and all their variations. Many of these devices are readily available in USB versions, and the number is likely to continue rising steadily.

Windows 2000 provides support for multiple monitors. This great new feature can improve productivity. It enables you to connect additional monitors to your workstation so that you can stretch your desktop and windows across several monitors, increasing the number of applications you can view at any given time.

System Bus

When we discuss the system buses, we refer mainly to four different systems:

- PCI bus
- CardBus

- IEEE 1394 (also known as FireWire or i.LINK)

- USB bus

These four systems provide specific functions for PC users. The PCI bus is perhaps the most common. As a standard to replace the legacy ISA bus, it vastly improved the transfer rate of information for high-speed devices. Network cards, modems, SCSI cards, and other PCI cards all perform better in a PCI model than in an ISA version.

The CardBus standard provides hardware support for laptop users. CardBus supports add-in cards, much as the PCMCIA standard did, but it provides better performance and greater support for the Plug-and-Play standard.

The IEEE 1394 bus, or FireWire, is a multipurpose standard that supports all sorts of devices. Theoretically, you can support up to 64,000 devices off a FireWire port. Common FireWire devices include digital video cameras, still cameras, scanners, printers, and removable media drives.

USB is another new technology that provides support for multiple devices connected to the computer through a single port. Although it supports a similar array of hardware, the technology is significantly different. Its maximum limitation for connected devices is 127. This number is much smaller than FireWire; however, it's hard to envision any PC with even this many connected peripherals.

Microsoft has committed to providing support for these important technologies from the ground up. This is an important achievement for Microsoft because it allows the end users maximum flexibility in purchasing hardware to meet their computing needs. Windows 2000 is definitely more technology friendly than Windows NT 4, both in its hardware support and in the efforts Microsoft has made with WDM technology. With all the hardware that Windows 2000 can support, Microsoft has provided an excellent set of tools to manage hardware. Utilities such as Device Manager and System Information provide a wealth of information regarding installed devices. The Add/Remove Hardware Wizard also makes adding new hardware a simple and straightforward matter.

Introducing Device Manager

Device Manager is one of the Microsoft Management Console (MMC) snap-ins. Go to Start|Settings|Control Panel, double-click on Administrative Tools, and then double-click on Computer Management. You'll find Device Manager under the System Tools node. The layout of Device Manager is much more user-friendly in Windows 2000 than it was in Windows NT 4 (see Figure 9.1). In NT 4 you had to use Windows NT Diagnostics, which was useful but limited compared to the familiar Device Manager found in Windows 95. Microsoft wisely adopted the familiar Device Manager layout for Windows 2000. Device Manager lists the installed hardware on your computer. You also can manage and trouble-shoot hardware here, as well as manage devices in hardware profiles and device drivers.

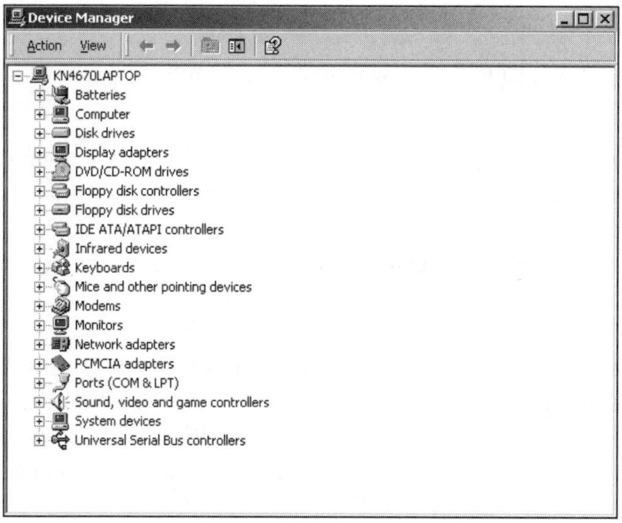

Figure 9.1
Windows 2000 Device Manager.

As a graphical depiction of your hardware, Device Manager allows you to quickly ascertain the status of installed devices. Any device that is not installed and functioning properly will display a visual indicator.

Tip: To install, uninstall, or configure devices, you must be logged in with an administrative account.

You can access Device Manager in several ways:

- Right-click on My Computer, choose Manage, and select Device Manager in the console tree of Computer Management.

- Select Start|Settings|Control Panel|System. From the Hardware tab of System Properties, click on the Device Manager button.

- From a command prompt, type "devmgmt.msc".

Viewing Your System Configuration

After you install Windows 2000, it's an excellent idea to look at Device Manager. Looking at this utility gives you an opportunity to examine your installed devices to make sure everything on your system was properly detected and configured. Device Manager shows you a list of device classes, such as Batteries, Disk Drives, and Display Adapters. Beneath each class, you can find any devices in that category installed on your system. By default, Device Manager hides all devices that are not Plug and Play, as well as devices that have installed drivers but are not currently attached to the system. Unidentified devices are also hidden. Follow these steps to display the hidden devices:

1. Open Device Manager.

2. Click on View.

3. Select Show Hidden Devices. Your display will immediately refresh to show the new devices.

Device Manager's initial window will quickly inform you of any devices that are not functioning properly on your system. Device Manager uses the familiar outline view, with expandable and collapsible entries. By default, all categories will be collapsed; however, any problematic devices are listed with a warning icon indicating a fault condition with the device. The branches of these devices will be expanded.

Tip: You will typically see one of three icons when viewing the status of a device in Device Manager. A normal icon indicates the device is working properly. You may also see an exclamation point over the device icon, indicating that the device is configured incorrectly or its drivers are not installed. A red "X" indicates that the device is disabled due to hardware conflicts. You will need to find available resources for the device and set it to use them manually.

As an example, in Figure 9.2 the V.90 Internal Modem is not working properly, as denoted by the X over the modem icon.

Setting View Options

Quickly organizing the information in Device Manager in different viewing formats can be useful. Device Manager offers four different view options, which allow you to see your information categorized in four different ways:

- Devices By Type

- Devices By Connection

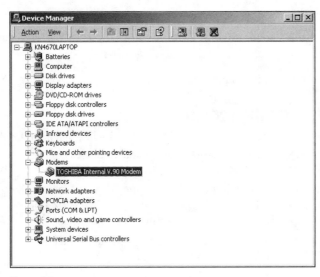

Figure 9.2
Device Manager shows any items not functioning properly.

- Resources By Type

- Resources By Connection

These view options can quickly help you determine available resources or problematic devices. For instance, if you need to see which devices are using a specific IRQ, you might want to change your view setting to Resources By Connection or Resources By Type.

Printing in Device Manager

One of the most important jobs any administrator performs is documenting. A hard copy of important information is always useful at some point. For this reason and many more, keeping a hard copy of the devices on your Windows 2000 Professional computer can be a wise move. And luckily, Microsoft has made printing this information relatively easy. In Device Manager, a Print option is available from the drop-down View menu. Selecting this option will bring up the dialog box shown in Figure 9.3.

From the Print dialog box, you can select one of three report types:

- System Summary

- Selected Class Or Device

- All Devices And System Summary

If you are printing this information for your records, the last option will provide you with the most comprehensive information and is the best choice. You can create a file by selecting the Print To File option, which will create a file on your hard drive with your device information. In other instances, it is advantageous just to select the device you need information on.

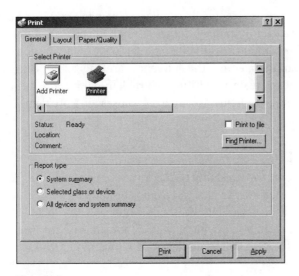

Figure 9.3
Using the Print dialog box in Device Manager, you can print information regarding your system's hardware.

System Summary is perhaps a misleading name. It actually provides a great deal of information in a single location. System Summary includes the following information:

- Windows version, service pack number, and build number

- Registered owner and registered organization

- Computer name

- Machine type

- System BIOS name, date, and version

- Processor type and number of processors

- Amount of memory installed

- Installed drives and their capacities

- IRQ, DMA, and memory usage summary

- Resource summary

Selecting a specific device displays the device's resource usage and related driver files, including their size and location. The All Devices And System Summary option gives you a combination of the first two options.

Tip: If you do not have a Generic/Text Only printer installed on your PC, now is a great time to install one. If you select Print To File, the information in the file is formatted for the selected printer. Selecting the Generic/ Text Only option creates plain text output that is easy to read. You can add this printer by choosing Add Printer from the Printers folder and installing the Generic/Text Only printer.

If all the computers in your network are identically configured, you do not need to print a separate complete summary for each PC. In this instance, a single report usually suffices for documentation purposes. For computers with different hardware configurations, print a complete summary for each variation, even if the differences are only slight. One single difference, such as a video card, can create a multitude of problems with some software. Excellent documentation will assist you in identifying likely causes for a problem when you begin troubleshooting.

Determining Device Status

A great feature of Device Manager is the capability to check the status of a device. Earlier we mentioned Device Manager's capability to give you a quick visual indication of a device's status. To receive more detail regarding the item's status, you can double-click on the listing in Device Manager. You can also highlight a device and click on the Properties button. The Properties page for the item will be displayed, as shown in Figure 9.4.

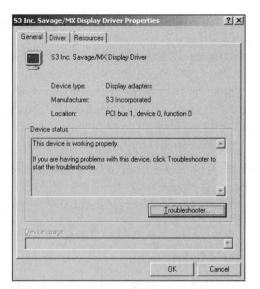

Figure 9.4
The Properties page for the display adapter shows the device is working properly.

The Properties page indicates the device type, manufacturer, and location as well as its status. If the device is disabled or if the driver was unable to load, those issues will be indicated here as well. You can also see a Driver tab.

This Properties page tab gives you the option to see detailed driver information, such as the name and path to the device's drivers, as shown in Figure 9.5. You also can uninstall or update the driver via the appropriate buttons. The driver provider, date, version, and digital signer are also indicated on this Properties page.

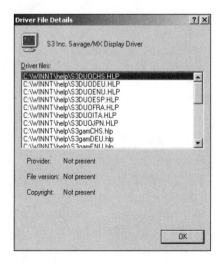

Figure 9.5
Clicking on the Driver Details button on the Driver tab gives you in-depth driver information.

Both the Driver and Resources tabs are excellent for in-depth troubleshooting as well. Whereas the Driver tab can help you track down out-of-date and incompatible drivers that may be causing problems, the Resources tab assists you in nailing down those troublesome hardware resource conflicts. On the Resources tab, as shown in Figure 9.6, the resources in use by the device as well as resource conflicts are displayed. You also have the option here to manually set resources for devices. This capability is particularly useful for non–Plug-and-Play devices. By using the Conflicting Device List, you can find the hardware that is using resources that the currently viewed device is trying to use as well.

You may find other tabs displayed on a device's Properties page as well. The additional tabs provide access to device-specific settings. If you are troubleshooting, check all these tabs so that you have the maximum amount of information to assist you in configuring and troubleshooting a device.

Modifying Configuration Parameters

Changing the settings of a device in Device Manager requires administrative privileges on the computer. If you are troubleshooting hardware, log on with administrative privileges so that you have maximum access to the information you require to resolve the issue. By using Device Manager, you can update and reinstall drivers, modify resource use, and disable and enable devices.

Working with Device Drivers

Often, you can resolve problems with hardware by updating the drivers. Typically, in these scenarios, your hardware is working fine and your computer is working fine, but the two

Figure 9.6
The Resources tab displays the resources in use by the selected device, as well as resource conflicts.

simply won't work together properly. You might be able to resolve this problem by updating the driver. Due to the inexhaustible combination of hardware that users have installed, it is virtually impossible to guarantee a driver will work flawlessly on every system. Manufacturers typically do a great job of making sure their drivers work with most installations and strive to resolve the problems encountered when drivers are released to the public. Because of these efforts, newer drivers than those shipping on the Windows 2000 CD or provided with your hardware are usually available. Newer drivers can resolve problems, as well as provide new features and even improve performance.

New drivers can be obtained from several sources. Your Microsoft-endorsed first stop should be the Windows Update site. You can access it by clicking on Start|Windows Update. This procedure takes you to Microsoft's Web site, which has the latest Microsoft-approved drivers, as well as security updates and patches, compatibility updates, Internet Explorer updates, and more. For the latest drivers, this site should be your first stop. You should also make regular visits here for all the other features it provides. Installation methods may vary, but often Windows Update will install the necessary files in the appropriate location on your PC.

When Windows Update does not have the driver you need, your next stop should be the manufacturer's Web site. PC manufacturers test drivers for the hardware bundled with their systems. If you're seeking a driver for preinstalled hardware, a PC manufacturer's Web site typically has the latest driver. Finding the appropriate driver is often as easy as finding your PC model. Drivers will typically be provided to you in one of three packages:

- A small program that installs the drivers for you

- A self-extracting executable (.exe) that copies multiple files to a location you specify

- A Zip file that requires you to have a program, such as WinZip, installed to open the file

The first option will typically take care of the entire setup process for you. The other two options will require you to initiate one of the Windows 2000 wizards to update the driver.

Reinstalling Drivers

For a variety of reasons, a driver may become corrupt. In these instances, you need to reinstall the driver. This simple process consists of the following steps:

1. In Device Manager, select the device for which you need to reinstall the driver, and click on Action|Properties or double-click on the device.

2. Click on the Driver tab and then click on the Update Driver button.

3. Click on Next, choose Search For A Suitable Driver For My Device (Recommended), and then click on Next.

4. Keep the boxes that are checked by default (see Figure 9.7) and click on Next again.

5. When the correct driver is found, click on Next to reinstall the driver.

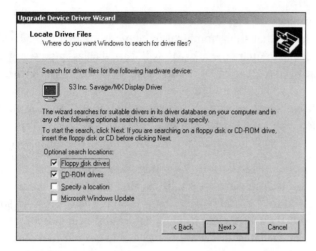

Figure 9.7
The Upgrade Device Driver Wizard enables you to choose the location to search for drivers.

Windows will search all the optional locations checked in Figure 9.7, as well as its driver database.

Windows 2000 stores all its drivers in a single file, Driver.cab, located in a subfolder of *%systemroot%*\Driver Cache. Windows will search *%systemroot%*\Inf to find a match for your hardware and install the appropriate driver you select. If a third-party driver that is appropriate is found in *%systemroot%*\Driver Cache, it will be installed instead of the driver shipped with Windows 2000.

If Windows finds multiple appropriate drivers, you are given the option to select one of the alternate drivers. Instead of choosing Next in Step 5 in the preceding steps, check the box Install One Of The Other Drivers (see Figure 9.8) and click on Next. Windows will present a list of the drivers it found, denoting the driver it prefers with an asterisk (*). You can highlight your preferred driver and click on Next to complete the driver's installation.

Installing a New Driver

You will often install a driver from a known location, such as a CD, floppy, network share, or location on your hard drive. You frequently use this method when downloading drivers from the Internet. In these instances, you will want to direct Windows 2000 to the location of the appropriate files. The steps are similar to those for updating a driver:

1. Double-click on the device in Device Manager and click on the Driver tab.

2. Click on the Update Driver button and then click on Next.

3. Keep the default settings and click on Next.

4. Choose Specify A Location, clear the other checkboxes, and then click on Next.

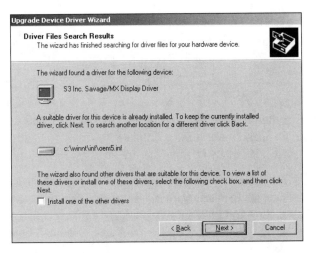

Figure 9.8
The Upgrade Device Driver Wizard allows you to select and install alternate appropriate drivers for your device.

5. Browse to the location of the device driver's files and click on Next.

6. Verify that the appropriate driver is selected and click on Next to complete the installation.

The location you browse to will contain an INF file. This text file contains the information Windows needs to properly install the file. If the location you browse to does not contain an INF file, this method will fail. Failure typically indicates that the location does not contain the correct files or that another installation method is necessary for this driver package. You should check your documentation and contact the driver provider for further information.

Installing a Driver from the List of Known Drivers

Windows provides you with several methods for driver installation. Another method is to select the driver from a list of drivers that Windows holds. You might need to select a different driver than the one that Windows chooses by default. This option allows you to browse all the available drivers for a device. To use this method, follow these steps:

1. Double-click on the device in Device Manager.

2. Select the Driver tab, click on Update Driver, and then click on Next.

3. Choose Display A List Of The Known Drivers For This Device So That I Can Choose A Specific Driver, and then click on Next.

4. Select Show All Hardware Devices Of This Device Class, and then click on Next.

5. Select the alternate driver you wish to install and click on Next to complete the installation.

Changing Resource Settings

The option to change resource settings for a device is available through its Properties page in Device Manager. Select the Resources tab and clear the Use Automatic Settings checkbox. In the Resource Settings list, select the resource for which you want to change the setting and click on the Change Setting button.

Be cautious when manually changing the resource settings. Changing them this way may create conflicts with other hardware and make it more difficult for Windows to allocate resources for Plug-and-Play devices. Manually setting resources is a last resort when you're configuring your devices.

You also may find that the checkbox for Use Automatic Settings is grayed out. A grayed option indicates that the device is Plug and Play, and Windows 2000 is handling the resource allocation. You may also find the checkbox grayed out when the device has no configurable resources.

Disabling and Enabling Devices

Device Manager facilitates disabling and enabling hardware. This feature is used in setting up hardware profiles and is also an aid in troubleshooting. To disable a device, open the device's Properties page. Under Device Usage, select Do Not Use This Device (Disable) and click on OK to disable the device and free its resources. To enable a disabled device, you can choose Use This Device (Enable) or click on the Enable This Device button. This button is available only if a device has been disabled.

Disabling a device is not the same as uninstalling it. You should disable a device only for troubleshooting purposes. If you do not intend to use the device again on your computer, you should completely uninstall it. Disabling a device does not remove Registry entries or other information from you computer.

Uninstalling Devices

If you no longer wish to use a device, you should uninstall it. If the device is Plug and Play, you can simply remove it from your system. Some devices, such as USB peripherals, can be removed while the computer is on. Other devices, such as PCI cards, should be removed only when the computer is powered down and unplugged. You can uninstall non–Plug-and-Play devices by right-clicking on the device in Device Manager and selecting the Uninstall option.

Using the System Information Tool

Another excellent source of system information is the System Information MMC snap-in. It provides a wealth of information about your system in a user-friendly format. You can open System Information by typing "msinfo32.exe" in the Run dialog box. You can also add it to your MMC console by opening an empty console and selecting the System Information snap-in from Console|Add/Remove Snap-in. System Information, shown in Figure 9.9, allows you to manage devices and gather information about your system.

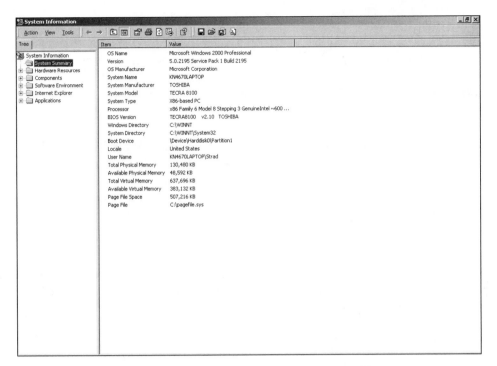

Figure 9.9
The System Information tool provides you with information regarding your system's hardware and software environment.

System Information categorizes the information it provides in the following nodes:

- *System Summary*—A summarization of information, including OS information, memory settings, and page file information.

- *Hardware Resources*—A listing of resource settings for DMA, IRQs, I/O addresses, and memory addresses.

- *Components*—Information regarding specific hardware, such as the modem, communication ports, storage, printing, and more.

- *Software Environment*—A list of items in memory, including drivers, environment variables, services, and other OS settings.

- *Internet Explorer*—Configuration settings for Internet Explorer, such as encryption strength, installation location, and file caching.

- *Applications*—Information regarding installed applications.

System Summary

System Summary provides an excellent listing of many aspects of your Windows 2000 installation and your PC hardware. This tool can be useful for providing system information to support personnel for troubleshooting purposes. It lists your OS version, including service pack number and your PC's manufacturer, model, and system type. The BIOS version is available, as well as directory paths for your Windows installation and the page file. Page file size is also listed, along with several different memory statistics: total physical memory, available physical memory, total virtual memory, and available virtual memory.

> **Tip:** *Don't see all these options? Be sure to click on View|Advanced. Many MMC consoles have an Advanced view that provides even more detailed information.*

You can also save this information in one of two formats: text file or System Information file. You can access these options by right-clicking on the System Summary folder. The Text File option saves the information in a plain text file that can be viewed and edited in Notepad, Wordpad, or any other plain text editor. If you choose to save the file as a System Information file, only System Information opens the file.

Hardware Resources

The Hardware Resources node provides detailed information regarding the resources on your computer. You can view the following resource information with this node:

- Conflicts/Sharing
- DMA
- Forced Hardware
- I/O
- IRQs
- Memory

The advantage System Information has over Device Manager is that it displays several important troubleshooting clues in one place. Conflicts/Sharing shows you all resources that are being shared among multiple devices, as well as all devices that are using the same resources and are in a conflict state. Because PCI devices can take advantage of IRQ sharing, devices listed here are not necessarily causing problems on your computer. They may simply be sharing the resource. IRQ sharing is a feature designed to allow you to add more hardware to your computer by allowing multiple devices to use a single IRQ.

Selecting DMA displays the devices and system components that use a DMA channel. You are shown the channel, device, and status. Any value beyond OK in the Status column is indicative of a problem and should be investigated.

Forced Hardware displays a listing of all devices that have manually set resources. Because these devices can severely restrict the capability of Windows to assign resources to Plug-and-Play devices, this list should be kept short. Use Device Manager to work with these devices if you can use automatic resource assignment with them. The information provided here includes the device and the PNP Device ID, an ID number assigned to the device by Windows.

I/O displays the Input/Output address ranges in use by hardware on your system. As with DMA, a Status column is displayed, and all items should display OK. If any other value is indicated, note the conflict and resolve it.

To see the IRQs in use, select IRQs. System Information details the devices in your system and the IRQ in use by that device. The Memory option is similar to I/O. You are shown the various memory ranges in use on your computer, the device using that range, and the status.

Components

The Components node of System Information, along with Hardware Resources, provides the most hardware information. This node details many aspects of your hardware environment, including the following:

- Multimedia
- Display
- Infrared
- Input
- Modem
- Network
- Ports
- Storage
- Printing
- Problem Devices
- USB

Problem Devices lists any hardware that is not operating. Disabled devices and devices in conflict, for instance, are displayed here. In Figure 9.10, you can see details regarding an installed modem. System Information clearly provides a depth of detail unavailable in any other Windows 2000 utility. This snap-in is an excellent place to research details of many hardware devices installed on your PC.

Software Environment

The Software Environment node details many aspects of your software environment. You can find information regarding drivers, environment variables, print jobs, network connections, and running tasks here. Also outlined are the loaded modules, services, program groups, startup programs, and OLE registrations. The most helpful aspect here for your troubleshooting purposes will be the Drivers node, which lists the driver name, description, and associated file. You'll also find the familiar Status option and information regarding the driver's type, start mode, current start status, and so on.

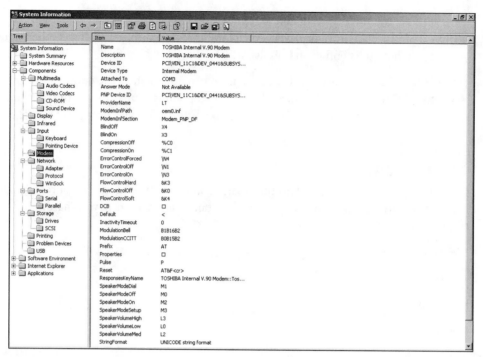

Figure 9.10
System Information provides excellent information regarding device details.

Internet Explorer

The Internet Explorer node displays information on Internet Explorer 5. If you have upgraded the IE version on your computer, this node may simply be named Internet Explorer. You'll find many settings and environment variables for your Web browser here.

Applications

The information shown in the Applications node varies. Most Microsoft applications, such as the Microsoft Office suite, are displayed here. A variety of information can be displayed, and it typically revolves around the Registry and customization settings for that particular application.

Installing New Hardware

I'll be the first to admit that I love buying and installing new hardware. Computer stores are my toy stores, and I think everyone enjoys making those purchases, whether it's a new item for the home or office. However, as a matter of good practice, if you are purchasing a new item, your first stop should be Microsoft's Web site, which details hardware compatibility (**www.microsoft.com/hcl/**). At this site, Microsoft provides you with the newest version of the Hardware Compatibility List (HCL), which details all the hardware that has been tested and certified by Windows Hardware Quality Labs. If you're working on a mission-critical server or workstation, checking the HCL is a hard and fast rule. On your personal computers and less critical machines, you may take the liberty of straying from strict adherence to the HCL, but keep in mind that you do so at the risk of losing Microsoft's technical support if any problems arise from using the nonsupported device.

As we've mentioned, Windows 2000 supports Plug-and-Play devices—finally! This capability will alleviate many of the problems you encountered setting up devices in Windows NT 4. However, especially for legacy machines that were upgraded to Windows 2000 from Window NT 4, you might need to change a BIOS setting for your hardware to work properly. For instance, often your BIOS includes a setting to indicate whether or not the installed OS is Plug-and-Play–compatible. With Windows NT 4, this setting should not be enabled; with Windows 2000, this setting should be enabled. If you are having a difficult time setting up hardware, you definitely should check this item. Many resource allocation problems can be traced to this setting.

9

Tip: *When starting, most newer computers will give you an indication of which key you need to press to enter the computer's BIOS or Setup. However, this is not always the case. In most cases, either the F1, F2, F10, Delete, or Esc key will take you there. If none of these keys work, you should be able to find documentation in the owner's manual or at the manufacturer's Web site.*

For Plug-and-Play compatibility, your motherboard is required to have a Plug-and-Play BIOS or an ACPI BIOS. With either of these two, Windows 2000 automatically detects, installs, and configures the hardware. If your Plug-and-Play device is not automatically detected, you can use the Add/Remove Hardware Wizard located in Control Panel.

Plug-and-Play Hardware

Most Plug-and-Play hardware is automatically found and installed by Windows 2000. Windows detects the hardware and installs the appropriate software. User interaction is minimal. However, you will encounter hardware that is not detected, and in these instances, you can use the Add/Remove Hardware Wizard. You can launch this applet from Control Panel. It allows you to add devices, troubleshoot devices that aren't working properly, and remove devices. This wizard is a great place to start when you're setting up most common peripherals, including DVD and CD players, scanners, modems, NICs, and many other multimedia devices. You can choose from two routes when using the Add/Remove Hardware Wizard: automatic or manual hardware installation.

Automatic Hardware Installation

By far, the easiest option is automatic hardware installation. You can use this option with Plug-and-Play devices that were not automatically detected by Windows. Non–Plug-and-Play devices can also use this method. Simply invoke the Add/Remove Hardware Wizard. Windows 2000 will query the hardware to determine the resources required. It will then compare these requirements with the available resources, negotiate a resolution to any conflicts arising with other Plug-and-Play devices, and install the appropriate software for the hardware.

To install a device using Automatic Hardware Installation, follow these steps:

1. With the PC powered off, install the device and make sure it is plugged in and powered on, if applicable.

Note: *Some devices do not require powering off the PC. Check your owner's manual.*

2. Open Control Panel and double-click on Add/Remove Hardware.

3. Click on Next on the wizard's welcome screen.

4. Select Add/Troubleshoot A Device and then click on Next to begin the search for new devices.

5. When the device is located, follow the wizard's instructions to complete the installation.

After the installation is complete, open Device Manager to confirm that the device is installed and working properly. If the wizard fails to find new Plug-and-Play hardware, the Choose A Hardware Device page is displayed, as shown in Figure 9.11. You are given the option to begin troubleshooting or to manually add a device.

If you choose to troubleshoot a device, you must select it from the list shown. The Windows 2000 Hardware Troubleshooter opens to assist you in determining the problem. We will cover the Hardware Troubleshooter in a later section of this chapter.

Manual Hardware Installation

Automatic installation makes hardware installation easier; however, not all hardware will install automatically. For example, Windows 2000 may fail to detect the device. And, sometimes automatic hardware installation is not desired. Typically, for security purposes,

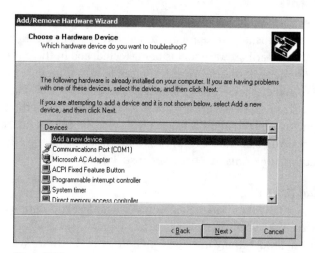

Figure 9.11
The Choose A Hardware Device page of the Add/Remove Hardware Wizard allows you to select a device category for troubleshooting or add a new device.

this feature may not be desirable. There are four requirements for devices to automatically install in the system context:

- The driver installation does not need a user interface.

- All driver files are on the computer.

- The driver package is digitally signed.

- The first pass of the installation is error-free.

To circumvent automatic hardware installation, you must cause one of these criteria to fail to be met. The simplest way to do so is to rename the Driver.cab file. Renaming the file will invalidate the second requirement and cause the installation to fail. This file is located at *%systemroot%*\Driver Cache\I386. When this file is renamed, the installation is no longer in the system context and is now in the user context. If the user is a member of the local administrator's group, the installation will proceed. However, if the user is not an administrator, the installation will fail.

Whether you wish to force manual hardware installation or your device simply remains undetected by Windows 2000, it is important to know the process to follow so that your device works properly in Windows 2000.

When you are aware that a device needs manual installation, prepare yourself by documenting the hardware resources the item will require before beginning the process. You often can find this information in the device's documentation.

Tip: You may also want to visit the manufacturer's Web site so that you can download the latest drivers, as well as any firmware updates that may exist for your product. Firmware updates are common for devices such as video cards, CD-Recorders, motherboards, and modems.

Follow these steps for manual installation of a device:

1. With your PC powered off, install the device on your computer. Be certain it is plugged in and powered on, if applicable. Then, start your computer.

Note: Some devices do not require you to power off your PC for installation. Check your owner's manual.

2. From Control Panel, launch the Add/Remove Hardware Wizard.

3. After the wizard completes its search for Plug-and-Play devices, it displays a list of devices. If your device is in this list, highlight it, click on Next, and follow the instructions of the wizard to complete the installation of your device. If it does not appear, select Add A New Device and click on Next.

4. Choose No, I Want To Select The Hardware From A List and click on Next.

5. Select your hardware type and click on Next.

6. Select the hardware manufacturer and model if listed and click on Next. Supply resources as appropriate and complete the wizard.

7. If your device is not listed and you have the driver, click on Have Disk and then click on Next. Browse to the location of the INF file for the hardware device and complete the wizard.

You can load drivers from your Windows 2000 CD, a network location, the manufacturer's CD or floppy, or via Microsoft Update.

Determining Available Resources

When you are aware of the resources required for a device, you can match them with the resources available in Windows 2000. Both System Information and Device Manager allow you to see free resources on your computer. To use Device Manager, follow these steps:

1. Open Device Manager.

2. Choose Resources By Connection from the View menu.

3. Expand the node for the resources your device requires, such as the IRQ and I/O node.

Armed with the free resources on your system and those required by the device, determine a workable set of resources for your hardware. You might need to set appropriate jumpers for your hardware, or you may have a setup disk that allows you to alter the resource settings in the hardware's CMOS.

Tip: No resources? Often, the hardware device may be limited to a certain set of IRQs, and none may be free. In this instance, you can often go into your BIOS and reserve an IRQ for a "legacy" device. This, or a similar option, will force Windows 2000 to move any Plug-and-Play devices off that IRQ and free it for your new hardware.

After the driver is installed and set to the appropriate resources in Device Manager, and the hardware is installed to the appropriate resource settings, the device should be functioning properly. However, keep in mind that if you install a device using jumpers to designate resource settings, it is in all likelihood not Plug and Play and not on the Windows HCL. These hardware devices, even if you manage to get them working happily in your system, may cause problems down the road when you add more devices. Avoid using legacy hardware on your Windows 2000 Professional workstation if at all possible.

Here's one point we cannot stress enough: Document! Whenever you make changes to your computer's BIOS and whenever you install legacy devices, be certain to keep a hard copy of the configuration changes you make. Often, when you're dealing with such devices, the resource juggling performed can be intricate. If the workstation ever needs to be rebuilt, you will not have to go through as much trouble finding a compatible set of resources for your devices. This is especially true when you have multiple legacy devices on the workstation.

Confirming Installation

After successfully installing a device following the steps outlined in the preceding sections, you should confirm that it is working properly. Some devices, such as sound cards or video cards, give immediate feedback. With other devices, further confirmation is required. Access Device Manager and double-click on the device. Its device status should indicate that it is working properly. If the device is not working properly, you should begin troubleshooting it to determine the root cause of the problem.

Troubleshooting Hardware

When you need to troubleshoot a device, you should consider some initial points. It is often tempting to jump right in and start modifying settings, switching jumpers, swapping out hardware, and trying new drivers. You may very often fix problems by using this approach; however, it is rarely the most efficient approach to use. The best approach is planned and methodical. Attempting too many fixes at one time may resolve the issue but will leave you unaware of the exact nature of the problem.

You can take the following steps (shown in Decision Tree 9.1) to begin your troubleshooting journey. Of course, we can't outline the best steps for every situation. Use these tips as a guideline in developing a troubleshooting strategy that works for you:

- Determine the nature of the problem. Is the problem hardware or software related? Is the problem affecting similar PCs? Multiple PCs?

- Determine when the problem began. Has the system been changed, modified, or altered recently? Can you backtrack your steps so that the problem disappears? Be sure to document your changes throughout this process.

- Is the problem consistent and repeatable? Is the failure random or part of a sequence of events? Often, you can determine where to investigate first if you can answer these questions.

- Get expert help. Seek information on the problem both at Microsoft's Knowledge Base (**http://support.microsoft.com**) and the manufacturer's Web site. You can find common problems that affect many users at these sites. Often, you are not alone.

- Check the device for proper driver installation. Often, the incorrect driver is installed, or the driver is not installed properly. Removing and reinstalling a driver can be a quick fix. You may also find another driver is not working properly, which affects the device you are trying to configure.

- Use Event Viewer. Although you should always check Event Viewer regularly to resolve problems, its importance is heightened when you're troubleshooting. Search for any errors and fault conditions that may provide you with more information, including drivers failing to start.

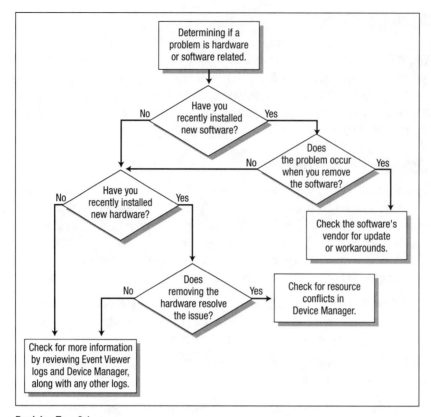

Decision Tree 9.1
Troubleshooting hardware.

Although you will not resolve every problem by following these guidelines, you will develop good habits and resolve more problems more quickly than when you use a haphazard method. Windows 2000 provides you with an array of tools to help you narrow down the cause of your hardware configuration problems.

Using Device Manager

Device Manager will be your first stop when determining why an installed device is not working. The codes listed by Device Manager can be helpful in resolving the problem. You can check the Device Status portion of a failed device's Properties page to get an error code, as you can see in Figure 9.12. The information is often limited; however, you can easily find more information regarding the code's meaning. A quick foray to the Knowledge Base at **http://support.microsoft.com** can help. A search for Q125174 will return an article listing the Device Manager error codes, their causes, and possible steps to resolution.

You might see some of these common error codes:

- *Code 1*—Typically, this code indicates the driver needs to be updated. Windows 2000 has not had a chance to configure the device. You might be able to resolve the problem by using the Add/Remove Hardware Wizard.

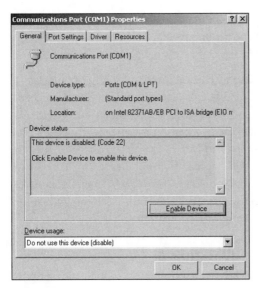

Figure 9.12
Checking status in a device's Properties dialog box.

- *Code 2*—The driver was unable to load. You might need to update your BIOS, reinstall the driver, or get a newer driver.

- *Code 3*—The driver may be bad. Try updating the driver using the Update Driver button.

- *Code 4*—This code suggests that either the driver is bad or the Registry is corrupt. Try running scanregw.exe if replacing the driver doesn't resolve the issue.

- *Code 5*—This code is indicative of driver issues. Update the driver, or remove the device and try adding it through the Add/Remove Hardware Wizard.

- *Code 6*—The device needs resources in use by another device. Follow the procedures outlined for resolving hardware resource conflicts.

- *Code 7*—The drivers need to be reinstalled if the device is not working. If reinstallation does not resolve the problem, remove the device from Device Manager and add it through the Add/Remove Hardware Wizard.

Device Manager can also reveal other information regarding the failed device. If a device is not functioning properly, its representative icon will be modified. The different icons you may see are as follows:

- *A red "X"*—Indicates a disabled device. This device is present in the system and consuming resources but does not have a protected mode driver loaded.

- *A black exclamation point in a yellow circle*—Indicates a problem with the device's state. It may be functioning or nonfunctioning; however, further investigation is required.

- *A blue "i"*—Indicates that the device is using manually set resources. The Use Automatic Settings box is unchecked on the Resources tab. This does not mean the device is not working properly.

Also, check the Resources tab for the device. This tab lists any conflicting devices and thus may point you to a quick solution for the fault condition. However, also keep in mind that some devices, such as sound cards and video cards, do not indicate in Device Manager all the resources they are using. This lack of information is typical with legacy devices and can cause conflicts that will not be displayed in Device Manager. To see whether this type of device is causing an issue in your system, disable the sound card and use the standard VGA video driver. If this approach resolves your issue, the legacy devices you are using are likely the culprits in your hardware problems. This problem is common with some S3 video adapters and older SoundBlaster cards and compatibles.

Windows 2000 Hardware Troubleshooter

The General tab of the device's Properties page also contains a Troubleshooter button. This button will open the Windows 2000 Hardware Troubleshooter, which takes you through a methodical approach to resolving hardware issues.

The Troubleshooter is an excellent tool because even the most seasoned professional can occasionally overlook simple steps and common causes for hardware failure. The Hardware Troubleshooter, shown in Figure 9.13, begins by asking you what problem you are experiencing.

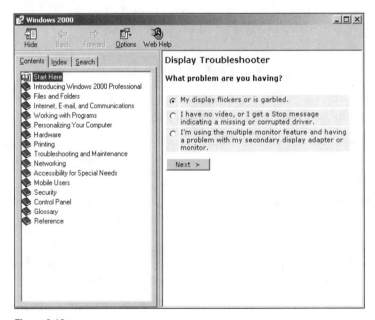

Figure 9.13
Reviewing Hardware Troubleshooter options.

The Troubleshooter proceeds through a decision tree process, which can often end in a resolution to the problem. Along the way are helpful links to open tools you will need, such as Device Manager. You can also back up or start over if you feel you are going down the wrong path.

Device Problems Troubleshooting Wizard

Along with the Device Manager's Hardware Troubleshooter, you can use the Device Problems Troubleshooting Wizard. You can access this troubleshooter through the Add/Remove Hardware Wizard by following these steps:

1. Open Add/Remove Hardware and click on Next on the welcome screen.

2. Select Add/Troubleshoot A Device and click on Next.

3. Windows will search for Plug-and-Play devices. The Choose A Hardware Device window is displayed next. Select the nonfunctioning device and click on Next.

4. When the device status is displayed, click on Finish to launch the Hardware Troubleshooter.

The wizard detects the status of the failed device and attempts to guide you through a fix for the problem. For instance, if the device is merely disabled, the wizard attempts to enable it for you. In other scenarios, it will launch the Hardware Troubleshooter detailed in the preceding section.

Enabling and Disabling Devices in Device Manager

You can use Device Manager's capability to disable devices to troubleshoot conflicting hardware and startup difficulties. Device Manager can be an excellent tool to troubleshoot devices that are using resources unreported by Windows 2000. If the conflicting devices are causing difficulty during startup, hold the F8 key during the Windows 2000 boot process. Then, select the Safe Mode option from the menu to load Windows 2000 with a minimal set of drivers. After you add new hardware, if you cannot boot normally yet can boot into safe mode, you most likely have a resource conflict. If you can boot normally but the device is failing to work properly, you can still use this method to discover which devices are conflicting.

Windows 2000 Fails to Boot

If Device Manager fails to indicate which devices are in conflict, you have two choices to determine the cause of the problem. You could pull hardware out of your computer, swapping items until the conflict becomes apparent. This approach can be very tedious. The preferred choice is to use Device Manager to enable and disable devices. To troubleshoot this issue, boot into safe mode, log on, and open Device Manager.

In Device Manager, select View and choose Resources By Connection. Your most common conflicts arise with devices attempting to share an IRQ. Expand the IRQ node to see the devices that require an IRQ. The following items are standard and should not be disabled:

- System Timer (IRQ 0)

- Keyboard (IRQ 1)

- Floppy Disk Controller (IRQ 6)

- CMOS/realtime clock (IRQ 8)

- Mouse (IRQ 12)

- Numeric Data Processor (IRQ 13)

- IDE Controllers (IRQ 14 and 15)

Use prudence when disabling other devices. Although you could disable the Microsoft ACPI-compliant system on some computers, it is likely not the cause of your problem. However, when all else fails, you might need to resort to disabling such devices. Start with more common sources of conflicts, however. You can disable communication ports, sound cards, network cards, and modems, and any other add-in cards you have installed.

Warning! If you are using a SCSI card and Windows is installed on SCSI drives, do not disable the card. Disabling it will likely make Windows 2000 unbootable and require more in-depth troubleshooting to resolve.

After you determine a likely set of devices to disable, follow these steps:

1. Double-click on an item to disable. Under Device Usage, select Do Not Use This Device (Disable). Repeat this step for all the devices to be disabled.

2. Close Device Manager and restart your computer.

3. If your computer starts normally, you have narrowed down the problem. It is likely that one of the devices you disabled was creating problems with booting Windows. Restart and go back into safe mode. Enable two devices in Device Manager, including any new hardware device that was installed, that you suspect may be causing the problem. Restart your computer.

4. If your computer again boots normally, return to safe mode and enable two more devices. Repeat this step until your computer fails to boot.

5. When the computer fails, go back into safe mode, disable one of the last two devices enabled, and reboot to narrow down which device is causing the conflict.

If your computer never fails to boot, you have experienced Windows voodoo—the unexplained resolution of a problem that should not yet be resolved. You have returned your system to the same state in which it would not boot, yet now it starts normally.

If, after you disable these devices, the computer does not start normally, you may need to consider other possibilities for the failure to start. You may also need to uninstall any newly added devices to resolve the issue and find the cause.

When you find the conflicting hardware, you have a couple of options to resolve the conflict. Your best option will depend on the hardware you are adding:

- If you're using a legacy device, try a Plug-and-Play version.

- If it is an ISA/EISA card, consider a PCI version instead.

- If you have unnecessary hardware on your PC, physically remove and uninstall it from Windows.

- Try a driver update for the device.

- Check your BIOS settings. Make sure no unnecessary resources are reserved for legacy devices.

- Disable IRQ reservation for your VGA and USB devices. It may not be necessary for you to use those devices; however, you should re-enable the IRQ reservation if it causes other problems with needed hardware.

Sometimes, especially with legacy devices, you might need to try a variety of resource settings and combinations. Even though the documentation indicates that any compatible settings will work, actually getting legacy devices to work in a mainly Plug-and-Play environment is an exercise in juggling resources.

Misidentified Hardware

If you look in Device Manager and see that your device is present but misidentified, you should make two quick stops. First, confirm that your device is listed as Windows 2000 compatible on the Hardware Compatibility List. Additionally, especially if the device is not listed on the HCL, confirm that the manufacturer supports the device in Windows 2000. Only items listed on the HCL are certified to work in Windows 2000. Your manufacturer may still provide support, even if the item is not on the HCL. When at all possible, use strictly HCL-supported hardware to minimize your troubleshooting difficulties.

To have Windows 2000 correctly identify a device, open Device Manager in Windows 2000 to locate the device and follow these steps:

1. Double-click on the device class for your device and double-click on the device itself to open its Properties page.

2. Click on the Driver tab and then click on the Update Driver button.

3. In the Upgrade Device Driver Wizard, click on Next.

4. Select Display A List Of The Known Drivers For This Device So That I Can Choose A Specific Driver and click on Next.

5. If you see the correct make and model for your device, highlight it and click on Next. Complete the wizard to finish the installation of the device.

6. If your device isn't listed, select Show All Hardware Of This Device Class to see whether your device is in this more inclusive list. If so, highlight it, click on Next, and complete the wizard to finish installation.

7. If your device still is not listed, you will need to provide the driver for this device. You can typically download the driver from the manufacturer's Web site. Choose Have Disk, browse to the location of the manufacturer's INF file, and complete the wizard.

8. When you're finished, restart the computer if prompted. Then, check in Device Manager to make certain your device is now listed and functioning properly.

Nonfunctioning Hardware

If you've installed hardware and find it is not working, you can take some steps to resolve the problem. As always, you should first check the HCL and manufacturer's Web site to confirm your device was intended to work in Windows 2000. After you do so, you can begin the troubleshooting process:

1. Go back over the installation of the device. Be sure that all cables are firmly seated, there are no bent pins on any cables or connectors, and the device is powered on if applicable.

2. Check the readme.txt file and all documentation provided with the device for known incompatibilities that might apply to your system.

3. Reread the installation instructions to ensure that all steps were followed.

4. Check the status of the device in Device Manager. To do so, open Device Manager and double-click on the device to open its Properties page.

5. If the device is disabled as indicated in the Device Status list, click on Enable Device to see whether that resolves the problem.

6. Use the Troubleshooter button to help resolve the issue.

7. Try reinstalling the driver from the Driver tab.

8. Check the Resources tab for conflicts.

9. Try the device on another computer or swap out the device with a known working device on this computer.

After you perform some or all of these steps, restart your computer to see whether the problem is resolved. With any luck, one of these steps resolved the problem. However, you might need to contact the manufacturer for additional steps as well, if the problem still persists.

Troubleshooting Unknown Devices

In Device Manager, you may see hardware identified as an unknown device beside a yellow question mark. Determining the cause of these entries can be challenging. Often, Device Manager provides no indication of what is causing the problem. The most common causes are an installed device with no driver, a driver intended for use with Windows 95/98, an unrecognized device ID, or faulty hardware/firmware.

No Device Driver

In Device Manager, double-click on the device and check the Device Status. If you see either Error Code 1 or Error Code 10, typically, you can resolve the problem by installing the device's driver. These errors can occur frequently with USB and FireWire devices. Although most USB and FireWire devices do not need additional device drivers, some newer devices may not be properly identified. If the device does not fit in an existing class of devices as well, an additional driver will be required. Check the device's documentation as well as the manufacturer's Web site for updated drivers.

Incorrect Driver

Windows 95 and 98 use virtual device drivers (VXDs), which are not compatible with Windows 2000 and will not work properly. A device using a VXD file may appear under Other Devices and will not function properly. Typically, a VXD file is installed as a driver file only if the INF file is incorrectly written. In this instance, contact the device manufacturer for driver files that are written for Windows 2000.

Unrecognized Device ID

If you install a Plug-and-Play device, it uses a special ID that identifies it to Windows 2000. This ID lets Windows 2000 know what device is being installed so that it can load the appropriate drivers. The identifier includes the vendor ID, device ID, subsystem ID, subsystem vendor ID, or revision ID. If this ID is not present or is unrecognized, the device will be listed as unknown.

Additionally, some software can create these devices. One example is Compaq Insight Manager, which creates a virtual device that monitors and communicates with your hardware. If you upgrade a computer that has Insight Manager to Windows 2000, you may find these virtual devices listed. The older versions of the software do not work properly in Windows 2000. Other drivers can also create virtual devices. An older Iomega Parallel Port driver for the Parallel Port Zip drive allows a parallel port drive to emulate a SCSI device and can create unknown devices in Device Manager. Make sure you use the most recent drivers to avoid this issue.

Faulty Hardware or Firmware

A device ID is provided by a hardware device. Software programs can emulate these device IDs, but older versions do not provide the device ID information to Windows 2000 in the expected format. When Windows 2000 looks for a device ID to identify the device, the software program indicates to Windows that a device is present, but Windows 2000 cannot identify the device. This unknown device is typically a virtual device, and does not represent hardware actually installed in your computer. To determine whether the device you see was created by software, try these solutions:

- Start your computer in safe mode by holding the F8 key while booting and selecting the Safe Mode option. Look in Device Manager in safe mode to see whether the device is still present. If it is not, the device was very likely created by software, not a piece of hardware. However, this technique is not 100 percent conclusive; use it to direct your further troubleshooting.

- If you have an idea of certain programs that may be causing the problem, remove any icons launching the software from the Startup folder and reboot. Also, end the running programs if they appear in your taskbar tray. Check Device Manager to see whether this step removed the device. The offending program may also be launched from one of the Registry's Run keys as well.

- Use System Information to help diagnose the problem. In System Information, expand Software Environment and check the Startup Programs folder. One of these items may be the offender, and you can discover the exact Registry location here to disable the program. Just take care in editing the Registry and be certain to make a backup before editing.

- Check the event log for errors that may indicate where the problem lies. Especially, take note of any programs that are also running at startup. You can uninstall the program to see whether uninstalling resolves the mystery device. If the program is the culprit, uninstalling and rebooting should remove it from Device Manager.

In System Information, use the Components node and the Problem Devices category to check for any devices listed there. The following information regarding items is listed under Problem Devices:

- The Device column lists the device or name of the device driver associated with the device.

- The PnP Device ID column lists the device IDs, such as PCI ID, ISA ID, another bus type ID, or Unknown.

- The Error Code column lists the error code for the problem. The error code may help you determine what created the device.

Another source of information is the setupapi.log file. It can help identify what created the unknown device, as long as the device name is meaningful. It may provide a clue as to the bus type or connection the device is using. It may also be misleading, however, if the device ID is misleading Windows 2000.

Hardware Devices

If the device is not a hardware device but a physical device on your system, you can pursue other avenues for troubleshooting as well. One method to determine the cause is to remove hardware devices from your PC one device at a time. This approach can be very time consuming and is not always 100 percent reliable. It can, however, provide useful information regarding the culprit and, in many circumstances, may be your only option.

Check the driver to see whether it is digitally signed. If it is not digitally signed, Windows 2000 generated an error message. Depending on your settings, this may be the cause, and digitally signed drivers may still be listed as unknown devices.

Some USB devices created with an earlier version of the USB specification can create ghost devices. These ghost devices appear only when the device is connected. By disconnecting the device, you can determine whether this is indeed the problem. If it is, seek out updated drivers or newer firmware for the device, or purchase a new model. The device may work fine, so your personal judgment should be the deciding factor.

Another source of ghost devices can be drivers installed for devices that are already detected. A close perusal of Device Manager can usually resolve this problem. Simply remove the unnecessary device driver. Plug-and-Play devices are typically not listed when you use the Add/Remove Hardware Wizard. You may assume the device is not installed and manually install a driver.

Following these guidelines should help you locate and resolve most issues with phantom and unidentified devices. The following section provides some excellent steps when you're troubleshooting specific devices.

Troubleshooting Specific Hardware

In the first portion of this chapter, we gave you several tips on how to set up hardware and resolve problems. However, you also should be aware of hardware-specific tips that depend on the hardware device you are installing. Unfortunately, each installation presents unique issues, so these tips are general guidelines for these device categories. In the following sections, we'll look more in depth at the following hardware devices:

- DVD drives
- Keyboards
- Modems
- Mice
- Multiple monitors
- Power Management
- Sound cards and speakers
- Zip drives

DVD Drives

Windows 2000 supports DVD drives but has several requirements. To use a DVD drive, you must have the following:

- DVD-ROM drive, either an IDE or SCSI version

- DVD decoder, either a hardware decoder—a physical card inserted in an available PCI slot—or a software decoder

- Video card and driver that support Directshow and Macrovision copy protection

- Sound card for audio

- DVD player tool, which Windows provides if it detects a supported decoder

Windows 2000 does not supply software decoders. You might need to update your decoder to a Windows 2000 version if it does not work properly. Check with your computer manufacturer and DVD equipment manufacturer to determine whether your devices meet Windows 2000 specifications, and also check the HCL.

You must deal with many common issues when you work with DVD drives. Be sure to check the following:

- Some decoders work only with certain display adapters. Contact the manufacturers to determine whether all your equipment is compatible. Prior to a purchase, you might want to contact a manufacturer to determine which supporting equipment it recommends.

- Make sure that direct memory access is enabled for your DVD-ROM. Some decoders require that DMA be enabled.

- Some decoders require or perform better with an AGP card. Check the requirements of your decoder.

- If you're using DVD with a laptop, check to see whether you need a BIOS upgrade for the DVD player and video to function properly.

- If this installation is an upgrade from Windows 9x, update the version of your software decoder through the manufacturer.

- If you receive an error regarding analog protection, update your drivers or contact the hardware manufacturer to see whether it is Windows 2000 compatible.

- If your video card says it supports DVD, it may still require a software or hardware decoder. Contact the video card manufacturer to determine if this is true for your card.

- Your USB speakers might not work with your DVD device; most decoders require a sound card. Use speakers connected to your sound card or purchase a decoder compatible with USB speakers.

- If you receive an error stating that the video cannot be shown on the computer monitor, the problem may have several causes. Try lowering the color depth, resolution, and refresh rate in Display Properties|Settings. You may also need to close Microsoft NetMeeting if it is running.

Keyboards

Losing the ability to use items such as keyboards and mice presents unique challenges when troubleshooting. You rely heavily on your ability to interact with the computer to resolve problems. The failure of these devices can be frustrating. If you find that your keyboard is no longer responsive, be sure to check the following:

- Check the obvious. Make sure that the keyboard is firmly plugged in. If you are using extension cables, check each connection as well. If checking these connections doesn't resolve the problem, try removing the extension cable temporarily and see whether plugging the keyboard directly into the computer resolves the problem. Reboot if the keyboard appears loose and plugging it in firmly does not return functionality.

- If you are using a USB keyboard plugged into a USB hub, be sure the hub is on and powered. If possible, remove the hub and plug the keyboard directly into the computer. You should power off to perform these steps because disconnecting a USB hub while the system is powered may cause a crash.

- If a mouse or any other devices are plugged in through the keyboard, remove them.

- If you are using a keyboard switchbox, remove it and try connecting the keyboard directly to the computer.

- Try a different keyboard if one is available.

- Try the Num Lock key to see whether a keyboard light is activated. If it is not, this is typically a sign that the keyboard is not properly connected or has failed. Try this keyboard on another computer. If it works there, you may have a faulty port on the computer.

- Try entering your computer's BIOS. If you are able to, chances are good your keyboard works, and the problem lies within Windows 2000. If this is the case, check Device Manager in safe mode to see whether you can spot any misbehaving devices. You may also want to remove any recently installed software or undo any recent changes to the system.

- Check for stuck keys. On some keyboards, when certain keys are stuck, you are prohibited from typing. Your keyboard may have something sitting on a key, or worse, you may have a stuck key. If a key is stuck, you might be able to pop off the key cap and clean it to alleviate the problem. If you spill soda or other liquids on the keyboard, do not attempt to clean the keyboard in your dishwasher or otherwise immerse it in liquid. A safer course of action is to purchase a new keyboard. A keyboard that is washed may function temporarily, but its life span has been greatly shortened by this treatment.

Considering how inexpensive keyboards are, purchasing a few spare keyboards can be a very wise investment. After you confirm you have a good connection, try rebooting the computer. Windows 2000 will redetect the keyboard, and you can test functionality again.

If the problem appears to lie in the keyboard port, you will need to have this problem fixed by a professional or the manufacturer if the computer is still under warranty. If the problem is in the cabling or keyboard, having an extra keyboard on hand will be a lifesaver.

Modems

Modems are one of the most popular peripherals. They are also perhaps the most hated. Whether the problem is getting the modem detected or getting connected, modems have developed a bad reputation. With Windows 2000, the problem can be exacerbated. Be certain to check the HCL to see whether your modem is Windows 2000 compatible. With Windows' strict guidelines for hardware, many modems may not work or may work with reduced functionality and more generic drivers. Be warned: Although you may get an unlisted modem to work in Windows 2000, doing so may not be worth the price and frustration. You are strongly urged to make the investment and purchase a Windows 2000–compatible modem, especially if you need this modem for any mission-critical work, or if the modem will connect to mission-critical hardware.

Modem Detection

If your modem doesn't appear to be detected, the first requirement is to determine what exactly "not detected" means. Open Device Manager and see whether your modem is listed under Modems or Other Devices. If it is listed, it is detected but possibly requires more configuration. See the next section for tips on getting it to work. If it is not listed, it might have other problems. Work through the following checklist:

- If you are using an external modem, be certain it is plugged in and powered on before starting your computer.

- Check the cable connecting the modem to the computer for bent or missing pins.

- Try another cable if one is available.

- Connect your modem to both serial ports on your PC to see whether that trick resolves the issue.

- Check your BIOS to see whether the necessary serial port is enabled.

- If you are using an internal modem, be sure it is well seated in an appropriate slot.

- Try placing the internal modem in another slot of the same type, in case you're having issues with a particular slot.

After you try each of the preceding items for your modem, click on the Action menu in Device Manager and select Scan For Hardware Changes. Then, see whether your modem is listed in Modems or Other Devices, indicating it is now detected. If it is still undetected, you may have a faulty modem or cable. The best option here is to attempt to use an identical modem on this computer or confirm that the modem is good by setting it up on another computer.

If your modem is now detected, you can complete the installation if necessary, or Windows 2000 may have completed it for you. Check the modem's status in Device Manager to see whether further intervention is required.

Modem Unable to Dial

If your modem is detected but you cannot connect, different troubleshooting steps are required. First, verify that your modem and PC are communicating as follows:

1. Open Device Manager and expand the Modems node.

2. Double-click on your modem.

3. Click on the Diagnostics tab.

4. Select the Query Modem button.

Windows 2000 will attempt to gather information regarding the modem. If it fails to gather information, the modem is not properly installed, and you should check the steps in the preceding section. If, on the other hand, the Modem Information Command and Response columns in the Diagnostics tab are now populated, Windows is successfully talking to your modem, which typically indicates that the problem is actually with the phone line and is not caused by a modem failure or driver issue. Begin checking the following common issues:

• Check the phone jack by plugging a normal phone into it to see whether it has a dial tone.

• Confirm that the phone cord from the wall goes into the appropriate jack on the modem.

• Swap phone cords to confirm that you are not using a bad phone cord.

After you complete each of these steps, attempt to connect to a service provider and see whether you can successfully dial a number and hear the remote location ring or answer your call.

Warning! Before you connect your modem to the jack, be certain that you are connecting the appropriate type of modem to the appropriate type of jack: digital to digital and analog to analog. Most modems you purchase are analog. Most office phone systems are digital. If your office has multiple lines, chances are it's digital. The two differing types of lines are not compatible, and you can damage your modem and computer by attempting to interconnect the two technologies.

If, after following these steps, you are still unable to dial a number, you might want to swap out the modem or test it on another machine.

Mice

Mouse failures, like keyboard failures, can be highly irritating. You can take several steps to ensure a long life for your mouse. When you're selecting a mouse, although prices vary, be sure to purchase a mouse from a quality manufacturer. Check the box and ensure that the mouse has at least a three-year warranty. I've owned some mice longer than the computer they were attached to. In fact, I recently put out to pasture my very first mouse, purchased in 1987. Although your mouse may not last as long, you can do several things to lengthen its useful life span:

- Always use your mouse on a clean surface. Keep the mouse pad free of dust and dirt.

- For a mouse with a ball, regularly remove the ball and clean it according to the manufacturer's instructions.

- The inner gears and wheels of the mouse may become dusty as well. Clean them, too, according to the manufacturer's guidelines.

Most problems with inoperative or erratically behaving mice can be resolved by cleaning the mouse. However, other issues may be causing problems also. Check for any of the following conditions:

- As with a keyboard, be sure to remove any extensions or switchboxes when checking functionality.

- Try the mouse on another computer to see whether it works there; this solution may point to a problem with the mouse port.

- As always, check Device Manager to see whether everything is functioning properly, such as the USB port for a USB mouse.

- If you're using a serial mouse, confirm that the serial ports are enabled in the BIOS.

- If you're using a USB mouse connected to a hub, connect it directly to a PC to see whether the hub is at fault. Be sure the hub is powered on and plugged in as well.

- If the mouse is wireless, confirm that nothing is blocking the communication path required by the device.

- Check all components against Microsoft's HCL. Some USB hubs in particular are not fully compatible with Windows 2000.

If the mouse is a PS/2 device, make sure it is well connected and reboot. Windows 2000 seeks hardware installed on PS/2 ports on startup. If the device was disconnected or loose, it may not have been detected, and rebooting may be necessary to make it functional again.

Also, make sure you are using the latest drivers for your mouse. Windows 2000 will typically not allow incompatible versions of software to be installed. However, if you upgraded Windows 2000 from an earlier version of Windows, older, incompatible software may have been brought into the equation. Check with the manufacturer of the mouse for newer software and drivers that are Windows 2000 compatible.

Table 9.1   Keyboard shortcuts.

Keys	Action
F3	Searches for a file or folder
Ctrl+O	Opens an item
Alt+Enter	Views the properties of the selected item
Alt+F4	Closes the active item or quits the active program
Alt+Tab	Switches between open items
Alt+Esc	Cycles through items in the order they were opened
F6	Cycles through screen elements in a window or on the desktop
Shift+F10	Displays the shortcut menu for the selected item
Ctrl+Esc	Displays the Start menu
Alt+Underlined letter (in a menu name)	Displays the corresponding menu
Underlined letter in a command name on an open menu	Carries out the corresponding command
F10	Activates the menu bar in the active program
Right arrow	When the menu bar is active, opens the next menu item to the right or opens a submenu
Left arrow	When the menu bar is active, opens the next menu item to the left or closes a submenu
F5	Refreshes the active window

When you must navigate Windows without a mouse, you may find several keyboard shortcuts useful; they are listed in Table 9.1.

Multiple Monitors

Using multiple displays is a great feature of Windows 2000, but only if you can get it working. You must follow several steps to ensure that your multiple monitors get up and running properly. The first is to double-check that all your video adapters are on Microsoft's HCL. After you confirm their presence on the HCL, install your display adapters into your computer and start Windows 2000. Then, follow these steps:

1. Check Device Manager to make sure that all your devices are working properly. In Device Manager, expand the Display Adapters node to check for any problems.

2. If all adapters are listed and working properly, right-click on your desktop and choose Properties. Click on the Settings tab. If you see multiple monitors listed, highlight the grayed monitor icon and select the Extend My Windows Desktop Onto This Monitor checkbox. This option should enable the monitors for you.

3. If adapters are not working properly, check the device's status on its Properties page. Resolve any hardware conflicts by using the methods mentioned earlier in this chapter.

4. If you installed multiple adapters at one time, try installing only one additional adapter at a time.

Warning! The primary adapter must be able to function in VGA mode. Additionally, a secondary adapter must be able to have VGA mode disabled.

Power Management

Windows 2000 supports Power Management; however, it may not be functioning on your system. If your computer supports Power Management through Advanced Power Management (APM), your first step should be the BIOS of your computer. APM can be disabled in the BIOS. If it is, your computer won't detect it, and APM will be disabled. If APM is disabled, re-enable it and reinstall Windows 2000.

If you still do not have APM support, Windows 2000 may not support your BIOS. Windows considers certain BIOS versions to be troublesome with APM support and will not install the support. Check the biosinfo.inf file to see whether your BIOS is listed. You can also run one of the support tools, named apmstat.exe, on your installation CD. When you run this command at a command prompt with the **-v** switch, it will give you information regarding APM support on your computer.

If your BIOS is not compatible, you might be able to contact your BIOS manufacturer and upgrade your BIOS.

Some computers may have trouble coming out of standby mode. If you are experiencing difficulty in this situation, check your BIOS setup. You should change these settings to the same or greater values than those listed in Windows 2000 Power Options Properties. If changing the settings does not resolve the problem, check to make sure you are using Windows 2000 drivers for all your hardware. Some Windows NT 4 drivers can cause this problem. Disable these drivers to see whether the issue disappears. If it does, re-enable the drivers one at a time to determine which device is at fault.

With the initial release of Windows 2000, Power Management has two known bugs:

- If your power scheme changes from Home/Office to Portable/Laptop inexplicably, this may be a bug. If Windows is installed on a system with APM disabled, Home/Office is the default power scheme. If you enable APM and modify the Home/Office scheme and then reinstall or upgrade, the default scheme changes to Portable/Laptop. Check your settings and switch back if necessary.

- If your power scheme settings change, the problem could be caused by enabling or disabling APM support in Power Options Properties. If you switch back and forth between the two options, your power scheme settings may change from your settings on some systems.

Sound and Speakers

Speakers and sound—they definitely brighten the computing environment. Configuring these devices can cause a host of problems, though. If you are using digital USB speakers, for instance, and cannot hear CD audio, you might need to enable digital CD audio playback. To do so, follow these steps:

1. Open Control Panel and click on System.

2. On the Hardware tab, click on Device Manager.

3. Expand the DVD/CD-ROM Drives node, and highlight your drive.

4. From the Action menu, choose Properties.

5. Select Enable Digital CD Audio For This CD-ROM Device.

6. Click on OK and restart your computer.

Additionally, an upgrade to Windows 2000 may leave your sound card undetected. If you have this problem, you can manually add the device by following these steps:

1. Right-click on My Computer, click on Properties, and then click on the Hardware tab.

2. Click on the Hardware Wizard button and then click on Next.

3. Select Add/Troubleshoot A Device and click on Next.

4. Click on Add A New Device, click on Next, and then click on Next again.

5. Under Hardware Types, select Sound Video And Game Controllers and click on Next.

6. Select the manufacturer and model of your sound card, click on Next, and then click on Next again.

7. Confirm that the resources are selected correctly, click on OK, and then click on Finish.

8. Restart your computer to complete the installation.

Zip Drives

Zip drives are a popular storage medium, due to their capacity, portability, and ease of use. They have been around for several years, and include 100MB and 250MB capacity models, as well as versions that connect to your PC through ports such as your parallel port, SCSI ports, and USB, as well as versions designed for IDE controllers. Some common issues interfere with the detection, operation, and functionality of these drives.

Parallel Port Zip Drives

When working with Zip drives, you should first confirm that you have the model you think you do. Check the back of the Zip drive and confirm that it has two 25-pin ports, one male and one female. The port on the right should have a printer icon over it. If your drive has two identical ports on the back, it is likely the SCSI model and will require a SCSI connection on your PC.

If you are troubleshooting, we recommend you follow these steps. Although they may not be necessary for use of the drive, the most important step is to get the drive working properly. Following these steps will resolve a number of issues that may or may not be causing you problems in getting your drive detected and working:

1. Enter your computer's BIOS and set the Parallel Port Mode to EPP or bi-directional. This step puts your parallel port in the most compatible mode for Zip drive detection.

2. Check the Zip drive cable for bent or broken pins. Replace it if any are found. Any bent pins may prevent detection or proper data transfer.

3. With your PC powered off, connect the Zip drive to your computer with the provided cable. This cable meets more exacting standards than some available off the shelf.

4. At this time, do not connect anything to the passthrough port on the Zip drive, such as a printer. The devices can interfere with communication to your Zip drive if they demand constant control over the port.

5. Power on your PC and then plug in your Zip drive. You should see a light on the front of your Zip drive. This step checks for proper power, and when you turn on your PC first, you can avoid problems with some computers that check the parallel port on boot and can "confuse" the Zip drive.

6. Log on to Windows 2000 and look for your Zip drive in the My Computer box.

7. If the drive appears, one of the previous steps resolved the issue. If it does not appear, try using it on another computer to determine whether it's a drive or computer error.

SCSI Zip Drives

The most important factor in getting a SCSI Zip drive working is proper installation of the SCSI card. Each SCSI device must have a unique ID, so be sure the ID you use for the Zip is free. After you do so, properly terminating your drive is the only other step required.

Here's a quick tutorial in SCSI termination: Multiple SCSI devices are connected in a "chain"—one device is linked to another device. The SCSI card itself is part of the chain and may support internal devices, such as a hard drive or internal Zip SCSI drive. It also may support external devices, such as an external Zip or a scanner. The rule of termination is that both ends of the chained devices must be terminated. If you have internal and external devices, the last item at each end must be terminated. A switch, jumper, or terminator block can set termination; consult your owner's documentation to see which method is recommended for your device. If you have only an internal chain or an external chain, the card itself must be terminated. Most cards auto-terminate themselves if they recognize they are one end of the chain; however, if you are unsure, check the documentation for your card. If you are having problems getting your SCSI Zip drive detected, be sure to check the following items:

- Be sure the drive is powered on at boot and a light is on the drive.

- Terminate the Zip drive and connect it directly to the SCSI card to see whether another device is interfering.

- Try changing the ID of the Zip drive.

- Check all cables for bent pins and replace the cable if necessary.

- Confirm that all devices have unique IDs and are terminated properly.

These steps should assist you in locating the cause of most installation failures for your SCSI Zip drive.

9

Summary

We have taken a long journey through the realm of hardware and Windows 2000. Although we have explored a great deal, we still have a great deal more to explore. Windows 2000 provides advances in driver technology that result in better drivers for end users and easier driver writing for hardware manufacturers. The Win32 Driver Model simplifies the process so that driver writers can concentrate on improving compatibility, features, and performance of their end product.

Device Manager is a superb tool to gather information about your system. Using it, you can see resources, check problem devices, alter configurations, and more, from a single interface. You can quickly uncover items that are not functioning properly and begin steps to locate the problem.

System Information does not enable you to alter the hardware and drivers like Device Manager; however, it provides a scope and depth of information unparalleled in Windows 2000. Although it is unlikely to be your first stop when troubleshooting, it is definitely useful when you're troubleshooting those more difficult problems.

With Plug and Play, installing hardware is much easier. Along with Plug and Play, Windows provides the Add/Remove Hardware Wizard to get other hardware up and running. And if you run into problems, it can also help you troubleshoot the causes. Additionally, Windows provides the Hardware Troubleshooter to track down causes of malfunctioning hardware.

Finally, this chapter covered several steps for getting hardware to work when the first attempt fails. We covered general steps and went in depth on other common peripherals, such as keyboards, multiple monitors, and Zip drives.

In the next chapter, we discuss the installation of printers, including local and network printers. We also cover common troubleshooting methods for printers.

Chapter 10

Windows 2000 Printing Solutions

Introduction to Printing

Although we have been hearing the term *paperless society* for many years, we will always need to create a hard copy of a document or spreadsheet to view it in print. In fact, improvements are constantly being made in the speed, clarity, and color of the hard-copy documents being produced. These documents are created using the printing capabilities included in Windows 2000 Professional.

To see your document in print, however, you will need to install a printer. It can be attached directly to your computer, in which case it is called a *local printer*, or it may be a *network-shared printer* that you have permissions to connect to. After you have installed the printer, you can send your documents to it to create a hard copy. You can manage any document you send to the printer, and anyone given the appropriate permissions to manage documents on the printer also can manage it. You also can customize printer settings to help you manage how documents are handled for printing when they are received at the printer. Furthermore, you can audit your printer activity, which is helpful in determining who is using the printer and how often it is being used. This auditing information can be beneficial in justifying the purchase of additional print devices.

Reviewing Printing Terminology

The implementation of printing in Microsoft Windows 2000 environments is sometimes confusing because of the terminology used when discussing the different components involved. To effectively manage the printing capabilities available to you in Windows 2000, you must have a thorough understanding of the components and terminology used to describe them.

The most commonly used term when referring to creating a hard-copy document is the term *printer*. In Windows 2000, a *printer* is the software that controls the *print device*, which is the physical device that produces the actual hard-copy document. The printer is a combination of the printer driver, the print queue, and the support files required to create the hard-copy document.

By default, when you decide to print a document in Windows 2000, your Windows application passes the information to the operating system, which *spools* the data to a specified printer. This process of *spooling* is the temporary placement of the information headed for the printer onto the hard drive. When the printer is ready to process the information to create the actual hard-copy document, the *spooler* sends the information to the printer at a speed the printer can handle. This spooling process allows you to return to work on your applications sooner.

When you are printing multiple documents, they are placed in a *queue*. This queue is a stack of spooled jobs waiting to be sent to a print device.

A printer *driver* is a file that resides on your hard disk to assist in creating the hard-copy document. The printer driver translates your text file to commands that the printer understands. These commands include actions such as performing a line feed, performing a page feed, printing the different characters, and using specific fonts and graphics. The commands tell your printer exactly how to generate the hard-copy document of your file. With so many different manufacturers and models of printers, these commands can be different, which is why you have to obtain a specific printer driver for each type of printer you are using.

Accessing the Printers Folder

You manage printers through the Printer folders, shown in Figure 10.1. You can access the Printers folder by choosing one of the following sequences:

- Start|Settings|Printers (the quickest and easiest way)

- Start|Settings|Control Panel|Printers

- My Computer|Control Panel|Printers

- Start|Programs|Accessories|Windows Explorer|My Computer|Control Panel|Printers (the longest and most difficult way)

After you open the Printers folder, you can view the printers you have already installed. You can use the Add Printer icon to install additional printers. The printers you have installed also can be deleted or managed through this folder. With the appropriate permissions, you can also manage the queues of the installed printers by double-clicking on a printer. Commands located on the menus allow you to manage the printers and drivers used by the printers. Management activities include the installation, configuration, connection, disconnection, and removal of printer drivers and printers.

Examining Printing Features

The many printing capabilities in Windows 2000 Professional provide a dynamic, flexible, and powerful opportunity for you to create hard-copy documents. A brief overview of the Windows 2000 Professional printing features is listed here:

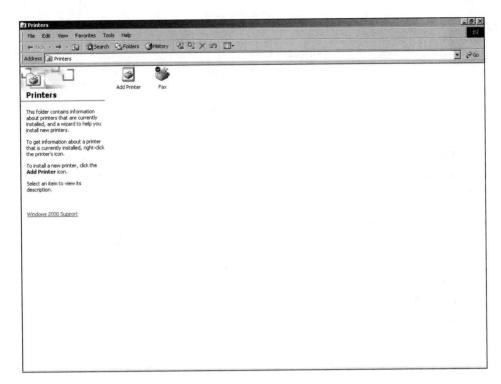

Figure 10.1
The Printers folder.

- You can easily add, modify, or remove printers directly from the Printers folder.

- You can install multiple printers for one print device, or you can configure one printer to use multiple print devices. Both options allow you to create custom schedules, permissions, and priorities for your devices.

- After installing a printer, you can easily share it on the network so that multiple users can print to it. These shared devices can have descriptive names, which can be easily identified by your users.

- You can define schedules, priorities, ownership, and permissions; you also can implement auditing on your network-shared printers.

- You can install multiple printer drivers on a network-shared printer, allowing multiple client types to use the printer. Most client types do not have to install the printer drivers manually because the drivers are automatically installed when the clients connect to the shared printer.

- You can easily manage the print job queue. For example, you can rearrange the order of print jobs, delete print jobs, pause printing, and resume printing.

Adding a Printer

When you want to install a printer on your computer, first check to see whether the print device is listed on the Hardware Compatibility List (HCL). The most current HCL is located on Microsoft's Web site at **www.microsoft.com/hcl/**. If the print device is not listed on the HCL, contact the hardware manufacturer and ask whether Windows 2000 printer drivers are available for the device.

Tip: If no printer driver is available for the specific print device, check to see whether a driver that is listed on the Windows 2000 HCL might be compatible with your print device. Note that the substitute driver might not contain all the functionality the required driver contains.

Before you add a new printer using the Add Printer Wizard located in the Printers folder, you should prepare yourself to answer the following prompts that you will encounter during the wizard process:

- Is it a local or network printer?

- If it is a local printer, are you going to share it?

- What printer driver or drivers will need to be installed?

- What is the name of the printer?

- Will you set it as your default printer?

Adding a Local Printer

After accessing the Printers folder, you can add a local printer by using the Add Printer Wizard. The wizard opens when you double-click on the Add Printer icon. The initial welcome screen explains that you can use the wizard to add a printer or connect to a printer that has already been installed. Click on Next to move to the Local Or Network Printer screen.

Note: If you add and configure a Plug-and-Play printer using USB, IEEE 1394, LPT, or infrared, you do not need to have administrative privileges. However, if the printer is not Plug-and-Play–compliant and you are connecting it directly to your computer, you must be logged on as an administrator or a member of the Administrators group.

The Local Or Network Printer screen presents a choice of adding a local or network printer. If you select Local Printer, you can take advantage of the Plug-and-Play option available to you in the Windows 2000 Professional environment to easily add an attached printer to your Printers folder. Add a checkmark to the Automatically Detect And Install My Plug And Play Printer checkbox, as shown in Figure 10.2, and click on Next. If your printer is attached through the Universal Serial Bus (USB), it should be detected immediately. If the printer is not attached through the USB, Windows 2000 Professional will attempt to automatically detect it on your defined ports. If the printer is detected using the Plug-and-Play feature, your printer is installed for you. If the printer is not detected,

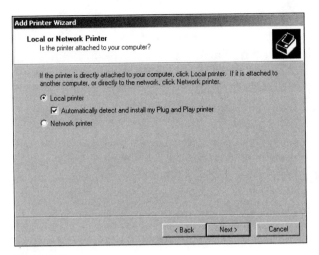

Figure 10.2
Adding a local printer using Plug-and-Play.

you will need to run the wizard again and deselect the option for automatic detection and then click on Next to proceed to the Select The Printer Port screen.

Note: *The Plug-and-Play detection process occurs when your computer is turned on and can also be invoked using the Add/Remove Hardware applet available in Control Panel.*

On the Select The Printer Port screen, shown in Figure 10.3, you select the printer port that has the printer attached to it. (A *port* usually refers to the connector on the computer where a peripheral device can be attached.) The most commonly used parallel printer port for an attached printer is LPT1 (Line Printer 1). However, if you know the print device is connected to another port, such as LPT2, or to a serial port, such as COM1 (Communications1) or COM2, you select that port.

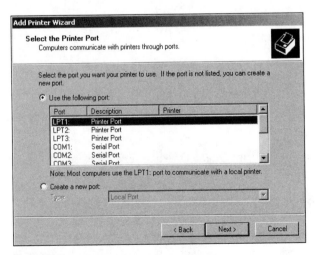

Figure 10.3
Selecting the printer port.

On the Select The Printer Port screen, you also can define a new port. When creating a new port, you can add a local, standard TCP/IP, or LPR port. This new local port can be used to attach a printer to your system if all the existing ports are already in use. A standard TCP/IP port is primarily used for directly attached network printers that support the TCP/IP protocol. An LPR port is best suited for servers that need to communicate with host computers such as VAX machines or Unix.

Tip: *If the LPR Port option is not available, you will need to install Print Services For Unix. You install it from the Add/Remove Programs applet within Control Panel. Choose Add/Remove Windows Components and then select the Other Network File And Print Services option to locate the Print Services For Unix.*

To add a local port, follow these steps:

1. Click on Create A New Port, select Local Port from the Type drop-down menu, and then click on Next.

2. Type the name of the port and then click on OK.

3. Finish adding the printer by completing the remaining steps in the Add Printer Wizard.

To add a standard TCP/IP port, follow these steps:

1. Click on Create A New Port and then select Standard TCP/IP Port from the Type drop-down menu.

2. Click on Next to invoke the Add Standard TCP/IP Printer Port Wizard.

3. Click on Next to open the Add Port dialog box.

4. Enter the printer name or IP address and the port name for the device.

5. If prompted, enter any additional port information required.

6. Click on Finish to add the new standard TCP/IP port.

To add an LPR port, follow these steps:

1. Click on Create A New Port and then select LPR Port from the Type drop-down menu.

2. Click on Next and provide the following information on the resulting screen:

   - Enter the Domain Name System (DNS) or IP address of the host for the printer you are adding.

   - In the Name Of The Printer Or Print Queue On That Server box, type the name of the printer as it is identified by the host.

3. Follow the instructions on the screen to install the TCP/IP printer.

Tip: *You also can add ports by using the Print Server Properties dialog box. You access this dialog box by opening the Printers folder, clicking on the File menu, and selecting Server Properties. In the Server Properties dialog box, you click on the Ports tab and then on the Add Port button.*

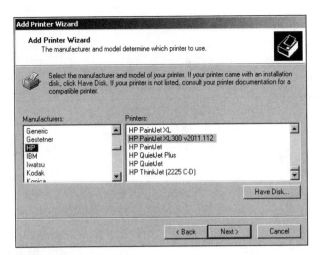

Figure 10.4
Identifying your printer manufacturer and model.

The next dialog box of the Add Printer Wizard, shown in Figure 10.4, requires you to identify the manufacturer and model of the print device you are adding. If your printer model is not listed, or your printer came with an installation disk, you can click on the Have Disk button and specify the location of the printer information that is required to install the printer. When specifying the location, you need to specify the drive letter that contains the drivers and then click on OK. Multiple drivers may be available, so be sure to choose the correct one based on the manufacturer's recommendation.

Note: The Add Printer Wizard searches for a file with an .inf extension. This file type, which contains driver information, is the standard file type supplied by manufacturers.

The next screen prompts you for a name for the printer. Windows 2000 supports long file names; however, not all clients and applications accessing the printer support long file names. With this point in mind, you should try to limit the file name to fewer than 32 characters.

The next dialog box presents the big question: Do you want to share the printer on the network? If not, you can click on Do Not Share This Printer and then choose whether you want to print a test page to be sure everything is installed correctly. Finally, you click on the Finish button to complete the installation of the local printer. If you want to share a printer, continue on to the next section.

Sharing a Local Printer

You can choose to share a printer when adding it using the Add Printer Wizard or after you have installed it by using the Sharing tab of the local printer's Properties dialog box. Both options provide an easy way to share your local printer on the network.

Sharing a Local Printer Using the Add Printer Wizard

If you choose to share the printer during the Add Printer Wizard process, the first few screens appear similar to those you saw when you added a local printer in the previous section. However, as you proceed through the wizard, you will encounter some different prompts to assist you in sharing the printer.

Follow these steps to create a shared network printer using the Add Printer Wizard:

1. Open the Printers folder, double-click on the Add Printer icon to start the Add Printer Wizard, and then click on Next.

2. On the Local Or Network Printer screen, choose Local Printer, clear the Automatically Detect And Install My Plug-And-Play Printer box, and then click on Next.

3. On the Select The Printer Port screen, choose a port you want the printer to use or create a port as described in the previous section. Click on Next to open the list of printer manufacturers and models.

4. Select the appropriate manufacturer and model or click on the Have Disk button to specify the location of the printer information required to install the printer. Then click on Next.

5. On the Name Your Printer screen, type a name for the printer in the Printer Name box. Click on Yes if you want to set this printer as the default for Windows-based programs; otherwise, click on No and then click on Next.

6. On the Printer Sharing screen, click on the Share As option, type the network share name that will be seen by the users when they remotely access the shared network printer, and then click on Next.

Note: *This network share name is seen by users when they browse for shared network printers, or the users can type it in when they are adding a shared network printer, as discussed in the "Adding a Shared Network Printer" section later in this chapter.*

7. Optionally, you can provide the location of the printer and any comments regarding the printer in the Location And Comment screen, shown in Figure 10.5.

Tip: *The optional information in the Location And Comment screen is extremely helpful to users who are trying to locate and connect to shared network printers. This information can be used to verify that the users are connecting to the appropriate printer and whether any special features or restrictions are placed on the printer.*

8. When the Print Test Page screen appears, asking whether you would like to send a test page to the printer to verify that the printer was installed correctly, choose Yes or No.

9. The final wizard screen displays a summary of the information you supplied during the Add Printer Wizard process. Verify that the information is correct, and click on Finish or use the Back button to back up to make any necessary changes. Then

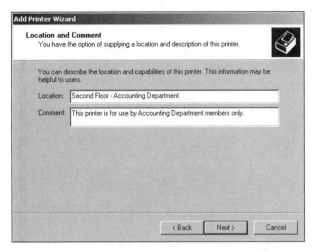

Figure 10.5
The location and comments of shared network printers.

return to the summary screen and click on Finish to complete the installation of the shared network printer.

You can use Decision Tree 10.1 to assist you in responding to the prompts you will encounter while adding a local printer.

Sharing a Local Printer Using the Sharing Tab

You may want to add a local printer and then test and configure it before you share it on the network. You can share a local printer after it has been installed by following these steps:

1. Open the Printers folder, right-click on the printer's icon, and choose Sharing or Properties from the shortcut menu to open the printer's Properties dialog box, as shown in Figure 10.6.

Note: The tabs that appear in the Properties dialog box depend on the printer you have installed.

2. If the Sharing tab is not selected, click on it.

3. Click on Shared As to generate a share name based on the printer name. You can leave the default name, or you can modify it.

Warning! To allow MS-DOS or Windows 3.x clients to use the printer, use eight or fewer characters with no more than a three-character extension when creating the printer name.

4. If clients who are accessing the printer are using different operating systems, you will need to install the required drivers for the different operating systems. To install other drivers, click on the Additional Drivers button and select the appropriate

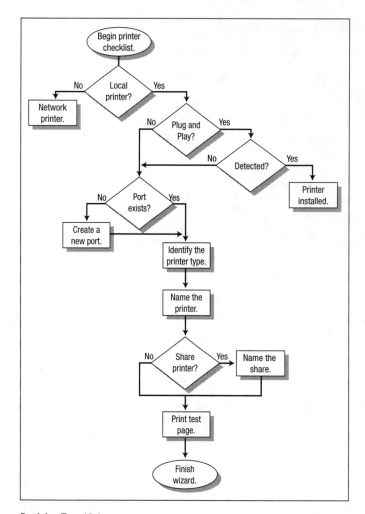

Decision Tree 10.1
Adding a local printer.

operating system drivers, as shown in Figure 10.7. When you're done, click on OK to return to the Properties dialog box.

Note: *No driver options are available for MS-DOS, Windows, or Windows for Workgroup clients. These drivers must be added and updated manually at the client machine.*

Tip: *Adding operating system drivers can greatly ease management of printer drivers for both the adminis- trator and user because these drivers are automatically downloaded when the user connects to the printer. This process eliminates the need for the administrator to load the driver for each user.*

5. To provide the optional location and comment information, click on the General tab and enter the information in the Location and Comment boxes.

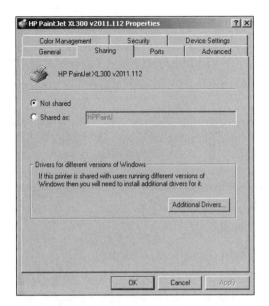

Figure 10.6
An installed printer's Properties dialog box.

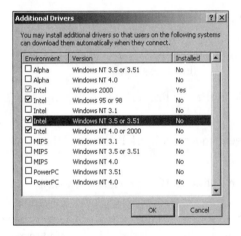

Figure 10.7
Available printer drivers.

6. Click on the OK button to share the printer. The printer's icon now has a hand under it indicating it is now a shared printer.

Both of the approaches described here are easy ways to share printers on the network so that users can connect to and use them. After you create the shared network printers, the users can add them to their Printers folder using the methods discussed in the next section.

You also might need to stop sharing a printer on the network. To prevent the sharing of your printer, open the Properties dialog box for your printer, click on the Sharing tab, and click on the Not Shared option.

Adding a Shared Network Printer

In Windows 2000 Professional, you can easily add a shared network printer to your Printers folder. However, certain requirements must be met before you can do so. These four requirements make it possible for your users to locate and connect to the shared network printer:

- The print device must be directly connected to the network. If the printer contains a direct network interface, the computer sharing the printer must be on the same network as the printer.

- The printer must be installed by completing all the steps in the Add Printer Wizard. This printer must also be functioning properly as a local printer.

- The printer must be shared on the network.

- The appropriate permissions must be set to allow the network users access to the printer.

You can add a shared network printer in a couple of ways in Windows 2000 Professional. The first way is to use the Add Printer Wizard, and the second way is to use the search capabilities of Active Directory. Let's look at how easily you can add a shared network printer using both of these options.

Adding a Shared Network Printer Using the Add Printer Wizard

Adding a shared network printer to your Printers folder is as easy as adding a local printer—maybe even easier. You use the same Add Printer Wizard located in the Printers folder to add the shared network printers. Just follow these steps:

1. Open the Printers folder, double-click on the Add Printer icon to start the Add Printer Wizard, and then click on Next.

2. On the Local Or Network Printer screen, choose Network Printer and then click on Next.

3. The Locate Your Printer screen, shown in Figure 10.8, provides a few ways to locate and connect to a shared network printer. You can supply the Universal Naming Convention (UNC) name, the Uniform Resource Locator (URL), or you can click on Next to browse the network for the shared network printer you are trying to add. The UNC name is specified using the following format:

   *printserver_name**printer_sharename*

   The URL name is specified using the following format:

   http://*printserver_name***/printers/***printer_sharename***/.printer**

4. If you clicked on Next to browse the network for the shared network printer, the Browse For Printer screen opens, as shown in Figure 10.9. On this screen, you can browse for available shared network printers, or you can type the shared network printer name using either the UNC or URL, as described in Step 3.

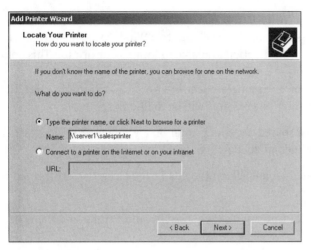

Figure 10.8
Locating your printer.

Note: After you select an available shared network printer, printer status information regarding the selected printer appears in the lower part of the window.

5. After you locate your printer, click on Next to move to the Default Printer screen. You can use this screen to set this printer as the default for your Windows-based applications.

6. The final screen displays a summary of the information you supplied during the Add Printer Wizard process. Verify that the information is correct, and click on Finish or use the Back button to back up to make any necessary changes. Then return to the summary screen and click on Finish to complete the installation of the shared network printer.

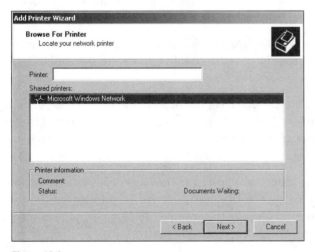

Figure 10.9
The Browse For Printer screen.

Adding a Shared Network Printer Using Active Directory

If your Windows 2000 Professional machine belongs to a Windows 2000 Active Directory domain, you will have an additional option available to locate your printer. This option—Find A Printer In The Directory—uses the capabilities of Active Directory to locate your printer. You don't need to know the name of the printer or its location. However, the more you know about the printer, the easier it will be to find the printer.

Follow these steps to install a shared network printer on a Windows 2000 Professional machine that belongs to a Windows 2000 Active Directory domain:

1. Open the Printers folder, double-click on the Add Printer icon to start the Add Printer Wizard, and then click on Next.

2. On the Local Or Network Printer screen, choose Network Printer and then click on Next.

3. On the Locate Your Printer screen, click on Find A Printer In The Directory to open the Find Printers dialog box.

4. You can use the Find Printers screen to choose how you want to search Active Directory for a printer. Each of the three tabs provide different search capabilities depending on the information you know about the printer you are trying to locate:

   - *Printers tab*—Used to search for a shared network printer by name, model, or location

   - *Features tab*—Used to find a shared network printer based on its installed features

   - *Advanced tab*—Used to search for a shared network printer based on any criteria published in Active Directory for shared network printers

5. After you locate a printer from the list of shared network printers returned, double-click on it to close the Find Printers screen and return to the Add Printer Wizard.

6. If this is not the first printer you have installed, you are asked whether your Windows applications should use this printer as the default. Choose the appropriate response and then click on Next.

7. You will then receive a summary screen of the answers you provided as you were prompted throughout the Add Printer Wizard process. If you are satisfied with your responses, click on Finish. If you are unsatisfied, click on the Back button to make the required modifications.

Adding local printers, sharing them, and allowing users to connect to shared network printers are fairly easy tasks to perform. However, some special printing features available to you in Windows 2000 Professional make the printing functionality more robust than what was available in previous Windows operating systems.

Examining Windows 2000 Special Printing Features

Up to this point, we have discussed the actions required to add local and network printers, and also how to share local printers so that users can access them remotely. Windows 2000 Professional provides other functionality that allows you to manage your printing environment more efficiently. Defining printer pools, defining multiple printers for the same print device, using fax and Internet printers, and printing using infrared technology all add robustness to the printing capabilities available in Windows 2000.

Multiple Printers and Multiple Print Devices

In Windows 2000 Professional, you can assign multiple names to a single print device that is being shared with others. This capability provides you the flexibility to have different people access the same device using different names, assign printing priorities to different users, make one printer available for local use while another is for network use, and specify different hours that the printers are available. On the flip side, you can provide a single printer name for multiple print devices, creating a printer pool for load balancing and efficiency.

Multiple Printers for a Single Print Device

The process of creating multiple printers for the same print device allows you to fine-tune the network's access to the printer. For example, each printer associated with the print device can have different priority settings and a different schedule of availability. This provides you, as the administrator, with more control of how and when the print device is accessed. To implement multiple printers on the same print device, you simply perform the same task for each instance; however, you must provide a different name for each instance.

The first instance of the printer requires the most time and effort to install. Adding subsequent instances of the printers to the same print device becomes faster because Windows 2000 Professional remembers the last printer you installed. Windows 2000 will automatically select the same manufacturer and model when you install subsequent printers to the same print device. However, it will prompt you to see whether you want to keep the existing driver or replace it with a new one. If the first instance is behaving as expected, keeping the existing one is recommended, unless you have obtained and tested a newer printer driver.

Warning! *If you don't give the new printer a different name, Windows 2000 will not actually create the new printer.*

During the installation of the subsequent printers, be sure to choose the same printer driver as you did for all other instances. Furthermore, be sure that all the other printer settings are configured as they should be. These additional printers allow you to choose which instances are shared on the network and which ones aren't. This is possible even though you are connecting to the same print device.

Multiple Print Devices for a Single Printer

Using multiple print devices for a single printer improves throughput of your printed documents. Your users connect to the same shared network printer, but you establish connections to multiple print devices through that one printer. This feature, called *printer pooling,* allows all your users to send a print job to a single printer, and the first available print device will create the printed document.

Warning! *All the print devices should be located in close proximity. Otherwise, your users must check every print device defined in the printer pool to locate their documents.*

All the print devices must be identical—the same make, model, and amount of memory—for printer pooling to work. Follow these steps to implement printer pooling:

1. Open the Printers folder, right-click on the printer's icon, and choose Properties from the shortcut menu to open the Properties dialog box.

2. Select the Ports tab and click on the Enable Printer Pooling checkbox.

3. Select all the ports that are connected to the attached print devices, as shown in Figure 10.10.

Note: *If the ports you need are not available, you can add them by using the Add Port button.*

4. When all ports are selected, click on OK to apply the changes. Any print job sent to this printer will be directed to the first available port.

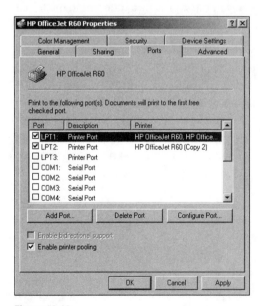

Figure 10.10
Creating a printer pool.

Tip: You may be able to create a printer pool with different print devices if they emulate a common printer. You can install the driver for the emulation and make any necessary adjustments to the print devices.

If properly configured, both printer pooling and multiple printers can be beneficial to you and the users who generate printed documents frequently.

Fax Printers

Fax printers are used for printing faxes. Unlike other printers in Windows 2000, fax printers cannot be shared on the network with other users. Although Windows 2000 Professional allows you to send and receive faxes using more than one fax device, all faxes are filtered through only one fax printer.

Fax printers are managed from the Printers folder. Figure 10.11 contains the Properties dialog box for the fax printer created for you by default. This dialog box has four tabs:

- *General*—Allows you to specify locations, add comments, and rename the fax printer

- *Sharing*—Simply states Sharing Is Not Supported As Previously Mentioned (Should Probably Be Removed)

- *Security*—Allows you to set permissions, define owners, and control auditing

- *User Information*—Allows you to provide information that will be used on the cover page

The Advanced Options tab of the Fax applet located inside Control Panel allows you to create multiple instances of the fax printer. Each instance can have completely customized

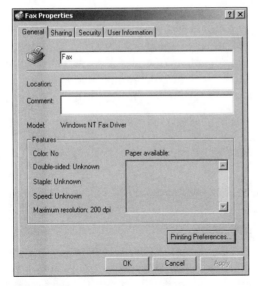

Figure 10.11
The Fax Properties dialog box.

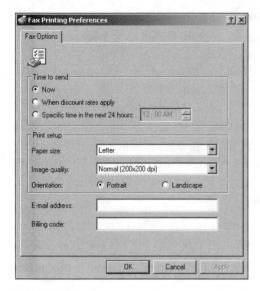

Figure 10.12
The Fax Printing Preferences dialog box.

printing preferences, which you access from the General tab by clicking on the Printing Preferences button. Some of these customizations, shown in Figure 10.12, include paper size, orientation, and the time of day to send faxes.

Internet Printers

Windows 2000 Professional enables you to connect to printers over the Internet or intranet using the Internet Printing Protocol (IPP). These printers have to be created and shared for such access. Internet printers that have been properly configured for such access are extremely useful for printing documents. Using printers connected this way, you don't need to print a hard copy of a document and then fax it to another location. Instead, you can print the document directly to an Internet printer that has been configured using IPP, as long as you have the correct permissions to access the printer.

Internet printing can be configured on a Windows 2000 Server running Internet Information Server 5 (IIS 5). IIS 5 is installed by default during the installation of Windows 2000 Server, and can be configured to use IPP to allow Internet connections to be made to the printer. After the Windows 2000 Professional client has added the URL of the printer installed on the IIS computer, users can easily print documents to that printer.

Printing Using Infrared Technology

Infrared printers can be installed to allow you to print to a printer using the infrared printing capability (IrLPT) provided with the Windows 2000 operating systems. If you add an infrared printer, Windows 2000 detects and automatically installs the required drivers for the infrared printer. This installation is completed without shutting down or restarting your computer.

To install a Plug-and-Play–compliant infrared printer, first make sure that the infrared-enabled computer and infrared printer are both turned on. You then position the two infrared devices to within one meter of each other to establish a wireless infrared connection. After several seconds, the computer will recognize the infrared-capable printer, and the printer icon will appear in the status area of your taskbar. After the two infrared devices recognize each other, the appropriate drivers are automatically installed on the computer, and the printer icon will appear in your Printers folder.

If the infrared printer is not Plug-and-Play compliant, or if your computer does not have a built-in infrared transceiver (so you have an infrared transceiver attached to your computer using a serial [COM] port), follow these steps:

10

1. Open the Printers folder using one of the ways discussed earlier.

2. Double-click on Add Printer to start the Add Printer Wizard and click on Next.

3. Click on Local Printer, verify that the Automatically Detect My Printer checkbox is cleared, and then click on Next.

4. Follow the instructions on the wizard screens to finish setting up the local printer by selecting the appropriate printer port, printer manufacturer, and model and typing a name for your printer.

When you are finished, the printer icon appears in the Printers folder and is available for use while the two infrared devices are within range.

Securing Your Printing Environment

After you install your printers and share them, you can control who can access them (especially those expensive color printers) and what they can do with the printers. You'll probably want to monitor the activity of the printers also. You do so by implementing security permissions and auditing in your Windows 2000 environment.

Setting Printer Permissions

Security permissions define exactly what tasks your users can perform when connected to a printer in Windows 2000 operating system environments. These permissions can range from the users submitting and managing their own documents to creating, configuring, and deleting network printers. These permissions are managed through the Security tab of your printer's Properties dialog box.

Note: *By default, only administrators and the owner of the printer have full access to the printer.*

Table 10.1 lists the default print permission levels and the tasks that can be performed with each permission level. As you can see, the users who receive the Manage Printers permission can perform any task involved with printers. The Manage Documents permission is less powerful, but it allows users to manage documents they submit to the printer as well as documents submitted by other users. Finally, the Print permission allows users to print and manage only documents they submitted.

Table 10.1   Default print permission levels and associated tasks.

Tasks	Print	Manage Printers	Manage Documents
Print	X	X	X
Control document settings		X	X
Change printing order of documents		X	
Change printer properties and permissions		X	

Table 10.2 lists the default print permissions and who receives them by default.

Note: *Printer permissions should be assigned only to groups, not individual users. Therefore, make all users members of a group before attempting to grant permissions to them.*

To set printer permissions, follow these steps:

1. Open the Printers folder using one of the methods previously discussed.

2. Right-click on the printer for which you want to set permissions and choose Properties from the shortcut menu to open the Properties dialog box.

3. Click on the Security tab to view the current permissions.

4. To modify existing printer permissions, select the group from the Name area and then clear or check the Allow or Deny checkbox within the Permissions area, as shown in Figure 10.13.

5. To add a new group to the printer permissions list, click on the Add button to open the Select Users, Computers, Or Groups dialog box, shown in Figure 10.14.

Tip: *The Name list will display only the accounts in the context you've logged on to. For instance, if you log on to the local computer, you will see only the accounts for the local computer. However, if you log on to the domain, you will see all the accounts for the domain. Use the Look In box to view other available users and groups that can be managed.*

Table 10.2   Default print permissions assigned to built-in user groups.

User Groups	Print	Manage Printers	Manage Documents
Administrators	X	X	X
Power Users	X	X	X
Everyone	X		
Creator/Owner	X		X

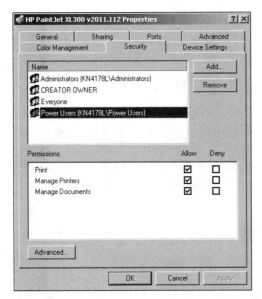

Figure 10.13
Modifying printer permissions.

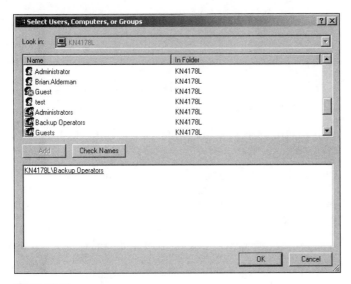

Figure 10.14
Adding new security groups.

6. To add a group, select the group name in the Name list, click on Add, and then click on OK to return to the Properties dialog box.

7. To remove a group, select the name of the group on the Security tab of the printer's Properties dialog box, click on Remove, and then click on OK.

Warning! Remember how the group permissions function. If a user is in multiple groups with different permissions, the system grants the highest-level permission. So, if Stacy is a member of one group with Print permission and a member of another group with Manage Printers permission, she'll always have Manage Printers permission. Permissions are not cumulative when one of the groups she belongs to has Deny permission to the printer. The Deny will always override all other cumulative permissions.

Changing Printer Ownership

By default, the user who creates the printer is considered its owner. The owner has Manage Printers permission on the printer and can completely manage the printer. If the user leaves the company or no longer wants to manage the printer, you will have to change the ownership of the printer. Only an administrator or a user with Manage Printers permission can change the ownership of a printer. To change ownership, follow these steps:

1. Log on to the Windows 2000 Professional machine as the user who will become the owner of the printer.

2. Open the Printers folder.

3. Right-click on the printer you want to take ownership of and choose Properties from the shortcut menu to open the Properties dialog box.

4. Select the Security tab and then click on the Advanced button to open the Access Control Settings dialog box for the printer.

5. Click on the Owner tab to display the dialog box, shown in Figure 10.15.

6. In the Change Owner To section, select the account name that you want to own the printer and click on Apply or OK.

The individual you selected is now the owner of the printer and has Manage Printers permission for the printer.

Printer Auditing

With all aspects of Windows 2000 Professional, you'll want to ensure that you have a secure and efficient environment. Auditing your printers can provide you information regarding who is using the printers, how often, and whether any unauthorized attempts have been made to access your printers.

Warning! To implement printer auditing, you must be logged on as an administrator.

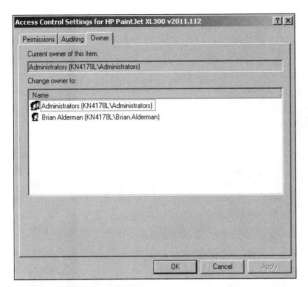

Figure 10.15
Changing a printer's ownership.

Auditing is a two-step process. First, you have to enable it, and then you have to define the objects you want to audit. In Windows 2000, you enable auditing using the Group Policy add-in as follows:

1. Choose Start|Run to open the Run dialog box.

2. In the Run dialog box, type "gpedit.msc" and press Enter to open the Group Policy window.

3. In the tree pane, locate the Audit Policy folder by following these steps:

   • Expand Computer Configuration by clicking on the plus sign.

   • Expand Windows Settings.

   • Expand Security Settings.

   • Expand Local Policies.

   • Click on the Audit Policy folder to display the audit policies in the detail pane.

4. Select Audit Policy Change, and then select Action|Security to open the Local Security Policy Setting dialog box, as shown in Figure 10.16.

5. Check the Success or Failure checkbox, or both, and click on OK.

6. Verify that auditing has been enabled for both Success and Failure in the detail pane of the Group Policy window, as shown in Figure 10.17.

7. Close the Group Policy window.

Figure 10.16
Enabling auditing using the Local Security Policy Setting dialog box.

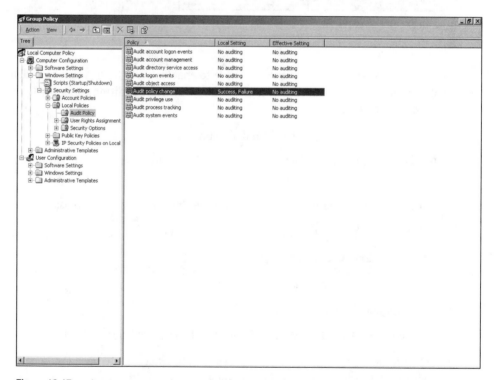

Figure 10.17
Verifying that auditing is enabled.

Auditing is now enabled on this local machine. The second set of steps requires you to choose what objects to audit. For instance, to audit a specific printer, follow these steps:

1. Open the Printers folder to access the defined printers.

2. Right-click on the printer you want to audit and choose Properties from the shortcut menu to open the Properties dialog box.

3. Select the Security tab and then click on the Advanced button to open the Access Control Settings dialog box for the printer.

4. Select the Auditing tab and then click on Add to open the Select Users, Computers, Or Groups dialog box.

5. Select a user or group and click on OK to open the Auditing Entry for the selected printer.

6. Click on the Successful and/or Failed checkbox for each item that you want to audit and then click on OK. Notice the entries made in the Access Control Settings dialog box shown in Figure 10.18.

7. Highlight an account in the Auditing Entries list to display some basic information for the type of audit. To modify settings of the selected account, click on the View/Edit button.

8. Click on OK on each dialog box to close it.

Tip: *This auditing information is stored in the Security log of the Event Viewer. You can access the Event Viewer through the Administrative Tools.*

Now that you have taken a look at some of the hidden special features regarding printing, you need to be familiar with the numerous options available to you for managing and customizing printers in Windows 2000 Professional.

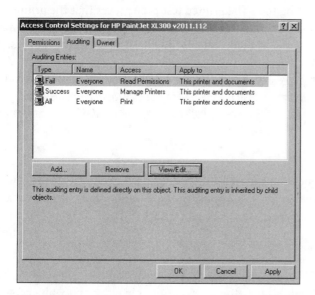

Figure 10.18
Access Control Settings containing auditing entries.

Customizing Your Printer

After you add and share your printers, you can customize them by using the Properties dialog box of each printer. You access the Properties dialog box like most Windows 2000 Professional objects—through the shortcut menu.

Your printer's Properties dialog box contains several tabs, including General, Sharing, Ports, Advanced, Security, and Device Settings. Optionally, you might have a Color Management tab if you're using a color printer. You use each different tab to customize your printer.

Tip: For more information on any of the items located on each tab, you can click on the ? in the upper-right corner of the Properties dialog box and then click on the item in question for a brief explanation of the item's purpose.

Using the General Tab

We briefly discussed the General tab earlier in the chapter when explaining how to share a local printer that had already been added but had not yet been shared. You use this tab to modify the local printer name and provide a location and comment for users browsing the network when adding a shared network printer to their Printers folder. The General tab also lists some of the features available on the printer. Two additional buttons are available for use: Print Test Page and Printing Preferences.

Print Test Page

When you first see the Print Test Page button, you may think, "Why bother when I can send any document to the printer to see whether it prints correctly?" However, you can use this test page as a troubleshooting tool. The printed test page proves that the printer can print both graphics and text. The printed text contains valuable information regarding the printer. This information includes a list of files supporting the printer and the file versions.

Tip: After you install a printer, print a test page and place the printed document in a safe place. This page can be useful in troubleshooting problems that may arise in the future. For instance, during troubleshooting, you can compare this list of files and versions that work correctly with the currently installed files and versions that are not working correctly.

Printing Preferences

You use the Printing Preferences button to define your printed layout. On the Layout tab of the Printing Preferences dialog box, you specify the Orientation (Portrait, Landscape, or Rotated Landscape), the Page Order (print Front To Back or Back To Front), and the Pages Per Sheet. For instance, if you set this last option to 2, two pages of the document will be printed on one sheet of paper.

On the Paper/Quality tab, you specify your Paper Source (trays or manual feeds), Media (quality of paper), and Color options (whether it can print only black-and-white copies or color copies as well).

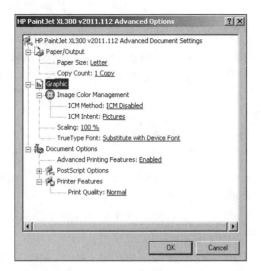

Figure 10.19
Advanced printer settings.

Both the Layout and Paper/Quality tabs have an Advanced button you can use to define the printer's environment. These options, shown in Figure 10.19, describe how the printer performs—for instance, type of paper loaded, default number of copies to generate, print quality, color quality, scaling options, font types, PostScript printer settings, and spooling functionality.

Note: The Sharing tab was discussed earlier in this chapter in the "Sharing a Local Printer Using the Sharing Tab" section.

Configuring Port Settings

The Ports tab displays which port the printer is using. You can add a port by double-clicking on the Add Port button and providing the information discussed in the "Adding a Local Printer" section earlier in this chapter.

Deleting a Port

You also can delete a port setting on the Ports tab. To delete a port, simply select the port from the list and click on the Delete Port button. Note that Windows 2000 Professional will not allow you to delete system ports, such as the physical parallel port LPT1.

If you delete a port and you later determine you need it, you should be able to add it again by using the procedure discussed earlier in this chapter. However, if that approach doesn't work, you will need to edit the Registry directly to add the port.

Warning! Editing the Registry to recover a port is not a task for just anyone and may render your system inoperable. Be sure that only experienced users edit the Registry of your Windows 2000 Professional operating system.

Configuring a Port

A port setting is used to determine how long Windows 2000 Professional waits before it decides that the printer attached to the parallel port is not responding and you need to be notified an error occurred. You use the Transmission Retry number to adjust the amount of time the system will wait for a printer to prepare itself to accept data to be printed. The default is 90 seconds.

This setting applies to all printers that use the same printer driver, not just to the one you have selected. To configure this time-out value, follow these steps:

1. On the Ports tab, select the port you want to configure and click on the Configure Port button to open the Configure Port dialog box.

2. Enter the time for the Transmission Retry in seconds and click on OK.

Tip: You also enable printer pooling on the Ports tab. If you are using printer pooling, you will have multiple ports assigned to one printer. However, you will have to make this modification to only one of the system ports (LPT1, LPT2, and LPT3), and it is automatically applied to the other system ports.

Using the Advanced Tab

The Advanced tab, shown in Figure 10.20, provides a powerful way to control and configure your printers. On this tab, you can define schedules, set priorities, configure spooling, and define separator pages.

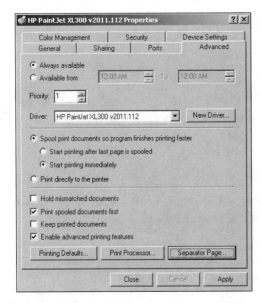

Figure 10.20
The Advanced tab of the printer's Properties dialog box.

Scheduling Print Jobs

By default, your newly created printer is always available. However, if you would rather it be available only at certain times, you can create a schedule by following these steps:

1. Click on the Available From option (clearing Always Available).

2. In the From time box, click on the up or down arrow to select a starting time or type in the starting time.

3. In the To time box, click on the up or down arrow to select an ending time or type in the ending time.

4. If you are finished configuring the printer, click on OK.

Note: *If a print job is sent to the printer while it is scheduled to be unavailable, that job will remain in the print queue until the schedule of the printer makes it available.*

You may be wondering how and why you would schedule a printer's availability to prevent users from accessing it during certain times of the day. You can use this option to ensure that users who require access to the printer are not blocked from it by someone who doesn't have the same urgency to access it. For example, the Accounts Payable department prints checks beginning at noon every Friday. You want to ensure that nobody else uses the printer during this time because the corporate checks are loaded in the printer. You would set up a schedule for Accounts Payable to have exclusive access to the printer during that time frame, preventing anyone else from printing to that printer.

Although you can set user logon and printer hours, you must set the printer hours for all groups that are accessing a particular printer. For instance, if you allow the administrators access to a printer at any time, you can't restrict a group from accessing it between 6 A.M. and 6 P.M. However, there are some exceptions to this rule:

- You can adjust the users' logon hours so they are forcibly disconnected when their logon hours expire.

- You can set up multiple printer names: one name for the times when the printer is available for use and another name for the times when the printer is unavailable. Those who connect to the printer name with the limited hours will be able to use the printer only during those hours.

Setting Printer Priorities

You can configure your shared network printer to control who receives priority access to the printers. You can also configure multiple names for the printer, each with its own priority assigned to it. You can then assign each group access to the appropriate printer name according to the priority you want to assign.

You can also set priorities by documents. Your document priorities affect where the document goes in the print queue. When a high-priority document enters the queue, it cuts in front of the lower-priority jobs that are in the queue. As soon as the print device becomes available, the high-priority print job is printed.

Priorities are assigned using numbers from 1 through 99, with 99 being the highest priority and 1 being the lowest priority. The default priority value for print jobs is 1.

For example, to modify the priorities of a WordPad document, follow these steps:

1. Open an existing document or create a document using WordPad.

2. Choose File|Print to open the Print dialog box.

3. Right-click on the printer you want to use and choose Properties from the shortcut menu to open the Properties dialog box.

4. Select the Advanced tab and raise the priority value to a higher number.

5. Click on OK.

6. Click on Print after you return to the Print dialog box.

Updating Printer Drivers

You also can use the Advanced tab to add new drivers for existing printers on your machine. From the Driver drop-down menu, simply choose the printer for which you want to add a new driver. After you select the printer, click on the New Driver button to begin the Add Printer Driver Wizard. This wizard steps you through the prompts required to add a new printer driver.

Spooling

Spooling is the temporary placement of the information headed for the printer onto the hard drive. You use the Advanced tab to control the spooling process. The default spooling process is set to spool the documents to the printer before they are printed. You configure this setting by clicking on the Spool Print Documents So Program Finishes Faster radio button. This option increases users' productivity because it allows them to get back to the tasks they were performing while the printing occurs in the background.

With the default option turned on, you can further optimize your printing by choosing one of the two following options:

- *Start Printing After Last Page Is Spooled*—Specifies that the print device should not begin printing until the entire document has been spooled. Until the entire document is printed, the printing application is unavailable to the user. However, using this option ensures that the entire document is available to the print device.

- *Start Printing Immediately*—Specifies that the print device should begin printing after the first page of the document is spooled. The printing application becomes available to the user much sooner than with the previous option.

When the Spool Print Documents So Program Finishes Faster option is selected, you can use four optional settings to manage the spooling process. These settings are helpful in managing the spooling and print queue in Windows 2000 Professional:

- *Hold Mismatch Documents*—Directs the spooler to check the printer setup and compare it to the document setup before sending the document to the print device.

Note: *A mismatched document waiting in the queue will not prevent matched documents from printing.*

- *Print Spooled Documents First*—Specifies that the spooler should process documents that have completed spooling when deciding which document to print next.

10

Tip: *Choose this option if you want to maximize printer efficiency.*

- *Keep Printed Documents*—Specifies that the spooler should not delete documents after they are printed. The documents can easily be resubmitted if necessary and must be removed manually.

- *Enable Advanced Printing Features*—Specifies that metafile spooling is turned on and options such as Page Order, Booklet Printing, and Pages Per Sheet are available, depending on your printer.

You also have the option of sending print jobs directly to the port connected to the printer. However, if you choose to implement this option, you cannot use your printing application until the print job is complete. For example, to send a WordPad document directly to the printer port, follow these steps:

1. Open an existing document or create a document using WordPad.

2. Choose File|Print to open the Print dialog box.

3. Right-click on the printer you want to use and choose Properties from the shortcut menu to open the Properties dialog box.

4. Select the Advanced tab and click on the Print Directly To The Printer option.

You can use the Print Directly To The Printer option to turn off spooling entirely. This capability is helpful for troubleshooting the printing process if you suspect that spooling is the problem.

Warning! *Although printing directly to the printer is helpful if you are experiencing spooling problems with your printer, this process will result in slower printing.*

The Printing Defaults button opens a dialog box that presents the same information and two tabs discussed earlier in the "Printing Preferences" section.

You use the Print Processor button to specify the print processor and default data type. Most likely, you will not need to change either of these. However, a few programs require a specialized print processor and particular data type to print. In this dialog box, you specify these special settings.

Managing Separator Pages

Separator pages are extra pages printed before the main document in an effort to help you organize your print jobs. These pages identify the owner of the print job, record the print time and date, print a message to owners of the print job, and record the print job number.

Separator pages are especially helpful in sorting documents if you have numerous people using the same shared network printer. Windows 2000 Professional stores several separator page files as SEP files in the *%systemroot%*\system 32 folder. Table 10.3 lists the four separator pages included with Windows 2000 Professional.

Warning! The separator page files included with Windows 2000 Professional may not work with all printers.

To specify a particular separator page, follow these steps:

1. Click on the Separator Page button located on the Advanced tab of your printer's Properties dialog box.

2. Click on Browse to open a Separator Page listing of the System32 directory, or you can type in the pathname of a specific SEP file.

3. Select one of the separator page files with the .sep extension, click on Open, and then click on OK to close the Separator Page dialog box.

4. Click on OK to close the printer's Properties dialog box and begin using the specified separator page.

When specifying the separator page, you can just specify the file name if you are already in the correct path to find the file. However, if you are not in the correct path to locate the file, you will need to specify the entire pathname.

Table 10.3   Windows 2000 default separator pages.

File Name	Compatibility	Description
SYSPRINT.SEP	PostScript	Prints a blank page before each print job
PCL.SEP	PCL	Switches a dual-language printer to Printer Control Language (PCL) mode
PSCRIPT.SEP	PostScript	Switches a dual-language printer to PostScript mode
SYSPRTJ.SEP	PostScript	Prints a blank page before each print job sent to a PostScript printer

Warning! The SEP file must be physically located on the computer that controls the printer for which you are specifying the separator page so that it can update the Registry. It cannot be located on a shared network folder. The error "Could not set printer: The specified separator file is invalid" is most likely a sign that the SEP file is not located on a local hard drive.

You can create your own separator page file by following these steps:

1. Click on Start|Programs|Accessories|Notepad to open the Notepad text editor.

2. Choose File|New to open a new document.

3. Enter a single character that you most likely won't use anywhere else in the document, such as $ or #, on the first line and then press Enter.

4. Enter the variables listed in Table 10.4 that specify what you want printed on your separator page. Each variable must be listed on a separate line. Then press Enter.

Table 10.4   Printer separator page variables.

Variable	Effect
BS	Prints text in block characters with pound signs (#) until you insert a $U. (Avoid using this variable because printing text in this format takes a lot of room.)
$D	Prints the date the job was printed, using the format defined on the Date tab of the Regional Options dialog box.
$E	Ejects a page from the printer. Use this code to start a new separator page or end the separator page file.
$F*pathname**filename*	Prints the contents of the file specified by *pathname/filename*, starting on a blank line. This does not include formatting.
$H*nn*	Sets a printer-specific control sequence, where *nn* is a hexadecimal ASCII code sent directly to the printer. See your printer documentation to determine the available numbers.
$I	Prints the job number.
$L*xxxx*	Prints all the characters (*xxxx*) following it until another escape code is encountered. This variable is used for comments to the users.
$N	Prints the login name of the person who submitted the job to the printer.
$*n*	Skips *n* number of lines (from 0 to 9), with 0 moving only to the next line.
$T	Prints the time the job was printed, using the format defined on the Time tab of the Regional Options dialog box.
$U	Turns off block-character printing.
$W*nn*	Sets the line width of the separator page. The default width is 80 characters, and the maximum is 256 characters. Characters beyond this width are truncated.

5. Choose Files|Save As to open the Save As dialog box.

6. In the Save As Type box, choose All Files from the drop-down menu and save the file with an .sep extension.

Warning! *If you save the file with an extension other than .sep, you will not be able to load it as a separator page.*

The following separator page file is used to generate a one-line separator page:

```
$
$N
$D
$T
$L This is a new separator page file.
$E
```

The output on the separator page will look something like this:

```
Stacy 09/20/2001 This is a new separator page file. 23:20:10
```

To disassociate a separator page from a printer, click on the Separator Page button located on the Advanced tab of your printer's Properties dialog box. Then delete the document part of the pathname and click on OK.

Securing Your Printer

You use the Security tab to manage permissions, ownership, and auditing options of printers in Windows 2000 Professional. These options were discussed in the "Securing Your Printing Environment" section earlier in this chapter.

Managing Your Device Settings

On the Device Settings tab, you configure and manage miscellaneous characteristics of the actual output generated when you print a document. These characteristics include paper type, font management, PostScript memory, and timeout options, as shown in Figure 10.21.

For instance, many printers support multiple trays, such as upper and lower trays. You can assign a form (which defines the paper size and margins) to your printer's trays. When a form is matched to a tray, you can select the appropriate form when you print. The printer prints from the tray to which that form is assigned.

Other options include the available PostScript memory, the protocol the printer will use for print jobs, whether the printer will be reset either before or after a PostScript job is submitted, job and wait timeout periods (in seconds, from 0 to 32,767), as well as minimum and maximum font size the PostScript driver will download while generating the document.

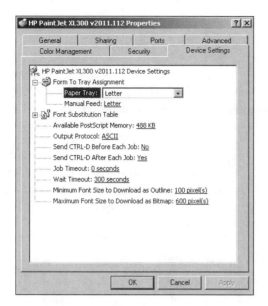

Figure 10.21
Printer Device Settings configuration options.

Using the Color Management Tab

If you have a color printer, you will have an additional tab called Color Management you can use to associate color profiles with your color printer. A color profile contains the data needed for translating the values of a color gamut, including information about color, hue, saturation, and brightness. Color profiles control the color on your printer based on the printer configuration and media being used.

Two options are available: Automatic and Manual. If you choose Automatic, Windows 2000 will automatically select the best color profile from the list of associated color profiles. This recommended setting is the default. However, you may choose Manual, which enables you to specify the default color profile from the list of associated color profiles for all output generated from this device.

Removing a Printer from Your Printers Folder

Now that you have a thorough understanding of how to add and configure printers, you can remove a printer from the Printers folder if you find it necessary. Just follow these steps:

1. Open the Printers folder.

2. Right-click on the icon for the printer you want to delete and choose Delete from the shortcut menu. (Even quicker yet, after selecting the printer, press the Delete key.)

3. Before Windows actually deletes the printer, it will display at least one confirmation box verifying that you really want to delete the printer. You may see a second confirmation box if print jobs are waiting in the printer's queue.

Warning! Deleting a shared network or local printer removes that printer from every user profile on the system. However, the related font files and driver files are not deleted from the disk.

So far we have discussed how to add, configure, and delete printers. We have also taken a peek at some of the special printing features available to us through Windows 2000 Professional. It's time to look at how to utilize these printers created in the Printers folder.

Printing a Document

After you have added and configured the printer, the hard part is over. Now, you get to use the printers you have defined in your Printers folder and manage your documents in the print queue.

Submitting a Print Job

You can submit a print job in many ways in Windows 2000 Professional. For example, you can submit a job from within your applications; using the Print option located on the shortcut menu of a document; using the Send To option, which is also located on the shortcut menu of a document; or using drag-and-drop.

Printing from within an Application

Your options for printing from within an application vary from application to application. However, behind the scenes, the file is sent to a disk file instead of directly to the printer. The file is then spooled to the correct printer by the spooler, which coordinates the flow of data and keeps you abreast of the progress of the print job. After the print job is queued up, you can view its status, rearrange the order of the documents, or delete the document from the queue.

Regardless of the program you choose to print from, follow these steps to submit your document to the printer:

1. Verify that the printer and page settings are configured correctly. Some applications provide Printer Setup, Page Setup, or other options to verify your printer settings.

2. Open the document you want to print; then choose File|Print to open a Print dialog box similar to the one shown in Figure 10.22.

3. Select the printer you want to use and specify any other appropriate options, such as the page range, number of copies, and collation of the pages. Then click on OK. This step will return an error if a problem occurs with the printer. Printer problems include the printer being out of paper, a port conflict, or any other error that would prevent the printer from printing the document.

Note: Yet another place you can configure options available for the specified printer is the Layout and Paper/Quality tabs of the Print dialog box.

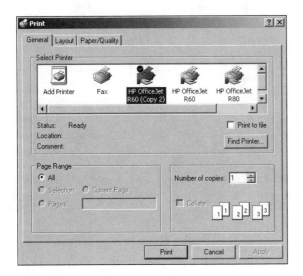

Figure 10.22
Controlling your print job.

Printing from the Shortcut Menu of a Document

The shortcut menu of a document may provide a couple of ways for you to print the document without having any printer icon visible to you. These options depend on the source application the document requires in order for it to open. Furthermore, when you use the shortcut menu to print, the file opens in its source program and starts printing immediately. After the document is spooled, the document closes automatically.

You can use the Print option on the shortcut menu to print a document. Simply right-click on the document, and if the Print option is available, click on it. This action will print the document using the process described in the preceding section.

The second shortcut isn't as easy to utilize. In fact, it requires you to take some steps to implement the printer on the Send To option. You can use this approach on documents for which the shortcut menu does not contain the Print option, thus enabling you to print from the shortcut menu. Follow these steps to add a printer to the Send To shortcut menu option:

1. Go to Start|Programs|Accessories and click on Windows Explorer to open it.

2. Click on the Documents and Settings folder located on the drive where Windows 2000 Professional is installed.

3. Double-click on the folder of the user for whom you are modifying the Send To option.

4. Double-click on the SendTo folder.

Note: The SendTo folder is hidden by default. If it is not visible, click on Tools\Folder Options, click on the View tab, and then click on Show Hidden Files And Folders.

5. Open the Printers folder containing the printer you want to add to the Send To option.

6. Drag the printer from the Printers folder to the SendTo folder.

7. Click on Yes when the Shortcut warning box informs you that you cannot move or copy this item to this location and it asks whether you want to create a shortcut item instead.

You can now right-click on a document, select the Send To option, and send the document to a printer that you added to the SendTo folder. Figure 10.23 shows an example of a Send To menu that contains a printer.

Printing Using Drag-and-Drop

Another easy way to print documents is to drag the document onto a printer's icon or window. However, this method works only with documents that have an association with a specific program. To verify whether the document has an association to a specific program, right-click on the document. If the shortcut menu includes an Open option (not Open With), the file has an association.

Follow these steps to print a file using drag-and-drop:

1. Arrange your desktop so that you can see the files you want to print and the printer's window or the printer's icon.

2. Drag the files you want to print onto the printer's icon or into the printer's window. After you do so, the following actions automatically take place:

   • The file is loaded into the source program associated with the file.

   • The Print command is executed.

   • The file is spooled and directed to the printer.

Note: The file is not removed from its original location; it's just printed.

This method is the easiest for printing if you have the documents and printers readily available. To provide easier access to the most frequently used printers, create a shortcut to the printers on your desktop. You can drag your documents or multiple documents over to the shortcut when you need to print them.

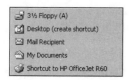

Figure 10.23
A Send To menu containing a printer.

Warning! *The only drawback to using the drag-and-drop method is that you don't have the option of modifying the default printer settings.*

Managing Your Print Queue

After submitting your jobs to the print queue, you have quite a few options available for controlling the documents while they reside in the queue. These options include reordering the print jobs, deleting a print job, canceling all print jobs, pausing and resuming a print job or all print jobs, and redirecting the print jobs.

Getting to Know Your Print Queue

10

You can use the print queue to check the status of your print job, determine how busy the printer is, or check to see how many print jobs are in the queue in the event you want to manage the printer.

You display your print queue by double-clicking on the printer's icon in the Printers folder. Another way to perform configuration tasks is to right-click on the printer's icon inside the Printers folder. Figure 10.24 shows a local print queue that is paused; it contains three print jobs. Pausing a printer is one of many options you can use to manage your printers in Windows 2000 Professional.

After you submit a print job to the print queue you can open the print queue to review the contents of the queue. The print queue contains the information listed in Table 10.5 about each print job in the queue.

The printer information is not constantly refreshed. If you display the print queue and want to update the information, you can periodically refresh it by pressing the F5 button. This manual refresh prevents additional traffic that would be involved if Windows 2000 Professional polled each workstation for print queue information.

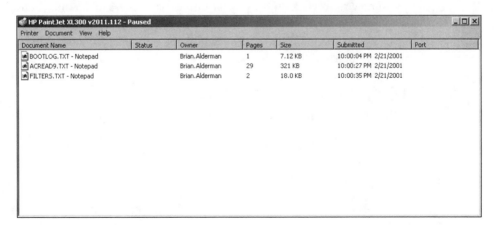

Figure 10.24
Print job information of a printer.

Table 10.5 **Print queue information.**

Column Name	Description
Document Name	Name of the file being printed and possibly the source program
Status	Whether the job is printing, paused, or being deleted
Owner	The name of the user who sent the print job to the queue
Pages	The number of pages to be printed
Size	The size of the document in megabytes
Submitted	The date and time the job was sent to the printer
Port	The port that a local printer is connected to

Pausing and Resuming Print Jobs

You can pause and resume individual print jobs or all print jobs on a specific printer. This capability is useful when you need to add paper or ink cartridges. However, not everyone can pause and resume printers. You need to be an administrator of the printer to manage printing to this degree. Users that have the Print permission can pause and resume only their print jobs.

You pause individual documents by right-clicking on the document in the queue and clicking on Pause in the shortcut menu. While the print job is paused, it will not print; however, the printer will continue printing other print jobs by jumping over the paused job and locating jobs that are not paused. In the Status area of the print queue, you will see the word *paused* while a job is paused. When you are ready to allow the job to print, you can again right-click on the print job and click on Resume on the shortcut menu.

To pause and resume all jobs for a printer with the print queue already opened, you can choose Printer|Pause Printing from the print queue's menu bar. If the print queue is not open, you can simply right-click on the printer inside the Printers folder and choose Pause Printing from the shortcut menu. You can also double-click on the printer icon (located on the taskbar when an item is printing) to open the print queue and then choose Pause Printing from the Printer option.

Deleting Print Jobs

In the event that you (or your users) decide you do not want a file to print, you can delete the document from the queue. Follow these steps to delete a document from a print queue:

1. Open the printer's window.

2. Select the file.

3. Choose Document|Cancel, or right-click on the document and click on Cancel, or press the Delete key.

Redirecting Print Jobs

If your printer completely fails and your documents are stuck in the print queue, you can transfer all documents, except the one printing, to another printer of the same type. To redirect documents, you must have the Manage Printers permission on both printers. To redirect documents, follow these steps:

1. Open the Printers folder.

2. Double-click on the printer that holds the documents you want to redirect.

3. On the Printer menu, click on Properties.

4. Click on the Ports tab of the Properties dialog box and perform one of the following tasks:

   - To send documents to another printer on the same printer server, click on the port to which the other printer is assigned and then click on OK.

   - To send documents to another printer on a different print server, click on Add Port, click on Local Port, and then click on New Port. Type the name of the print server and the share name of the printer.

All documents in the queue, with the exception of the document that was printing, will print on the other print server.

Summary

Windows 2000 Professional provides many options for printing. As an administrator, you will find that the management and configuration of printers can be time-consuming. However, if the printers are implemented correctly, they can provide numerous benefits to your organization, including lower hardware costs, increased user productivity, and ease of use for your end users.

Printing is just one resource you need to manage properly to provide a dynamic, secure, and optimized environment in Windows 2000 Professional. You also need to be familiar with other resources to maintain this flexible, secure, and efficient Windows 2000 Professional environment. Chapter 11 will thoroughly describe ways to create and maintain this environment.

Chapter 11

Administering Resources Using Windows 2000 Professional

Administering Resources

Printers are among the many resources you are responsible for administering in a Windows 2000 Professional environment; you must install, configure, and maintain them. The administration techniques used to manage your resources vary, depending on whether you are in a *workgroup environment* or have implemented a Windows 2000 domain configuration also known as a *client/server environment*.

This chapter discusses the administration of your local and network resources, which include printers, file shares, and applications shared in both Windows and non-Windows environments. Furthermore, this chapter considers the support of non-Windows clients. For instance, you may have Novell servers and clients, Unix servers and clients, and Macintosh clients either sharing resources or requiring access to network shared resources.

Understanding a Workgroup Environment

Depending on the number of users involved in your computer environment and how you want to manage your resources, you might install Windows 2000 Professional in a workgroup. A *workgroup* (also known as a *peer-to-peer network*) is a small collection of computers (usually fewer than 10 with a recommended maximum of 15) that are managed individually. These computers communicate directly with each other without the use of a server managing the network resources. This network does not include the security and features provided by a network server. However, you can still use many of the networking tools and features in Windows 2000 to share files, hardware resources, CD-ROMs, and printers.

Workgroups are generally easier to maintain and are less expensive than server-based models. The term *peer-to-peer* is derived from the fact that each computer is equal, and each computer shares its resources without the use of a server. The user of each computer determines what data he or she will share on the network. Windows 2000 Professional is an ideal operating system for use in a workgroup environment.

Creating a Workgroup

When configuring a peer-to-peer network, you need to have special hardware installed on each computer, and you also must install certain services and configure certain protocols. Five steps are required when you're establishing a peer-to-peer network that you are going to use to share resources in a secure environment:

1. Set up the hardware.

2. Configure the connection to the network.

3. Configure the connection to the workgroup.

4. Share the network resources.

5. Configure the security settings.

Setting Up the Hardware

The hardware requirements for a computer in a workgroup are fairly standard. A network adapter must be installed on your computer. This adapter will be used to make the connection to the network. It can be located on the computer's motherboard, or it can be a separate device in one of your computer's slots, as described in Chapter 9.

The adapter establishes a connection to the Windows 2000 local area network (LAN). You can locate and configure your network adapter in the Network And Dial-Up Connections folder inside Control Panel. When you start your computer, the network adapter is detected, and it automatically establishes a connection to the LAN.

Note: A local area connection is the only type of connection that is automatically created and activated until you disconnect it. After it is disconnected, it is no longer automatically activated.

You must also determine the physical layout of the computers and the kind of cabling used to establish a connection between the computers. A *hub*—a common connection point containing multiple ports used to connect the segments of your LAN—connects your computers so that they can share data. The hub acts as a distribution center for the entire network.

A primary advantage to using a hub is that, if a failure occurs in a single cable or computer, the rest of the computers in the LAN are not affected. Many types of hubs are available, and your choice of cabling and network type will determine the type of hub you purchase and connect. After you install the necessary hardware on each machine and connect the computers to the hub, you can configure each one with the required services and protocols.

Note: Be sure the hub provides enough ports for you to connect all computers in your LAN.

Configuring Your LAN Connection

One of the main reasons you establish a connection to the network is to access resources and information that have been shared on the network or to share resources and information that reside on your computer with the network.

To communicate with other computers, including accessing the information and resources on the network, your computer must have the required *network protocols*—a defined set of commands and rules used to send information over the network, providing the link between your computer and the network. Chapter 14 provides a thorough description of the different network protocols available in Windows 2000.

During the installation of Windows 2000 Professional, the TCP/IP network protocol is installed by default. After installing the appropriate networking components, you need to configure your connection to the workgroup.

11

Configuring the Workgroup

Each computer in a workgroup must be identified with a unique name before joining the workgroup. This unique name is displayed to the users browsing the network for available resources. It can be any name you want to assign, but it must have fewer than 15 characters and they must all be uppercase.

Warning! TCP/IP will recognize computer names up to 63 characters in length in a domain environment. However, not all network protocols will recognize computer names with this many characters.

After you assign a name to a computer that belongs in a workgroup, you can rename it by following these steps:

1. Open the System applet located in Control Panel.

2. Click on the Network Identification tab and then click on the Properties button to display the Identification Changes dialog box, as shown in Figure 11.1.

3. In the Computer Name area, type the new name of the computer and then click on OK.

Tip: A workgroup name cannot be the same name as a computer name, and it cannot contain any of the following characters:

*( ) ; : " < > * + = \ / ? , !*

After you assign a unique name to the computer, your next step is to join a workgroup. To do so, follow these steps:

1. Open the System applet located in Control Panel.

2. Click on the Network Identification tab and then click on the Properties button to display the Identification Changes dialog box, as shown in Figure 11.1.

3. Within the Member Of area, click on the Workgroup radio button.

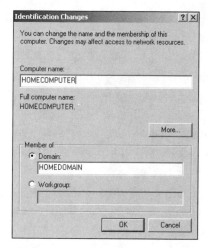

Figure 11.1
Renaming the computer in the Identification Changes dialog box.

4. Type the name of the workgroup that you want to join, and click on OK.

5. Restart your computer to apply the changes and join the workgroup.

After you name your computer and join the workgroup, your next step is to decide whether you want to share any resources on the network.

Sharing Network Resources

Each user in a workgroup decides which resources and documents he or she wants shared on the network as a shared resource. A *shared resource* is any resource made available to users on the network, including files, folders, applications, and printers.

Workgroup users can choose from numerous methods for discovering what resources are shared on the network and connecting to shared resources, including mapping a network drive, browsing the network, and using the Run command located on the Start menu. These options apply to both workgroup and client/server environments. We'll discuss them in more detail in the "Connecting to Shared Resources" section.

Securing Your Resources

After sharing your resources, you should take the necessary steps to protect your applications and data. Windows 2000 includes features that allow you to control access to your data, identify the people on the network, and set policies that define how people can use the resources. The steps required for securing your resources apply to both workgroup and client/server environments and are discussed later in this chapter in the section titled "Securing Your Shared Rexources."

To secure access to a computer that belongs in a workgroup, you control the password functionality of that computer. One option you can configure is whether the users will be required to supply usernames and passwords when they log on.

Tip: Automatic computer logon is helpful if you are in a low-risk security environment and only one person uses the computer.

Anyone logged on as the administrator or a member of the Administrators group can use the Users And Passwords option located in Control Panel. You can take the following steps to configure a computer for a required password or disable a logon password:

1. Double-click on the Users And Passwords applet located in Control Panel.

2. On the Users tab, do one of the following:

   • Click on the Users Must Enter A Username And Password To Use This Computer checkbox to require that the users provide information when they log on.

   • Clear the Users Must Enter A Username And Password To Allow The Users To Automatically Log On checkbox. You will have to provide the username and password of the user account that will be used to perform the automatic logon when the computer starts.

11

Note: The Users Must Enter A Username And Password To Use This Computer checkbox does not appear if your computer is connected to a domain.

As you can see, workgroups are useful in smaller computing environments, but they also introduce many limitations in an environment containing many computers. The implementation of client/server networks, commonly referred to as *domains*, provides complete flexibility and security, and can expand to include an unlimited number of computers. However, before you can implement a client/server environment, you need to understand the different types of servers available to you in a client/server network.

Understanding the Different Server Types

Companies that use client/server networks can configure networks containing different server types. When you are deciding on the type of server to install, you need to understand what each server type is used for and how it fits into the Windows 2000 client/server network. Two types of servers are available: disk servers and file servers.

Disk Servers

A *disk server* creates a centralized storage area for your data and files. This type of server is connected to the network like any other computer and appears as another local hard disk on your computer.

You save information to the disk server like you would any other local drive on your computer. However, retrieving information from a disk server becomes a bit more complicated and slower.

When retrieving information from your local hard drive, you have to access either the file allocation table (FAT) on a FAT16 or FAT32 volume or master file table (MFT) on an NT

File System (NTFS) volume to locate exactly where the file is stored. After retrieving the file location, the read/write heads are moved to the location of the file on the hard drive, and the file is copied into memory, which is where you actually access the file.

This same process is used whenever you locate a file on the disk server, but now these tables are much larger and because they are stored on the disk server, the appropriate table (FAT or MFT) must be copied to your machine before it can begin to locate your files. But, what if multiple changes are made to your files and they end up being moved? Your local table has a pointer to a location other than the place they are really stored. Reassessing the information and retrieving your files will take much longer.

A resolution for this problem of slow data retrieval on your disk server is to divide your disk server's hard drives into multiple volumes. Each volume is reserved for a particular workstation. Furthermore, all the information you want to share with other users is stored on a read-only volume, allowing users to view the information but preventing updates to it, therefore preventing updates to the FAT or MFT.

File Servers

File servers are similar to disk servers in that they provide a centralized storage area for your files and disks. However, file servers maintain their own FAT or MFT, so the search of these tables is performed on the remote server. The FAT and MFT files don't need to be downloaded to each workstation every time they change on the server. This enhancement provides great performance and accuracy to your workstations when you're requesting data from a server.

You'll find another advantage of file servers over disk servers—besides the centrally stored and maintained FAT and MFT files. You can provide a larger storage area for all your workstations because you don't have to divide the disk on the file server into numerous smaller volumes.

Note: You still can manage the amount of disk space and level of access by applying disk quotas and permissions on your NTFS 5 volumes on the file server.

Dedicated vs. Nondedicated File Servers

Often, you will hear the terms *dedicated* and *nondedicated* when referring to the types of file servers available on your network. The difference between these two types of file servers is as follows:

- *Dedicated file server*—Contains its own hard drive and functions only as a file server; no other tasks are performed by this server. This type of file server allows the operating system to allocate all its memory to file server functions.

- *Nondedicated file server*—Contains its own hard drive but also performs other tasks besides functioning as a file server. These other tasks may include running an application on the computer, such as SQL Server or Exchange, or functioning as a domain controller. In this environment, the memory is shared among the different functions the server performs.

Configuring a dedicated file server has several advantages over configuring a nondedicated file server. These advantages, listed here, will greatly improve your network's performance:

- *Speed*—A dedicated file server is faster because all the processes and memory are allocated to the file server's functions.

- *Efficiency*—Because a dedicated file server has to respond only to file server functions, it is not interrupted to perform other tasks.

- *Safety*—With the machine functioning just as a file server, there is less chance of a user or application crashing the machine.

Using a dedicated file server also has disadvantages. The most critical and obvious disadvantage is cost. You have to purchase a fairly hefty machine that contains only files and data, maintain the integrity of the files and data, and maintain the appropriate level of security for the information stored on the file server. You cannot easily justify the cost when it comes to asking for the funds to purchase this type of server.

Another disadvantage of a dedicated file server is that, if it crashes, you may lose a lot of data. An implementation of fault tolerance using RAID 1 or RAID 5, however, can alleviate this problem. File servers also require a stringent data backup strategy that will assist in the recovery of a system or disk crash. (See Chapter 17 for more information on backing up data.)

Now that you have an understanding of the different types of servers used in a client/server network, let's look at the features of a client/server network.

Understanding a Client/Server Environment

Windows 2000 Professional is the ideal client operating system for use in a client/server environment. It provides the full functionality of Windows 2000 for end users and also takes advantage of the functionality a Windows 2000 server provides.

A client/server environment offers these four key advantages over a peer-to-peer environment:

- *Centralized administration of your resources*—The network administrator is responsible for controlling the availability of resources and access to the resources.

- *Security*—Security is managed and enforced by network administrators, ensuring that the users provide usernames and passwords that uniquely identify them. This information is used to determine what resources the users have access to and what level of access they have to those resources.

- *Easier to upgrade*—The flexibility of this environment is significantly higher because you can access more information on the network, and there is more software available for client/server configurations.

- *Expandable in size*—Client/server environments can contain hundreds of machines in a LAN configuration. A WAN configuration can have thousands of machines. This number is significantly larger than the recommended maximum number of 15 computers in a workgroup.

You will find some downsides to the client/server network. For instance, it is more costly because you have to install and manage servers, and they are more difficult to manage in comparison to a workgroup environment. You can use Decision Tree 11.1 to help you decide whether you should implement a workgroup or domain environment.

The concepts of client/server networks aren't exactly new to the computer industry. The mainframe and terminal configurations available before the PCs became so popular used a similar architecture. The biggest difference is that, instead of having a *dumb terminal* (a machine that does not perform any tasks on it) as the client, you have a client PC that can perform some processing.

Configuring a Client/Server Network

To configure your computer to participate in a client/server networking environment, you have to join a domain. A Windows 2000 computer can be a member of only one domain; it can be either a Windows 2000 domain or a Windows NT 4 domain. A computer account

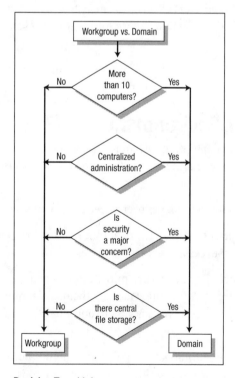

Decision Tree 11.1
Choosing between a workgroup and domain.

must exist in the domain you're joining so that the Windows 2000 computer can join. This computer account can be created either before you join the domain or while you are joining the domain.

Creating a Computer Account

To create a computer account in a Windows 2000 domain, you can add the computer account to the Active Directory database using the Active Directory Users And Computers Microsoft Management Console (MMC) snap-in. When you install Active Directory, it automatically creates a domain controller and installs the MMC snap-in. When you're creating the computer account using the Active Directory Users And Computers snap-in, follow these steps:

1. Log on as a member of the Domain Admins group.

2. Click on Start|Programs|Administrative Tools|Active Directory Users And Computers to open the Active Directory Users and Computers interface, as shown in Figure 11.2.

3. Choose New from the Action menu and then click on Computer to open the New Object - Computer dialog box, as shown in Figure 11.3.

4. Type the name of the new computer in the Computer Name box.

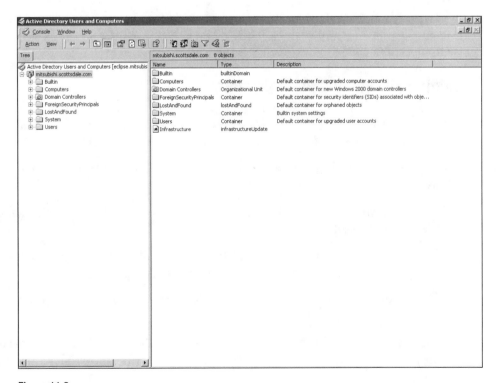

Figure 11.2
Opening the Active Directory Users and Computers snap-in.

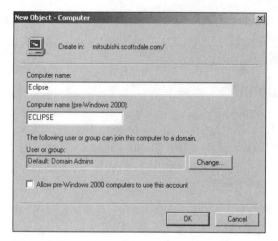

Figure 11.3
Creating a new account in the New Object - Computer dialog box.

Note: You can also supply a pre-Windows 2000 computer name for backward compatibility.

5. After you type in the required information, click on OK.

After creating the computer account in the domain, you can join the computer to the domain. After joining the domain, you are no longer part of a workgroup or peer-to-peer environment but are now in a client/server network.

Joining a Windows 2000 Domain

Your Windows 2000 Professional computer can join either an NT 4 domain or a Windows 2000 domain. After you create a computer account in the domain that you want to join, follow these steps to join a Windows 2000 domain:

Note: You must be a member of the computer's Local Administrators group to join a Windows 2000 domain.

1. Click on Start|Settings|Control Panel and double-click on the System applet to open the System Properties dialog box.

2. Click on the Network Identification tab to view your full computer name and the name of the domain or workgroup you currently reside in.

3. Click on the Properties button to open the Identification Changes dialog box, as shown earlier in Figure 11.1.

4. Under the Member Of area, click on the Domain radio button and type the name of the domain that you want to join. Then click OK to return to the System Properties dialog box.

Warning! *You will be prompted for a username and password so that you can join the computer to the domain. Obtain this information from a network administrator before you execute these steps.*

5. Click on OK to close the System Properties dialog box.

6. Restart your computer to apply the changes and join the Windows 2000 domain.

When your system restarts, your computer is now a member of the Windows 2000 domain that you specified in Step 4. Membership gives you full functionality to participate in the client/server network and allows you to take advantage of the client/server technology discussed earlier.

Joining a Windows NT Domain

The migration from Windows NT 4 domains to Windows 2000 domains can be a slow process. The migration timetable will depend on business needs, expenses, and available resources. You may upgrade your computer to Windows 2000 Professional and then want to join a Windows NT 4 domain. You can join this domain by following the steps discussed when joining a Windows 2000 domain, or you can use the Network Identification Wizard by following these steps:

1. Click on Start|Settings|Control Panel and double-click on the System applet to open the System Properties dialog box.

2. Click on the Network Identification tab to view your full computer name and the name of the domain or workgroup you currently reside in.

3. Click on the Network ID button to start the Network Identification Wizard and then click on Next after reviewing the welcome screen to move to the Connecting To The Network dialog box, shown in Figure 11.4.

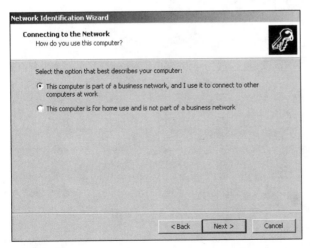

Figure 11.4
Specifying the role of your computer in the Connecting To The Network dialog box.

4. Select the appropriate role of this computer—either home use or business use—and then click on Next.

5. If you are connecting to a domain, select My Company Uses A Network With A Domain. If you are connecting to a workgroup, select My Company Uses A Network Without A Domain. Click on Next to display the Network Information box, which lists the information required for you to connect your computer to the network.

6. After you obtain the required information, click on Next to open the User Account And Domain Information dialog box, as shown in Figure 11.5.

7. After you supply the required username, password, and domain information, click on Next to continue to the Access Level Wizard.

Tip: *At this point, the wizard checks to see whether the computer name exists; if the name does not exist, the wizard will create the computer account. This step may take a couple of minutes, depending on where your domain controllers are located.*

8. To define the level of access the users of the local computer should have, choose one of the following three radio buttons:

   • *Standard Users*—Allows users to make modifications to the computer, install applications on the computer, but not read files they do not own.

   • *Restricted Users*—Allows users to save documents they modify but does not give rights to make modifications to the computer or install applications.

   • *Other*—Allows you to insert the users into a different group. They will inherit the rights and permissions the group has been given.

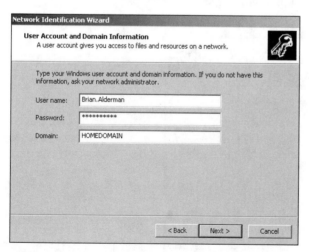

Figure 11.5
Entering account information in the User Account And Domain Information dialog box.

A Common Problem When Joining an NT 4 Domain

A common problem that occurs when you join a Windows 2000 Professional client to a Windows NT domain is that you get this error message: "No domain server was available to validate your password." This error is generated because the Windows 2000 Professional client cannot resolve the NETBIOS computer name to an IP address. This prevents Windows 2000 from communicating with the NT 4 domain controller using TCP/IP.

When you use TCP/IP as your networking protocol to communicate between clients and servers in a Windows NT 4 domain, the computer name has to be resolved to an IP address because IP does not understand these NETBIOS names, only the IP addresses of those computers. So, you have to provide a way for the NETBIOS computer name to be translated to an IP address.

To verify that you are experiencing this problem, use the **ping** command from the command prompt to see whether you can ping the IP address of the Windows NT 4 domain controller. If you are able to, the problem is name resolution, and it must be fixed so that you can join the domain.

You can fix this name-resolution problem by installing and configuring a Windows Internet Name Service (WINS) or editing your local LMHOSTS file. Both will provide the name resolution required to locate a domain controller in your Windows NT 4 environment. Your network administrator should configure WINS or edit the LMHOSTS file. However, if you feel lucky and want to try it yourself, you can check the Windows NT Server or Windows 2000 Server online documentation at Start|Help for information on what steps to take to resolve NETBIOS names to IP addresses.

9. Click on Next to open the final wizard dialog box. After clicking on Finish in this dialog box, you will be prompted to reboot the machine to join the specified domain.

Now that we have looked at the difference between a workgroup and domain and looked at the steps required to join either one of them, it's time to discuss how to manage resources in Windows 2000. The management of resources includes how to share and control access to your resources.

Introducing Windows 2000 Professional Resources

Windows 2000 Professional is the perfect operating system for end users to work with both local and remote resources. Files, folders, and printers are the primary resources you will be maintaining. Chapter 10 provided an in-depth look at the management of printers in Windows 2000. This chapter focuses on managing files and folders.

As a Windows 2000 Professional user who spends most of your time working with files and folders, you'll see that these four primary categories are involved with file and folder management:

• *Organizing*—Involves creating, modifying, copying, moving, and deleting files and folders.

- *Locating*—Involves storing the files in a manner that will make it easy for you to locate them. If you have so many of them that you can't remember exactly where everything is stored, you can search for them using criteria such as file extension, date, size, and even wildcard characters.

- *Maintaining*—Involves compressing, defragmenting, and possibly sharing files and folders on the network.

- *Securing*—Involves applying permissions, encryption, and auditing.

An understanding of these different file and folder management concepts will make your experience with Windows 2000 Professional easier, more efficient, and safer. The organization of files and folders has not changed much over the past few releases of Windows operating systems. However, locating files and folders in Windows 2000 has changed enough that spending some time on this topic is worthwhile.

To locate files and folders in Windows 2000, you have a couple of choices. You can search for files and folders on your local machine or any machine you have connected to by following these steps:

1. Click on Start|Search|For Files Or Folders to open the Search Results dialog box.

Tip: *You can also open this dialog box by choosing Search from the File menu in My Computer after you click on an available drive. Alternatively, you can click on the Search button inside Windows Explorer.*

2. Type the name of the file or folder you are looking for in the Search For Files Or Folders Named section of the Search Results dialog box.

Tip: *If you are not positive about the file name, you can use wildcards to search for files. For instance, B*.txt will return all TXT files that begin with the letter B. By default, the search text you enter is not case sensitive. For example, this statement will return all files beginning with either an uppercase or lowercase b.*

3. You can also search for files that contain certain text by specifying the text you are searching for in the Containing Text box. You can use this feature by itself or in conjunction with the file names you specified.

4. Use the Look In box to specify what drive, folder, or network connection you want to search using the criteria you supplied.

5. Optionally, you can narrow your search by selecting one or more of the following options from within the Search Options:

   - *Date*—Specify a date range for the file's creation, modification, or last-accessed date from the drop-down menu.

   - *Type*—Select the file type you are looking for from the drop-down menu.

   - *Size*—Specify the minimum or maximum size of the file in kilobytes.

- *Advanced Options*—Specify whether you want to search subfolders, use case sensitivity, or search slow files.

6. After you supply your search criteria, click on the Search Now button to begin the search.

Figure 11.6 contains the criteria and results for a search of all files that begin with the letter *B*, have the file extension .txt, and contain the text *science fiction*. In this case, you will search all subfolders.

When you are part of a Windows 2000 domain you also can search the Windows 2000 Active Directory directory services database. Follow these steps to search the Active Directory database:

1. Open My Network Places.

2. Double-click on Entire Network, click on Entire Contents, and then double-click on Directory.

3. Right-click on an Active Directory domain and click on Find.

4. Supply the search information about the Active Directory object you are searching for. These objects include users, computers, printers, shared folders, and so on.

After locating your file or folder, you might want to perform maintenance tasks such as compressing the file or folder. Compressed folders and files save disk space, and their compression and decompression are transparent to you.

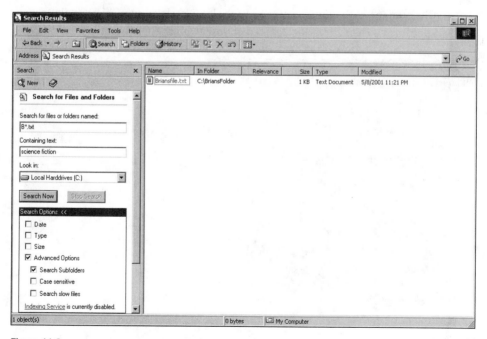

Figure 11.6
Viewing criteria in the Search Results dialog box.

Compressing Volumes, Files, and Folders in Windows 2000

These days, disk space is cheaper than ever. You wouldn't believe what I paid for a 20MB hard drive several years back. Certainly, back then the ability to save disk space was much more important than it is today. However, it is always nice to know you have free space available to you. Compressing your volumes, folders, and files will help you maintain free space on your hard drives.

Note: You can use the Windows 2000 compression option only on NTFS volumes. This option is not available on FAT or FAT32 volumes.

You can reduce your space consumption on NTFS volumes in two ways: by using the Properties dialog box of the volume, folder, or file or by using a command-line utility called compact.exe. Regardless of which method you choose to compress your files, your executables are reduced by around 40 percent of their original size, and your text-based files are reduced by 40 to 50 percent of their original size.

Compressing Entire NTFS Volumes

The easiest way to compress your volumes, folders, and files is to use the Properties dialog box. You can do the following to compress an NTFS drive in Windows 2000:

1. Open My Computer and right-click on the NTFS volume that you want to compress. Select Properties to open the NTFS volume's Properties dialog box.

2. Click on the Compress Drive To Save Disk Space checkbox at the bottom of the volume's Properties dialog box, as shown in Figure 11.7, then click on OK.

3. Click on one of the radio buttons in the Confirm Attribute Changes dialog box that appears and then click OK. You can choose from these two available options:

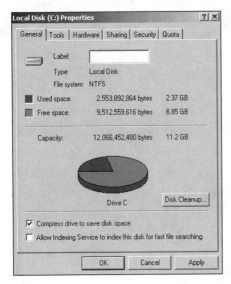

Figure 11.7
Choosing to compress a drive on the NTFS volume's Properties dialog box.

- *Apply Changes To C:\ Only*—Compresses only the root of the drive
- *Apply Changes To C:\ Subfolders And Files*—Propagates the compression attribute to all files and subfolders on the drive

4. Click on OK to begin the compression of your selected NTFS volume.

Compressing Individual Folders and Files

You can also compress individual folders and files on an NTFS volume in Windows 2000. This way, you can selectively compress your extremely large folders and files. The steps for compressing folders and files are similar to those for compressing the entire drive. Just follow these steps to compress a specific folder or file:

1. Open Windows Explorer and locate the folder or file that you want to compress.

2. Right-click on the folder or file and then click on Properties to display the Properties dialog box, as shown in Figure 11.8.

3. Click on the Advanced button to open the Advanced Attributes dialog box. Click on the Compress Contents To Save Disk Space checkbox, as shown in Figure 11.9. Then click on OK.

Warning! The encryption and compression settings are mutually exclusive in the Advanced Attributes dialog box. This means that only one of these attributes can be set at a time. Most often in Windows, you will see radio buttons when you can use only one of the available options. However, this dialog box is an exception.

4. When the Confirm Attribute Changes dialog box appears, click on the appropriate radio button to specify whether you want the subfolders and files compressed also.

Figure 11.8
Viewing the Properties dialog box.

Figure 11.9
Setting options in the Advanced Attributes dialog box.

5. Click on OK to begin the compression of your folder or file.

If you enjoy working with command-line utilities or want to implement compression in a batch file, you can use the compact.exe command-line utility.

Using the Compact.exe Command-Line Utility

If you prefer to use command-line utilities to manage your Windows 2000 environment, the compact.exe file will be your tool of choice to implement and maintain file compression in Windows 2000.

You can execute the **compact** command without supplying any parameters to display the compression state of the current directory. Using this command is a quick way to determine whether the files contained within the directory are compressed and whether new files added to the directory will be compressed. Figure 11.10 displays the results of the **compact** command entered in the C:\BriansFolder directory.

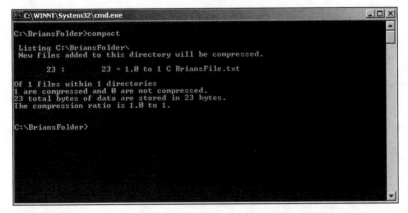

Figure 11.10
Using the **compact** command without switches.

The **compact** command can do plenty more for you besides displaying the current compression status. The following list describes the switches available for use with this command:

Warning! If you use multiple switches, you must provide a space between each of them.

- **/c**—Compresses the specified file or folder
- **/u**—Uncompresses the specified file or folder
- **/s:*dir***—Specifies to include the subfolders of the current directory or the directory specified in the command
- **/f**—Forces compression or uncompression of the specified file or folder

Note: The /f switch is useful if the system crashed while you were compressing a file, leaving the file partly compressed.

- **/a**—Displays the hidden or system files
- **/i**—Ignores any errors generated during compression or uncompression of files and folders
- **/q**—Displays only the important information
- ***filename***—Specifies the folder or file name to compress or uncompress

Tip: You can specify multiple file names separated by commas, or you can use wildcard characters to compress or uncompress multiple files.

You can use the following worksheet, also found on the accompanying CD-ROM, to document your compression strategy when you use the **compact** command. The following example shows how your worksheet might look.

Compressing folders or files using the compact command.							
Folder or File Name	**/c or /u**	**/s**	**/f**	**/a**	**/I**	**/q**	**Comments**
Graphics Folder	**/c**	y	n	n	y	n	Compress all the large BMP files
HugePicture	**/c**	n	y	n	n	y	Free up disk space

Now that we have discussed the different switches available to us when using the **compact** command, let's look at a couple of compression examples. To compress all EXE files in the temp folder and its subfolders, use the following:

```
compact /c /s:\temp *.exe
```

To force compression of all BMP files in the Pictures folder, you would use the following:

```
compact /c /f C:\Pictures *.bmp
```

The process of compressing and uncompressing your files is transparent to your users and saves you disk space. This compression option can be beneficial if you have large folders and files on your system. However, there is a trade-off if you get carried away with the compression capability because it has to uncompress the files whenever you access them and then recompress them when you are finished with them. This activity can result in performance degradation.

Warning! *If you compress your entire boot partition—which contains your operating system—every system file accessed must be uncompressed and then compressed again. The result is overall system performance degradation.*

Identifying Your Compressed Folders and Files

Windows 2000 enables you to easily identify which folders and files on your computer are compressed. You identify them by modifying the color of the name of the file or folder to a different color.

To easily identify your compressed folders and files in My Computer or Windows Explorer, follow these steps:

1. Click on Start|Settings|Control Panel, and then double-click on Folder Options.

2. Click on the View tab.

3. Click on the Display Compressed Files And Folders With Alternate Color checkbox.

4. Click on OK to apply the change.

Maintaining the Compression Attribute

When you copy a compressed file to another folder that also has the compression attribute turned on, it will maintain its compression state.

Note: *When you copy a compressed file from one compressed folder to another, Windows 2000 actually uncompresses the file, copies it to the new folder, and then reapplies the compression attribute inherited from the new folder.*

When you copy a compressed file to a folder that does not have the compression attribute turned on, the file will be stored in an uncompressed state. The file inherits the attributes of the target folder.

If you move a compressed file to an uncompressed folder on the same volume, however, the file retains its compression attributes, meaning it will remain compressed. But, if you move a compressed file to an uncompressed folder on a different volume, the file inherits the folder's compression attributes. Moving files between volumes is actually a copy-and-delete operation. A file is copied to the target folder and then deleted from the source folder.

Securing Your Files and Folders

To control who gets access and the type of access they get, you use permissions in Windows 2000. Windows 2000 permissions provide an easy yet very specific way to control the use of your resources. For instance, you may have a file on your machine that you want to ensure no one but yourself makes changes to. You could assign local permissions to the file, allowing only read access to everyone but yourself, thus preventing users from modifying the file although they can view it.

Note: NTFS permissions are assigned to a file that resides on an NTFS volume on your computer. These permissions are enforced whenever the file is accessed locally or if it is accessed remotely by connecting to a share on your machine over the network. These permissions are available only on an NTFS volume, not a FAT or FAT32 volume.

11

Understanding NTFS Special Permissions

Implementing permissions is a huge part of an administrator's job and can be accomplished easily using NTFS standard permissions; however, it can get a little more complicated if you use special permissions. Windows 2000 provides standard NTFS permissions that are defined using the special NTFS permissions. (Standard permissions are just a group of special permissions.) Let's look at the following list of available special permissions and their associated actions in Windows 2000:

Note: If a special permission contains two actions separated by a forward slash (/), the first action is used when applied to a folder; the second action is used when applied to a file.

- *Traverse Folder / Execute File*—Browse through the folder and subfolders to reach other folders and files / execute program files.

- *List Folder / Read Data*—View subfolder names and file names within the folder / view data files.

- *Read Attributes*—View NTFS attributes (hidden or read-only) of the folder or file.

- *Read Extended Attributes*—View extended attributes of the folder and file. These attributes vary from program to program.

- *Create Files / Write Data*—Create files within the folder / make changes to files, overwriting their existing content.

- *Create Folders / Append Data*—Create folders within a folder / make changes to the end of a file but do not overwrite its existing content.

- *Write Attributes*—Change NTFS attributes of a file or folder, such as hidden or read-only.

- *Write Extended Attributes*—Change extended attributes of a file or folder. The attributes available for change vary from program to program.

- *Delete Subfolders and Files*—Delete files and subfolders even if you have not been granted the delete permission on the file or subfolder.

- *Delete*—Delete the file or folder.

- *Read Permissions*—Read permissions of the file or folder, such as Read, Write, and Full Control.

- *Change Permissions*—Change permissions of the file or folder, such as Read, Write, and Full Control.

- *Take Ownership*—Take ownership of a file or folder. The owner can always change permissions, regardless of any permissions on the file or folder.

- *Synchronize*—Signal whether different threads wait to synchronize with the other threads. This permission applies to multithreaded and multiprocess programs only.

Now that you have an understanding of all the different special permissions, let's look at how to use them when applying standard permissions to files and folders.

Implementing NTFS File Permissions

File permissions are implemented at a file level on your NTFS volume. These permissions control exactly what actions can be performed on the file. To apply permissions to a file, follow these steps:

1. Right-click on the file that you want to set permissions on and click on the Properties option.

2. Click on the Security tab to see the default permission settings, as shown in Figure 11.11.

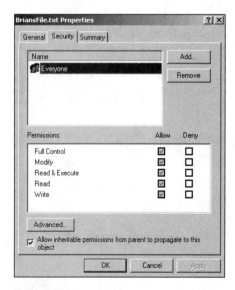

Figure 11.11
Viewing the Security tab.

Warning! By default, the Everyone group gets Full Control on your files and folders when they are created. The Everyone group includes all users who connect to your network, regardless of how they got connected. We recommend you remove this default setting and apply the Users group or the appropriate group you want to have access to the file.

3. Perform one of the following:

   - To apply permissions for a new user or group, click on Add. Search for or type the name of the user or group and then click on OK to close the dialog box and return to the Security tab.

   - To remove permissions from an existing user or group, click on the name of the user or group and then click on Remove.

   - To modify permissions for an existing user or group, click on the name of the user or group.

4. If you're applying permissions for a new user or group or modifying permissions for an existing user or group, click on Allow or Deny for each permission you want to change for the selected user or group.

5. Click on OK to close the Properties dialog box and apply the new permission settings.

Applying permissions to a file is not difficult but can be time-consuming. It is imperative that you understand the different permission settings available so that you apply the most restrictive permission yet still allow the user or group to perform the required action. The following standard permissions can be applied to a file:

- Full Control

- Modify

- Read & Execute

- Read

- Write

Each permission includes a group of special permissions. These standard NTFS permissions and their associated special permissions are listed in Table 11.1.

As you can see, when you are applying the standard permissions to a file, it contains several different special permissions. For instance, the Write standard permission includes the following special permissions:

- Create Files / Write Data

- Create Folders / Append Data

- Write Attributes

- Write Extended Attributes

Table 11.1 NTFS file permissions and associated special permissions.

Special Permission	Full Control	Modify	Read & Execute	Read	Write
Traverse Folder / Execute File	X	X	X		
List Folder / Read Data	X	X	X	X	
Read Attributes	X	X	X	X	
Read Extended Attributes	X	X	X	X	
Create Files / Write Data	X	X			X
Create Folders / Append Data	X	X			X
Write Attributes	X	X			X
Write Extended Attributes	X	X			X
Delete Subfolders and Files	X				
Delete	X	X			
Read Permissions	X	X	X	X	X
Change Permissions	X				
Take Ownership	X				
Synchronize	X	X	X	X	X

- Read Permissions

- Synchronize

Folder permissions are similar to file permissions, except that they provide the capability to list a folder's contents.

Implementing NTFS Folder Permissions

Folder permissions are implemented at a folder level on your NTFS volume. These permissions control exactly what actions can be performed on the folder and may also be applied to the contents of the folder. You apply permissions on a folder using the same steps you used to apply permissions to a file; see the "Implementing NTFS File Permissions" section of this chapter.

A slight difference between the file and folder permissions is the number of standard permissions available. When you're applying standard permissions at the file level, you can choose from five standard permissions. When you're applying standard permissions at the folder level, you can choose from any of the following six standard permissions:

- Full Control

- Modify

- Read & Execute

- List Folder Content

- Read

- Write

To apply the appropriate permissions to your folders, you need to understand what standard permissions are available to you and what special permissions are included when applying the standard folder permissions. Table 11.2 lists the available standard folder permissions and their associated special permissions.

Using the standard permissions is an easy way for you to apply numerous special permissions at one time to either a file or folder on an NTFS volume. However, what if you don't have a standard permission available to meet your specific needs? In this case, you can dig a little deeper and apply the special permissions individually using what are commonly referred to as *advanced permissions*.

Implementing NTFS Advanced Permissions

Advanced permissions customize the standard permissions. You can select the special permissions individually to create your own permission strategy. These permissions are not often used, but it is nice to know that you have the capability available to you.

To create advanced permissions, you need to locate the special permissions and selectively allow or deny them to the file or folder as follows:

1. Using either Windows Explorer or My Computer, locate the file or folder for which you want to set special permissions.

Table 11.2 NTFS folder permissions and associated special permissions.

Special Permission	Full Control	Modify	Read & Execute	List Folder Content	Read	Write
Traverse Folder / Execute File	X	X	X	X		
List Folder / Read Data	X	X	X	X	X	
Read Attributes	X	X	X	X	X	
Read Extended Attributes	X	X	X	X	X	
Create Files / Write Data	X	X			X	
Create Folders / Append Data	X	X			X	
Write Attributes	X	X			X	
Write Extended Attributes	X	X			X	
Delete Subfolders and Files	X					
Delete	X	X				
Read Permissions	X	X	X	X	X	X
Change Permissions	X					
Take Ownership	X					
Synchronize	X	X	X	X	X	X

2. Right-click on the file or folder and then click on Properties.

3. Click on the Security tab.

4. Click on the Advanced button to display the Access Control Settings dialog box, as shown in Figure 11.12, and then perform one of the following actions:

   - To apply special permissions for a new user or group, click on Add. Search for or type the name of the user or group and then click on OK to close the dialog box. The Permission Entry dialog box will appear.

   - To remove an existing user or group and their special permissions, click on the name of the user or group and then click on Remove. You do not have to perform Steps 5 through 7 when removing an existing user or group.

Note: If the Remove button is dimmed, you must clear the Allow Inheritable Permissions From Parent To Propagate To This Object checkbox on the Access Control Settings dialog box.

   - To view or modify special permissions for an existing user or group, click on the name of the user or group and then click on the View/Edit button.

5. If you're applying special permissions to a folder, choose the option that you want to apply the special permissions to by using the Apply Onto drop-down menu of the Permission Entry dialog box, as shown in Figure 11.13.

Note: For more information about this and other permission inheritance and propagation behaviors, see the section "Understanding Permission Inheritance and Propagation" later in this chapter.

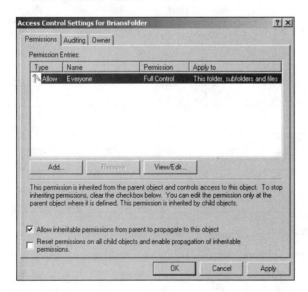

Figure 11.12
Setting advanced permissions in the Access Control Settings dialog box.

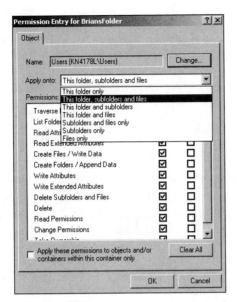

Figure 11.13
Choosing the objects to apply the special permissions to in the Permission Entry dialog box.

6. Select the appropriate permission strategy by selecting or deselecting Allow or Deny for each special permission required.

7. If you want to limit these special permissions to only the current folder, click on the Apply These Permissions To Objects And/Or Containers Within This Container Only checkbox and then click on OK to return to the Access Control Settings dialog box.

8. Select the Reset Permissions On All Child Objects And Enable Propagation Of Inheritable Permissions checkbox if you want the child objects of this parent object to inherit these changes. Then, click on OK to close the Access Control Settings dialog box.

9. Click on OK to close the object's Properties dialog box.

The implementation of permissions in Windows 2000 can be complicated, especially if users have user-level permissions and they are in security groups that also have permissions.

Determining a User's NTFS Permissions

When you combine the NTFS permissions from your user account with those in the security groups you belong to, you can have conflicting permissions. When you combine NTFS permissions, your resulting permissions are the cumulative permissions of all permissions involved. For instance, say Katy has been assigned Modify permissions to her user account on a folder called public. Katy also belongs to a security group called Marketing that has Read permissions. Katy will have Modify permissions when accessing the public folder because the Modify permission includes the Read permission.

Of course, understanding permissions can't be that simple; there has to be a little twist to it. The previous implementation of permissions is correct in all cases except when a Deny permission is involved. The Deny permission always overrides all allowed permissions. So, if we look at the scenario with Katy again and change the Marketing group permission from Read to Deny, we know that Katy will not be able to access the public folder.

Understanding how NTFS permissions are applied to your resources is extremely important so that you can avoid users getting unauthorized access to any proprietary or confidential information.

Applying security to files and folders using either standard or advanced permissions would be a tedious task if you had to perform these steps for every file and folder on your system. With an understanding of how to propagate permissions or prevent propagation of permissions, you will see that you don't need to perform this task on each and every file and folder on your computer.

Understanding Permission Inheritance and Propagation

Understanding how permissions are inherited and propagated will assist you in managing the permissions more efficiently, and you will soon discover that you don't have to perform the steps we have just discussed as often as you thought.

Child objects inherit permissions from parent objects. For instance, if you have a folder that contains subfolders and files, these subfolders and files are child objects of the parent folder. If you apply permissions to the parent folder then those permissions also apply to the child objects; the child objects inherit the permissions from the parent. Child objects inherit parent object permissions because the parent propagates these permissions to the child. The combination of propagation and inheritance makes permission management much easier in Windows 2000.

Let's look at some of the options mentioned in the previous section to see how those options assist you in the management of NTFS permissions.

Controlling Permission Propagation

The Permission Entry dialog box appears when you set permissions on your folders and files. When you're applying permissions to your folders, this dialog box contains two powerful options: Apply Onto and Apply These Permissions To Objects And/Or Containers Within This Container Only. These two options determine where and if you propagate these new permission settings.

Note: *These two options are dimmed when you're applying permissions to a file.*

The Apply Onto list provides several options for you to choose from; the options, shown here, determine where the permissions can be applied:

- This Folder Only

- This Folder, Subfolders And Files

- This Folder And Subfolders

- This Folder And Files

- Subfolders And Files Only

- Subfolders Only

- Files Only

After you determine where you want the permissions propagated to, your next step is to determine the effect of these permissions through the Apply These Permissions To Objects And/Or Containers Within This Container Only option. In other words, you need to determine how deep in the hierarchy of folders these permissions go. Table 11.3 shows the effects of all the Apply Onto options when the Apply These Permissions To Objects And/Or Containers Within This Container Only option is not checked. By default, this setting is not selected in Windows 2000 Professional. If you check the Apply These Permissions To Objects And/Or Containers Within This Container Only checkbox, the results of new permission settings would be as shown in Table 11.4.

As you can see, there is a huge difference when the checkbox is selected. The permission changes do not propagate any further than the current folder's subfolders and files in any

Table 11.3   Effects of the Apply Permissions checkbox being cleared.

Apply	Current Only	Subfolders Only	Files Only	All Subfolders	All Files
This Folder Only	X				
This Folder, Subfolders And Files	X	X	X	X	X
This Folder And Subfolders	X	X		X	
This Folder And Files	X		X		X
Subfolders And Files Only		X	X	X	X
Subfolders Only		X		X	
Files Only			X		X

Table 11.4   Effects of the Apply Permissions checkbox being checked.

Apply	Current Only	Subfolders Only	Files Only	All Subfolders	All Files
This Folder Only	X				
This Folder, Subfolders And Files	X	X	X		
This Folder And Subfolders	X	X			
This Folder And Files	X		X		
Subfolders And Files Only		X	X		
Subfolders Only		X			
Files Only			X		

Apply Onto scenario. You can easily control the propagation of permissions. However, you can get greater control of where the permissions get propagated by controlling the inheritance of permissions.

Controlling Permission Inheritance

You can further control permission propagation by deciding what folders and files inherit permissions from their parent objects. You achieve this control by using the Allow Inheritable Permissions From Parent To Propagate To This Object checkbox located on the Security tab of the Properties dialog box of your files and folders, as shown earlier in Figure 11.11. By default, this checkbox is selected, and the permissions are inherited from the parent object.

However, if you want to change the inherited permissions, you can perform one of the following three tasks:

- Make the change on the parent object from which the child object is inheriting.

- Select the permission on the child object that is opposite the permission on the parent object by using the Deny and Allow options.

- Clear the Allow Inheritable Permissions From Parent To Propagate To This Object checkbox.

If you clear the checkbox, you will be forced to make a decision. Windows 2000 needs to know what to do with the current permissions on the object, so it will present you with the Security dialog box shown in Figure 11.14. This Security dialog box presents you with the following three choices:

- *Copy*—Copies the previously inherited permissions from the parent object and also allows you to make explicit permission changes to the object.

- *Remove*—Removes the previously inherited permissions from the object, keeping only the permissions explicitly applied to the object. You have complete control over the permissions on that object.

- *Cancel*—Retains the previously inherited permissions from the parent object and closes the Security dialog box without making changes to it.

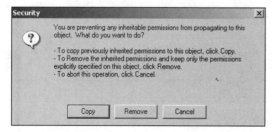

Figure 11.14
Changing inheritable permissions in the Security dialog box.

We suggest you maintain the default behavior by allowing the permissions to propagate throughout the directory structure. Having the opportunity to block the propagation by using the Allow Inheritable Permissions From Parent To Propagate To This Object checkbox is a nice feature, but it can lead to difficulty when you're troubleshooting resource access problems.

Introducing Shared Resources

The sharing of resources is one of the primary reasons for connecting to either a workgroup or a client/server network. Sharing resources reduces the need to have multiple copies of folders, files, data, printers, and applications. You can share one instance of a data file on your network instead of trying to maintain multiple copies of the data file on each user's machine and then trying to keep them synchronized.

An important part of an administrator's job is sharing and securing resources in a Windows 2000 environment. You can share resources using Windows Explorer or the Computer Management snap-in. Using Windows Explorer is the easiest way to manage your shared resources; however, Computer Management provides some additional functionality not available through Windows Explorer.

Note: A share can be created on a resource located on any Windows 2000 supported file system, including FAT16, FAT32, NTFS, CDFS, and UDF (Universal Disk Format that supports DVD volumes).

Preparing to Share Your Resources

The capability to share your resources on the network requires that your system be configured to allow remote connections to these shared resources. Specifically, the File And Printer Sharing For Microsoft Networks component must be installed and enabled, which occurs by default.

Note: This Windows 2000 component is equivalent to the Server service in Windows NT 4.

If you need to remotely configure the File And Printer Sharing For Microsoft Networks component on a Windows 2000 server, follow these steps:

1. Open Network And Dial-Up Connections by clicking on Start|Settings|Network And Dial-Up Connections.

2. Right-click on a local connection, usually Local Area Connection, and then click on the Properties option on the shortcut menu.

3. Perform one of the following:

   • If you are on a LAN, locate the Components Checked Are Used By This Connection box on the General tab and then click on File And Printer Sharing For Microsoft Networks to highlight it. Next, click on the Properties button.

   • If you are configuring a dial-up, VPN, or incoming connection, locate the Components Checked Are Used By This Connection box on the Networking tab and then click on File And Printer Sharing For Microsoft Networks. Then, click on the Properties button.

4. Perform one of the following:

- Click on Minimize Memory Used to optimize the server for a small number of clients.

- Click on Balance to optimize the server for a combination of file and printer sharing and other services.

- Click on Maximize Data Throughput For File Sharing to dedicate the maximum resources to the file and printer services.

- Click on Maximize Data Throughput For Network Applications to optimize server memory for distributed applications, such as SQL Server.

5. To allow LAN Manager 2.x clients to view the shared resources on your machine, click on the Make Browser Broadcasts To LAN Manager 2.x Clients checkbox.

Note: *Windows 2000 Professional does not have the optimization options listed in Steps 4 and 5; these steps only apply to Windows 2000 Server computers.*

6. Click on OK to apply the changes and close the Properties dialog box.

If the File And Printer Sharing For Microsoft Networks component is not enabled, you will not be able to share resources. If you are unable to share a folder, ensure that the File And Printer Sharing For Microsoft Networks component is enabled by placing a checkmark in the checkbox, as shown in Figure 11.15.

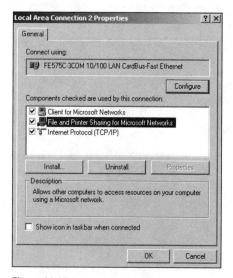

Figure 11.15
Enabling the File And Printer Sharing For Microsoft Networks component.

Creating Resource Shares in Windows 2000

The first step in managing your shared resources is to decide what resources you want shared and then share them. Sharing resources is a simple process that any administrator can perform. You can follow these steps to share a folder through Windows Explorer:

1. Open Windows Explorer by clicking on Start|Programs|Accessories|Windows Explorer.

2. Right-click on the folder you want to share and click on Properties on the shortcut menu to open the folder's Properties dialog box. Then, click on the Sharing tab. If the Sharing tab is not available to you, open the Services snap-in and locate the Server service. Start the Server service if it is not running.

Tip: *Alternatively, you can open the Sharing tab by right-clicking on the folder and then choosing the Sharing option. This method automatically makes the Sharing tab active when the Properties dialog box is opened.*

3. Click on the Share This Folder radio button to begin the process of sharing the folder using the available options, as shown in Figure 11.16.

Note: *By default, the name of the folder becomes the share name; however, you can modify this name now, or you can come back and rename it later.*

4. In the Share Name textbox, make any modifications to the default share name that you want to make.

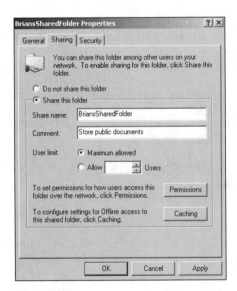

Figure 11.16
Sharing folders on the Sharing tab of the folder's Properties dialog box.

Tip: You can create a hidden share by typing "$" at the end of the share name. This character will prevent the share name from being listed when users are browsing the network. Only users who know the name of the share will be able to connect to it. For instance, to hide a folder called HiddenShare, type "HiddenShare$" in the Share Name box.

5. Optionally, you can provide a description of the share in the Comment box. This information is displayed to users when they browse for shares on the network.

6. Optionally, you can limit the number of simultaneous connections made to the share, or you can leave the number set to the Maximum Allowed. This option is useful when you are experiencing performance degradation because of the number of simultaneous connections or if you do not want to exceed the number of purchased licenses.

Note: The maximum number of simultaneous connections permitted on a Windows 2000 Professional machine is 10. You will not be able to set the Allow option to a number greater than 10.

Note: The Permissions and Caching buttons are discussed later in this chapter in the section titled "Caching Your Shared Resources."

7. After you click on the OK or Apply button, the folder is shared on your network.

Tip: You can easily identify shared folders on your local drive by the little blue sleeve and hand icon that is attached to the bottom of the folder.

A folder or file can have multiple share names, allowing you to create shares to the folder for different users and apply permissions for those users. Follow these steps to create an additional share name on an existing share:

1. Open Windows Explorer by clicking on Start|Programs|Accessories|Windows Explorer.

2. Right-click on the folder you want to share and click on Properties on the shortcut menu to open the folder's Properties dialog box. Then, click on the Sharing tab.

3. Click on the New Share button to open the New Share dialog box, as shown in Figure 11.17, and supply the following information:

    • The name of the new share

Figure 11.17
Adding information in the New Share dialog box.

- Comments about the new share

- The number of simultaneous connections

- Permissions for this share name

After you share the folder a second time, you will have another button to choose from the Sharing tab, as shown in Figure 11.18. The Remove Share button removes a share name from a resource that has been shared multiple times. You can access the share name that you want to stop sharing by using the drop-down menu of the Share Name box.

After you share your resources, your next step is to decide who gets access to the share and the type of access these users have to the share. By default, the Everyone built-in group is granted Full Control, meaning users in this group can do anything they want with the resource. In most situations, the default permissions will have to be modified to ensure that the resource is not accidentally modified or deleted.

Securing Your Shared Resources

After you share your resources, it is important to ensure that only the users you want to access the resources are accessing them and these users are accessing them with the appropriate level of permissions. A big part of shared resource management is understanding and assigning permissions.

Note: *Shared permissions are enforced only when the resources are accessed from the network. NTFS permissions are used on NTFS volumes to control access to files and folders when a user is logged on locally and can be used in conjunction with share permissions.*

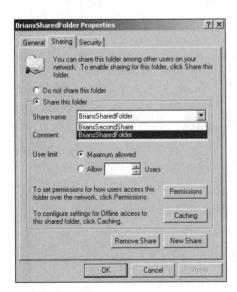

Figure 11.18
Accessing the Sharing tab containing the Remove Share button.

Table 11.5   Windows 2000 standard folder and file share permissions.

Action	Full Control	Change	Read
View file and subfolder names	X	X	X
Traverse to a subfolder	X	X	X
View data in files, run programs	X	X	X
Add files and subfolders to a shared folder	X	X	
Change data in files in a shared folder	X	X	
Delete files and subfolders	X	X	
Change NTFS permissions	X		
Take ownership of files or subfolders (NTFS only)	X		

Table 11.5 lists the available standard folder and file share permissions you have and what actions are associated with the permissions listed.

Note: The standard printer permissions that you apply to a shared printer were discussed in Chapter 10.

You can follow these steps to set your standard share permissions in a Windows 2000 operating system environment:

1. Open Windows Explorer and locate the shared folder that you want to set permissions for.

2. Right-click on the shared folder and click on Properties on the shortcut menu to open the folder's Properties dialog box. Then, click on the Sharing tab.

3. Click on the Permissions button on the Sharing tab to open the Permissions dialog box, as shown in Figure 11.19.

4. To set the shared permissions, click on Add to open the Select Users, Computers, Or Groups dialog box, shown in Figure 11.20. Locate the name of the users and groups under the Name section and double-click on each user or group you want to set permissions for. When you're done click on OK.

Note: To remove permissions, select the user or group in the Name section and then click on the Remove button.

5. In the Permissions dialog box, select the user or group that you want to set permissions for and click on the appropriate Allow or Deny option that you want to set for this user or group.

6. After you set permissions for each group and user, click on OK to apply the new permission settings.

By using the standard share permissions, you can easily secure your shared resources. These standard share permissions are derived from more specific permissions provided by

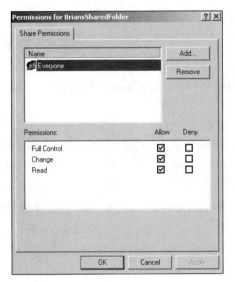

Figure 11.19
Setting shared permissions on the Permissions dialog box.

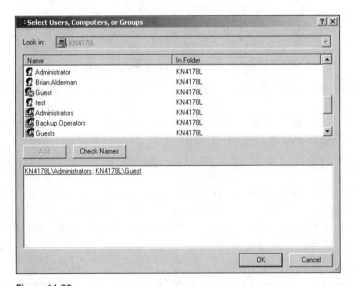

Figure 11.20
Adding users and groups to share permissions in the Select Users, Computers, Or Groups dialog box.

Windows 2000. For instance, the Read share permission includes the following Windows 2000–specific permissions:

- View file and subfolder names
- Traverse to a subfolder
- View data in files and run programs

Similar to the implementation of NTFS permissions, your shared permissions are cumulative unless a Deny permission is involved, in which case they are denied. Unlike NTFS permissions, which apply to users who access the resource either locally or remotely, share permissions are taken into consideration only when the resource is accessed over the network. They are not taken into consideration if the resource is accessed locally.

Stopping Resource Sharing

You might have a reason to stop sharing your resources to the network. Perhaps the information is outdated or obsolete, and it is no longer accessed by anyone. Follow these steps to stop sharing a folder or drive on your computer:

1. Open Windows Explorer or My Computer and then locate the shared drive or folder that you want to stop sharing.

2. Right-click on the shared drive or folder and click on the Sharing option.

3. On the Sharing tab, click on the Do Not Share This Folder option.

4. Click on OK to apply the changes and remove the share from the network.

After you stop sharing your resources, they are only available locally. Therefore, only users who log on to the machine locally will be able to access them.

Examining Windows 2000 Special Shared Folders

When you install Windows 2000, some special shared folders are created for system and administration use. Your system configuration determines which shared folders are created. These special shared folders are hidden from view when you are exploring your hard drives through My Computer or Windows Explorer.

The following special shared folders are available in Windows 2000:

- *Drive Letter$*—A hidden shared folder is created for every volume on your Windows 2000 machine. It allows administrators to connect to the root directory of each volume on your machine. For instance, if you have a machine that has C, D, and E drives, C$, D$, and E$ special shared folders are created automatically.

- *ADMIN$*—This hidden shared folder is available for remote administration of your computer. It allows you to connect to the path of the Windows 2000 system root (the directory that contains your Windows 2000 operating system files).

- *IPC$*—This folder is used for remote administration of your computer's shared resources.

- *PRINT$*—This folder is used for remote administration of your printers.

- *NETLOGON$*—This folder is used by the Net Logon service of your Windows 2000 server computer to process your domain logon request.

Note: *The Net Logon service is available only on Windows 2000 server machines.*

- *FAX$*—This folder is used by fax clients in the process of sending a fax. This folder stores fax cover pages to temporarily cache files on the machine.

Managing Your Shared Folders

Your shared folders, including the user-defined, hidden, and special folders, are easily viewed and managed through the Shared Folders utility located in the Computer Management snap-in, as shown in Figure 11.21.

Note: *The Shared Folders utility replaces the Server applet located in Control Panel in NT 4.*

The Shared Folders utility provides the following functionality:

- You can create, view, and set permissions for shares running on Windows NT 4 and Windows 2000.

- You can view a list of your files currently opened by remote users. You can also close one or all of the open files.

- You can view a list of users currently connected to your computer. You can also disconnect one or all of the connected users.

- You can configure Services for Macintosh to allow PC users and Macintosh users to share resources through a computer running Windows 2000 server.

The information provided is arranged into three columns: Shares, Sessions, and Open Files On Your Local Computer. The following functionality and information are available in Shared Folders:

- *Shares*—Provides information about the shared resources, including the following:

    - *Shared Folder*—Directory, printer, or named pipe

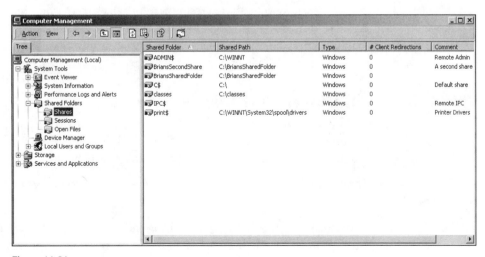

Figure 11.21
Accessing the Shared Folders utility.

- *Shared Path*—The physical location of the shared resource

- *Type*—Windows, Macintosh, or NetWare network connection

- *# Sessions*—The number of users currently connected to the shared resource

- *Comment*—A brief description about the resource

- *Sessions*—Provides information about user connections, including the following:

  - *Users*—The names of users currently connected

  - *Computer*—The name of the user's computer

  - *Type*—Windows, Macintosh, or NetWare network connection

  - *Open Files*—The number of resources opened by this user

  - *Connected Time*—The hours and minutes the connection has been established

  - *Idle Time*—The hours and minutes since the user last initiated any action

  - *Guest*—Whether the user connected as a guest (displays yes or no)

- *Open Files*—Provides information about open files, including the following:

  - *Open File*—List of the open files

  - *Accessed By*—The name of the user accessing the open files

  - *Type*—Windows, Macintosh, or NetWare network connection

  - *# Locks*—The number of locks on the open files

  - *Open Mode*—The permission granted when the resource was opened

This utility is useful for managing your shared resources. It enables you to view information about your shared resources and also disconnect users who are accessing your resources. You should be very familiar with the functionality of this utility when sharing and managing resources on your Windows 2000 machines.

Connecting to Shared Resources

Similar to needing a service running to share a resource, you also need a service running to access shared resources. The Client For Microsoft Networks is a Windows 2000 service that allows your machine to access shared resources on a Microsoft network.

Note: The Client For Microsoft Networks service replaces the Workstation service in Windows NT 4.

This component is installed and enabled by default during the installation of the Windows 2000 operating system. However, if you need to configure the service, follow these steps:

1. Open Network And Dial-Up Connections by clicking on Start|Settings|Network And Dial-Up Connections.

2. Right-click on a local connection, usually Local Area Connection, and then click on the Properties option on the shortcut menu.

3. Perform one of the following:

   - If you are on a LAN, locate the Components Checked Are Used By This Connection box on the General tab and then click on Client For Microsoft Networks to highlight it. Next, click on the Properties button.

   - If you are configuring a dial-up, VPN, or incoming connection, locate the Components Checked Are Used By This Connection box on the Networking tab and then click on Client For Microsoft Networks. Next, click on the Properties button.

4. In the Name Service Provider list, click on an RPC name service provider. The default is Windows Locator.

5. If you choose DEC Cell Directory Service, type the network address of your provider in the Network Address box.

6. Click on OK to close the Client For Microsoft Networks dialog box. Then, click on OK again to close the connection's Properties dialog box.

After you ensure that the Client For Microsoft Networks service is running, you can access shared resources on your Microsoft network. You connect to a network resource in one of the following three ways:

- Browsing My Network Places

- Mapping a network drive using a GUI

- Mapping a network drive using the command prompt

Choosing a method to connect to network resources is determined by how much information you know about the shared resource and also the number of resources you have already connected to or anticipate connecting to. Let's look at the three different ways you can connect to a shared network resource.

Browsing My Network Places

If you don't know what resources are available on the network, you can browse to see what has been shared on your network. After double-clicking on My Network Places, you can double-click on Computers Near Me to view shared resources located in your workgroup.

If you are part of a domain, you can double-click on the Entire Network icon after you open My Network Places. Double-clicking on this icon will present all the shared resources in your domain. You can double-click on the machines located in the domain to view the resources available to you. After you obtain the location and name of the shared resource you want to connect to, you can map a network drive to it.

Mapping a Drive Letter to a Shared Resource

The process of mapping a drive letter to a shared resource is the most commonly used method for accessing shared resources in Windows 2000. Just follow these steps:

1. Open My Computer or Windows Explorer.

2. Choose Map Network Drive from the Tools menu to open the Map Network Drive dialog box, as shown in Figure 11.22.

3. In the Drive pull-down menu, select the drive letter that you want to use to map to the shared resource.

Note: *You can also type the drive letter if you have a specific letter you want to use and know it is not being used.*

4. In the Folder pull-down menu, type the UNC name of the share you want to map the drive letter to, or click on the Browse button to locate the resource on your network.

Tip: *If you want to automatically connect to the mapped drive every time you log on, select the Reconnect At Logon checkbox.*

5. Click on the Finish button to complete the process of mapping a drive letter to a shared network resource.

When you're mapping a network drive using the Map Network Drive dialog box, you can choose to map a drive to the shared resource using a user account other than the one you used to log on to Windows 2000. By default, when you attempt to map a drive to the shared network resource, it uses your current logon credentials. However, you might want to map to a drive using a logon account that has been granted permissions to the shared resource.

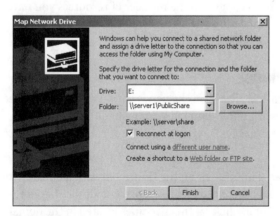

Figure 11.22
Specifying a drive letter in the Map Network Drive dialog box.

Say a network administrator named Jeff has logged on locally using his nonadministrative account. He needs to connect to a network share called Admintools that allows only administrators to connect to it. Jeff can click on the Connect Using A Different User Name option and open the Connect As dialog box, as shown in Figure 11.23. Here, he can supply the administrative account credentials that will be used to connect to Admintools.

Connecting to a Shared Resource Using the Run Command

The problem with mapping a shared resource to a drive letter is that you may run out of drive letters. Letter *A* is usually assigned to your floppy drive, and *C* is usually assigned to the first partition of your first hard drive. This leaves only 24 drive letters available for mapping a drive letter to shared network resources.

11

Tip: *In previous versions of Windows, the letter B was reserved for a second floppy drive. However, Windows 2000 allows you to map the letter B to a shared network resource if it is not used by a second floppy drive.*

You can overcome this limitation by mapping to a network share using the **Run** command like this:

1. Click on Start|Run to open the Run dialog box, as shown in Figure 11.24.

2. Type the UNC name of the resource you want to connect to, or if you do not know what it is, click on the Browse button to locate it.

3. Click on OK to establish the connection to the shared resource.

This process establishes a connection to the shared resource you specified in the Open section of the Run dialog box without consuming a drive letter.

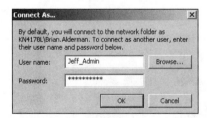

Figure 11.23
Supplying user credentials in the Connect As dialog box.

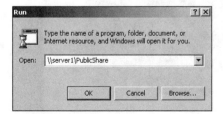

Figure 11.24
Connecting to a shared resource using the Run dialog box.

Managing Your Shared Resources Using the Command Prompt

As with many actions you perform through the GUI of Windows 2000, you have the option of viewing and connecting to network shares using the command prompt. The **net view** and **net use** commands are available for viewing and connecting to network resources, respectively.

Using the net view Command

The **net view** command locates machines, resources, and domains on your network. This command is similar to browsing in My Network Places or using the Browse button on the Map Network Drive dialog box and the Run dialog box to browse for shared folders.

For instance, you can use the **net view** command without any parameters to display a list of machines in your workgroup or domain, as shown in Figure 11.25.

You can pass parameters with the **net view** command to customize the information being returned to you. Use the following parameters to generate specific results:

- **\\\computername**—Returns a list of the available resources on the computer name

- **\\\computername /domain:domainname**—Returns a list of the available resources on the computer name in the domain you specified

- **/domainname**—Returns a list of all the domains on the network

The **net view** command is helpful for locating shared resources, but you cannot access them with it. You use the **net use** command to connect to printers and shared folders from the command line.

Using the net use Command

The **net use** command enables you to review your current connections and connect to additional shared resources. You use the **net use** command without any parameters to

Figure 11.25
Viewing the results of a **net view** command.

view your current connections. For instance, if you want to list all shared resources you are currently connected to, you enter the following command:

```
C:\ net use
```

After you decide you want to connect to a shared resource, you also use the **net use** command, but this time you pass parameters with it. For example, if you want to connect to the PublicShare on Server1, you use the following command:

```
C:\ net use \\Server1\PublicShare
```

Warning! *If the name you are providing contains a space, you have to surround it with double quotation marks; for example, \\"server 1"\sharename.*

11

Like the **net view** command, the **net use** command has many commonly used parameters. They are as follows:

- **/home**—Connects you to your home folder
- **/persistent:yes**—Specifies that the drive is automatically mapped every time you connect to the network
- *Sharename* **/delete**—Disconnects you from the mapped drive specified

Now that we have shown you how to connect to the shared resources available to you on your network, you need to be familiar with how to access the information when you are disconnected from the network. You can do so by caching your shared folders.

Caching Your Shared Resources

Of course, you can access shared resources while you're connected to the network, but what about people who use laptops and travel frequently? They don't have the luxury of always being connected to the network that contains the shared resources. In this case, the ability to cache resources is very important.

Caching resources makes those resources available offline. When your users need to access the resources, they access them from a reserved area of disk space on their local machine that is called a *cache*. These cached documents are available for use regardless of whether the user is connected to the network.

Another great reason to cache documents is performance. The file resides locally, so you can retrieve that file from your local hard drive instead of having to copy it over the network to your machine to work on each time you want to modify it.

In Chapter 8, we discussed offline files and folders and how to configure both the network share that holds the primary copy and the clients that hold the cached copy. We also discussed the three types of file caching: manual caching for documents, automatic caching for documents, and automatic caching for programs.

The Synchronization Manager synchronizes the information that has changed in your local cache with those folders that reside on the network share. In this way, caching shared files makes mobile computing more efficient on Windows 2000.

Understanding Shared Resources and Non-Microsoft Operating Systems

Nowadays, most larger networks are heterogeneous environments. This means that not everything on the network is running a Microsoft operating system. For instance, Novell servers may contain resources that everyone on the network needs access to. Furthermore, Novell or Macintosh clients may want access to Windows resources. The capability to share information among all operating systems creates a more dynamic and efficient environment.

Windows 2000 makes it easy for you to share information among the different operating systems. We'll begin by looking at how Microsoft clients can access non-Microsoft shared resources; then we'll look at how non-Microsoft clients can access shared resources on Microsoft operating systems.

Accessing Resources on NetWare Servers

After realizing that you have resources running on a NetWare server that you want your Microsoft clients to access, you have to first install the appropriate services and transport protocols and then connect to the shared resource.

Installing Client Service For NetWare

The first step to configuring access to your Novell resources is to install the Client Service For NetWare. You can follow these steps to install the Client Service For NetWare service, which includes the NWLink IPX/SPX/NetBIOS Compatible Transport Protocol, on your Windows 2000 operating system:

Warning! *When you install the Client Service For NetWare service, it is installed for all connections. If you want to remove it for a certain connection, view the properties for that connection and clear the Client Service For NetWare box.*

1. Open the Network And Dial-Up Connections applet inside Control Panel.

2. Right-click on the connection that you want to install the Client Service For NetWare service on and then click on Properties.

3. Click on Install on the General tab.

4. Click on Client on the Select Network Component Type dialog box, as shown in Figure 11.26, and then click on Add.

5. Click on Client Service For NetWare in the Select Network Client dialog box. Then, click on OK.

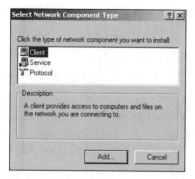

Figure 11.26
Choosing the type of network on the Select Network Component Type dialog box.

11

Tip: *To ensure that the Client Service For NetWare has been installed correctly, type "net view / network:nw" at the command prompt. You should see a list of available NetWare servers.*

Connecting to a NetWare Server

After installing the Client Service For NetWare service, you can map to NetWare resources. These resources can be either NetWare volumes or printers. Follow these steps to connect to a NetWare volume:

1. Double-click on My Network Places.

2. Perform one of the following:

   • Double-click on NetWare or Compatible Network.

   • Double-click on Entire Network and then double-click on NetWare or Compatible Network to display the NDS and individual computers.

3. Double-click on a tree or volume to locate the volume or drive that you want to connect to.

4. Double-click on the volume or folder to open it. Or, to map a drive to the volume or folder, click on the volume or folder and then choose Map Network Drive from the Tools menu.

The other resource you will want to connect to is a printer attached to a NetWare server. To do so, you can follow these steps:

1. Click on Start|Settings|Printers to open the Printers dialog box.

2. Double-click on Add Printer and then click on Next.

3. Click on Network Printer and then click on Next.

4. In the Name section, type the UNC name of the NetWare printer.

Note: *If you are logged on to an Active Directory domain, you can also locate the printer by using the Find A Printer In The Directory option.*

5. Follow the instructions for the Add Printer Wizard and then click on Finish to add the connection to the NetWare printer.

Now it's time to look at how non-Microsoft clients are able to connect to shared resources on Windows 2000 machines.

Accessing Resources on Windows Machines

Windows 2000 resources can be accessed by Microsoft clients and non-Microsoft clients, including Macintosh and NetWare. You must configure their accessibility on your Windows 2000 machine before they can access your resources.

NetWare Clients Accessing Windows 2000 Resources

NetWare users who need access to Windows 2000 resources can access a Windows 2000 server running the File and Print Services for NetWare (FPNW). This software is not provided with Windows 2000 Professional or Server but is included in the Services for NetWare product.

FPNW enables a Windows 2000 computer to look like a NetWare file and print server to NetWare clients. The NetWare clients can gain access to shared volumes, drives, and printers on the Windows 2000 server.

Macintosh Clients Accessing Windows 2000 Resources

Windows 2000 provides support for Macintosh client access to shared files and shared printers. However, you need to install two separate services to allow access to both the shared files and shared printers.

To allow Macintosh clients access to your shared folders, you need to install the File Server for Macintosh (MacFile) service. This service allows administrators to designate a directory as a Macintosh-accessible volume, ensure that Macintosh file names are legal NTFS names, and ensure the correct permissions have been set.

To allow Macintosh clients access to your shared printers, you need to install the Print Server for Macintosh (MacPrint) service. This service enables Macintosh clients to send and spool documents to printers attached to the Windows 2000 server. Macintosh clients are able to send documents to any printer on an AppleTalk network.

Integrating Windows 2000 with Unix

You also can share resources between Unix and Windows 2000 if you install a separate product called Services For Unix (SFU). SFU provides fully integrated interoperability components that make it easy to integrate Windows 2000 operating systems into existing Unix networks.

SFU provides password synchronization, a Network Information Service (NIS), and an NIS To Active Directory Wizard. This wizard assists in mapping usernames and network file system (NFS) server, client, and gateway software.

Summary

This chapter provided details on the advantages of client/server networks over workgroups. Centrally managing resources and providing single logon information for your users are two key advantages of using domains.

NTFS permissions control both remote and local access to your resources, and your share permissions control only remote access. A combination of the two permissions provides the most secure environment for controlling remote access to your resources.

Before users can access remote resources, you have to ensure the correct services are running on both the client and server. Furthermore, you have to share the resources and assign the appropriate permissions to them.

11

If you are in a heterogeneous environment, you must install additional services, and in some cases, you may have to purchase additional software for these services.

After sharing and securing your resources, you need to decide what your users will have for software and what they will be able to do with their desktop environment.

Now that you know what is involved with joining either a workgroup or domain, and you know how to manage your local resources and access remote resources, you need to be familiar with how to manage your users. Managing users involves local policies and group policies. Chapter 12 provides in-depth information regarding users, groups, security identifiers, local policies, and group polices.

Chapter 12

User and Group Management

Managing Users and Groups in Windows 2000 Professional

After successfully installing Windows 2000 Professional, you can log on as the local administrator and start using all the built-in features of the operating system. Depending on the environment, you may find it useful to create additional users and groups so that you can better manage a computer and its resources. Understanding the process of creating and managing users and groups will give you more administrative control over what actions your users and groups are allowed to perform and what resources they have access to.

You can install Windows 2000 Professional in a single user configuration, but often you will not be the only person using that computer. If you have multiple users logging on to the same computer, you must understand how to create and manage multiple user accounts so that each individual user who logs on to that computer uses his or her own account.

You also need to be aware that Windows 2000 Professional installs with some built-in user accounts. You will probably be using these accounts in your daily duties, so you will need to understand how they are used and be familiar with the permissions that are assigned to them by default.

Groups are an entirely separate area of administration, but when you're looking at the "big picture," you will find that users and groups are bound together so tightly that it will be equally important for you to understand how to use the built-in groups and create additional groups when the built-in groups do not meet your needs. Fortunately, Windows 2000 Professional provides several management and administration tools to assist you in the management of your users and groups. These tools include the following:

- Local Users And Groups

- Users And Passwords

- Active Directory Users and Computers Microsoft Management Console (MMC) snap-in (in a domain environment)

Depending on the environment, all or just some of these tools can be used to create, manage, and administer users and groups in Windows 2000 Professional.

For the purposes of this chapter, we have broken down the interrelated topics of users and groups into their component parts so that you can gain a better understanding of how to manage each of them separately, as well as how to combine them for a more effective management strategy. We will begin by looking at user account administration, and then we'll shift our focus to group management.

Introducing User Accounts

Every task that you perform when using Windows 2000 Professional begins with logging on to the computer using a built-in account or a user account that you have created. Windows 2000 Professional can be configured to automatically log on every user using the same user account when booting the computer, or it can be configured so that every user who attempts to log on to the computer is required to enter a username and password after the boot process has completed.

Understanding the Automatic Logon Feature

The choice you make about logging on is critical, and the decision usually depends on the level of security you are trying to implement. Configuring a computer with the automatic logon feature means that anyone who has physical access to the computer can gain access to all the computer's contents and quite possibly any network that the computer is connected to. This setting is appropriate only for a computer that is physically secure, so you must take the appropriate steps to ensure that unauthorized users cannot remotely access the Registry.

If you choose the automatic logon feature, every user will be logged on using the built-in Local Administrator account. For obvious reasons, this is not the most secure choice because every user logging on to that computer can manage the entire computer, including taking ownership of other users' files and changing anything having to do with the computer configuration.

This option is not available by default for a Windows 2000 Server or a Windows 2000 Professional client in a domain environment. However, a Registry entry can turn on this feature regardless of the operating system or computing environment.

To enable automatic logon (on any type of Windows 2000 computer), you need to perform the following procedure in the Windows 2000 Registry:

Warning! *This procedure will allow any user to log on automatically to the domain. This capability can cause serious security problems and should be used with caution. Anyone booting this system with this Registry modification will be logged on to the system with the user's security credentials that are entered in the Registry.*

1. Start Regedt32.exe from the Start|Run command and locate the following Registry key:

   ```
   HKEY_LOCAL_MACHINE\SOFTWARE\Microsoft\Windows NT\CurrentVersion\Winlogon
   ```

2. Enter the domain name, account name, and password, using the values you want to use for the automatic logon. You need to assign the following values: DefaultDomainName, DefaultUserName, and DefaultPassword.

3. If the DefaultPassword value does not exist, you will need to create it by using the following procedure:

   a. Select Add Value from the Edit menu. The Add Value dialog box will appear.

   b. In the Value Name textbox, type "DefaultPassword". In the Data Type pull-down menu, select REG_SZ.

   c. Click on OK.

   d. In the String Editor box, type in the password. Notice that the password is stored in clear text. Using clear text is a huge security risk because this Registry key can be read remotely by every member of the Authenticated Users group. Click on OK and save your changes.

Tip: *If you do not specify a DefaultPassword string, Windows 2000 automatically changes the value of the AutoAdminLogon key from 1 (true) to 0 (false). This value effectively disables the AutoAdminLogon feature.*

4. If the AutoAdminLogon value does not already appear in the list, open the Edit menu and click on Add Value. Type "AutoAdminLogon" in the Value Name textbox. Select REG_SZ in the Data Type pull-down menu. Enter "1" in the String textbox and save your changes.

5. Exit Regedt32.exe.

6. Shut down Windows and then restart your computer to implement your changes. You should now be able to log on automatically.

Note: *If you enable the automatic logon feature and then want to log on as a different user, hold down the Shift key after logging off or after restarting Windows.*

For increased security you may choose to configure the computer so that it requires each user to enter a username and password in order to log on. In Figure 12.1, you can see the Users Must Enter A User Name And Password To Use This Computer checkbox setting for requiring that each user provide a username and password when logging on to the computer. You can access this dialog box by double-clicking on the Users And Passwords icon located in Control Panel.

When you want to increase security, a better method for administering computers is to use the built-in Administrator account to create accounts for all the other users and then

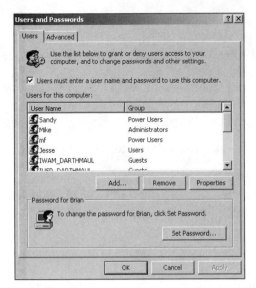

Figure 12.1
Changing settings in the Users And Passwords dialog box.

assign only the permissions required to each individual user account. This way, each user has access only to the files he or she owns, along with any shared applications that have been installed on that computer.

The choice you make here is entirely up to you; a general guideline would be to use the auto-logon feature when the physical security features of that computer do not allow unauthorized access or perhaps on a standalone machine in a home environment. For every other installation, and especially in a domain environment, you would probably choose to require a username and password.

Every Object Is Unique

The creation of user accounts is going to be one of the keys for allowing access to resources on both the local computer and throughout an entire domain. Every time you create an object (user account, group, and so on), Windows 2000 assigns that object a unique number that is then always used when that object attempts to access a resource. This unique number, called a security identifier (SID), is similar to the concept of assigning a Social Security number to each new child that is born.

Using the SID is also similar in that when you are performing any kind of "official personal business," the first question you are often asked is "Can you verify your Social Security number for me?" Just like your Social Security number uniquely identifies you to an official agency, the object's SID uniquely identifies that object to the operating system whenever that object attempts to access a resource. The internal processes of Windows 2000 actually refer to the object's SID rather than the actual user or group name.

The fact that SIDs are unique to each object raises some important issues in the area of object management. Perhaps the most important issue is that, due to a SID's uniqueness, deleting an object deletes the associated SID. This means that even if you create a new object with the same name and characteristics as the object you previously deleted, the operating system does not recognize it as the old object; it only recognizes it as the new object because of the unique SID created every time you create a new object. A SID ensures that no other object can "impersonate" another object to gain access to the resources that are available to that SID.

Now that you understand why SIDs are so important, it's time to discuss the types of user accounts that you will encounter when you begin creating user accounts.

User Account Types

Windows 2000 Professional allows for several types of user accounts. For proper administration, you must understand all of them, including how, when, and where they can be used. The types of user accounts you will find in Windows 2000 include local user accounts and domain user accounts. In addition, the operating system itself creates two built-in user accounts by default when you install Windows 2000 Professional. They are the Local Administrator account and the Guest account.

Local User Accounts

Local user accounts are created on the local computer, and they allow access only to resources on the computer they are created on. This is true because a local user account resides in the Security Accounts Manager (SAM) database on just that computer, and other computers will not recognize that account for resource access. This means if you have 10 computers and you want to have access to resources on each of them, you would have to create 10 separate accounts, one on each computer, and use that local account when accessing resources on the associated computer.

Using this type of account has many disadvantages, including the requirement for you to maintain 10 passwords, one for each computer. Having so many passwords is often a common source of security breaches, and it is therefore recommended that you limit your use of this method and instead use domain user accounts.

Note: *SIDs are not limited to user accounts. Every group and computer account you create is assigned a unique SID that is also referenced when the group or computer is used to access resources.*

Domain User Accounts

Domain user accounts are created just one time, and they then allow access to resources throughout the entire domain as long as the appropriate permissions have been applied. Domain user accounts reside in the Windows 2000 Active Directory directory service and are replicated to all the other domain controllers within the same domain. This requires that you have a Windows 2000 Server acting as a domain controller, and it allows a user to log on to the domain from any computer on the network with a single user account and password.

Built-in User Accounts

The two built-in accounts allow for performing administrative tasks (in the case of the Local Administrator account) or for gaining temporary access to network resources (in the case of the Guest account). You cannot delete either of these accounts, but you can rename them. The Guest account is disabled by default and does not have a password assigned to it, so you should assign it a strong password if you do plan to enable it. For obvious reasons, you cannot disable the Local Administrator account.

A common method for increasing security and protecting the Administrator account is to rename it using your standard naming convention. After you rename the Administrator account, create another account with the name Administrator and possibly assign it to a group that has limited or no access privileges. Then, set up auditing on this account and/ or group so that you can track who is attempting to log on to the system using an account named Administrator.

You may also consider changing the description on the default Administrator account because it clearly spells out what the account is capable of doing, and renaming this account does not change the default description. If an unauthorized user were able to gain access to the administrative tools, he or she would be able to see these descriptions and could view which account has the Administrator description even though you have renamed it.

To rename the default Administrator account or modify the description of it, open the Local Users and Groups located in Computer Management, double-click on Users, and right-click on the Administrators account. Select Rename on the shortcut menu to rename the account, or select Properties to change the description of the account.

The Local Administrator and Guest accounts reside in the local SAM database. If you are using a domain environment, you will also find a Domain Administrator account and a Domain Guest account stored in Active Directory.

User Account Names

Whenever you create a new user account, you must enter a unique name for it. Depending on the size and needs of your organization, naming it could be as simple as using the user's first and last names. However, in a large organization, you will often have an established user account naming convention that allows for users who have the same name. The convention often uses a combination of the following:

- Full first name with last name initial

- First name initial with full last name

- Full first name with middle initial and full last name

These conventions ensure that each username is unique across the entire organization. You will need to determine what the requirements are based on your needs, or you may have to follow a preexisting user naming convention.

Regardless of the convention you use, you will find that following some general guidelines can streamline your efforts in this area. Therefore, you might want to consider the following when naming user accounts:

- Local user account names must be unique on the computer you create them on.

- In a domain environment, user logon names must be unique in the Active Directory, and user account full names must be unique within the domain you create them in.

- Windows 2000 recognizes only the first 20 characters you enter as the logon name, and although you can use a combination of special and alphanumeric characters, you cannot use the following characters:

  " / \ [ ] : ; | = , + * ? < >

Note: *A user account name cannot consist of just spaces or periods.*

12

- Determine a naming convention for users with the same name that allows for easy identification of special classes of employees, such as prefacing the user account name for contractors with the letter *C* and a dash (such as *C-JonFoster*). You can also use this convention for any temporary employees. A common method would be to use the letter *T* and a dash (such as *T-JonFoster*).

Password Guidelines

The username itself does not provide any additional security, which is why a strong password policy is so important for controlling access to the local computer and to the network. The level of security that is required will determine what type of password policy is required, and you can follow some general guidelines to implement a password policy that allows for the level of security you are looking for:

- Always assign a strong password to the Administrator account to prevent unauthorized access.

- Assign a strong password to the Guest account when enabling it.

Note: *A complex password (as defined by Microsoft) is a password that has at least eight characters and contains at least each of the following: one uppercase letter, one lowercase letter, a number, and a special character. What is considered a strong password varies depending on the environment, administrator, and needs of each organization.*

- Educate users about the importance of using a strong password. Passwords can be up to 127 characters but anything over 6 to 8 characters usually results in the user writing down the password and keeping it near his or her computer.

Tip: *Windows 95/98 support passwords up to a maximum of 14 characters. If your Windows 2000 network has computers using Windows 95/98, you might want to consider using passwords that are no longer than 14 characters; otherwise, you might not be able to log on to your network from a Windows 95/98 computer.*

- Use a combination of alphanumeric characters and uppercase and lowercase letters.

- Depending on the environment, use the Local Security Policy to implement a strong password policy on the local machine or the Default Domain Policy to set a strong password policy across the entire domain. Figure 12.2 shows the Local Security Settings console with the Minimum Password Length Policy setting open. To open the Local Security Settings console click Start|Settings|Control Panel. Double-click on Administrative Tools, and then double-click on the Local Security Policy icon. Expand Account Policies, then double-click on Password Policy. The local policy is effective when you're setting a password policy on a standalone machine.

Figure 12.3 shows the Default Domain Group Policy opened to the Account Policies node, where you can configure the domain password policy, the account lockout policy, and the Kerberos policy settings. When configuring the Account Policies for a network, you should set them only at the domain level because they will be ignored at any other level. For instance, if you set Account Policies at the site or organizational unit level, they will be ignored.

Creating Local User Accounts

After determining the conventions you will use for your local user accounts, you can then begin the process of creating these accounts using the Computer Management console. You will be able to create local user accounts only on a computer that is

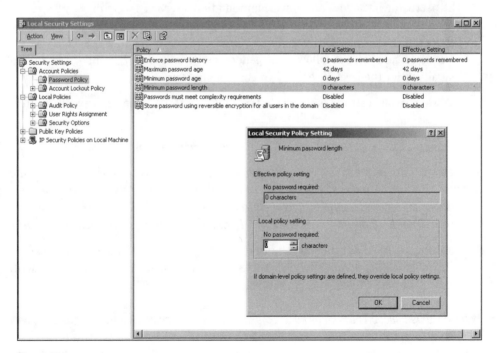

Figure 12.2
Setting the Local Security Policy.

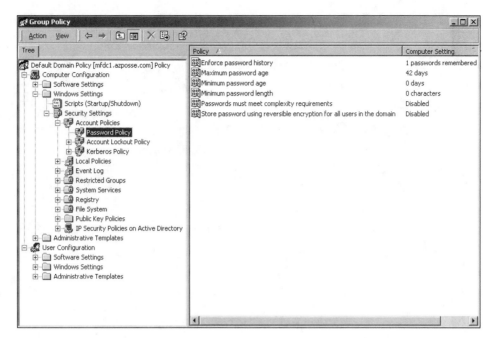

Figure 12.3
Viewing the Default Domain Group Policy.

running Windows 2000 Professional or on a standalone or member server that is
running Windows 2000 Server or Windows 2000 Advanced Server. Windows 2000
domain controllers do not allow for the creation of local user and group accounts; you
will not even have access to the Local Users And Groups node when you are working
with the Computer Management console on a Windows 2000 domain controller.

Tip: Only members of the Administrators and Account Operators groups have the right to create user accounts.

To create a local user account, perform the following steps:

1. Click on Start|Settings|Control Panel. Open the Administrative Tools folder, and then
   open Computer Management.

2. In the Computer Management console, expand System Tools and then expand Local
   Users And Groups.

3. Right-click on the Users folder and select New User. Figure 12.4 shows the Computer
   Management console expanded to the appropriate folder and the New User dialog box,
   where you will enter the username, the full name, and an optional description that
   can be used to further identify the user by job title, department, location, and so on.

4. After you enter this information, enter the user's password and confirm it by entering
   it again in the appropriate fields.

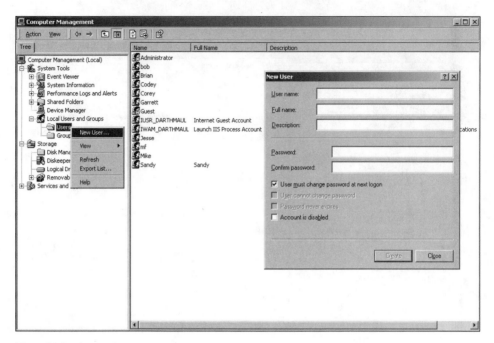

Figure 12.4
Creating a user in the New User dialog box.

5. Select the checkboxes that are appropriate for the way you want to manage the user's password. The following provides additional information on the options that you have in this area:

- The default is to force the user to change his or her password the first time he or she logs on. Deselecting the User Must Change Password At Next Logon checkbox gives you access to the next two options, described below.

- The User Cannot Change Password option is useful for shared accounts in which you would not want one user changing the password because the other users would then have problems logging on. You also can use this setting on a high security network where the IT staff is controlling passwords and you do not want any of your users to have the ability to change their assigned passwords.

- The Password Never Expires option can open security holes, and it is recommended that you never use this option. (Part of a strong password policy is forcing your users to periodically change their passwords.)

- You can also disable the account by selecting the Account Is Disabled checkbox. This capability can be useful when you're precreating accounts for users who have not begun working at your organization, or when a user goes on an extended leave of absence and you do not want to delete the account but also do not want another user logging on using this account.

- One more checkbox does not appear until after the account has been created: Account Is Locked Out. This checkbox appears on the General tab of a user account's Properties dialog box only after creation of the account (perhaps because an account that you have just created could not possibly be locked out). This checkbox is always dimmed until a user is locked out for violating the username and password restrictions. If a user is locked out, an administrator must log on and deselect this checkbox so that the user can log on again using this account. Figure 12.5 displays the checkbox for an account that has been locked out.

Note: Account lockouts are not configured to occur by default. An administrator must configure this setting in a Local Security or Group Policy for account lockouts to occur.

6. In the New User dialog box, click on Create to create the user account and then create additional accounts as required, or click on Close to close the dialog box.

Using the Users And Passwords Utility

Another tool you might find useful for performing common administrative tasks, such as deleting a user account or renaming an account, is the Users And Passwords utility located in Control Panel. This tool offers limited capabilities when compared to the Local Users And Groups node of the Computer Management console, but using it is often the easiest method for performing those tasks that it does support. Some of these common tasks are as follows:

- Creating a user account

- Adding a user account to a group

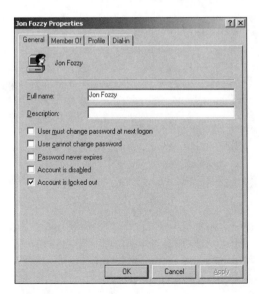

Figure 12.5
Viewing the user account's Properties page displaying the Account Is Locked Out checkbox.

- Renaming an account

- Deleting a user

- Setting passwords

- Requesting or viewing a digital certificate

Perhaps one of the most secure settings is located in the Secure Boot Settings area on the Advanced tab of the Users And Passwords dialog box. As shown in Figure 12.6, this checkbox sets the requirement that all users of this computer must press the Ctrl+Alt+Delete key sequence to open the Logon dialog box. Pressing Ctrl+Alt+Delete before logging on guarantees that the authentic Windows 2000 logon prompt appears.

Tip: *Requiring the use of Ctrl+Alt+Delete increases security and can prevent certain Trojan Horse programs from damaging the computer.*

Selecting the Advanced button in this dialog box opens the Local Users And Groups utility as a standalone tool.

Certificates

A digital certificate is a collection of data (information) signed by a Certification Authority that binds a public encryption key to the entity that holds the corresponding private encryption key. The certificate ensures data confidentiality and user authentication across an untrusted network such as the Internet. Digital certificates are often used in e-commerce transactions as well as on or between LANs to verify that a user or computer is who it says it is (authentication) and to encrypt the data that is transmitted.

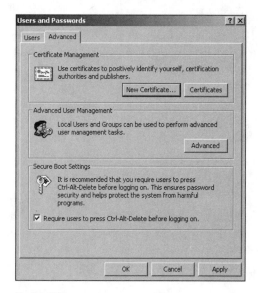

Figure 12.6
Choosing settings on the Advanced tab of the Users And Passwords dialog box.

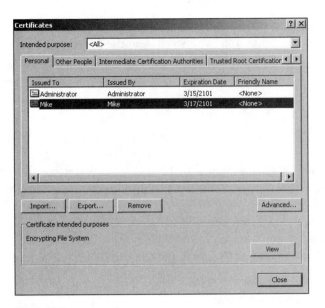

Figure 12.7
Viewing certificates in the Certificates dialog box.

Selecting the Certificates button on the Advanced tab will open the Certificates dialog box, as shown in Figure 12.7. Certificates are organized into the following four categories:

- *Personal*—This tab displays the certificates that have been issued to the associated user account. Selecting the Advanced button on this tab opens the Advanced Options dialog box, where you can modify the purpose of the certificate and choose the format to be used when exporting the certificate.

- *Other People*—This tab displays the certificates that have been issued to other individuals or organizations.

- *Intermediate Certification Authorities*—This tab displays the Intermediate Certification Authorities that issue various types of certificates, including personal certificates, publisher certificates, or certificates for other Intermediate Certification Authorities. Intermediate Certification Authorities issue and validate personal digital certificates.

Note: These certificates must be validated by a root certificate in the Trusted Root Certification Authorities.

- *Trusted Root Certification Authorities*—This tab displays the certificates that are issued by root certification authorities that you explicitly trust.

You can double-click on any certificate to view its associated information. The Certificate dialog box is organized into three panes:

- *General*—This is the default display for viewing the certificate's purpose. This information includes who issued the certificate, who the certificate was issued to, and the period for which the certificate is valid.

- *Details*—This view displays the actual fields of the X.509 certificate, any extensions, and additional properties of the certificate. You can also click on the Edit Properties button to modify the Friendly Name and Description fields and specify what the certificate can be used for. On this tab, you can also select the Copy To File button to export the certificate.

- *Certification Path*—This view displays the certification path up to the issuer of the certificate.

Built-in Group Accounts

A disadvantage of the Users and Passwords utility is that you cannot use it to create groups and, as you can see in Figure 12.8, you can add a user to only one group. To access the Group Membership tab, click Start|Settings|Control Panel, then double-click on Users And Passwords. Right-click on the user account you wish to modify and select Properties to open the Properties dialog box. If you need to create a new group or add a user account to more than one group, use Local Users And Groups in the Computer Management console.

As you can see from Figure 12.8, Windows 2000 Professional provides the following built-in groups of accounts with preset permissions:

- *Standard User*—These users, who belong to the Power Users group, can change computer settings and install applications, but cannot access documents that have been created by other users.

- *Restricted User*—These users, who belong to the Users group, can run programs and save their documents. They cannot change computer settings, install applications or programs, or view documents that have been created by another user.

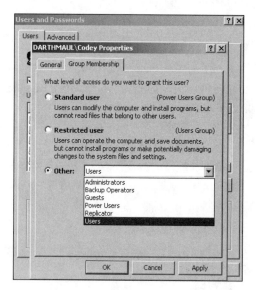

Figure 12.8
Choosing a user on the Group Membership tab of a user account's Properties page in the Users And Passwords utility.

- *Other*—This area contains a list of all the built-in groups, including Administrators, Backup Operators, Guests, Power Users, Replicator, and Users.

Creating Domain User Accounts

As you have seen, local user accounts allow access only to resources on the computer they are created on. If you are looking for access to resources throughout your network, a better solution is to use domain user accounts. With domain user accounts, you create the account just once on a Windows 2000 domain controller, and after you assign the appropriate permissions, that account can be used to access resources anywhere in the domain.

To create domain user accounts from a computer running Windows 2000 Professional, you will need to install the appropriate administrative tools on that computer. The tools required to manage your domain user accounts are located in the I386 folder on the Windows 2000 Server and Windows 2000 Advanced Server CD-ROM. As you can see in Figure 12.9, double-clicking the ADMINPAK.MSI Windows Installer package file will launch the Windows 2000 Administration Tools Setup Wizard, which you will then use to install the Windows 2000 administration tools. You can install the tools on a Windows 2000 domain controller, a computer running Windows 2000 Professional, or a Windows 2000 member server in order for you to remotely manage a Windows 2000 domain controller.

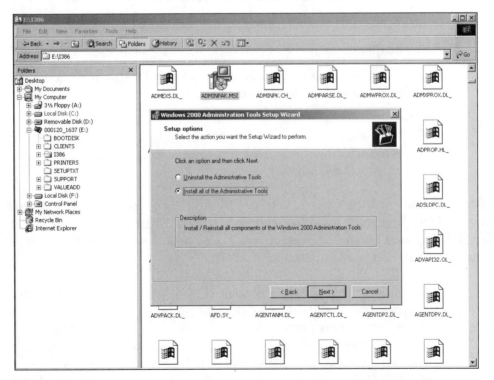

Figure 12.9
Starting the Windows 2000 Administration Tools Setup Wizard.

Tip: When creating user accounts, you should be aware that any plain folder in the Active Directory Users and Computers console is called a container. A container is not an organizational unit (OU), and you cannot apply Group Policy to a container; you can apply Group Policy only at the local, site, domain, or OU level. Therefore, you should create the additional organizational units that are required by your organization and then create your user accounts in these OUs so that you can apply Group Policy to them.

Use the following worksheet to document your user account information. This worksheet is useful for deciding what information you want to enter when creating a new user account. The completed worksheet can assist you in identifying conflicting user accounts, and determining whether you have created a username strategy that accommodates duplicate names. The completed worksheet below provides an example of its use. A blank worksheet can be found on the accompanying CD-ROM. Print as many copies as necessary when preparing to create your user accounts.

Documenting new user account information.				
First Name	**Initials**	**Last Name**	**Logon Name**	**Pre-Windows 2000 Logon Name**
Brian	J.	Alderman	brian.alderman@homedomain.com	homedomain\brian.alderman
Erik		Eckel	erik.eckel@homedomain.com	homedomain\erik.eckel

To create a domain user account, perform the following steps:

1. Select Start|Programs|Administrative Tools|Active Directory Users And Computers.

2. Expand the domain you want to add the new user account to and select the appropriate folder you wish to create the account in.

3. Right-click on the folder, point to New, and then click on User to open the New Object - User dialog box, as shown in Figure 12.10. Here, you will enter the information that identifies this user account. Table 12.1 describes the information you will be able to enter in this window.

Tip: Another recommendation is to enable the Advanced Features option from the View menu the first time you open the Active Directory Users and Computers console. This option adds several advanced administrative capabilities, such as allowing you to view the permissions that have been assigned to that account and any digital certificates that have been issued to that account.

4. After you enter the required information, click on Next to advance to the screen shown in Figure 12.11. Here, you will set the password requirements for this user account. You will be required to enter the password and then enter it again to confirm it. In this window, notice that you have all the same options that you had when creating a local user account. Figure 12.11 also displays some of the informational messages you may receive based on the combination of parameters you choose when defining the password setting.

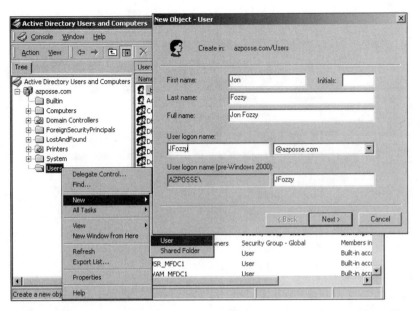

Figure 12.10
Creating a new user account using the New Object - User dialog box.

Table 12.1   User properties.

Field	Description
First Name	The user's first name.
Initials	The user's middle initial. This entry is optional.
Last Name	The user's last name.
Full Name	The user's full name, which must be unique within this container.
User Logon Name	The user's logon name, which must be unique in the Active Directory.
User Logon Name (Pre-Windows 2000)	The user's logon name, which must be unique within the domain and is used to log on from computers running previous versions of Microsoft Windows operating systems.

Tip: The User Must Change Password At Next Logon option overrides the User Cannot Change Password option, and the Password Never Expires option overrides the User Must Change Password At Next Logon option. Windows 2000 will warn you when you set either of these two incompatible options for the same user account and will automatically deselect the incompatible option before it allows you to proceed.

After you install the Windows 2000 Administration Tools, you can use the Active Directory Users and Computers console on your Windows 2000 Professional computer to create and manage your domain user accounts.

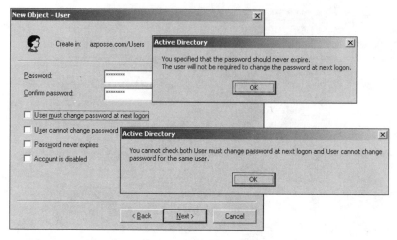

Figure 12.11
Confirming a password in the New Object - User dialog box.

Using the Run As Command

One very important utility that every administrator needs to be aware of is the **Run As** command (also known as the "secondary logon" feature). Whenever you are creating user accounts, or performing any administrative tasks for that matter, it is recommended that you log on under the context of a regular user account and then use the **Run As** command to perform the required administrative tasks. Logging on as an administrator opens up the local computer, and therefore the entire network, to Trojan Horse viruses and other equally destructive hacker attack methods. The possibility is very high that you may download a virus while surfing the Internet, and if you are logged on as an administrator, the virus will run under the context of the Administrator account. This can wreak havoc on your system or network.

Any user with multiple accounts can use the **Run As** command to launch a program under the context of another user account. To use the **Run As** command, hold down the Shift key and right-click on the tool you wish to run under a different context. This action opens the dialog box shown in Figure 12.12. Here, you enter the user account, password, and domain name for the account you wish to launch the program with. Note that items such as Windows Explorer, the Printers folder, and desktop items are launched indirectly by Windows 2000 and therefore cannot be started with the **Run As** command. Where it is supported, the **Run As** command can also be used from the command prompt or the Run dialog box, which you can access from the Start menu.

Setting Domain User Account Properties

After creating domain user accounts, you might want to further customize these accounts by setting some user account properties. User account properties include settings such as home folders, personal properties, and logon options. Depending on the options you select in the Active Directory Users and Computers console, you will see up to 15 tabs on the Properties dialog box for each user account. Table 12.2 explains the purpose of each tab.

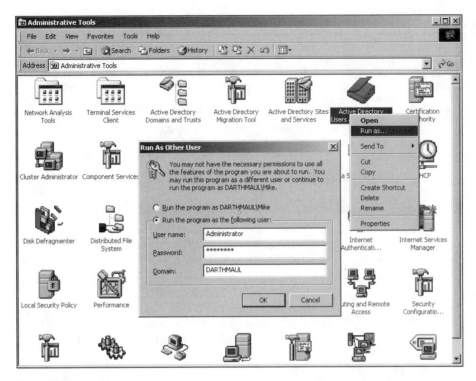

Figure 12.12
Logging on as a different user in the Run As dialog box.

Table 12.2 Domain user account properties.

Tab	Purpose
General	Displays the user's name, description, office location, telephone number, email address, and home page information
Address	Displays the user's street address, post office box, city, state or province, ZIP code, and country
Account	Displays the user's logon name and allows you to set various options, such as the hours that a user is allowed to log on, the computers that a user is allowed to log on to, and various password and account expiration options
Profile	Displays the user's profile path and home folder path as set up by the administrator
Telephones	Provides the ability to enter various phone numbers and other descriptive information about the user
Organization	Displays the user's title, department, company, manager, and direct reports
Member Of	Displays the groups that the user account is a member of
Dial-in	Allows you to set various parameters for the user's remote access permissions, callback options, and more
Environment	Allows you to set terminal server settings for the application(s) that will start when a user makes a connection to a Windows 2000 server
Sessions	Allows you to set terminal server settings that control the user session on a terminal server

(continued)

Table 12.2 Domain user account properties *(continued)*.

Tab	Purpose
Remote Control	Allows you to set terminal server settings for allowing remote control of the user session
Terminal Services Profile	Allows you to configure a profile that is used only during terminal server sessions
Published Certificates	Lists the X.509 certificates that have been issued to the user account
Object	Displays the Fully Qualified Domain Name (FQDN) of the user object, along with information about when it was created and modified
Security	Displays the Discretionary Access Control List (DACL) for the object with the Access Control Entries (ACE)

The last three tabs are available only after you select the Advanced Features option from the View menu.

As an administrator, you will want to enter as much information as you can in these areas because all of them can be used when searching the Active Directory for a particular user account or property. As an added benefit, unused properties do not consume any space in the Active Directory.

Let's continue our discussion by looking at some of the most commonly used properties, and then we'll let you explore some of the other properties on your own.

Setting User Account Properties

You access a user account's Properties dialog box by right-clicking on a user account in the Active Directory Users and Computers console and selecting Properties. Selecting the Account tab will bring up the screen displayed in Figure 12.13. Here, you can set various

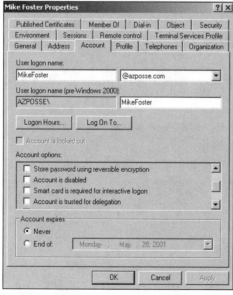

Figure 12.13
Setting account information on the Account tab of a user account's Properties dialog box.

parameters that allow you a very granular degree of control over what this account can do. You can use this tab to specify additional password options that are not available during the creation of the user account and set an expiration date and time for the account. This capability can be very useful if you have contract or temporary employees at your organization, and you want to ensure that their accounts cannot be used to log on to the network after they have left the organization.

Some of the advanced password settings are worthy of discussion, so Table 12.3 describes the additional password options that do not appear when you're creating a new user account.

Setting Logon Hours

Selecting the Logon Hours button on the Account tab will open the window displayed in Figure 12.14. Here, you can specify the hours that a user is able to log on to the network. By default, users have permission to log on to the domain 24 hours a day, 7 days a week, so this feature is useful when you have shift workers and you want them to be able to log on to the network only during their regularly scheduled working hours. A blue box

Table 12.3   User account password options.

Option	Description
Store Passwords Using Reversible Encryption	Use this option when you have users logging on to your Windows 2000 network from Apple computers. You should also use this option when configuring Challenge Handshake Authentication Protocol (CHAP) as the remote access authentication method.
Smart Card Required For Interactive Logon	Use this option to securely store public and private keys, passwords, and other types of personal information for this user account. You must have a Smart Card reader attached to the user's computer, and the user must have a personal identification number (PIN) to be able to log on to the network using a Smart Card.
Account Is Trusted For Delegation	Use this option to enable a user to assign responsibility for management and administration of a portion of the domain namespace to another user, group, or organization.
Account Is Sensitive And Cannot Be Delegated	Use this option if this account cannot be assigned for delegation by another account.
Use DES Encryption Types For This Account	Use this option if you need the Data Encryption Standard (DES). DES supports multiple levels of encryption, including MPPE Standard (40-bit), MPPE Standard (56-bit), MPPE Strong (128-bit), IPSec DES (40-bit), IPSec 56-bit DES, and IPSec Triple DES (3DES).
Don't Require Kerberos Preauthentication	Use this option if the account uses another implementation of the Kerberos protocol other than the Windows 2000 implementation. The Kerberos Key Distribution Center (KDC) uses ticket-granting tickets (TGTs) for obtaining network authentication in a domain, and the time at which the Key Distribution Center issues a ticket-granting ticket is critical to the Kerberos authentication process. Windows 2000 provides its own method for time synchronization, so this may be required when the client is not a Windows 2000 computer or is not using the Windows 2000 Kerberos implementation.

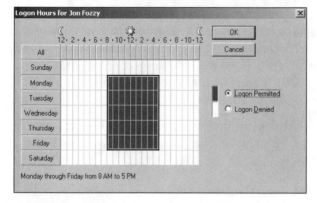

Figure 12.14
Specifying logon times in the Logon Hours For *User* dialog box.

indicates the hours that a user can log on; a white box indicates the hours that a user will not be able to log on.

Tip: *Be aware that this setting will not disconnect a user who is already logged on, but it will prevent him or her from making any new connections to other computers in the domain.*

Setting Logon Workstations

In addition to specifying the hours that a user is able to log on (or not log on), you can specify the computers that a user can log on to by selecting the Log On To button on the Account tab. Selecting this button will bring up the window shown in Figure 12.15. By default, any user with a valid user account can log on to the network from any computer that is running Windows 2000 (domain controllers are the only exception).

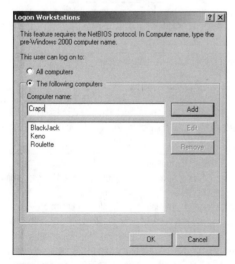

Figure 12.15
Choosing computers to log on in the Logon Workstations dialog box.

Warning! *You can specify only the computers that a user is able to log on to; you cannot specify the computers that a user cannot log on to. This means that after you enter a computer name in this area, the user account can no longer be used to log on to any other computer in the domain that does not appear in this list. In this window, notice that specifying only the computer(s) that a user can log on to requires the use of the NetBIOS protocol on the network.*

Using the Profile Tab

The Profile tab of a user account's Properties dialog box is one of the most-used tabs when setting up the properties for your user accounts. On this tab, you can configure home folders and user profiles that are stored on a network server rather than on the user's local machine. In a domain environment, these features can be very useful, and the following sections discuss the use and configuration of the settings available on this tab.

12

Creating Home Folders

Home folders provide a central network storage area where users store their documents. The benefit of using home folders is that, as an administrator, you can perform a backup of all the users' data from a central location rather than have each individual user attempt to back up all his or her own files on the local computer. Another great benefit of using home folders is that they are not part of the user's user profile, so they will not affect a user's logon performance. This reduces the amount of time required for a user to log on.

To use home folders, you must first ensure that your storage server has sufficient space to store all your user data; then, you must create and share a folder on that server to host the users' home folders. After you create and share the folder with the appropriate permissions, you then specify the path to the user's home folder by entering a Universal Naming Convention (UNC) path to the home folder on the Profile tab of the user account's Properties dialog box, as shown in Figure 12.16. The path needs to be in the form *server_name**home_folder_share_name*\%*username*%. Using the %*username*% variable will ensure that the operating system creates a unique name for each individual user's home folder (named after the user), and it will assign the appropriate permissions to allow only that user to have access to the folder.

Creating User Profiles

In addition to creating home folders, you can further tailor your user accounts by creating user profiles. The user's environment is primarily determined by the user profile that is created the very first time he or she logs on to a computer. It contains all the user-defined settings, such as the display resolution and desktop settings. The following types of profiles can exist on a computer running Windows 2000:

- *Default user profile*—This template is used to create all other user profiles. Every user profile begins with the application of the default user profile when a user first logs on to a computer running Windows 2000.

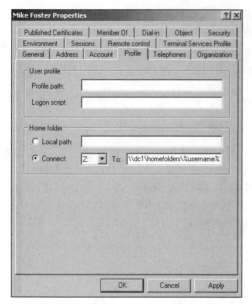

Figure 12.16
Setting a user's home folder on the Profile tab of a user account's Properties dialog box.

- *Local user profile*—This profile is created the first time a user logs on to a computer. It is stored on the local computer and is specific only to the local computer. When multiple users are logging on to the same computer, Windows 2000 will use the default user profile as a template and then create an individual local user profile for each user logging on to the computer.

- *Roaming user profile*—This type of profile is created by an administrator and stored on a network server. Storing it on the server ensures that the user's profile is available regardless of which computer a user logs on to, and it is saved back to the network server whenever a user makes a change to his or her profile and then logs off.

- *Mandatory user profile*—This type of profile also is created by an administrator, and it does not allow a user to modify the settings specified by the administrator. Any changes a user makes while logged on are discarded when the user logs off. This feature can be useful when you do not want a user, or a group of users, making changes to the profile.

To create a roaming user profile, perform the following steps:

1. Create a shared folder on a network server.

2. Provide the users with the Full Control permissions to the folder.

3. Access the Profile tab for a user account's Properties dialog box and enter the UNC path that points to the shared folder in the form *server_name**shared_folder_name*\%*username*%.

This process works just like creating home folders because it will create the user profile folder based on the user account name and then allow only that user to access the folder.

On this tab, notice that you can also provide a local path for the home folder and enter a logon script that will run when the user logs on.

To create a mandatory user profile, you will follow a similar procedure to the one discussed previously. The steps include the following:

- Creating and sharing a folder to store the profile

- Creating a new user account

- Specifying the user's profile folder

- Logging on as that user

- Configuring the settings the way the user wants them and then logging off

These steps create the user profile in a file named Ntuser.dat in the user's folder, located by default in the path C:\Documents and Settings*user_name*. You will then want to log on as an administrator, open Windows Explorer, navigate to the appropriate user's profile folder, and rename Ntuser.dat file to Ntuser.man.

Tip: *Renaming the user profile makes it read-only so that no changes can be made to it.*

You can use Decision Tree 12.1 to assist you in deciding whether you are going to use a local, roaming, or mandatory user profile.

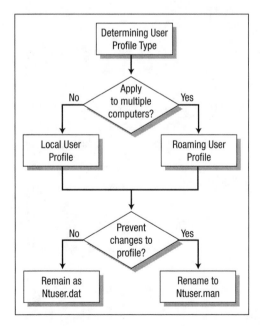

Decision Tree 12.1
Determining your user profile type.

Before creating mandatory user profiles, you need to be aware that the My Documents folder is part of the user's profile, and if you create mandatory user profiles, any changes made to the My Documents folder will not be saved when the user logs off. The solution for this problem is to use the Group Policy folder redirection feature to store the My Documents folder in a separate location from the mandatory user profile. Figure 12.17 displays the Default Domain Group Policy opened to the My Documents Properties folder redirection dialog box, where you can specify the location where Windows 2000 stores the My Documents folder. The default is No Administrative Policy Specified.

After specifying one of the folder redirection policies, you must specify either a UNC path (for a Basic redirection of everyone's folders to the same location) or folder redirection policies for groups. These settings become available on the Target tab after you specify one of the nondefault policies. Specifying a Basic redirection policy also gives you access to the various Settings tab options, as shown in Figure 12.18. These options allow you to control how the My Documents redirected folder is treated when the policy is applied or removed and whether you wish to include the My Pictures folder along with the My Documents folder.

You need to be careful when configuring these settings. If the redirection policy you set specifies that the folder be redirected back to the local user profile location upon removal of the policy but does not specify that the contents be moved during redirection, the contents of the folder will no longer be visible to the user upon removal of the policy. This

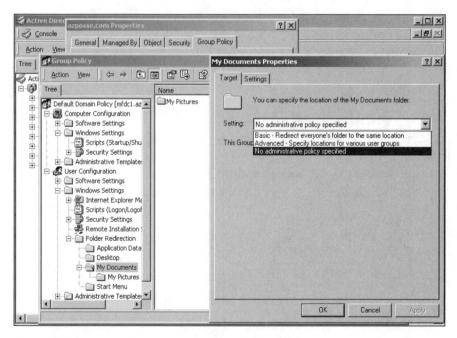

Figure 12.17
Setting the My Documents folder redirection feature located in the Default Domain Group Policy.

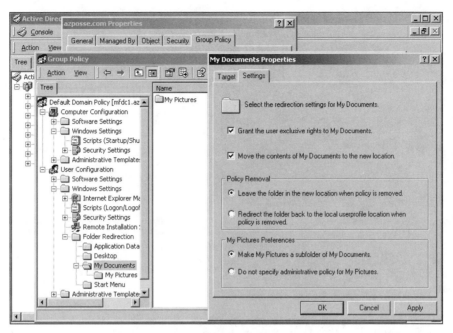

Figure 12.18
Configuring settings on the Settings tab of the My Documents Properties dialog box.

means that the user's files will remain at the location that was specified when the policy was in effect, and the user will not have access to those files.

Setting Advanced User Account Properties

In this section, we will explore several of the other tabs on a user account's Properties page, starting with the General tab. As you can see in Figure 12.19, the General tab is the place you can specify the user's first name, initials, last name, display name, description, office name or location, multiple telephone numbers, email address, and Web page. The benefit of filling in each of these areas is that this information will then be stored in Active Directory and can be used when conducting searches of the Active Directory to find specific values.

The next tab, the Address tab, is where you can specify many address properties, including the street address, city, state or province, ZIP or postal code, and the user's country or region. If you use the drop-down menu next to the Country/Region field, you will see that Microsoft has provided an extensive list of countries and regions throughout the world.

The Telephones tab can be used to provide complete information regarding methods for contacting the user. You can enter multiple phone numbers for the user's home, pager, mobile, fax, or IP phone, and you can enter any other contact information for the user that you deem pertinent in the Notes box.

The Organization tab is the place you can enter the user's job title, department, company, manager, and any other person/organization that the user reports directly to.

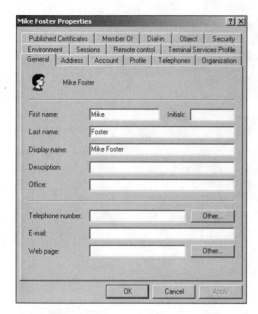

Figure 12.19
The General tab of a user account's Properties dialog box.

The Environment tab is specifically used for Terminal Services client settings. As you can see in Figure 12.20, you can use this tab to specify the program(s) that can be used when a user connects to a terminal server. Specifying a program, or programs, on this tab limits the user to using only those programs when he or she connects to the terminal server. In Figure 12.20,

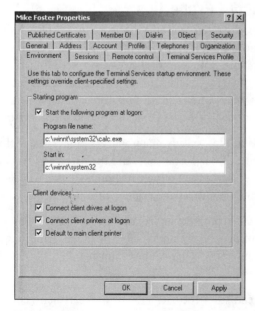

Figure 12.20
The Environment tab of a user account's Properties dialog box.

the user has been allowed to use only the calculator program, and if he or she closes the calculator program, the terminal server will disconnect the user and end the session. This feature can be very useful when you want to allow access to only a limited number of programs through your terminal server. Notice that on this tab you can also specify settings for client drives and printers that will be connected during a terminal server session.

The Sessions tab allows you to configure specific time settings that determine how long a client can remain connected to a terminal server session. In Figure 12.21, notice that you can specify settings for ending a disconnected, active, or idle session and choose what actions to take when a user reaches his or her session limit or breaks the terminal server connection, and how the terminal server responds when a client attempts to reconnect to the terminal server.

Microsoft recommends configuring the End A Disconnected Session setting for 10 minutes and configuring the Idle Session Limit to 5 minutes to free terminal server resources in the event your users do not follow established procedures for conducting terminal server sessions. The Allow Reconnection setting works only for clients running Citrix ICA Client for Windows client software (more information on this client software is available at **www.citrix.com**).

The Remote Control tab displays the default remote control settings for terminal server clients. The default is to allow remote control with the user's permission. This tab also has a setting that allows support personnel to interact with the session; it can be changed to allow only viewing of the user's session. These features can be very useful when you're troubleshooting a user's terminal server session because they allow help desk support

12

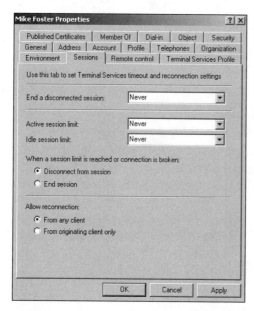

Figure 12.21
The Sessions tab of a user account's Properties dialog box.

personnel to interact and even control the user's session. This setting can also be useful for training purposes.

You use the Terminal Services Profile tab, displayed in Figure 12.22, to specify a user profile and home directory that is relevant only to the terminal server environment. The home directory can be a local directory located on the terminal server itself or a remote directory stored on a network server. Every administrator needs to pay particular attention to the Allow Logon To Terminal Server checkbox, which is checked by default. This setting allows every user who has an account on the terminal server to connect to the terminal server. As a security or performance enhancement, you might want to deselect this checkbox for those users whom you do not want to be able to make a connection to your terminal server.

The Published Certificates tab displays the X.509 digital certificates that have been issued to this account. These certificates have been issued by a Certificate Authority (CA) for various security purposes, including for use with the Encrypting File System (EFS), secure email, and possibly authentication.

On the Member Of tab you can quickly add or remove a user account to or from a group. Notice that on this tab you can also set the primary group membership for Macintosh users or when you are using POSIX-compliant applications.

You use the Dial-in tab to control a user's access to a remote access server. Figure 12.23 displays the default settings that are set to deny remote access. If you wish to allow

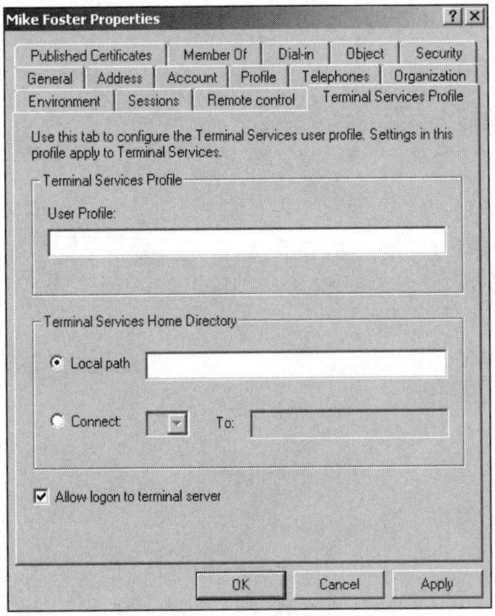

Figure 12.22
The Terminal Services Profile tab of a user account's Properties dialog box.

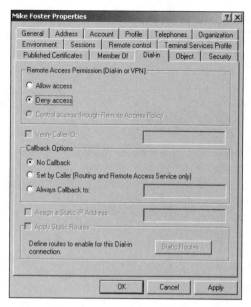

Figure 12.23
The Dial-in tab of a user account's Properties dialog box.

remote access, you would have to change this setting to either Allow Access or Control Access Through Remote Access Policy.

The Control Access Through Remote Access Policy setting becomes available only after you switch the domain from mixed mode to native mode. The Callback Options are the only other options available in a mixed mode domain. In this example, the domain is running in mixed mode. If the domain were running in native mode, all these options would be available.

When you're running in native mode, you can also configure this tab so that the remote access client can be assigned a static IP address for the remote session and also enter static routes that will be added to the remote access server's routing table when the remote user makes the connection.

Note: *For you to be able to use the Caller ID option, all the hardware between, and including, the remote user and remote access server would have to support this feature.*

The Object tab, shown in Figure 12.24, displays the Fully Qualified Domain Name of the object (in this case, the user), along with its class, creation date, the date it was last modified, and the corresponding Update Sequence Numbers (USNs).

The Security tab displays the Discretionary Access Control List for the user account with the Access Control Entries listed as individual entries in the Name window and the associated permissions in the Permissions window. In Figure 12.25, notice that you have

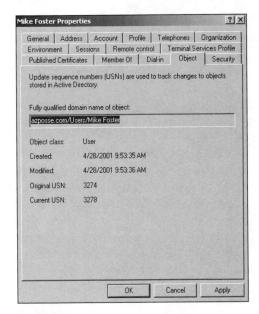

Figure 12.24
The Object tab of a user account's Properties dialog box.

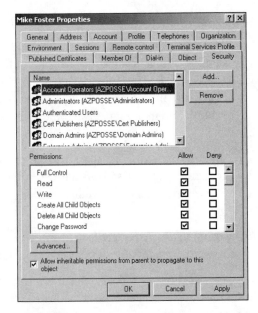

Figure 12.25
The Security tab of a user account's Properties dialog box.

the option of deselecting the Allow Inheritable Permissions From Parent To Propagate To This Object checkbox. Deselecting this box brings up a dialog box in which you can copy the permissions that are being inherited, or you can remove all the permissions that are propagating from the parent. You need to be careful when selecting the second option because doing so removes all the assigned permissions and you would then have to reapply permissions to the object.

Selecting the Advanced button near the bottom of this window will bring up the Access Control Settings dialog box for the user account. This dialog box has three tabs. The first one is the Permissions tab, displayed in Figure 12.26. On this tab, you can add, remove, view, and edit the permissions that are associated with this object. Selecting the View/Edit button on this tab will bring up the Permission Entry dialog box, where you can further tailor the permission settings via the Object and Properties tabs.

12

The Auditing tab allows you to configure auditing for the user account. This security configuration allows you to track changes that are made to this account. Selecting the View/Edit button on this tab will bring up the Auditing Entry dialog box, where you can further define the type of auditing you wish to perform via the Object and Properties tabs.

Tip: *No audit policy is established by default. If you wish to enable an audit policy, you must configure it manually.*

On the Owner tab, you can view the current owner of the object as well as change the owner. In Figure 12.27, notice that the current owner is displayed in the top field, and the user accounts that can take ownership are displayed in the bottom Name window.

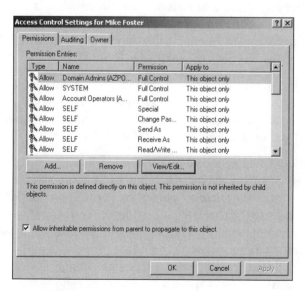

Figure 12.26
The Permissions tab of a user account's Access Control Settings dialog box.

Figure 12.27
The Owner tab of a user account's Access Control Settings dialog box.

Copying Domain User Accounts and Using Account Templates

Setting account properties on an individual account basis could end up taking a lot of administrative effort. If you're a proactive administrator looking to reduce administrative overhead, you will also be concerned with how to create user accounts for users who have many of the same account properties. Creating such accounts can be useful when you have various classifications of employees, such as sales or marketing employees, that all require some common account properties. When you copy an existing user account, several of the account properties are copied over to the new account. The properties that are copied over, along with those that are not, are explained in Table 12.4.

You should be aware that copying an existing user account does not copy any of the permissions that have been directly assigned to the user account that is being copied. To copy an existing user account, open the Active Directory Users and Computers console, right-click on the user account you wish to copy, and select Copy.

Copying existing user accounts will reduce your administrative overhead, but quite often you will have employees who are members of a specific group, such as your sales employees, and they will all require some common account properties. For this, you may choose to create an account template that can then be used for creating user accounts that contain all the common properties required by that department or functional unit. An account template begins by creating a generic user account that will be used as the template for creating copies for all the users who require the same settings. The idea here is to create a template for each classification of employee; doing so can also be very useful when you have contract or temporary employees who all require the same account options, such as logon hours or other restrictions.

Table 12.4 Properties copied when copying domain user accounts.

Tab	Properties Copied to the New Domain User Account
General	None.
Address	Everything except the street address.
Account	Everything except the logon name, which is copied from the Copy Object - User dialog box.
Profile	Everything except the profile path and home folder entries, which are modified to reflect the new user's logon name.
Telephones	None.
Organization	Everything except the title.
Member Of	Everything.
Dial-in	None; the default settings apply to the new user account.
Environment	None; the default settings apply to the new user account.
Sessions	None; the default settings apply to the new user account.
Remote Control	None; the default settings apply to the new user account.
Terminal Services Profile	None; the default settings apply to the new user account.

12

You create the template the same way you create any other user account. After you create the account, you configure the properties in the exact configuration you need and then save it for future use.

Tip: It is often a good idea to place a nonalphanumeric character (such as an underscore) as the first character in the user account name. This account will always appear near the top of the list inside the Active Directory Users and Computers console details pane.

You will also want to disable the template account when you create it so that it cannot be used to log on to the network. When you create a new user account by copying the template, you just have to remember to enable the new account so that it can be used.

After you create your user accounts, you also can perform some additional management tasks in the Active Directory Users and Computers console by right-clicking on the user account and making the appropriate selections. Figure 12.28 shows the options that will be available to you when you right-click on an existing user account. You can copy the user account, make it a member of a group, disable it, reset the password, move it, delete it, rename it, open the user account's home page, and send email to the user.

One option on the fly-out menu is not as readily identifiable as the others: Name Mappings. A *name mapping* is a special Windows 2000 feature that enables an MS-DOS or Windows 3.x user to gain access to an NTFS- or FAT-formatted partition or volume. Windows 2000 allows share names that contain up to 255 characters for file sharing. MS-DOS and Windows 3.x are restricted to share names that contain up to 8 characters followed by a period, with an extension of up to 3 more characters. Each file or folder that does not

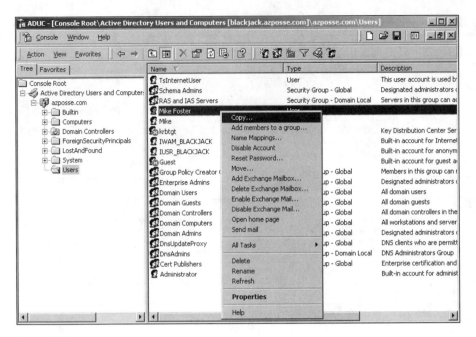

Figure 12.28
User account options.

conform to this MS-DOS "8.3" file-naming convention is automatically given a second name that does. These clients cannot read the long file names used by Windows 2000.

Name mapping ensures that each MS-DOS and Windows 3.x user connecting to the file or directory over the network sees the name in the 8.3 format. Windows 2000 users see the long name. You can also use name mapping to allow a non–Windows 2000 Kerberos realm user or an external (nonenterprise) user who has an X.509 certificate that has been issued by a trusted CA to gain access to your Windows 2000 domain. This certificate-based authentication method is often used in extranet business partner relationships when you want to allow a user from another organization that does not have an account in the Active Directory to be able to access your Windows 2000 domain resources.

Name mappings can also be used by Microsoft's built-in Web server, Internet Information Services (IIS), to authenticate clients requesting access to the Web server. You can associate (or map) client certificates to a Windows user account on your Web server. After you configure a name mapping, each time a user logs on with a client certificate, your Web server will automatically associate that user to the appropriate Windows user account. This allows for automatic authentication of users who log on with client certificates, without requiring the use of either Basic, Digest, or Integrated Windows authentication.

Basic authentication sends usernames and passwords in clear text and is supported by almost any browser. However, sending passwords in clear text can be a security issue so Microsoft has developed two additional methods for authenticating with the Web server.

Digest authentication uses a one-way hash algorithm to encrypt the password so it is more secure than Basic authentication, but it only works in an environment that contains a Windows 2000 domain controller and the clients must be running IE 5 or later. The other option is Integrated Windows authentication. With this authentication method the password is never sent over the network. Instead, the current Windows user information is used to validate access to the Web server. The drawbacks are that it is best suited for an intranet environment where the user and the Web server are located in the same domain, it does not work across HTTP proxy connections, and the clients must be running IE 2 or later.

You can map a single client certificate to a single Windows user account (one-to-one mapping) or multiple client certificates to a single user account (many-to-one mapping). For example, if you have several different departments or organizations using the same Web server, each with its own Web site, you could use a many-to-one mapping to map all the client certificates for each department or organization to its own Web site. This way, each site would provide access only to its own clients. You can find additional information on using name mappings with Internet Information Server in the IIS Help file.

12

Setting User Account Exchange Properties

This section is designed to introduce you to the three additional Exchange Server tabs that will appear on the user account's Properties pages after the installation of the Active Directory Connector (ADC) on a Windows 2000 domain controller, followed by configuring a Connection Agreement with a Microsoft Exchange Server. The Active Directory Connector is located on the Windows 2000 Server CD-ROM in the VALUEADD\MSFT\ MGMT\ADC folder.

The Active Directory Connector (ADC) and the Microsoft Management Console (MMC) are the Windows 2000 Server software components that allow you to synchronize and manage communications between the Windows 2000 Active Directory and Exchange Server 5.5 directory service. The ADC uses the Lightweight Directory Access Protocol (LDAP) to provide an automated way of keeping the separate directory information stored in these two directory services synchronized and consistent. Without the ADC, you would have to manually enter new data, transfer existing data between, and provide updates to both directory services.

The ADC provides a single interface for administration of these two separate directory services and provides bi-directional or one-way synchronization of the data stored in these two directories. It also replicates only changes made to directory objects at the attribute level so as to limit the amount of replication traffic transmitted over the network.

Note: This section is just a brief overview and is not designed to be an exhaustive discussion of Exchange Server or the configuration of an Exchange Server or the Active Directory Connection Agreement. You can find a wealth of additional information on configuring Connection Agreements on the Microsoft Windows 2000 and Exchange Server Web sites.

Figure 12.29 displays the Exchange General tab, on which you can configure basic email attributes, depending on whether users are mail-enabled or mailbox-enabled. The attributes on this tab include an alias, the user's email address, message size limits, and delivery restrictions.

The E-mail Addresses tab allows you to configure multiple email addresses, including adding new addresses, removing existing addresses, and viewing the properties of existing addresses.

The Exchange Advanced tab, shown in Figure 12.30, allows you to configure advanced email attributes, including Protocol Settings, Exchange Custom Attributes, and the Internet Locator Service (ILS) settings. The Protocol Settings allow you to configure the various protocols that are supported for secure collaboration between the Exchange Information Store and remote clients. Supported protocols for your mailbox-enabled users include the following:

- Hypertext Transfer Protocol (HTTP) is one of the underlying protocols used on the World Wide Web. It defines how email messages are formatted and sent, and how Web servers and browsers respond to various commands. You must enable HTTP on a mailbox so that it is accessible through a Web browser using Outlook Web Access (OWA).

- Internet Message Access Protocol 4 (IMAP4) is an Internet messaging protocol that enables a client to access and manipulate email stored in his or her mailbox on the Exchange Server instead of having to download the entire message to the user's

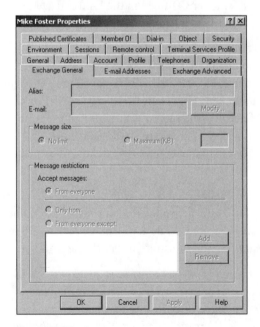

Figure 12.29
The Exchange General tab of a user account's Properties dialog box.

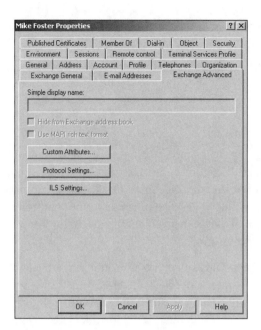

Figure 12.30
The Exchange Advanced tab of a user account's Properties dialog box.

computer. IMAP4 also allows a user to access public folders, multiple email folders, and to search through a mailbox.

- Post Office Protocol 3 (POP3) is an Internet messaging protocol that enables POP3 clients to download email from the server; it works well for computers that are not able to maintain a continuous connection to the Exchange Server. With POP3, the messages are simply downloaded to the client, and the messages are managed on the client. It does not allow the users to manipulate messages on the Exchange Server. POP3 also provides access only to the user's Inbox; it does not support access to public folders.

Custom Attributes allow you to configure and track various values for recipients, such as when you are using an employee identification numbering system.

The Internet Locator Service (ILS) feature allows NetMeeting users to locate the mailbox owner to set up an online meeting. Also, notice the checkbox that allows you to hide this account's email address from the Exchange address book so that users cannot view it.

Introducing Groups

Creating user accounts allows you to assign appropriate permissions to those accounts so that they can be used to access network resources. The questions are:

- Do you really want to spend all the time required to set permissions on each individual user account?

- Is there a better way?

The answers to these questions are no and yes. Instead of assigning permissions to each individual user account, you could add all the user accounts that require the same permissions to a group and then assign the permissions just once to the group. In this way, every member of the group will have the same permissions just by virtue of belonging to the group.

Understanding Groups

Now that you understand that using groups will simplify administration by allowing you to grant permissions once rather than multiple times, the next step is to understand how groups can be used in Windows 2000 Professional. One of the first key areas you need to be aware of is that the use of groups in Windows 2000 has changed somewhat from the way groups were used in Windows NT 4. The first step will be to understand these differences so that you can plan an effective group strategy.

Windows NT 4 consisted of two key groups whose membership could be controlled by the administrator, the Administrators group, and the Users group. For an additional group called Everyone, the membership was controlled by the operating system or domain. By default, every user who was authenticated by the domain was a member of the Everyone group. An administrator could increase the level of access control by removing the Everyone group from the Discretionary Access Control Lists for resources.

Windows 2000 now has three groups whose membership is controlled by the administrator: Users, Power Users, and Administrators. The operating system or domain now controls the membership of another group called Authenticated Users. This group is the same as the Everyone group, except that it does not contain anonymous users or guests. Whereas the Everyone group in Windows NT 4 could be used to assign permissions, the Authenticated Users group is not used to assign permissions. Instead, an administrator primarily assigns permissions to the Users, Power Users, and Administrators groups. To implement higher security on a Windows 2000 computer, you will want to make only Authenticated Users members of the Users group.

Understanding Workgroup and Domain Group Characteristics

The next issue you need to be aware of is that groups operate differently based on whether you are operating in a workgroup or in a domain.

Groups in a workgroup will have the following characteristics:

- They can be created only on a computer running Windows 2000 Professional or on a standalone or member server running Windows 2000 Server/Advanced Server.

- They reside in the local Security Accounts Manager database on the local computer.

- They can be used to grant permissions to resources and rights for system tasks only on the computer that you create the group on.

Groups in a domain will have the following characteristics:

- They are created only on domain controllers.

- They reside in the Active Directory directory service.

Note: *You cannot create local groups on Windows 2000 domain controllers. Local groups are not the same as domain local groups.*

- They can be used to grant permissions to resources or grant rights for system tasks on any computer in the domain.

As an administrator, you must understand the difference between *user rights* and *permissions*. User rights grant specific privileges and logon rights to users and groups in your computing environment. User rights differ greatly from permissions because user rights apply to user accounts, whereas permissions are attached to objects. For instance, the logon rights that can be assigned to a user account are as follows:

- Access This Computer From A Network

- Log On Locally

- Log On As A Batch Job

- Log On As A Service

- Deny Access To This Computer From The Network

- Deny Logon As A Batch Job

- Deny Logon As A Service

- Deny Local Logon

Note: *The special user account called LocalSystem has almost all the available privileges and logon rights assigned to it because all the operating system processes are associated with this account, and these processes require a complete set of user rights.*

The following list shows the privileges that can be assigned to a user account. These privileges can be managed with the User Rights policy:

- Act As Part Of The Operating System

- Add Workstations To A Domain

- Back Up Files And Directories

- Bypass Traverse Checking

- Change The System Time

- Create A Token Object

- Create Permanent Shared Objects

- Create A Pagefile

- Debug Programs

- Enable Trusted For Delegation On User And Computer Accounts

- Force Shutdown From A Remote System

- Generate Security Audits

- Increase Quotas

- Increase Scheduling Priority

- Load And Unload Device Drivers

- Lock Pages In Memory

- Manage Auditing And Security Log

- Modify Firmware Environment Values

- Profile A Single Process

- Profile System Performance

- Replace A Process-Level Token

- Restore Files And Directories

- Shut Down The System

- Take Ownership Of Files Or Other Objects

- Unlock A Laptop

One of the most critical areas to understand about these privileges is that some of them can override the permissions that have been directly set on an object. For example, when a user is logged on to a domain as a member of the Backup Operators group, this user has the right to perform backup operations for all domain servers. This right requires the user to have the ability to read all the files on those servers, even files on which permissions have been set to explicitly deny access to all users, including members of the Backup Operators group. In this case, the user right to perform a backup will take precedence over all file and directory permissions.

When you understand rights and permissions and the fact that groups are used differently and behave differently based on whether you are operating in a workgroup or a domain, you can then look at how you go about implementing them in these two environments. We'll start by looking at how to implement groups in a workgroup.

Implementing Groups in a Workgroup

Because you are creating groups on the local computer, all the groups you create in a workgroup are local groups. You can create local groups only on a Windows 2000 member server, standalone server, or a computer running Windows 2000 Professional. You can create additional local groups as required, but you also need to understand that some default local groups are created during the installation of the operating system so all computers running Windows 2000 will have local groups. It is often advantageous to follow these simple guidelines when creating local groups:

- In a domain environment, do not create additional local groups because they do not appear in the Active Directory; therefore, they must be managed on the local computer they are created on.

- Local groups can be used to control access to resources only on the local computer that they are created on.

- Local groups can contain local user accounts only from the same computer you create the local group on.

- A local group cannot be a member of any other group.

- You must be a member of the Administrators group or Account Operators group to create a local group.

The built-in groups have a set of predetermined rights assigned to them that determine the system tasks that a member of these groups can perform. The built-in local groups that you will find in a workgroup environment include the following:

- *Built-in local groups*—Members of these groups will have various rights to perform system tasks, such as changing the system time or backing up and restoring files. You will find these groups listed in the Groups folder in the Local Users And Groups area of the Computer Management console:

  - *Administrators*—The Administrators group is the only built-in group that is automatically granted every built-in right and ability in the system. Membership in this group means that you have full control over the computer. The membership of this group should be tightly controlled, and this account should not be used for daily end-user–oriented tasks. You should use this account only when performing necessary administrative tasks, such as installing the operating system, service packs, drivers, and system services; backing up or restoring the system; and managing the security and audit policy. If you are still using legacy applications, this account will usually be required when you're performing the installation so that the application will run under Windows 2000. Only members of the Administrators group can add a user to the Administrators, Backup Operators, or Replicator group.

  - *Backup Operators*—Members of the Backup Operators group cannot change security settings on a computer, but they can log on to the computer and shut it down. They can also back up and restore files on the computer, regardless of any permissions that protect those files. This can be a security issue because being able to back up and restore files requires permissions to read and write to those files. This means that the default permissions granted to Backup Operators also make it possible for them to use the group's permissions for other purposes, such as reading another user's files or installing a Trojan Horse program. As an administrator, you should be careful when assigning users to this group and possibly consider setting a Group Policy so that Backup Operators can run only a backup program.

- *Power Users*—Power Users have fewer permissions than administrators but more permissions than members of the Users group. Members of this group can perform any operating system task except those tasks that are reserved for the Administrators group. Power Users can stop and start system services that are not started by default. The Windows 2000 Power Users group default security settings are comparable to the Windows NT 4 Users group default security settings. This means that any program a member of the Users group can run in Windows NT 4, a member of the Power Users group can run in Windows 2000. (This capability ensures backward compatibility with Windows NT 4.) Power Users will be able to create user accounts but can administer only the accounts they create. They will also be able to create and administer local groups and remove user accounts from the Power Users, Users, and Guests groups. They will not be able to modify the membership of the Administrators or Backup Operators groups; they cannot take ownership of other users' files; and they cannot back up or restore data, install device drivers, or administer auditing.

  As an administrator, you should be careful when assigning users to this group because a Power User can install or modify programs. This capability can be a security issue because a Power User can log on, make a connection to the Internet, and download a Trojan Horse program or pose other security risks.

Note: *Domain controllers do not have a Power Users group.*

- *Users*—Membership in the Users group allows users to perform most common computer tasks, such as running applications, using local and network printers, and locking the local workstation. They can also create local groups and modify only the local groups they create. To prevent Trojan Horse attacks, users cannot install programs that can be run by other users, and they will not be able to run most legacy programs written for previous Windows operating systems because previous versions of Windows either did not support file system and Registry security or shipped with lower default security settings. They can run certified Windows 2000 programs that have been installed by an administrator. They cannot modify system-wide Registry settings, operating system files, or program files. Users cannot install local printers or share directories. They can shut down workstations but not servers.

- *Guests*—Membership in the Guests group allows occasional or one-time users to log on to a workstation's built-in Guest account with limited rights and permissions assigned. These users can shut down workstations but not servers.

- *Replicator*—This special group supports directory replication functions. The Replicator group should have only one member, and it should be a domain user account that is used to log on to the Replicator services of the domain controller. An administrator (or other user) should never add user accounts to this group.

- *Special identities groups*—These groups are also called "special groups," and the operating system handles their membership. Even an administrator cannot view or modify the membership of these groups. A user becomes a member of one of these groups by performing some action on the network. When a user logs on to the local machine, he or she automatically becomes a member of the Interactive special group. When a user accesses a resource over the network, he or she becomes a member of the Network special group. If you have installed a Windows 2000 Terminal Server in application server mode, any user who logs on to the terminal server will become a member of the Terminal Server User special group.

12

Note: *If you install a terminal server in remote administration mode, a user logging on to the terminal server will not be a member of the Terminal Server User special group.*

When you understand the built-in local groups and the fact that you can create additional local groups as required, the next step is to look at a proven strategy for using local groups in a workgroup. One issue you should be aware of is that you can go about setting up a group strategy in many ways, so we are going to discuss only the strategy that is recommended by Microsoft. There are two reasons for describing this method. The first is that it has been proven to work; the second is that if you use any method other than the recommended one, you may find that Microsoft will not offer support if you do experience any problems.

When you're implementing groups in a workgroup, Microsoft recommends using the ALP strategy. It works like this:

- After creating your user accounts, you place the Accounts (A) in the Local group (L) on the computer that is hosting the resources.

- You then grant Permissions (P) or rights to the local group on the computer that is hosting the resources.

The ALP strategy does have its limitations, and perhaps the most obvious one is that an administrator can grant permissions only to resources that reside on the local computer. This is often a very good reason to choose the domain model when you're setting up a network. We'll see how this model allows for much more flexibility in the next section, but for now, we'll continue on our current path by looking at how to create local groups.

To create a local group, perform the following steps:

1. Open the Computer Management console and expand Local Users And Groups.

2. Right-click on the Groups folder and select New Group. Figure 12.31 displays the New Group dialog box, where you will enter various information, including the group

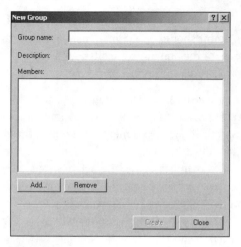

Figure 12.31
Creating a local group in the New Group dialog box.

name. Group Name is the only required field, and it can be up to 256 characters but does not accept a backslash (\).

3. Click on Add to add a new user to the group or Remove to remove an existing member.

4. Click on Create to create the group and then create additional groups or click on Close to return to the Computer Management console.

As you have seen in this section, using local groups in a workgroup has many limitations, and you will not even have access to the Local Users And Groups node when you are creating groups on a domain controller. If you are looking to fully exploit all the features of groups in Windows 2000, you will want to implement a domain environment that allows you to take full advantage of the available options. In the next section, we'll look at how to implement groups in a domain.

Implementing Groups in a Domain

Implementing groups in a domain offers several advantages over implementing groups in a workgroup. Creating domain groups on a domain controller allows for centralized administration, and domain groups also allow for more advanced options for administering these groups. Having these advanced options makes domain groups more complex, so the first step is to understand the following two group types you will find in an Active Directory environment:

- *Security groups*—These groups are the only group type you can assign permissions to and are normally used for security-related purposes. Security groups also share the characteristics of distribution groups, so you can send email to the group and all members of the group will receive the email.

- *Distribution groups*—These groups are used by applications for non-security–related functions, such as a list used for sending an email message to a group of users. You cannot assign permissions to a distribution group.

Note: Distribution groups reside in the Active Directory, and therefore only applications that are designed to work with the Active Directory (such as Microsoft Exchange 2000) can use distribution groups.

In addition to the two group types are the following three group scopes that determine where in the domain a group can be used and what it can be used for:

- *Global group*—You use global groups to organize users who share the same network access requirements. A global group can be used to grant permissions to resources that are located in any domain, but it does have several restrictions. You can add members to a global group only if they come from the same domain you created the global group in, and you must be running the domain in native mode to be able to nest one global group inside another group.

12

Note: A native mode domain contains only Windows 2000 domain controllers and has been set to run in native mode inside the Active Directory Domains And Trusts console or inside the Active Directory Users and Computers console.

- *Domain local group*—You use domain local groups to grant permissions only to domain resources that are located in the same domain that you create the domain local group in. Domain local groups have an "open membership" characteristic, which means you can add members to a domain local group from any other domain. You cannot nest domain local groups in another group, which means that you cannot add a domain local group to any other group.

- *Universal group*—You use universal groups to grant permissions to resources that are located in any domain. Universal groups also have an "open membership" characteristic, which means you can add members to a universal group from any domain. A universal group can be nested within another domain local group or universal group.

Note: Universal groups are available only when your domain is operating in native mode.

Based on the preceding information, many new Windows 2000 users ask the question "Why don't I just use universal groups for all my group needs?" This is a valid question, and the reason you don't use universal groups for everything has to do with replication. Universal group membership is stored on a special domain controller called a Global Catalog server. The universal group membership is replicated to every other domain controller that hosts a Global Catalog server role as part of the Active Directory replication process.

The issue here is that every time you make a change to the membership of a universal group this change has to be replicated forest-wide. This means every time you add or remove a user or group to a universal group this change has to be replicated throughout the entire forest, which can add a significant amount of replication traffic based on how often changes are made. The solution is to add only global groups as members of a universal group because the global groups you add or remove will no doubt change much less often than individual user account memberships. You can then add user accounts to the global groups that belong to the universal group without creating additional replication traffic.

Just like a workgroup, a domain also has some built-in groups that have a set of predetermined rights assigned to them; these rights determine the system tasks that a member of the built-in group can perform.

Built-in Domain Local Groups

Built-in domain local groups have predefined rights and permissions that allow a member to perform tasks on a domain controller and in the Active Directory. These groups exist only on domain controllers, and as you can see in Figure 12.32, you will find these groups listed in the Built-in container located in the Active Directory Users and Computers console.

Table 12.5 provides additional information on the function and capabilities of each of the built-in domain local groups.

One additional nondefault group that you need to be aware of is the Pre-Windows 2000 Compatible Access group. This special backward-compatibility group reduces the default Windows 2000 security settings so that all users, including anonymous users, have Read access on all Active Directory objects (including all users and groups in the domain).

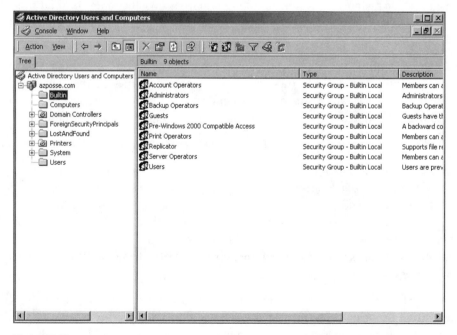

Figure 12.32
Viewing objects in the Built-in container in the Active Directory Users and Computers console.

Table 12.5   Built-in domain local groups.

Group	Description
Account Operators	Membership in this group allows a user to have limited capabilities to manage various account creation and management functions. This means that members of the Account Operators group can administer domain user and group accounts.
Administrators	Membership in the Administrators group allows a user to have full control over the computer. By default, it is the only built-in group that is automatically granted every built-in right and ability in the system.
Backup Operators	Membership in the Backup Operators group allows a user to back up and restore files on the computer, regardless of any permissions that protect those files. Backup Operators can override security restrictions for the sole purpose of backing up and restoring files. Members of this group cannot change the security settings on a computer, but they can log on to the computer and shut it down.
Guests	This group is primarily used to allow occasional or one-time users to log on to a workstation's built-in Guest account that is granted limited abilities by default. You should be aware that members of the Guests group can also shut down the system.
Print Operators	Membership in this group allows a user to manage printers. Print Operators can administer domain printers.
Replicator	This group is used primarily for directory replication functions. The Replicator group should have only one member, and it should be a domain user account that is used to log on to the Replicator services of the domain controller. You should not add the user accounts of actual users to this group.
Server Operators	Membership in this group allows a user to have limited management capabilities for managing servers. Server Operators can administer domain servers.
Users	Membership in the Users group allows users to perform most common tasks, such as running applications, using local and network printers, and shutting down and locking the workstation. Users can run certified applications but not most legacy applications. Users are prevented from making accidental or intentional system-wide changes. Members of this group can also create local groups, but the users will be able to modify only the local groups that they created. Members of the Users group cannot share directories or create local printers.

The purpose of this group is to nest the Everyone group in the Pre-Windows 2000 Compatible Access group to either allow or disallow anonymous (null) connections to the Active Directory database. This may be required under certain circumstances because Windows NT 4 clients use null connections to perform various actions. Without the Everyone group nested, certain Windows NT 4 null credential actions do not work.

This option is generally chosen as an operating system configuration item during the installation of Windows 2000 Server domain controllers, but it can also be added after the installation via the command prompt. To add this group during the installation of a Windows 2000 domain controller, you choose the Permissions Compatible With Pre-Windows 2000 Servers option on the Permissions page when you run the Active Directory Installation Wizard (Dcpromo.exe). If you do not want to lower the default security settings, you should choose the Permissions Compatible Only With Windows 2000 Servers option on the Permissions page.

Regardless of the option you choose, the built-in Pre-Windows 2000 Compatible Access group will be added in the Access Control Lists (ACLs) throughout Active Directory. The difference is that with the first option, permissions compatible with pre-Windows 2000–based servers are selected, and the Everyone group is nested in the Pre-Windows 2000 Compatible Access group. If you choose the second option, the Everyone group is not nested. To add this group after the installation of a Windows 2000 Server domain controller, open a command prompt and enter the following command:

```
Net localgroup "Pre-Windows 2000 Compatible Access" Everyone /add
```

Include the quotation marks in the command, or it will not run properly.

As an administrator, you need to carefully weigh the security implications of allowing this group to have the ability to read all Active Directory object attributes. In a pure Windows 2000 environment, you should not allow this group to have access privileges to the Active Directory, but you might need to allow for this group when you have down-level clients in your Windows 2000 domain. This is also a requirement when you have Windows NT 4–based Remote Access Service (RAS) member servers in your Windows 2000–based domain and you want to allow the NT 4 RAS member server to be able to access the remote access credentials stored in the Windows 2000 Active Directory. This is required in order for the NT 4 RAS member server to be able to authenticate remote access dial-in users because it allows the RAS server to use Windows NT LAN Manager (also called Challenge/Response or NTLM) security to read user account properties.

Several existing applications, including Microsoft BackOffice applications such as Structured Query Language (SQL) Server, and some third-party applications depend on this type of access to function correctly. If you add this group and find that you no longer require it or you want to remove it later, you can run the following command from a command prompt:

```
Net localgroup "Pre-Windows 2000 Compatible Access" Everyone /delete
```

Tip: *You have to reboot all the Windows 2000 domain controllers after adding or removing the Everyone group to the Pre-Windows 2000 Compatible Access group; otherwise, it will not take effect throughout the entire domain. If you reboot only the domain controller on which you perform this action, only that domain controller will be affected.*

All these built-in groups have a domain local scope and are primarily used to assign a set of default permissions to users who will have some type of administrative control in that domain. As an example, the Administrators group in a domain has total administrative authority over all the accounts and resources in that domain.

Table 12.6 shows the rights that can be assigned to these groups.

Table 12.6   Assignable rights.

Right	Description
Access this computer from the network	Allows a user to connect to the computer over the network. This right is assigned by default to members of the Administrators, Everyone, and Power Users groups.
Back up files and file folders	Allows a user to back up files and folders. This right overrides file and folder permissions. This right is assigned by default to members of the Administrators and Backup Operators groups.
Bypass traverse checking	Allows a user to move between folders to access files, even if the user has no permission to access the parent file folders. This right is assigned by default to members of the Everyone group.
Change the system time	Allows a user to set the time for the internal clock of the computer. This right is assigned by default to members of the Administrators and Power Users groups.
Create a pagefile	Allows a user to modify the parameters of a paging file. This right is assigned by default to members of the Administrators group.
Debug programs	Allows a user to debug various low-level objects such as threads. This right is assigned by default to members of the Administrators group.
Force shutdown from a remote system	Allows a user to shut down a system remotely. This right is assigned by default to members of the Administrators group.
Increase scheduling priority	Allows a user to increase the execution priority of a program. This right is assigned by default to members of the Administrators and Power Users groups.
Load and unload device drivers	Allows a user to install and remove device drivers. This right is assigned by default to members of the Administrators group.
Log on locally	Allows a user to log on at the local keyboard/console. This right is assigned by default to members of the Administrators, Backup Operators, Everyone, Guests, Power Users, and Users groups.
Manage auditing and security log	Allows a user to specify the types of resource access (such as file access) that will be audited, along with having the ability to view and clear the security log. This right does not allow a user to set a system-wide audit policy. Members of the Administrators group can always view and clear the security log. This right is assigned by default to members of the Administrators group.
Modify firmware environment variables	Allows a user to modify system environment variables that are stored in nonvolatile RAM. This right is assigned by default to members of the Administrators group. The computer must support this type of configuration.
Profile single process	Allows a user to perform performance sampling on a process. This right is assigned by default to members of the Administrators and Power Users groups.
Profile system performance	Allows a user to perform performance sampling on the computer. This right is assigned by default to members of the Administrators group.
Restore files and file folders	Allows a user to restore backed-up files and file folders. This right overrides file and directory permissions. This right is assigned by default to members of the Administrators and Backup Operators groups.

12

(continued)

Table 12.6   Assignable rights *(continued).*

Right	Description
Shut down the system	Allows a user to shut down a computer. This right is assigned by default to members of the Administrators, Backup Operators, Everyone, Power Users, and Users groups.
Take ownership of files or other objects	Allows a user to take ownership of files, folders, printers, and other objects that are installed in or attached to the computer. This right overrides permissions that have been assigned to protect objects. This right is assigned by default to members of the Administrators group.

Special Identities Groups

These groups are also called "special groups," and the operating system handles their membership. Even an administrator cannot view or modify the membership of these groups. A user becomes a member of one of these groups by performing some action on the network. When a user logs on to the local machine, he or she automatically becomes a member of the Interactive special group. When a user accesses a resource over the network, he or she becomes a member of the Network special group.

Predefined Global Groups

These groups allow an administrator to control all the domain users. These groups exist on all domain controllers, and as you can see in Figure 12.33, they can be viewed in the Users container located in the Active Directory Users and Computers console.

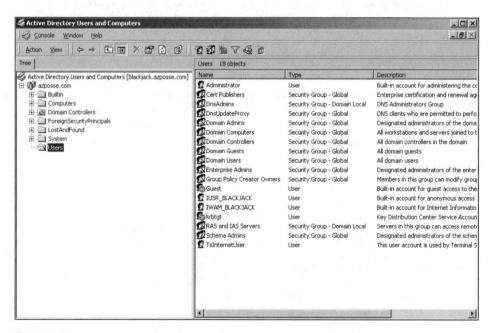

Figure 12.33
Viewing groups in the Users container in the Active Directory Users and Computers console.

Table 12.7   Predefined global groups.

Group Name	Description
Cert Publishers	By default, members of this group can manage the publishing of digital certificates.
DNSUpdateProxy	This special security group, new to Windows 2000, is used for dynamic DNS update-related functions. By default, any object created by a member of this group has no security, and the first user/computer (that is not a member of the DNSUpdateProxy group) to modify the set of DNS records associated with a client becomes its owner. Adding all DHCP servers as members of this special built-in group helps to resolve some DNS update concerns about maintaining secure updates. At the same time, this solution introduces some additional security holes because any DNS names registered by a computer running the DHCP server service that is also a member of this group are nonsecure. As such, an administrator needs to carefully weigh the security factors surrounding the addition of members to this group.
Domain Admins	By default, the Domain Admins group in a domain is a member of the Administrators group in the same domain. Members of the Domain Admins group have broad administrative rights throughout the entire domain. Windows 2000 does not place any accounts in this group automatically.
Domain Computers	By default, any computer account you create in the domain is automatically added to the Domain Computers group.
Domain Controllers	By default, Windows 2000 places any Windows 2000 domain controllers that you create in this group.
Domain Guests	By default, the Domain Guests group is a member of the Guests group in the same domain and automatically has as its member the domain's default Guest user account.
Domain Users	By default, any user account you create in a domain is automatically added to the Domain Users group.
Enterprise Admins	By default, any user account that is a member of the Enterprise Admins group has permission to administer every domain in the forest. You should be very careful when adding users to this group because they will have full administrative control over the entire forest. User and computer accounts that are members of the Enterprise Admins group are automatically granted permission to log on to all the domain controllers in the forest.
Group Policy Admins	By default, any user account that is a member of this group can modify Group Policy settings.
Schema Admins	By default, any user account that is a member of this group can modify the schema.

12

Table 12.7 provides additional information on the function and capabilities of each of these groups.

Creating Additional Local Groups

After you have an understanding of the built-in domain local and predefined global groups, along with the fact that you can create additional local groups as required, the next step is to look at a proven strategy for using groups in a domain.

Note: You can set up a group strategy in many ways, so we are going to discuss only the strategy that is recommended by Microsoft (which is similar to the workgroup strategy that has already been discussed).

The strategy recommended by Microsoft is called the AGDLP strategy. It works like this:

• After creating your user accounts, you place the accounts (A) in the domain global groups (G).

- You then place the global groups into the domain local group (DL) on the computer where the resource resides.

- You then grant permissions (P) or rights to the domain local group on the computer that is hosting the resource(s).

The AGDLP strategy offers a much greater degree of control and more flexibility than that offered by the ALP strategy used in a workgroup environment. This strategy allows you to grant permissions to resources that reside on any computer in the domain. This capability is often a very good reason to choose the domain model over the workgroup model when setting up a network.

To create a domain group, perform the following steps:

1. Open the Active Directory Users and Computers console and expand the domain name.

2. Right-click on the folder you wish to create the new group in and select New|Group. Figure 12.34 displays the New Object - Group dialog box, where you will enter various information, including the group name, pre-Windows 2000 group name (which is used to support down-level Microsoft operating systems), group scope, and group type.

3. Click on OK to create the group and return to the Active Directory Users and Computers console.

After creating a group, you will probably choose to add members to the group. To do so, perform the following steps:

1. Open the Properties dialog box of the group you wish to add members to.

2. Select the Members tab and then click on Add.

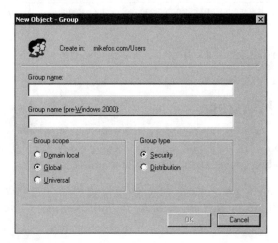

Figure 12.34
Creating a domain group in the New Object - Group dialog box.

3. In the Select Users, Contacts, Computers, Or Groups dialog box, double-click on the account name you wish to add and then click on OK.

4. Click on OK to close the group's Properties dialog box.

Something every administrator needs to be aware of is the resultant effect of adding a user to a group when that user is already logged on. In this case, the user will not receive all the rights and permissions assigned to that group until he or she logs off and then logs back on. The user must log on again because every user who logs on to the network is given an "access token" as part of the logon process; this token determines the access privileges for both the user's account and the privileges for any groups that the user belongs to. For the changes to take effect, the user must obtain a new access token that reflects the new group membership. Because access tokens are granted only at logon, the user must log off and then log back on to obtain the updated access token.

12

Using Restricted Groups

One additional capability that provides an important new security feature in Windows 2000 acts as a governor for group membership. Restricted Groups automatically provide security memberships for default Windows 2000 groups that have predefined capabilities, such as Administrators, Power Users, Print Operators, Server Operators, and Domain Admins. You can also add additional groups that you consider sensitive or privileged to the Restricted Groups security list.

As an example, the Administrators group is automatically part of the Restricted Groups group because it is a default Windows 2000 group. Say this group contains two users— Jon and Mike—and then Mike adds Brian to the group using the Active Directory Users and Computers console to cover for him while he is on vacation. However, no one remembers to remove Brian from the group when Mike comes back from vacation. Over the course of time, not removing these members can result in extra members who should not have these rights belonging to the Administrators group. As an administrator, you can configure security settings on the Restricted Groups to prevent this situation. Because only Jon and Mike are listed in the Restricted Groups node for Administrators, when Group Policy settings are applied, Brian is automatically removed from the group. Figure 12.35 displays an example of using Restricted Groups to restrict the membership in the Administrators group to a single user account (MikeFoster).

By configuring Restricted Groups, you can ensure that group memberships are maintained as specified. Any groups or users not specified in Restricted Groups are removed from the specific group automatically by the operating system.

Tip: It is recommended that Restricted Groups be used primarily to configure membership of local groups on workstation or member servers.

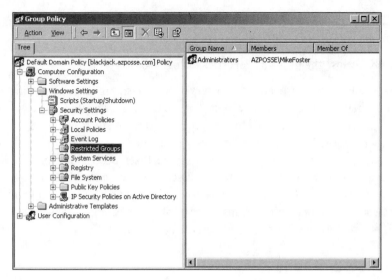

Figure 12.35
Restricting membership in the Restricted Groups node in the Default Domain Policy.

As you have seen in this section, using groups in a domain environment has many advantages when compared to using groups in a workgroup. You can centrally manage all your domain groups from one location (the Active Directory Users and Computers console), and you have to create the group only once to allow for domain-wide access.

Summary

The information presented in this chapter will allow you to create a secure and robust Windows 2000 environment. The Users and Passwords utility provides limited functionality, so you most likely will use Local Users and Password to manage your local user accounts and groups on a Windows 2000 Professional machine.

As your need for more dynamic access to shared network resources increases, you will use Active Directory Users and Computers to manage your domain global groups and user accounts.

You should take advantage of the built-in groups provided with Windows 2000, but if you need additional groups you can create them. The Restricted Groups group policy is a great tool for ensuring that members being added to your Domain Admins, Enterprise Admins, and Schema Admins are carefully managed.

After you create your users and groups either locally or on the domain controller your users can access Windows 2000. However, most users want the capability to customize their work environment. This customization can be saved and reapplied whenever they log on. Although, you may not need to customize certain areas of their work environment, as an administrator you can restrict what their customization options are or prevent them from saving their customization options.

Chapter 13 discusses the options available for customization, how these changes are saved, and how you can configure Windows 2000 to apply these changes regardless of what computer they log on to. Furthermore, you can prevent them from making changes, or prevent them from saving changes they do make while they are logged on so the changes are not applied the next time they log on.

12

Chapter 13

Configuring Your Windows 2000 Professional Desktop

Configuring Your Desktop

Configuring your desktop involves many considerations, including how your desktop looks, how to secure your desktop, and how to manage your applications. Some companies want a consistent desktop look for all their users. Furthermore, they may want all users of a particular department to have similar permissions to department-specific resources, and they may want these users to run the same applications on their desktops.

Administrators can manage these requirements manually by visiting each workstation, or they can automate these requirements by using user profiles, local policies, or group policies. By using the features available in Windows 2000, your network administrators can easily manage and maintain an entire enterprise. Let's begin with the different customizable options available in Windows 2000.

Understanding Your Desktop Environment

Your *desktop environment* is the screen you see on your monitor after you log on to Windows 2000. It is the door to access your local and remote resources and to run programs. Your desktop should contain the essential features required to work efficiently in your computing environment. The desktop is created with default settings that you can modify unless you have been restricted from doing so.

Configuring Windows 2000 Professional Default Desktop Settings

When you install Windows 2000 Professional, your desktop is configured with the following six default features:

- *Taskbar*—Use this option to access the Start button and open a document, start a program, locate a file, or access the Help feature. By default, the taskbar appears at the bottom of your screen. However, you can click on it and drag it to the top, right, or left of the screen. After you open a document or program, a button appears on the taskbar for each open window. You can use these taskbar buttons to easily switch from one open window to another. You can also use these buttons to minimize your windows (remove them from the desktop but not close them).

The Quick Launch bar is an area on the taskbar that contains mini-icons. Clicking on a mini-icon allows you to easily launch a program with a single mouse click. If this area containing mini-icons does not show up on your taskbar, you can turn it on by right-clicking on an empty area of the taskbar, selecting Toolbars, and then selecting Quick Launch, which will place a checkmark next to it.

Tip: *To quickly minimize all windows on your desktop, you can click on the Show Desktop mini-icon located on the taskbar immediately to the right of the Start button. To view the windows again, re-click on the Show Desktop button. Other Quick Launch mini-icons that are loaded on your taskbar during a default installation include Internet Explorer and Outlook Express.*

- *My Documents*—Use this folder as the default location to store your documents, graphics, and other files, including Web pages. Each user who logs on locally to the computer receives a My Documents folder. Because all users have their own My Documents folders, they are easily prevented from accessing objects contained within your My Documents folder.

- *My Computer*—Use this folder to quickly see the contents of your hard, floppy, CD-ROM, and mapped network drives. This folder also provides you with access to Control Panel, where many of your computer configuration settings are made.

- *My Network Places*—Use this folder to locate shared network resources on the entire network that your computer is connected to. After you access a document on a computer, FTP server, or Web server, a shortcut is automatically created in My Network Places. You can manually create shortcuts to other computers, FTP servers, or Web servers by using the Add Network Place Wizard.

Tip: *If your computer belongs to a workgroup, you can double-click on Computers Near Me to locate computers that are in the same workgroup.*

- *Recycle Bin*—Use this feature to view the files, folders, Web pages, and graphics that you have deleted. They will reside here until you right-click on the Recycle Bin and click on Empty Recycle Bin.

- *Internet Explorer*—Use this feature to browse the World Wide Web and your local intranet after establishing a connection to the Internet or intranet.

The taskbar contains many options, but the most useful option is the Start menu. The elements found on your Start menu come from many places:

- *Previous versions of Windows*—If you performed an upgrade from an earlier version of Windows, your old program groups appear as folders.

- *Windows 2000 Setup*—During the installation of Windows 2000, the setup program adds several standard folders that contain a collection of programs. One of these folders is called Startup. You can add programs to this folder if you want them to execute when you start your computer.

Note: *To have a program start each time you start Windows 2000, locate the program and drag it to the Startup folder.*

- *Software installations*—The setup program for most software that you install will add folders to the Programs menu.

- *Shortcuts to programs*—You can create shortcuts to programs by dragging the program to the Start menu or by right-clicking on the taskbar and using the Advanced tab on the Taskbar And Start Menu Properties dialog box.

Most users want or need to modify their desktop settings to create an individualized environment. These modifications may include additional desktop icons, additional taskbar icons, a different background on the desktop, and possibly shortcuts to frequently used applications.

Customizing Your Windows Desktop

A desktop with the default setting gives you just the six features discussed in the preceding section. However, if you want to be more productive, you can customize your desktop to provide quicker access to your documents and applications. You can also customize how it looks by changing the background, colors and fonts, screen resolution, and monitor refresh rate.

Some of the settings most often customized are located in the Display applet in Control Panel. You can access the Display Properties dialog box, shown in Figure 13.1, by double-clicking on the Display applet. You can also access this dialog box by right-clicking on any area on your desktop that does not have an open window and then clicking on the Properties option on the shortcut menu.

You can use the six tabs of the Display Properties dialog box to customize your desktop. For example, you can perform the following five common tasks to customize the various display settings on your computer:

- Choose a desktop background

- Change the look of individual desktop items or choose a desktop scheme that is applied to all desktop items

- Specify how many colors are displayed on your monitor

- Change your screen resolution

- Use multiple monitors to improve productivity

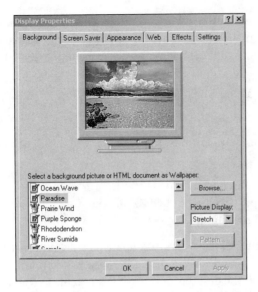

Figure 13.1
The Background tab of the Display Properties dialog box.

If you want to perform these tasks, you must understand what options are available on each tab so that you can use the numerous options effectively.

Using the Background Tab

On the Background tab of the Display Properties dialog box, you can set the desktop to display a pattern or a picture. The background picture you specify can have any of the following file extensions:

- .bmp

- .dib

- .gif

- .jpg

- .htm

Note: *To display a Web page with the .htm file extension, you first have to save the document to your hard drive. Then click on the Browse button to locate it on your hard drive.*

Follow these steps to set or change the background of your desktop:

1. Open the Display Properties dialog box.

2. On the Background tab, perform one or more of the following actions:

    - Locate and click on the background picture you want to apply from the Select A Background Picture Or HTML Document As Wallpaper section.

Warning! *Some of the wallpaper options require you to activate the Active Desktop option before the wallpaper is applied. Click on Yes to enable Active Desktop when you receive a dialog box informing you that the wallpaper you selected requires Active Desktop, or click on No and choose a different wallpaper. If you choose Yes, Active Desktop will remain enabled even if you apply a wallpaper setting that does not require Active Desktop. Use the Web tab of the Properties page to disable Active Desktop. Active Desktop is discussed in more detail later in this chapter.*

- From the Picture Display list, choose Center, Tile, or Stretch to position the wallpaper selection on your desktop. If you select Center, the Pattern button will be activated. You can then click on the Pattern button to open the Pattern dialog box, where you can select the pattern of your background from the Pattern area. (The pattern background will only appear if there is space around your wallpaper, or if you choose no wallpaper at all.) Optionally, you can click on the Edit Pattern button to modify the pattern you selected.

13

Note: *The Picture Display option is not available if you choose to display an HTM file.*

3. Click on Apply to display the new background setting without closing the Display Properties dialog box, or click on OK to display the background setting and close the Display Properties dialog box.

Defining Your Screen Saver Options

Screen savers prevent static text or pictures from being burned into your monitor and damaging it. Screen savers can also secure your computer by implementing password protection.

On the Screen Saver tab, shown in Figure 13.2, you can define which screen saver you want to use, modify the screen saver options, define the time the computer must be idle before it kicks in, and secure your machine by requiring a password before you are able to access the machine.

Follow these steps to set or change your screen saver options:

1. Open the Display Properties dialog box and click on the Screen Saver tab.

2. From the Screen Saver drop-down menu, select the screen saver that you want to automatically start after your computer is idle for a specified amount of time.

3. Use the Wait option to set the number of idle minutes before the screen saver automatically starts. This number can be from 1 through 9999.

4. Click on the Settings button to configure the selected screen saver settings. These settings will vary based on the screen saver you selected. Figure 13.3 shows the settings for the 3D Pipes screen saver.

5. Optionally, you can click on the Preview button so that you can see exactly how the screen saver is going to look when running in full-screen mode.

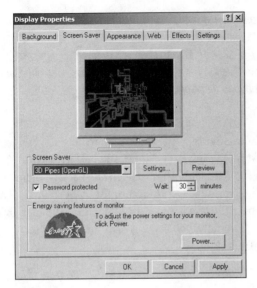

Figure 13.2
The Screen Saver tab of the Display Properties dialog box.

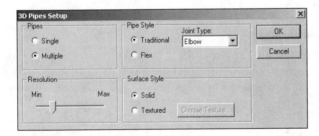

Figure 13.3
The 3D Pipes Setup dialog box.

Tip: You can select the Password Protected checkbox to secure your files and folders. After you select this checkbox, your computer will be locked when the screen saver is activated. When you are ready to use the computer, you will be prompted for a password to unlock it. This password is the same one you used when you logged on to the computer.

Changing the Appearance of Your Desktop Items

You use the Appearance tab to change the colors and fonts in the windows that display your documents and programs on your screen. You can use predefined schemes or create custom schemes to modify the appearance of your windows.

Follow these steps to modify the appearance of your windows in Windows 2000:

1. Open the Display Properties dialog box and click on the Appearance tab to display the Appearance options, as shown in Figure 13.4.

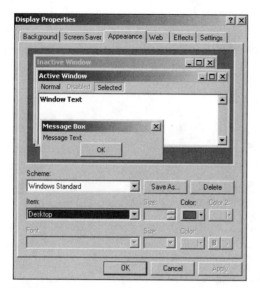

Figure 13.4
The Appearance tab of the Display Properties dialog box.

2. From the Item drop-down menu, choose the item for which you want to change the appearance. For instance, choose Menu, Window, Desktop, and so on.

3. To apply a predefined color and font scheme, select a scheme from the Scheme drop-down menu.

4. To apply a customized scheme, use the Color and Size options to create the new scheme. Then, click on the Save As button and type a name for the new scheme. This new scheme is then made available in the Scheme list.

Note: The Font area will not be available for items in the Items list that do not display text.

Configuring Your Web Options

Using the Web tab is one way to enable Active Desktop. After you enable it, you will receive dynamic updates from the Web addresses that you have added to this tab. You can configure your Active Desktop entries by clicking on the Properties button and displaying the Web tab, as shown in Figure 13.5.

You use the New and Delete buttons to add or remove Active Desktop entries from your desktop, respectively. You can clear the Show Web Content On My Active Desktop checkbox to disable Active Desktop on your computer.

You also can enable Active Desktop functionality in a couple of other ways:

• Right-click on a blank area on the desktop, click on Active Desktop, and then click on Show Web Content.

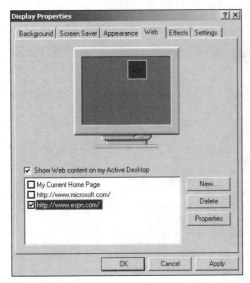

Figure 13.5
The Web tab of the Display Properties dialog box.

- Open Folder Options in Control Panel and then click on Enable Web Content On My Desktop under Active Desktop on the General tab.

Note: To disable Active Desktop, you can clear the options previously discussed.

Using the Effects Tab to Modify the Visual Effects on Your Desktop

The Desktop Icons section on the Effects tab shown in Figure 13.6 enables you to modify the default icons used on your desktop. To change a default icon, click on the icon that you want to change. Then, click on the Change Icon button to display the available system-supplied icons. If other icons are not listed, you can click on the Browse button to locate them.

On the Effects tab, you can also modify the visual effects of your desktop. Figure 13.6 shows the six options available to help customize the visual effects of your Windows 2000 environment. You can use any of the following options to customize your desktop environment:

- *Use Transition Effects For Menus And Tooltips*—Enables your animations, such as scrolling and fading of menus and windows when you open or close them.

- *Smooth Edges Of Screen Fonts*—Specifies that you want to smooth the edges of large fonts to make them more readable.

Note: The Smooth Edges Of Screen Fonts option is supported only on computers that have a video card and monitor that support 256 colors.

- *Use Large Icons*—Increases the size of the icons that represent folders, files, and shortcuts on your desktop. These larger icons use more memory than the smaller icons.

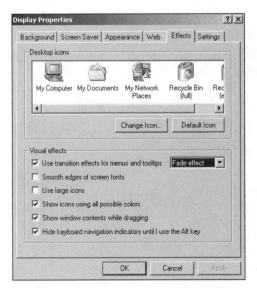

Figure 13.6
The Effects tab of the Display Properties dialog box.

- *Show Icons Using All Possible Colors*—Specifies that you want to use all the colors supported by your display adapter and your color palette settings.

- *Show Window Contents While Dragging*—Specifies whether to display the entire contents of your window while moving it on your screen or just an outline of the window.

- *Hide Keyboard Navigation Indicators Until I Use The Alt Key*—Specifies whether to display the drawing of keyboard shortcuts. This includes the underlined characters in menus and control screens and the dotted rectangles around active objects. The underlined characters and dotted rectangles are automatically activated when you start using the Tab, Alt, or arrow keys to navigate in Windows 2000.

Using the Settings Tab

On the Settings tab, you can change the number of colors supported by the monitor that is connected to your video adapter. You can also define your screen area size by dragging the Screen Area pointer toward Less or More to decrease or increase the screen resolution (the amount of screen area, measured in pixels, that makes the items appear smaller or larger), respectively. Figure 13.7 shows the Settings tab options you can use to change your screen area.

Note: A higher screen resolution reduces the size of the objects on your screen but increases the size of your desktop real estate. Your screen resolution options are determined by the type of monitor and display adapter you are using.

To change the number of colors your monitor can display, you select the desired setting from the Colors list. A High Color setting will allow more than 65,000 colors, whereas a

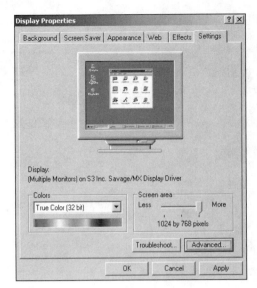

Figure 13.7
The Settings tab of the Display Properties dialog box.

True Color setting will allow more than 16 million colors. However, increasing the number of colors you want your monitor to display also increases the number of processing resources required.

By clicking on the Advanced button, you can access additional configuration options, including the capability to set smaller or larger display fonts. Follow these steps to change the size of your display font:

1. Open the Display Properties dialog box, click on the Settings tab, and then click on the Advanced button.

2. On the General tab, select the font setting you want to use for system fonts from the Font Size list.

3. If you choose Other from the Font Size list, you can create custom options in Custom Font Size by selecting one of the percentage options. Alternatively, you can click on the ruler and drag the pointer.

4. Click on OK to apply the settings.

You can use the Troubleshoot button to assist you in troubleshooting problems with your display components, including your monitor, video card, and drivers.

Supporting Multiple Monitors

Windows 2000 supports the use of up to 10 monitors on your computer. This capability provides additional desktop space that may result in increased productivity. Using multiple monitors allows you to easily work on multiple tasks by moving the windows from one monitor to another or by stretching a window across multiple monitors.

For instance, you can edit image or text documents on one monitor while viewing Web activity on another monitor. You can also use multiple monitors to view large documents on multiple screens. This feature is extremely helpful when you're using programs such as Excel that have numerous columns that require you to constantly scroll to other columns when you're viewing them on one monitor. You now can spread an Excel spreadsheet across many monitors, thus reducing or eliminating the need to scroll out to see all the data.

When you use multiple monitors, one of them serves as the primary monitor that will contain the logon box after you start your computer. Most programs will display their windows on the primary monitor when you first open it. You then can move these windows to another monitor.

The monitors can be attached to individual graphic adapters or to a single graphic adapter that supports multiple output. You can configure the resolution and color settings for each monitor attached to your computer by going to the Settings tab of the Display Properties dialog box, clicking on the monitor that you want to configure, and using the steps discussed in the "Using the Settings Tab" section earlier in this chapter.

13

Understanding Active Desktop

You can use Active Desktop to make your desktop look and work like a Web page. After you enable Active Desktop, you can display Web information directly on your desktop. This Web information can be updated automatically, making your desktop active. For example, you can add a sports or investment channel to your desktop to receive the latest information on your desktop.

After you turn on Active Desktop, you can add Web content by following these steps:

1. Right-click on an area of unused space on your desktop and then select Active Desktop to open the Active Desktop shortcut menu.

2. Click on New Desktop Item to open the New Desktop Item dialog box, in which you can begin the process of adding new Web content.

3. In the Location box, type the Uniform Resource Locator (URL) of the Web content that you want displayed on your desktop or click on Browse to locate a Web page or picture.

4. Click on OK to add the Web content to your desktop.

After you enable Active Desktop, the following shortcut menu options are available to update and configure your Active Desktop items:

- *Show Desktop Icons*—Displays icons on your desktop.

- *Lock Desktop Items*—Secures the size and location of your Active Desktop items. When this feature is enabled, the Active Desktop items cannot be moved or resized.

- *Synchronize*—Immediately updates Web page content on your desktop.

Some users use Active Desktop to keep current on Web activity. Of course, as you may have already figured out, some overhead is involved with maintaining the Active Desktop. The constant updates will increase processor usage and consume network bandwidth.

Customizing the Start Menu and Taskbar

You can modify the Start menu and taskbar to include additional applications for easy access to your most frequently used programs. The Start menu and taskbar are easily accessible, and they both provide a way for you to organize your desktop environment, much like folders that are used to organize your documents.

Opening the Taskbar And Start Menu Properties Dialog Box

You can easily customize your Start menu in Windows 2000 by using the Taskbar And Start Menu Properties dialog box that is opened when you right-click on an empty area on the taskbar and click on Properties. This dialog box contains two tabs: General and Advanced. Using these two tabs, you can customize options available on the Start menu and taskbar and remove the history of recently accessed documents, Web sites, and programs.

The General Tab

The General tab of the Taskbar And Start Menu Properties dialog box contains five options, as shown in Figure 13.8. You select or deselect these options to change some of the basic settings available on the taskbar and Start menu.

The five options on the General tab are as follows:

- *Always On Top*—This default setting keeps the taskbar visible to you, even when you have another window maximized.

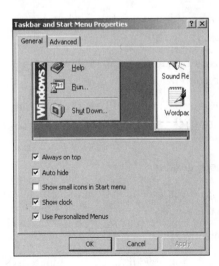

Figure 13.8
The General tab of the Taskbar And Start Menu Properties dialog box.

Note: *The taskbar is not visible if a screen saver is running.*

- *Auto Hide*—This option automatically hides the taskbar until you move your mouse pointer to the place where the taskbar is hidden. This capability is useful when you have limited desktop space on your screen.

- *Show Small Icons In Start Menu*—This option reduces the size of the icons located on the Start menu. It also removes the Windows 2000 operating system banner that is displayed on the left side of the Start menu.

- *Show Clock*—This default setting displays the clock on the right side of your taskbar.

- *User Personalized Menus*—This option configures Windows 2000 to automatically remember the menu items you use most often. When you access the Start menu and traverse through the items, the menu will display only those items recently used. To access all the menu items, you roll your pointer over the double arrows.

The Advanced Tab

You can set some of the basic Start menu and taskbar settings on the General tab, but the Advanced tab of the Taskbar And Start Menu Properties dialog box provides more specific customization options. Figure 13.9 displays some of the Advanced tab customization options.

You can use the following five buttons on the Advanced tab to customize the Start menu:

- *Add*—Use this button to add a shortcut to the Start or Programs menu. This button uses the Create Shortcut Wizard to add the new item to the appropriate menu.

- *Remove*—Use this button to remove a shortcut from either the Programs or Start menu. After you click on this button, the Remove Shortcuts/Folders dialog box is displayed. You locate the item you want to remove and click on the Remove button to remove it.

Figure 13.9
The Advanced tab of the Taskbar And Start Menu Properties dialog box.

- *Advanced*—Use this button to open Windows Explorer in the Start Menu folder. You can use this option to add or remove items from your Start menu.

Note: *By default, the Advanced button opens Windows Explorer in the %systemroot%\ Documents and Settings\username\Start Menu folder. The username is the name you used to log on to the computer.*

- *Re-sort*—Use this button to reorder the items listed on the Programs menu so that they are displayed in the default order.

- *Clear*—Use this button to remove the list of recently accessed programs, documents, and Web sites from the Documents list on the Start menu and the Web addresses from the Address drop-down menu in your Web browser.

The Start Menu Settings area of the Advanced tab presents some optional settings you can use to define the objects you want listed and how specific items are displayed when you open them. The following settings are available:

- *Display Administrative Tools*—Displays the Administrative Tools menu on the Programs menu

- *Display Favorites*—Displays the Favorites menu on the Start menu

- *Display Logoff*—Displays the Logoff option on the Start menu

- *Expand Control Panel*—Displays the contents of Control Panel instead of the Control Panel window

- *Expand My Documents*—Displays the contents of My Documents instead of the My Documents window

- *Expand Network And Dial-up Connections*—Displays the contents of Network And Dial-up Connections instead of the Network and Dial-up Connections window

- *Expand Printers*—Lists the contents of the Printers menu instead of the Printers windows

- *Scroll The Programs Menu*—Scrolls the contents of the Programs menu instead of displaying the contents in columns

After you make your choices, click on Apply to apply the changes and leave the Taskbar And Start Menu dialog box open, or click on OK to apply the changes and close the Taskbar And Start Menu dialog box.

Now that you have an understanding of the different ways to change the visual settings of your taskbar and Start menu, it's time to look at how you can add and remove shortcuts on the these menus.

Adding a Shortcut to Your Taskbar or Start Menu

You can easily add a shortcut to your taskbar or Start menu by using the drag-and-drop method. Simply locate the item you want to add, and click and hold the mouse button down as you drag it to the taskbar or Start menu. After you reach your destination, release the mouse button to drop the item.

You can also add a shortcut or submenu to the Start menu by following these steps:

1. Click on Start|Settings|Taskbar & Start Menu.

2. Click on the Advanced tab.

3. Click on the Add button to open the Create Shortcut Wizard.

4. Follow the prompts of the wizard to add the shortcut to the Start menu.

13

Adding a Submenu to Your Start Menu

Adding shortcuts creates a pointer to an existing folder, file, program, or computer. However, you may want to add a submenu to the Start menu to help you organize your different shortcut options. For instance, you may want to create a submenu called Word Processing and move WordPad, Notepad, and Word shortcuts within the submenu. To do so, just follow these steps:

1. Open the Advanced tab of the Taskbar And Start Menu dialog box as described previously.

2. Click on the Advanced button to open Windows Explorer.

3. Choose New from the File menu and then click on Folder.

4. Type a name for your new submenu item and then press Enter.

After you create the new submenu, you can use the drag-and-drop method to add shortcuts to programs on the new submenu. You then can access the submenu and shortcuts created within the submenu from the Start menu.

If multiple users are sharing a computer, you may want to create a submenu on the Start menu that will be accessible for a group of users. To do so, just follow these steps:

1. Log on to the computer using an administrator's account.

2. Right-click on Start and then click on Open All Users.

3. Locate and double-click on the folder that you want to add as a submenu.

4. Choose New from the File menu and then click on Folder.

5. Type a name for the new submenu and then click on an empty space on your desktop.

Note: *If you are logged on as an administrator, you can cut, copy, move, rename, or delete shortcuts that were created for a group of users.*

Working with Shortcuts on Your Start Menu and Submenus

During the discussion of ways to customize the taskbar and Start menu, I have referred to the objects added as *shortcuts*. Shortcuts are pointers to the original item that resides on the hard drive. They provide quick access to the original files and programs, and you can organize your shortcuts for quicker access.

You can easily add, rename, move, and delete shortcuts on the Start menu and submenus. You can manage your shortcuts directly from the desktop by using any of the following approaches:

- You can drag any shortcut icon to the Start button and then drop it on the location you want it to appear on the Start button.

- You can drag and drop any shortcut icon directly from the Start button to any location on your desktop.

Tip: *If you want to delete a shortcut icon, you can drag and drop it directly to the Recycle Bin. Deleting the icon will not affect the original item located on the hard drive.*

- You can rearrange the order of your shortcuts and folders on the Start menu. You can also drag and drop these items to different locations using Windows Explorer.

- You can rename a shortcut located on the Start menu by right-clicking on it, clicking on Rename, and then typing the new name.

You can also delete a shortcut on your Start menu or a submenu by following these steps:

1. Open the Taskbar And Start Menu Properties dialog box.

2. Click on the Advanced tab to display the Advanced configuration options.

3. Click on Remove to display the Remove Shortcuts/Folders dialog box.

4. Locate and select the item that you want to delete and click on Remove.

5. Click on Close to close the Remove Shortcuts/Folders dialog box.

6. Click on OK to close the Taskbar And Start Menu Properties dialog box.

Now that you've learned about the shortcuts that you can apply on the taskbar and Start menu, it's time to look at ways to create shortcuts on your desktop.

Adding and Removing Shortcuts on Your Desktop

Shortcuts can also be placed on your desktop for easy access. Folders, files, programs, and computers that you use frequently can be accessed easily from your desktop as well. Follow these steps to create a shortcut on your desktop:

1. Open Windows Explorer or My Computer.

2. Locate and click on the folder, file, program, or computer for which you want to create a desktop shortcut.

3. Choose Create Shortcut from the File menu.

4. Drag and drop the shortcut from Windows Explorer or My Computer to your desktop.

Tip: *To make modifications to the desktop shortcut, simply right-click on the shortcut icon and click on Properties.*

After you add a shortcut icon to your desktop, you can easily remove it by dragging and dropping it in the Recycle Bin, or you can right-click on the shortcut icon and click on Delete on the shortcut menu.

Using the Windows 2000 Accessibility Options

13

Windows 2000 provides features that can be used to modify the appearance and behavior of your Windows 2000 desktop environment, thereby improving accessibility for mobility-impaired, vision-impaired, and hearing-impaired users. These accessibility options are built into the Windows 2000 operating system and do not require any additional hardware or software:

- *Magnifier*—Enlarges a portion of your viewing screen so that it is easier to read.

- *Narrator*—Reads the contents of the screen aloud, using text-to-speech technology. This feature is useful for people who are vision-impaired.

- *On-Screen Keyboard*—Allows you to type on screen using a pointing device.

- *Utility Manager*—Enables administrators to check an Accessibility program's status, start or stop an Accessibility program, and specify when to have the Accessibility programs start.

You can use Accessibility Options located in Control Panel to easily configure the display, keyboard, and mouse functions on your computer. You can also use the Accessibility Wizard to assist you in configuring your options and programs to fit your specific needs.

Note: *The Accessibility tools included with Windows 2000 provide a minimum level of functionality for physically challenged users. Most users with physical challenges will require additional utility programs with more functionality.*

Using the Accessibility Options in Control Panel

You have numerous options available to you when using the Accessibility Options dialog box, as shown in Figure 13.10. The five tabs provide the options to configure the following Accessibility functions:

- *StickyKeys*—Enables simultaneous keystrokes while you are pressing only one key at a time. This feature is useful when you use the Alt, Ctrl, and Shift keys.

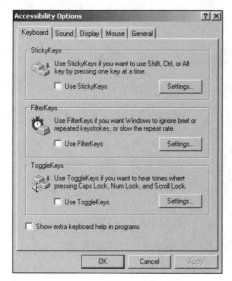

Figure 13.10
Windows 2000 Accessibility Options dialog box.

- *FilterKeys*—Adjusts the response of your keyboard to actions such as repeated keystrokes.

- *ToggleKeys*—Provides sound when certain locking keys are pressed, including Num Lock, Caps Lock, and Scroll Lock.

- *SoundSentry*—Presents a visual display for your system sounds.

- *ShowSound*—Instructs your programs to display captions for sounds and program speech.

- *High Contrast*—Uses alternative colors and fonts to improve screen contrast.

- *MouseKeys*—Enables you to use the keyboard for your pointer functions.

- *SerialKeys*—Allows you to use alternative input devices to replace your keyboard and mouse.

Table 13.1 lists the keyboard shortcuts that you can use to turn on and off the Windows 2000 Accessibility options.

Along with the built-in Accessibility features in Windows 2000, you can obtain additional third-party products for MS-DOS and other Microsoft Windows operating systems to provide the following functionality:

- Applications that alter or enlarge the color of information on the screen

- Applications that describe information in synthesized speech or Braille

- Software and hardware utilities that change your mouse and keyboard behavior

Table 13.1   Accessibility Options keyboard shortcuts.

Keys to Press	Results When Pressed
Right Shift key for eight seconds	Switches FilterKeys on and off
Left Alt+Left Shift+Print Screen	Switches High Contrast on and off
Left Alt+Left Shift+Num Lock	Switches MouseKeys on and off
Shift five times	Switches StickyKeys on and off
Num Lock for five seconds	Switches ToggleKeys on and off
Windows key+U	Opens the Utility Manager

- Applications that enable you to enter text using a mouse or your voice

- Phrase or word prediction software that allows you to type more quickly using fewer keystrokes

- Alternate input devices, such as puff-and-sip devices (which communicate with the computer using mouth actions, requiring no use of hands) or single switches (which are attached to your computer and allow you to communicate with minimal movement) if you are unable to use a keyboard or mouse

Using the Accessibility Wizard

You use the Accessibility Wizard to customize your computer with the tools provided to help meet your hearing, mobility, and vision needs. However, like most Windows 2000 wizards, the Accessibility Wizard assists you in the configuration of your tools. After you install the Accessibility tools, you can access them by using the Accessibility menu located in Control Panel.

You open the Accessibility Wizard by clicking on Start|Programs|Accessories|Accessibility Wizard. Follow the instructions on each screen to identify and configure the Accessibility options that you want to apply to the desktop.

Using the Utility Manager to Manage Your Accessibility Options

The Utility Manager provides the capability to start and stop as well as check the status of an Accessibility program. If you have administrator's permissions and rights, you can also configure an Accessibility program to start when Windows 2000 starts.

The built-in programs accessible from the Utility Manager are Narrator, Magnifier, and the On-Screen Keyboard. The Narrator and text-to-speech programs start automatically when you open the Utility Manager.

You can configure other Accessibility programs to start automatically when you open the Utility Manager by following these steps:

1. Click on Start|Programs|Accessories|Accessibility|Utility Manager to open the Utility Manager, as shown in Figure 13.11.

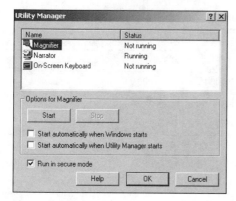

Figure 13.11
The Utility Manager dialog box.

2. Select the program you want to start automatically from the Name column.

3. Under Options, click on the Start Automatically When Utility Manager Starts checkbox. To disable it from starting, clear the checkbox.

Now that you know how to customize your desktop, you may be curious about where the changes are stored and how you can reuse them. The following sections introduce user profiles and explain what they do and how important they are in Windows 2000.

Introducing User Profiles

User profiles store information about your customized desktop environments. This information includes display settings, network and printer connections, and other settings. Both the system administrator and the user can define a desktop environment. The type of user profile determines what and when desktop characteristics are applied to your computer.

Windows 2000 supports three types of user profiles: local, roaming, and mandatory. You can use the following information to determine which type of profile is appropriate for your environment:

- *Local user profile*—This type of profile is created the first time you log on to a computer and is stored on the hard drive. Any changes you make to the local profile are saved and applied when you log on to that specific computer.

- *Roaming user profile*—This type of profile is created by a system administrator and is stored on a shared network resource. This profile is not stored locally like the local user profile, so you can use it on any computer on your network.

- *Mandatory user profile*—This type of profile is also a roaming user profile, but you cannot save any changes made to it while you're logged on to the computer. If you want to make a change to a mandatory profile, you must be a system administrator.

Understanding Local User Profiles

Local user profiles are specific for each user who logs directly on to a machine. This type of profile contains the settings the user configured the last time he or she logged on to the machine and are applied each time they log on to that machine.

Each user who logs on to the machine receives his or her individual user profile the first time he or she logs on to the machine. For instance, say that Kenny logs on to the computer and sets up a background of his favorite automobile. When he logs off from the computer, the automobile background setting is saved in his local user profile.

Jessie walks up to the same machine, logs on, connects to a few shared network resources, and sets her background to her favorite automobile. Her settings are also saved when she logs off from the computer. Now, when either Kenny or Jessie logs on to the computer, he or she will get his or her favorite automobile as the background setting.

These configuration settings are saved in a separate folder for each user. The default location for local user profiles is *%systemroot%*\Documents and Settings*Username* folder that is created the first time the user logs on to the computer.

Note: *The* Username *of the preceding directory path is the name used to log on to the computer.*

Inside these individual folders are other folders that represent the various configuration settings—Desktop, Cookies, My Documents, and Favorites. For instance, the Desktop folder contains most of the things that are on your desktop, including files, folders, and some of the default desktop icons. Figure 13.12 displays the contents of my Desktop folder.

Note: *Not all your icons will appear in the Desktop folder—Recycle Bin, Outlook, and Internet Explorer do not.*

After a user profile is created, you can use it to create other profiles. You may also want to delete a user's profile so that he or she can start with a clean slate, or if you discover a user no longer needs a local profile.

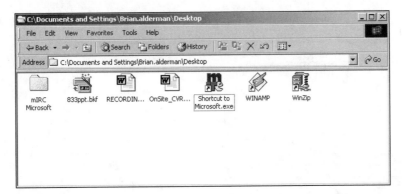

Figure 13.12
Sample contents of a Desktop folder.

Copying User Profiles

If a new user is going to use your computer and you already have a profile configuration that you want that person to use, you can copy an existing user profile to create a user profile for the new user by following these steps:

1. Click on Start|Settings|Control Panel and double-click on System to open the System Properties dialog box.

2. Click on the User Profiles tab and then locate the user profile that you want to copy in the Profiles Stored On This Computer Section, as shown in Figure 13.13.

3. Click on the user profile and then click on the Copy To button to open the Copy To dialog box.

4. In the Copy To dialog box, under Copy Profile To, type the location for the new profile. Optionally, you can click on the Browse button to select the location.

5. Click on the Change button to open the Select User Or Group dialog box, as shown in Figure 13.14. Then, click on the name of the new user from the Name list.

6. Click on OK to create the new user's profile on your computer.

Deleting User Profiles

When an employee no longer accesses a computer, you might want to delete that user's profile to save disk space. You can use the following steps to delete a user profile:

1. Open the System applet in Control Panel.

2. Click on the User Profiles tab to display the user profiles on your computer.

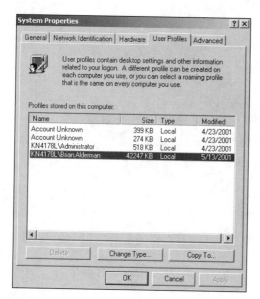

Figure 13.13
The User Profiles tab of the System Properties dialog box.

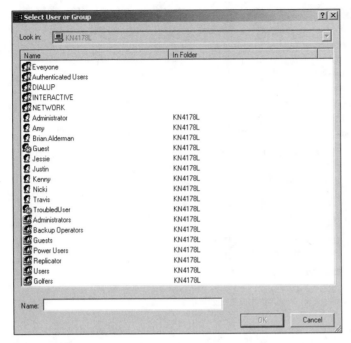

Figure 13.14
The Select User Or Group dialog box.

3. Click on the user profile that you want to delete and then click on the Delete button.

4. Click on Yes in the Confirm Delete box to confirm that you want to delete the user profile.

Note: You must be logged on as an administrator to copy or delete a user profile in Windows 2000.

Understanding Roaming User Profiles

Roaming profiles are much more powerful than local profiles because they follow you around the network. You can define a single roaming profile that contains configuration settings and store it on a centralized server. This profile is applied to your desktop regardless of what computer on the network you log on to.

The profile path specified on the centralized server is identified using the Universal Naming Convention (UNC). A UNC name begins with two backslashes, followed by the computer network name, a single backslash, the share name, another single backslash, and the profile name. An example of a profile pathname is \\Server1\Profiles*Username*.

Use the following steps to set up a roaming profile:

1. Open Users And Passwords in Control Panel.

2. Right-click on a user's account and click on Properties.

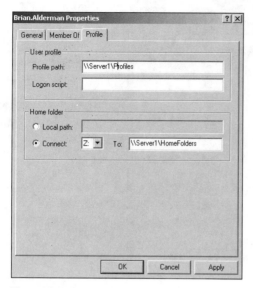

Figure 13.15
A user's Properties dialog box.

3. Click on the Profile tab, as shown in Figure 13.15.

4. Type the UNC location of the user's roaming profile, click on Apply, and then click on OK.

5. Go to each user's machine in the workgroup and create a user account. Enter the same profile pathname as the one you specified in Step 4.

Tip: You can also supply the name of a logon script and specify either a local home folder directory location or a network home folder directory location.

Switching between a Local and Roaming User Profile

Windows 2000 provides you the flexibility to easily switch between a local user profile to a roaming user profile or vice versa. This capability allows you to easily modify the target machines of a user's profile.

Follow these steps to switch between local and roaming user profiles:

1. Open the System applet in Control Panel.

2. Click on the User Profiles tab of the System Properties dialog box.

3. Locate the user profile that you want to change under the Profiles Stored On This Computer section and click to select it.

4. Click on the Change Type button to open the Change Profile Type dialog box.

Creating a Mandatory Profile

Windows 2000 mandatory user profiles are managed by users who have been granted administrator permissions and rights. Although users can make modifications to their desktop while logged on, the modifications are not saved when they log off. Mandatory profiles prevent users from permanently modifying their desktop environment.

Administrators create these profiles to present a consistent or job-specific desktop. Each time users log on to the network, the mandatory user profile is downloaded to the computers they are logging on to.

Follow these steps to create a mandatory profile:

1. Open *%systemroot%*\Documents and Settings*Username*.

2. Right-click on the Ntuser.dat file to open the shortcut menu and click on Rename.

3. Type ".man" to rename the file to Ntuser.man.

13

Your user profile is now a mandatory profile, prohibiting other users from saving any changes they made while logged on to the computer.

As we mentioned previously, a user profile is created for an individual user when he or she logs on, but before the user profile can be created, an administrator needs to create the user account to allow that user to log on to the computer.

Creating Local User Accounts

Windows 2000 Professional provides two ways for you to add new local user accounts to your computer: by using the Users And Passwords or Local Users And Groups utility. Both utilities require the user who is creating the account to be a member of the Administrators group.

Creating a Local User Account with the Users And Passwords Utility

The Users And Passwords utility in Control Panel allows you to add users to a computer and to a group. We encourage the use of groups in Windows 2000 when granting permissions and user rights. All members of groups receive the permissions and user rights assigned to the groups they belong to.

Follow these steps to add a new user to the computer:

1. Open Users And Passwords in Control Panel to open the Users And Passwords dialog box, as shown in Figure 13.16.

2. Click on the Add button to open the Add New User dialog box.

3. Enter a name and domain for the new user in the Add New User dialog box and then click on Next.

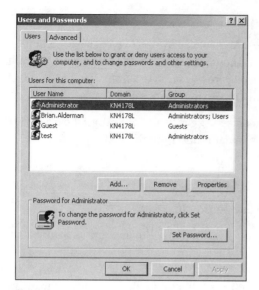

Figure 13.16
Users And Passwords dialog box.

4. Choose the level of access that you want to grant to the new user from the group options, as shown in Figure 13.17:

- *Standard User*—This user, who belongs to the Power Users group, can modify the computer and install applications but cannot read files that he or she does not own.

- *Restricted User*—This user, who belongs to the Users group, can use the computer and save documents but cannot install applications or make potentially damaging modifications to system settings and files.

- *Other*—Use the drop-down menu to select the group type of permissions you want to apply to the user. When you choose a group, a description of the permissions is displayed below the Other box. The groups available to choose from include

Figure 13.17
Setting the level of permissions for the new user.

Administrators, Backup Operators, Guests, Power Users, Replicator, Users, and any other local groups that you have created on your local computer.

Note: In Users And Passwords, you can add a user to only one of these three levels of access.

5. Click on Finish to create the new user account.

As you can see, the Users And Passwords utility provides limited functionality for creating users, setting passwords, and adding users to groups. If you need a more powerful utility to manage your users and groups, you can use the Local Users And Groups utility.

Use the following worksheet to document your user account information. This worksheet is useful for deciding what information you want to enter while creating a new user account. The completed worksheet here provides an example of its use. You can find a blank worksheet on the accompanying CD-ROM. Print as many copies as necessary when preparing to create your user accounts.

13

Documenting new user account information.

Username	Domain Name	Access Level	Group	Comments
David W.	HomeDomain	Standard	Power Users	Junior Administrator
Beth W.	HomeDomain	Restricted	Users	Nonadministrative user
Justin T.	HomeDomain	Other	Backup Operators	Performs nightly backups
Nicki T.	HomeDomain	Other	Replicator	Manages replication process

Introducing Local Users And Groups

The Local Users And Groups utility is available on computers running the Windows 2000 Professional operating system or a member server running Windows 2000 Server. Windows 2000 domain controllers do not offer the Local Users And Groups utility. Users and groups created on a domain controller are referred to as domain or global users and groups. Domain or global users and groups are managed through the Active Directory Users and Computers snap-in.

The big difference between the two types of users and groups is that local users and groups can be granted permissions and rights from your local computer only by the local administrators. Domain or global users and groups can be granted permissions and rights by any network administrator.

Creating a New User Account Using Local Users And Groups

You create user accounts using Local Users And Groups located in Computer Management. Computer Management is accessed using the steps discussed in previous sections, but here you open Users. Follow these steps to add a new user account to a computer using Local Users and Groups:

1. Open Computer Management by clicking on Start|Settings|Control Panel.

2. Double-click on Administrative Tools and then double-click on Computer Management.

3. Double-click on Local Users And Groups and then click on Users.

4. Choose New User from the Action menu to open the New User dialog box.

5. Type the information requested—username, full name, and description—in the New User dialog box, as shown in Figure 13.18.

Note: A username must be unique on the computer on which you are creating the account. The name can be up to 20 uppercase or lowercase characters but cannot contain any of the following characters:

*" / \ [ ] : ; | = , + * ? < >*

6. Type a password in the Password box and then retype the password in the Confirm Password box.

Note: You can type a password containing up to 127 characters on a Windows 2000 computer. However, for backward compatibility with other operating systems, you might want to restrict the password length to 14 or fewer characters.

7. Select or clear the password setting checkboxes for the following:

- User Must Change Password At Next Logon (selected by default)

- User Cannot Change Password (dimmed by default)

- Password Never Expires (dimmed by default)

- Account Is Disabled (cleared by default)

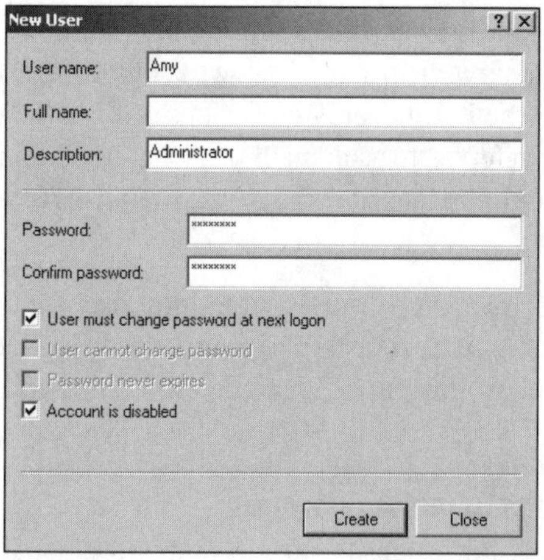

Figure 13.18
The New User dialog box.

Note: *If the User Must Change Password At Next Logon checkbox is selected, the User Cannot Change Password and Password Never Expires options are dimmed. Also, if either the User Cannot Change Password or Password Never Expires checkboxes are selected, the User Must Change Password At Next Logon option is dimmed.*

8. Perform one of the following:

   • To create another user, click on Create and repeat Steps 4 and 5.

   • If you are finished creating user accounts, click on Create and then click on Close.

As you can do with groups, you can also rename a user account. When you do so, you retain all its other properties—such as its group memberships, description, password, account information, and assigned permissions and rights—because it retains its original security identifier (SID). Managing local user accounts and groups may include disabling or re-enabling an account, resolving an account that is locked out, and resetting passwords. The Local Users And Groups shown in Figure 13.19 contains user accounts that are disabled.

After you create the accounts, your users can log on and generate their own user profiles. They can make changes to their desktop, taskbar, and Start menu to customize their work environment. However, you can use group policies to restrict the modifications that your users can make.

Using Group Policies to Control the Desktop Environment

Windows 2000 introduced group policies as a replacement for the system policies used in previous NT operating systems. Group policies are much more powerful and robust in comparison to system policies. You can use the Group Policy tool to define and control

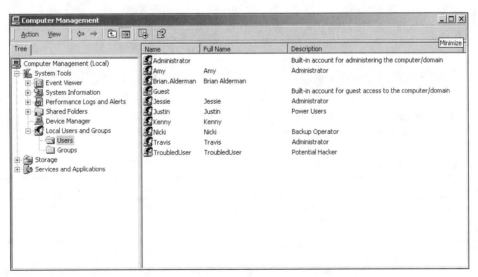

Figure 13.19
Local Users And Groups containing disabled accounts.

how programs, the operating system, and network resources work with the computers and users on your network.

Understanding Windows 2000 Group Policy

In an Active Directory environment, you apply group policies to users or computers based on their membership in sites, domains, and organizational units (OUs). Administrators can manage the five key components listed in Table 13.2 in a Windows 2000 networking environment.

Group policy settings defined by a network administrator are stored in a *group policy object*—a document created using the Group Policy snap-in that contains a collection of group policy settings that affect users in a site, domain, or organizational unit.

Windows 2000 Professional contains a limited version of Group Policy called Local Security Policy; it allows you to control the following local security configuration options:

- *Audit Policy*—Determines which security events are written to the Windows 2000 Security log located in Event Viewer. These events could be failed attempts, successful attempts, or both.

- *User Rights Assignment*—Determines which users or groups have logon or system task permissions on the computer.

- *Security Options*—Enables or disables security settings for the computer—for instance, digital signing of data, the name of the default built-in accounts (Guest and Administrator), CD-ROM and floppy drive access, driver installation, and logon prompts.

These local policies apply only to users and groups on the computer they are defined on. However, you can import these settings to a group policy object in Active Directory. After you do so, they will affect the local security settings of any computer accounts to which you apply the group policy.

Enhancing Windows 2000 Professional Group Policies

This limited version of the Group Policy implementation on Windows 2000 Professional does not provide the capabilities to really manage a user's desktop environment. If you want to maintain a user's environment, you need to use the full version of Group Policy

Table 13.2   Primary group policy components.

Component	Description
Administrative Templates	Sets Registry-based policy
Security Settings	Manages security for domains, computers, and users
Software Installation	Assigns or publishes software to Windows 2000 computers or users
Scripts	Specifies scripts to execute during computer startup/shutdown and user logon/logoff
Folder Redirection	Places a user's special folders, such as My Documents, on a shared network drive

by installing the Group Policy Editor. You can add it to your Windows 2000 Professional computer by performing one of the following:

• Adding the Group Policy snap-in to your Microsoft Management Console (MMC)

• Running the gpedit.msc utility using the Run command

Both of these options enable you to take advantage of the full version of Group Policy on your local computer, therefore allowing you to control the user's ability to perform certain tasks.

Adding the Group Policy Snap-in to Your MMC
The Group Policy Editor used to manage your group policies can be added to your MMC, thus allowing easy access to the editor and making it easy to manage your group policies. Follow these steps to add the Group Policy Editor snap-in to the Computer Management MMC:

1. Select Run from the Start menu and type "mmc /a" to open an empty MMC in author mode.

2. Select Add/Remove Snap-In from the Console menu to display the Add/Remove Snap-In dialog box.

3. Click on Add to display a list of available snap-ins in the Add Standalone Snap-In dialog box.

4. Locate Group Policy and double-click on it. Leave the Group Policy Object set to Local Computer and click on Finish.

5. Close the Add Standalone Snap-In dialog box and return to Add/Remove Snap-In dialog box.

6. Click on OK to close the Add/Remove Snap-In dialog box.

7. Expand the Local Computer Policy option in the console tree of the new MMC to display the User Configuration and Computer Configuration options, as shown in Figure 13.20.

After adding the Local Computer Policy to the MMC, you can configure any of the numerous user- and computer-level desktop settings on that computer.

Accessing Group Policy Using a Command-Line Utility
You can also access the Group Policy Editor using a command-line utility called gpedit.msc. This utility opens the same interface that we just discussed. You open the Group Policy Editor from the Run command by typing "gpedit.msc" to display the same window shown in Figure 13.20.

After opening the Group Policy Editor, you can configure desktop settings at the computer level or user level. If you configure them at the computer level, the settings apply to

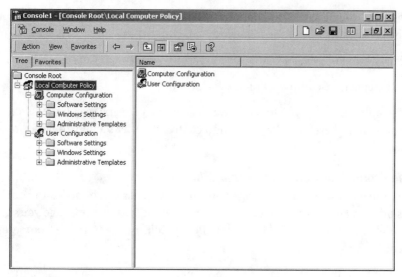

Figure 13.20
Local Computer Policy MMC option.

everyone who logs on to that computer. The user settings apply to the specific user you apply them to.

By default, all the policies are turned off. As you can see, numerous policies are available, so we will not discuss them in detail. You can look through the different policies and implement them by enabling them. If you want to turn off a policy setting, you can disable it.

Warning! *Be careful of the wording used to describe the policies. For instance, if you want to disable the Add/Remove Programs option in Control Panel, you need to enable that option. In effect, you are enabling a disable to receive the desired results.*

You use a specific profile's Properties dialog box to change the configuration setting in the Group Policy Editor. After you choose the desired option—Not Configured, Enabled, or Disabled—the setting is reflected in the Group Policy window, as shown in Figure 13.21.

The administrators who configure the group policies determine what options the users have to work with on their desktops. After an administrator determines the options and implements them using Group Policy, it is up to the user to configure his or her desktop using the options available to him or her. Most desktop configurations are changed through Control Panel and saved to a user profile when the user logs off the computer.

Using Control Panel to Configure Your Desktop

Now that you know the importance of user profiles, user accounts, and group policies, it's time to explore Control Panel in a little more detail. We have already discussed the Display and Accessibility options, providing you with a better understanding of how these

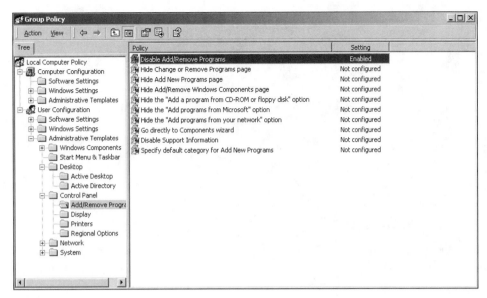

Figure 13.21
Group Policy settings.

features work behind the scenes, so we'll now look at a few additional options you can use to customize your work environment.

Exploring the Folder Options

You use Folder Options to change the appearance of your desktop and folder content, as well as how your folders are opened. For instance, you can have your folders open in the same window on your desktop instead of opening a new window for each folder.

To open the Folder Options dialog box, as shown in Figure 13.22, use one of the following methods:

• Click on Start|Settings|Control Panel and then double-click on Folder Options.

• Open Windows Explorer or My Computer and choose Folder Options from the Tools menu.

After you open the Folder Options dialog box, you can use the General and View tabs to customize how your folders are displayed and what is displayed in them.

Configuring Your Folder View Using the General Tab

On the General tab of the Folder Options dialog box, you can customize the appearance of the contents and subfolders of My Computer, My Network Places, My Documents, and Control Panel. Four sections on the General tab allow you to customize your folder content view:

• *Active Desktop*—Enables or disables the Active Desktop feature. After you click on the Enable Web Content On My Desktop option, your Active Desktop is turned on. To turn it off, simply click on the Use Windows Classic Desktop option.

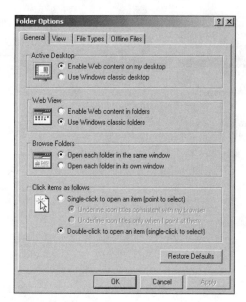

Figure 13.22
The General tab of the Folder Options dialog box.

- *Web View*—Makes your folders appear as if they are a Web page. You enable the Web view by clicking on the Enable Web Content In Folders option. You turn off this view by clicking on the Use Windows Classic Folders option.

Note: When you click on Enable Web Content In Folders, descriptive hyperlinked text appears on the left side of your folders. For instance, when you click on a file, the attributes (hidden, system, read-only, and so on) associated with it, the date it was last modified, an explanation of it, and its size are displayed.

- *Browse Folders*—Sets whether your folders are opened in a separate window or over-write the contents of the previous window's contents. Click on the Open Each Folder In Its Own Window option if you want a new window opened for each folder you open. Click on the Open Each Folder In The Same Window option to overwrite the previous window's content.

- *Click On Items As Follows*—Define the number of mouse clicks required to open an item on your desktop. If you select Single-Click To Open An Item (Point To Select), clicking opens the item you are pointing to. If you choose Single-Click, you can also choose how you want icon titles to be underlined. If you select Double-Click To Open An Item (Single-Click To Select), you have to double-click on the item you are pointing to in order to open it.

You use the General tab to define your folder views, but you use the View tab to determine what is displayed in the folders that you open.

Configuring Your Folder Contents Using the View Tab

The View tab of the Folder Options dialog box consists of two sections: Folder Views and Advanced Settings. In the Folder Views section, you can set all folders on your computer to be the same as the current folder by clicking on Like Current Folder. Clicking on Reset All Folders sets all folders back to the default setting applied to them when Windows 2000 was initially installed.

In the Advanced Settings section, you can specify various display options for your desktop, folders, and files. The 10 options that you can configure, their default settings, and descriptions are listed in Table 13.3.

Table 13.3   Advanced settings on the View tab of the Folder Options dialog box.

Advanced Setting	Default	Description
Display Compressed Files And Folders With Alternate Color	Off	Specifies whether to show compressed files and folders in blue when they are viewed through My Computer or Windows Explorer.
Display The Full Path In The Address Bar	Off	Specifies whether to display the complete path of the open folder or file in the address bar of the window.
Display The Full Path In The Title Bar	Off	Specifies whether to display the complete path of the open folder or file in the title bar of the window.
Hidden Files Or Folders	Do not show	Specifies whether to display files or folders that contain the hidden attribute.
Hide File Extensions For Known File Types	On	Specifies whether to display the three-letter file extensions for specific common files.
Hide Protected Operating System Files (Recommended)	On	Specifies whether to display critical operating system files when displaying the contents of the folder.
Launch Folder Windows In A Separate Process	Off	Specifies whether each folder is opened in a separate memory space. When you open a folder in a separate memory space, you can decrease performance but also increase the stability of Windows 2000.
Remember Each Folder's View Settings	On	Specifies whether each folder's settings are retained when the window is closed and reopened.
Show My Documents On The Desktop	On	Specifies whether to display My Documents on your desktop.
Show Pop-Up Description For Folder And Desktop Items	On	Specifies whether a description of the desktop item or folder is displayed when selected.

Warning! *The default setting for Hide Protected Operating System Files is highly recommended. If you choose to disable this setting, you must verify your choice in a confirmation dialog box to ensure that you really want to disable it.*

After you configure these settings, you may decide you want to set them back to the defaults that were specified when you installed the operating system. You can easily do so by clicking on the Restore Defaults button on the View tab.

Configuring Miscellaneous User Settings

Some additional settings that are often personalized when users access Windows 2000 include the keyboard, mouse, and sounds. Configuring any of these features will create a more efficient and productive user environment.

Personalizing Your Keyboard Behavior

You use the Keyboard option inside Control Panel to specify keyboard options such as repeating characters, cursor blink rate, input locales, and hardware. You use the Keyboard Properties dialog box, as shown in Figure 13.23, to configure these different options.

To change the way your keyboard responds to your keystrokes and to change the cursor blink rate, you can make the following adjustments on the Speed tab:

- Use the Repeat Delay slider to configure how much time elapses before characters repeat when you are holding down a key.

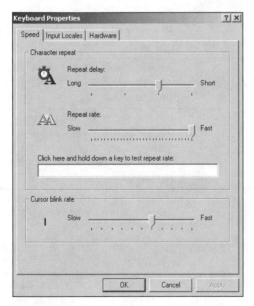

Figure 13.23
Keyboard Properties dialog box.

- Use the Repeat Rate slider to configure how quickly the characters repeat when you are holding down a key.

- Use the Cursor Blink Rate slider to adjust the cursor blink rate speed.

On the Input Locales tab, you can specify your keyboard layout, the Caps lock configuration, and the hot keys for input locales. You use the Hardware tab to view a list of display devices, set the properties for the devices, and troubleshoot your keyboard.

Personalizing Your Mouse Behavior

On the Mouse Properties dialog box, as shown in Figure 13.24, you configure mouse buttons, configure the double-click speed of your mouse, set the mouse pointers, and set the motion speed of the mouse.

On the Buttons tab, you can set the mouse buttons for right-handed and left-handed settings. These settings allow you to define which button you use most often when working with folders and files in Windows 2000. You also can set whether you double-click or single-click to open an item. The Test Area of the Double-Click Speed section allows you to test the effects of your changes to the double-click option.

On the Pointers tab, you can define a pointer scheme to use as a visual notification indicating what the operating system is doing during different operations. You can create your own scheme from the different pointers available and then save it to a new scheme name and use the new scheme for your desktop environment.

The Motion tab provides a slider to set how fast your mouse pointer moves and whether it accelerates as you move your mouse faster. You can also set your mouse pointer to automatically jump to the default button in your dialog boxes when they are opened.

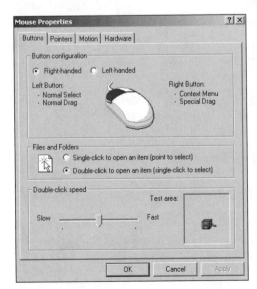

Figure 13.24
The Mouse Properties dialog box.

The Hardware tab displays information about your pointing device. Here, you can also change the properties of your pointing devices and troubleshoot them by using the Troubleshoot button.

Personalizing Your Sound Effects in Windows 2000

On the Sounds And Multimedia Properties dialog box, shown in Figure 13.25, you can assign sound effects to the different events on your operating system, adjust the volume, configure the different sound options, and configure the properties of the attached sound hardware.

The sounds supported by Windows 2000 include a brief piece of music, a simple beep, or entire songs. Different sound effects can be assigned to specific Windows 2000 events. For instance, you can have a sound effect play when you receive new mail and either the same sound effect or a different one play when you open a window.

You use the Sounds tab to assign sounds to individual program events, or you can assign an entire scheme to the numerous different events. Follow these steps to assign specific sound effects to system events:

1. Open the Sounds and Multimedia applet in Control Panel to display the Sounds And Multimedia Properties dialog box.

2. Under Sound Events on the Sound tab, locate and click on the specific event for which you want to assign a sound.

3. Using the Name drop-down menu or the Browse button, locate the sound that you want to associate with the selected event.

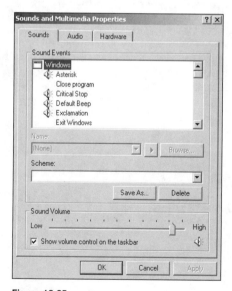

Figure 13.25
The Sounds And Multimedia dialog box.

Tip: *To test a sound, click on the right arrow button to play it. If you choose a long-running sound, you can stop it by clicking on the box button.*

4. After you assign all the sound effects to the system events using Steps 2 and 3, click on OK to apply the changes.

You can also adjust the volume or assign a predefined scheme to your system events by using the Sound Volume and Scheme sections, respectively.

Use the Audio tab to assign a device to the Sound Playback, Sound Recording, and Music Playback sections. Each has a Volume button, so you can tailor the sound effects for the different devices. The Advanced tabs allow you to use sliding bars to adjust the hardware acceleration and quality options of your sounds.

Similar to the previous options we discussed, you can use the Properties button to further configure the different sound devices on your machine. If you should encounter problems with any of the sound devices, you can use the Troubleshoot button to try to resolve the problems.

13

As you can see, you have many options to create a comfortable desktop environment. Depending on the group policies applied, you can completely personalize your desktop environment to meet your specific needs. Your user profile maintains your configuration settings so that they are saved for later use, and if you implement a roaming profile, it will follow you around the network on any machine you log on to.

After configuring your desktop environment, you need to look seriously at the applications available to you by default and also look at how to install additional software on your Windows 2000 Professional computer.

Working with Windows 2000 Programs

You use applications to execute commands, communicate with other programs, and share information with other programs. Understanding some of the fundamental skills required when using applications in Windows 2000 will assist you in quickly completing tasks, thereby improving your productivity. For instance, you can have several programs running tasks simultaneously in Windows 2000.

After you install Windows 2000, numerous programs are available for your use. You use these programs to perform your day-to-day tasks, maintain and troubleshoot your computer, or access entertainment. Table 13.4 describes some of the most commonly used programs that ship with Windows 2000 Professional.

You can install additional programs that are not shipped with Windows 2000 Professional by using the Add/Remove Programs applet in Control Panel.

Table 13.4   Windows 2000 Professional's most commonly used programs.

Program Name	Description
Address Book	Provides a convenient place to store contact information, including names of people, businesses, and mailing lists
Backup	Creates a copy of the data on your hard drive
Calculator	Use in Standard view for simple calculations, or Scientific view for statistical and advanced scientific calculations
CD Player	Plays audio compact discs from the CD-ROM drive connected to your computer
Computer Management	Contains administrative properties and tools used to manage local and remote computers
Device Manager	Provides information about your computer's hardware and configuration and how it interacts with your computer's programs
Disk Management	Provides a graphical interface you can use to manage your hard drives and volumes
Event Viewer	Maintains information about programs, security, and system events on your computer
Group Policy	Provides the primary tool for defining and controlling your programs, operating system, and network resources
Internet Explorer	Enables you to search and view information on the World Wide Web
Local Users and Groups	Manages the local users and groups on your computer
Notepad	Provides a basic text editor you can use to create or edit files requiring formatting
Performance	Provides Performance Logs and Alerts and System Monitor tools you can use to collect and view real-time data about hardware and other activity on your computer
Services	Manages the services on your computer, including custom names and descriptions
Shared Folders	Enables you to create, view, and set permissions on your shared files and folders
Synchronization Manager	Controls when your offline files are synchronized with files on the network
System Information	Collects and displays your system configuration information
Windows Task Manager	Provides information about your computer's performance and programs and processes running on your computer
Windows Update	Scans your computer for outdated system files and automatically replaces them with the most recent versions
WordPad	Creates or edits text files that contain formatting or graphics

Using Add/Remove Programs to Install Applications

Add/Remove Programs manages the installation and removal of programs on your computer. The applet walks you through the steps required to add a new program, modify an existing program, or remove a program.

You also can use Add/Remove Programs to add programs that you chose not to install during the original installation of Windows 2000 Professional. They include Indexing Services, networking options, and any other optional Windows 2000 programs.

You can use the Add/Remove Programs applet to add programs that are shared on the network, located on a CD, or on a floppy disk. Regardless of the location of the program you are adding, the steps are similar. Just do the following to add a program to your Windows 2000 environment:

1. Click on Start|Settings|Control Panel and then double-click on Add/Remove Programs to open the Add/Remove Programs dialog box.

2. Click on Add New Programs and then click on CD or Floppy.

3. Click on Next on the Install Program From Floppy Disk Or CD-ROM screen. The application will search your floppy and CD-ROM drives for an application (install.exe or setup.exe) it can use to install the program. Then, the Run Installation Program screen appears.

4. If the application is unable to locate an installation program, you can click on Browse to manually search for the program that you want to install.

5. After you locate the correct installation program, click on Finish to begin the installation of the program.

You can use similar steps to add a program that is located on the network; however, you must choose the appropriate category to display the programs you are authorized to install in the Add Programs From Your Network section of the Add/Remove Programs dialog box. Select the program that you want to install and click on Add to start the installation of the program.

Configuring Microsoft Windows Update

Although the Windows Update feature is one of the programs installed by default in Windows 2000, you may have to reinstall it if you removed it or if it is damaged. You can add the Windows Update feature from the Add/Remove Programs dialog box. After you click on the Windows Update feature, you can locate and download new features, device drivers, and system updates from the Windows Update Web site. The URL to access the latest and greatest updates is **http://windowsupdate.microsoft.com**.

This Web site provides step-by-step instructions on how to locate, download, and install the numerous options available to you. Figure 13.26 shows the Windows Update Web site just a few days after the release of Windows 2000 Service Pack 2.

In Figure 13.26, notice that you can also locate other product updates, support information, Microsoft Office updates, and other Microsoft Windows family Web pages.

Changing or Removing a Program in Windows 2000

After you install a program in Windows 2000, you may have to modify it or remove it completely from your configuration. These tasks can also be accomplished through the Add/Remove Programs applet.

Figure 13.26
Microsoft Windows Update Web Page.

Note: You can use the Add/Remove Programs applet to remove only programs that were written for Windows operating systems. To remove programs that were not written for Windows, check the program documentation on how to remove them.

Follow these steps to change or remove a program written for Windows operating systems:

1. Open the Add/Remove Programs dialog box as previously described.

2. Click on Change Or Remove Programs to display a list of installed programs, as shown in Figure 13.27.

Tip: If you want to rearrange the order in which the applications are presented, you can click on the Sort By drop-down menu and sort them by name, size, frequency of use, or date last used.

3. Click on the program that you want to change or remove and then click one of the following buttons:

   • Click on Change/Remove or Change to change a program.

   • Click on Change/Remove or Remove to remove a program.

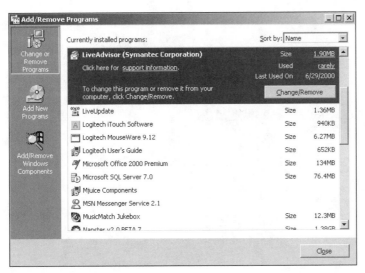

Figure 13.27
Choosing which programs to change or remove.

Warning! *Most programs present a confirmation dialog box providing you an opportunity to change your mind and cancel the removal of the program. However, some programs are immediately removed without the confirmation dialog box. Be extremely cautious when clicking on the Change/Remove button.*

4. Click on Close to close the Add/Remove Programs dialog box.

You also can use the Add/Remove Programs applet to manage your Windows 2000 operating system components.

Adding and Removing Windows 2000 Components

The Add/Remove Windows Components option on the left side of the Add/Remove Programs dialog box enables you to change or remove the different components of the operating system. As you can see in Figure 13.28, these same components were available to you during the installation of Windows 2000.

Note: When you choose to install certain Windows components, they may require additional configuration before they can actually be used. If components need to be configured, they will be displayed when you click on Add/Remove Windows Components. To configure a component in the list, click on Configure and follow the instructions.

At this point, you may be asking yourself whether there is an easier way to manage your programs and applications in Windows 2000. Fortunately, you can use a component called Windows Installer to simplify the process of installing applications in Windows 2000.

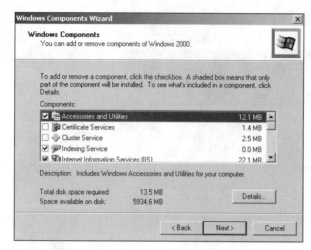

Figure 13.28
The Windows Components Wizard dialog box.

Introducing Windows Installer

Windows Installer manages the installation and removal of applications in Windows 2000. It manages the applications by applying a set of centrally defined setup rules during the installation of your program. These setup rules define how the application is installed and configured.

Windows Installer also acts as an extensible software management system. The capability to manage and maintain the software after it has been installed is a huge feature of Windows Installer. You also can use Windows Installer to perform the following tasks:

- Add and delete software components

- Monitor file resiliency

- Maintain basic disaster recovery using rollbacks

- Support multiple sources for installation of software components

Understanding the Windows Installer Technologies

Windows Installer is divided into two key parts that work in conjunction with each other to install and maintain your applications. These two parts include a client-side installer service called Msiexec.exe and a package file that has an .msi file extension. This package file contains the information required by Msiexec.exe to perform the installation.

Installer Program

The Msiexec.exe program is a component of the Windows Installer operating system service. This program uses a Dynamic Link Library (DLL) called Msi.dll to read the contents of the MSI file and apply transformations that are contained in an MST file.

The installer service performs the following installation-related tasks:

- Copies files to the hard drive

- Modifies the Registry

- Creates shortcuts on the desktop

- Displays dialog boxes to request installation preferences from the user

When Windows Installer is running, it uses the file association capabilities of the operating system to automatically run Msiexec.exe when someone double-clicks on a file with the .msi extension. As you can see, these MSI files are required to install the software.

Note: MSI files are usually provided by the vendor of the software that you want to install using Windows Installer. Microsoft has created numerous MSI files for installing its products. Many third-party vendors are also creating MSI files to allow easy installation of their software on a Windows 2000 operating system.

Installation Package Files (MSI Files)

The MSI files contain a relational type database that stores the data and instructions required to install or remove the software under different installation scenarios. For instance, if the software has already been installed on the computer, the steps required to perform the installation are different from the steps required to install the software on a computer that does not already contain the software.

Because the database in the MSI file is relational, a change in one place automatically propagates throughout the entire database. This propagation of changes through the relational database provides an efficient and consistent change to the installation process.

Numerous tables reflect the overall layout of the entire group of applications, including the following:

- Available features

- Components

- Relationships between the components and features

- Required Registry settings

These interrelated tables make up a database that contains the information necessary to install a group of features of a specific application. Table 13.5 describes the groups of related tables you will find in an MSI file.

The MSI file containing these groups performs a consistent installation across many computers. However, if you want to create custom installations on your computers, you must use transform files.

Table 13.5   Tables found in an MSI file.

Group Name	Description
Core table group	Describes the basic features and components of the application and installer package
File table group	Contains the files associated with the package
Registry table group	Contains the entries that need to be made to the Registry
System table group	Contains information about the columns and tables of the installation database
Locator table group	Used to search the installer configuration data, Registry, INI files, or directory tree for the unique file signature
Program installation group	Contains properties, shortcuts, bitmaps, and other information required for the installation
Installation procedure group	Manages the tasks performed during the installation by custom and standard actions

Using Transform Files (MST Files)

You can modify the installation process by applying transform files to the installation database, thereby modifying the elements of the database. For instance, if you need to install a version of Microsoft Office that supports the English native language on some machines and French native language on others, you use an MST file.

Windows 2000 will use the contents of the MST file to change the installation package to reflect the required changes at installation time, thereby dynamically modifying the behavior of the installation process. Similar to patches, these customization files are stored in cache on the local computer and applied to the base package file whenever Windows Installer needs to perform a configuration change to the installation package.

Note: *Transform packages are applied during the initial installation of the package. They cannot be applied to a package that has already been installed.*

Now that you understand how the installer packages work together, let's take a closer look at some of the features provided by the Windows Installer technology.

Using the Features of Windows Installer

As you have already seen, Windows Installer and the MSI package files provide an easy way to perform software installation and removal. Windows Installer provides an easy way to create resilient applications in your Windows 2000 environment. Now, let's dig a bit deeper into what Windows Installer provides:

- *Restores original computer state upon installation failure*—Keeps track of all system changes during the installation of the package. If the installation fails, it can automatically restore or roll back the system to its original state.

- *Helps prevent certain forms of inter-application conflicts*—Enforces the installation rules that reduce conflicts with shared resources between existing applications.

Note: *These types of conflicts can be caused when a new software installation updates a DLL used by an existing application.*

- *Reliably removes existing programs*—Reliably removes any program that was installed using Windows Installer. Furthermore, it removes all associated Registry entries and application files, unless they are used by other applications.

- *Diagnoses and repairs corrupted applications*—Applications that were installed using Windows Installer can query Windows Installer to determine whether there are any missing or corrupted files used by the application. If problems are detected, Windows Installer will automatically replace the missing or corrupted files.

- *Supports on-demand installation of application features*—Can install a minimal subset of an application and then install additional components to the application as the users access those features.

- *Supports unattended application installation*—Installation packages can be configured to be installed without any user intervention.

All these features are provided through the Windows Installer technology included in Windows 2000. We have already mentioned that MSI files are installed automatically when a user double-clicks on them. Similar to most of the topics we have discussed, a command-line version of Windows Installer also is available; it can be used to install your package files.

Installing a Package File from the Command Line

You can use the command line to create a batch file that will install the package at a particular time, or you can simply enter the command and required parameters at the command line. Follow these steps to install a package from the command line:

1. Click on Start|Programs|Accessories|Command Prompt to open the command window.

2. Type the following command at the command prompt:

```
msiexec /I packagefilename
```

Note: *Alternatively, you can use the Product Code to specify the package file you want to install. The Product Code is the globally unique identifier (GUID) of the package file.*

As you can probably guess, numerous switches and options are available to you when you use the command-line utility to install a package. For a detailed explanation of all the switches available, search the online documentation for "command-line options." The switches that you use at the command line or inside a batch file are not case sensitive, making it easier to create lengthy commands.

If you experience problems performing an installation using Windows Installer, you can check the Windows 2000 Application Log in Event Viewer for details. You can also create an installation log file from the command line by supplying a path and name of a log file, along with the **/L** switch and appropriate flag specifying what information you want logged.

Another way you can install MSI files is through software packages that are made available to users for installation as part of their Active Directory Group Policy Object (GPO). These GPOs contain a collection of settings that customize and control a user's desktop environment.

As you can see, the Windows Installer capabilities are extremely dynamic and powerful. You can have your users install the software package files by double-clicking on the MSI package file, using the command-line interface, or using a GPO to distribute the package files. You can use Decision Tree 13.1 to decide which is the best method for you to use when determining how your domain users will install their programs.

Summary

This chapter discussed numerous customization options available in Windows 2000, including the background, the display settings, and taskbar and Start menu options. You also learned how to set up multiple monitors. Then, you looked at the power of implementing Active Desktop on your Windows 2000 operating system and configuring your folder views as well as your mouse and keyboard settings.

Of course, to customize your desktop, you need to create user accounts, log on to the computer, and generate a local user profile. After you customize your desktop, you can save the settings to the local user profile. However, if you want the customized desktop to be available on every machine you log on to, you must change it from a local profile to a roaming profile.

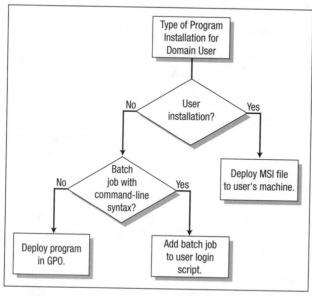

Decision Tree 13.1
Choosing your program installation type.

Applications allow you to perform your job more effectively and efficiently. The installation of Windows 2000 provides numerous applications, but sometimes you require additional software. The easiest way to install this software is through Windows Installer, which you invoke from the command line, by double-clicking on an MSI file, or by using a GPO.

After you configure your desktop and create a comfortable work environment, you will want to access the network to take full advantage of the Windows 2000 operating system and shared resources. First, you must become familiar with the networking capabilities available in Windows 2000 Professional. Chapter 14 provides in-depth information regarding the numerous networking features available to you.

13

Chapter 14

Windows 2000
Professional Networking

Making the Connection

It is no secret that information technology's true power is harnessed when computers are connected. Without local area networks (LANs), wide area networks (WANs), and the Internet, the advantages and benefits of groupware applications, email, file sharing, and Web services are lost.

Fortunately, Windows 2000 Professional simplifies networking. A new wizard makes it easier than ever for you to configure a variety of network connections. The Network Connection Wizard provides IT professionals with step-by-step directions for the following:

- Dialing up private networks

- Dialing up to the Internet

- Creating a virtual private network (VPN) connection

- Accepting incoming connections

- Connecting directly to another computer

Windows 2000 Professional also boasts significant new enhancements that improve its networking capacities. Support exists for many new networking technologies not previously found in Windows platforms, including Internet Protocol Security (IPSec), which you can use to encrypt data traffic on a LAN. Windows 2000 Professional also provides support for Network Address Translation (NAT), which permits multiple systems to access the Internet and external network resources using a single Internet IP address.

The actual interface you use to configure and administer network connections is streamlined, too. Accessed by default from Control Panel or the Start menu, networking settings can be easily edited, with separate icons and networking settings devoted to each connection created on a system.

All these enhancements and improvements add up to simplified but powerful networking capabilities in Windows 2000 Professional. Let's begin our examination of Windows 2000 Professional networking by quickly reviewing the basics.

Networking 101

The Open Systems Interconnection (OSI) model, ratified by the International Organization for Standardization (ISO) in 1978, standardizes network communications. The OSI model dictates the operations that occur at each level, or layer, of communication. Protocols often work together, creating a protocol stack, to complete connections and communications.

Although many IT professionals discount the real-world significance of the OSI model, it's important to note the role the model plays in network communications. In fact, its impact is both relevant to your enterprise and otherworldly, having impact beyond earth's confines.

Consider the International Space Station (ISS), a 16-nation effort to build the largest orbiting scientific program in history. With the first component launched in November 2000, the ISS will include some 100 computer systems when it is completed sometime in 2006. A variety of disparate operating systems, including Microsoft Windows and Sun Solaris Unix—not to mention the use of Russian, Asian, North American, and European systems components—maintain life-support systems, conduct experiments, and record data.

IBM ThinkPads serve as onboard workstations, and PC Cards provide necessary networking connections. The OSI model helps ensure that the protocols used to link these different operating systems and system components, including different software programs, work properly to permit seamless communication. The interconnection model performs the same role for your enterprise.

The OSI Model

The OSI model has seven layers, as shown in Figure 14.1. Specific functions occur at each layer.

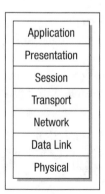

| Application |
| Presentation |
| Session |
| Transport |
| Network |
| Data Link |
| Physical |

Figure 14.1
The OSI model has seven layers, starting with the Physical layer on the bottom and concluding with the Application layer at the top.

Application Layer

The Application layer is responsible for enabling network access to applications. Processes that operate at this layer of the OSI model provide applications with the capability to send and receive data packets across a network. Common Application layer protocols include the Simple Mail Transfer Protocol (SMTP) and File Transfer Protocol (FTP).

Presentation Layer

The Presentation layer works closely with the Application layer to ensure that data being passed from lower OSI levels to the Application layer can be read by the Application layer. Redirectors, such as Microsoft Server Message Blocks (SMBs), operate at this OSI layer. Popular Presentation layer protocols include Simple Network Management Protocol (SNMP) and FTP.

Session Layer

The Session layer assumes the responsibility for creating, maintaining, and ending communications between applications and processes between systems. Communications are conducted using these sessions, hence the name. It's also at the Session layer that a system verifies the identity of the other system with which it is communicating.

Transport Layer

The Transport layer manages the actual transmission of data between two systems. It is also responsible for confirming the proper delivery of data. Data packets are assembled and disassembled at the Transport layer. Transmission Control Protocol (TCP) and Sequenced Packet Exchange (SPX) operate at the Transport layer, along with NetBIOS Extended User Interface (NetBEUI).

Network Layer

The Network layer assumes responsibility for routing a transmission's data packets. The Network layer also translates logical addresses and names into physical addresses. Common Network layer components include Internet Protocol (IP), network interface card (NIC) drivers, and Internetwork Packet Exchange (IPX).

Data Link Layer

The Data Link layer ensures error-free data transfer between two systems. Originally created as a single layer, the Data Link layer was later broken into two distinct sections: the Logical Link Control (LLC) and Media Access Control (MAC) layers.

The LLC manages service access points (SAPs) and packages data for reading by the layers above and below. It resides above the MAC layer, which is charged with regulating the NIC's electronic voltage. The MAC layer also shares access to the NIC.

Network Device Interface Specifications (NDIS), device drivers, and network bridges operate at the OSI's Data Link layer.

Physical Layer

The Physical layer is occupied with the actual bytes and bits that travel across a physical connection between two systems. It's at this layer that hardware connections come into play. Repeaters operate at this layer.

By ensuring protocols and components work within the OSI model confines, disparate systems can share data. However, more than just a networking model is required to exchange information.

Services, Clients, and Protocols

To connect to a network and share files, a system must possess these three components:

• A *service*, which enables the sharing of files, printers, and other resources on a network

• A *client*, which enables communication between Windows 2000 Professional and other workstations and servers

• A *protocol*, which provides the language two systems will use to exchange information and data

In most Microsoft networking environments, a common triumvirate exists. The three most popular networking components, installed when Typical Settings is selected as the Networking Components option during Windows 2000 Professional setup, are as follows:

• *File and Print Sharing for Microsoft Networks*—Fulfills the role of the service

• *Client for Microsoft Networks*—Provides the client component

• *Internet Protocol (TCP/IP)*—Specifies the protocol in use

However, Windows 2000 Professional supports many other services, clients, and protocols. We'll examine each supported component later in this chapter. But first, let's quickly review common network infrastructures.

Network Types and Topologies

Two types of network environments exist: *peer-to-peer* and *domain*. In peer-to-peer, or workgroup, environments, each workstation provides client and server services. Generally, 10 or fewer systems are connected, so security is not a pressing issue. Each member of the workgroup acts as a server by sharing files and resources, while also simultaneously acting as a client by connecting to other systems and using resources those systems make available.

Domains, on the other hand, boast dedicated servers that provide authentication, file and print sharing, mail, application, and Web services. Domains are the preference of most enterprises because administration is greatly simplified. In domains, both client and server administration can be conducted centrally. Security is much more easily controlled in domain environments, too.

Network infrastructures can be further simplified. If you're an IT professional, you may remember from your earliest training that the following types of network topologies are used:

- *Bus*—Consists of a single linear cable connecting multiple systems
- *Ring*—Consists of a single cable with no terminated ends
- *Star*—Uses a hub or switch to connect multiple systems on different cables

Hopefully, you're not still using a bus topology, which is now mostly obsolete. The Thinnet and Thicknet cabling just doesn't provide the bandwidth and reliability category-five cabling does.

Token ring networks, although still in place in large organizations, are considerably slower than 100Mbps star networks, which are increasingly taking over in today's corporate environments. Soon, though, 100Mbps networks will seem slow compared to gigabit Ethernet, which is just around the corner.

14

Variations of the different network topologies exist. For example, in star bus configurations, several linear cables connecting systems are attached using a hub. A star ring variation also exists, in which different star topologies are connected using hubs.

The network type and topology you select depend on many factors. Although such a discussion is outside the scope of this text, network infrastructure design plays a critical role in networking. Whenever you add systems or install a new network, you should always give careful attention to network design.

After you make network infrastructure decisions, you can proceed with the actual installation of network components.

Installing Network Components

The most common networking components are typically installed when Windows 2000 Professional is set up. Occasionally, however, network components become corrupted, new network interface cards are added, or another reason necessitating the installation of networking components will arise. Often, too, you will need to install networking components other than the defaults.

Installing Network Services

The following services are supported in Windows 2000 Professional:

- *File and Printer Sharing for Microsoft Networks*—Permits file and print resource sharing on a network
- *QoS Packet Scheduler*—Processes and manages packet traffic on a network
- *SAP Agent*—Provides a NetWare service for use on Microsoft networks to advertise servers and network addresses

Installing Network Services

Follow these steps to install any of the network services:

1. Click on Start|Settings|Network And Dial-up Connections.

Tip: An alternative to clicking on Start|Settings|Network And Dial-up Connections is to right-click on My Network Places and select Properties.

2. Select the local area connection where you wish to install the network service.

3. Click on Properties in the resulting connection's Status dialog box.

4. Click on Install, select Service from the Select Network Component Type dialog box (shown in Figure 14.2), and then click on Add.

5. Click on the service you want to install (File And Printer Sharing For Microsoft Networks, QoS Packet Scheduler, or SAP Agent).

6. Click on OK.

After the service is installed, it will appear in the connection's Properties dialog box. A network connection's Properties dialog box, with the common Microsoft triumvirate of networking components installed, is shown in Figure 14.3. Ensure that the checkbox for the service is checked. Complete the installation by closing the open dialog boxes.

Uninstalling any of the services is simple. Just select it from the connection's Properties dialog box and click on Uninstall.

Tip: You will have to reboot the system to make the deletion of the QoS Packet Scheduler or SAP Agent take effect.

Additional services can be installed, but you'll have to provide the required drivers. Select Have Disk during the fourth step when installing services that are not provided by default.

Figure 14.2
You add protocols, services, and clients by using the Select Network Component Type dialog box.

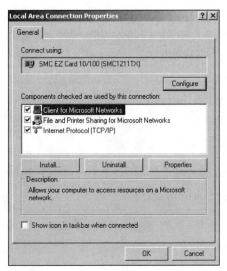

14

Figure 14.3
Network clients, services, and protocols are installed, uninstalled, and configured from a connection's Properties dialog box.

Installing Network Clients

Windows 2000 Professional supports a pair of network clients, by default. They are Client for Microsoft Networks, used to connect to Microsoft servers, and Client Service for NetWare, which is used to connect to NetWare servers. Do not let the name fool you, though; Client Service for NetWare is, indeed, a client component.

Installing Client for Microsoft Networks

Clients are installed similarly to services in Windows 2000 Professional. Follow these steps to install Client for Microsoft Networks:

1. Click on Start|Settings|Network And Dial-up Connections.

2. Select the local area connection where you wish to install Client for Microsoft Networks.

3. Select Properties from the connection's Status dialog box.

4. Click on Install, select Client from the Select Network Component Type dialog box, and then click on Add.

5. Select Client For Microsoft Networks.

6. Click on OK.

The new client will appear in the connection's Properties dialog box. Ensure that the box for the service is checked. Then, complete the installation by closing the open dialog boxes.

Removing the client is easy. Just highlight it on the General tab of the connection's Properties dialog box and click on Uninstall. You will have to confirm the uninstall action and reboot your system before the client will be removed.

Installing Client Service for NetWare

As mentioned in the preceding section, clients are installed similarly to services in Windows 2000 Professional. You can follow these steps to install Client Service for NetWare:

1. Click on Start|Settings|Network And Dial-up Connections.

2. Select the local area connection where you wish to install Client Service for NetWare.

3. Select Properties from the connection's Status dialog box.

4. Click on Install, select Client from the Select Network Component Type dialog box, and then click on Add.

5. Select Client Service for NetWare.

6. Click on OK.

The new NetWare client will appear in the connection's Properties dialog box. Ensure that the checkbox for the service is enabled.

The Select NetWare Logon box will appear after the client is loaded. You will have to provide the following:

• The name of the preferred server

• A default tree and context, should you wish to use them

• Whether a login script is to be run

After you provide the necessary information required by your NetWare servers, close the open dialog boxes. You will need to reboot the system to complete the installation.

To remove the client, highlight it on the General tab of the connection's Properties dialog box and click on Uninstall. You will have to confirm the uninstall action and reboot your system before the client will be removed.

Additional clients can be installed, but you'll have to provide the required drivers. Select Have Disk during the fourth step when installing clients that are not provided by default.

Installing Protocols

Windows 2000 Professional supports the following protocols by default:

• Internet Protocol (TCP/IP)

• NetBIOS Extended User Interface (NetBEUI)

• NWLink

• AppleTalk

- Data Link Control (DLC)

- Network Monitor Driver

Installing Internet Protocol (TCP/IP)

The Internet Protocol (TCP/IP) is by far the most commonly used protocol. In addition to being routable, it supports organizations of all sizes equally well. Follow these steps if you must manually add TCP/IP:

1. Click on Start|Settings|Network And Dial-up Connections.

2. Select the local area connection where you wish to install the protocol.

3. Select Properties from the connection's Status dialog box.

4. Click on Install, select Protocol from the Select Network Component Type dialog box, and then click on Add.

5. Select Internet Protocol (TCP/IP).

6. Click on OK.

14

In default Internet Protocol (TCP/IP) installations, the protocol is configured to receive an IP address and other configuration settings automatically. Internet Protocol (TCP/IP) uses Dynamic Host Configuration Protocol (DHCP) to obtain IP address, subnet mask, default gateway, and Domain Name Service (DNS) settings from a server.

If a network has a server available to provide these settings, no rebooting is required. The protocol will broadcast its request for these settings. A server running DHCP will answer the request and send back necessary IP addressing information, thereby enabling network access on the client machine.

Uninstalling Internet Protocol (TCP/IP) is simple. Highlight the protocol in the window labeled Components Checked Are Used By This Connection on the General tab of the connection's Properties dialog box. Click on Uninstall and confirm that you wish to remove the protocol. Remember, you will need to reboot the system to complete the deletion of Internet Protocol (TCP/IP).

Note: Later in this chapter, we will explore manual configuration of Internet Protocol (TCP/IP).

Installing NetBEUI

NetBEUI is a small, fast, and efficient protocol. Although it is not routable, it is a broadcast-based protocol. Therefore, it is not well suited for medium or large enterprises or an environment in which routing is required.

The odds are you will not use NetBEUI in new network deployments. Rather, most future NetBEUI installations are likely to arise when you're replacing machines or adding new systems in an existing LAN that is already using NetBEUI.

NetBEUI is installed just like Internet Protocol (TCP/IP). Just follow these steps:

1. Click on Start|Settings|Network And Dial-up Connections.

2. Select the local area connection where you wish to install the protocol.

3. Select Properties from the connection's Status dialog box.

4. Click on Install, select Protocol from the Select Network Component Type dialog box, and then click on Add.

5. Select NetBEUI Protocol.

6. Click on OK.

NetBEUI will appear as installed. Ensure that the checkbox for the protocol is enabled and close any open dialog boxes.

To remove NetBEUI from your system, highlight NetBEUI on the General tab in a connection's Properties dialog box. Click on Uninstall and confirm you wish to remove the protocol.

Installing NWLink

Another supported protocol in Windows 2000 Professional is NWLink, which is labeled NWLink IPX/SPX/NetBIOS Compatible Transport Protocol in Windows 2000 Professional. This protocol is Microsoft's version of the Internetwork Packet Exchange/Sequenced Packet Exchange (IPX/SPX) protocols used by Novell systems.

When the NWLink IPX/SPX/NetBIOS Compatible Transport Protocol is installed, Windows 2000 Professional systems running it can communicate with NetWare systems running IPX/SPX. NWLink also permits NetWare systems to access resources on Windows 2000 networks.

NWLink is installed in the same manner as Internet Protocol (TCP/IP):

1. Click on Start|Settings|Network And Dial-up Connections.

2. Select the local area connection where you wish to install the protocol.

3. Select Properties from the connection's Status dialog box.

4. Click on Install, select Protocol from the Select Network Component Type dialog box, and then click on Add.

5. Select NWLink IPX/SPX/NetBIOS Compatible Transport Protocol.

6. Click on OK.

To remove the protocol, highlight it on the connection's Properties dialog box and click on Uninstall. You will have to reboot the system to make the deletion take effect.

Installing AppleTalk

Apple computers communicate on Ethernet networks using AppleTalk, which is known for being "chatty," or generating excessive network traffic. The Windows 2000 Professional AppleTalk protocol permits Windows 2000 Professional machines to access resources on Apple Macintosh systems. Regardless of the organization you work for, it always seems there's at least one user that insists on using a Macintosh system, thereby necessitating additional work on your part. Generally, you'll find such staffers in the marketing and graphics departments.

Note: A Windows 2000 Server running Windows 2000 Services for Macintosh must be present on the network when you're using AppleTalk on Windows 2000 Professional.

AppleTalk is installed and deleted using the same steps as other protocols:

1. Click on Start|Settings|Network And Dial-up Connections.

2. Select the local area connection where you wish to install the protocol.

3. Select Properties from the connection's Status dialog box.

4. Click on Install, select Protocol from the Select Network Component Type dialog box, and then click on Add.

5. Select AppleTalk Protocol.

6. Click on OK.

AppleTalk is easily deleted. Highlight it on the General tab of a connection's Properties dialog box and click on Uninstall. After you confirm that you wish to delete the protocol, you will have to reboot the system to make the change take effect.

Installing DLC

Data Link Control (DLC) is a nonroutable protocol. Thus, it cannot be used for WAN applications and it isn't used to enable communication between systems. However, DLC plays an important role when you're connecting many Hewlett-Packard printers to a network. DLC is mostly used on Windows 2000 Professional machines to enable them to communicate with mainframe computers.

Tip: DLC, like any protocol, should be used only when necessary. The more protocols installed on a system, the slower the system may respond to and return network requests.

Follow these steps to install the DLC protocol:

1. Click on Start|Settings|Network And Dial-up Connections.

2. Select the local area connection where you wish to install the protocol.

3. Select Properties from the connection's Status dialog box.

4. Click on Install, select Protocol from the Select Network Component Type dialog box, and then click on Add.

5. Select DLC Protocol.

6. Click on OK.

Delete DLC by selecting it on the General tab of a connection's Properties dialog box and clicking on Uninstall. Then, confirm you wish to delete the protocol.

Installing the Network Monitor Driver

Windows 2000 Professional also supports the Network Monitor Driver, which is used to enable the collection of network-related statistics for a system. It works by monitoring the activity of a system's NICs. You can read the statistics the Network Monitor Driver collects by using the Network Monitor Agent Service. You also can review the network statistics by using the Systems Management Server (SMS) and Network Monitor.

Note: *For more information on Windows 2000 Professional system monitoring, see Chapter 15.*

You install the Network Monitor Driver by following the same steps used for any other protocol:

1. Click on Start|Settings|Network And Dial-up Connections.

2. Select the local area connection where you wish to install the protocol.

3. Select Properties from the connection's Status dialog box.

4. Click on Install, select Protocol from the Select Network Component Type dialog box, and then click on Add.

5. Select Network Monitor Driver.

6. Click on OK.

You delete the Network Monitor Driver by following the same steps used to remove any other protocol. Just highlight it on the General tab of a connection's Properties dialog box and select Uninstall.

Additional protocols can be installed, but you'll have to provide the required drivers. Select Have Disk during the fourth step when installing protocols that are not provided by default.

Understanding and Configuring Network Bindings

After your networking components are installed, you must determine how to configure network bindings. Protocols are linked with NIC drivers in a process called *binding*. Multiple protocols can be bound to the same NIC. A single protocol can also be bound to multiple NICs. All the network components that work together with a NIC are referred to as a *protocol stack*.

At the lowest binding level is the network adapter card, which physically passes data packets onto the network. The highest binding level is reached when data is passed to workstation or server services. A system's different protocols and the NIC's driver work between those binding layers to ensure proper network communications. The Transport Device Interface (TDI) layer, meanwhile, helps protocols communicate properly with file system drivers.

The NIC works closely with its software drivers, as shown in Figure 14.4. These drivers must meet the Network Device Interface Specifications (NDIS) standard. Windows 2000 Professional works to bind all networking components properly and relies upon NDIS version 5–compliant minidrivers to ensure trouble-free communications.

Network connection bindings are easily viewed and configured. You can view a Windows 2000 Professional system's binding order by following these steps:

1. Right-click on My Network Places and click on Properties.

2. Click on Advanced from the Network And Dial-up Connections menu bar.

3. Select Advanced Settings.

14

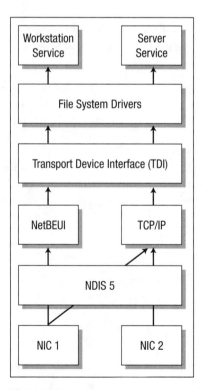

Figure 14.4
Network communication requires a carefully orchestrated dance between several different component layers, and protocols can be bound to more than a single interface, as shown.

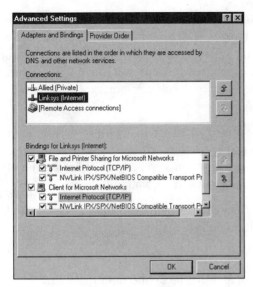

Figure 14.5
Windows 2000 Professional lists binding order information for each configured network connection.

Binding information is displayed on the Adapters And Bindings tab in the window labeled Bindings For *local area connection*, as shown in Figure 14.5. You can highlight a NIC in the Connections window to display its binding information.

Protocol bindings are listed for each installed client and service. If the checkbox next to a protocol is checked, it means the protocol is bound to that NIC. Check the box to bind a protocol to the network adapter. Uncheck a protocol's box to unbind it from the NIC.

You can adjust the binding order by highlighting a protocol that is listed under a client and clicking on the up or down arrows to change the order. Because Windows 2000 Professional tries the protocol listed first when establishing network connections, the most often-used protocol should be placed at the top. The least-used protocol should be placed at the bottom of the binding order.

Configuring Network Connections

Windows 2000 Professional supports several types of network connections. All the following can be configured on Windows 2000 Professional systems:

- Local area network connections

- Private network dial-up connections

- Dial-up Internet connections

- Virtual private networks

- Inbound connections

- Direct computer links

LAN connections are the most often-configured network type in an enterprise, so let's explore LAN implementations first.

Using LAN Connections

The two types of LAN implementations are workgroups and domains. In workgroups, of course, client systems connect to one another. Each client provides both server and client services, sharing its own resources with other systems. In domain environments, clients connect to servers that share resources, authenticate clients, and provide other services.

When Windows 2000 Professional is installed, the setup program asks whether the system will be joining a workgroup or domain. The information necessary to complete each configuration is different.

When joining a workgroup, you must provide the workgroup's name and a full computer name. When joining a domain, you must also provide a full computer name in addition to the domain name. When you're joining a Windows 2000–powered domain, a computer account must also have been added in Active Directory. If the computer account is not created first, administrator permissions will be required to create the computer account when you attempt to join the domain.

14

You check a system's configuration by right-clicking on My Network Places, selecting Properties, and clicking on Network Identification from the Advanced menu of the Network And Dial-up Connections box. The Network Identification tab, shown in Figure 14.6, will list the system's computer name and its workgroup or domain membership information.

You use the Network Identification Wizard, accessed by clicking on the Network ID button on the Network Identification tab, to change a system's network membership.

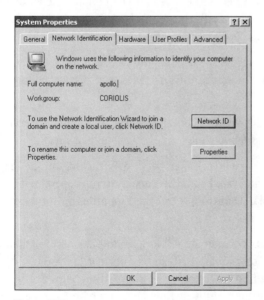

Figure 14.6
You use the Network Identification tab to view and edit a system's network membership.

Using the Network Identification Wizard, you can connect a computer to a network or change its network settings, while also adding a new user to a domain. Follow these steps to change a computer's network membership and add a new user to a domain:

1. On the Welcome To The Network Identification Wizard screen, click on Next.

2. Specify whether the computer is part of a business network or used at home and select Next. In this example, we will specify that the system is connected to other computers at work.

3. Specify whether the company network uses a domain and click on Next. In this example, we will select the radio button labeled My Company Uses A Network With A Domain.

4. The wizard's next screen recommends that you have the username, password, and user account domain on hand because that information is required to complete the following steps. The wizard also recommends that you have the computer name and computer domain information ready. Click on Next.

5. Provide a valid username, the user's password, and the domain name. Then, click on Next.

6. Provide the computer name and computer domain. Click on Next.

7. The wizard will request the name and password of an account that possesses the necessary permissions to join the system to the domain (if the account being added does not possess those permissions). Provide the account information and click on OK.

8. If the user does not exist in the domain, the wizard will provide a screen permitting you to add the user to the domain. Select either the Add The Following User or Do Not Add A User At This Time radio button. In this example, we will select the Add The Following User button and click on Next.

9. The wizard will ask which level of access the user should be provided. Specify either Standard User, Restricted User, or Other. For this example, we will select Standard User. Then, click on Next.

10. A screen will appear confirming the wizard's completion. Click on Finish to complete the operation. The system must be rebooted for the changes to take effect.

You can also manually change a system's network membership by clicking on the Properties button on the Network Identification tab. From the same System Properties dialog box from which you select the Network ID button, select the Properties button to open the Identification Changes dialog box, shown in Figure 14.7.

Change the computer name and update the domain or workgroup information and then click on OK. Should you wish to provide primary DNS suffix information, you can do so by clicking on the More button. Providing additional DNS information helps the system resolve host names being searched without a fully qualified domain name, such as

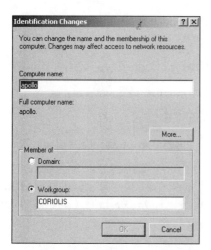

Figure 14.7
You use the Identification Changes dialog box to change a system's network membership.

14

www.microsoft.com. There is also an option to configure Dynamic DNS (DDNS). You should check the Register This Connection's Addresses In DNS box if you wish to configure the client system to participate in dynamic DNS updates.

Be sure to check the Change Primary DNS Suffix When Domain Membership Changes box if you wish to update the primary DNS suffix settings when the domain membership changes. Clicking on the More button on the Identification Changes dialog box also reveals a system's NetBIOS name.

Windows 2000 Professional boasts another networking wizard. The Network Connection Wizard creates different network connections. We will examine its capability to create dial-up connections first.

Creating and Configuring Dial-up Connections

Although the popularity of broadband Internet connectivity is growing quickly, and although such connections are usually configured as VPN links, more corporate users than you can count still rely on 56Kbps modems to dial connections to their corporate networks or Internet service providers (ISPs). Thus, as an IT professional administering Windows 2000 Professional systems, you must be familiar with the ins and outs of configuring dial-up connections.

Two types of dial-up connections can be configured: private network dial-up connections and Internet dial-up connections.

Dialing Up to a Private Network

You can select the Dial-Up To Private Network option on the Network Connection Wizard if you wish to use your modem or ISDN line to connect to a private or corporate network. Follow these steps to create such an outbound connection:

1. Click on Start|Settings|Network And Dial-up Connections and select Make New Connection.

2. When the welcome screen appears for the Network Connection Wizard, click on Next.

3. Select Dial-up To Private Network, as shown in Figure 14.8, and click on Next.

4. Enter the telephone number the modem should dial and select Next.

5. Specify whether the connection is to be used only by the current user logged in or by all of a system's users; then select Next.

6. Provide a name for the dial-up connection. Check the Add A Shortcut To My Desktop box if you want a shortcut to be created on your system's desktop. Click on Finish to complete the installation.

You dial the connection by double-clicking on its shortcut. Alternatively, you can select the connection by clicking on Start|Settings|Network And Dial-up Connections and selecting it from the available connections that appear.

Configuring a Private Network Dial-up Connection

When the connection is executed, the Connect *Connection Name* dialog box appears. (The dialog box displays the connection name in its title bar in place of *Connection Name*.) The username, password, and telephone number to be dialed appear. This dialog box also has a checkbox you can select to save the password so that you don't have to enter it each time the connection is used.

You can configure several settings for a private network dial-up connection. Click on the Properties button in the Connect *Connection Name* dialog box to access configurable settings, which reveals these five tabs:

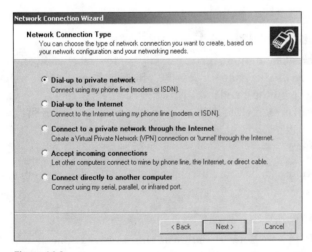

Figure 14.8
You use Windows 2000 Professional's Network Connection Wizard to create network connections.

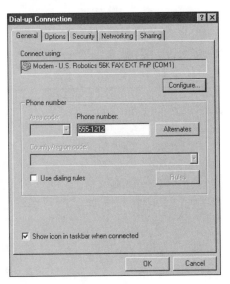

Figure 14.9
You use the General tab from a dial-up connection's dialog box to configure modem and telephone number settings.

- *General*—You use the General tab, shown in Figure 14.9, to select the modem the connection should use. On the General tab, you can also provide the telephone number the connection should dial. Also on the General tab is a checkbox that, when selected, results in an icon appearing in the system tray when the connection is in use. You also specify that dialing rules be used on the General tab.

- *Options*—On the Options tab, you can specify that display progress be shown when connecting, that the connection should prompt the user for a username and other account information, whether Windows domain information should be passed to the system being called, and whether the connection should prompt the user for a telephone number to dial. You also use the Options tab to specify redialing options and X.25 settings, as shown in Figure 14.10.

- *Security*—On the Security tab, shown in Figure 14.11, you can specify whether Typical or Advanced security options are to be used. In the drop-down box, you can specify how a user's identity should be validated. Available options include allowing an unsecured password, requiring a secure password, or using a smart card. Interactive logon and scripting settings are also configured from the Security tab. You also can specify several advanced security settings if you select Advanced Security Options. These settings include the use of the following:

  - Extensible Authentication Protocol (EAP)

  - Unencrypted passwords (PAP)

  - Shiva Password Authentication Protocol (SPAP)

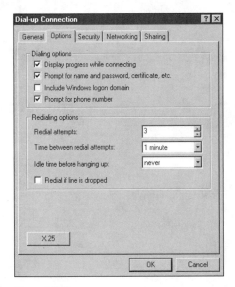

Figure 14.10
You configure dialing, redialing, and X.25 options from the Options tab of a dial-up connection's Properties dialog box.

- Challenge Handshake Authentication Protocol (CHAP)

- Microsoft CHAP (MS-CHAP)

From the Advanced Security Settings dialog box, which you accessed by specifying that Advanced security options be used, you can specify that the user's Windows logon name, password, and domain be used automatically when using MS-CHAP protocols and data encryption settings.

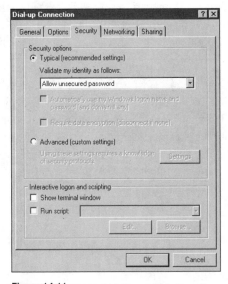

Figure 14.11
You configure security options for dial-up connections from the Security tab.

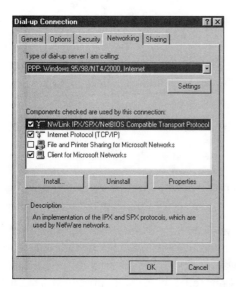

Figure 14.12
The Networking tab houses network component and dial-up server settings.

14

- *Networking*—On the Networking tab, shown in Figure 14.12, you can specify the type of dial-up server to be called. The options include PPP, Windows 95/98/NT4/2000, Internet, or SLIP/Unix Connection. Also, on this Networking tab, you can specify and edit the networking components used by the connection.

- *Sharing*—Internet Connection Sharing (ICS) settings are configured from the Sharing tab. This tab also has an option for enabling on-demand dialing, which permits a system to automatically dial another system to connect to external resources. Check the box if you want the dial-up connection to dial the external network when other systems require access to remotely located resources. More information on ICS is provided later in this chapter.

Dialing Up to the Internet

Often, you need to create Internet dial-up connections. Follow these steps to create connections to ISPs:

1. Click on Start|Settings|Network And Dial-up Connections and select Make New Connection.

2. When the welcome screen appears for the Network Connection Wizard, click on Next.

3. Select Dial-up To The Internet and click on Next.

4. The Internet Connection Wizard will appear. Three options are presented:

    - Sign up for a new Internet account

    - Transfer an existing Internet account

    - Set up an Internet connection manually by using a LAN connection

Select the first option because we are creating a dial-up connection to the Internet and click on Next.

5. The Internet Connection Wizard will provide a list of telephone numbers for connecting to the Microsoft Internet Referral Service in your area. Select a number and click on Next.

6. The modem will dial the Microsoft Internet Referral Service. Follow the prompts you are presented to create an Internet account and complete the creation of the Internet dial-up connection.

If a client system is to use a preexisting Internet account, select the second or third option in the fourth step. Then, follow the prompts the Internet Connection Wizard provides.

Most likely, a Windows 2000 Professional system will be operating in a LAN environment. In such cases, you should select the third option (I Want To Set Up My Internet Connection Manually or I Want To Connect Through A Local Area Network) in the fourth step. When this option is selected, the Internet Connection Wizard will prompt you for additional information. You will be asked to specify whether the system is connecting through a phone line or modem or through a LAN. You will also be prompted to specify whether a proxy server should be discovered automatically, an automatic configuration script should be used, or whether a manual proxy server exists. The last option the Internet Connection Wizard will present you is the opportunity to create an Internet mail account.

Internet dial-up connections are configured in the same manner as private network connections. Just select the connection, open its Properties tab, and configure the settings as necessary.

Creating and Configuring Virtual Private Networking

Increasingly, virtual private networks (VPNs) are being used to connect remote workers to corporate networks. VPNs add a measure of security by creating a secure tunnel for data packets to travel through when traversing the public Internet.

Follow these steps to create a VPN connection:

1. Click on Start|Settings|Network And Dial-up Connections and select Make New Connection.

2. When the welcome screen appears for the Network Connection Wizard, click on Next.

3. Select Connect To A Private Network Through The Internet and click on Next.

4. Specify whether Windows 2000 Professional should dial an initial connection. You should elect to dial the initial connection when the VPN will rely on a dial-up connection. If you wish to dial an initial connection and more than one exists, specify which connection should be dialed. Then, click on Next.

5. Specify the host name (such as **www.coriolis.com**) or IP address (such as 38.187.128.45) of the computer or network that you wish to connect with using the VPN. Click on Next.

6. Specify whether the connection is to be used only by the user currently logged in or all users. Then, click on Next.

7. The Completing The Network Connection Wizard confirmation screen will appear. Provide a name for the VPN connection you are creating, check the Add A Shortcut To My Desktop box if you wish to create a shortcut, and then click on Finish.

You connect to the private network using the VPN by double-clicking on the VPN's shortcut. Alternatively, you can access the VPN connection by clicking on Start|Settings| Network And Dial-up Connections and selecting the respective VPN. The Connect *VPN Name* screen will appear. Click on Connect to execute the connection.

VPN connections are configured in the same manner as private network and Internet dial-up connections. Just select the connection, open its Properties tab, and configure the settings.

You will find most VPN connection Properties settings identical to those found in private network and Internet dial-up connections. However, a few differences should be noted. The most important is located on the General tab, where, instead of selecting a modem or phone number to be dialed, you can edit the host name or IP address of the destination system. Another difference is the omission of the Prompt For Phone Number checkbox located on the Options tab.

14

Creating and Configuring Inbound Connections

Windows 2000 Professional systems can be configured to accept inbound connections. In such cases, the Windows 2000 Professional system serves as the host machine. Other systems can connect to a Windows 2000 Professional machine using a telephone line, the Internet, or a direct cable connection.

For the next example, we will create an inbound connection arriving from the Internet. Follow these steps to create such a connection:

1. Click on Start|Settings|Network And Dial-up Connections and select Make New Connection.

2. When the welcome screen appears for the Network Connection Wizard, click on Next.

3. Select Accept Incoming Connections and click on Next.

4. Specify which connection devices should be used for the incoming connection. Then, click on Next.

5. Specify whether VPN connections should be permitted. For this example, we will instruct Windows 2000 Professional to accept VPN connections. Click on Next.

6. Select which users should be permitted to connect to the computer using the incoming connection. Callback settings can be configured for each user. Just highlight the respective user and click on the Properties button. When user settings have been set, click on Next.

7. Specify which networking components are to be used by the connection and click on Next.

8. When the wizard's final screen appears, provide a name for the new connection and click on Finish to complete the creation of the incoming connection.

With the incoming connection configured, another system can connect to it over the Internet. For the connection to work properly, the remote system's user must possess the appropriate permissions to access the incoming connection. In addition, the remote user must know the system's host name or IP address.

Should you wish to accept inbound connections arriving by telephone or a direct cable connection, select the appropriate connection method during the fourth step above. Keep in mind that you will have to install a modem to accept connections via telephone.

To configure an incoming connection's Properties settings, select the connection by clicking on Start|Settings|Network And Dial-up Connections and clicking on the appropriate incoming connection you wish to edit. The *Connection Name* Properties dialog box appears immediately; it has the following three tabs:

• *General*—Use the General tab to view and edit the devices enabled for the incoming connection. You can also use the General tab to enable VPN connections and display an icon in the system tray when the connection is in use.

• *Users*—Use the Users tab to administer user permissions for the incoming connection. From the Users tab, you can also require that all users secure their passwords and data or that directly connected devices be permitted to connect without providing a password.

• *Networking*—The Networking tab, appropriately enough, configures network settings. You can use the Networking tab to view and edit the networking components that the incoming connection uses.

Creating and Configuring Direct Computer Connections

Occasionally, you may need to link two systems using a direct computer connection. Typically, a cable is attached connecting two systems' parallel or serial ports. Direct Cable Connections (DCCs) are not ideal. Transfer rates are slow, and both machines must be located close to one another (usually in the same room). In addition, only files can be transferred; printers cannot be shared using a DCC.

Parallel cables connecting two systems provide faster transfer rates than two machines with connected serial ports. For serial connections, null modem cables and RS-232 cables are the most popular direct cable connectors. If both systems support infrared ports, an infrared connection can be used, too.

When you're connecting two systems using a DCC, power both systems down before attaching the cables. When the physical connections are completed, power up the machines. Then, follow these steps to host a DCC:

1. Click on Start|Settings|Network And Dial-up Connections and select Make New Connection.

2. When the welcome screen appears for the Network Connection Wizard, click on Next.

3. Select Connect Directly To Another Computer and click on Next.

4. Specify which role the system will play: host or guest. Select Host if other systems will be accessing the system's resources. Select Guest if the system will be contacting another system to obtain resources that the other system is hosting. For this example, select Host and then click on Next.

5. Specify the device the direct connection should use. Then, click on Next.

6. Specify which users should have permissions to connect to the computer. When permissions have been set, click on Next.

7. Provide a name for the incoming connection (as incoming direct connections are called) in the wizard's confirmation screen and click on Finish to complete the process.

14

View and edit the *Incoming Connection Name* Properties by clicking on Start|Settings| Networking And Dial-up Connections and selecting the respective Incoming Connection. You will find the same three tabs for the DCC incoming connection as you do in other incoming connections.

You must also configure a system to act as a guest. Follow the same steps as you would to host a direct cable connection. However, be sure to specify guest instead of host.

You can view and edit DCC guest settings by clicking on Start|Settings|Networking And Dial-up Connections and selecting the respective DCC. Click on Properties from the Connect *Direct Connection Name* dialog box to open a Properties dialog box with these five tabs:

- *General*—Use the General tab to select the device that should be used to complete the connection. Also, on the General tab you can select a checkbox to display an icon in the system tray indicating the connection is in use.

- *Options*—The Options tab displays the same options found for a VPN connection. The other tabs are the same as with VPN connections, with one exception. On the Networking tab, instead of a drop-down box in which you specify the type of VPN server being called, the DCC's drop-down box contains options for specifying the type of dial-up server being contacted.

- *Security*—The information found on the Security tab is identical to that found on the VPN Security tab.

- *Networking*—The information found here is identical to that found on the VPN Networking tab, with the exception that different server options exist.

- *Sharing*—Again, the information found on the Sharing tab is identical to that found on the VPN Sharing tab.

Now that we've completed our discussion of the different network connections the Network Connection Wizard can create, let's examine how to fine-tune the settings for popular protocols, beginning with NWLink.

Configuring NWLink

The NWLink IPX/SPX/NetBIOS Compatible Transport Protocol can power communications between Windows 2000 systems. NWLink is most often used to provide NetWare clients access to resources on a Microsoft network and to provide connectivity for Windows systems on a NetWare network.

After you install the NWLink IPX/SPX/NetBIOS Compatible Transport Protocol, as demonstrated earlier in this chapter, you must configure three components. It is important to remember that the following components must be configured on each NIC that uses NWLink:

- *Frame type*—Determines how a NIC formats data

- *Internal network number*—Provides a unique number that identifies a specific system or virtual network segment

- *Network number*—Identifies the network

You configure these three components from a connection's Properties dialog box. To configure NWLink, just select NWLink IPX/SPX/NetBIOS Compatible Transport Protocol and click on the Properties button.

When you're using NWLink, Windows 2000, by default, autodetects the NWLink frame type the network is using. The client's frame type must match the NetWare server's frame type. Otherwise, Windows 2000 Professional systems may not connect properly to NetWare servers.

NWLink can operate using several frame types. The most popular frame type is 802.2. However, 802.3, Ethernet II, ArcNet, and Sub-Network Access Protocol (SNAP) are also compatible with NWLink. Should Windows 2000 autodetect more than one frame type operating on a network, the operating system defaults to using 802.2.

You can manually specify a frame type. Just follow these directions to view and edit the NWLink frame type:

1. Click on Start|Settings|Network And Dial-up Connections.

2. Select the local area connection for which you wish to adjust the NWLink settings.

3. Highlight NWLink IPX/SPX/NetBIOS Compatible Transport Protocol and click on Properties.

4. Click on the Frame Type drop-down box (shown in Figure 14.13) and select the appropriate frame type.

5. Click on OK and close the open dialog boxes.

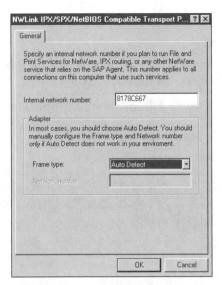

Figure 14.13
You configure NWLink settings from its Properties dialog box.

When you're using NWLink, you also must specify unique network numbers and internal network numbers. Just as with the frame type, Windows 2000 Professional automatically detects the network number in use. However, a unique internal number, set at 00000000 by default, must be supplied for each system when any of the following situations apply:

- File and Print Services for NetWare is in use and a single NIC is supporting multiple frame types.

- File and Print Services for NetWare is in use and multiple NICs use NWLink.

- SAP is in use.

Warning! *The internal network number cannot be all zeros. It must be set to a unique value.*

You change the internal network number and network number by following the same procedure used to adjust the frame type. Instead of configuring the frame type from the NWLink IPX/SPX/NetBIOS Compatible Transport Protocol Properties dialog box, you should supply the appropriate values for the internal network number and network number.

Troubleshooting NWLink

If you experience difficulty configuring NWLink, a few common troubleshooting options are available. You should begin troubleshooting NWLink connections by verifying that the client systems are running the correct frame type. To communicate with any NetWare servers, the frame types must match. Otherwise, connectivity problems will result (unless a NetWare server provides routing services).

By default, NetWare 2.2 and 3.11 use the 802.3 frame type. NetWare 3.12 and later operating systems use the 802.2 frame type.

For each NIC that NWLink is bound to, always remember to ensure that the correct frame type and network number are configured. Such settings are easily verified.

Confirm that NWLink has been bound properly by double-checking a NIC's bindings. Right-click on My Network Places and select Advanced Settings from the Advanced menu. Network connections are displayed in the top window, and connection bindings are displayed in the bottom window.

You can view NWLink's specific settings by editing a connection's NWLink properties. To do so, click on Start|Settings|Network And Dial-up Connections, select the connection you wish to check, highlight NWLink, and click on Properties.

Alternatively, you can open a command window in Windows 2000 Professional and type "ipxroute config". The command triggers the NWLink IPX Routing and Source Routing Control Program, version 2.0. The command lists NIC information, including the network, node, and frame type in use. Figure 14.14 displays a sample **ipxroute config** screen.

Should you experience trouble with NWLink's network number, you can manually specify the network number to be used by editing the Windows 2000 Professional Registry. Two values in the HKEY_LOCAL_MACHINE\SYSTEM\CurrentControlSet\Services\Nwlinkipx\Parameters\Adapters*NIC* Registry key must be adjusted:

- *NetworkNumber*—Lists the network number in hexadecimal format. If a 0 REG_MULTI_SZ value is present, Windows 2000 Professional will autodetect the network number to be used.

- *PktType*—Instructs Windows 2000 Professional on the frame, or packet, type to be used. It, too, uses a REG_MULTI_SZ value. Six values can be provided, as described in Table 14.1. For example, you would enter a REG_MULTI_SZ data type with a value of 2 to specify the use of the 802.2 frame type.

Figure 14.14
The NWLink IPX Routing and Source Routing Control Program provides NWLink configuration information.

Table 14.1   Frame (or packet) types supported by Windows 2000.

Registry Value	Frame Type
0	Ethernet II
1	Ethernet 802.3
2	Ethernet 802.2
3	SNAP
4	ArcNet
FF	Autodetect mode

Configuring TCP/IP

TCP/IP is the most widely used protocol. Entire network infrastructures are designed and built with this protocol in mind. Configuration can be minimal or extensive. The complexity of configuring Windows 2000 Professional connections using TCP/IP ultimately depends on the design of the network the client machine is joining.

Configuring TCP/IP on a Windows 2000 Professional system can be as simple as selecting Typical Settings during installation of the operating system. By default, Windows 2000 Professional tries obtaining an IP address automatically. Using the Dynamic Host Configuration Protocol (DHCP), when booting, so-configured Windows 2000 Professional machines send a packet out on the network requesting an IP address. A DHCP server pulls the packet off the network and, if permissions are properly configured, the server sends back an IP address to be used by the client system.

The DHCP server performs other actions, too. It also serves the client machine with other critical information. The DHCP server provides the addresses of DNS servers, a default gateway for connection to external networks, and a subnet mask (used to help the client system determine whether an address is local or external).

Often, though, you might need to manually enter these network settings. Follow these directions to view and edit a connection's Internet Protocol (TCP/IP) configuration:

1. Click on Start|Settings|Network And Dial-up Connections.

2. Select the local area connection for which you wish to adjust the Internet Protocol (TCP/IP) settings.

3. Highlight Internet Protocol (TCP/IP) and click on Properties. The Internet Protocol (TCP/IP) Properties dialog box will appear.

Four radio buttons appear on the General tab, along with an Advanced button (see Figure 14.15). The first pair of radio buttons specifies whether an IP address should be obtained automatically or whether provided settings should be used.

Select Obtain An IP Address Automatically if you want Windows 2000 Professional to use DHCP services for its addressing information. This is the default setting.

14

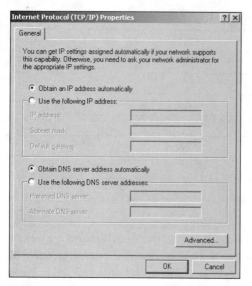

Figure 14.15
On the Internet Protocol (TCP/IP) Properties General tab, you can specify whether an IP address or DNS server address should be obtained automatically.

Select Use The Following IP Address if you wish to manually provide IP addressing information. If this radio button is selected, you must provide the following:

- IP address

- Subnet mask

- Default gateway

The IP address, subnet mask, and default gateway information must be supplied in a dotted-decimal format. For example, addresses must be entered in octets, substituting the appropriate values, like this: 192.168.5.3.

The second set of radio buttons specifies DNS settings. If Windows 2000 Professional should receive the addresses of DNS servers automatically, select the Obtain DNS Server Address Automatically radio button. If you wish to manually specify the DNS servers to be used by the Windows 2000 Professional system, select Use The Following DNS Server Addresses. You must then provide the preferred DNS server address in dotted decimal octet format. You should also provide an alternate DNS server address.

Clicking on the Advanced button opens the Advanced TCP/IP Settings dialog box. You can configure a host of settings on these four tabs. From the IP Settings tab (shown in Figure 14.16), you can add, edit, and remove IP addresses and default gateways. You also can set the interface metric, which is used to set a "cost" for routing data on the network connection. The lower the value, the lower the cost, or number of hops, required for data to reach its ultimate destination. The default setting is 1.

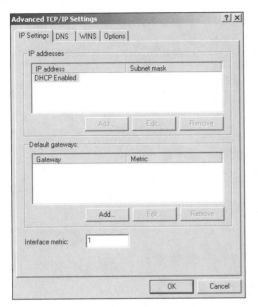

Figure 14.16
On the IP Settings tab, you can add and remove IP addresses and default gateways.

On the DNS tab, as shown in Figure 14.17, you can add, edit, and remove DNS servers. DNS servers, of course, resolve friendly Internet names and addresses, such as **www.microsoft.com**, to dotted-decimal and octet-formatted IP addresses.

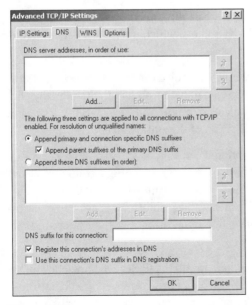

Figure 14.17
You can configure a connection's DNS settings on the DNS tab.

14

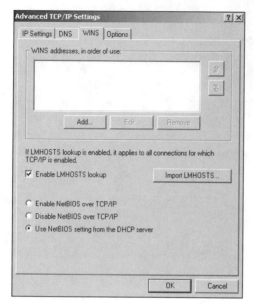

Figure 14.18
Configure WINS settings from the WINS tab.

On the WINS tab (shown in Figure 14.18), you can add, edit, and remove WINS address information. In addition, LMHOSTS lookup settings are configured here, as are NetBIOS over TCP/IP settings. You can enable or disable NetBIOS over TCP/IP or specify that NetBIOS settings be received from the DHCP server.

Remember, NetBIOS by itself is not routable. Enabling NetBIOS over TCP/IP permits encapsulation of NetBIOS traffic in TCP/IP packets, which makes it possible to route NetBIOS traffic.

LMHOSTS files are an older technology used to resolve friendly NetBIOS names to IP addresses. You can import a static LMHOSTS database from another system by clicking on the Import LMHOSTS button. If you elect to import an LMHOSTS file, you can use the resulting dialog box to navigate to the location of the static LMHOSTS file.

You can use the Options tab to specify optional settings, as shown in Figure 14.19. IP Security and TCP/IP filtering are two of the most common options configured from this tab. IP Security enables protection and authenticity verification of IP packets on a network. TCP/IP filtering provides limited firewall capabilities by permitting control of TCP/IP traffic. You configure either option by highlighting it in the Optional Settings window and clicking on Properties.

To configure IP Security (IPSec), for example, highlight IP Security and click on the Properties button. The resulting IP Security dialog box features two radio buttons that specify whether IPSec should be used. You must also specify an IP Security policy to use from these three options:

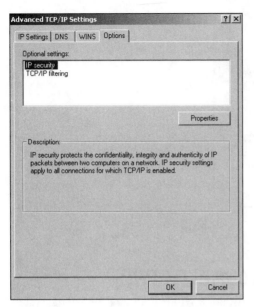

Figure 14.19
You can configure IP Security and TCP/IP filtering on the Options tab.

- *Client (Respond Only)*—Permits unsecured communications; uses the default response rule to communicate with servers that request IP Security

- *Secure Server (Require Security)*—Does not permit unsecured communication with untrusted clients; requires Kerberos security

- *Server (Request Security)*—Always requests Kerberos security for all IP traffic but permits unsecured communications with clients that do not respond to security requests

TCP/IP filtering provides basic firewall capabilities by permitting or denying all or specific TCP and UDP port traffic and IP protocols. You can configure TCP/IP filtering by highlighting TCP/IP Filtering and clicking on the Properties button. Be sure to check the Enable TCP/IP Filtering (All Adapters) box to turn on IP filtering.

Permitting all TCP and UDP port traffic and IP Protocols is the default setting, as shown in Figure 14.20. You can, however, deny specific TCP and UDP port traffic and IP Protocols by selecting the respective Permit Only radio buttons and adding the appropriate TCP and UDP ports and IP Protocols. You can also remove TCP and UDP port and IP Protocol restrictions. If you have opted to restrict traffic in the past, highlight the TCP or UDP port or IP protocol you wish to open to traffic and click Remove.

Note: *For more information on Windows 2000 Professional security, see Chapter 16.*

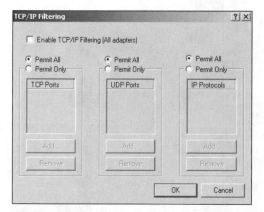

Figure 14.20
You can configure which ports and protocols should be permitted using TCP/IP filtering.

Troubleshooting Internet Protocol (TCP/IP)

If all IP settings appear to be set correctly, but a Windows 2000 Professional system's network connections still fail to operate properly, it is probably time to troubleshoot IP settings. Always check your physical connections first. Disconnected cables—whether unplugged from a NIC or a hub, switch, or router—are often the culprit.

If you have verified that the system's NIC is working properly and all the cable connections are in order, you need to troubleshoot IP settings. There are different schools of thought as to the best approach. Some IT professionals believe it is best to begin testing the destination system, whereas other experts believe you should check the basics first.

We believe it best to begin with the absolute fundamentals. First, verify that your servers, routers, switches, and hubs are all online and that no power interruptions have occurred. It is silly to expend significant time checking client settings if you have not first confirmed that other components on the network are functioning properly.

Tip: Always keep your eyes and ears open. If multiple clients complain of lost network connectivity at the same time, that is an obvious sign the issue does not lie with the client systems but a failed router, DNS server, gateway, switch, or hub.

Find a cable tester. You might have a failed cable connecting the client system. Also, check the NIC to ensure that it is receiving power and is functioning properly.

If your servers are operating normally and you believe the network connectivity problem lies somewhere else, begin troubleshooting by opening a command prompt and typing "ipconfig /all". Figure 14.21 shows sample results returned from an **ipconfig /all** command.

Verify that the Windows 2000 Professional client system is using a correct and valid IP address, subnet mask, and default gateway. Confirm, too, that the DNS server addresses are correct.

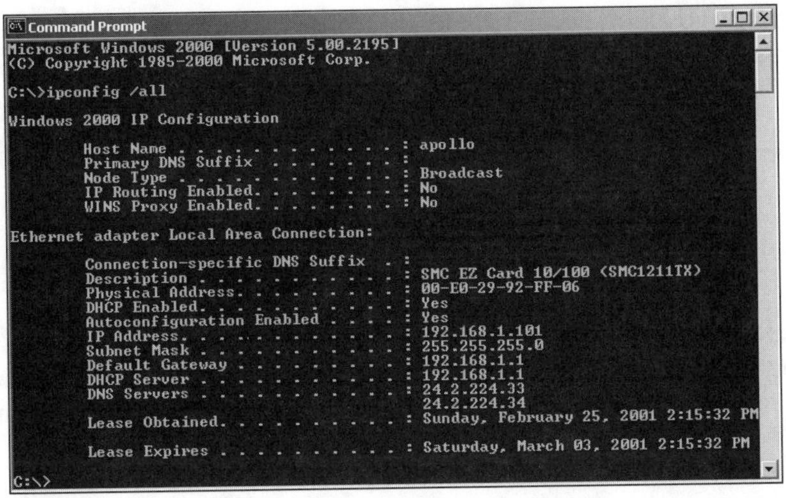

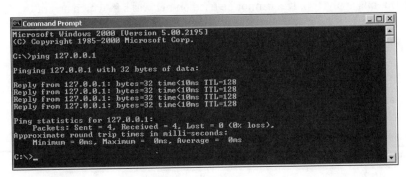

Figure 14.21
You can use the **ipconfig /all** command to view a system's current IP configuration.

Next, check the client system's TCP/IP protocol stack. Use the **ping** command to test your TCP/IP loopback address by opening a command prompt and typing "ping 127.0.0.1". If your local TCP/IP protocol stack is functioning properly, the **ping** statistics that are returned should result in no lost packets and four replies, as shown in Figure 14.22. If errors occur, it is likely that your protocol stack is corrupt. Try reinstalling the protocol to correct the problem.

If the client system passed the loopback test, you should next ping your local machine. Type "ping *w.x.y.z*", where *w.x.y.z* is your local system's IP address. The **ping** command should result in no lost packets and four replies. If it does not, the errors indicate that the network does not recognize your system's address. This is a sign that the client system is using a bad IP address or that a physical connection or hardware device is malfunctioning. Two possible culprits are a bad NIC or patch cable. Try replacing them first.

Figure 14.22
The **ping 127.0.0.1** command should result in no lost packets; otherwise, a problem may exist with the TCP/IP protocol stack.

If you can ping yourself, try pinging the default gateway. If you cannot ping the gateway, it is likely that the gateway has failed. Check to see that it is online and functioning properly. If you can ping the gateway, but you cannot reach an Internet address using its friendly name, such as **www.coriolis.com**, it is likely that the DNS server or servers being used by the Windows 2000 Professional system are not operating properly.

Review Decision Tree 14.1, which lists the steps for troubleshooting TCP/IP issues, if you experience network connectivity issues.

Configuring Internet Connection Sharing

In many organizations, you might need to share IP addresses. Several options are available. You can create a pool of private addresses that your servers provide to client machines. However, if you have Windows 2000 Professional systems deployed in small or remote offices, you have two additional options. You can implement Internet Connection Sharing (ICS), or you can turn to an alternative hardware solution.

ICS permits multiple systems to access external resources using only a single routable Internet IP address. Powered by Network Address Translation (NAT), ICS provides a miniature version of DHCP to other internal systems, which are given private IP addresses.

The Internet Assigned Numbers Authority (IANA) has reserved three IP address ranges for private use. These IP addresses, listed in Table 14.2, are not distributed to companies as routable, public Internet IP addresses. Organizations use these private IP address ranges to conserve the number of routable, public Internet addresses received from the InterNIC.

However, ICS possesses several limitations. It relies on a limited DHCP service, which cannot be further configured. In addition, external systems cannot directly access resources on the systems possessing private addresses. Although some IT professionals may see that as a security benefit, others will see it as a curse. Sharing files and other resources is made difficult, and hosting a Web server on a system possessing a private address is out of the question.

Other restrictions apply, too. ICS cannot be used on networks in which any of the following apply:

• Multiple subnets exist.

• The network possesses DNS or DHCP servers.

• Static IP addresses exist.

Table 14.2   IP address ranges reserved for private use.

Private IP Address Range	Subnet Mask
10.0.0.0 through 10.255.255.255	255.0.0.0
172.16.0.0 through 172.31.255.255	255.240.0.0
192.168.0.0 through 192.168.255.255	255.255.0.0

14

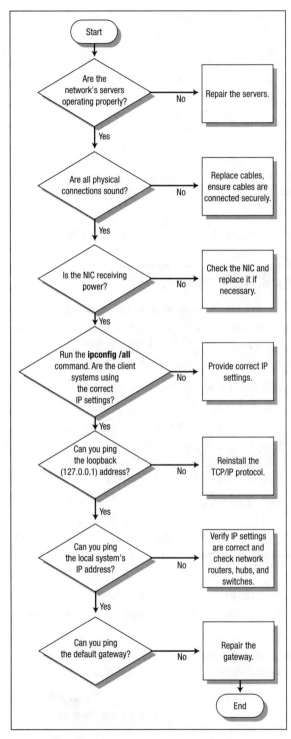

Decision Tree 14.1
Ensure that you approach network connectivity issues in a logical fashion.

For these reasons, ICS is best used only in small offices or home office environments. In some cases, ICS may work well in branch locations, too.

To be able to run ICS, at least one system on the network must have Internet connectivity and a routable Internet address (not a private address). The same system must also possess two NICs. One network adapter will be used for the external network connection to the Internet; the other NIC will connect to the internal network.

The host system, or the machine with both NICs, uses NAT to provide address translation services. The host system extends DHCP services (albeit in miniature form) to other clients on the network, providing them with a subnet mask, DNS proxy services, and an IP address in the 192.168.*x*.*y* range.

The host system routes external network requests received on the internal-homed NIC out to the external network via the external-homed NIC. When responses to the internal

Understanding Network Address Translation

NAT's strength is its capability to provide IP address translation services for multiple machines using just a single public (and routable) Internet IP address. Using a single Internet IP address, a system running NAT can provide DHCP, DNS, WINS, and proxy services to 253 other systems. NAT works by distributing IP addresses from the 192.168.*x*.*y* address range and using a miniature version of DHCP.

The following three components are responsible for NAT's capability to share addresses and provide translation services:

- *Addressing*—A system running NAT provides DHCP and DNS services to internal network systems. When an internal machine configured to use DHCP logs on, the NAT computer answers its DHCP request by serving up a private IP address in the 192.168.0.2 to 192.168.0.254 range, a 255.255.255.0 subnet mask, the default gateway's address, and a DNS server address.

- *Name resolution*—The system hosting NAT becomes the internal network's DNS server. Internal systems send the NAT host their name resolution requests. The NAT system forwards name resolution requests to the real DNS server, receives a response from the real DNS server, and then passes the real response to the internal machine with the private network address that instigated the name resolution request.

- *Translation*—The system hosting NAT serves as a network translator. The NAT host receives and translates IP addresses and TCP and UDP port numbers of the data packets the internal systems send between themselves and external resources.

Although NAT can translate common protocols, it has limitations. NAT works with FTP, TCP/IP, NetBIOS over TCP/IP, PPTP, UDP, and some other protocols. However, it cannot translate IPSec or Kerberos data traffic.

NAT can also be used by itself, without Internet Connection Sharing, to share IP addresses on a network. However, a Windows 2000 server is required because additional routing capabilities are needed for proper network communications.

network requests are received, the host system routes the responses received from the external network to the requesting client.

Follow these steps to enable ICS:

1. Click on Start|Settings|Network And Dial-up Connections.

2. Select the internal network connection through which you want other local network systems to access external resources.

3. Click on Properties.

4. Click on the Sharing tab (shown in Figure 14.23).

5. Check the box labeled Enable Internet Connection Sharing For This Connection.

6. Click on OK and then confirm that you wish to change the LAN adapter's address and enable Internet Connection Sharing.

7. Click on Close.

For each client system that will share the connection you just configured, configure each client connection to automatically obtain an IP address.

When you execute the preceding steps, Windows 2000 Professional performs several actions. First, it changes the IP address for the NIC from its current setting to 192.168.0.1. This system becomes the host, with a subnet mask of 255.255.255.0.

The external NIC is enabled, and a static route of 0.0.0.0, which points to the external NIC, is added to the system's routing table. Systems on the internal network that request an IP

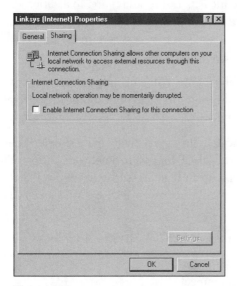

Figure 14.23
You can configure ICS on the Sharing tab, which you access through a network connection's Properties dialog box.

address are given an address in the 192.168.0.2 through 192.168.0.254 range, with a subnet mask of 255.255.255.0. The IP address 192.168.0.1 is assigned proxy services responsibilities.

When ICS is enabled, you can configure several settings by clicking on the Settings button on the connection's Sharing tab. The resulting Internet Connection Sharing Settings dialog box has two tabs: Applications and Services. On the Applications tab, you specify the applications to be enabled for systems that share the Internet connection. On the Services tab, you specify which services should be provided to the external network. Options include the following:

- FTP Server

- Internet Mail Server (SMTP)

- Post Office Protocol (POP) version 3

Alternatives to ICS are available for sharing IP addresses. However, instead of relying on a software solution, you may wish to consider a hardware answer.

Using Alternative Hardware Solutions

Many small or remote offices have discovered the benefits of alternative hardware solutions to meet the challenges of sharing network connections. Several companies have introduced relatively inexpensive hardware devices that perform address translation tasks, while also adding the benefits of switching, firewall services, and routing capabilities.

Often referred to as Ethernet or broadband routers, peripherals from companies such as Cisco, Linksys, SMC, and others provide 100Mbps switching, firewall and proxy services, the capability to configure routing for specific data traffic, and more. In addition to permitting a single IP address to be shared with as many as 253 other systems, these devices provide a secure method for external systems to access resources on machines configured with internal or private IP addresses.

These broadband routers also provide other benefits. While helping protect systems from vulnerabilities that inevitably arise with always-on Internet connections, they also provide internal machines with DHCP and DNS services.

Although these devices may sound complicated, they are actually quite simple. When a client system that has been configured to use DHCP logs on to a network, the broadband router answers the DHCP request by serving up an IP address (usually in the 192.168.0.2 through 192.168.0.254 range), a subnet mask, the address of a DNS server, and a default gateway address.

Several such devices are available, most for less than $200. Here's a short list of current models:

- 3Com Home Internet Gateway and OfficeConnect Routers

- Allied Telesyn Cable/DSL Routers

- Cisco SOHO Series Routers

- Equinox Internet Broadband Gateways

- Farallon NetLINE Broadband Gateways

- Linksys Broadband EtherFast Cable/DSL Routers

- NetGear Fast Internet Access Cable/DSL Routers

- Netopia R-Series Routers

- SMC Networks Barricade Cable/DSL/ISDN Routers

Summary

True computing power results when systems connect to one another. This is true whether they are in the same room or across the globe. The OSI model helps ensure that different systems can share information efficiently.

Windows 2000 Professional further simplifies the networking process with the inclusion of new wizards and administrative interfaces. You will find support for new protocols, enhanced network configuration, and strengthened security features when you're networking systems powered by Windows 2000 Professional.

Whether you need to create dial-up accounts, configure VPN links, accept incoming connections, or share Internet addresses, Windows 2000 Professional provides wizards and interfaces that can power such connections and more. Windows 2000 Professional also works well with alternative hardware solutions that help expand networking capabilities.

Of course, networks do not always run smoothly, so we reviewed the many configuration settings for different protocols, network connection types, and services and clients that Windows 2000 Professional supports. Sometimes you need to troubleshoot networking issues, as well. Although you should always check physical network connections first, as an IT professional, you must be able to identify common client networking issues and know how to solve them quickly.

When connectivity errors arise, first ensure that a client system is configured with the proper address information. If a Windows 2000 Professional system has correct IP address information yet still experiences trouble connecting to other resources, try pinging the local machine and then the default gateway. By following an organized troubleshooting tree, you should quickly be able to determine the culprit plaguing the network.

When you have a network operational and running smoothly, you will want to ensure that it continues performing well. The first step in maintaining a network's performance is the establishment of a baseline for standard performance. When the baseline is determined, the network should be monitored to ensure that it is performing properly. In the next chapter, we will examine Windows 2000 Professional monitoring and optimization.

Chapter 15

Monitoring and Optimization

Monitoring and Optimizing Windows 2000 Professional

All computer systems require constant monitoring and continuous management of tasks and resources. Windows 2000 Professional is no exception. However, it provides numerous tools to assist you in the management of your tasks and resources, as well as tools to monitor and maintain an optimized environment. An optimized operating system will improve both efficiency and productivity in your Windows 2000 Professional environment.

Numerous options are available to assist you in managing, optimizing, and troubleshooting the Windows 2000 Professional operating system. These tools include driver signing, task scheduling, hardware profiles, event logs, and the Disk Management utility.

Ensuring that you only install recognized (safe) files, perform regularly scheduled maintenance tasks, optimize your hard drives, and monitor your Windows 2000 Professional environment will help you to create and maintain an optimized and stable Windows 2000 Professional configuration. To ensure system functionality, one of the first things you should do is verify that the files and drivers you add are not going to wreak havoc in your Windows 2000 environment.

Ensuring Stable Files in Windows 2000 Professional

You need to be sure that you have a stable Windows 2000 Professional environment. A stable environment is one that is constantly available and is minimally affected by incompatible or incorrect hardware, software, or device drivers. A device driver, commonly referred to as a *driver,* is a program that allows a specific device, such as a printer, network card, or modem, to communicate with Windows 2000 Professional. For example, without serial port drivers, Network Connections cannot use a modem to connect to a network.

Although a hardware device may be installed on your system, Windows 2000 cannot use that device until you have installed and configured the appropriate driver. If a device is listed in the Hardware Compatibility List (HCL), a driver is usually included with Windows 2000. Your device drivers load automatically (for all enabled devices) when your computer is started and thereafter run invisibly to you.

Code Signing in Windows 2000

Drivers are very powerful, so if the wrong one is loaded, it may render your system—or at least the component associated with the driver—unusable. Windows 2000 introduces a new feature called *code signing* that provides the capability to ensure that a correct and safe driver is being loaded, using a digital signature by Microsoft. Furthermore, code signing verifies that your operating system files have been digitally signed by Microsoft to ensure their quality. Verifying signatures can help reduce the risk of an incorrect driver or operating system file corrupting your Windows 2000 Professional operating system.

A Microsoft digital signature provides you with assurance and ease of mind that a specific file has met a certain level of testing and that the file has not been modified or overwritten by another program's installation process.

Setting File Signature Verification Options

Depending on how your computer is configured, Windows 2000 either ignores device drivers that do not contain a digital signature; displays a warning when it detects device drivers that are not digitally signed, which is the default; or prevents you from installing device drivers that do not contain a digital signature.

To set the file signature verification options, follow these steps:

1. Click on Start|Settings|Control Panel. After opening Control Panel, click on the System applet.

2. Click on the Hardware tab and then click on the Driver Signing button to open the Driver Signing Options dialog box, as shown in Figure 15.1.

3. Under File Signature Verification, choose one of the following options:

   - *Ignore*—Installs all device drivers on the computer, regardless of whether they have a digital signature

   - *Warn*—Displays a warning message when an installation program attempts to install a device driver that does not contain a digital signature

   - *Block*—Prevents an installation program from installing device drivers without a digital signature

Tip: If you are logged on as a member of the Administrators group or as the administrator, you can click on Apply Setting As System Default to apply the selected setting as the default for all users who log on to the computer.

Windows 2000 Professional includes three features to ensure that your device drivers and system files remain in their original, digitally signed state:

- Windows File Protection

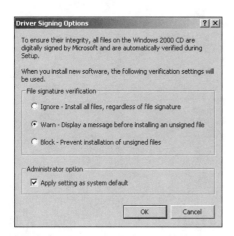

Figure 15.1
Setting the file signature verification options.

- System File Checker

- File Signature Verification

Windows File Protection

In Windows operating systems prior to Windows 2000, software installed on your operating system may have overwritten your shared system files, such as your dynamic link libraries (with the .dll extension) and executable files (with the .exe extension). When these files are overwritten, system performance can degrade or become unpredictable, and your programs may behave strangely. This behavior can potentially lead to an operating system failure.

Windows 2000 Professional includes Windows File Protection to prevent the replacement of protected system files, including SYS, OCX, DLL, TTF, EXE, and FON files. The Windows File Protection feature runs in the background and automatically protects all files installed by the Windows 2000 setup program.

Windows File Protection detects attempts by other applications to move or replace a protected system file. It also verifies the file's digital signature to determine whether the new file is the correct Microsoft version. If the file is not correct, Windows File Protection replaces the file either from the backup stored in the dllcache folder or from the Windows 2000 CD. If Windows File Protection cannot locate the appropriate file, it prompts you for the location of the file. This feature will also write an event to the event log noting the attempt to replace the file.

Warning! The dllcache folder is located in the %systemroot%\winnt\system32 folder. Be sure not to make any modifications to it or its contents.

By default, Windows File Protection is always enabled and allows protected system files to be replaced only when you're installing the following:

- Operating system upgrades using Winnt32.exe

- Windows Update

- Windows 2000 Services Packs that use Update.exe

- Hotfix distributions using Hotfix.exe

System File Checker

The System File Checker, *%systemroot%*\system32\dllcache\sfc.exe, is a command-line utility that scans and verifies the versions of all protected system files after you restart your computer. If the System File Checker detects that a protected file has been replaced, it retrieves the correct version of the file from the dllcache folder and then replaces the modified file with the original, protected file.

Tip: *If the dllcache folder becomes corrupt or unusable, use the **scannow**, **scanonce**, or **scanboot** parameter to repair the contents of the directory.*

For instance, the following command will immediately scan all protected system files and replace all incorrect file versions without prompting you. See Table 15.1 for a list and description of the **sfc** parameters available.

```
Sfc.exe /scannow /quiet
```

Note: *You must be logged on as an administrator or as a member of the local Administrators group to run the System File Checker.*

Table 15.1   sfc.exe parameters.

Parameter	Description
scannow	Scans all protected system files immediately
scanonce	Scans all protected system files once
scanboot	Scans all protected system files every time the computer is restarted
cancel	Cancels all pending scans of protected system files
quiet	Replaces all incorrect file versions without prompting the user
enable	Returns Windows File Protection to the default operation, prompting you to restore protected system files when files with incorrect versions are discovered
purgecache	Purges the Windows File Protection file cache and scans all protected system files immediately
cachesize=x	Sets the size, in MB, of the Windows File Protection file cache

File System Verification

Sometimes, during the installation of new software, your system files are overwritten by unsigned or incompatible versions, causing system corruption. The system files provided with Windows 2000 Professional use a Microsoft digital signature to identify them as the original, unmodified system files. This digital signature also identifies files that have been approved by Microsoft for use with Windows 2000. The File Signature Verification utility identifies unsigned files on your computer and provides the following information about the files:

- File name

- File location

- File type

- File version number

- File modification date

Now that you have an idea of the information that the File System Verification utility provides you, it is time to look at how to configure the utility to check for the appropriate digital signatures and write the information to a log file for later review.

Checking System and Nonsystem Files for Digital Signatures

To begin the process of checking the system and nonsystem files for digital signatures, you must first start the File Signature Verification utility. You do so by clicking on the Start button on the taskbar and then on the Run command to open the Run dialog box. Next, you type "sigverif" to open the utility. To begin the process of checking digital signatures for both your system and nonsystem files, follow these steps:

1. Click on the Advanced button to display the Advanced File Signature Verification Settings dialog box.

2. If the entire Search dialog box is not shown, click on the Search tab and select one of the following options, as shown in Figure 15.2:

   - *Notify Me If Any System Files Are Not Signed*—Checks only the Windows 2000 system files for the digital signature.

   - *Look For Other Files That Are Not Digitally Signed*—Provides some additional option boxes to specify the nonsystem files to be searched. You can specify a specific type of file to search based on the file extension or allow it to search all files as specified in the Scan This File Type box. You also need to specify the directory or volume that contains the nonsystem files you want to search.

   Note: *You can add a checkmark to the Include Subfolders checkbox if you want the utility to search the subfolders of the directory you specified in the Look In This Folder box.*

3. Click on OK and then click on Start if you are ready to begin the verification process.

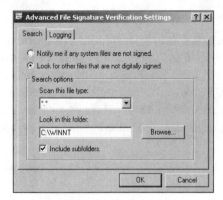

Figure 15.2
Specifying which files to search.

Writing Digital Signature Information to a Log File

Now that you understand the information provided when using the File System Verification utility, it is time to configure whether the information is written to a log file. You can write the digital signature information to a log file by following these steps:

1. Start the File Signature Verification application using the steps described in the preceding section.

2. Click on the Advanced button to open the Advanced File Signature Verification Settings dialog box.

3. Click on the Logging tab, as shown in Figure 15.3.

4. Click on Save The File Signature Verification Results To A Log File.

5. Select one of the following options:

   • *Append To Existing Log File*—Adds new search results to the end of an existing log file

   • *Overwrite Existing Log File*—Replaces the existing log file with a new log file

6. In the Log File Name text box, specify a name for the log file. (The search results are written to this file.)

7. Click on OK and then click on Start to begin the verification process.

Code signing is one way to ensure that your Windows 2000 Professional machine is stable and does not become unusable because of inappropriate file modifications. Other options are available to you to ensure stability of your system and your resources. For instance, you can use the Task Scheduler to schedule processor-intensive activities to occur during off-peak hours.

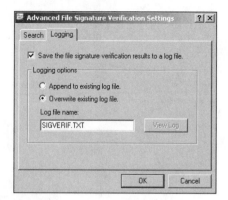

Figure 15.3
Specifying the logging options of your file verification.

Scheduling Tasks

15

Using Scheduled Tasks, you can schedule any program, script, or document to run at a time that is more convenient or when the processor is not being heavily utilized. The Task Scheduler service runs in the background and is started every time you start Windows 2000. You use this service to manage the tasks you scheduled using the Scheduled Tasks applet in Control Panel. This applet allows you to do the following:

- Schedule a task to run daily, weekly, monthly, or at certain times (such as at logon)

- Change the schedule for a task

- Stop a scheduled task

- Customize how a task runs at a scheduled time

Warning! Confirm that the system date and time on your computer are accurate because Task Scheduler relies on this information to run scheduled tasks. To verify or change this information, double-click on the time indicator on the taskbar.

Now, let's look at creating, configuring, and managing tasks in Windows 2000 Professional.

Creating a Scheduled Task

You will probably want to begin by creating a task to perform an action for you. This action may be to run anti-virus software, perform a backup, or perform a disk cleanup. Whatever the action may be, you initially schedule it by using the Add Scheduled Task option available inside the Task Scheduler. Choosing this option will fire up the Schedule Task Wizard, which steps you through the process of scheduling a task.

After you see the welcome screen and click on Next, you are prompted for the name of the file you want to schedule. You can choose from the list of files presented, but if you can't locate the one you want within the list, you can browse the computer to locate the file.

After you highlight the program you want to schedule and click on Next, the wizard presents the next screen on which you can name the task and schedule its frequency. Your frequency choices include the following:

- Daily

- Weekly

- Monthly

- One Time Only

- When My Computer Starts

- When I Log On

- When Idle

After you select the frequency and click on the Next button, you select the time, day, and month for the task to actually run. However, these options will vary, depending on the choice you made on the preceding screen. After you click on Next, you are prompted for the username and password that will be used to run the task.

The final wizard screen provides you with summary data and the opportunity to open the advanced properties for the task. Clicking on the Open Advanced Properties For This Task When I Click Finish checkbox opens the Properties dialog box for the task you are creating. However, the Properties dialog box does not appear until after you click on the Finish button to complete the wizard. The different Properties tabs for the task are discussed in the next section.

Use the following worksheet to document your scheduled tasks. This worksheet is useful for deciding what tasks need to be created and the details of each task. The completed worksheet can assist you in identifying conflicting schedules or whether there are excessive tasks running at the same time that may cause performance degradation. The completed worksheet below provides an example of its use. A blank worksheet can be found on the accompanying CD-ROM. Print as many copies as necessary when planning your scheduled tasks.

Worksheet 15.1   Documenting your scheduled tasks.

Task Name	File Name	Username	Frequency	Time	Comments
Back up C drive	ntbackup.exe	Administrator	Daily	12:00 A.M.	Back up to tape.
Antivirus	Nmain.exe	Administrator	At login	N/A	Executes after login.
Freecell	Freecell.exe	brian.alderman	Daily	8:00 A.M.	Runs every hour on the hour.

Modifying a Scheduled Task

Often, you will have to modify a task you have previously scheduled to run. This modification can include a change to the schedule, security, or settings. Follow these steps to access, modify, and save a task:

1. Open the Scheduled Tasks applet inside Control Panel by double-clicking on it to display the Scheduled Tasks window, as shown in Figure 15.4.

Tip: You can modify the order of columns as well as which columns are displayed by opening the View menu and then clicking on Choose Columns.

2. Right-click on the task you want to modify and then click on Properties to display the properties associated with this task. Figure 15.5 displays the four tabs you can use to modify the task.

3. Click on the appropriate tab and make your changes. The various changes you can make are described in the following sections.

15

Modifying General Information about a Task

On the Task tab shown in Figure 15.5, you can modify general information regarding a task. This information includes the directory pathname of the file associated with the task and any parameters required to run the task. You enter this information in the Run text box.

Warning! If the directory pathname contains spaces, you must enclose it in double quotation marks for it to be recognized.

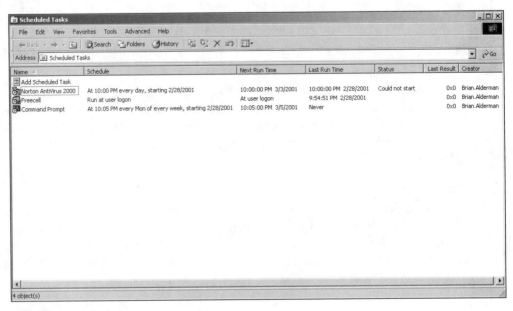

Figure 15.4
Viewing the Scheduled Tasks window.

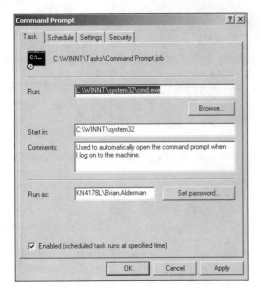

Figure 15.5
Checking task property options.

In the Start In box you can specify the folder that contains the program file or related files. Sometimes, programs need to use files from other locations. You use this box to specify the folder where these other files are located so that the program can locate them.

The Comments area provides space for you to type a description or other information about the task. This information can be useful for less obvious tasks or in an environment where multiple administrators are creating scheduled tasks.

In the Run As text box, you can supply the account and password that are used to run the task. This information includes the domain name or computer name that contains the account.

Notice also that you can choose to enable or disable the task on this tab. You can control this action by checking the Enabled (Scheduled Task Runs At Specified Time) box when you want it to run or clearing it when you don't want it to run. This capability is useful in an environment where you might want to temporarily disable a task but do not want to delete it.

Scheduling Your Task

Your task is defined to run at specific times using a schedule. However, some tasks may require multiple schedules. If a task requires multiple schedules, you can click on the Show Multiple Schedules box on the bottom of the Schedule tab, as shown in Figure 15.6. On this tab, you can create, modify, and delete a schedule associated with your task. The first drop-down box displays the schedule(s) of your task.

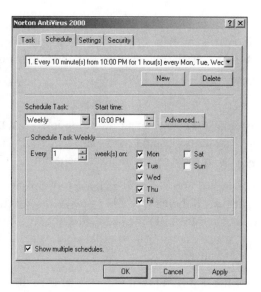

Figure 15.6
Scheduling your task.

After you select the schedule you want to modify, you can change the frequency of the task inside the Schedule Task box. Remember that the frequency can be daily, weekly, monthly, and so on, as discussed earlier in the "Creating a Scheduled Task" section.

After you choose the frequency, your Schedule tab dynamically changes to provide the appropriate selections based on your choices. You then specify the exact parameters for the schedule you are modifying. Figure 15.6 shows a weekly schedule for running anti-virus software.

You can choose the Advanced button to define a start date and optionally an end date for the scheduled task. This Advanced Schedule Options dialog box, shown in Figure 15.7,

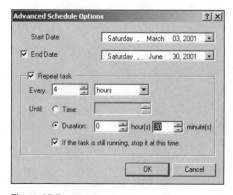

Figure 15.7
Setting advanced scheduling options.

also gives you the option of scheduling the task to run repeatedly at defined time intervals. Furthermore, you can set a duration period on how long you want the task to run. If the task is still running when the duration is exceeded, you can have it end the task by selecting the If The Task Is Still Running, Stop It At This Time checkbox.

Modifying Task Settings

You use the Settings tab for further customization of some of the task options. This tab has three parts: Scheduled Task Completed, Idle Time, and Power Management. In each of these areas, as shown in Figure 15.8, you can further define the task's behavior.

In the Scheduled Task Completed area, you can define what to do if the task runs too long. For instance, if the task runs longer than 72 hours (probably a problem with the task), you can stop it. You can also set an option to delete the task if it is not scheduled to run again. This capability can be useful if you are creating a task that is going to run one time only and you want to be sure it is removed afterward.

In the Idle Time area, you define whether the task should truly start up at the scheduled time. For example, if the task is scheduled to start at noon, but mouse or keyboard activity occurs, you might want to have the task hold off and not start immediately. If you select the Only Start The Task If The Computer Has Been Idle For At Least box, the task will not start until no mouse or keyboard activity is detected for the defined amount of time. If the task does not start at noon because the idle time has not been met, you can also specify a retry interval for the computer to attempt to start the task. After the retry interval is reached it will check to see whether the configured idle time has been met. Another option available in this area is to force the task to end if the computer ceases to be idle.

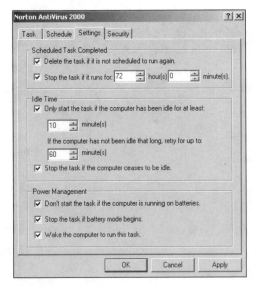

Figure 15.8
Modifying scheduled task settings.

In the third area of the Settings tab, you can define the behavior of the task if the computer is not using power from an AC source but from the computer's battery. You might not want to consume battery power to run a task. You can configure your computer not to start the task or to stop the task if the computer switches to battery mode. If your computer is in sleep mode, you can configure the task to wake the computer at the scheduled task time so that the task can be performed. You can independently turn on or off each of these options for each task.

Configuring Security Settings

The Security tab is used for assigning permissions for the task. This tab is used throughout the Windows 2000 Professional environment for managing permissions of resources, controlling ownership, and auditing. The Security tab is also used to determine whether you are going to inherit permissions from the parent object or customize your own permissions. You will customize these settings based on the security requirements of your task.

Stopping and Deleting a Task

You can stop a task that is currently executing by opening the Scheduled Tasks window and highlighting the task you want to stop. Right-click on the task to display the shortcut menu and click on the End Task option.

You can also remove a task from the Scheduled Tasks window. You do so by opening the window and highlighting the task you want to remove. After you highlight the task, right-click on it to open the shortcut menu and click on the Delete option. You then see a confirmation box asking whether you are sure you want to move the task to the Recycle Bin. Click on Yes to remove the task.

Tip: You can also delete a task by highlighting it in the Scheduled Tasks window and pressing the Delete key.

Managing Your Scheduled Tasks

Your Scheduled Tasks window contains the tasks you have created. We have looked at managing individual tasks, so now we are going to look at managing all the tasks in the Scheduled Tasks window. Managing tasks includes temporarily pausing all tasks, stopping all tasks, identifying missed tasks, and managing the Task Scheduling service. You can manage all these actions by using the Advanced menu in the Scheduled Tasks window.

You can pause the Task Scheduler if you do not want any of your scheduled tasks to run at the same time you are installing software or running a conflicting application. To pause all tasks currently located in the Scheduled Tasks window, open the Advanced menu and click on Pause Task Scheduler. When you are ready to restart the Task Scheduler, open the Advanced menu again and click on Continue Task Scheduler.

Warning! Tasks that are scheduled to run while the Task Scheduler is paused are not run until their next scheduled time.

You can stop the Task Scheduler services by opening the Advanced menu and clicking on Stop Using Task Scheduler. Choosing this option will prevent your scheduled tasks from running.

Warning! After choosing this option the Task Scheduler will not start automatically when you restart Windows 2000.

You can also be notified if a task that is scheduled to run does not run. You turn on this service by clicking on the Notify Me Of Missed Tasks menu item. When this service is enabled, an entry is made in the scheduler log file notifying you the task did not run. The scheduler log file is located in *%systemroot%*\winnt and is called schedlog.txt by default. It contains information regarding the starting of the Task Scheduler service, including each task that starts, finishes, or fails. You can view this log by opening the Advanced menu and clicking on the View Log option. The default log file size is 32KB and uses the First In First Out (FIFO) method for recording events. When the end of the log is reached, it will begin overwriting the events at the beginning of the log file.

The Task Scheduler service uses either a local system account or user account to start the service. You can manage this account by opening the Advanced menu and clicking on AT Service Account. This will provide you the opportunity to select the account type and also type the user account name and password for the account that will be used to start the service.

Note: AT is a command-line utility used in previous versions of Windows. The Task Scheduler graphical user interface replaces the AT command-line service.

Using the Task Scheduler is a great way to run redundant tasks without having to manually fire them off. Schedules can be defined so that tasks run during off-peak hours to improve performance. Managing the storage of your resources is another important task of a Windows 2000 administrator.

Managing Your Hard Drives

The management of your hard drives is critical for maintaining both performance of your system and access to your resources. The Disk Management utility is a Microsoft Management Console (MMC) snap-in used to manage the hard drives on your system. This graphical disk management tool replaces the Disk Administrator available in Windows NT.

Starting the Disk Management Utility

The Disk Management interface is the primary interface you use to manage all your drives. You can use it to create and format partitions, change drive letters, and perform other tasks directly related to the management of your hard drives, including configuring fault tolerance.

To open Disk Management, click on Start|Settings|Control Panel, double-click on Administrative Tools, and then double-click on Computer Management. In the console tree

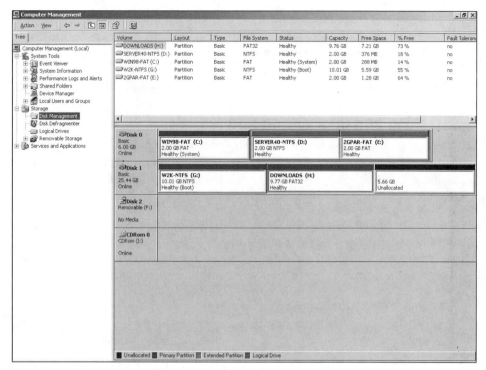

Figure 15.9
Locating the Disk Management utility.

under Storage, click on Disk Management. The path to locate Disk Management is shown in Figure 15.9.

Note: *You must be logged on as an administrator or a member of the Administrators group to be able to use the Disk Management utility.*

The Disk Management utility provides many new features that the Disk Administrator did not provide, including the following:

- Support for partitions, logical drives, and dynamic volumes.

- Local and remote disk management, allowing you to manage any remote Windows 2000 computer on which you are a member of either the Server Operators built-in group or the Administrators group.

- Simplification of tasks and an intuitive user interface. Disk Management provides numerous shortcut menus to show you which tasks you can perform on the selected object. This utility is also "wizardized," providing you assistance with tasks such as creating partitions and volumes and upgrading disks from basic to dynamic.

Tip: *Dynamic disks and volumes are not supported on portable computers. If you are attempting to upgrade a disk on a laptop, the upgrade option will not be available.*

- Online disk management, allowing you to perform online administrative tasks without having to shut down the system or interrupt your users. For example, you can create, extend, or mirror a volume without restarting the system. You can also add disks without restarting the system. In fact, most of your configuration changes take effect almost immediately; you don't need to save or commit the changes before they take effect.

Installing and Configuring a New Disk

After you add a new disk to your Windows 2000 Professional computer, you need to partition the disk and format the partition with the appropriate file system. The options available for partitioning the disk are discussed in detail in the "Disks and Volumes" section of Chapter 4.

With Plug-and-Play technology, the new disk should be recognized without any further steps. However, if the disk is not seen while you are in the Disk Management utility, you can open the Action menu and click on Rescan Disks. If Disk Management still does not recognize the new disk, you might need to restart your computer.

Creating Simple Volumes

To partition the disk by creating simple volumes, you need to decide what size your volumes are going to be and then take the following steps to create them on your drive:

1. In the Disk Management window, select the new disk and choose Create Partition from the Action menu. Choosing this option will start the Create Partition Wizard.

2. Select the type of partition you want to create, either primary or extended. (Extended partitions are used to exceed the four-partition limit imposed by primary partitions.) By default, Windows 2000 will use all available free space on the disk when you create a primary partition. To create other partitions on your disk, set the size of the partition to the size you have decided, leaving free space for additional partitions you can create later.

3. After setting the size, click on OK to create the simple volume.

4. To format the partition, click on the drive and select Format from the Action menu.

5. Select the file system you want to use: FAT, FAT32, or NTFS. If you are unsure of which file system to select, choose FAT because it is recognized by all operating systems and can be easily converted to NTFS.

Note: *Review the "Supported File Systems" section in Chapter 4 for information regarding the different file systems.*

6. After you select the file system, you can enable or disable the QuickFormat feature. This feature tells Windows 2000 Professional whether to first scan the partition for bad sectors. A QuickFormat of the partition will be much faster than if you do a format that performs a scan for bad sectors on the disk. A QuickFormat is normally

used on a new hard drive, because it is not concerned with disk fragmentation or areas of the drive that have been marked unusable.

7. Click on OK, then click on OK again to confirm your choice and begin the formatting process.

8. When the formatting process is complete, Windows 2000 Professional assigns a drive letter to the new volume, and the volume is ready for use.

Creating Spanned Volumes

After you create simple volumes, you can create a larger volume by adding disk space from other drives to it. When you extend a volume to another disk, it becomes a spanned volume but appears as one volume to Windows 2000. To create a spanned volume, you need to add free disk space from at least two disk drives, and they must be dynamic disks. You can create a spanned volume using between 2 and 32 dynamic disks. The data will be written to the first disk until that area of space is consumed. It will then start writing to the next disk in the spanned volume, and so on. If you decide to delete the spanned volume or if one of the drives included in the spanned volume goes bad, you lose all data associated with the spanned volume.

15

Warning! The simple volume needs to be formatted with NTFS before you can extend it to create a spanned volume.

The steps required to create a spanned volume are as follows:

1. Open Administrative Tools in Control Panel; then click on Computer Management to open the Computer Management window.

2. Expand Storage in the console tree and then click on the Disk Management folder.

3. Hold down the Ctrl key and select the drives or parts of drives you want to include in your spanned volume.

4. Choose Create Volume Set from the Action menu.

5. Windows 2000 Professional will prompt you for the total spanned volume size from all of the drives used to create the spanned volume. Enter the size for the spanned volume.

6. To prepare to format the volume, click on the Partition menu and select Commit Changes Now.

7. Locate and right-click on the newly created spanned volume, select NTFS as the file system to use, and leave the QuickFormat box unchecked. Then click on OK to format the spanned volume.

8. To save the new changes made to your system, run the Windows Backup utility to create a new Emergency Repair Disk (ERD).

Creating Striped Volumes

You create striped volumes in Windows 2000 the same way you create spanned volumes. If you decide to delete a striped volume or if one of the drives included in the striped volume goes bad, you lose all data associated with the striped volume.

Follow these steps to create a new striped volume:

1. Open Disk Management inside of Computer Management, and decide what areas of free space are going to be used in your striped volume.

2. Hold down the Ctrl key and select the drives or parts of drives you want to include in your striped volume.

3. Choose Create Striped Volume from the Action menu.

4. Windows 2000 Professional will prompt you for the total striped volume size. Input the size you want your volume to be.

5. To prepare to format it, click on the Partition menu and select Commit Changes Now.

6. Right-click on the striped volume, select NTFS as the file system to use, and leave the QuickFormat box unchecked. Then click on OK to format the striped volume.

7. To save the new changes made to your system, run the Windows Backup utility to create a new Emergency Repair Disk.

Warning! Both the spanned volume and striped volume are non–fault-tolerant. To ensure data recovery, be sure to back up the volumes regularly.

Managing Volume Properties

Each volume you create has an associated Properties sheet, or dialog box, that you can use to view information; the property sheet also provides tools for maintenance and administration of the volume. Volume sharing, security, and quotas can also be managed using the Properties dialog box. To access and view properties for a volume, from within Disk Management, right-click on the volume and select Properties to open a Properties dialog box similar to the one shown in Figure 15.10.

Using the General Tab

The General tab holds information about many general aspects of a volume in Windows 2000 Professional. You use this tab to assign a label to the volume for easier identification. This tab also provides information regarding the type of disk and file system. It also provides both visual and textual information regarding the total size of the partition as well as the amount of used and free space available on the volume.

The General tab also provides a Disk Cleanup button you can click to clean up the selected drive. Disk Cleanup can free disk space by deleting temporary files, uninstalling

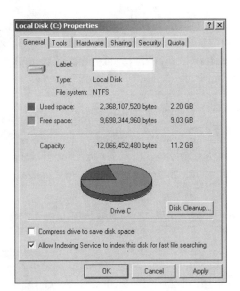

Figure 15.10
Viewing properties in the volume's Properties dialog box.

unnecessary programs, removing the contents of the Recycle Bin, and deleting Internet cache files.

You also can select two available checkboxes. The Compress Drive To Save Disk Space checkbox enables compression on the NTFS drive. By default, only files in the root directory are compressed automatically. To have Windows 2000 compress all folders on this drive, select the Apply Changes To *Drive Letter*: Subfolders And Files In The Confirm Attributes Changes checkbox that appears after you check the Compress Drive To Save Disk Space checkbox and then click OK or Apply.

The Allow Indexing Service To Index This Disk For Fast File Searching checkbox specifies that the contents of the drive be indexed to enable faster searches. Indexing enables you to search for information (such as text in a document) or properties (such as the size of the document). The entire contents of the drive are not indexed unless you select the Apply Changes To *Drive Letter*: Subfolders And Files In The Confirm Attributes Changes checkbox that appears after clicking OK or Apply.

Using the Tools Tab
The Tools tab contains three areas you can use to maintain your drive. The Error-Checking area contains a button called Check Now that opens the Check Disk tool. This tool scans the selected drive for damage.

Warning! *The disk is not available for use when it is being scanned. Also, the disk-checking process can take a long time for a drive that contains an extremely large number of files.*

The Backup area contains a button labeled Backup Now. Clicking on this button opens the Backup dialog box, as shown in Figure 15.11. You use this dialog box to select wizards that help you back up and restore files and folders or prepare for automated system recovery. You can also create a schedule of your backups and system recovery, as well as create an Emergency Repair Disk.

In the third area, Defragmentation, you can start the process of defragmenting your drive. Clicking on the Defragment Now button opens the Disk Defragmenter, which locates fragmented files and folders on local volumes. Fragmented files are parts of files that are scattered over different areas of the disk. Fragmentation occurs as files on a disk are deleted and new files are added.

Note: We will discuss Disk Defragmenter in more detail later in this chapter.

Using the Hardware Tab

The Hardware tab of the Properties dialog box contains information about your floppy, hard disk, and CD-ROM drives. You can select any of the drives listed and click on the Properties button to receive additional information about the drive, as shown in Figure 15.12. The Troubleshooter button in this Properties box provides online assistance for troubleshooting the selected drive.

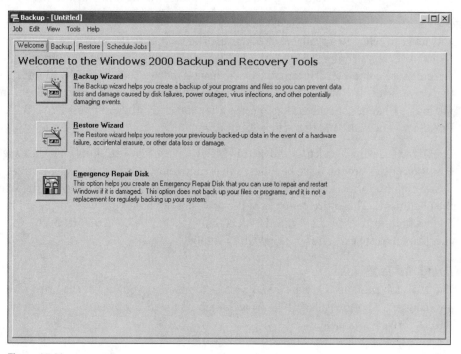

Figure 15.11
Choosing a backup method from the Backup dialog box.

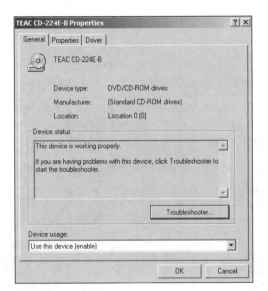

Figure 15.12
Accessing local drive properties.

Using the Sharing Tab

You use the Sharing tab to share resources, set network access permissions, provide comments, and specify the caching options for offline use. This option was discussed in detail in Chapter 11.

Using the Security Tab

You use the Security tab to define the local NTFS permissions for the resource, including the standard and individual special permissions. You also use this tab to configure auditing and define the owner of the resource. We will go into more detail about this tab in Chapter 16.

Using the Quota Tab

You use the Quota tab to track and control disk space usage for your volumes. You can configure Windows 2000 to do the following:

- Prevent further disk space use and log an event when a user exceeds a specified disk space limit

- Log an event when a user exceeds a specified disk space warning level

The implementation of disk quotas is new in Windows 2000 and applies only to the version of NTFS used in Windows 2000. Numerous options are available for configuring disk quotas, which are discussed later in this chapter. The next section discusses some of the settings available for each of the volumes located on your Windows 2000 Professional operating system.

Managing Volume Settings

Information about the number of disks, types of disks, and partitions is managed through Disk Management. We already talked about using the Rescan Disks option located on the Action menu to check for new disks added to your machine without having to reboot.

You can also use the Action menu to delete partitions, mark partitions as active, or change the drive letter or path of a partition. These options give you dynamic control of your disk environment without having to restart your machine.

An *active partition* is identified during the startup of a machine as the partition that contains the files required to boot the system. The active partition is the system partition we discussed in Chapter 4. The system partition must be a primary partition that has been marked as active for booting your system and must be located on the disk that the computer accesses when starting up the system. However, only one partition can be active at a time, regardless of the number of operating systems installed.

Understanding NTFS Mounted Drives

Disk Management is also used for mounting a local drive in an empty folder on a local NTFS volume. You can then format the mounted drive with any file system supported by Windows 2000. Windows 2000 assigns a drive path rather than a drive letter to the drive. Mounted drives eliminate the 26-drive restriction that is imposed by drive letters on a computer. Windows 2000 ensures that the drive paths retain their association to the drive, so you can add or rearrange your storage devices without the drive path failing.

Managing Drive Letters

The functionality to dynamically change a drive letter or path also is managed through Disk Management. To change a drive letter or path for a volume, right-click on the partition that you want to change the drive letter of and then click on Change Drive Letter And Path. Choosing this option opens the Change Drive Letter And Path dialog box for the volume you clicked on.

You can click on the Add button to add a drive letter or mount a local drive to an empty folder on an NTFS volume instead of assigning a letter. Clicking on Add opens a dialog box called Add A Drive Letter Or Path. If you are mounting a volume, click on Mount In This NTFS Folder, and type the path or click on Browse to locate the path. If you are adding a drive letter, you can use letters *C* through *Z*.

Tip: If you do not have two floppy disk drives, you can assign the letter B to a network drive.

By clicking on the Remove button, you can delete the drive letter or path. By clicking on the Edit button, you can modify the drive letter of the volume. However, to modify a drive path, you must remove it and then create a new drive path using the new location.

Warning! You cannot edit or remove the boot or system partition drive letter.

The Status column in the Disk Management interface provides an excellent indication of whether there is a problem with a disk. This column always provides a description in the graphical view of your disk. If you discover problems with a disk, you can use Table 15.2 to help diagnose and correct the problems.

After you add your drives, you might want to control how much space each user is consuming on each of the volumes. This capability is made possible by implementing disk quotas.

Introducing Volume Disk Quotas

Disk quotas are used to monitor volume use by an individual user. Each user's utilization of disk space does not affect the disk quotas for other users of the same volume. For instance, if you set a quota limit of 100MB on volume D and a user creates a file that is 100MB, that user is unable to create any additional files on that volume. However, that restriction does not prevent any other user who has not exceeded his or her disk quota from creating additional files on volume D.

Disk quotas are based on file ownership and are enforced regardless of where the files reside on the volume. For instance, if the user from the preceding paragraph moves files from one folder to another folder on volume D, this user is still prevented from creating additional files because she has reached her threshold of 100MB. The volume space consumed by the user has not changed. However, if the user copies files to a folder on volume E, she has reduced her disk space usage on volume D and is again able to create new files on volume D.

Note: *To administer disk quotas on a volume, you must be a member of the Administrators group on the computer that contains the drive.*

Table 15.2   Disk Management status descriptions.

Status	Description
Online	The disk is accessible and there are no known problems. This option is available on both basic and dynamic disks.
Online (Errors)	I/O errors have been detected on a section of the disk. This option is available only on dynamic disks.
Offline	The disk is not accessible and may be corrupted, powered down, or disconnected.
Foreign	The disk has been moved from another computer to your computer. However, the disk has not been set up for use on your computer.
Unreadable	The disk is not accessible and may have experienced I/O errors, corruption, or a hardware failure.
Unrecognized	The disk contains an Original Equipment Manufacturer's (OEM) signature that is not recognized by Windows 2000 and cannot be used.
No Media	The media have not been inserted into the CD-ROM or removable drive. This option is available only for CD-ROM or removable disk types.

You enable disk quotas on a drive by following these steps:

1. Open Disk Management, right-click on the disk volume for which you want to enable disk quotas, and then click on Properties.

2. In the Properties dialog box, click on the Quota tab.

Warning! *The Quota tab will not appear if you are not a member of the Administrators group or if the volume is not formatted with Windows 2000 NTFS.*

3. Click on the Enable Quota Management option and then click on Apply to enable the quotas, as shown in Figure 15.13. Notice the traffic light turns yellow while calculating current quota information. The light is green when the disk quota option is enabled.

4. Select the Limit Disk Space To option to activate the fields to define the disk space limit and warning levels.

5. Type numeric values in the text fields and use the drop-down menus to define the space limit and warning level units. You can choose from KB, MB, GB, TB, PB, or EB. Then, click on Apply to activate the quota entry.

Warning! *When you first enable disk quotas, the default limit of disk space is 1KB. Be sure to modify this setting; otherwise, your users will have very limited capabilities.*

After enabling disk quotas, you can set a few options to manage the behavior of Windows 2000 regarding these disk quotas. It is important to understand the options available to you so that you can correctly configure your Windows 2000 Professional environment.

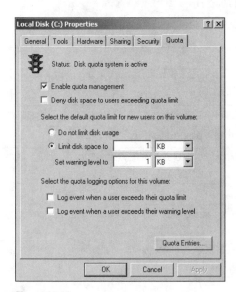

Figure 15.13
Enabling disk quota management.

The next big decision is to choose what action to take if users exceed their disk quota limits. If you click on the Deny Disk Space To Users Exceeding Quota Limit checkbox, any user who exceeds his assigned quota limit will not be able to write additional data to the volume without first moving or deleting some of his existing files from the volume.

Warning! *The quota limit is also checked when a user is installing software. If the required disk space for the application is not available, the software will not install.*

When the disk quota is exceeded, you can choose to log quota options for the volume. For instance, to log an event when a user exceeds her quota limit, select the Log Event When A User Exceeds Their Quota Limit checkbox. If you want to log an event when a user exceeds the warning level, you select the Log Event When A User Exceeds Their Warning Level checkbox. These events are logged to the system log of the Event Viewer.

Note: *For compressed files, the disk quota size is calculated, and counted towards the users overall disk quota, using the noncompressed size of the file.*

Decision Tree 15.1 steps you through the actions required to enable disk quotas on your Windows 2000 NTFS volume. Use this when configuring disk quotas on your volume.

Implementing Individual Disk Quotas

The logging that you turned on is implemented at a volume level and applies to all users who own files on that volume. You also might need to configure individual user disk quota entries. You do so by clicking on the Quota Entries button on the Quota tab. When you click on this button, the Quota Entries window, as shown in Figure 15.14, is displayed. You use this window to manage the individual quota entries.

This window lists individual user quota entries that have been added to it. This dialog box allows you to customize the settings for users who have special needs. For instance, you are most likely not going to put a quota limit on your administrators. Also, if some users perform all your software installations and upgrades and need unlimited disk space or a much higher amount of disk space, you will define individual entries for them.

You set up these individual settings by following these steps:

1. Open My Computer.

2. Right-click on the volume for which you want to add a new disk quota entry and then click on Properties.

3. Click on the Quota tab of the Properties dialog box.

4. Click on the Quota Entries button on the Quota tab.

5. Select the Quota menu and then click on New Quota Entry.

6. In the Select Users dialog box, select the domain or workgroup that you want to use to locate the user from the drop-down menu in the Look In area.

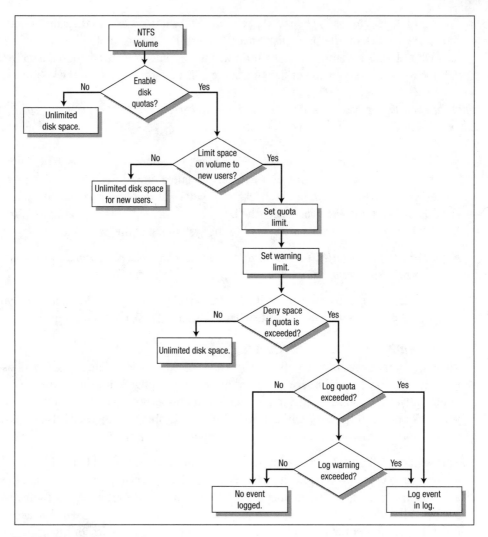

Decision Tree 15.1
Enabling volume disk quotas.

7. Locate the user, double-click on the username for which you want to add a quota entry, and then click on Add.

8. In the Add New Quota Entry dialog box, specify one of the following:

- *Do Not Limit Disk Usage*—Tracks disk space usage but does not prevent the user from writing to the volume.

- *Limit Disk Space To*—Activates fields for limiting both disk space and setting warning levels. Provide a numeric value and the disk space limit unit from the drop-down menu.

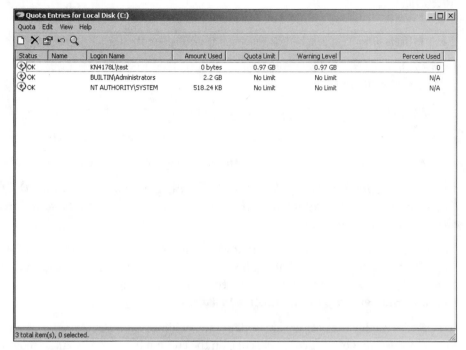

Figure 15.14
Managing disk quotas in the Quota Entries window.

The list of individual disk quota entries can get quite large, and locating individuals can become difficult when you're managing their quotas. However, you can arrange the order of the users to provide a more efficient way to locate them.

Managing Your Individual Disk Quota Entries

Sorting your individual disk quota entries provides for easier management of your users' quotas and allows you to generate a disk quota report. Follow these steps to sort your disk quota entries:

1. Use the steps discussed previously to access the Quota Entries window.

2. From the View menu of the Quota Entries window, click on Arrange Items and then choose one of the following ways to arrange the quota entries:

   - *By Folder*—Sorts entries by folder location

   - *By User Name*—Sorts entries according to the user's full name, which can include first name, middle initial, and last name

   - *By Logon Name*—Sorts entries by logon name

   - *By Status*—Sorts entries by disk quota status as follows:

     - Users under the quota warning level

- Users over the warning level but under the disk quota limit

- Users who have reached or exceeded their disk quota limit

- *By Amount Used*—Sorts entries according to the actual amount of space the users have used on the volume

- *By Quota Limit*—Sorts entries according to the specified disk space limits

- *By Warning Level*—Sorts entries according to specified warning levels

- *By Percent Used*—Sorts entries by the percentage of disk space limit used

Note: *An alternative way to sort the entries is to click on a column's title in the Quota Entries window to sort based on the entries in that column. To reverse the sorted order, click on the column title again.*

After you sort the results in the order that you want them to appear, you can generate a report. You open the program that is going to store the information, such as Excel, and then highlight each row you want in your report. You then drag the rows to the application you opened and save the information to a file.

You can also modify the position and order of the columns in the Quota Entries window. To change the order of your columns, click on the column header you want to move and drag it to a new position in the list. To change the size of a column, position the mouse pointer between the columns and click and drag to the size you prefer. Your positioning and sizing changes are saved when you close the Quota Entries window and are restored the next time you open it.

Disabling Individual Disk Quota Entries

When a user no longer requires access to a volume that has quotas enabled, you can remove that user's warning level and quota limit by deleting his or her entry from the Quota Entries window. However, you can do so only after all the folders and files owned by that user have either been removed or deleted from the volume, or the ownership of the files has been transferred to someone else.

To delete an individual's disk quota entry, follow these steps:

1. Access the Quota Entries window as discussed earlier.

2. In the Quota Entries window, locate and click on the entry for the user you want to delete. Then, from the Quota menu, click on Delete Quota Entry.

3. If the Disk Quota dialog box appears, click on Yes. Then, click on the files that you want to take action on. Choose one of the following buttons to specify the action you want to take:

- *Delete*—Deletes selected files from the volume

- *Take Ownership*—Gives you ownership of the files you have selected

- *Move*—Moves the selected files to a different volume

4. Click on Close to complete the action and disable the individual disk quota entry.

Using disk quotas is a great way to manage your resources and prevent disk space hogs from consuming too much space. The cost of hard drives has dropped considerably in recent years. But, if you want to force your users to clean up their files occasionally, instituting disk quotas is a great way to enforce that behavior.

Optimizing Windows 2000

Optimizing Windows 2000 improves performance of your operating system and applications. As an administrator, you can improve performance in many ways. For example, you can control the services and devices enabled, configure additional processors, manage disk fragmentation, and manage your computer's memory and processor time.

15

Understanding Hardware Profiles

Hardware profiles are a set of instructions that tell Windows 2000 which services and devices to start when you start your computer. They can also be used to customize the settings for these devices and services. When you install Windows 2000 Professional, a default hardware profile called Profile 1 is installed. By default, every device on your machine is enabled in Profile 1 when you install Windows 2000 Professional.

Note: *For laptops, the default profiles are either Docked Profile or Undocked Profile, depending on the status of the machine during the installation.*

Hardware profiles are especially beneficial when you are using portable computers. Most portable computers are used in multiple locations with a different configuration per location. These different configurations can be managed using hardware profiles. For instance, you can use a hardware profile called Docking Station Profile when your laptop is docked at a docking station that contains additional components such as a network adapter and CD-ROM drive. You can then have another hardware profile called Undocked Profile for when the laptop is not docked, meaning no network card or CD-ROM is available.

You manage hardware profiles by double-clicking on System in Control Panel and then clicking on the Hardware tab, which contains a Hardware Profiles button. Click on the Hardware Profiles button to configure the hardware profiles for your computer. You can have numerous hardware profiles, and you can define one as the default to be used if you do not choose another one when you boot the system.

After you create different hardware profiles, you can designate which devices are enabled or disabled by using the Device Manager. When a device is disabled, it will not be loaded when the computer is started. Furthermore, you can use the hardware profiles to configure which services you want started or not started, thus improving overall performance on your system.

Creating a Hardware Profile

When you decide to create another hardware profile, follow these steps to create and name it, as well as identify which devices and services are applied to the hardware profile:

1. Open the System applet in Control Panel.

2. On the Hardware tab, click on the Hardware Profiles button.

Tip: *You must be logged on as an administrator to the local computer to copy or create hardware profiles.*

3. Under Available Hardware Profiles, click on Profile 1 (Current).

4. Click on Copy, type a name for the new hardware profile, and then click on OK. Figure 15.15 shows two hardware profiles for a laptop that sometimes is docked in a docking station and other times is not.

5. You can customize the new profile by enabling or disabling the devices for it through Device Manager.

Tip: *To open Device Manager, double-click on the System applet in Control Panel and click on the Device Manager button on the Hardware tab. For more information about Device Manager, choose Help from the Action menu inside Device Manager.*

You use the Services utility inside the Administration Tools of Control Panel to define the services that will be used by the different hardware profiles. For instance, when you are not docked, you don't need to retrieve an IP address from the DHCP server. So, you might

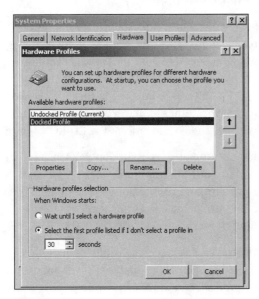

Figure 15.15
Creating hardware profiles.

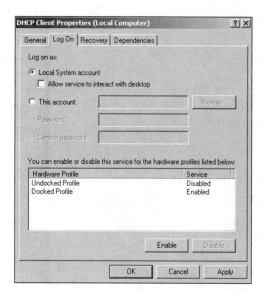

Figure 15.16
Disabling services within a hardware profile.

want to disable the DHCP client service when using the undocked hardware profile. Figure 15.16 shows the DHCP Client Properties dialog box used to disable the service for the undocked hardware profile.

To access this dialog box, open the Administration Tools located in Control Panel. Double-click on the Services option to open the Services window. Right-click on the service you want to configure and click on Properties. Then, click on the Log On tab, where you can configure the service associated with the available hardware profiles.

Defining Your Default Hardware Profile

Your default hardware profile is the one used if you do not choose a different one when your computer is starting. After you have configured a second hardware profile, you are presented with a hardware profile menu from which you can choose the hardware profile you want to use.

You can manage the default hardware profile and the time allowed to choose a hardware profile by using the System Properties Hardware Profiles interface, as shown in Figure 15.17. By default, you have 30 seconds to make a choice. However, you can modify the time allowed to anywhere between 0 and 999 seconds, or choose to force the user booting the system to make a decision by selecting the Wait Until I Select A Hardware Profile option.

If no hardware profile is chosen, Windows 2000 uses the default profile that appears at the top of the Available Hardware Profiles list. You can modify this list by selecting an existing profile and then clicking on the up or down arrow to change the order of the profiles, leaving your preferred default profile at the top of the list.

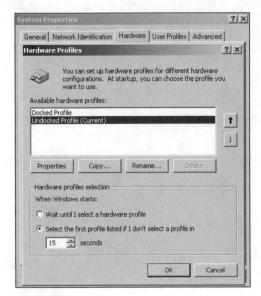

Figure 15.17
Managing hardware profiles.

After you define and configure your hardware profiles, you can choose the most appropriate profile to optimize your Windows 2000 Professional environment. However, optimization involves many aspects of Windows 2000 Professional, including the processor speed and number of processors.

Managing Multiple Processors

Windows 2000 offers support for multiple processors, providing much better performance for both the operating system and your applications. The operating system and applications can run multiple tasks on the separate processors. However, your application must be designed to take advantage of multiple processors.

For instance, the operating system must be able to divide the workload being sent to the processors into manageable slices and control when and how these slices are sent to the processors. The capability to divide the workload is also beneficial in a single processor environment. An operating system that has this capability is referred to as a *multitasking operating system*. The two types of multitasking operating systems are *cooperative* and *preemptive*.

Cooperative multitasking means each application shares the processor cooperatively with other applications. Windows 95 and Windows 98 support older 16-bit applications using cooperative multitasking in a virtual machine, but 32-bit applications that were written for Windows 9x use preemptive multitasking. Each application takes turns running its instructions on the processor, periodically releasing the processor to the other applications. Table 15.3 shows the different Windows 2000 operating systems and the number of processors supported.

Table 15.3   Processor support in Windows 2000.

Windows 2000 Version	Number of Supported Processors
Professional	2
Server	4
Advanced Server	8
Datacenter Server	32

This process has a couple of downsides to it. The first is that there is no hierarchical structure on who has access to the processor, and the operating system also has to wait for access to the processor. The second is that each application must release the processor when it is finished. If it doesn't, it may cause the system to freeze up or crash.

Windows NT and Windows 2000 use an enhanced preemptive multitasking scheme. This scheme defines the central portion of the operating system as the *kernel*. The kernel is responsible for scheduling applications to use the processor and always gets precedence over the other applications. The kernel also can remove an application from the processor, either forcing it to wait for another turn at the processor or stopping the application completely. In this environment, if a program hangs or crashes, the kernel can remove it from memory without affecting the rest of the system.

15

Because the Windows 2000 kernel has complete control of the applications being run and control over what application gets access to the processor, it doesn't matter to the applications how many processors are available.

Using Task Manager

Task Manager provides performance information about your Windows 2000 Professional system. It presents a snapshot of processes and programs that are currently running on your computer. Task Manager also provides a summary of both memory and processor usage.

Tip: You can open Task Manager by right-clicking an empty area on the taskbar and then clicking on Task Manager. You also can access Task Manager by pressing Ctrl+Alt+Del and clicking on the Task Manager button.

You can use Task Manager to monitor applications, processes, and performance statistics that affect your computer's performance. Using Task Manager, you can quickly review the status of programs that are running and end programs that have unexpectedly stopped running. You can also monitor the activity of running processes.

The Task Manager contains three tabs: Applications, Processes, and Performance (see Figure 15.18). The information on these tabs can assist you in optimizing and trouble-shooting your system. For instance, the Applications tab shows the status of programs that are currently running or that have stopped responding on your computer. You can start a new application, switch to a running application, or end an application by using the buttons located on this tab.

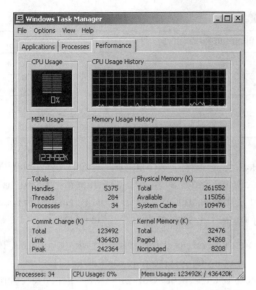

Figure 15.18
Accessing the Task Manager dialog box.

The Processes tab displays information about the processes running on your computer. A process is an executable program, such as PowerPoint, or a service, such as Event Log. One process that is always running and consumes most of your CPU time is the System Idle Process, which consumes CPU time when no other applications are using the CPU.

Tip: You can customize the Processes tab by clicking on the Select Columns option from the View menu.

The Performance tab displays a dynamic overview of your computer's performance. The information provided on the Performance tab includes the following:

• Graphs for memory and CPU usage

• Totals for the number of processes, handles, and threads that are currently running on the computer

• Totals for physical, commit, and kernel memory

Note: The Show Kernel Times option located on the View menu adds red lines to the CPU Usage and CPU Usage History graphs. This red line displays the amount of CPU resources consumed by the kernel.

Assigning Applications to a Processor

You can set up applications to use a specific processor installed on your system. If you have multiple processors installed on your machine, you can follow these steps to map a specific processor to a process:

Note: This functionality is only available on a computer that contains multiple processors.

1. Open the Task Manager by pressing Ctrl+Alt+Delete on your keyboard. In the Windows Security dialog box that appears, click on the Task Manager button.

Tip: *You can also open Task Manager by right-clicking an empty area on the taskbar and then clicking on Task Manager.*

2. In Task Manager, click on the Performance tab to view the processor and memory percentage being used.

3. Click on the Processes tab. Notice that most of the CPU usage is consumed by the System Idle Process. This special process keeps the processor busy when no other applications are using it.

4. Scroll down the list of processes to see all the processes running. Locate the process called spoolsv and right-click on it.

5. On the shortcut menu, click on the Set Affinity option and select the processor to be assigned to the SPOOLSV process. This procedure ensures that the SPOOLSV process will always use the CPU you assigned to it.

15

Note: The processors are numbered beginning with 0 and incremented by 1. Your first processor is CPU0; the second, CPU1; and so on.

As you can see, multiple processors can greatly improve the performance of your operating system and applications. Your processes can be assigned to specific processors, providing you better control over how your applications run.

Note: Microsoft BackOffice applications such as SQL Server also provide settings to allow you to further configure performance and processor affinity.

Managing fragmentation on your disks is another administrative function you can perform to optimize performance in your Windows 2000 Professional environment. If your users are making many changes to their files on the volume, these changes can cause fragmentation, which in turn reduces response time for both reading and writing files on your hard drive.

Using the Disk Defragmenter

Fragmented files are parts of files that are scattered over different areas of the hard drive. Fragmentation occurs as files on a disk are deleted and new files are added to the disk, but the disk does not have a large enough contiguous section of free space to store the file. Fragmentation slows disk access and degrades the overall performance of disk operations, although usually not severely.

Disk Defragmenter locates the fragmented files and folders on local volumes and moves the pieces of each file or folder to one location on the volume so that each one occupies a contiguous section on your disk drive. This process of locating and consolidating your files and folders is called *defragmentation*. Disk Defragmenter can defragment FAT, FAT32, and NTFS volumes.

After you defragment your files and folders, the time required to access them is more efficient because they are located in one contiguous location. Saving files also becomes more efficient because the free space on the hard drive is also consolidated.

Tip: *Generally, volumes on file servers need to be defragmented more often than those on client machines.*

To open Disk Defragmenter, click on Start|Settings|Control Panel, double-click on Administrative Tools, and then double-click on Computer Management. In the console tree under Storage, click on Disk Defragmenter. The location of Disk Defragmenter and the Disk Defragmenter interface are shown in Figure 15.19.

Note: *You must be logged on as a member of the Administrators group or as the administrator to analyze or defragment your volumes.*

The Disk Defragmenter window contains two main areas. The upper area lists the volumes on the local computer; the lower area displays a graphical view of how fragmented the selected volume is.

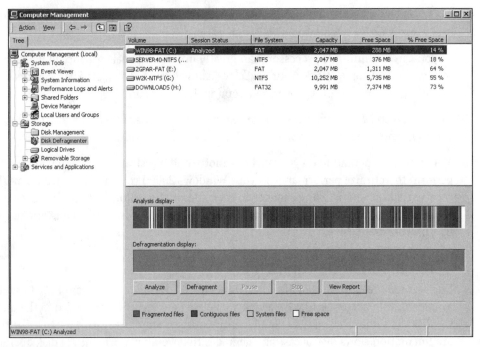

Figure 15.19
Viewing the Disk Defragmenter interface.

A great feature of Disk Defragmenter is that you can analyze your drives to check for the amount of fragmentation without performing the actual defragmentation process. This way, you can see whether the defragmentation process is necessary.

Follow these steps to analyze a volume in Windows 2000:

1. Open Disk Defragmenter.

2. Click on the volume that you want to check for fragmented files and folders and then click on the Analyze button.

3. After the analysis is complete, a dialog box appears telling you whether you need to defragment the volume. Figure 15.20 shows the results of an analyzed volume.

Tip: For more information about the files and folders that were analyzed, click on View Report.

Table 15.4 explains the colors used to indicate the condition of your volume after the analysis has been completed. After defragmenting your volume, you can compare the Analysis Display area to the Defragmentation Display area to see the improvement in your volume.

15

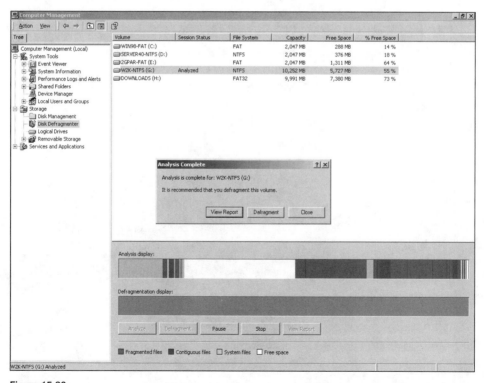

Figure 15.20
Viewing volume fragmentation analysis results.

Table 15.4   Understanding the results of a volume analysis.

Color	Description
Red	Shows areas of fragmented files
Blue	Shows areas of contiguous, or nonfragmented, files
White	Shows areas of free space on the volume
Green	Shows NTFS-specific system files that cannot be moved by Disk Defragmenter

If the analysis indicates that you need to defragment the volume, you can do so by clicking on the Defragment button located in the Disk Defragmenter. After the defragmentation is completed, your Disk Defragmenter interface will look similar to Figure 15.21.

Tip: Click on the View Report button to view detailed information about the files and folders that were defragmented.

The amount of time required to perform the defragmentation depends on several factors, including the size of the volume, amount of fragmentation, number of files that reside on the volume, and available local system resources.

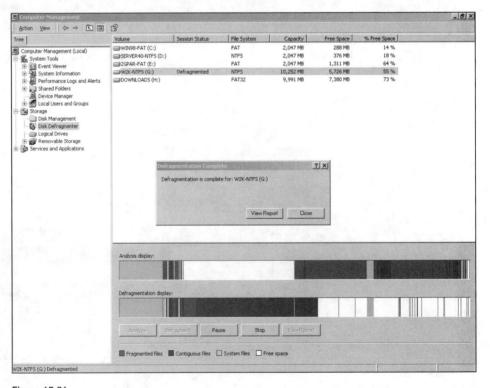

Figure 15.21
Viewing volume defragmentation results.

Warning! *The defragmentation application included with Windows 2000 cannot be scheduled. It is an interactive process and has to be initiated manually using the steps discussed here.*

You can use Decision Tree 15.2 when you are experiencing performance degradation and suspect fragmentation as the cause for the degradation. Use these steps to analyze and optionally defragment your volumes.

Introducing the System Monitor

System Monitor is the most powerful tool you have to measure the performance of your computer. The information gathered using System Monitor includes the activity of your

15

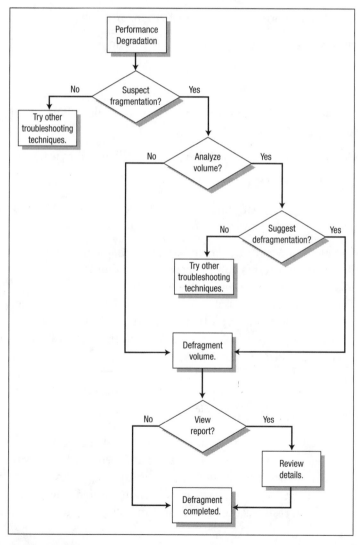

Decision Tree 15.2
Deciding whether to defragment your volumes.

system services and usage of your hardware. You can review this information to help identify bottlenecks on your system.

Note: A bottleneck is caused by excessive demand on certain resources. The four re-sources to be most concerned with are memory, processor, disk, and network activity.

System Monitor provides many benefits to you when you are trying to optimize your system. Using System Monitor, you can do the following:

- Collect and view real-time performance data on your local computer or from remote computers

- View data previously gathered in a counter log

- Display the gathered data in a printable report, histogram, or graph

- Create reusable monitoring configurations that can be used in other Microsoft Manage-ment Consoles

- Create performance views using HTML pages

The System Monitor is similar to the Performance Monitor available in Windows NT 4. To open the System Monitor interface, follow these steps:

1. Click on Start|Settings|Control Panel and then double-click on Administrative Tools.

2. Double-click on the Performance icon to open the Performance window.

3. Click on System Monitor in the left-hand pane to activate it. System Monitor will start with the default blank graph view, as shown in Figure 15.22.

After you open System Monitor, you can add counters to the graph by clicking on the plus (+) sign on the toolbar. Clicking on this button opens the Add Counters dialog box, as shown in Figure 15.23. This dialog box provides the available objects and counters that can be monitored. You choose the appropriate object from the Performance Object drop-down menu and then choose the counters for that object from the Select Counters From List list box. Table 15.5 contains a list of the key counters and critical thresholds you should monitor when trying to identify system bottlenecks.

*Tip: If the physical disk and logical disk objects do not exist, you must enable them by using the **diskperf -Y** command at the command prompt and then restart your system.*

When you follow the process to add counters, after a short period of time you will notice counter values being added to the graph area. The names and associated information for the counters you added are shown in the columns, beneath the graph area, known as the *legend*. Figure 15.24 contains the four counters most often monitored. Each counter is a different color so that you can easily identify it. %Disk Time is highlighted with a more obvious white color.

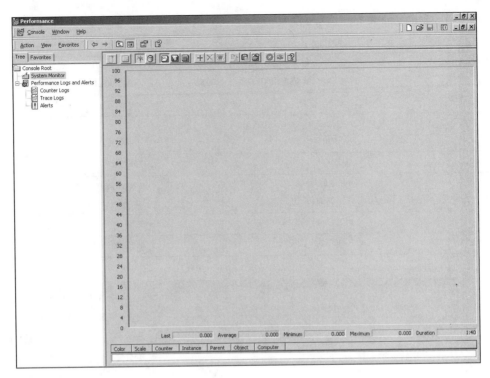

Figure 15.22
The System Monitor interface.

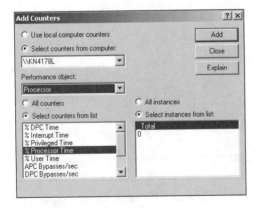

Figure 15.23
Adding counters in the Add Counters dialog box.

Table 15.5   Critical performance counters.

Object	Counters	Bottleneck Threshold
Physical Disk	%Disk Time	90%
	%Disk Reads/sec and Disk Writes/sec	Manufacturer Specific
Logical Disk	%Free Space	<5%
Memory	Pages/sec	20
	Available Bytes	<4MB
Paging File	%Usage	99%
Processor	Interrupts/sec	Depends on processor
	%Processor Time	85%
System	Processor Queue Length	2
Network Segment	%Network Utilization	Depends on type of network

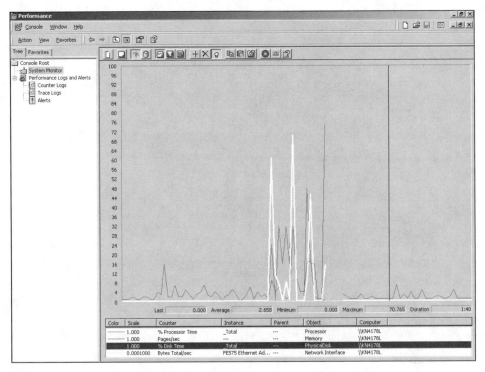

Figure 15.24
Viewing counters in the active System Monitor.

Tip: To highlight a specific counter in the graph, click on the counter in the legend area and then press Ctrl+H. The highlight provides easier identification of the counters in the graph area. You turn off this feature by pressing Ctrl+H again.

Tip: To print the performance data from one of the graph modes, you can press Alt+Print Screen to copy the content you are viewing and then paste it into the Paint program. Next, choose the Print option from the File menu in Paint to create a hard copy of the graph.

Using Performance Logs and Alerts

You use the Performance Logs and Alerts MMC snap-in to configure your performance logging and alerts. You can have multiple instances of logs and alerts running at the same time. Alerts detect when a counter exceeds or falls below a defined threshold and take an action. This action can be to send a message, run a program, or start a log after that threshold has been reached.

Logging can occur automatically based on a user-defined schedule or manually on demand. You can view this logged data by using System Monitor, or you can export it to spreadsheet programs, such as Excel, to analyze it and generate reports.

15

Creating a Counter Log

Counter logs also record data about hardware usage and the activity of the system services from both local and remote computers. To create a new counter log, follow these steps:

1. Open the Performance window as described earlier.

2. Expand Performance Logs And Alerts by double-clicking on it in the console tree. Then, click on Counter Logs to display existing logs in the details pane.

Tip: A red icon associated with a counter log indicates it is stopped; a green icon indicates it is currently running.

3. Right-click a blank area of the details pane and click on New Log Settings in the shortcut menu.

4. In the Name dialog box, type the name of the counter log and click on OK.

5. On the General tab of the newly defined counter log dialog box that appears, click on Add and select the counters you want to log.

Tip: To obtain a description of a counter, select it and then click on the Explain button.

6. If you want to modify the default file and schedule information, make the changes on the Log Files and Schedule tabs, respectively, and then click OK.

7. To save these file settings, right-click on the file in the details pane, click on Save Settings As, and supply a file name with a .htm extension.

Note: Saving the information to an HTM file allows you to view the counters using a Web browser.

To modify the counters of an existing log file, access the counter logs as previously described. Double-click on the log file you want to modify to open the Properties dialog box, as shown in Figure 15.25. Then, on the General tab, modify the counters by adding new ones from the list of available counters, or remove them by selecting the counters and clicking on the Remove button.

Creating a Trace Log

Trace logs also record data about hardware usage and the activity of the system services from both local and remote computers. However, trace logs differ from counter data logs in that they measure data continuously rather than take periodic samples of the data. To create a new trace log, follow these steps:

1. Open the Performance window as described earlier.

2. Expand Performance Logs And Alerts by double-clicking on it in the console tree. Then, click on Trace Logs to display existing logs in the details pane.

3. Right-click a blank area of the details pane and click on New Log Settings.

4. In the Name dialog box, type the name of the trace log and click on OK to create it. Figure 15.26 shows an example of a trace log.

Note: By default, the log file is created in the PerfLogs folder in the root directory by appending a sequence number to the file name you provided and adding the .etl file extension. You can modify these default options on the Log Files and Advanced tabs.

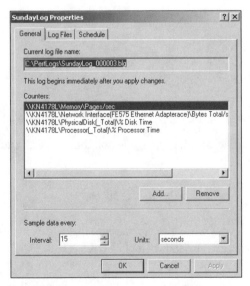

Figure 15.25
Modifying counters in the Counter Log File Properties dialog box.

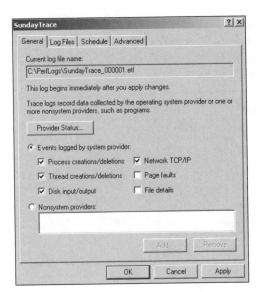

Figure 15.26
Viewing trace log properties.

Creating an Alert

Alerts can create a proactive troubleshooting environment. You can use alerts to notify you of potential problems before they actually occur. Follow these steps to create an alert:

1. Open the Performance window as previously described.

2. Expand Performance Logs And Alerts by double-clicking on it in the console tree. Then, click on Alerts to display existing alerts in the details pane.

3. Right-click a blank area of the details pane and click on New Alert Settings.

4. In the Name dialog box, type the name of the alert and click on OK.

5. Click on the General tab in the dialog box that appears and add the counters and threshold limits as well as provide a comment about the alert, as shown in Figure 15.27.

6. Click on the Action tab and define what action should be taken when the threshold is reached. Figure 15.28 shows the actions available.

Tip: We suggest you always select the Log An Entry In The Application Event Log checkbox and review it daily.

7. Click on the Schedule tab and define when to begin scanning for threshold violations.

Task Manager and Performance Logs and Alerts are the primary tools for reviewing and configuring the performance of your system. Describing optimization of your Windows 2000 Professional environment could in itself require an entire book. Therefore, we focus on the key areas and tools available for optimizing your Windows 2000 installation. Now, it is time to look at Windows 2000 Professional troubleshooting tools that you can use to help detect, analyze, and resolve problems.

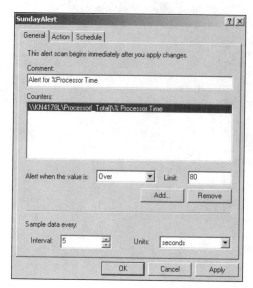

Figure 15.27
Adding counters and limits on the General tab.

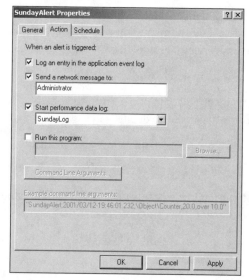

Figure 15.28
Defining an action on the Action tab.

Troubleshooting Tools in Windows 2000 Professional

No matter how well you understand Windows 2000 Professional or how much time you spend planning the installation and configuration of it, and even more time optimizing it, there are always going to be times when things just are not working the way they should be. At these times, you need to put on your analytical cap and figure out just what is wrong. The good news is that, with tools such as Device Manager, Event Viewer, and interactive troubleshooters, help is never too far away.

Troubleshooting tools are useful when you need to identify a hardware or software problem or to perform maintenance tasks on your computer. These types of problems are often difficult to identify unless you have some tools available to assist you.

Troubleshooting Hardware with Device Manager

You use Device Manager to view and manage hardware installed on your computer. Device Manager can assist you in the following ways:

- Modify hardware configuration settings

- Identify device drivers that are loaded for each device

- Determine whether the hardware is working properly

- Install updated device drivers

- Identify device conflicts and manually configure hardware settings

- Disable, enable, and uninstall devices

Warning! *Modifying hardware settings can disable your hardware and may cause your computer to be inoperable or behave erratically.*

Viewing Devices and Resource Settings

When you have to troubleshoot hardware resources, you can view these devices and resources using the Device Manager utility. Follow these steps to open the Device Manager and choose the format of the output of the devices:

1. Click on Start|Settings|Control Panel.

2. Double-click on the System applet.

3. Click on the Hardware tab and then click on the Device Manager button to display the Device Manager window shown in Figure 15.29.

4. Click on View and then choose one of the following output formats:

   - *Devices By Type*—Displays devices by the type of device installed

   - *Devices By Connection*—Displays devices by connection type, such as COM1

   - *Resources By Type*—Displays the status of all allocated resources by type of device using the resource

   - *Resources By Connection*—Displays the status of all allocated resources by connection type

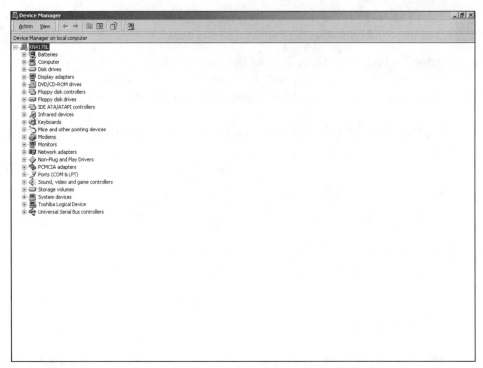

Figure 15.29
The Device Manager window.

Tip: To include hidden devices, such as non–Plug-and-Play devices, open the View menu and click on Show Hidden Devices. A checkmark next to Show Hidden Devices indicates that the hidden devices are being displayed.

You can also print a report containing information about your devices. You can generate the report by clicking on the Print option on the View menu. Under Report Type on the Print dialog box, select one of the following:

- *System Summary*—Prints a summary of devices that are installed on your computer

- *Selected Class Or Device*—Prints a report for the device or hardware type you have selected

- *All Devices And System Summary*—Prints a report for each device or hardware type that is installed on your system and a summary of your system

Configuring Device Properties and Settings

When you install a Plug-and-Play device, Windows 2000 automatically configures the device so that it will work properly and not conflict with any other devices installed on your system. Part of this configuration process is to assign the following system resources: unique interrupt request (IRQ) line numbers, direct memory access (DMA), channel, input/output (I/O) port addresses, and memory address ranges.

Occasionally, two devices require the same resources, causing a device conflict. If this happens, you can manually change the resource settings to ensure that each setting is unique. When you install non–Plug-and-Play devices, the resource settings for the device are not automatically configured. Depending on the type of device, you might have to manually configure it with the settings provided with the device documentation.

Warning! You should avoid changing resource settings manually. When you do so, you are creating static settings. These static settings reduce the flexibility required when adding dynamic devices.

Updating Device Drivers

Updated device drivers are often released to provide enhancements or fixes to older device drivers. You use Device Manager to update the device drivers by following these steps:

1. Open Device Manager as previously discussed.

2. Double-click on the type of device you want to update, right-click on the specific device, and then click on Properties.

3. On the Driver tab, click on the Update Driver button to start the Update Device Driver Wizard. Then, follow the instructions contained in the wizard.

Tip: To update all drivers at once, use the Windows Update option located on the Start menu. This option will connect you to the Microsoft Web site. You can then click on Product Updates to download current drivers, patches, help files, and Internet products to keep your system configuration current.

Using Event Viewer

You use Event Viewer to gather information about software, hardware, and system problems and to monitor Windows 2000 security events. Windows 2000 Professional records events to three types of logs:

- *Application log*—Contains events logged by programs or applications. For example, Excel might record a file error in this log.

- *System log*—Contains events logged by Windows 2000 system components. For example, Event Viewer might log a failure of a service to start or a system component to load.

- *Security log*—Contains events such as valid or invalid attempts to log on or events related to resources such as creating, modifying, or deleting files.

Tip: By default, security logging is turned off. You can enable it by using a Group Policy. Furthermore, as administrator, you can set auditing policies in the Registry that will cause the system to halt when this log is full. This capability is useful for preventing illegal access to your system and resources.

The Event Log service starts automatically when you start Windows 2000. Application and system logs can be viewed by all users, but a security log can be accessed only by an administrator. To open Event Viewer, open Control Panel, double-click on the Administrative Tools icon, and then double-click on Event Viewer.

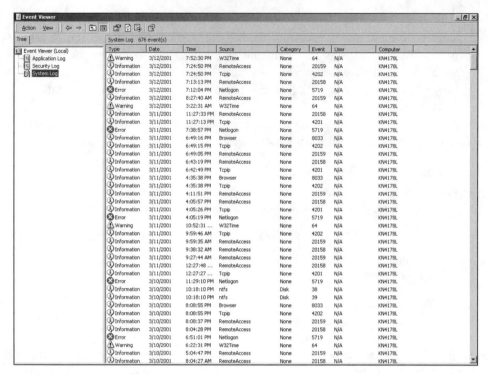

Figure 15.30
Accessing the system log of Event Viewer.

Figure 15.30 displays the events from the system log of the Event Viewer. The following five types of events can be written to the Event Viewer:

- *Error*—Indicates a significant problem, such as a loss of data or functionality

- *Warning*—Indicates a possible future problem, although it is not currently significant enough to prompt an error

- *Information*—Describes the successful operation of a program, service, or driver

- *Failure Audit*—Indicates that an audited security access attempt has failed

- *Success Audit*—Indicates that an audited security access attempt has succeeded

Note: *Failure Audit and Success Audit events are the only types of events written to the security log.*

Using Event Viewer to Troubleshoot Problems

For the most part, Event Viewer is considered a reactive tool used to troubleshoot problems. It contains events that have already taken place. You should carefully monitor event logs to help you predict and identify sources of problems. These logs can also confirm problems with software. If a program halts, you can use the appropriate log to determine the activity that occurred prior to the problem.

The following are four ideas of ways to diagnose different types of problems using your event logs:

- *System problems*—If an event appears to be related to the system, search the system log for similar events or to determine how often the event is occurring.

- *Note event ID numbers*—These numbers match a text description contained in a message file and can be used to understand what occurred in the system.

- *Hardware problems*—If a hardware component appears to be the problem, filter the system log to display only those events generated by that component.

- *Archive logs in log format*—You can save the events to log format (EVT), text format (TXT), or comma-delimited (CSV) format. This flexibility provides you with several ways to search the events.

Customizing the Event Log

Numerous options are available for customizing the logs, including the capability to sort the order of events, filter events, set logging options, and manage the size of the log.

To change the sort order of the events, open the event log you want to view and click on the column heading you want to sort by. To reverse the sort order, click on the column heading a second time. To sort chronologically, click on Newest First or Oldest First on the View menu.

To filter certain events, open the log you want to filter and click on the Filter option on the View menu. Specify the characteristics you want on the Filter tab, as shown in Figure 15.31. If you want to turn off event filtering, click on All Records on the View menu.

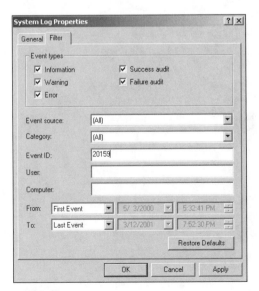

Figure 15.31
Specifying filtering characteristics.

You can set your event logging options by clicking on the Properties option on the Action menu. Click on the General tab to display the logging options available for customization. These options, shown in Figure 15.32, include the log name, log size, action to take when the log fills up, and a button to clear the log.

Working with Windows 2000 Troubleshooters

Windows 2000 Troubleshooters are built into the online help and can be used to help you diagnose and solve technical problems occurring with the operating system, specific software, and hardware. These troubleshooters provide a series of questions for you to answer to assist you in solving the problem.

Using the Troubleshooters

The Windows 2000 Professional Troubleshooters provide the best results when you follow these guidelines:

- You should resize the Help window and move it to the right side of your screen, leaving the left half of the screen to follow the troubleshooter instructions.

- Click on Hide on the Help toolbar to hide the navigation pane of the Help window.

- Follow the troubleshooter steps exactly to avoid an incorrect configuration.

- Some of the Help steps require you to restart your computer or close the trouble-shooter window. If this occurs in a single computer environment, perform the following:

  - Print the current troubleshooter step by clicking on Print on the Help toolbar and then clicking on OK. Double-click on all headings within the step you are printing to ensure that all the procedures are open.

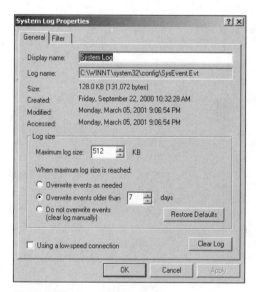

Figure 15.32
Setting event log customization options.

- Write down how you answered each question in the troubleshooter so that you can return to the same location after you restart your computer or after you reopen the troubleshooter window.

Windows 2000 provides numerous troubleshooters, including Client Services for NetWare, Display, Hardware, Internet Connections, Modem, MS-DOS Programs, Multimedia and Games, Networking TCP/IP, Print, Remote Access, Sound, System Setup, and Windows 3.x Programs.

Several tools are available for troubleshooting Windows 2000 Professional, and you should become familiar with each of them to ensure that you are aware of the best way to resolve any problem that arises with your system. Understanding your options for troubleshooting will make it much easier for you to manage your Windows 2000 Professional environment.

Maintaining an optimized and trouble-free environment is great, but if your system is not secure, you are opening it up for potential corruption. As an administrator of your own client machine, you need to ensure that you maintain a secure Windows 2000 environment. **15**

Summary

This chapter introduced the many options available to you when trying to create a safe environment or troubleshoot a corrupt environment. The signing of files, the use of the System File Checker, and Digital Signatures can all be used as proactive measures for safeguarding your system.

You can schedule tasks to manage your environment and use the Disk Defragmenter to optimize the I/O of your system. Furthermore you can set performance alerts to notify you if a resource is nearing a critical threshold.

The Task Manager, System Monitor, and Windows 2000 Troubleshooters are all used for locating and resolving system problems on your Windows 2000 operating system.

This information can assist you in creating an optimized and trouble-free environment, but a major concern that is discussed in the next chapter involves securing your Windows 2000 Professional environment.

Chapter 16

Security

Introducing Security in Windows 2000 Professional

In the last few years, security issues have become among the most important issues facing network administrators. A series of high-profile denial of service (DoS) attacks, notable credit card thefts from e-commerce sites, and the regular defacement of Web sites have made security a top priority for many administrators. What is even more frightening is that a vast number of security breaches go unnoticed, and many occur not from the outside, but from within your own company. Experts speculate that the majority of security breaches actually occur at the hands of a company's own employees. Additionally, most of these breaches go unnoticed, and in the few instances when they are noticed, they remain unreported.

In light of these considerations, you need to implement a security policy and standards on your network to keep both your data safe from prying eyes and your network infrastructure safe and sound from eavesdropping and malicious DoS attacks. It is also important to have standards in place to secure your data for your remote users. In fact, you would be wise to encrypt all communications that take place between your workstations and your servers.

Windows 2000 provides several resources for the security-minded administrator. You can encrypt traffic with Internet Protocol Security (IPSec). You also can track and log resource access. Users need authentication to access your network and its resources; for that reason, Kerberos v5 is supported. Data can be encrypted with the Encrypting File System (EFS), and remote access can also be secured. However, incorrectly configuring these tools may be worse than not configuring them at all. You therefore need to understand your tools and how they are best deployed to secure your network.

Creating a Security Plan

You should create a security plan before you begin implementing security. Although this advice might seem to be common sense, many administrators skip this crucial step or leave it until they have more time. This excess time never arrives, in most cases. An excess of security also is rarely found. When you are implementing a security plan, having more security, not less, is almost always advantageous.

Security should also be visible—and invisible. When you make your network security visible, your users know that you take security seriously. Your network and workstation security should make itself evident to the users. As a start, Windows 2000 can require your users to log on so that their identities are authenticated. Users may also receive warnings when they access restricted resources on the network. This visible verification informs your users that they are attempting to engage in prohibited activity. When Windows 2000 informs your users that their attempted access was noticed, they are discouraged from attempting such activities in the future.

Invisible security is also vital to your network. Invisible security includes EFS and IPSec, for example. EFS encrypts files, so that only their owner can view them. The encryption itself is invisible to the user. Similarly, IPSec encrypts traffic traveling between computers. It is also invisible to users but will immediately be apparent to anyone attempting to gain unauthorized access to a resource.

Most security breaches do not happen because the necessary tools to stop the breaches are too expensive or unavailable. They happen because the steps to keep out intruders and protect the data are incorrectly followed—or worse yet, simply not implemented. Because creating a security plan is not easy, the plan should be well thought out. You should include the input of your company's senior management to ensure your security policies are supported throughout the company. Additionally, you should not create a security policy that, while maintaining strict security, creates a network environment that is cumbersome and unusable.

Consider the following points when creating your security plan:

- *Security goals*—Define what you want to secure.

- *Security risks*—Outline the points in your network that are vulnerable to attack, such as a Web server on the Internet, payroll records, or important servers that could be brought down by a DoS attack. Rank them by their importance, their risk level, and the nature of the risk.

- *Security strategy*—List measures that you can take to eliminate and reduce your security risks.

- *Security policy*—Define the group policy settings or local security settings that will be in place on your network.

- *Security groups*—List the security groups you will need in your organization or on your local PC to maintain security and ease administration of your network.

- *Authentication procedures*—Discuss and outline the methods for ensuring proper authentication for network users. This step may include an implementation plan for smart cards and other supported devices under the Extensible Authentication Protocol (EAP).

- *Data security*—Outline the measures you will take to secure your data, through encryption both on your hard drive and across your network.

- *Administrative security*—Create policies to govern the administration of the network and the data that ensure logs are monitored and all access, even at the administrative level, is justified and appropriate.

- *Public key policies*—Consider the use of a public key infrastructure for your clients, as both an internal and external security feature.

- *User education*—Many components of your plan may change the way your employees currently work. It is vital for you to educate your users so that they understand how their work will be affected. They may need to learn new technologies, such as how to use smart cards. Your security plan should address the need for user training. Additionally, by devoting time to training, you let your employees know that the company takes security seriously and the training is worth your time and theirs.

The preceding are simply starting points for you to consider. Your exact network needs may vary significantly. Test your policy in a lab environment that allows you to see the impact of your proposed policies. You might also choose to introduce your policy in a smaller segment of your network before implementing it on the entire enterprise. Although introducing features and policy changes to your network on a large scale is often tempting, these actions can be disastrous, with disruption in production and unintended results.

16

Mobile Computing Considerations

Laptops have changed forever the face of enterprise computing. The cost of laptops has dropped, and they are now approaching the price range of desktops. With the portability and power of laptops, many companies are finding them invaluable assets for increasing employee productivity. They create new challenges for the security-minded administrator, however. Laptops have made the headlines, as high-profile people in various national security agencies, in the U.S. and abroad, have lost their laptops and, with them, national security secrets.

The single most important task you can perform as an administrator is to educate your users. Laptops can be easily stolen, so employees should be aware that their laptops are prized targets of thieves. They may be stolen for their value or the value of the data they contain. EFS is an ideal technology to protect your mobile data. EFS encrypts your data so that thieves cannot easily recover the information on your laptop. Even if the laptop does not contain sensitive data, it may contain enough information for a thief to log on to your network and do more damage. Therefore, your data should be secured via EFS.

Additionally, laptop users often connect to your network remotely. It is important that their connection method be secure. Windows 2000 supports IPSec to encrypt the data being transmitted. Additionally, through the use of a virtual private network (VPN), data being transmitted over the Internet is also secure.

Security Attacks

Your network may be attacked in more ways than you are familiar with. Computer criminals vary widely in their sophistication. Your modest efforts will keep out most people; however, thorough preparation and planning are required to keep out more determined criminals who may use any of the following methods:

- *Data interception*—When data travels across the network or Internet, it can be intercepted by packet sniffers and decoded. A packet sniffer, such as Network Monitor, which is provided with Windows 2000 Server, is a software tool that allows you to see the data in raw form as it passes through your network. Free packet sniffers are readily available on the Internet for download. An internal breach can also occur if a disgruntled employee decides to sniff packets on your local network. By default, most transmissions on a network are in plain text—email messages, FTP passwords, and instant messaging communication, for instance.

- *Denial of service*—A denial of service attack denies legitimate users access to network resources. Often, routers are overwhelmed with bogus packets of information from computers across the Internet. DoS attacks are becoming increasingly popular. They require little technological savvy to execute. Several tools freely available on the Internet (such as Trinoo, Tribal Flood Network, Smurf, and Stacheldracht) allow novices to implement powerful denial of service attacks. These attacks have brought down major Web sites such as CNN.com, eBay, Yahoo, and Amazon.com.

- *Identity fraud*—This type of attack occurs when an intruder gains access to a username and password for a legitimate network user. The trespasser may use packet sniffing or social engineering (see below) to get the credentials.

- *Macro viruses*—Viruses are becoming increasingly prevalent. Macro viruses take advantage of programming capabilities built into popular word processing and spreadsheet programs. The macro virus Melissa gained attention a few years ago. It overwhelmed email servers as a denial of service attack but also was capable of sending out confidential documents, thereby compromising data.

- *Mobile code*—Java and ActiveX, which are cross-platform languages, can be downloaded from the Internet. If the author of a program created using one of these languages has malicious intentions, the program could have a devastating impact. Because of the prevalence of Java and ActiveX on the Internet, users have become accustomed to installing them, without fully understanding the programs' true functions. The very fact that the vast majority of mobile code applications are benign is enough to create a false sense of security that lulls people into installing and running dangerous code.

- *Data manipulation*—Hackers can manipulate packets of information traveling the network, altering the information for their own purposes. Data can also be corrupted on your network by viruses or malicious users.

- *Misuse of privileges*—Administrators have a great amount of power. Their privileges can be abused, however. Even those administrators with lesser power can misuse their rights on the system to compromise data or access restricted resources.

- *Replay attack*—A savvy user could record an exchange of information between two hosts on the network and replay the exchange to impersonate the valid user. The information could be altered for use with other attacks.

- *Social engineering*—For years, social engineering has been used to gain illicit access to networks. This type of attack involves a hacker's ability to convince a user with access to divulge information regarding the network. This information can aid the hacker's quest to gain unauthorized access to information. The hacker may contact an employee and pretend to be a member of the IT department, for instance, and request account and password information.

- *Trojan horse*—Any program that masquerades as a useful utility or harmless program but actually performs other tasks, such as revealing passwords and logon information to a hacker, falls into this category. A particularly clever example was a software email reader called ProMail. This email reader did everything a user would expect from an email program. However, users were unaware that ProMail was actually harvesting email logon, password, and server information and sending it to a Web-based email account.

16

Part of a well-thought-out security plan will consider all these forms of attack. Not every attack type will apply to your network; however, for those that do, you need to formulate a strategy in your security plan to minimize the risk and the possible effects of such attacks.

Security Concepts

You can employ several solid strategies when dealing with security attacks and developing a security plan. Windows 2000 implements several concepts to ensure that your data and networks are protected from intruders. The two main facets of Windows 2000 security are *authentication* and *authorization*. Authentication is the first step toward network access. A user's identity is authenticated using one of several methods. When the user's identity is authenticated, the second facet of security, authorization, can be determined. Based on a user's identity, access to network resources can be controlled.

In a domain environment, a central domain controller provides authentication. A Windows NT 4 or Windows 2000 server is required to create a domain, which eases administration. In a workgroup, each Windows 2000 computer authenticates the user attempting to log on. Workgroups work best for 10 or fewer computers. The first step of security involves confirmation of a user's right to access the system by verifying their identity.

Windows 2000 Authentication

Authentication provides the first measure of defense in your security plan. Windows 2000 provides several methods to ensure that authorized people attempting to access your network will be granted access. Each user is assigned a username and password. Windows 2000 supports extra levels of authentication as well, such as smart card technology. Windows 2000 also supports Kerberos v5 to encrypt traffic. This extra level of authentication provides an extra layer of protection for your network.

Authentication helps prevent two of the attacks mentioned earlier:

- *Identity fraud*—Exchanges are encrypted, so it is more difficult to intercept an identity and use it to gain unauthorized access to resources.

- *Replay attack*—Time stamping of authentication protocols makes a replay attack useless.

Single Network Logon

To simplify administration, Windows 2000 gives users a single logon, which allows them to access a range of resources, from printers to files to applications. Considering the vast number of resources that may be available on your network, requiring a different password for each resource would actually be a security risk. Your end users would not be able to keep track of all the various passwords and would invariably write them down. When a password is written down, the chance that an unauthorized user will learn the password increases dramatically.

Increasing Authentication Effectiveness

Using Windows 2000, you can strengthen the authentication facet of the security model. As mentioned previously, Windows 2000 supports the Extensible Authentication Protocol. When you hear the acronym *EAP*, think *smart card*—currently the most common implementation of EAP in Windows 2000. With standard Windows 2000 authentication, a user simply enters a username and password to prove his or her identity. A smart card adds a new layer of security to this authentication. The user must have a username, password, and the smart card to be authenticated. Imagine a private club to which you belong: To gain entrance to the club and its weekend shuffleboard tournament, you must get by the doorman. The doorman requires you to give your name and password. Additionally, he has to see your membership card, and you're given a new membership card weekly. Without all this identification, you can't get by the doorman, and you won't get to show off your shuffleboard prowess.

A commonly used smart card has an LCD display with a six-digit number that changes every 60 seconds. To be authenticated, the user must enter his or her name, PIN code, and this number. Without the card, gaining access would be nearly impossible. Other smart cards require a card reader installed on each computer. The user must enter his or her password and logon name and swipe the card through the card reader before access is allowed.

Biometric authentication is also part of EAP. Once the realm of spy movies, now retina scans, fingerprint scans, voice prints, and more can be required for authentication. These solutions are expensive; however, they make it extremely difficult for an intruder to break into your network.

Authentication of Program Code

Invariably, end users download software from the Internet or install unauthorized software on the company computer. Windows 2000 and Internet Explorer can help combat this problem. Although software may seem harmless, the Internet is full of malicious software in the form of viruses and Trojan horses. Software and code can be digitally signed. This digital signature will verify that the code has not been altered since it was published.

However, having a digital signature is not a guarantee that the code is safe because, for instance, the publisher may have accidentally published virus-infected software. Additionally, the publisher might actually have had ill intent and purposefully published infected software. In either case, your browser can be configured to block the download of unsigned code.

Tip: When you're browsing the Internet and confronted with a Security Warning dialog box asking whether you wish to install software, never select the Always Trust Content From Publisher checkbox. Always choose each download on a case-by-case basis. Even VeriSign, a company that provides certificate authority services, can make a mistake. By selecting this option, you're giving carte blanche authority to the software company to install its software without your explicit approval for each package on your PC.

16

By enforcing code authentication on your network, you can lessen the threat of certain security risks:

- *Macro viruses*—If code signing is used and a macro virus is added after the signing, code authentication reveals the tampering.

- *Mobile code*—You can block unsigned code from being installed.

Authorization

As mentioned earlier, the next step after authentication is authorization. After a user logs on to the network, his or her rights to access resources are determined by the permissions set on those resources. NT File System (NTFS) permissions on resources define the user's rights to access the resources. Because resource access is critical, you can see why authorization is an incredibly important part of Windows 2000 security.

Encryption

We have discussed several layers of protection that Windows 2000 implements to secure your network. You can think of the security model as an onion: Every layer of security you peel back reveals another layer. Encryption provides another layer of security for your network, and Windows 2000 fully supports encryption.

Symmetric key encryption uses the same key to both encrypt and decrypt the data. The benefits of symmetric key encryption include the capability to quickly process large amounts of data. A drawback, however, occurs if one key is compromised. In this event, all keys need to be replaced.

A better method of encryption is *public key encryption*. With this type of encryption, you have two keys: a private key and a public key. The private key must be kept secure and safe, while the public key can be distributed freely. Data is encrypted with the public key, and decrypted with the private key. This model is used when you connect to secure Web sites. Windows 2000 uses public key encryption as the basis for several layers of its security model, such as digital signing and EFS. To fully deploy encryption, Windows 2000 relies on a public key infrastructure (PKI), which consists of digital certificates, Certificate Authorities (CAs), and registration authorities. These various components of the public key infrastructure validate the identity and authenticity of each party involved in a transaction.

Data Integrity

When you purchase a box of cereal expecting to pour out a bowl of corn flakes and instead find you have a bowl full of puffed rice, you may be somewhat disappointed. What you purchased is not what you received. It is also not what the maker intended. You have the same expectations with your data. You want the data you receive to be identical to what the creator intended, and maintaining data integrity ensures this will be so. From frames traversing the network to files on your hard drive, maintaining the integrity of your data is important. Tools such as digital signing can use public key technology to ensure that your data is not maliciously or accidentally altered from its original form.

Data Confidentiality

Although maintaining data integrity is important, doing so can be useless if the data is confidential, and the confidentiality is not maintained. Therefore, encrypting data as it passes from one point to another on your network is important. Symmetric key encryption allows you to do that. Passwords, emails, and other vital information travel through your network in plain text. Any eavesdropper with minimal technical skill can learn network passwords and company secrets. To eliminate this threat, you can use encryption to make the passing traffic unintelligible to eavesdroppers. Data confidentiality is a critical component of the onionlike model of security for protecting your network.

Nonrepudiation

Another important facet of your security plan is *nonrepudiation*. If someone contends he or she sent a message, nonrepudiation confirms who sent the message and ensures that the sender is who he or she claims to be. When you make a credit card purchase, you often have to show your driver's license as well. You make a transaction, and you confirm your identity. PKI is responsible for identity confirmation in Windows 2000.

Establishing and confirming the identity of the sender are vital for secure communication between parties. Establishing a PKI provides nonrepudiation. PKI gives a private key with a unique digital signature to a user. When a message is sent with this private key, the recipient uses the sender's public key to read it. This key exchange ensures the identity of the sender and provides security against repudiation.

Managing Windows 2000 Security

You would be amazed at how many companies do not pay proper attention to security. Security is vital to every company. For example, you lock the doors to the office when you leave for the weekend. Not doing so would be ludicrous. But, you too often forget to lock all the doors on your network. Windows 2000 provides significant security tools. However, although you might have a lock on the door, if you don't use it, it's useless.

Security Policy is a part of Group Policy and is also available on standalone computers. In a domain environment with Active Directory installed, you would use Group Policy to enforce your domain security settings. With standalone workstations, you can use Local Security Policy to manage security settings.

Audit logs are another method of tracking security issues. Auditing creates logs of activities on your computer. By reviewing these logs, you can identify attempts at abusing your network and computer. Auditing can provide the smoking gun and can be legal evidence should criminal mischief occur. Audit logs also are often untouched by hackers because the logs can be difficult and time-consuming to erase.

Using Security Configuration And Analysis, administrators can analyze security settings in place on a computer. This tool allows you to compare a template to the settings in effect on a computer. With the results of the analysis, you can find the differences between your desired security configuration and your actual security configuration. This information will guide your troubleshooting and configuration adjustments.

16

Other Security Factors

Security on your network is not simply related to your operating system. Several other factors play an important part as well. It would be shortsighted to configure Windows 2000 for security and then consider your network secure.

Physical security is a factor as well. Depending on the importance and role of a PC on the network, you might need to secure it physically to a desk or lock it in a secure room. Although retrieving data often is the objective of hackers, simply physically damaging your PC will deny you the service of that equipment and may bear a significant cost in downtime. Analyze the importance of all the equipment on your network; consider what would happen if you removed a piece of equipment. If doing so would cause a great loss of productivity for network users, it is likely that piece of equipment should be physically secured.

Another important security factor that is often overlooked is user education. You can put locks on the doors and password-protect the desktop, but if users write down their passwords and leave doors unlocked, your efforts are useless. By educating your users, you can prevent many security breaches. If you stress the importance of your security, your users will become more security conscious. Raise the level of consciousness toward security throughout your network, and your network becomes more secure—no software patch required.

When you educate your users about common security problems, they can actually alert you to potential issues. For example, I once oversaw a wide area network (WAN) that covered an entire state. Because our staff was large, and we had many branch offices, all employees at branch offices didn't know everyone in our MIS department by sight. We implemented ID badges for all MIS staff to help branch office employees recognize us. One day I received a phone call from a branch office. Someone had arrived to pick up the office manager's laptop for routine maintenance. The receptionist was wary because the person did not have an ID badge. I informed her this person wasn't from our department, and when she turned back to him, the stranger had left. If we had not put in place the ID policy, we could have lost valuable equipment, data, and time. A cautious receptionist, thanks to some user education and good policy, saved the day.

User education can help in many areas:

- *Social engineering*—Educate your users that they should never reveal certain information over the phone, such as passwords or usernames. Teach them to be suspicious when someone claiming to be with your department calls for information.

- *Ineffective passwords*—Teach your employees the importance of choosing good passwords. Explain that the best passwords are words that can't be found in the dictionary. Additionally, good passwords include upper- and lowercase letters, along with numbers and symbols. Let the employees know how easily someone can hack into the network if they don't protect their accounts. Also, explain that, with weak passwords, if their accounts are compromised, a hacker can impersonate them in email and destroy their data.

- *Workstation security*—Employees often write down passwords or leave their workstations unlocked. These practices are just as bad as using ineffective passwords or none at all. Explain how easily someone can find passwords stored around the workstation. Teach your users to lock their workstations if they are going to be away from their desks for more than a minute or two. You may even want to demonstrate how quickly a workstation can be compromised by installing a key-logging program, which often takes less than a minute.

Authenticating Users

Windows 2000 Professional supports user authentication, which ensures that the individual using a workstation is authorized to log on to your network. User authentication identifies an individual and, along with authorizing that person, also enables you to track the user's activity on the network and set appropriate limits to network access.

You can separate the purpose of authentication in the security model into two categories:

- *Interactive logon*—With the correct credentials, a user is allowed to access a local computer or the network. The user is allowed to interact with the computer and possibly other computers on the network.

- *Resource authentication*—A user's credentials determine whether that user is allowed to access network resources and services. His or her credentials are authenticated by one of three methods included with Windows 2000: Kerberos v5, smart cards, or NT LAN Manager (NTLM).

When you log on to Windows 2000, you may be presented with two options: to log on locally or to log on to a domain. When you log on locally, your credentials are checked in the local Security Accounts Manager (SAM). When you log on to a domain, a domain controller authenticates your credentials. If you are logging on to a domain, you also can use a smart card, NTLM, or Kerberos v5 authentication.

Smart Cards

Smart cards are a tamper-resistant way to store credentials associated with a user account to further authenticate a user's right to log on; they are a critical component of the PKI infrastructure and Windows 2000 security. Typically, logging in requires knowledge of a username and password. Each user will also need their own smart card.

This type of authentication provides a high level of security. Smart cards are not part of the network like a server, so they cannot be accessed remotely and hacked or broken into. They are also highly portable—typically the size of credit cards. The exact manner in which smart cards provide security can vary. There are three types of cards:

- *Stored-value card*—As the name implies, this card stores a value on it that is decremented when it's used. The value may relate to money or tokens. Stored-value cards are rarely used in network security.

- *Contactless card*—Also known as a proximity card, this card is read by sliding it through a reader or, more commonly, from a short distance, such as by waving it in front of a special reader. These cards often contain an electronic chip and an antenna.

- *Integrated circuit card (ICC)*—This card is well suited for network security. The integrated circuit generates access codes and can be used with information provided by the user to create another layer of security for authentication.

ICCs are the most suitable for authentication because they can provide digital signing and key exchange. They are basically miniature computers.

Smart cards can provide many enhancements to your network beyond the way you and your users log in. Smart cards can secure network traffic such as email, and other network communication. They can also authenticate remote user login and remote network access.

When you use a smart card, a hardware device becomes part of the equation as well: You will need to attach a smart card reader to the computers. Adding such a device can entail a significant up-front expense; however, the enhancement to your network security may be well worth the cost.

NT LAN Manager

Windows NT 4 relied on NTLM for network authentication. NTLM relies on a challenge/response method of authenticating a user's identity. Although Windows 2000 supports NTLM, it does so for backward compatibility with pre–Windows 2000 clients. Windows 95, 98, Me, and NT 4 support NTLM for authentication.

When you install Windows 2000 in a domain environment, it is installed in mixed mode, which simply indicates that Windows NT 4 domain controllers exist or will be implemented. If neither of these two assumptions is true, you are urged to convert to native mode on your domain controllers. Native mode limits NTLM authentication and provides the heightened level of security today's networks require.

NTLM is used in a variety of situations in mixed mode:

- Whenever a Windows client of any sort is authenticated on an NT 4 domain controller

- Whenever a Windows NT 4 Workstation client is authenticated with a Windows 2000 domain controller

- When users in an NT 4 domain are authenticated on a Windows 2000 domain

Eliminating the use of NTLM whenever possible is one of your major goals when implementing security. Therefore, you should strive to use Windows 2000 clients and domain controllers throughout your network.

NTLM provides three methods for challenge/response authentication:

- *LAN Manager (LM)*—This is the weakest form of NTLM security. It provides backward compatibility to client computers running Windows for Workgroups, Windows 95, and Windows 98. LAN Manager provides share-level security in these scenarios.

- *NTLM version 1*—More security is provided with NTLM version 1 than in LM's challenge/response authentication. It allows Windows 2000 clients to connect to Windows NT domain servers when the domain controller is running Windows NT 4 with Service Pack 3 or below.

- *NTLM version 2*—This version of NTLM is the most secure. It is used for Windows 2000 Professional machines that are connecting to Windows NT 4 domain controllers running Service Pack 4 or higher in an NT 4 domain. It is also used for mixed mode Windows 2000 domains that include Windows NT 4 servers.

Microsoft added tremendous strength to Windows 2000 by adding Kerberos v5 support. Windows 2000 has taken a huge step forward in plugging the security holes that plagued Windows NT 4. Assuredly, several security holes will be found in Windows 2000, and many already have been discovered. Kerberos, however, definitely pushes Microsoft security to the forefront.

Kerberos v5

Kerberos v5 provides authentication within a domain. The Kerberos v5 security protocol is an Internet standard; it handles authentication for users and computers. Kerberos v5 encrypts passwords that are sent across the network. This capability provides an extra level of protection against packet sniffers that may be in use.

Kerberos, which was created at MIT, uses *secret key cryptography*. It enables clients to prove their identity to a server, and vice versa, even when the network connection is not secure. When identity on both sides is established, all communications can be encrypted with Kerberos. This encryption ensures protection of both the initial password and the data.

Tip: You can download more information regarding Kerberos, including source code, from MIT's Web site, *http://web.mit.edu/kerberos/www/*.

Kerberos v5 provides several benefits over NTLM:

- *NTLM requires connection to a domain controller for client authentication.* This requirement can slow down the process. With Kerberos, any server can authenticate the client on its own by reviewing the client's credentials. After the client's credentials are authenticated, they are valid for the remainder of that network session.

- *Kerberos provides two-way authentication.* NTLM authenticates only the client. Kerberos authenticates both the client and server. This is an important second level of authentication. NTLM works on the *assumption* that the server is genuine. Kerberos *ensures* that the server is genuine.

- *Trust relationships are simplified.* Windows 2000 trusts, unlike those in Windows NT 4, are two-way, *transitive* trusts. A transitive trust occurs when Domain A trusts Domain B, and Domain B trusts Domain C. This arrangement would result in Domain A trusting Domain C. Trusts no longer must be created among all the domains through-out your enterprise, creating a web of trusts. Your credentials, when authenticated, are accepted throughout the entire tree and forest.

- *Kerberos, unlike NTLM, is a standard.* Kerberos can be used with other operating systems; it is not simply a Microsoft security feature. This standard improves the capability of Windows 2000 to interoperate with other network operating systems.

Warning! If you intend to set up Kerberos v5 on Windows 2000 to interoperate with other operating systems, such as Unix, you need to set up a test lab environment to ensure that your design will work in your production environment. Microsoft has made a change in the data authorization field of the protocol, which may limit the roles that other operating systems can play in your security scheme.

Kerberos v5 authentication assumes that initial communications are not secure. This assumption, which is often true, follows the sage advice of erring on the side of safety. Communications are considered to take place on an open network, where a hacker could easily monitor traffic. Additionally, because of the ease with which a hacker can spoof your identity, the Kerberos motto is to trust no one.

Kerberos relies on the *shared secret* method of authentication. If two individuals share a secret and tell no one else, they can verify each other's identity by asking the other individual to divulge the secret, to see whether that person truly knows it. Before communicating any information to each other, they can each confirm the secret and thus the identity of the person on the other end of the line.

The catch, however, is confirming the secret. If the secret is simply stated over the network, a third person could capture the data, learn the secret, and impersonate either party. In fact, because the basic assumption is that other people are actively monitoring traffic, you must assume that this could happen. Therefore, each person must be able to show he or she knows the secret without sending it over the wire.

To handle this challenge, Kerberos uses secret key cryptography. Each person in the example shares a cryptographic key. Using this key, the two people verify each other's identity. The shared key is symmetric: A single key is able both to encrypt and decrypt. The Key Distribution Center (KDC) hands out keys in Windows 2000, and Kerberos relies on the KDC to implement security.

All three authentication methods are active by default. However, Local Security Policy allows you to disable use of the weaker methods of authentication.

Administering Groups, Rights, and Permissions

Groups provide a quick and easy way to administer security in a network. Using groups, you can quickly administer rights for large numbers of users to access resources on your network. You can just as quickly secure resources in the same manner. (For more information on groups, see Chapter 12.)

Windows 2000 has several preconfigured groups. When you're setting up your computers, you need to know the rights and settings for these built-in groups:

- *Guests*—Members of this group can shut down the system but otherwise have very limited abilities. The Guest user account is disabled by default.

- *Users*—This group includes most user accounts. In NT 4, users had quite a bit of read and write access to your system. In Windows 2000, this access has been restricted. Members of this group cannot read other users' data, nor can they install applications that modify system directories.

- *Power Users*—This group has not changed much from Windows NT 4. Members of this group have read and write permissions to more directories than the Users group. They therefore can install more applications and perform some administrative-level tasks.

- *Backup Operators*—These group members can back up and restore files on the computer. They cannot read all the files, but they are not limited by permissions in their ability to back up the files. They can restart the computer as well, but they cannot change security settings.

- *Administrators*—Members of the Administrators group can perform almost any task on the computer. Administrators can make system-wide changes and have more control over the computer than any other account.

User rights can be divided into two categories:

- *Privileges*—These rights allow users to perform specific actions on the network, such as backing up files or taking ownership of objects.

- *Logon rights*—These rights define how users can log on to the system. Domain controllers, for instance, prohibit users from sitting down at the keyboard and logging on, known as *logging on locally*.

Privileges

When restrictive permissions are set on an object, privileges can override them. For instance, the privilege granted to backup operators that allows them to access all files overrides restrictions set by a user who attempts to deny them access. You can set privileges in the Local Security Settings console on your Professional workstation, as shown in Figure 16.1. Table 16.1 describes the privileges that can be assigned to a user.

16

Logon Rights

Logon rights can also be managed with User Rights Assignment settings, which you can access in the Local Security Settings console under Local Policies. Logon rights define the methods a user can use to log on to a computer. Table 16.2 defines the rights that can be assigned in this category.

If you deny a user, for instance, the right to access a computer from a network and the right to log on locally, the user would effectively be denied access to the computer.

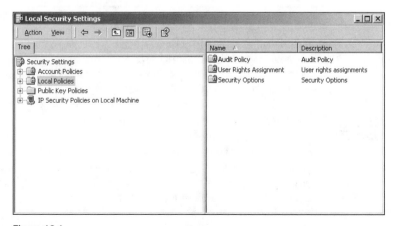

Figure 16.1
The Local Security Settings console allows you to view and edit the security settings on your workstation.

Table 16.1   User-assignable privileges.

Privilege	Description
Act as part of the operating system	This privilege allows a process to be authenticated as a user and thus access any resources available to that user. Keep in mind that, potentially, access is not limited to what is associated with the user by default. The calling process may also request that arbitrary additional accesses be put in the access token. The calling process can also create an anonymous token that can provide complete access. This token does not provide a primary identity for tracking events in the audit log. Typically, an administrator should assign this privilege to low-level authentication services, if it is ever assigned at all. Processes that require this privilege should use the LocalSystem account, which already includes this privilege, rather than use a separate user account with this privilege specially assigned.
Add workstations to a domain	This privilege allows the user to join a computer to a domain. The user specifies the domain to join, either during setup or from System Properties on the computer that is joining the domain. This action creates an object in the Computer container of Active Directory.
Back up files and directories	With this privilege, the user can bypass file and directory permissions to back up data. This is basically the same as granting the user the following permissions on all files and folders on the local computer: Traverse Folder/Execute File, List Folder/Read Data, Read Attributes, Read Extended Attributes, and Read Permissions. Also, note the privilege "Restore files and directories."
Bypass traverse checking	Typically, if a user has no access to a folder, he or she cannot pass through it while browsing a directory structure. This permission allows the user to pass through when browsing or navigating the Registry. Although the user can pass through the directory, the directory's contents cannot be viewed.
Change the system time	This privilege allows the user to modify the time of the internal clock on his or her computer.
Create a pagefile	The pagefile is used by the operating system. This privilege permits the user to create and change the pagefile's size. The user makes pagefile modifications by specifying the changes to the paging file size for a given drive on the Performance Options dialog box, which can be found on the Advanced tab of the System Properties Control Panel applet.
Create a token object	This privilege is also rarely used by a user account. It allows a process to create a token that is used to access any local resources when the process uses **NtCreateToken()** or other token-creation application programming interfaces (APIs). As with other similar privileges, typically, the administrator will use the LocalSystem account for a process requiring this privilege because the LocalSystem account has the privilege by default. Using the built-in account is better administratively than using the privilege because creating a new account to serve the same purpose as an existing account creates unnecessary administrative overhead.
Create permanent shared objects	This privilege grants to a process the capability to create a directory object in the Windows 2000 Object Manager. This privilege is typically used by kernel-mode components that plan to extend the Windows 2000 object namespace. Because components running in kernel mode already have this privilege assigned to them, an administrator does not need to specifically assign this privilege.

(continued)

Table 16.1   User-assignable privileges *(continued)*.

Privilege	Description
Debug programs	This privilege permits the user to attach a debugger to any process. Assign it carefully, and only when absolutely necessary, because it provides a great deal of access to sensitive and critical system operating components.
Enable computer and user accounts to be trusted for delegation	By granting this permission, an administrator allows the user to set the Trusted For Delegation setting on a user or computer object. The user or object that is granted this privilege must have write access to the account control flags on the user or computer object. A server process either running on a computer that is trusted for delegation or run by a user who is trusted for delegation can access resources on another computer. This access uses a client's delegated credentials, as long as the client account does not have the Account Cannot Be Delegated account control flag set. Misuse of this privilege or of the Trusted For Delegation settings could make the network vulnerable to sophisticated attacks using Trojan horse programs that impersonate incoming clients and use their credentials to gain access to network resources.
Force shutdown from a remote system	Granting this privilege allows the user to shut down a computer from a remote network location.
Generate security audits	This privilege allows a process to make entries in the security log for object access auditing and generate other security audits. The security log in Event Viewer traces unauthorized system access.
Increase quotas	This privilege is powerful because of its potential for abuse. It allows a process with write property access to another process to increase the processor quota assigned to that other process. This privilege is useful for system tuning but also can be used as a denial of service attack.
Increase scheduling priority	This privilege permits a process with write property access to another process to increase the execution priority of that other process. Using Task Manager, a user with this privilege can modify the scheduling priority of a process.
Load and unload device drivers	The abilities assigned by this privilege are more likely to be useful to the average administrator than several of the others listed here. This privilege allows a user to install and uninstall plug-and-play device drivers. If the device drivers are not Plug and Play, they are not affected by this privilege and must be installed by administrators. This privilege can be dangerous. Device drivers run as trusted programs, and this trust could be misused to install Trojan horses or other malicious programs.
Lock pages in memory	Another privilege that an administrator will not likely use often, it allows a process to keep data in physical memory. The system is unable to page the data to virtual memory on disk. Exercising this privilege could significantly affect system performance. This privilege is obsolete and is therefore never checked.
Manage auditing and security log	This privilege grants access to a user to specify object access auditing options for individual resources such as files, Active Directory objects, and Registry keys. Remember, object access auditing is not performed until an administrator enables it under audit policy settings under Group Policy or under Group Policy defined in Active Directory. Note that this privilege doesn't grant access to the computer-wide audit policy. However, it does allow the holder to view and clear the security log from the Event Viewer.

16

(continued)

Table 16.1   User-assignable privileges *(continued)*.

Privilege	Description
Modify firmware environment values	The holder of this privilege can modify any system environment variables either through System Properties or by using a process.
Profile a single process	Granting this privilege allows a user to use Windows 2000 performance monitoring tools. Using these tools, the user can monitor the performance of nonsystem processes.
Profile system performance	This privilege allows a user to use Windows 2000 performance monitoring tools to monitor the performance of system processes.
Remove computer from a docking station	If the user is using a laptop connected to a docking station, this privilege allows the user to undock the laptop using the Windows 2000 user interface.
Replace a process-level token	When an administrator grants this privilege, a process is allowed to replace the default token associated with a subprocess that has been started.
Restore files and directories	Similar to the backup privilege, this privilege allows a user to bypass file and directory permissions when restoring backed-up files and directories. Without this privilege, the user might be unable to restore many files and directories. It also allows the user to set any valid security principal (either a user or a computer) as the owner of an object.
Shut down the system	This privilege is necessary to shut down the system. By default, this privilege is not given to users on a Windows 2000 server, so the user won't be able to shut down the computer.
Synchronize directory service data	This privilege is necessary to allow a user to synchronize Active Directory information.
Take ownership of files or other objects	With this privilege, a user is allowed to take ownership of any securable object in the system, including Active Directory objects, files and folders, printers, Registry keys, processes, and threads.

Table 16.2   User-assignable logon rights.

Logon Right	Description
Access this computer from a network	This right allows a user to connect to the computer over the network. Administrators, Everyone, and Power Users have this right by default.
Log on as a batch job	Granting this right permits a user to log on using a batch-queue facility. By default, this privilege is granted to Administrators.
Log on as a service	This right allows a security principal to log on as a service, as a way of establishing a security context. For instance, the LocalSystem account always retains the right to log on as a service. Also, any service that runs under a separate account must be granted this right. Sometimes, backup programs might need their own service account; this account would be granted this right. By default, this right is not granted to anyone.
Log on locally	This right permits a user to log on at the computer's keyboard. This right, which is limited, is given only to Administrators, Account Operators, Backup Operators, Print Operators, and Server Operators by default.
Deny access to this computer from the network	The user is denied the right to connect to this computer over the network.

(continued)

Table 16.2   User-assignable logon rights *(continued)*.

Logon Right	Description
Deny logon as a batch job	The user is denied the right to log on using a batch-queue facility.
Deny logon as a service	The user is denied the right to log on as a service.
Deny logon locally	The user is not permitted to log on at the computer's keyboard.

You need to have a good understanding of all these abilities. When you're installing software or creating user accounts, occasionally the software will give itself or a user account certain privileges. To maintain security, you should document these instances and verify that the levels of rights and privileges accorded any user in your network are appropriate and necessary.

Default File System Permissions

The default file system permissions in Windows 2000 are listed in Table 16.3. You should be familiar with these permissions. As you can see, a large number of directories grant the Full Control permission to Everyone. This permission can be a significant security risk. However, you should change permissions in a lab environment first to ascertain that the proper access is given. For example, if users don't have write access to certain directories, some software they use, such as Microsoft Office, will not function properly. Figure 16.2 shows the Security tab of the Drive Properties dialog box, where NTFS permissions are set. Right-click on a file, folder, or drive, and then choose Properties to bring up the Security tab.

16

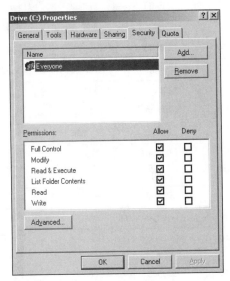

Figure 16.2
NTFS file permissions are set on the Security tab of the Drive Properties dialog box.

When you install Windows 2000 on an NTFS partition, the permissions shown in Table 16.3 are set by default. If you convert the drive to NTFS by using the **convert** command, the default permissions will be Everyone with Full Control. A default installation to drive C: is assumed.

Table 16.3 Default NTFS file system permissions.

Path	Administrators	Creator/Owner	Everyone	Server Operators	System
C:\	Full Control	Full Control	Change	-	Full Control
C:\Program Files and subfolders	Full Control	Full Control	Change	Change	Full Control
C:\Temp	Full Control	Full Control	Change	-	Full Control
C:\Documents and Settings	Special (RWXD)	-	List (RX)	-	Full Control
C:\Documents and Settings\ Administrator and subfolders	-	Full Control	Special (RWX)	-	Full Control
C:\Documents and Settings\ All Users and subfolders	-	Full Control	Special (RWX)	-	Full Control
C:\Documents and Settings\ Default User and subfolders	-	Full Control	Special (RWX)	-	Full Control
C:*%SystemRoot%*	Full Control	Full Control	Change	Change	Full Control
C:*%SystemRoot%*\Addins	Full Control	Full Control	Change	Change	-
C:*%SystemRoot%*\ Connection Wizard	Full Control	Full Control	Change	Change	Full Control
C:*%SystemRoot%*\Config	Full Control	Full Control	Change	Change	Full Control
C:*%SystemRoot%*\CSC	Full Control	Full Control	Change	Change	Full Control
C:*%SystemRoot%*\CSC\D1	Full Control	Full Control	Change	Change	Full Control
C:*%SystemRoot%*\CSC\D2	Full Control	Full Control	Change	Change	Full Control
C:*%SystemRoot%*\CSC\D3	Full Control	Full Control	Change	Change	Full Control
C:*%SystemRoot%*\CSC\D4	Full Control	Full Control	Change	Change	Full Control
C:*%SystemRoot%*\CSC\D5	Full Control	Full Control	Change	Change	Full Control
C:*%SystemRoot%*\CSC\D6	Full Control	Full Control	Change	Change	Full Control
C:*%SystemRoot%*\CSC\D7	Full Control	Full Control	Change	Change	Full Control
C:*%SystemRoot%*\CSC\D8	Full Control	Full Control	Change	Change	Full Control
C:*%SystemRoot%*\Cursors	Full Control	Full Control	Change	Change	Full Control
C:*%SystemRoot%*\Debug	Full Control	Full Control	Change	Change	Full Control
C:*%SystemRoot%*\ Downloaded Program Files	Full Control	Full Control	Change	Change	Full Control
C:*%SystemRoot%*\Driver Cache	Full Control	Full Control	Change	Change	Full Control

(continued)

Table 16.3   Default NTFS file system permissions *(continued)*.

Path	Administrators	Creator/Owner	Everyone	Server Operators	System
C:*%SystemRoot%*\ Driver Cache\I386	Full Control	Full Control	Change	Change	Full Control
C:*%SystemRoot%*\Fonts	Full Control	Full Control	Change	Change	Full Control
C:*%SystemRoot%*\Help	Full Control	Full Control	Change	Change	Full Control
C:*%SystemRoot%*\Inf	Full Control	Full Control	Change	Change	Full Control
C:*%SystemRoot%*\Installer	Full Control	Full Control	Change	Change	Full Control
C:*%SystemRoot%*\ Java and <subfolders>	Full Control	Full Control	Change	Change	Full Control
C:*%SystemRoot%*\Media	Full Control	Full Control	Change	Change	Full Control
C:*%SystemRoot%* Msagent and subfolders	Full Control	Full Control	Change	Change	Full Control
C:*%SystemRoot%*\ Msapps and subfolders	Full Control	Full Control	Change	Change	Full Control
C:*%SystemRoot%*\ Mww32 and subfolders	Full Control	Full Control	Change	Change	Full Control
C:*%SystemRoot%*\ Offline Web Pages	Full Control	Full Control	Change	Change	Full Control
C:*%SystemRoot%*\Registration	Full Control	Full Control	Change	Change	Full Control
C:*%SystemRoot%*\Repair	Full Control	Full Control	Read	Full Control	Full Control
C:*%SystemRoot%*\Registration	Full Control	Full Control	Read	Full Control	-
C:*%SystemRoot%*\ Security and subfolders	Full Control	Full Control	Read	Full Control	-
C:*%SystemRoot%*\Speech	Full Control	Full Control	Change	Change	Full Control
C:*%SystemRoot%*\System	Full Control	Full Control	Change	Change	Full Control
C:*%SystemRoot%*\System32	Full Control	Full Control	Change	Change	Full Control
C:*%SystemRoot%*\System32\ CatRoot	Full Control	Full Control	Change	Change	Full Control
C:*%SystemRoot%*\System32\ Com	Full Control	Full Control	Change	Change	Full Control
C:*%SystemRoot%*\System32\ Config	Full Control	Full Control	List	List	Full Control
C:*%SystemRoot%*\System32\ Dhcp	Full Control	Full Control	Read (RX)	Full Control	Full Control
C:*%SystemRoot%*\System32\ Drivers and subfolders	Full Control	Full Control	Read (RX)	Full Control	Full Control

16

(continued)

Table 16.3   Default NTFS file system permissions *(continued).*

Path	Administrators	Creator/Owner	Everyone	Server Operators	System
C:*%SystemRoot%*\System32\DTCLog	Full Control	Full Control	Read (RX)	Full Control	Full Control
C:*%SystemRoot%*\System32\Export	Full Control	Full Control	Read (RX)	Full Control	Full Control
C:*%SystemRoot%*\System32\GroupPolicy and subfolders	Full Control	Full Control	Read (RX)	Full Control	Full Control
C:*%SystemRoot%*\System32\IAS	Full Control	Full Control	Read (RX)	Full Control	Full Control
C:*%SystemRoot%*\System32\Inetsrv	Full Control	Full Control	Change	Change	Full Control
C:*%SystemRoot%*\System32\Mui and subfolders	Full Control	Full Control	Change	Change	Full Control
C:*%SystemRoot%*\System32\Npp	Full Control	Full Control	Change	Change	Full Control
C:*%SystemRoot%*\System32\NtmsData	Full Control	Full Control	Change	Change	Full Control
C:*%SystemRoot%*\System32\Os2 and <subfolders>	Full Control	Full Control	Change	Change	Full Control
C:*%SystemRoot%*\System32\Ras	Full Control	Full Control	Change (RWXD)	Full Control	Full Control
C:*%SystemRoot%*\System32\Rocket	Full Control	Full Control	Read (RX)	Full Control	Full Control
C:*%SystemRoot%*\System32\Wbem and subfolders	Full Control	Full Control	Change	Change	Full Control
C:*%SystemRoot%*\System32\Wins	Full Control	Full Control	Change (RWXD)	Change (RWXD)	Full Control
C:*%SystemRoot%*\Tasks	Full Control	Full Control	Change	Change	Full Control
C:*%SystemRoot%*\Temp	Full Control	Full Control	Change	Change	Full Control
C:*%SystemRoot%*\twain_32	Full Control	Full Control	Change	Change	Full Control
C:*%SystemRoot%*\Web	Full Control	Full Control	Change	Change	Full Control
Any other folders	Full Control	Full Control	Change	Change	Full Control

The following folders give the Full Control permission to Administrators, Creators/Owners, and the System. They give the Read (RX) permission to Everyone, and Change (RWXD) to Replicator and Server Operators:

- C:*%SystemRoot%*\System32\Rpcproxy
- C:*%SystemRoot%*\System32\Setup
- C:*%SystemRoot%*\System32\ShellExt

The spool folder, located at *%SystemRoot%*\System32\Spool, gives Read (RX) permission to Everyone and grants Full Control to Administrators, Printer Operators, Creators/ Owners, the System, and Server Operators.

Having this reference handy can be advantageous when you're troubleshooting access issues. You can actually use it to restore your system to its default state of rights and permissions.

The Registry has permissions as well. Running Regedt32.exe as opposed to regedit.exe sets Registry security, as shown in Figure 16.3. After you open your Registry, choose Permissions from the Security menu.

Table 16.4 displays the default Registry permissions. For security purposes, you may wish to tighten users' abilities to modify certain keys. If you choose to do so, be sure the system works properly and make a backup before you make any modifications.

Abbreviations used in the table are as follows:

- HKLM = HKEY_LOCAL_MACHINE

- SW = Software

- MS = Microsoft

- CV = CurrentVersion

- CCS = CurrentControlSet

- W NT = Windows NT

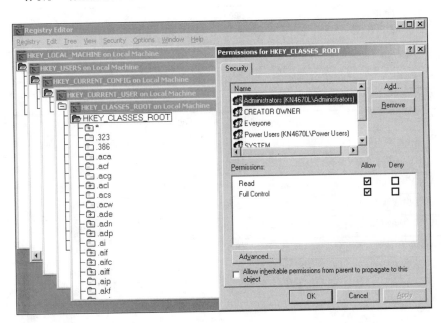

Figure 16.3
Regedt32.exe allows you to set Registry permissions.

Table 16.4   Default Registry permissions for power users and default users.

Key	Default Power User Permissions	Default User Permissions
HKEY_LOCAL_MACHINE		
HKLM\Software	Modify	Read
HKLM\SW\Classes\helpfile	Read	Read
HKLM\SW\Classes\.hlp	Read	Read
HKLM\SW\MS\Command Processor	Read	Read
HKLM\SW\MS\Cryptography\OID	Read	Read
HKLM\SW\MS\Cryptography\Providers\Trust	Read	Read
HKLM\SW\MS\Cryptography\Services	Read	Read
HKLM\SW\MS\Driver Signing	Read	Read
HKLM\SW\MS\EnterpriseCertificates	Read	Read
HKLM\SW\MS\Non-Driver Signing	Read	Read
HKLM\SW\MS\NetDDE	None	None
HKLM\SW\MS\Ole	Read	Read
HKLM\SW\MS\Rpc	Read	Read
HKLM\SW\MS\Secure	Read	Read
HKLM\SW\MS\SystemCertificates	Read	Read
HKLM\SW\MS\Windows\CV\RunOnce	Read	Read
HKLM\SW\MS\W NT\CV\DiskQuota	Read	Read
HKLM\SW\MS\W NT\CV\Drivers32	Read	Read
HKLM\SW\MS\W NT\CV\Font Drivers	Read	Read
HKLM\SW\MS\W NT\CV\FontMapper	Read	Read
HKLM\SW\MS\W NT\CV\Image File Execution Options	Read	Read
HKLM\SW\MS\W NT\CV\IniFileMapping	Read	Read
HKLM\SW\MS\W NT\CV\Perflib	Read (via Interactive)	Read (via Interactive)
HKLM\SW\MS\W NT\CV\SecEdit	Read	Read
HKLM\SW\MS\W NT\CV\Time Zones	Read	Read
HKLM\SW\MS\W NT\CV\Windows	Read	Read
HKLM\SW\MS\W NT\CV\Winlogon	Read	Read
HKLM\SW\MS\W NT\CV\AsrCommands	Read	Read
HKLM\SW\MS\W NT\CV\Classes	Read	Read
HKLM\SW\MS\W NT\CV\Console	Read	Read
HKLM\SW\MS\W NT\CV\EFS	Read	Read

(continued)

Table 16.4   Default Registry permissions for power users and default users (continued).

Key	Default Power User Permissions	Default User Permissions
HKLM\SW\MS\W NT\CV\ProfileList	Read	Read
HKLM\SW\MS\W NT\CV\Svchost	Read	Read
HKLM\SW\Policies	Read	Read
HKLM\System	Read	Read
HKLM\SYSTEM\CCS\Control\SecurePipeServers\winreg	None	None
HKLM\SYSTEM\CCS\Control\Session Manager\Executive	Modify	Read
HKLM\SYSTEM\CCS\Control\TimeZoneInformation	Modify	Read
HKLM\SYSTEM\CCS\Control\WMI\Security	None	None
HKLM\Hardware	Read (via Everyone)	Read (via Everyone)
HKLM\SAM	Read (via Everyone)	Read (via Everyone)
HKLM\Security	None	None
HKEY_USERS		
USERS\.DEFAULT	Read	Read
USERS\.DEFAULT\SW\MS\NetDDE	None	None
HKEY_CURRENT_CONFIG	= HKLM\System\CCS\HardwareProfiles\Current	
HKEY_CURRENT_USER	Full Control	Full Control
HKEY_CLASSES_ROOT	= Merge of HKLM\SW\Classes + HKCU\SW\Classes	

16

There is no perfect guideline in changing these settings to enhance your security. The situations in which you might modify them are so varied that no single suggestion will be valid for most users. Therefore, we recommend that you back up your Registry before making any modifications. In addition, thoroughly test the effects of your changes on the computer and test all facets of your software applications for unintended ill effects after making changes and before deploying your changes into a production environment.

Setting a Security Policy

In Windows NT 4, you used the Policy Editor to control security settings on workstations and servers. In Windows 2000, you control many of these same settings by using Security Policy. Some Policy Editor functions are now a part of Group Policy. Others can be found in Security Policy. The interface is considerably different, and the options and settings are greater in number and scope. You can access Local Security Settings by choosing Start|Settings|Control Panel, and then double-clicking on Administrative Tools. Local Security Settings combines four nodes of security policies:

- Account Policies

- Local Policies

- Public Key Policies

- IP Security Policies

Security Policy can be applied throughout a domain or at the local computer level. If the policy of the domain differs from the local policy, the domain policy overrides the locally defined policy. Security Policy allows you to create a single set of security settings that affect multiple users. This capability eases your administration overhead.

Windows 2000 Professional computers install Local Security Policy by default. This way, local settings can be implemented. To create domain-wide Security Policy, you will need to be in a domain environment with Active Directory installed.

Local Security Settings

Under the four categories described in the preceding section are seven more subcategories that define the settings applicable to the local computer. Domain security policy includes more options, such as settings for Kerberos. However, we'll take a closer look at these settings that apply to the local computer:

- Password Policy

- Account Lockout Policy

- Audit Policy

- User Rights Assignment

- Security Options

- Encrypted Data Recovery Agents

- IP Security Policies on Local Machine

The Account Policy category includes both Password Policy and Account Lockout Policy. Password Policy can be modified depending on the settings that are necessary for the level of security you wish to implement. You can specify a minimum and maximum password age, password length, complexity requirements, and a password history. A prudent combination will result in strong passwords used throughout your network. It is additionally important to educate your users regarding the characteristics of strong passwords.

Your policy should include a reasonable length for passwords. Typically, the optimal length for passwords is six to eight characters long. Although longer passwords are often stronger, they also are more likely to be written down. Encourage your users to use passwords that cannot be found in the dictionary. Passwords should include upper- and lowercase characters, numbers, and symbols to increase the complexity.

Account Lockout Policy defines the result when a user fails to provide a correct username and password. The account lockout duration can be defined, as well as the number of failed attempts before the account is locked out. You can also reset the counter for failed attempts, defining the amount of time that must pass before the counter is set to zero.

As with all security·policies, balance is required. If you allow only a single failed attempt, you definitely heighten the level of security in your network. However, you will also proportionately increase the number of calls to your help desk. Additionally, users can purposefully lock out other users. The overhead resulting from such a secure policy might not be worth the security. You must measure the cost effectiveness.

Under Local Policies, you will find Audit Policy, User Rights Assignment, and Security Options. By default, all auditing is turned off. If you wish to audit security events, you must turn on auditing here and then enable auditing on the object you wish to monitor. Settings in Audit Policy include account management, logon events, privilege use, and directory service access. Although you might be tempted to turn on all auditing, be sure that you will actually monitor the security events. Auditing without reviewing the information is useless and consumes system resources. Auditing is a powerful tool, however, so to proactively manage your network security, you should use it.

Keep in mind as well that you should audit successes and failures for many events. For example, if someone is trying to hack your administrator password, logging failures will be your first indication of their efforts. However, only by logging success will you immediately know if the hacker succeeded.

16

User Rights Assignment covers all the settings described in depth earlier in this chapter. By modifying these settings, you can add groups and individual accounts to policies that allow users to log on locally to a computer, for instance, or change the system time.

Security Options includes a wide variety of security settings. Settings include disabling the Ctrl+Alt+Del requirement for logon, which will force a smart card logon. You can prevent users from installing printer drivers, and you can create a logon banner and message here. One of the most important settings here is the LAN Manager Authentication Level. You can strengthen the level of LM authentication used by changing this setting to use NTLM version 2.

Public Key Policies contains the subcategory for Encrypted Data Recovery Agents. Any account in your network that is designated as a recovery agent can recover data encrypted with EFS, regardless of who encrypted the file. By default, the first administrator account created on the computer is listed here. You can add other accounts as necessary. All the settings' main nodes are shown in Figure 16.4.

Internet Protocol Security Policies

The Internet Protocol Security Policies category allows you to set IPSec policy. IPSec is a standard that allows network communication to be encrypted for security. When you secure the traffic, it is not vulnerable to casual monitoring by individuals who are sniffing traffic. IPSec policy includes settings to request or require IPSec-secured communications. You should carefully plan and monitor these communications to confirm that you've properly implemented IPSec policy in your network.

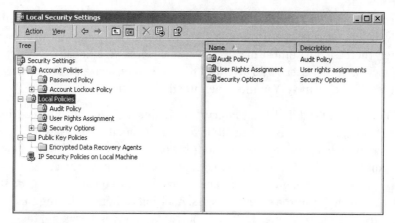

Figure 16.4
The Local Security Settings console controls many aspects of security on your network, from traffic encryption to data encryption.

Default Policy Settings

The default settings on a standard installation are provided in Tables 16.5 through 16.10. Resetting policies to their default settings can be helpful when you're tracking down security problems.

Table 16.5   Password Policy default settings.

Policy	Local Setting
Enforce password history	0 passwords remembered
Maximum password age	42 days
Minimum password age	0 days
Minimum password length	0 characters
Passwords must meet complexity requirements	Disabled
Store password using reversible encryption for all users in the domain	Disabled

Table 16.6   Account Lockout Policy default settings.

Policy	Local Setting
Account lockout duration	Not defined
Account lockout threshold	0 invalid logon attempts
Reset account lockout counter after	Not defined

Table 16.7   Audit Policy default settings.

Policy	Local Setting
Audit account logon events	No auditing
Audit account management	No auditing
Audit directory service access	No auditing
Audit logon events	No auditing
Audit object access	No auditing
Audit policy change	No auditing
Audit privilege use	No auditing
Audit process tracking	No auditing
Audit system events	No auditing

Table 16.8   User Rights Assignment default settings.

Policy	Local Setting
Access this computer from the network	Everyone
Act as part of the operating system	None
Add workstations to domain	None
Back up files and directories	Backup Operators
Bypass traverse checking	Everyone
Change the system time	Power Users
Create a pagefile	Administrators
Create a token object	None
Create permanent shared objects	None
Debug programs	Administrators
Deny access to this computer from the network	None
Deny logon as a batch job	None
Deny logon as a service	None
Deny logon locally	None
Enable computer and user accounts to be trusted for delegation	None
Force shutdown from a remote system	Administrators
Generate security audits	None
Increase quotas	Administrators
Increase scheduling priority	Administrators
Load and unload device drivers	Administrators

16

(continued)

Table 16.8   User Rights Assignment default settings *(continued)*.

Policy	Local Setting
Lock pages in memory	None
Log on as a batch job	None
Log on as a service	None
Log on locally	Computer\Domain\Guest
Manage auditing and security log	Administrators
Modify firmware environment values	Administrators
Profile single process	Power Users
Profile system performance	Administrators
Remove computer from docking station	Users
Replace a process level token	None
Restore files and directories	Backup Operators
Shut down the system	Users
Synchronize directory service data	None
Take ownership of files or other objects	Administrators

Table 16.9   Security Options default settings.

Policy	Local Setting
Additional restrictions for anonymous connections	Rely on default permissions (none set by default)
Allow server operators to schedule tasks (domain controllers only)	Not defined
Allow system to be shut down without having to log on	Enabled
Allowed to eject removable NTFS media	Administrators
Amount of idle time required before disconnecting session	15 minutes
Audit the access of global system objects	Disabled
Audit use of Backup and Restore privilege	Disabled
Automatically log off users when logon time expires (local)	Enabled
Clear virtual memory pagefile when system shuts down	Disabled
Digitally sign client communication (always)	Disabled
Digitally sign client communication (when possible)	Enabled
Digitally sign server communication (always)	Disabled
Digitally sign server communication (when possible)	Disabled
Disable Ctrl+Alt+Del requirement for logon	Not defined
Do not display last user name in logon screen	Disabled

(continued)

Table 16.9   Security Options default settings (continued).

Policy	Local Setting
LAN Manager Authentication Level	Send LM and NTLM responses
Message text for users attempting to log on	None
Message title for users attempting to log on	None
Number of previous logons to cache (in case domain controller is not available)	10 logons
Prevent system maintenance of computer account password	Disabled
Prevent users from installing printer drivers	Disabled
Prompt user to change password before expiration	14 days
Recovery Console: Allow automatic administrative logon	Disabled
Recovery Console: Allow floppy copy and access to all drives and all folders	Disabled
Rename administrator account	Not defined
Rename guest account	Not defined
Restrict CD-ROM access to locally logged-on user only	Disabled
Restrict floppy access to locally logged-on user only	Disabled
Secure channel: Digitally encrypt or sign secure channel data (always)	Disabled
Secure channel: Digitally encrypt secure channel data (when possible)	Enabled
Secure channel: Digitally sign secure channel data (when possible)	Enabled
Secure channel: Require strong (Windows 2000 or later) session key	Disabled
Send unencrypted password to connect to third-party SMB servers	Disabled
Shut down system immediately if unable to log security audits	Disabled
Smart card removal behavior	No Action
Strengthen default permissions of global system objects (for example, Symbolic Links)	Enabled
Unsigned driver installation behavior	Not defined
Unsigned non-driver installation behavior	Not defined

16

Table 16.10   IP Security Policies on Local Machine default settings.

Policy	Description	Assigned
Client (Respond Only)	Communicate normally (unsecured). Use the default response rule to negotiate with servers that request security. Only the requested protocol and port traffic with that server is secured.	No
Secure Server (Require Security)	For all IP traffic, always require security using Kerberos trust. Do not allow unsecured communication with untrusted clients.	No
Server (Request Security)	For all IP traffic, always request security using Kerberos trust. Allow unsecured communication with clients that do not respond to request.	No

Security Setting Defaults by Policy

You might often wonder why certain settings are set by default. With many settings, Microsoft appears to be seeking maximum compatibility, not security. Several would be considered security issues, including the ability to shut down the system without having to log on. This could easily lead to a denial of service attack because anyone could shut down an important workstation, and there would be no record of a user performing the action. The following policies are enabled by default:

- Allow system to be shut down without having to log on

- Automatically log off users when logon time expires (local)

- Digitally sign client communication (when possible)

- Secure channel: Digitally encrypt secure channel data (when possible)

- Secure channel: Digitally sign secure channel data (when possible)

- Strengthen default permissions of global system objects (for example, Symbolic Links)

Again, while you consider the implications of these policies, note the policies that are disabled by default. Passwords do not need to meet complexity requirements by default. Additionally, the last logged-in username is displayed. Displaying this name is considered a security risk because it gives a hacker half the information he or she needs to break into your system. Several policies that strengthen your system's security are disabled by default.

Group Capability Comparison

Often, administrators wonder exactly what capabilities are granted to members of different groups. The following list details the different rights granted to members of the Administrators group compared to members of the Power Users group. Administrators can perform the following actions that Power Users cannot:

- Install the operating system

- Install or configure hardware device drivers (Power Users can install printer drivers only)

- Install system services

- Install Service Packs and Windows Updates

- Upgrade the operating system

- Repair the operating system

- Install applications that modify Windows system files

- Configure password policy

- Configure audit policy

- Manage security logs

- Create administrative shares

- Create administrative accounts

- Modify groups or accounts created by other users

- Remotely access the Registry

- Stop or start any service

- Configure services

- Increase quotas

- Increase execution priorities

- Remotely shut down the system

- Take ownership of arbitrary objects

- Assign rights to members of the Users group

- Override a locked computer

- Format a hard disk drive

- Modify system-wide environment variables

- Access the private data of members of the Users group

- Back up and restore files

16

Power Users have several abilities that regular users do not. Remember that although these users can create user accounts, the user accounts do not have more rights than the Power User. This group can do the following:

- Create local users and groups

- Modify users and groups that they have created

- Create and delete nonadministrator file shares

- Create, manage, delete, and share local printers

- Change system time (default user right)

- Stop or start manually started services

These rights and the permissions mentioned earlier in the chapter allow Power Users to install many applications, as long as the applications don't modify system files or the HKLM\System Registry key. Power Users can also run certain legacy applications that modify the Registry incorrectly. Regular users would receive error messages and would not be able to run the applications. Be sure you trust your Power Users, however. Power Users could plant Trojan horse programs that may create security risks. Additionally, they have enough authority to make changes that affect many other users of the system.

Using Security Templates

Windows 2000 has increased the simplicity of implementing security with security templates, which are predefined security settings. You can use security templates to apply security settings to a computer. By using such a template on multiple computers, you can ensure consistent settings across your network. You can import a template into a database and compare it to the settings on a specific computer as well. Before you use security templates in a production environment, be sure to test them in a test environment.

Security Console

One of the first steps in adding security templates is to create a dedicated security console. You can do so by following these steps:

1. Open a blank MMC file by clicking on Start|Run, typing "MMC", and clicking on OK.

2. Click on Console|Add/Remove Snap-in.

3. Click on Add and double-click on both Security Configuration And Analysis and Security Templates.

4. Click on Close and then click on OK.

These steps will put your security analysis tool and security templates in a single location. Your console will look like the one shown in Figure 16.5. Be sure to save this console. The Security Configuration And Analysis snap-in enables you to import and export templates and compare those settings to the settings on the local computer. The first step in performing the comparison is to open a security database by following these steps:

1. In the console you just created, right-click on Security Configuration And Analysis and then click on Open Database.

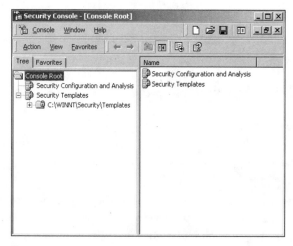

Figure 16.5
The Security Console allows you to manage many security settings from a single location.

2. Highlight a database and click on Open. Or, you can create a new database by typing a database name, clicking on Open, selecting a template file, and then clicking on Open again.

The next step is to right-click on Security Configuration And Analysis and choose Analyze Computer Now. A comparison will be made between your current settings and the settings in the template file. Choosing Configure Computer Now will resolve the differences between the template and the local computer.

If you run Windows 2000 applications, you most likely will not need to modify any permissions assigned to groups, and the default groups will provide the necessary rights for users to perform their jobs. Typically, when your system uses older applications, the Power Users group will be necessary. We cannot stress enough that you should not use the Power Users group unless absolutely necessary, due to the security risks involved.

Security Templates

Windows 2000 provides five basic levels of security templates. The important point to remember is that you need to apply them sequentially up to the highest level of security you desire. The higher security templates do not include the settings made by the lower-level security templates.

Basic

The Basic template applies the default settings outlined earlier. If you have a Windows NT computer that was upgraded to Windows 2000, this template brings the upgraded computer in line with the default Windows 2000 settings (many security settings from an upgraded computer are not changed). You can also use this template to lower your security settings if the need arises.

Optional Component File Security

The Optional Component File Security templates apply security settings to the optional components that may be installed during setup. (During setup, optional components are the choices that are not selected by default.) If optional components are installed, be sure to apply these templates as well. Because optional components are typically installed, you should make adding these templates a part of your security checklist.

Compatible

The Compatible template weakens security settings so that applications will work without necessitating the addition of users to your Power Users group. This template will weaken the default permissions so that users can access legacy programs.

Warning! Using this template weakens your security settings and makes your Windows 2000 installation significantly less secure.

Secure

The Secure template creates a more secure workstation. All members of the Power Users group are removed, for instance, and passwords are required to be more secure. The Secure template is not concerned with users' ability to run legacy applications, so the applications may not run properly. However, it does not modify permissions. Be sure to test this template in a lab environment before deploying it on your network. Users with the right permissions, however, will still be able to run these applications.

High Secure

The High Secure template increases the security level of your workstations significantly. Server Message Blocks (SMB) packet signing is required, for instance. Unsigned driver installation is blocked as well. Most security settings are set at the most restrictive, most secure setting. This template does not take into consideration any other aspects of workstation performance except security. Ease of use, interconnectivity with other clients, and performance are not considerations in this template—security rules. If you use a High Secure template in a mixed environment with Windows 9x and NT worksta-tions, you will likely experience significant problems because it takes advantage of many Windows 2000 technologies that aren't available in those older operating systems.

Using IPSec

IPSec encrypts network traffic to protect data. This secured communication allows important traffic to pass over an insecure network. The encryption takes place at the IP network layer, so encryption rarely interferes with applications. The key that encrypts the traffic is encrypted at each computer, so even the shared key isn't passed across the network.

To use IPSec, you must implement an IPSec security policy. Your policy will depend on the requirements of your network. You can view your current policy under Local Security Settings. To view your current settings, open Local Security Settings under Administra-tive Tools. Click on IP Security Policies On Local Machine. See Table 16.10 earlier in the chapter to review the settings for this selection.

You can activate one of these polices by right-clicking on the policy and choosing Assign from the shortcut menu. By right-clicking on the policy and choosing Properties, you can further refine the policy through the Properties dialog box.

When you're defining a policy for your network, it is important to realize that the encryp-tion process is demanding on your CPU. You should monitor your computers in a test lab environment, watching the processor load to see whether it becomes a bottleneck. It might be better to use alternative resources to handle IPSec encryption, such as a special network interface card (NIC), or upgrade the CPU on the affected PCs. The crucial step in your deployment is to thoroughly test IPSec in a test lab that closely simulates the processing load.

You can specify the levels of authentication between computers as well as the amount of confidentiality required by configuring the appropriate settings. You can also dictate the lower level of security that is acceptable between computers. Non-IPSec-enabled clients can be prevented from communicating with IPSec-enabled clients as well. All communications can be encrypted, or plain text communication may be permitted.

IPSec can be ideal for providing security in the following situations:

- Communication between workstations over an intranet, when those communications are confidential or sensitive in nature

- Communications between a client and server, when the server holds confidential information, such as files and documents of a sensitive nature

- All remote access communications, whether by dial-up or VPN

- WAN communications between routers

When correctly applied, an IPSec policy can significantly improve the security of your network.

Using the Encrypting File System

16

Securing network communications is important, but securing data on your drives is also important. Although NTFS permissions apply a certain level of security, your ability to encrypt data takes this security to a new level. The Encrypting File System encrypts data on your hard drive using symmetric key encryption along with public key technology. EFS is available only on drives formatted in NTFS. Only the owner can open encrypted files; however, the first administrator account on the PC is designated as a recovery agent, and this account can also recover the file if necessary. If the recovery agent is removed, no one can access the file but the owner. Additionally, other accounts can be designated as recovery agents if you so desire.

How EFS Works

EFS is set with an encryption attribute. When this setting is enabled, the file is encrypted. EFS saves the file as encrypted ciphertext. If a user is authorized to access the file, EFS decrypts the file for the user in the background, and the user is presented with a plaintext version of the file. If the file is modified and saved, EFS steps in and saves the file in encrypted ciphertext. No one else can view or modify the encrypted files. EFS provides confidentiality to prevent access to the files even from disk tools that view the disk content.

You can encrypt information by encrypting the files or the folder containing the files. It is recommended that you encrypt information at the folder level as opposed to the file level. For instance, when you open MS Word, a temporary file is created. If you encrypt the original file, the temporary file is not encrypted and could be read. However, if you encrypt the folder, the temporary file, created in the same folder, will be encrypted as well. Therefore, it's wiser to encrypt folders instead of files. To encrypt a file or a folder, follow these steps:

1. Right-click on the file or folder and choose Properties to open the Properties dialog box.

Figure 16.6
The Advanced Attributes dialog box allows you to set the encryption attribute to protect your data.

2. Click on the Advanced button to open the Advanced Attributes dialog box, as shown in Figure 16.6.

3. Under Compress Or Encrypt Attributes, select Encrypt Contents To Secure Data.

Note that you cannot select both Compress and Encrypt. If a file needs compression and encryption, opt for Encrypt when security is at stake and buy a larger hard drive if significant space must be saved using compression. Encryption is a new feature of Windows 2000 and NTFS 5; it is not compatible with older versions of NTFS.

EFS and Public Key Technology

EFS requires the user to have a valid EFS user's certificate. A recovery agent with a valid EFS recovery certificate must be available as well if the data might need to be recovered in the event of employee termination, for instance. No Certificate Authority is required to issue the certificates; EFS creates its own and issues them to the user and default recovery agent. The Microsoft Cryptographic Application Programming Interface (CryptoAPI) and Microsoft Cryptographics Service Provider (CSP) create the private key for EFS.

EFS encryption follows these steps:

1. A bulk symmetric encryption key is generated.

2. The file is encrypted with the key.

3. The bulk encryption key is encrypted with the EFS user's public key.

4. The bulk encryption key is stored in a special header of the file called the data decryption field (DDF).

EFS uses the user's private key to decrypt the bulk encryption key and then decrypt the file whenever necessary. Only the user has the private key, so only the user is able to decrypt the bulk encryption key that is necessary to access the file.

If the user's private key is lost or damaged, the designated recovery agent is able to decrypt and recover the file. EFS allows the recovery agent to access the file by following these steps:

1. The bulk encryption key is encrypted using the public key from each recovery agent.

2. The encrypted key is stored in the data recovery field (DRF) that is a part of the file, like the DDF.

The data recovery field can contain multiple instances of information to allow for multiple recovery agents. The DRF is rewritten every time the file is viewed, opened, copied, or moved. Recovery agents can be designated under Encrypted Data Recovery Agents, which is located under Public Key Policies in the Local Security Policy console.

Encrypted Data Recovery

In many circumstances, another individual may need to recover data. If an employee encrypts files and is terminated, for instance, an administrator may need to recover the encrypted data. Cipher is a command-line utility that you can use if a recovery agent account, a certificate, and a private key exist. Cipher comes with Windows 2000 Professional and can be run from the command prompt. To use it, log on as the recovery agent and decrypt the file using Cipher. The recovery agent must be listed in the DRF, as indicated earlier. Also, the private key must be installed on the computer for you to be able to use Cipher.

16

Recovery Key Security

With a recovery key, data can be easily decrypted. Therefore, you must secure your recovery keys. You can take several steps to secure the recovery keys. You can disable the default recovery account and export the recovery agent's certificate and private key. This information can be placed in a secure location. This way, even if a laptop is stolen, the data will be safe if it is encrypted. No one will be able to access the data.

Recovery Key Expiration

If a file is unchanged for a long time, the certificate might expire. To ensure access to all your files, you should institute a method of archiving your data. You can save the crucial information to recover the data by exporting the certificate and private key. Just as you do with any backup media, you should store them in a safe location. When exporting a key, you must also provide a password to access the private key. The password is encrypted as well, so it cannot be easily recovered.

Recovering data with an expired certificate requires the archived information you created. You must import the expired certificate and key from the archive to the local computer. Efsinfo will provide the recovery agent information you need to recover the encrypted information. Efsinfo is a Resource Kit utility, but can also be downloaded separately from Microsoft's site at **www.microsoft.com/windows2000/techinfo/reskit/tools/existing/efsinfo-o.asp**.

Summary

Security is a broad topic, enough to fill an entire book. In this chapter, we discussed various new technologies implemented in Windows 2000 to secure your network. You can secure your communications with IPSec, and you can secure your data with EFS. Windows 2000 also provides new tools, such as security templates, to make your computer configuration easier. Rights and permissions also play an important role in maintaining security in your network. However, amazingly enough, most networks do not use these tools. And unused tools are ineffective. If you are going to secure your network, you must use the provided tools, carefully analyze your network, and secure it. Often, the most persuasive argument for ensuring security is a revelation to upper management regarding the risks to data if it is not properly secured.

Taking care of your network security is important, and so is taking care of your network's data. The next chapter will guide you through backing up and restoring your data.

Chapter 17

Fault Tolerance and System Recovery

Understanding the Risks of System Management in Windows 2000 Professional

Windows 2000 Professional is considered a stable, reliable, and resilient operating system. But, nothing is perfect, and the Windows 2000 Professional operating system is no exception. Even if the Windows 2000 Professional operating system were considered bulletproof, what about the hardware and the users who access the operating system? Are they bulletproof as well? We all know the answer to that question is no.

Creating a bulletproof environment isn't possible, so you need to protect your operating system, user data, and system data from corruption. You also need to implement a strategy to avoid or minimize the loss of data and the amount of time required to return your system to a consistent state.

This chapter introduces ways to create an environment that allows for minimal loss of data and time; it also introduces recovery procedures in the event you experience problems with the operating system, system files, or user data files.

You can protect your Windows 2000 Professional operating system, user data, and system data in the following ways, thereby minimizing the overall impact of an unexpected problem:

- Implementing Redundant Array of Inexpensive Disks (RAID) on your hardware

- Performing backups of your system and user data

- Understanding your recovery options

- Properly configuring your system

Implementing RAID in Windows 2000

Windows 2000 provides three levels of RAID: level 0, level 1, and level 5. However, only one of these levels, RAID level 0, is available in the Windows 2000 Professional operating system. RAID levels 1 and 5 are available only in Windows 2000 Server operating systems.

What does this mean to you? It simply means that no Windows 2000 Professional fault-tolerant RAID implementation is available.

We do have some good news for you. Windows 2000 Professional supports a hardware RAID implementation that allows you to create RAID 1 (disk mirroring) and RAID 5 (striping with parity) using the physical controllers of the hard drives.

Normally, enabling a fault-tolerant RAID implementation is one of the first steps you would take to reduce the risk of losing your system and user data and protect your operating system. Even though these fault-tolerant RAID levels are not available in Windows 2000 Professional, it is important that you understand them in case you encounter them elsewhere.

RAID level 0 is the only supported RAID level in Windows 2000 Professional. It is implemented using the striped volumes that were discussed in Chapter 15. Striped volumes do not provide fault tolerance in any way, but do improve performance. However, striped volumes introduce the risk of losing more data than when the data is not striped across multiple drives because all data included on a striped volume is lost if any of the hard drives fail.

RAID level 1 provides Windows 2000 fault tolerance by creating mirrored volumes that duplicate your partitions on two different physical drives. The redundant information provides fault tolerance if one of the drives fails. The other drive contains the data, so the system can continue to function. RAID level 1 is primarily used for protecting your system and boot volumes.

RAID level 5 provides Windows 2000 fault tolerance by distributing the data and parity information across at least three physical drives. The parity information—a calculated value that is used to re-create the information after a disk failure—and the remaining data are used to re-create the data that was lost on the failed drive.

Note: *Although you cannot create RAID level 1 or RAID level 5 volumes on Windows 2000 Professional, you can use Windows 2000 Professional to create the fault-tolerant drives on a remote Windows 2000 Server machine.*

In the event you administer a RAID environment on a remote Windows 2000 Server from your Windows 2000 Professional machine, you need to have a general idea of what options are available to you. Table 17.1 contains a list of RAID commands and a brief description of what they provide.

Protecting Your Data in Windows 2000 Professional

Without the implementation of RAID in Windows 2000 Professional, it is more important than ever that you be sure to regularly make copies of your data. You can use these copies to replace the data on a hard drive that goes bad or replace data that is accidentally or intentionally corrupted or deleted.

Table 17.1   RAID commands in Windows 2000.

Command	Description
Create Volume	Creates a striped, mirrored, or RAID 5 volume.
Delete Volume	Removes a striped, mirrored, or RAID 5 volume and deletes all the data contained in the volume.
Break Mirror	Breaks a mirrored volume. The data is not deleted, but data redundancy is no longer available, thus preventing fault tolerance.
Repair Volume	Repairs a mirrored or RAID 5 volume that resides on basic disks.
Reactivate Disk	Repairs a dynamic disk that is marked Missing or Offline.
Rescan Disk	Updates disk configuration information without having to reboot.
Restoring Disk Configuration	Updates a Windows 2000 configuration on a computer that also contains an earlier version of Windows. After you run this option, Windows 2000 will recognize the existing volume sets, stripe sets, mirror sets, and stripe sets with parity.

The Windows 2000 Backup utility creates a copy of data that resides on your hard drive. This utility is extremely powerful and provides many options to you for protecting your data.

17

Implementing Windows 2000 Backup Operations

The Backup utility creates a duplicate copy of the data on your hard disk by copying it to another storage device, such as a tape or another hard drive. You then can use this copy to replace the lost data.

The Backup utility enables you to do the following:

- Back up specific folders and files on your hard drive.

- Restore folders and files that have been backed up to your hard drive or any other drive you can access.

- Make a copy of your computer's System State, which includes your system files, boot files, the Registry, and other critical files pertaining to the services running on your machine—for instance, Active Directory, File Replication, and Certificate Services.

- Create a schedule for your files that are backed up regularly, allowing you to automate the task.

- Create an Emergency Repair Disk (ERD) to help you repair corrupted or replace deleted critical system files.

You can use the Backup utility to back up and restore data on either FAT or NTFS volumes. However, it is not recommended that you back up a Windows 2000 NTFS volume and restore it to a FAT volume. This procedure can cause data loss and loss of the Windows 2000 folder and file special features. For instance, disk quota, Encrypting File System

(EFS), permission, mounted drive, and Remote Storage information are specific to Windows 2000 NTFS volumes and will be lost if you restore these files to a FAT partition.

This chapter drills down into each of these options to ensure that you are familiar with the tasks involved and how to perform each task. You need to become familiar with the tasks before you have to perform them in a real-world environment. Nothing is worse than trying to restore critical files while your boss is hovering over you and asking you questions. You certainly want to look knowledgeable and experienced while the boss is around.

To open the Backup utility, as shown in Figure 17.1, click on Start on the taskbar, choose Programs|Accessories|System Tools, and then click on Backup.

As you can see in Figure 17.1, plenty of options are available to you through this utility, including the ability to run Backup and Restore Wizards, create an ERD, start an immediate backup without the wizard, and create a schedule for the backup process. We'll look into each of these options in the upcoming sections.

Understanding the Backup Operation

Performing a backup isn't really difficult, but it does require that you be familiar with the process and options available to you. You can back up information to a file on a hard disk, floppy disk, or any other type of removable or nonremovable media such as tapes or

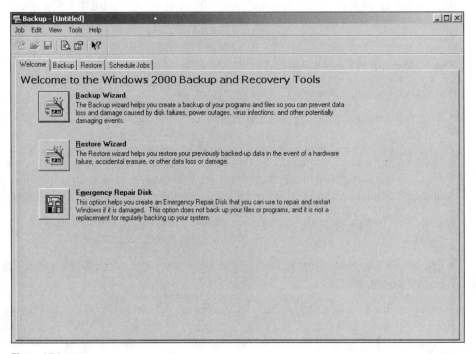

Figure 17.1
Selecting your Backup utility option.

compact discs. When you back up data to a file, you have to specify the file name. The default file extension of the backup is .bck, but you can use any file extension you wish.

When backing up data to tape, you must have a tape device attached to your computer. You manage the tapes by using the Removable Storage service located in the Computer Management console. The Removable Storage and Backup utilities work together, but you have to use Removable Storage to perform certain maintenance tasks, such as preparing your tapes and ejecting them.

Follow these four simple steps to create a backup:

1. Locate and select the drives, folders, and files you want to back up.

2. Select the type of media or location to which you want to back up the information.

3. Select your backup options.

4. Begin the backup operation.

Note: You must be a member of the Backup Operators built-in group or an administrator to perform a backup.

Now, let's look at these four steps in more detail. As you can see in Figure 17.2, you use a hierarchical view of your disks to locate and select the drives, folders, and files you want

17

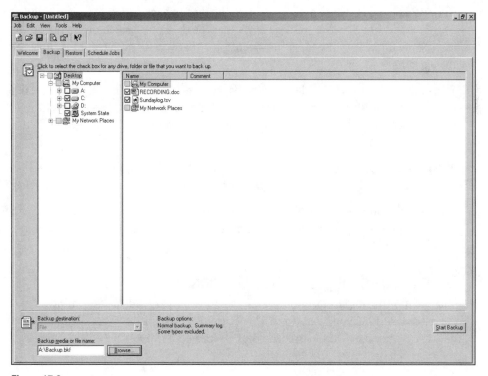

Figure 17.2
Selecting the folders and files to back up.

to back up. You can navigate through this structure the same as you would through Windows Explorer: Click on the plus signs to see underlying objects and click on the minus signs to collapse objects.

Note: You cannot select portions of the System State objects to be backed up. The System State information is backed up and restored as a unit to ensure consistency.

After you select the information you want backed up, you choose the storage media type or tape device to which you want to back up the information. The storage media type can be a hard drive, Zip drive, or any other type of removable or nonremovable device that you want to back up to. When you perform a backup operation, you create a *backup set*, which is the file or one or more tapes that contain the files, folders, and other data you are backing up.

Note: The tape device option will not be available if you do not have a tape device installed on your machine.

The most common types of tape drives include Digital Audio Tape (DAT), Digital Linear Tape (DLT), and Quarter-Inch Cartridge (QIC). Regardless of the type of tape drive you use, be sure to check the Hardware Compatibility List to ensure the tape drive is supported in Windows 2000.

In the third step, you customize your backup operation by specifying the options in the Options dialog box. These options include the type of backup, whether you should create a log file, and whether you want to verify that the data was backed up correctly. You also can specify file types—based on file extension—that you do not want to include in the backup.

Your final step is to actually kick off the backup operation. After you specify the different options, you can start the backup of the selected files, or you can create a schedule for the backup operation. This scheduled backup is submitted to the Task Scheduler and can be managed from there.

Note: These steps provide a brief overview of what is required to perform a backup of your folders and files. You will find more detailed explanations later in this chapter.

Numerous options are available to you when you're performing a backup. Understanding all the options is imperative to creating an efficient, effective, and optimal backup strategy in Windows 2000.

Options, Options, and More Options

You can use the numerous options available to you when you're performing a backup to customize your backup operations. This customization creates a backup set that contains only the required data and also promotes a speedy recovery in the event you lose data or the system fails.

To access the Options dialog box, follow these steps:

1. Click on Start on the taskbar, choose Programs|Accessories|System Tools, and then click on Backup to open the Backup utility.

2. From the Tools menu, click on Options to open the Options dialog box.

3. Click on the tab that contains the backup options that you want to customize and make the appropriate changes.

The five tabs available in the Options dialog box are:

- General

- Restore

- Backup Type

- Backup Log

- Exclude Files

These tabs require an in-depth explanation so that you have a thorough understanding of their capabilities. This information will allow you to create an accurate customized backup operation.

17

General Backup Options

On the General tab, you can select general customization options to be applied to your backup operation. These eight options, listed here, allow you to define the backup operation behavior when backing up to both a disk drive and tape drive. The configuration of these options may affect performance during a backup or restore operation:

- *Compute Selection Information Before Backup And Restore Operations*—You can select this option to estimate the number of bytes and files that will be backed up or restored during the current operation. The information calculated and displayed will greatly depend on the files you selected to be backed up or restored.

- *Use The Catalogs On The Media To Speed Up Building Restore Catalogs On Disk*—You can use this option to specify that you want to use the *on-media catalog* (information stored on the storage media containing a list of files and folders that have been backed up on the backup set) to build the *on-disk catalog* (information stored on the local disk drive containing a list of files and folders that have been backed up on the backup set). This option can be used to optimize the restore process.

***Warning!** You should not select the preceding option if you suspect that the data stored on your media is damaged. However, when this option is not selected, the building of your on-disk catalog may take a significant amount of time. Increasing the time could drastically decrease the effectiveness of your restore process.*

- *Verify Data After The Backup Completes*—You can select this option to check the backed-up data against the original data located on your hard drive to be sure that it is the same. If it is not the same, you might have a problem with the file or media you are backing up to.

Tip: *We always leave the Verify Data After The Backup Completes option selected. Although it may slow down the backup operation somewhat, it ensures that the data you backed up is not corrupt in the event you have to restore from that file or media.*

- *Back Up The Contents Of Mounted Drives*—You can select this option to specify whether you want to back up the data that is contained on the mounted drive. If you do not select this option, only the information regarding the mounted drive path is backed up; the data is not.

- *Show Alert Message When I Start Backup And Removable Storage Is Not Running*—This option is useful if you want to be notified that the Removable Storage service is not running when you start the Backup utility. If you primarily back up to a file and save that file to a removable disk, floppy drive, or your hard disk, you don't need to check this box.

- *Show Alert Message When I Start Backup And There Is Compatible Import Media Available*—This option is useful if you want to be notified that new media is available in the media pool when you start the Backup utility. If you primarily back up to a file and save that file to a removable disk, floppy drive, or your hard disk, you don't need to check this box.

- *Show Alert Message When New Media Is Inserted Into Removable Storage*—When this option is selected, you will receive notification when new media is detected by the Removable Storage service. If you primarily back up to a file and save that file to a removable disk, floppy drive, or your hard disk, you don't need to check this box.

- *Always Move New Import Media To The Backup Media Pool*—When this option is selected, any new media detected by Removable Storage is automatically moved to the Backup media pool (a logical collection of storage media reserved by the Windows 2000 Backup utility). If you primarily back up to a file and save that file to a removable disk, floppy drive, or your hard disk, you don't need to check this box.

The configuration we use for a disk backup is shown in Figure 17.3. This configuration may not be the quickest way to perform a backup, but it provides information regarding backups and ensures the integrity of the backups.

Restore Options for Existing Files

You use the Restore tab, as shown in Figure 17.4, to define the behavior Windows 2000 will take when restoring a file from a backup to a system that already contains that file. The three options on this tab are as follows:

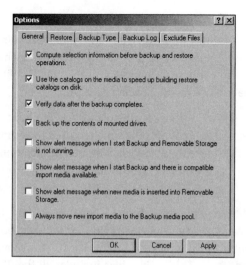

Figure 17.3
Configuring the General tab of the Backup utility's Options dialog box.

Figure 17.4
Choosing restore options for existing files.

- Do Not Replace The File On My Computer (this option, the default, is recommended)
- Replace The File On Disk Only If The File On Disk Is Older
- Always Replace The File On My Computer

Note: *We think that Microsoft should add one more option here that prompts you to decide while performing the restore whether you want to replace the file or let it remain untouched.*

Backup Types

On the Backup Type tab of the Options dialog box, you can define the type of backup you want to create. This tab, shown in Figure 17.5, provides a drop-down menu from which you can set the default type of backup. As you choose each different backup type, Windows 2000 Professional provides a brief explanation of what that backup type provides.

The Windows 2000 Professional operating system provides support for five different types of backups. The type of backup you choose directly affects the time required to complete the backup and amount of space required to store it. Often, you will include a combination of backup methods to create the most efficient backup strategy for your environment. The five backup types are as follows:

- *Normal backup*—Copies all selected files and marks each file as being backed up, thus clearing the archive attribute. This type of backup is normally the first backup you perform. The incremental and differential backups depend on this backup to recover your system or user data to a consistent state. This backup type includes all the files you selected to back up.

- *Copy backup*—Copies all selected files but does not mark each file as being backed up; thus, it does not clear the archive attribute. This backup type is useful if you want to back up files between the normal and incremental backups without affecting the normal backup operation of those backups.

Tip: *Using a combination of normal backups and incremental backups is the most efficient backup method. This combination requires the least amount of storage space but may require a bit more recovery time if the data is spread across multiple disks or tapes.*

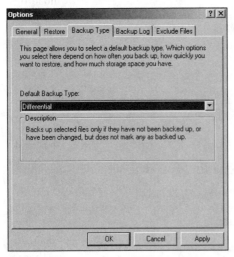

Figure 17.5
Specifying your backup type.

- *Differential backup*—Copies files created or changed since the last normal or incremental backup. This type of backup does not clear the archive attribute, indicating that it has not been backed up. We often refer to this type of backup as a *cumulative* backup. It will continue backing up files that have been created or changed until you back up those files using a normal or incremental backup. A normal backup must be restored before the differential backup can be restored.

- *Incremental backup*—Copies only those files created or changed since the last normal or incremental backup. This type of backup clears the archive attribute, indicating that it has been backed up. A normal backup must be restored before the incremental backup can be restored.

- *Daily backup*—Copies all selected files that were created or modified the day the backup is performed. The archive attribute is not cleared, indicating that it has not been backed up. This means it will be backed up again if you perform a normal, incremental, or differential backup.

Logging Your Backup Operations

On the Backup Log tab, you can specify the type of log, if any, that you want generated when you perform a backup. This information can be helpful in determining whether any problems occurred during the backup process. You can choose from these three logging options:

- *Detailed*—Logs specific information regarding both the backup and restore operations. This information includes the names of all files and folders backed up or restored, failure to access a file, the loading of the tape, and the start of an operation.

- *Summary*—Logs only critical operations, including the loading and unloading of the tape, the beginning of the backup or restore operation, and whether any problems occurred while accessing files.

- *None*—Indicates that no information is logged when performing your backup or restore operation.

Excluding Files from Your Backup Operations

The last Options dialog box tab allows you to define which file types you want excluded from your backup operation. The Exclude Files tab is shown in Figure 17.6; this tab is broken into two areas: Files Excluded For All Users and Files Excluded For User *Currently Logged In*.

In the Files Excluded For All Users area, some default files are automatically excluded from your backup operation. They include the page file, temporary files, and power management files. You can exclude additional files from the backups by clicking on the Add New button to open the Add Excluded Files dialog box, as shown in Figure 17.7. In this dialog box, you can choose additional files that are listed in the System Registry by selecting them from the Registered File Type section. You can also specify the path that contains the file types you want excluded from the backup. If this path contains subfolders that have file types you want excluded, be sure to click on the Applies To All Subfolders checkbox.

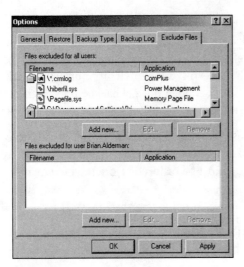

Figure 17.6
Excluding files from your backup operation.

Figure 17.7
Excluding files in the Add Excluded Files dialog box.

You can also choose to list files that you own and want excluded from the backup or restore operation. Use the Files Excluded For User section of the Exclude Files tab to list these files. You can list additional file types by clicking on the Add New button to open the Add Excluded Files dialog box, where you can add file extensions that you have created to the list of files you want excluded from the backup. Here again, you can specify the path that contains the file types you want excluded from the backup. If this path contains subfolders that have file types you want excluded, be sure to click on the Applies To All Subfolders checkbox.

Now that you understand the backup options, the next step is to decide the backup strategy you want to implement. This strategy will directly reflect your restore process when you're ready to perform a restore operation. It is important to create an efficient, tested, and documented backup strategy.

Designing Your Backup Strategy

Your backup strategy should be designed to have the least amount of impact on your system and the users in the event you have a failure that requires you to restore data to your system. One of the first questions many people ask is how often they should back up data. Unfortunately, the answer to that question is not the same for everyone. But, you can take these factors into consideration when creating your backup strategy:

- The frequency that your data changes (daily, weekly, monthly) and how many changes occur in that time frame.

- The cost of lost data. Can you afford to lose any data?

- The cost to replace the files, including time involved restoring the files and the loss to the business during the restore process.

- The importance of these files to your daily operations. Can you survive without them?

17

These key factors will influence your decision of how often you should back up your files in Windows 2000 Professional. The decision considerations we focus on the most are how much data we can afford to lose and how long it will take to restore the files and bring the system back to an operable state.

Tip: There is a trade-off: If you want a fast and efficient restore process with minimal to no data loss, you are most likely going to have to implement a backup strategy that requires more time.

For instance, say you perform a normal backup every Sunday at midnight. On Tuesday at 4:00 P.M. you lose a hard drive that contains critical data. Because your latest backup was done at midnight on Sunday any changes that occurred between midnight on Sunday and 4:00 P.M. on Tuesday are lost.

Let's consider another example. Say you perform a normal backup every Sunday at midnight and an incremental backup every evening at 6:00 P.M. On Tuesday at 4:00 P.M. you lose a hard drive that contains critical data. You can now restore the normal backup from Sunday night and then the incremental backup from Monday evening. In this case, you lose only Tuesday's changes.

Let's take the preceding example a step further. Take the same backup strategy from the preceding paragraph, but this time, say you have a disk failure on Thursday at 4:00 P.M. You will now have to restore the normal backup from Sunday and then the incremental backups from Monday, Tuesday, and Wednesday evening in chronological order. This means you will have to perform four restore operations. Furthermore, you still lose the data from Thursday.

Now, let's modify the preceding example. You perform a normal backup on Sunday at midnight and then a differential backup every evening at 6:00 P.M. If you have a disk failure on Thursday, you will have to restore the normal backup from Sunday night and then the differential backup from Wednesday evening. Remember that the differential backup is cumulative and will contain all the changes made since the last normal or incremental backup. The restore operation will be more efficient because you need to restore only the normal backup and then the differential backup from Wednesday evening. Obviously, as the week progresses, the time required to perform the differential backup will increase. However, the time required to perform the restore process will decrease because you will have to perform only two restore operations. But again, you will lose the data from Thursday.

What if losing any data is unacceptable? In this case, you can implement a similar backup strategy, but more backup operations have to occur. You perform a normal backup on Sunday at midnight, a differential backup every evening at 6:00 P.M., and now you are going to perform an incremental backup at 9:00 A.M., noon, and 3:00 P.M. This time, you lose a hard drive containing critical data on Thursday at 4:00 P.M. The restore strategy will be to restore the normal backup from Sunday night; the differential from Wednesday evening; and then the incremental backups from 9:00 A.M., noon, and 3:00 P.M. on Thursday. In this case, you lose only one hour's worth of changes. The restore process will take a little longer because you are performing five restore operations, but you will save critical data.

The design of your backup strategy needs to take many factors into consideration, and as you can see, the two primary considerations are the time to restore the data and the amount of data you can, or cannot, afford to lose. The time to perform the backup should not be a factor when you're designing your backup strategy. The efficiency and cost of the

Documenting your backup strategy.					
Job Name	**Files Backed Up**	**Backup Type**	**Frequency**	**Time**	**Comments**
Backup C Drive	C:\	Normal	Daily	12:00 A.M.	Back up to tape.
System Info	System State	Normal	Daily	12:00 A.M.	Back up to tape.
SQL Server Master	Master.mdf	Normal	Daily	9:00 P.M.	Back up to removable media.
SQL Server Sales	Sales.mdf	Normal	Daily	10:00 P.M.	Back up to tape.
SQL Server Sales Log	Sales.ldf	Incremental	Hourly	6:00 A.M.–6:00 P.M.	Back up to local hard drive.

restore operation should be the two factors influencing your backup strategy. You can use the following worksheet, also found on the accompanying CD-ROM, to document your backup strategy. The following example shows how your worksheet might look.

Performing a Backup Operation

You can perform a backup in Windows 2000 in many ways. You can create a backup by using the Backup Wizard in the Backup utility, you can perform a manual backup by using the Backup tab in the Backup utility, or you can perform a command-line backup by using the **ntbackup.exe** command.

We'll walk through the options available for each of these methods so that you can determine which is the best method available to you for performing a backup operation.

Using the Backup Wizard

Using the Backup Wizard is probably the easiest way to perform a backup in Windows 2000 Professional, and it is a nice way to become familiar with the backup capabilities. The Backup Wizard prompts you for information regarding the backup operation and steps you through the process of creating the backup job, which can be run immediately or scheduled to run at a later time.

To create a backup job using the Backup Wizard, follow these steps:

1. Click on the Backup Wizard button on the Welcome tab in the Backup utility to open the welcome screen and then click on Next.

2. In the What To Back Up screen, choose one of the following backup options:

   • Back Up Everything On My Computer

   • Back Up Selected Files, Drives, Or Network Data

   • Only Back Up The System State Data

3. Then, click on Next.

Note: Your choice here determines the next screen that will be presented. If you choose to back up everything or back up only the system data, the Where To Store The Backup screen appears. If you choose to back up selected drives, the Items To Back Up screen appears, containing the hierarchical structure of your disks, as shown in Figure 17.8. You use this dialog box to select the drives, folders, and files you want to back up. You then move to the Where To Store The Backup screen.

In the Where To Store The Backup screen, shown in Figure 17.9, you specify the backup media type and backup media or file name. If the Backup Media Type drop-down menu is dimmed, no other media types are available to choose from. For instance, you do not have a tape drive attached to the computer that you can use to create a backup. After you click on Next, the summary screen of the Backup Wizard lists the responses to the prompts you answered.

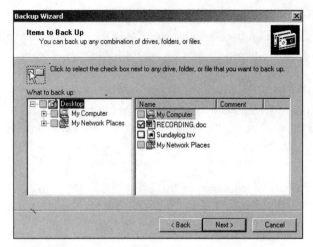

Figure 17.8
Choosing items to back up in the Items To Back Up screen.

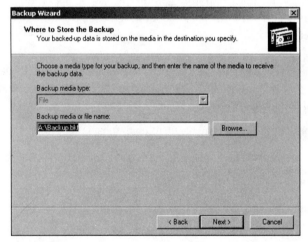

Figure 17.9
Choosing a location in the Where To Store The Backup screen.

You aren't finished yet. You can click on the Advanced button to customize the backup job you are defining. The Advanced dialog box prompts you to do the following:

- Indicate the type of backup.

- Verify the backup.

- Use hardware compression (if supported).

- Append or replace the information on the existing media with the information you are backing up.

- Restrict access to the data you are backing up.

- Provide backup and media label names.

- Indicate when to back up the data (now or later). You can create a schedule for this backup operation.

You are again presented with the summary screen of the Backup Wizard for a final review. If you want to change any of your options, you can click on the Back button to return to a screen and make the modification. You then continue clicking on Next to return to the summary screen.

Creating a Manual Backup

After you become familiar with the options available to you when creating a backup, you can create a backup job by using the Backup tab inside the Backup utility. This approach provides you complete flexibility in creating and scheduling your backup operation but is not driven by a wizard.

Follow these steps to manually create a backup job in Windows 2000 Professional:

1. Open the Backup utility by using the steps discussed earlier.

2. Click on the Backup tab and then choose New from the Job menu.

3. Select the folders and files you want to back up by putting a checkmark in the checkbox on the left of the objects located in the area named Click To Select The Check Box For Any Drive, Folder, Or File That You Want To Back Up.

4. From the Backup Destination drop-down menu, choose a file or tape device that you want to back up your files to.

Note: *If you do not have a tape device installed on your computer, File is selected by default.*

5. In the Backup Media Or File Name box, type the backup file name or choose the tape that you want to use for the backup operation.

6. Customize the backup operation by clicking on the Tools menu and then clicking on Options. After you customize the backup, click on OK.

Note: *We discussed these options earlier in this chapter in the section titled "Options, Options, and More Options."*

7. When you are ready to begin the backup, click on the Start Backup button and make any last-minute modifications in the Backup Job Information dialog box.

8. If you want to set any advanced options, such as hardware compression or data verification, click on Advanced. After you choose the advanced options, click on OK.

9. Click Start Backup to begin the backup operation.

The Create Backup Wizard and the backup you create manually are both generated using a graphical user interface (GUI) available in Windows 2000 Professional. But, if you like to

17

use command-line utilities to create batch files, you can also use a backup command to back up your data.

Using ntbackup in a Batch File

In Windows 2000 Professional, you can perform backup operations by using the **ntbackup** command, which you can enter interactively, or you can create a batch file containing the **ntbackup** command along with the appropriate parameters. However, when you're using batch files to back up your data, you must be familiar with a couple of restrictions:

- You can back up entire folders only, not individual files.

- Batch files do not support the use of wildcard characters; that is, *.txt will not back up all files with a .txt extension.

You can use numerous parameters with the **ntbackup** command to create a customized command-line backup operation. These parameters are supplied when you use the **ntbackup** command interactively or from within a batch file. To create an accurate and efficient backup, you must be familiar with these switches. Table 17.2 contains some of the most commonly used parameters, along with brief descriptions.

*Note: You cannot perform a restore operation by using the **ntbackup** command.*

*Tip: The following switches default to the settings already set using the GUI version of Backup, unless you specify otherwise when executing **ntbackup**:*

/V /R /L /M /RS /HC

Table 17.2   ntbackup command parameters.

Parameter	Description
Systemstate	Specifies that you want to back up the System State data.
Bks *file name*	Specifies the backup selection file that contains the folders and files you want backed up.
/J "*job name*"	Specifies the job name to be used in the log file. (This parameter usually contains a description of the job and date and time you backed up the data.)
/T "*tape name*"	Appends or overwrites to the tape name specified. Do not use this parameter with **/P**.
/N "*media name*"	Specifies the new tape name. This parameter cannot be used with **/A**.
/A	Performs an append operation. You must use **/T** or **/G** with this parameter.
/V:yes|no	Verifies the data after the backup has completed.
/R:yes|no	Restricts access of this tape to the owner or members of the Administrators group.
/L:f|s|n	Specifies the type of log file—**Full**, **Summary**, or **None** if no log file is to be created.
/M *backup type*	Specifies the type of backup operation to perform.
/RS:yes|no	Specifies whether to back up the Removable Storage database.
/HC:on|off	Uses hardware compression on your tape drive if it is available.

Let's look at an example of how to use the **ntbackup** command at the command line and in a batch file. For this example, we'll perform a normal backup named "Job 1 Backup" of the remote share named "\\server1\D$". The name of the tape is "Command Line Backup 1", with the description "Testing command line backup":

```
ntbackup backup \\server1\D$ /M normal /j "Job 1 Backup" /d "Testing command
 line backup" /n "Command Line Backup 1" /v:yes /r:no /l:s /rs:yes
```

Here, the backup job will be verified, it has no access restrictions, the log will contain summary information, and it will also back up the Removable Storage database.

Scheduling a Backup Operation

Regardless of the backup method you use, you can perform the backup immediately, or you can schedule it to execute at a later time. In fact, you can set up a recurring schedule for the backup job.

When you define the backup operation using either the Backup Wizard or the Backup tab inside the Backup utility, you have the option to schedule the backup operation. You can configure this schedule to be a one-time deal, or you can set it up as a recurring task. If you choose to create a batch file containing the **ntbackup** command, you can schedule the batch file to run on a recurring schedule as well.

17

No matter what approach you take to create the backup operation, the scheduled job is handled by the Schedule Task component of Windows 2000 Professional. This component is responsible for handling all tasks that are scheduled in the Windows 2000 Professional operating system.

Backing Up System State Data

One of the most critical backups you will perform involves backing up the System State data. In Windows 2000 Professional, this backup creates a copy of your critical system components, including the following:

- *Boot files*—The files required to start up the Windows 2000 operating system, such as ntldr.exe and ntdetect.com, as well as the critical operating system files.

- *Registry*—A hierarchical structured repository containing information about your computer's configuration. This information includes the following:

  - Property settings about your applications and folders

  - The hardware you have attached to your computer

  - The communication and serial ports being used

  - Profiles for each user accessing the machine

- *COM+ Class Registration Database*—Information used by developers to create and use Component Object Models (COM) in Windows 2000.

You can back up the System State data in two ways: by using the Backup Wizard or the Backup tab, both of which are located in the Backup utility. If you use the Backup Wizard, the screen immediately after the welcome screen asks what data you want to back up. Choose Only Back Up The System State Data, as shown in Figure 17.10.

If you choose to back up the System State data by using the Backup tab, you simply click on the checkmark in the box to the left of the System State option, as shown in Figure 17.11. You cannot choose specific objects within the System State data. You have to back up all the objects as a whole. Backing up the System State data this way will help reduce the chance of system corruption because of inconsistent files.

Tip: When you back up the System State data, copies of your Registry files also are stored on the local hard drive in the %systemroot%\repair\regback folder. If your system is bootable, you can use these Registry files to perform a faster recovery of your Registry.

During the process of a backup operation, the Backup Progress dialog box provides you with information regarding the backup and then gives you summary information regarding the backup operation. The information provided at the end of a backup, as shown in Figure 17.12, includes the following:

- Progress of the backup operation

- Name of the media being accessed

- Status of the backup operation

- Time elapsed and remaining for the backup operation

- Number of files and the size (in bytes) of information backed up

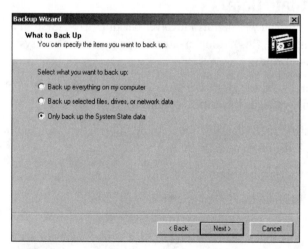

Figure 17.10
Using the Backup Wizard to back up the System State data.

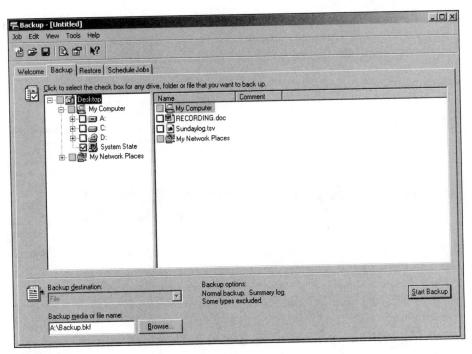

Figure 17.11
Using the Backup tab to back up the System State data.

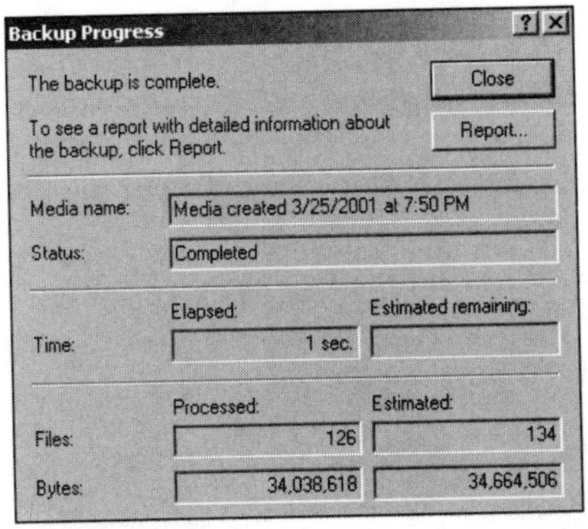

Figure 17.12
Viewing the completed Backup Progress dialog box.

Performing a Restore Operation

Similar to when you are performing a backup, you have a few options in Windows 2000 Professional when performing a restore operation. Here, you can also use a wizard, called the Restore Wizard, or you can perform a restore by using the Restore tab located in the Backup utility.

The huge difference between performing backup and restore operations is that a restore operation is usually required to salvage lost or corrupted user data or lost or corrupted system data. Normally, the pressure is on when you are performing a restore operation. The system or the users' data is unavailable, ceasing productivity and possibly causing you to lose money by the minute.

Tip: We highly recommend that you perform test restore operations frequently to ensure that you are prepared should a crisis arise. You can test your restore operation by restoring your files to a location other than where they originally resided.

Restoring User Data Using the Restore Wizard

Using the Restore Wizard to restore information that you backed up is a simple process. You fire up the Restore Wizard from within the Backup utility and then select the folders or files you want restored by clicking on the appropriate checkboxes (similar to what you did when choosing which files to back up). After you click on the Next button, the wizard presents the summary information of the restore operation, as shown in Figure 17.13. This screen also includes an Advanced button you can use to customize the restore operation.

Working with the Advanced Restore Options

To ensure a consistent and reliable restore operation, you must be familiar with the Advanced options you have available to you. These options significantly affect the success and efficiency of your restore operation.

The first advanced restore option determines where the information is restored. As you can see in Figure 17.14, you have three options to choose from:

- *Original Location*—Restores files to the location from which they were originally backed up.

Figure 17.13
Viewing the summary of your restore operation.

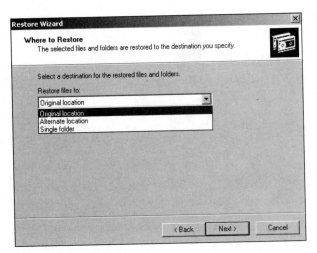

Figure 17.14
Choosing a restore destination in the Where To Restore dialog box.

- *Alternate Location*—Restores files to a location other than the one from which they were originally backed up. This option is great for restoring your information to a secondary machine, providing redundancy.

- *Single Folder*—Restores the original information to a single folder. This option is useful when you want to test your backups for validity and readability.

On the next Restore Wizard screen, you can choose how to restore the information from the backups if the files already exist in the location you are trying to restore them to. This screen also provides the three choices we discussed earlier in this chapter in the section titled "Restore Options for Existing Files."

The actual Advanced Restore Options are shown in Figure 17.15. These options, described next, allow you to define how to handle the security and special system files:

- *Restore Security*—Restores all security settings for your folders and files. These settings include ownership, auditing, and NTFS permissions. This option is available only for NTFS volumes that have been backed up and that are restored to an NTFS volume.

- *Restore Removable Storage Database*—Restores the Removable Storage database that resides in the *%systemroot%*\system32\Ntmsdata directory. You select this option only if you are using Removable Storage media, such as floppy disks, tapes, and so on.

- *Restore Junction Points, Not The Folders And File Data They Reference*—Restores the junction points; however, it does not restore the data and files the junction points reference.

Note: *Junction points are created when you mount a drive in Windows 2000. A junction point is a physical location on your hard drive that points to another storage device or location on the same disk.*

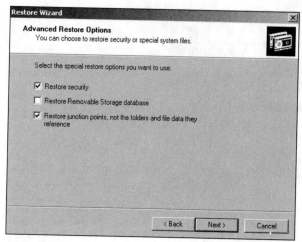

Figure 17.15
Choosing settings in the Advanced Restore Options dialog box.

After you select the appropriate Advanced options, the final wizard screen summarizes the options you chose throughout the Restore Wizard. You can use the Back button to return to previous screens to make modifications to your restore options.

After you click on the Finish button, the Enter Backup File Name dialog box appears, as shown in Figure 17.16. Here, you specify the file you want to restore. After the restore operation is complete, the Restore Progress dialog box specifies the media name, status, elapsed time, files, and number of bytes of information that were restored.

This step completes the restore operation using the Restore Wizard. However, similar to the backup operation, a restore operation can also be completed using the Restore tab of the Backup utility.

Manually Restoring User Data

Restoring volumes, folders, and files using the Restore tab in the Backup utility provides flexibility to the restore process. It actually provides more flexibility than when you restore using the Restore Wizard.

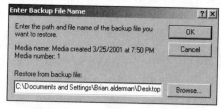

Figure 17.16
Indicating the file you want to restore in the Enter Backup File Name dialog box.

Follow these steps when performing a restore using the Restore tab of the Backup utility:

1. After opening the Backup utility, click on the Restore tab.

2. In the Click To Select The Check Box For Any Drive, Folder, Or File That You Want To Restore area, choose the folders and files to be restored by clicking in the box to the left of the folder or file.

Tip: *This procedure is similar to the one you used to select the volume, folders, and files when you performed the backup operation.*

3. Choose the location that you want to restore the files to by clicking on the appropriate option in the Restore Files To drop-down menu. Your three choices are as follows:

   • *Original Location*—Restores files to the location from which they were backed up. You can now jump to Step 5 of this operation.

   • *Alternate Location*—Restores files to a location that you specify. This option maintains the folder structure of the backed-up data.

   • *Single Folder*—Restores files to a specific folder without maintaining the folder structure of the backed-up data.

4. If you chose Alternate Location or Single Folder in Step 3, type a path for the folder in the Alternate Location area or click on Browse to locate the folder that you want to restore the backed-up information to.

5. Choose Options from the Tools menu to specify what action to take if you are restoring files to a location that already contains these files. Your choices include the following:

   • Do Not Replace The File On My Computer

   • Replace The File On Disk Only If The File On Disk Is Older

   • Always Replace The File On My Computer

6. Click on OK to set your restore options.

7. Click on Start Restore to open the Confirm Restore dialog box.

8. Click on the Advanced button to further customize your restore operation in the Advanced Restore Options dialog box, as shown in Figure 17.17. Your options include the following:

   • *Restore Security*—Restores all security settings for your folders and files. These settings include ownership, auditing, and NTFS permissions. This option is available only for NTFS volumes that have been backed up and that are restored to an NTFS volume.

17

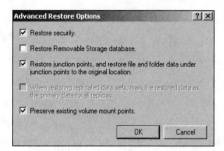

Figure 17.17
Setting options in the Advanced Restore Options dialog box.

- *Restore Removable Storage Database*—Restores the Removable Storage database that resides in the *%systemroot%*\system32\Ntmsdata directory. You select this option only if you are using removable storage media, such as floppy disks, tapes, and so on.

- *Restore Junction Points, And Restore File And Folder Data Under Junction Points To The Original Location*—Restores your junction points on your hard drive and the data pointed to by the junction points.

- *When Restoring Replicated Data Sets, Mark The Restored Data As The Primary Data For All Replicas*—Restores your File Replication Services (FRS) data and replicates the data to your other servers.

Note: This option is only available when you configure File Replication Services in a Windows 2000 environment.

- *Preserve Existing Volume Mount Points*—Prevents the restore operation from writing over the existing volume mount points on the volume you are restoring data to.

9. Click on OK in the Advanced Restore Options dialog box to return to the Confirm Restore dialog box. Click on OK to begin the restore operation.

Note: If you are restoring information from a tape, you should update the on-disk catalog (the list of files and folders that have been backed up in the backup set) for the tape before you perform the restore operation.

As you already know, the System State backups contain numerous critical files that can be used to bring your computer back to a consistent state. You must thoroughly understand this critical restore operation before you perform the restore operation of the System State data.

Restoring System State Data

Understanding how to restore the System State data is not very difficult; however, understanding what a critical operation it is and the impact it can have on your system is important. The steps to perform the restore operation of the System State data are the same as performing a restore of the user data. However, if you are not familiar with the impact, you might end up rendering your system unusable.

To restore the System State data, you open the Backup utility and then click on the Restore tab or the Restore Wizard button. If you choose to restore by using the Restore Wizard, you need to place a checkmark in the box next to the System State option in the What To Restore dialog box. If you choose to manually restore the System State data by using the Restore tab, you place a checkmark in the box next to the System State option in the Click To Select The Check Box For Any Drive, Folder, Or File That You Want To Restore area.

Note: *You can restore the System State data only to a local computer, meaning a computer you are directly logged on to. You cannot perform the restore operation on a remote computer.*

Next, you have to choose where to restore the System State data. You must be very aware of the end result of the restore operation based on the location you have chosen. The location, original or alternate, of the restore may or may not greatly affect your system. For instance, if you choose to restore the System State data to the original location, the Backup utility will delete the current System State data and replace it with the data you are restoring. In Windows 2000 Professional, this means that the boot files, operating system files, Registry, and COM+ Class Registration database from the restore operation become the files used on the computer.

Note: *If you are restoring the System State data on Windows 2000 Server, the Certificate Services database is also restored if it is functioning as a Certificate Server. If you are restoring the System State data on a domain controller, the Active Directory directory services database and the SYSVOL directory are also restored.*

If you choose to restore the System State data to an alternate location in Windows 2000 Professional, only the Registry and system boot files are restored. Notice that the COM+ Class Registration database is not restored.

Note: *If you are restoring the System State data on Windows 2000 Server to an alternate location, the Certificate Services database is not restored. Furthermore, restoring to an alternate location on a domain controller does not restore the Active Directory directory services database or the SYSVOL directory.*

The ability to perform a restore operation in Windows 2000 should be limited to very few individuals. By default, any administrator or anyone who is a member of the Backup Operators group can perform a backup or restore. Be extremely cautious when adding user accounts to these groups.

Warning! *A restore operation of the System State data in Windows 2000 Professional is a relatively easy process. However, performing a restore operation of the System State data on a domain controller becomes quite complex and can greatly affect your entire domain. Be sure you have a thorough understanding of the difference between an authoritative and nonauthoritative restore when you are restoring the System State data in a Windows 2000 Active Directory environment.*

Granting Permissions to Perform Backup and Restore Operations

After you design your backup and restore strategy, create your scheduled tasks to perform the recurring backup operations, and test your restore strategy, you might decide to delegate the backup and restore operations to other individuals. Doing so will reduce your workload and provide you more time to perform other tasks, such as implementing security policies.

You add these individuals to the Backup Operators group on a Windows 2000 Professional operating system by following these steps:

1. Click on Start on the taskbar and click on the Settings|Control Panel option.

2. Double-click on Administrative Tools and then double-click on Computer Management.

3. Click on Local Users And Groups in the console tree of the MMC.

4. In the details pane, double-click on Groups to display the Backup Operators group, as shown in Figure 17.18.

5. Double-click on the Backup Operators group to open the Backup Operators Properties dialog box.

6. Click on the Add button to open the Select Users Or Groups dialog box.

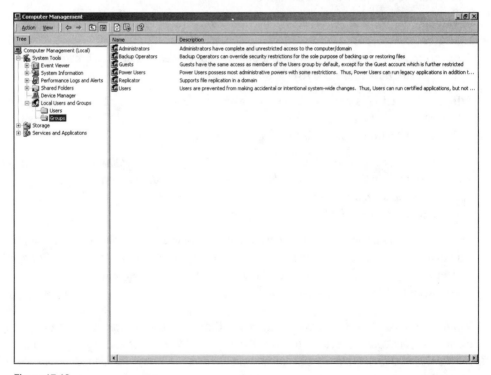

Figure 17.18
Locating the Backup Operators group.

7. Under the Name section, locate the name of the user that you want to add to the Backup Operators group and double-click on that name. Click on OK to return to the Backup Operators Properties dialog box.

8. Click on OK to add the user to the Backup Operators group.

The user is now able to perform any of the backup or restore operations discussed in this chapter. Not all system problems can be resolved using the backup and restore strategy, however. For instance, if you add to your system a driver that is not recognized, you might not be able to log on to the system. You may even find yourself in a situation in which you can't boot up to perform a restore operation. The next section discusses other options you have available to recover your system.

Implementing Windows 2000 Professional System Recovery

Numerous options are available to you to resolve a system failure. The option you choose will depend on the problem with the system. Of course, reinstalling Windows 2000 Professional will always work, but you will want to try less drastic options available to you first.

17

Configuring System Startup and Recovery Options

One of your first tasks as a Windows 2000 Professional administrator is to ensure that you configure your system to respond in the event you experience a critical system problem. For instance, what if you experience a Blue Screen of Death (BSOD) caused by a critical error with the operating system or a piece of hardware installed on your computer? You can set configuration options to tell your system how to respond to a fatal exception or stop error.

The Startup And Recovery dialog box provides options for you to define the behavior of Windows 2000 in the event the system stops unexpectedly. Using this dialog box, you can do any of the following:

• Write an event to the System Log of Event Viewer

• Send an Administrative Alert

• Automatically reboot the computer

• Dump the contents of system memory to a file that is used for debugging

Advanced users can use the system memory's log file to determine the cause of the stop error.

Follow these steps to specify what actions Windows 2000 will take in the event that the system stops unexpectedly:

1. Open the System applet located inside Control Panel.

2. Click on the Advanced tab of the System Properties dialog box, as shown in Figure 17.19.

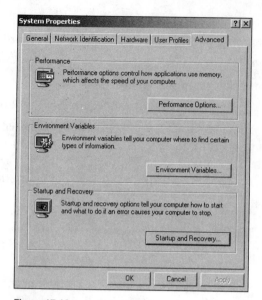

Figure 17.19
The Advanced tab of the System Properties dialog box.

3. Click on the Startup And Recovery button to open the Startup And Recovery dialog box, as shown in Figure 17.20.

4. Under the System Failure section, choose any combination or all the actions that you want to occur in the event of an unexpected system failure. These options include the following:

- *Write An Event To The System Log*—Indicates that any information relevant to the event is recorded in the System Log of Event Viewer.

Note: This option is available only on Windows 2000 Professional. This action occurs automatically on a Windows 2000 Server operating system.

- *Send An Administrative Alert*—Indicates that the system administrator will be notified.

Note: Both of the preceding options require at least 2MB of free space on the computer's boot volume.

- *Automatically Reboot*—Indicates that the computer will automatically attempt to restart.

5. Beneath the Write Debugging Information section, specify how much information and where the information should be recorded when a system failure occurs. Your options are as follows:

- *Small Memory Dump*—Records only the most useful information that will help identify the problem. This option requires Windows 2000 to create a new file each

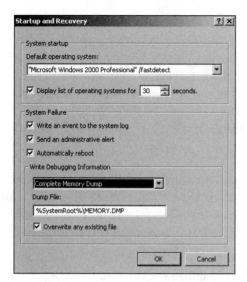

Figure 17.20
The Startup And Recovery dialog box.

time the system fails unexpectedly. The paging file must be located on your boot volume and must be a minimum of 2MB in size.

- *Kernel Memory Dump*—Records only the kernel memory, speeding up the process when recording information after the system fails unexpectedly. The required space for the paging file is between 50MB and 800MB, and it must be located on your boot volume.

- *Complete Memory Dump*—Dumps the entire contents of system memory when a system failure occurs. The boot volume must have enough free space to hold the entire contents of all the physical RAM plus an additional 1MB. For instance, if you have 512MB of RAM, you would need to maintain at least 513MB of free disk space on the boot volume.

Note: *The Dump File location will always be on the boot volume. The boot volume is specified using the wildcard name %systemroot%. Unlike the Dump File location, the default name of the dump file, MEMORY.DMP, can be modified.*

Recovering from a System Failure

Understanding the recovery process in the event of a system failure will significantly reduce the amount of time required to resolve the problem and return the system to production. The steps you take to repair the system depend on what caused the problem. In the following sections, we'll look at a few problems that can occur along with what steps you can take to resolve them.

Using the Last Known Good Configuration

If the problem you are experiencing has occurred since you added a new driver for your hardware, you might be able to resolve the problem by using the Last Known Good Configuration. This option replaces the Registry information that was updated during the installation of the driver. When you choose this option, Windows 2000 restores only the Registry information that was previously stored in the Registry key HKEY_LOCAL_ MACHINE\System\CurrentControlSet. Changes made to any other Registry keys will not be restored.

Warning! *This option will not help you if you have already logged on to the machine. After you log on to the machine, the Registry information that was used as a backup for the restore of the Registry key is updated.*

Restoring this Registry key requires you to start your Windows 2000 operating system using the Last Known Good Configuration option as follows:

1. Click on the Start button on the taskbar and then click on Shut Down.

2. Click on Restart and then click on OK.

3. When the system is restarting, you see a screen with the message "Please select the operating system." It also advises you to press F8 for troubleshooting and advanced startup options. Press this key now.

4. After you press F8, use the arrow keys to select Last Known Good Configuration and then press Enter to return to the preceding screen.

Warning! *If you are using the arrow keys on the keypad the Num Lock option must be turned off before you can use them to select this option.*

5. Select the Windows 2000 Professional operating system and press Enter.

After choosing the Windows 2000 Professional operating system, you will boot up into it. The Windows 2000 Security dialog box in which you log on to Windows 2000 then appears. When you log on, the HKEY_LOCAL_MACHINE\System\CurrentControlSet Registry key will be restored from the previously saved configuration, overriding the driver information causing problems.

This process is beneficial for recovering from a driver problem as long as you are still able to boot up and log in. However, if the problem is so severe that you are unable to get to this point, your next step will be to try using safe mode.

Using the Safe Mode Options

If your computer is damaged to the point where you are unable to start it normally, you might be able to start it in safe mode. Windows 2000 uses default settings such as a VGA monitor, Microsoft mouse driver, no network configuration options, and only the device drivers required to start Windows 2000. For instance, say that after you install software, your computer will not start. You can attempt to start your computer in safe mode to avoid the detection of the software and possibly eliminate the problem and be able to start the computer.

Each of the several safe mode options provides or eliminates certain functionality. You should be familiar with the following different safe mode options:

Tip: *Always begin using the most basic option, which is safe mode. If this one fails, the rest of them most likely will fail also.*

- *Safe Mode*—Starts your Windows 2000 operating system using only the basic drivers and files required to boot the system. This option loads the mouse (except serial mice), monitor, keyboard, base video, storage devices, and the default system services.

Warning! *If your computer does not start correctly using one of the safe mode options, you might need to use the Emergency Repair Disk that is discussed in the next section to repair your system.*

- *Safe Mode With Networking*—Starts your Windows 2000 operating system using only the basic drivers and files required to boot the system and make network connections.

- *Safe Mode With Command Prompt*—Starts your Windows 2000 operating system using only the basic drivers and files required to boot the system. After you log on to Windows 2000, the command prompt is displayed instead of the Windows desktop environment. You can use command prompt utilities to troubleshoot the problem you are experiencing.

- *Enable Boot Logging*—Starts your Windows 2000 operating system and logs all drivers and services that are loaded, or not loaded, to a file called ntbtlog.txt. This file is located in the *%windir%* directory. The Safe Mode, Safe Mode With Networking, and Safe Mode With Command Prompt options add a list of all services and drivers to this file. You can use this file to determine which files and services are logged or not logged to assist you in determining the startup problem.

- *Enable VGA Mode*—Starts your Windows 2000 operating system using the basic VGA driver. You can use this option for troubleshooting a video card driver that is preventing Windows 2000 from starting correctly. This driver is always used when you start Windows 2000 in Safe Mode, Safe Mode With Networking, or Safe Mode With Command Prompt.

- *Last Known Good Configuration*—Starts your Windows 2000 operating system using the Registry information saved during the last shutdown of Windows 2000. This option is useful when you're troubleshooting incorrect configurations of drivers. It will not fix problems generated because of missing files or drivers, however.

- *Directory Service Restore Mode*—This option is available only on a Windows 2000 Domain Controller. It restores the SYSVOL directory and the Active Directory directory service.

17

- *Debugging Mode*—Sends debugging information across a serial cable to another computer when you start your Windows 2000 operating system. Advanced support technicians use this option to assist in troubleshooting critical errors.

Note: Additional options may be available if you are using or have used Remote Installation Services to install Windows 2000 on your computer.

Now that you have an understanding of the different safe mode options available to you, you can follow these steps to start your computer and choose the appropriate safe mode option for your particular situation:

1. Click on the Start button on the taskbar and then click on Shut Down.

2. Click on Restart and then click on OK.

3. When the system is restarting, you'll see a screen with the message "Please select the operating system." It also advises you to press F8 for troubleshooting and advanced startup options. Press this key now.

4. After you press F8, use the arrow keys to highlight the safe mode option of your choice and then press Enter to return to the preceding screen.

5. Select the Windows 2000 Professional operating system and press Enter.

Using the safe mode options is a great way to diagnose problems with your system. They can also be used to eliminate those problems. After adding a new device or updating a driver, you can use safe mode to remove the device or driver you added and eliminate the problem. If the problem does not occur while you're operating in safe mode, you can rest assured that the default settings and minimum device drivers are not the cause of the problem.

Unfortunately, safe mode will not resolve every problem, especially when you're repairing system files. When system files are damaged or corrupted, you will have to take another approach: using the Windows 2000 Recovery Console or the Emergency Repair Process.

Starting the Windows 2000 Recovery Console

The Recovery Console is a command-line console that provides you with a limited set of administrative commands that you can use to repair your computer. For example, you can use it to format drives, read and write data on a local drive, start and stop services, and repair a Master Boot Record (MBR). The Recovery Console is most beneficial in situations in which you need to repair your system by replacing a corrupted or damaged file from either a CD-ROM or floppy disk to your hard drive. It is also very helpful if you need to reconfigure a service that is preventing you from successfully starting your computer.

Warning! The Recovery Console utility is very powerful and should be used only by advanced users who have a thorough understanding of the Windows 2000 environment. Only administrators have the required permissions to use the Recovery Console.

You have two options available to you to start the Recovery Console:

- *Using the Windows 2000 Setup disks*—You use this method if you are unable to start your computer.

Tip: *You also can use the Windows 2000 Professional CD if you have a bootable CD-ROM drive.*

- *Using the* **/cmdcons** *switch with the* **Winnt32.exe** *command*—You can use this method only if you are able to successfully start your computer. You take this proactive step prior to any system problems.

After you start the Recovery Console, you have to choose the Windows 2000 Professional operating system that you are attempting to fix, and you have to log on to that operating system as an administrator.

Note: *You can retrieve help on the available Recovery Console commands by typing "help" at the Recovery Console command prompt.*

To install the Recovery Console as a startup option on your boot menu, follow these steps:

1. While you're running Windows, insert the Windows 2000 Professional CD into your CD-ROM drive to activate the autorun program.

2. When you are prompted to install or upgrade to Windows 2000, click Exit on the screen shown in Figure 17.21.

3. Click on Start|Run and then type "cmd" to open the command prompt.

4. Type the following information at the command prompt to switch to your CD-ROM drive and install the Recovery Console:

```
C:> E:    (where E is the letter of your CD-ROM drive)
E:> \I386\winnt32.exe /cmdcons
```

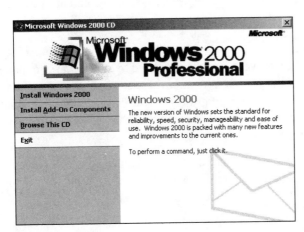

Figure 17.21
Exiting from the Windows 2000 Professional startup screen.

5. The Windows 2000 Setup dialog box then appears. It provides information about the Recovery Console, disk space requirements, and asks whether you want to continue with the installation. Click Yes to continue with the installation of the Recovery Console.

6. The Windows 2000 Professional Setup dialog box will present a progress bar during the installation of the Recovery Console. This installation concludes with a Windows 2000 Professional Setup screen advising you that the installation of the Recovery Console has completed successfully. Furthermore, it explains how to access the Recovery Console and retrieve help on the different Recovery Console commands available to you.

If you encounter serious system problems preventing you from starting the system and you have not already performed the preceding steps to install the Recovery Console, you can use another method to access the Recovery Console. Using the method shown here enables you to run the Recovery Console on a system that will not start:

1. Insert the Windows 2000 Professional 3.5-inch Setup Disk 1 into your disk drive, or if you have a bootable CD-ROM drive, insert the Windows 2000 Professional CD into your CD-ROM drive.

2. Restart your computer.

3. Follow the directions as discussed previously, choosing the options to repair your Windows 2000 installation and then choose to start the Recovery Console.

Note: If you are using the 3.5-inch Setup disks, you will be prompted to insert the additional disks.

Installing the Recovery Console enables you to recover from critical system problems. To access the Recovery Console, you must restart your computer and select the Windows 2000 Recovery Console option when presented the list of available operating systems. After you start the Recovery Console, you can choose from several commands to help recover your system.

Using the Recovery Console

After you successfully access the Recovery Console, you need to know what commands can assist you in the recovery of the system. You enter these commands at the command prompt and can retrieve help on them by typing "help" at the command prompt inside the Recovery Console. Table 17.3 contains an alphabetized list of the Recovery Console commands along with brief descriptions of the commands.

The commands in Table 17.3 are extremely powerful and useful when you are recovering from a system failure. You will want to be familiar with them in the event you are unable to boot your machine but have to solve a critical system problem.

Table 17.3 Recovery Console commands.

Command	Description
attrib	Changes the attributes of a directory or file. These attributes include read-only, hidden, system, and compression. You supply a plus or minus sign to turn them on or off, respectively.
batch	Executes the commands contained inside the text file supplied with the batch command. For example, **batch C:\locate.txt** will execute the commands contained in the text file called locate.txt.
chDir (cd)	Displays the name of the current directory if used by itself. Or, you can change to a different directory by passing the new directory name along with the **cd** command.
chkdsk	Creates and displays a status report regarding the fragmentation of a disk. You can use the **/r** parameter to check the disk for bad sectors and also recover any readable information from the disk.
cls	Clears the command prompt screen, leaving only the command prompt and flashing cursor.
copy	Copies a file from one location to another. The parameters you pass along with the **copy** command specify the location and name of the file being copied (source) and the name and location where you want the file copied to (destination).
delete (del)	Deletes a file from the location you specify using the parameters you pass with the **delete** command. The parameters can include the drive letter, directory name, and file name.
dir	Returns a list of files and subdirectories within a directory you pass in the parameters list. The parameters determine the drive and directory you want the list of files from.
disable	Disables a Windows 2000 device driver or system service. The parameters you pass determine which service or driver is disabled. The startup type for the service or driver is set to SERVICE_DISABLED.
diskpart	Manages the partitions on your hard drive. You can create and delete partitions on a hard drive by passing the appropriate parameters.
enable	Enables a Windows 2000 driver or system service. The parameters you pass determine the service or driver you want to enable. The startup type for the service or driver is set to SERVICE_AUTO_START.
exit	Closes the Windows 2000 Recovery Console and restarts your computer.
expand	Extracts a file from a compressed file. You use this command to extract a driver file from a compressed or cabinet (.cab) file on the Windows 2000 CD. You can use parameters to review the files without actually extracting or expanding them.
fixboot	Fixes the boot partition. This command writes a new boot sector onto the system partition that is passed as a parameter.
fixmbr	Repairs the Master Boot Record of the partition boot sector. A new Master Boot Record is written to the hard drive you specify as a parameter.
format	Formats the drive with the file system you specify. Both the drive and file system type are passed as parameters.
help	Provides online assistance about the Windows 2000 Recovery Console. You can use **help** along with the command name—for example, **help extract**. Or, you can enter the command name followed by **/?**. Using **help** with the command name is the best way to get a thorough understanding of all the commands and the available parameters for each command.
listsvc	Lists the drivers and services available on your computer.
logon	Logs you on to an installation of a Windows 2000 operating system. You will be prompted for the local administrator's password when you choose from the list of operating systems presented to you.

17

(continued)

Table 17.3   Recovery Console commands (continued).

Command	Description
map	Displays a list of drive letters and the physical device names they are mapped to. This information is useful when you're using the **fixboot** or **fixmbr** commands.
mkdir (md)	Creates a directory or subdirectory on the drive letter you specify in your parameters. You use the **path** parameter to specify the new directory name.
more	Displays the contents of a text file. You can use the **type** command as well. Both of these commands allow you to view the contents without modifying them. The text file you want to view is passed as a parameter.
rename (ren)	Changes the name of a single file. The original and new file names are passed as parameters with the command.
rmdir (rd)	Deletes a directory in Windows 2000. You pass the location of the directory including the drive letter and pathname. However, the directory cannot be deleted if it contains files or other directories.
set	Displays and sets Recovery Console environment variables. This command is not enabled by default but can be enabled using Security Templates.
systemroot	Sets your current directory as the *%systemroot%* folder, which identifies where the Windows 2000 installation files are located.
type	Displays the contents of a text file. You can also use the **more** command. The information contained within the file is displayed but not modified.

Deleting the Recovery Console

After you solve your system problems and feel confident things are running smoothly again, you might decide to delete the Recovery Console. Follow these steps to delete the Recovery Console from your Windows 2000 Professional operating system:

1. Restart your computer. During the restart, notice that you have a version of Windows 2000 Professional with a Recovery Console suffix.

2. Open My Computer and then double-click on the volume that contains your installation of the Recovery Console.

3. On the Tools menu, click on Folder Options to open the Folder Options dialog box.

4. Click on the View tab, which contains the Folder Views And Advanced Settings options.

5. Click Show Hidden Files And Folders and clear the Hide Protected Operating System Files checkbox, leaving the settings shown in Figure 17.22. Click on OK.

6. Locate the \Cmdcons folder in the root directory and highlight it. Press the Delete key to delete the directory.

7. Locate the Cmldr file in the root directory and highlight it. Press the Delete key to delete the file.

8. Locate the Boot.ini file in the same directory, right-click on it, and then click on Properties.

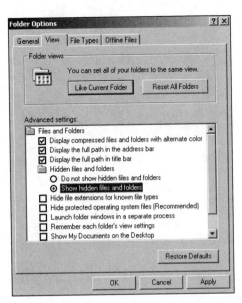

Figure 17.22
Setting options on the View tab of the Folder Options dialog box.

17

9. Deselect the Read-only attribute and then click on OK.

10. Right-click on the Boot.ini file and choose Open With from the shortcut menu. Scroll down to locate Notepad, click on it, and then click on OK.

11. Remove the Windows 2000 operating system entry that contains the Recovery Console suffix. The entry will look similar to the following line:

```
C:\CMDCONS\BOOTSECT.DAT="Microsoft Windows 2000 Recovery Console" /cmdcons
```

Warning! *An incorrect modification to the Boot.ini file may prevent your system from restarting. Be extremely cautious when modifying this file.*

12. On the File menu, click on Save and then click on Exit to close the file.

Tip: *Microsoft recommends that you turn the Read-only attribute back on using the procedure discussed in Step 9. You may also want to hide your system files by reversing the procedure discussed in Step 5.*

You can use the Recovery Console to solve most smaller system problems. However, if things are really bad, you may have to take the next step: performing an Emergency Repair Process.

Understanding the Emergency Repair Process

You can use the Emergency Repair Process to repair problems with system files and the partition boot sector on your boot volume and solve problems in a multiboot environment.

This process requires that you are proactive in creating an Emergency Repair Disk that is used to kick off the Emergency Repair Process.

Creating an Emergency Repair Disk

You create an ERD by using the Windows 2000 Backup utility. After you create the ERD, the disk will contain information about your current system configuration. To create an ERD, you must have a blank 1.44MB floppy disk available.

Warning! *The repair process depends heavily on the information that is saved in the* %systemroot% \repair *folder. This folder must not be deleted or modified.*

Follow these steps to create your ERD:

1. Open the Backup utility by choosing Start|Programs|Accessories|System Tools|Backup to display the Welcome tab, as shown earlier in Figure 17.1.

2. You can perform either of the following two tasks to create the ERD:

   - Click on the Emergency Repair Disk button on the Welcome tab of the Backup utility.

   - Click on the Backup tab and select the Create An Emergency Repair Disk option from the Tools menu.

3. Both options will open the Emergency Repair Diskette dialog box, as shown in Figure 17.23.

4. Selecting the Also Backup The Registry To The Repair Directory checkbox also saves Registry files to the *%systemroot%*\repair folder. We recommend that you select this checkbox when creating your ERD.

Tip: *Creating an ERD should not be considered a one-time operation. Any time you make significant changes to your system, including hardware, partitions, system files, or anything that updates the Registry, you should update your ERD.*

You need to create and maintain the ERD when administering your Windows 2000 environment. Understanding the steps involved to recover your system using the Emergency Repair Process will make the recovery much easier and efficient.

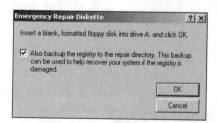

Figure 17.23
Choosing to back up the Registry in the Emergency Repair Diskette dialog box.

Using the Emergency Repair Process

The Emergency Repair Process is the last step you can take to try to "save" your system before you consider reinstalling Windows 2000. This section provides explicit detail on how to use the ERD when performing an Emergency Repair Process to recover your system.

Warning! *The Emergency Repair Process may not even begin unless you have created an ERD. Be sure to create one and keep it updated.*

The following steps are required to recover your system using the Emergency Repair Process:

1. Start your computer using either the Windows 2000 Setup disks or a Windows 2000 bootable CD.

Note: *Your hardware and BIOS must support bootable CDs in order for you to boot your system using the Windows 2000 CD.*

2. After your computer starts, the Setup program will prompt you for information it needs to perform the Emergency Repair Process. Answer the prompts as follows:

   a. Press Enter to start the installation of Windows 2000. This action is required to perform the repair on your system.

   b. Press R to perform a repair of an existing Windows 2000 installation.

   c. Press R again when asked whether you want to use the Emergency Repair Process or the Recovery Console to repair the installation.

3. You now must decide the type of repair you want to perform: fast or manual.

   - *Fast Repair requires you to press F.* Choose this repair process if you want Setup to automatically attempt to repair the Registry, startup environment, system files, and partition boot sector. The Registry is restored to its state when you first installed Windows 2000. This repair doesn't require any additional user intervention.

Warning! *Any changes made to the Registry since you installed Windows 2000 will be lost because you restored the Registry created when the Windows 2000 Setup was first run.*

   - *Manual Repair requires you to press M.* Choose this repair process if you want Setup to repair specific system files, startup environment components, and the partition boot sector. You must decide which options Setup attempts to repair.

Warning! *Unlike the Fast Repair, the Manual Repair option does not let you repair problems with your Registry. If the Registry needs repairs, you can use the Recovery Console.*

4. Start the repair process by using the ERD that you created using the Backup utility and the original Windows 2000 CD.

17

Note: *If you do not have an ERD, the Emergency Repair Process will attempt to locate your Windows 2000 installation and try to repair it.*

5. If your Emergency Repair Process is successful, your computer will automatically restart, and you should have a stable Windows 2000 environment.

Warning! *If the Emergency Repair Process does not repair your system and you have already attempted to repair it using the Recovery Console, you might have to reinstall Windows 2000.*

As you can see, numerous options are available to you to recover your system in the event you have a system failure. You can use the Last Known Good Configuration, safe mode, Recovery Console, and the Emergency Repair Process. Which one you choose depends on the state of your computer and what problem you are trying to fix. Use Decision Tree 17.1 when performing a system recovery on a computer that will not start.

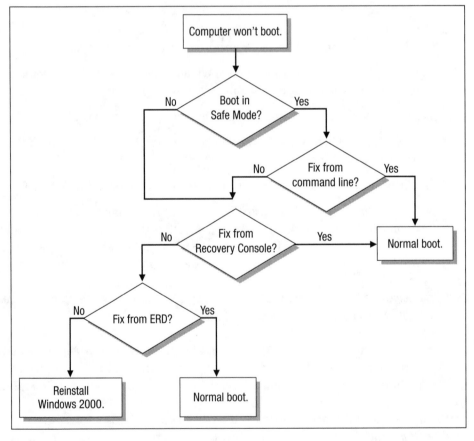

Decision Tree 17.1
System recovery options for a nonbootable computer.

Forcing a Blue Screen Event

Up to this point, we have discussed ways to avoid, minimize, and recover from critical system crashes. Now, we're going to show you a way to safely cause your system to display a blue screen. You can use this procedure to test your Windows 2000 recovery options and ensure that they work as expected and see how a blue screen will affect the software running on your machine.

The easiest way to force a blue screen is to hack the Registry. Remember, we have mentioned a few times that hacking the Registry can be harmful to your system and may render it unusable. We are going to show you a way to safely generate a blue screen.

As always, before you modify the Registry, you should back it up. You can use this backup to restore a corrupted Registry. After you back up the Registry, you can edit it by using REGEDT32.EXE. You open the Registry Editor by clicking on the Start button, clicking on the Run option, and then typing "REGEDT32".

After you open the Registry, you have to navigate to the following Registry location: HKEY_LOCAL_MACHINE\SYSTEM\CurrentControlSet\Services\i8042prt\Parameters. You need to create a new Registry key called CrashOnCtrlScroll using the DWORD type and specify a value of 1, as shown in Figure 17.24. To activate the new Registry key, you need to restart your system.

17

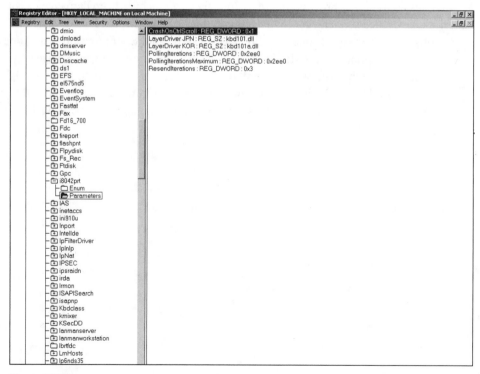

Figure 17.24
Creating the CrashOnCtrlScroll Registry key.

Note: You have just defined a sequence of keystrokes that can be executed to crash your system and create a blue screen.

After you restart your system, you can press Ctrl+ScrollLock+ScrollLock to cause an immediate blue screen to occur.

Warning! *You must press the Ctrl key located on the right side of your keyboard. Using the Ctrl key on the left side of the keyboard will not cause the system to fail.*

After adding the Registry key, you can test how your system will react to a system exception that causes your system to crash. You can use the simulated crash to test your system recovery procedures.

Summary

There are numerous ways to ensure that your user data and system data are always available or are at least easily recoverable. Performing regular backups of the user data ensures that your users always have access to their data. Remember, your backup strategy should be directly affected by the amount of data you can or cannot afford to lose and the length of time required to perform the restore operation. Most times, a longer backup process will result in a more efficient restore process.

Your system recovery process should include how you recover from damaged or corrupted driver files, failed services, corrupted Registry files, and corrupted system files. The options for recovering include choosing Last Known Good Configuration, using one of the safe mode options, using the Recovery Console, and performing an Emergency Repair Process. If you cannot recover your system by using any of these methods, you might have to reinstall Windows 2000 to get your computer running again. However, this reinstallation may require you to reinstall all of your other applications as well.

Appendix A

Other Windows 2000 Professional Resources

Retrieving Additional Information about Windows 2000 Professional

The chapters in this book discussed numerous aspects regarding the installation, configuration, optimization, and management of your Windows 2000 Professional operating system.

As you probably have discovered, there are many responsibilities involved when you are maintaining your installation, and not all of these areas are easy to administer. An entire book could be written about performance, optimization, and troubleshooting to provide you the details required to understand and manage every aspect of each of these topics.

This appendix provides you some additional resources that you can use when administering a Windows 2000 Professional computer. This additional information can be acquired from other books, CD-ROMS, and Web sites.

Other Windows 2000 Professional Reference Books/CD-ROMs

There are a number of books available that cover different aspects of Windows 2000 Professional. These books discuss some of the topics in more depth than what we are able to provide in this book. Some books provide labs, or processes, that you can use to practice the different steps, if you have a configuration that allows you to do so. Other books specialize in preparing you for the Microsoft exam that you can take and pass to obtain a Microsoft certification. Each of the following sections contains information about the book that introduces the section.

Windows 2000 System Administrator's Black Book

This book provides you with an intermediate to expert level view of the functionality available in Windows 2000. After discovering the benefits of Windows 2000 and exploring its numerous new features, you will want to take advantage of this book. *Windows 2000 System Administrator's Black Book* contains real-world experience from two administrators.

I suggest you review this book if you are familiar with Windows NT 4 and are seeking a book that provides you a nice contrast and comparison between Windows NT 4 and Windows 2000.

Another great thing about this book is that it focuses on the utilities found in the Windows 2000 Resource Kit. Furthermore, it provides you Windows 2000 Server topics including Active Directory, fault tolerance, and other topics not supported in Windows 2000 Professional. This is a must-have book for more advanced users who are supporting a combination of Windows 2000 Professional and Server operating systems.

Windows 2000 Security Little Black Book

Like all operating systems, Windows 2000 requires that you create and maintain a secure computing environment. The security tips and methods that are discussed in this book provide you a wealth of information on how to secure your Windows 2000 operating system.

Security is not a subject to take lightly and the author of this book provides you in-depth ideas and secrets for securing your Windows 2000 operating system.

I like the fact that this book covers the key areas of the Windows 2000 operating system that you will want to secure in order to create a safe computing environment, including group policy, encryption, smart cards, Active Directory, and other areas that you need to be familiar with to create and maintain a secure computing environment.

MCSE Windows 2000 Professional Exam Cram

If you are looking to pass the Microsoft Windows 2000 Professional exam (70-210), this book should be in your arsenal of weapons. It provides thorough explanations of concepts and how they correlate to the exam objectives.

Although it provides the required details to pass the exam, it was written at a level that makes it easy to read and comprehend. This team of authors has produced a book that provides clear and concise information that you can use to prepare to easily pass the 70-210 exam. I strongly advise you to use this excellent study guide when preparing for the Windows 2000 Professional exam.

Introducing Microsoft Windows 2000 Professional

If you are fairly new to the Microsoft Windows environment, this is a great preview of the Microsoft Windows family. This book can be used to plan for deployment, and to get that first look at Microsoft Windows 2000 Professional.

I recommend this book if you are new to Windows 2000 but have some experience with previous versions of Microsoft operating systems. Topics covered include key system features and services; a comparison of the functionality and performance of Windows 2000 Professional with other Windows clients, including Windows NT Workstation and Windows 98; and a guide that focuses on preparing for and capitalizing on the business advantages of the technology, with an emphasis on reducing the total cost of ownership.

Microsoft Windows 2000 Professional Resource Kit

If you are familiar with the power and features of Microsoft resource kits, you will be happy to know there is one available for Windows 2000 Professional. This kit contains over 1,700 pages of explicit technical information, along with over 200 utilities and tools on the CD.

You'll find the resource kit provides everything you need to maximize the reliability and efficiency of Windows 2000 Professional, as well as reduce your total cost of ownership. The tools and information will teach you how to reduce deployment costs; configure an optimized TCP/IP network; protect your local and shared resources; analyze and optimize your disk, memory, and processor usage; and use troubleshooting strategies and procedures to solve common operating system problems.

Along with the Help files, the CD-ROM provided with the resource kit contains over 200 utilities and tools for setting up, automating deployment, managing your desktops, monitoring your system, and solving problems. You can run and manage these tools through the familiar Windows Explorer interface.

Web-Based Assistance for Windows 2000 Professional

As often as technology changes, it is nice to have access to content that is frequently updated. Accessing information on the Web can provide you with the most current information on a particular topic or problem.

The following list contains the primary topics available to you on the Web, and allows you to easily retrieve additional information about Windows 2000:

- Windows 2000 information

- Online product support for Windows 2000

- Downloads

- Hardware and software compatibility

- Deployment guides

- Resource kits

- Accessibility

Let's take a look at each of these topics in more detail so you know which site will provide the information you are looking for.

Warning! As technology changes, so does the information on the Web sites. The Web pages and links in this section are subject to change without notification. If you are unable to locate a particular Web page, try again at a later time. Search for the topic using the Search feature on the Microsoft Web site, or contact Microsoft via phone or email regarding the status of the Web page.

Basic Windows 2000 Information

The Windows 2000 home page contains information and links to other information regarding the entire Windows 2000 operating system family. You can access this page at **www.microsoft.com/windows2000/**.

The home page lists the Web site links for all of the different Windows 2000 operating systems. It also contains the latest service packs, and links to articles that discuss benefits, features, and operating system functionality comparisons. There are links to dozens of Microsoft Web sites that provide information about particular subjects.

It also provides a search function so you can search the entire Microsoft Web site for a specific topic. This can be extremely helpful if you are searching for help or additional information on a specific Windows 2000 option.

This site also provides information on the latest releases and information about upcoming releases of the Windows 2000 products like Windows XP (short for experiences) and Windows 2002.

Online Product Support for Windows 2000

This Web page provides additional technical information that you can use as an administrator to analyze, troubleshoot, and resolve problems that may occur during the operation of Windows 2000. You can access the Support page at **www.microsoft.com/windows2000/support/**. This page provides fast access to numerous support options available for Windows 2000.

After you access this page you can click on any of the following links to retrieve additional information regarding the support option:

- *Top Issues and FAQs*—This site is updated weekly with a list of the top issues reported by Windows 2000 users to the Microsoft Windows 2000 Support team. You can view this list to see if anyone else has experienced and reported the problem you are seeking support information on.

- *Search Support*—Gives you access to numerous support resources available for Windows 2000. You can enter keywords that you want to search, and choose the type of information you want included in your search.

- *Contact Support*—Provides a list of all of the Web page links, phone numbers, and contacts available to Windows 2000 users.

- *Newsgroups*—Provides a list of Web sites that communicate online with other Windows 2000 users. You can focus on a specific topic by browsing the different categories based on a certain area of expertise.

- *Troubleshooters*—Helps you diagnose and solve technical problems that you experience in Windows 2000.

- *Online Product Documentation*—Allows you to review the entire online Help documentation of the four Windows 2000 operating systems: Professional, Server, Advanced Server, and Datacenter Server.

- *Diagnostic Solution Guide Pilot*—A new tool that you can use to quickly find the correct support information.

Downloads

This Windows Update site contains files that you can download to your desktop to install system updates, device drivers, and new features. The link to access this Web page is **http://windowsupdate.microsoft.com**.

This page provides the latest and greatest files and information on all of your Windows 2000 components, including Service Packs for your operating system or any of your products, such as Internet Explorer. You will also find information regarding other desktop products like Windows Media Player.

You can configure Windows 2000 to automatically track and notify you when there are updates available on the Web site that should be applied to your computer. The Product Updates option on this site allows you to configure your desktop to enable Active Desktop. After you enable Active Desktop, it will maintain the operating system by communicating with this Web site.

After you click on Product Updates you will receive a Security Warning dialog box similar to the one shown in Figure A.1. You must click on Yes to install and run the Microsoft Windows Update Active Setup distributed by Microsoft.

Hardware and Software Compatibility

The check hardware and software compatibility site provides a list of hardware and software that have been tested by Microsoft and deemed compatible with the Windows 2000 operating

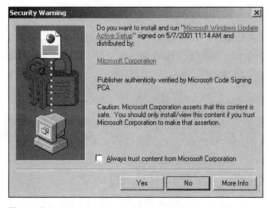

Figure A.1
The Security Warning dialog box.

system. This list is quite extensive, so it should be checked to ensure all components are recognizable to Windows 2000. To access this Web site, enter the following URL: **www.microsoft.com/windows2000/server/howtobuy/upgrading/compat/default.asp**.

This will present a Web page that allows you to choose whether you are looking for computers, hardware devices, or software compatibility information.

Computer Compatibility

Click on Computers if you want to search to see if your computer is compatible with Windows 2000. This page also provides you with important information regarding a BIOS update.

After you click on Computers, you are presented with a search screen that allows you to enter the manufacturer and model of the computer you want to search for. You then use the drop-down menu to choose the type of computer: desktop, laptop, server, clustering, or all.

Tip: *If you do not know the exact model of the computer, provide as much information as you know and it will generate a list for you. Although a vague search may yield a large list, you will still be able to verify whether your computer is supported by Windows 2000.*

Hardware Devices

Another component that you can search for is a hardware device. Hardware devices include printers, scanners, hard drives, and the like that are compatible with Windows 2000. The search may also return links that you can use to download drivers from the hardware manufacturer.

Note: *There is a specific Web site for hardware devices if you are using Windows 2000 Datacenter Server: **www.microsoft.com/windows2000/datacenter/hcl/**.*

This screen also allows you to enter a manufacturer and model of the hardware device you are searching for. Your options for device type include DVD, audio, modems, and monitors.

Software

The software component allows you to search for specific applications or products to ensure they are compatible with Windows 2000. You can search for a specific application, or you can choose to download the entire list in XML format.

Enter the company that developed the application or the application/product name. You can also choose to search for a specific product category such as arts and entertainment, data warehousing, or multimedia. If you want the result set in a language other than the default, you can choose to return the information in a different language.

Deployment Guides

When determining how you are going to deploy the Windows 2000 operating system, Windows 2000 Service Packs, or any other operating system–level applications on your computers, a number of deployment guides are available at **www.microsoft.com/ windows2000/techinfo/planning/default.asp**.

The guides will assist you in planning your deployment of the different components of Windows 2000. There is also information regarding system migration and interoperability with third-party systems.

If, after you begin planning a deployment strategy, you determine it is a very large project that requires additional resources, you can contact Microsoft Consulting Services (MCS). MCS works with enterprise customers to efficiently deploy Windows 2000 and also offers consulting engagements.

Resource Kits

The Resource Kit Web site provides selected material from the Windows 2000 Resource Kits discussed previously. Some of the tools are free to download and can assist you in managing your security features, Group Policy, Active Directory, and application deployment. You can access the site by using the following URL: **www.microsoft.com/windows2000/ techinfo/reskit/default.asp**.

This site also provides lab-based scenarios you can use to determine the most efficient method to deploy the Windows 2000 operating system in a large organization. Furthermore, there is a search tool you can use to locate most of the error and event log messages generated by Windows 2000. Each of these messages includes a detailed explanation and suggested user action.

Accessibility

The default installation of Windows 2000 provides some limited accessibility options. If the default accessibility options do not provide the appropriate level of functionality, you can visit **www.microsoft.com/enable/** for some additional information regarding compatible accessibility options.

This Web site contains the following five areas that discuss accessibility options in great detail:

- *Accessibility & Microsoft*—Introduces accessibility and Microsoft's effort to improve in this area.

- *News & Events*—Provides a free newsletter containing information regarding accessibility. There is also a calendar of events available so you can get involved with the accessibility enhancements in Windows 2000.

- *Products & Aids*—Discusses Microsoft's products, available accessibility aids, and documentation, along with the research being performed to enhance the current accessibility options.

- *Training*—Discusses ways to train individuals about accessibility options, the resources available for training, and some nifty tips and tricks on training accessibility.

- *Developing Technology*—Contains information on the software and hardware guidelines for accessibility, closed caption information, user documentation, and downloads that are available.

Many of the options we discussed in this appendix will be beneficial to you as you encounter different problems and situations with Windows 2000 Professional. As you can see, you are not alone—no matter how small or large your organization is, plenty of help is available.

Microsoft Knowledge Base

A very popular and helpful site that you want to be familiar with is the Microsoft Knowledge Base. This site provides detailed explanations of problems that have been reported to Microsoft along with a workaround or solution to the problem.

After accessing **http://search.support.microsoft.com/kb/**, you can search Microsoft's database. You can search the database using a variety of options, including specific keyword, file name, troubleshooting tool, article ID, or even the most recently reported problems.

This site is very powerful and is a must for anyone who supports Windows 2000. We recommend you use this site as one of your primary troubleshooting tools when resolving problems encountered with any Microsoft product.

Appendix B

Windows 2000 Frequently Asked Questions

Questions, Questions, and More Questions

Whether you are new to Windows 2000 or a veteran of this particular operating system, you are going to have questions about the different areas of Windows 2000. This appendix includes some of the most frequently asked questions (FAQs), beginning with simple questions and ending with more complex questions regarding Windows 2000. There is a broad range of questions and answers provided for you that we chose because we have heard them time and time again. We broke them down into different categories, making it easier for you to locate the question you may be asking.

The following six categories are used in this appendix:

- Understanding Windows 2000

- Installing and Upgrading

- System Configuration

- User Configuration

- Services

- Performance

Understanding Windows 2000

This first section enables a new user to establish an understanding of Windows 2000. This understanding provides a foundation for you and will be expanded as you move through the remaining sections of the appendix.

What Is Windows 2000 Professional?

Well, it was supposed to be Windows NT 5.0 Workstation, but Microsoft decided to rename it to Windows 2000 to be consistent with their other product lines, like Office 2000. Windows 2000 Professional is a desktop operating system that was designed for businesses of all sizes.

Windows 2000 Professional is the easiest Windows operating system yet, with high-level security and improved mobile user support. The operating system is designed to provide corporate-wide reliability with a lower total cost of ownership (TCO), while easing administration.

What Is New in Windows 2000 Professional?

Windows 2000 Professional is more compatible than any workstation you have previously used. It was designed for easier use, easier management, and increased compatibility, and it is more powerful than previous workstations.

Windows 2000 Professional makes it easier to work with files, locate information, customize your work environment, work on the Web, and work remotely. It is easier to manage because of the improved setup, administration, and support options.

Windows 2000 provides increased compatibility with other types of networks, and also with legacy hardware and software support. There is improved driver support for your hardware and multimedia technologies. There is also improved reliability, security, and performance with many new features included with Windows 2000 Professional.

What Is Active Directory?

Active Directory is a directory service that holds information about all of the resources on your network. As with any directory, the basic purpose of Active Directory is to store information about other information.

The Active Directory storage file called ntds.dit is located in the *%systemroot%*\ntds directory. Active Directory clients can easily query Active Directory for information about any resource on the network. If the directory gets too large, you can group the information by type or location.

Active Directory includes the following powerful features:

- Stores information in a secure format. Access to the information is determined by the resource Access Control List (ACL)—a list of resources that may access the object and what these resources can do with that object.

- Generates a global catalog providing a flexible mechanism for querying Active Directory.

- Replicates the directory information to all domain controllers, thereby improving accessibility, availability, and fault tolerance.

- Features an extensible design that allows new objects to be added, or you can expand the existing objects.

- Uses Domain Name System (DNS), rather than NetBIOS names, when naming and locating your domain controllers.

- Communicates over multiple protocols with the implementation of the X.500 foundation. These protocols can be LDAP versions 2 and 3, and HTTP.

What Are X.500 and LDAP?

X.500 is the most commonly used protocol for directory management. There are two main standards—the 1988 standard and the 1993 standard, which provides numerous improvements over the 1988 standard. The Windows 2000 implementation of the Active Directory directory services is based on the 1993 X.500 standard.

X.500 uses a hierarchical approach to objects in the namespace, with a root at the top of the namespace and children coming off from it. The domain names in Windows 2000 are DNS names instead of NetBIOS names. For instance, BRIANA.ORG is a DNS Windows 2000 domain name; a child domain of BRIANA.ORG could have a DNS name of TRAINING.BRIANA.ORG.

Although the directory service is based on X.500, the mechanism used to access Active Directory is Lightweight Directory Access Protocol (LDAP). X.500 is a part of the Open Systems Interconnect (OSI) model, but it does not translate well in a TCP/IP environment. LDAP is used to communicate with Active Directory using TCP/IP.

LDAP improves performance by reducing the number of functions available with a full X.500 implementation. LDAP is the primary mechanism for communicating with Active Directory, and it only performs the basic read, write, and modify operations.

B

What Is the Global Catalog?

The global catalog contains an entry for every object in the entire enterprise forest—one or more domain trees that do not necessarily form a contiguous namespace. For instance, BRIANA.ORG is a domain tree that is part of a forest that also contains another domain tree with a completely different namespace called ACME.ORG. You may see this type of environment when two companies merge and they both want to maintain their original namespace.

The global catalog server contains only a few key attributes of each Active Directory object. Searches of the entire enterprise forest can be done only on the attributes that are stored in the global catalog. However, searches in the user's own domain tree can be done on all of the objects' attributes.

Note: Only domain controllers can perform the role of global catalog servers.

What Is the Schema?

The schema is a blueprint of all of the objects and attributes in Active Directory. When you first create a domain, a default schema is created that contains the definitions of the different objects—users, computers, domains, and so on. You can have only one schema per forest, preventing you from having multiple definitions of the same object.

Your default schema definition is located in the schema.ini file. This file also contains the initial structure of the Active Directory database file ntds.dit. The file is an ASCII text file that can be viewed with a text editor.

Installing and Upgrading

The basic installation of Windows 2000 Professional is pretty straightforward. However, there are some options you should be familiar with that will reduce the amount of time it takes to perform the installation or upgrade, and to ensure the installation is accurate.

Why Do I Need Smartdrv in Order to Install Windows 2000 Professional?

Smartdrv.exe is an MS-DOS utility that is important to have on your computer during the installation of Windows 2000 Professional. The presence of this file will significantly decrease the installation time of Windows 2000 Professional when you perform the installation using the winnt.exe installation method.

Use the following steps to take advantage of the improved performance that smartdrv.exe offers:

1. Create a DOS bootable disk using the **format a: /s** command at the command prompt.

2. Use the **copy** command to copy smartdrv.exe and himem.sys to the bootable floppy.

3. Edit or create the autoexec.bat file on the floppy drive using your favorite text editor and add the following statement:

   ```
   A:\smartdrv.exe /q
   ```

4. Edit or create the config.sys file on the floppy drive using a text editor and add the following statement:

   ```
   device=himem.sys
   ```

5. Use the **Net Use** command to connect to the shared network drive that contains the installation files and start the installation using winnt.exe.

Note: *Himem.sys is needed by smartdrv and allows access to privileged areas of memory, improving performance of the installation.*

After you create your floppy disk and make the recommended changes, boot your computer from the floppy to begin the installation of Windows 2000 Professional utilizing the smartdrv.exe file.

Does Windows 2000 Professional Have to Be Installed on the C: Drive?

Absolutely not! You can install Windows 2000 Professional on any partition on your computer. However, the installation still places a few files on the active partition in order for Windows 2000 Professional to boot. The active partition is also referred to as the *system partition;* the partition on which you choose to install Windows 2000 Professional is referred to as the *boot partition*.

Can I Perform an Unattended Installation of Windows 2000 Professional?

Yes. You can create a text file that contains the responses to the questions asked during an installation of Windows 2000 Professional. You pass the name of the text file to the installation program, instructing the program to retrieve the answers to the questions from the text file.

This text file is normally called unattend.txt and is passed to the installation program by using the **/U:unattend.txt** switch when you begin the installation using the winnt.exe program. Because of the implications involved when using the text file, it has to adhere to a complex and strict format. However, there is an application called setupmgr.exe, located on the Windows 2000 Server CD, that can be used to generate the unattend.txt file using a Graphical User Interface (GUI).

How Do I Create the Windows 2000 Professional Installation Disks?

You may need to create the system setup disks if you need to perform an installation from them, or if you need to perform an emergency repair process using the Emergency Repair Disks (ERD). Use the following steps to create the Windows 2000 setup disks:

Note: *You will need four blank setup disks that should be labeled "setup disk one", "setup disk two", "setup disk three", and "setup disk four".*

1. Insert a blank, formatted 3 1/2" floppy disk into your floppy disk drive.

2. Insert the Windows 2000 CD-ROM into your CD-ROM drive.

3. Click on Start|Run to open the Run dialog box.

4. Type "d:\bootdisk\makebt32 a:" in the Open box of the Run dialog box (where *d* is the letter of your CD-ROM drive and *a* is the letter of your floppy drive).

5. Click on OK to begin creating the Windows 2000 setup disks and insert the appropriate disk when requested.

Note: *You can create the setup disks from any computer running any version of MS-DOS or Windows operating systems.*

How Do I Uninstall Windows 2000 Professional from an NTFS Partition?

The best way to uninstall Windows 2000 from an NTFS volume is to actually delete the volume that Windows 2000 was installed on. However, if you are in a dual-boot configuration, most of your other operating systems will not be able to access files on the NTFS volume.

Use the following steps to delete the NTFS volume that contains the Windows 2000 Professional installation:

1. Start the computer from the Windows 2000 setup disks.

2. When prompted to create or choose partitions, select the NTFS partition that contains the installation that you want to delete.

3. Press D to delete the volume, and then press L to confirm.

4. If Windows 2000 was not on the active partition, you need to replace the boot loader. You can do this by booting up using a Windows 98 startup disk, and then typing the following command at the command prompt:

```
SYS c:
```

*Note: If you deleted the active partition, you would have to identify a new active partition in order to use the computer. When you do so, it will create a new master boot record without any record of Windows 2000 so you won't have to execute the **SYS** command.*

5. Reboot your computer.

If you are in a dual-boot environment and both operating systems are installed on FAT partitions, you can boot to the alternate operating system and delete the FAT partition that contains the Windows 2000 operating system. You will also want to delete the boot.ini, ntldr.exe, ntbootdd.sys, and ntdetect.com files from the active partition.

System Configuration

Windows 2000 Professional is the most complex and powerful desktop operating system released by Microsoft to date. Its robustness also requires the need to understand how to customize the entire system. This section discusses some of the FAQs regarding your computer's configuration.

How Do I Decrease the Boot Delay Time?

On a dual-boot system with Windows 2000 Professional, you have 30 seconds to decide which operating system you want to boot to. If you do not choose an alternate system, the computer will boot to the configured default operating system. If the 30 second setting is too long of a setting for you, you can decrease it to a shorter period of time.

Use the following steps to easily decrease the boot delay time on your Windows 2000 computer:

1. Log on with an account that has administrator permissions.

2. Right-click on the My Computer icon and select Properties.

3. Click on the Advanced tab and then click on the Startup And Recovery button.

4. Set the desired amount of time in the Display List Of Operating Systems For section of the Startup And Recovery dialog box.

How Can I Create a New Hardware Profile?

Hardware profiles are used to determine which services, devices, and drivers are installed during the boot-up process. Depending on your configuration, you may want to prevent all of the services and devices from being installed, thereby optimizing the performance of your system.

Use the following steps to create a new hardware profile in Windows 2000:

1. Right-click on the My Computer icon and select Properties.

2. Click on the Hardware tab and then click on the Hardware Profiles button.

3. Click on Profile 1 (current).

4. Click on the Copy button and type a name in the Copy Profile dialog box.

5. Click on OK to create the new hardware profile and close the Copy Profile dialog box.

6. Click on OK to close the Hardware Profiles dialog box.

7. Click on OK to close the System Properties dialog box.

How Can I Remove Entries on the Add/Remove Software Applet That I Am Unable to Remove Using the Remove Software Option?

Sometimes you will install an application and it will show up in the Add/Remove Software list of an installed application. However, when you try to uninstall the application using the Add/Remove Programs applet in Control Panel, the uninstall of the application fails. You can remove these applications by editing the Registry using the following steps:

1. Start the Registry Editor by selecting Start|Run and then typing "regedt32".

2. Locate HKEY_LOCAL_MACHINE\Software\Microsoft\windows\currentversion\ Uninstall in the Registry.

3. Select the Registry key of the software that you want to remove and select Delete from the Edit menu.

4. Close the Registry Editor to save your changes.

How Can I Remove an Applet from Control Panel?

Each applet in Control Panel is associated with a CPL file located in the *%systemroot%* SYSTEM32 directory. To remove an item from Control Panel for all users on the computer, you can either delete the CPL file or rename it using a different file extension. Table B.1 contains an alphabetized list of the common CPL files and what applet they correspond to.

If you want to control who accesses the specific Control Panel applets and your boot partition is formatted with NTFS, you can remove the read permission for users that you do not want to access the applet. For instance, if you want to prevent Corey from using the Display option of Control Panel, you would remove the read permission from the desk.cpl file for his user account.

How Can I Run a Control Panel Applet from the Command Prompt?

Some people prefer to use the command prompt to run the Control Panel applets. To do this, type the command with the *control* statement followed by the applet name and any required parameters.

For instance, let's say that you want to run the Keyboard applet from the command prompt. We have already discovered it is part of the main.cpl file. To run this applet, issue the following command at the command prompt:

```
Control main.cpl keyboard
```

After you issue this command, the Control Panel Keyboard applet will display on your screen.

Table B.1   Common CPL files and their associated applets.

CPL File Name	Control Panel Applet
access.cpl	Accessibility Options
appwiz.cpl	Add/Remove Programs
desk.cpl	Display
inetcpl.cpl	Internet Options
intl.cpl	Regional Options
jmain.cpl	Fonts, keyboard, mouse, and printers
mlcfg32.cpl	Mail
mmsys.cpl	Sounds and Multimedia
nwc.cpl	Network and Dial-up Connections
timedate.cpl	Date/Time

How Can I Open a Document with an Application Other Than the Default Associated Application?

Most files that can be opened for viewing can be opened by right-clicking on the file and selecting Open. However, you may want to open the document with an application other than the one that has been associated with it.

To open a document with a different application, right-click on the document and then choose Open With.

How Do I Disable Task Manager?

Task Manager can be used to stop processes and applications, and to take a quick look at your system performance. You may want to remove this capability so your users don't stop something that they shouldn't.

Use the following steps to edit the Registry and disable Task Manager:

1. Start the Registry Editor by selecting Start|Run and then typing "regedt32".

2. Locate HKEY_CURRENT_USER\Software\Microsoft\windows\currentversion\Policies.

3. If the System key does not exist, create it by selecting the Add Key option from the Edit menu.

4. Add a value to the System key called DisableTaskMgr with a type of DWORD and a value of 1. The key should look like the one shown in Figure B.1.

5. Close the Registry Editor.

Alternatively you can set the NTFS permissions to prevent users from accessing Task Manager, or you can rename taskmgr.exe, which prevents all users on your computer from using it. You can rename the file by locating it in the *%systemroot%*\system32 folder, right-clicking on it, and clicking on Rename. You then supply a new name for the file—I suggest just changing the extension of the file from .exe to .sav.

How Can I Switch between 12-Hour Time and 24-Hour Time?

The display of your system's time is determined by the settings located in the Regional Options applet in Control Panel. The time setting can be displayed in a variety of ways; the most common request is to switch from the 12-hour time format to 24-hour time format, and vice versa. This can be easily performed using the following steps:

1. Click on Start|Settings|Control Panel and double-click on Regional Options to open the Regional Options dialog box.

2. Click on the Time tab to display the Time options shown in Figure B.2.

3. Specify the required time format in the Time Format pull-down window, using H for the 24-hour format and h for the 12-hour format.

4. Click on Apply or OK to save the new settings.

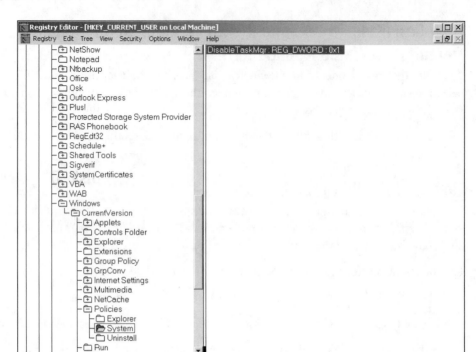

Figure B.1

The Registry key used to disable the Task Manager.

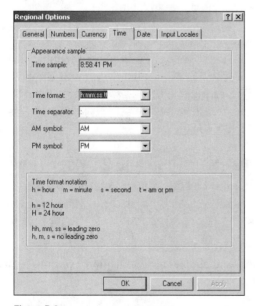

Figure B.2

The Time tab used to set the display format of the system time.

User Configuration

You will want to customize your desktop to create an efficient and easy-to-use computing environment. Windows 2000 allows users to configure their desktops any way they want, but you may want to prevent them from doing so if corporate policy requires every user to have a standardized desktop. Remember, these customizations are stored in the user's profile, so they can be reapplied every time they log on. Let's look at some of the FAQs regarding a user's desktop environment.

How Do I Create a Shortcut on the Desktop to a Disk, Directory, or File?

You have to access a specific disk or directory frequently, and you want the convenience of locating the disk or directory from your desktop. Use the following steps to create a shortcut on your desktop that points to a disk or directory:

1. Open Windows Explorer (Start|Programs|Accessories|Windows Explorer).

2. Locate and right-click on the disk, directory, or file that you want to create a shortcut to and drag it to your desktop.

3. Release the mouse button.

4. Click on Create Shortcut(s) Here on the shortcut menu.

The shortcut will now appear on your desktop.

How Do I Disable Active Desktop?

Active Desktop is a powerful Web-based desktop tool that can provide dynamic updates to your desktop. It is also a required component for some of your background pictures. Although you may enable Active Desktop by selecting a background picture that requires it, you may decide afterwards to disable it. Use the following steps to easily disable Active Desktop:

1. Right-click on any blank area of your desktop to open a shortcut menu.

2. Select Active Desktop from the shortcut menu and then click on Show Web Content to clear the checkmark next to it.

How Can I Create a Keyboard Shortcut to a Web Page?

You can actually save time required to access Web pages by creating a keyboard shortcut to the Web page. This keyboard shortcut allows you to press the defined keys to display the Web page instead of having to locate it through Internet Explorer.

1. Open Internet Explorer.

2. Connect to the Web page for which you want to create the keyboard shortcut.

B

3. Click on Add To Favorites on the Favorites menu. Change the name of the Favorite to whatever you want, and then click on OK.

4. Click on Organize Favorites from the Favorites menu.

5. Right-click on the Web page in your list of Favorites and click on Properties.

6. Click anywhere in the Shortcut Key box on the Web Document tab of the Properties dialog box.

7. Press either the Ctrl, Alt, or Shift key to display Ctrl + Alt in the Shortcut Key box. While holding the key, press any key on the keyboard to generate a keyboard shortcut to the Web page. An example of key combinations is shown in Figure B.3.

8. Click on OK to close the dialog box.

Services

There are numerous services available in Windows 2000 Professional supporting a wide range of functionality. For instance, to schedule tasks to execute at specific times, you need the Task Scheduler service running.

Windows 2000 Professional does not support all applications available to you in a Windows 2000 environment. For example, Windows 2000 Professional cannot act as a DNS server, DHCP server, or WINS server. It can, however, be a client of any or all of these services.

Figure B.3
The Web Document tab of the Web Page Properties dialog box.

How Do I Configure a DNS Client?

DNS is used to resolve hostnames or computer names to IP addresses so that two computers can communicate with each other. Before the two computers begin the communication process, they have to resolve or translate their computer names to IP addresses via DNS. The clients have to know the IP address of the DNS server before the resolution can take place. Use the following steps to configure your Windows 2000 Professional computer as a client to a DNS server:

1. Click Start|Settings|Network And Dial-up Connections and then right-click on the TCP/IP connection that you want to configure for DNS.

2. Select the Properties option on the shortcut menu to display the connection's Properties page.

3. On the General tab of the LAN connection that you want to configure, select Internet Protocol (TCP/IP), and then click the Properties button.

4. If you want to obtain the DNS server address from your DHCP server, select the Obtain DNS Server Address Automatically radio button.

   If you want to manually configure the DNS server addresses, select Use The Following DNS Server Addresses radio button, type an IP address for the preferred DNS server, and optionally type an IP address for the alternate DNS server.

5. Click on OK to close the open dialog boxes.

B

How Do I Configure a DHCP Client?

A DHCP client automatically receives TCP/IP information from a DHCP server, eliminating the need to manually configure TCP/IP. Use the following steps to configure a DHCP client:

1. Click on Start|Settings|Network And Dial-up Connections and then right-click on the TCP/IP connection that you want to configure to use DHCP.

2. Select the Properties option on the shortcut menu to display the connection's Properties dialog box.

3. On the General tab of the LAN connection that you want to configure, select Internet Protocol (TCP/IP), and then click on the Properties button.

4. Select the Obtain An IP Address Automatically radio button, and then click on OK.

5. Click on OK to close the open dialog boxes.

How Do I Configure a WINS Client?

A WINS client uses a WINS server to automatically register and resolve NetBIOS computer names to IP addresses. Similar to DNS, your NetBIOS computer names need to be resolved or translated to an IP address. Windows 2000 Professional clients need to be configured to communicate with the WINS server by supplying the WINS server IP address. Use the following steps to configure a WINS client:

1. Click on Start|Settings|Network And Dial-up Connections and then right-click on the TCP/IP connection that you want to configure to use WINS.

2. Select the Properties option on the shortcut menu to display the connection's Properties dialog box.

3. On the General tab of the LAN connection that you want to configure, select Internet Protocol (TCP/IP), and then click the Properties button.

4. Click on the Advanced button, and then click on the WINS tab.

5. Click on the Add button to open the TCP/IP WINS Server dialog box.

6. Type the IP address of the WINS server, and then click on Add.

7. Repeat Steps 5 and 6 to add more WINS servers.

8. Click on OK to close the open dialog boxes.

Performance

Performance is always an issue when it comes to computers, which is why technology changes so quickly. We are constantly hearing about faster processors, disks, and network cards. You need to be familiar with some of the most common questions about how to improve performance on a Windows 2000 Professional machine.

How Do I Move My Pagefile?

A pagefile is a file used by Windows 2000 to hold information that's moved out of memory. Windows 2000 uses the pagefile, which is commonly referred to as *virtual memory,* to make Windows 2000 think that there is more physical memory than there actually is. Moving data out of memory in this fashion is called *page swapping,* and is done to allow you to use more memory than the actual amount of RAM on your machine. Virtual memory increases performance when running multiple applications or an application that is memory intensive.

By default, pagefile.sys is located in the root of the drive that you installed Windows 2000 on. However, if you want to improve performance in Windows 2000, you can move the pagefile to a drive different from the one where the operating system files are stored.

The pagefile and the operating system files are constantly accessed to assist in completing the numerous tasks performed by the operating system. Moving the pagefile to a hard drive other than the drive containing the operating system files reduces contention to read and write information to the same disk, and improves performance. Use the following steps to relocate your pagefile in Windows 2000:

1. Right-click on your My Computer icon and click on Properties to open the System Properties dialog box.

2. Click on the Advanced tab, and then click on the Performance Options button to open the Performance Options dialog box.

3. Click on the Change button to open the Virtual Memory dialog box shown in Figure B.4.

4. Select the current pagefile disk and change the Initial Size to 0. Then click on the Set button.

5. Select a different disk and set the Initial Size and Maximum Size values to be at least 1.5 times the amount of RAM on your computer. Click the Set button.

6. Click on OK to close the open dialog boxes.

7. Restart the computer to implement the change.

How Can I Monitor the Performance of My Logical Drives?

By default the disk counters are only available for you to monitor the performance of your physical drives through System Monitor. If you want to monitor your logical drives, you must manually turn the logical drive counters on at the command prompt. Table B.2 contains a list of commands and a description of how they affect the disk counters. After you execute any of the commands listed, you must restart your computer for them to take effect.

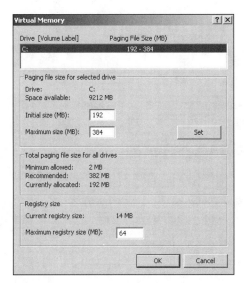

Figure B.4
Using the Virtual Memory dialog box to relocate the pagefile.

Table B.2   Disk performance commands.

Command	Description
Diskperf	Displays the status of both physical and logical disk performance counters.
Diskperf -y	Enables both the physical and logical disk performance counters.
Diskperf -yd	Enables the physical disk performance counters. (This is the default setting.)
Diskperf -yv	Enables the logical disk performance counters.
Diskperf -n	Disables both the physical and logical disk performance counters.
Diskperf -nd	Disables the physical disk performance counters.
Diskperf -nv	Disables the logical disk performance counters.

Warning! The disk performance counters can cause slight performance degradation in a disk I/O–intensive environment.

What Is the Best Way to Run My 16-Bit Applications?

By default, your 16-bit applications use a shared Virtual DOS Machine (VDM) that has its own memory space. There is one problem with running multiple 16-bit applications in a single VDM: If one application fails, all of them are affected, and they may all fail.

A safer way to run your 16-bit applications is to run each of them in its own memory space. This is achieved by using the following command at the command prompt:

```
Start /Separate application name
```

You can also start a 16-bit application in its own memory space by creating a shortcut to the application. Do so by performing the following steps:

1. Right-click on the application shortcut and select Properties.

2. Click on the Shortcut tab to display the shortcut to the application, as shown in Figure B.5.

3. Click on the Run In Separate Memory Space checkbox.

4. Click on OK to apply the changes and close the Shortcut Properties dialog box.

Note: If the Run In Separate Memory Space checkbox is dimmed out, the application you are accessing cannot be run in a separate memory space. This will occur with 32-bit applications.

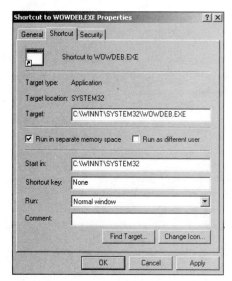

Figure B.5
The Shortcut tab of the Properties dialog box.

Appendix C

The Windows 2000 Professional Boot Process

A Five-Stage Launch

Windows 2000 Professional systems are initialized using a distinct five-stage boot process. The launch of the Windows 2000 Professional operating system begins when a system powers up.

Computers begin operation by conducting a Power On Self Test (POST). During the POST cycle, a system essentially replicates a human who is awakening in the morning after a long slumber. The computer checks for its arms and legs, head and neck, and toes and fingers. In other words, it conducts a scan to determine which hardware components are installed.

The POST procedure begins the first phase of the Windows 2000 Professional boot cycle. The boot process is completed when Windows 2000 Professional loads after you successfully log on to the system. In between, various other procedures and processes occur, all governed in a meticulous dance chaperoned by the Windows 2000 Professional Ntldr program and a select group of operating system files.

Microsoft identifies the five stages of the Windows 2000 Professional boot process as follows:

- Stage 1: Preboot Sequence
- Stage 2: Boot Sequence
- Stage 3: Kernel Load
- Stage 4: Kernel Initialization
- Stage 5: Logon

You need to understand which actions are taken in which stage. In addition, when you are troubleshooting boot issues, knowing which program files are responsible for performing which tasks can be quite beneficial.

Like most things in life, starting at the beginning is often best. We will begin the review of the Windows 2000 Professional boot process by examining the Preboot Sequence.

Stage One: The Preboot Sequence

In addition to learning the amount of memory a system possesses, during a system's POST procedure, systems possessing a Plug-and-Play BIOS prepare installed and detected hardware for operation. Next, the system identifies the device that will boot the system, which is usually a hard disk. Occasionally, the boot device can be a CD-ROM, floppy disk, or other drive.

This stage features (usually) a black screen and plain white text. The text displays the information a BIOS gathers as the Preboot Sequence begins.

After the boot device is identified, the system's BIOS seeks the Master Boot Record (MBR). The MBR searches for an active partition while scanning the system's partition table. When it finds the active partition, the MBR finds the boot sector on that partition and stores that sector in memory before executing it.

The Windows 2000 Professional Ntldr file executes next. Ntldr is the file responsible for controlling the boot process from the first stage until the fourth stage, when it hands off its duties to the Windows 2000 kernel.

These steps complete the Preboot Sequence. Figure C.1 charts the four steps that compose the first stage of the Windows 2000 Professional boot process.

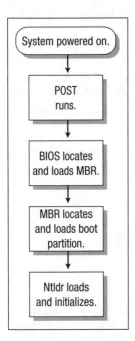

Figure C.1
Four steps comprise Windows 2000 Professional's Preboot Sequence.

Stage Two: Boot Sequence

In the next stage, the Boot Sequence, Ntldr begins its work by switching the microprocessor from real mode to a 32-bit mode. The 32-bit flat memory mode is required for Ntldr to continue.

Ntldr then starts minifile system drivers. These drivers enable the Ntldr file to read FAT- and NTFS-formatted hard disks.

The BOOT.INI file loads next. If only a single operating system is configured to run on the system, the NTDETECT.COM and NTOSKRNL.EXE files detect installed hardware. If multiple operating systems exist in the BOOT.INI file, a screen appears requesting that you select which operating system is loaded. After a specified period, a default is selected.

Making Sense of the BOOT.INI File

The BOOT.INI file is located on a hard disk's active partition. It is composed of two sections.

The first section, the boot loader, specifies the location of the system's boot partition. The location is identified using what is known as an ARC path. (ARC stands for Advanced RISC Computing.) A typical ARC path appears as follows:

```
multi(0)disk(0)rdisk(0)partition(1)\WINNT
```

The **multi** value indicates the hard disk controller (beginning with 0 for the first controller). The **disk** value indicates the SCSI ID, if a SCSI drive holds the boot partition. In such cases, instead of **multi**, **scsi** will appear in the ARC path. When **multi** appears, the disk value is always 0. When **scsi** appears, **rdisk** is always 0.

The **rdisk** value identifies the disk, and the **partition** value indicates the partition. Partition values, unlike **multi**, **disk**, and **rdisk** number values, begin with 1.

Thus, in the preceding example, the boot partition exists on the first hard disk controller, uses the first hard disk, and resides on the first partition. Further, the **\WINNT** string indicates the location of the Windows 2000 Professional system root folder.

The second BOOT.INI section is titled operating systems. It includes information required to start Windows operating systems installed on a system. A sample operating systems section looks like this:

```
multi(0)disk(0)rdisk(0)partition(1)\WINNT="Microsoft Windows 2000
  Professional" /fastdetect
```

The **/fastdetect** switch disables serial mouse detection. You can use other switches within the BOOT.INI file as well. The **/basevideo** switch boots a system using a standard VGA driver. The **/maxmem RAMSize** switch helps troubleshoot faulty RAM chips. In place of **RAMSize**, enter the amount of RAM you wish Windows to use. The **/noguiboot** switch eliminates the graphical boot status screen, and the **/sos** switch lists drivers as they load, which can be a great help when you're trying to identify a misbehaving driver.

C

NTDETECT.COM creates an inventory of all the hardware devices that are found and passes the list to the Ntldr file. The next significant event during the boot process is the presentation of the Hardware Profile/Configuration Recovery Menu screen, which appears so that you can select an appropriate hardware profile. If multiple hardware profiles do not exist, this step is skipped. In these cases, Ntldr continues using a default profile.

Selecting a hardware profile marks the last step in the boot process's second stage. Figure C.2 charts the Boot Sequence's four steps.

Stage Three: Kernel Load

After a hardware profile is selected, the Windows 2000 Professional kernel steps up to the plate for the next boot stage, known as Kernel Load. Several critical steps are performed at this stage. You can identify them by looking for vertical white rectangles at the bottom of the screen.

As the process is completed, load progress is tracked by vertical white rectangles that become a solid white line as the stage finishes. Above the white rectangles is a string of text that reads "Starting Windows."

First, NTOSKRNL.EXE loads. Then, the hardware abstraction layer, or HAL.DLL file, loads, as does the HKEY_LOCAL_MACHINE\SYSTEM Registry key.

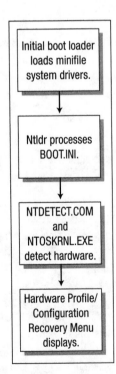

Figure C.2
The Boot Sequence is made up of four steps.

Ntldr selects a control set and uses it to initialize the system. Finally, low-level hardware drivers load according to the order specified in the Registry.

Tip: The HKEY_LOCAL_MACHINE\SYSTEM\CurrentControlSet\Control\ServiceGroupOrder subkey instructs the Ntldr file as to which order low-level hardware drivers, such as those for a system's CD-ROM and disk drivers, are to be loaded.

Figure C.3 charts the five tasks performed in the Kernel Load stage of the boot process.

Stage Four: Kernel Initialization

With Ntldr's duties complete, it passes control of the boot process to the NTOSKRNL.EXE file, which is initialized. Remember, NTOSKRNL.EXE was loaded early in the Kernel Load stage.

A graphical screen displaying load status appears. Blue squares on a white Windows 2000 splash screen track this stage's progress. Above the blue squares is a text string that reads "Starting up."

The Windows 2000 Professional kernel takes information regarding detected hardware and creates a new HKEY_LOCAL_MACHINE\HARDWARE Registry key. Next, NTOSKRNL.EXE creates a Clone control set.

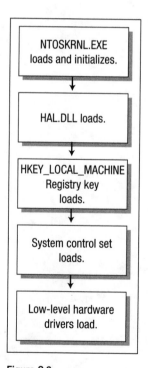

Figure C.3
During Kernel Load, the HAL loads, as do an important Registry key, the system control set, and low-level device drivers.

NTOSKRNL.EXE then initializes the low-level hardware drivers. It also checks the HKEY_LOCAL_MACHINE\SYSTEM\CurrentControlSet\Services\DriverOrServiceName\ ErrorControl Registry key for Start entry 0x1 values. If it finds them, it loads them, upon which they are initialized.

The SMSS.EXE file, known as the Session Manager, then starts Windows 2000's subsystems and services. It also executes other startup functions, as instructed by the Registry.

Figure C.4 charts the four steps that occur during Kernel Initialization.

This marks the last step in the Kernel Initialization stage.

Stage Five: Logon

The final stage, Logon, begins with the Windows subsystem triggering WINLOGON.EXE. WINLOGON.EXE starts LSASS.EXE, the Local System Authority, which displays the Windows Logon dialog box.

The Windows 2000 Professional Service Controller then kicks into gear. It starts the Workstation and Server services. After you provide an appropriate username and password (if required) and successfully log on to the system, the startup process is considered complete.

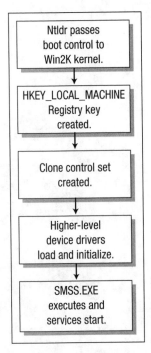

Figure C.4
During the Kernel Initialization stage, four important tasks are completed.

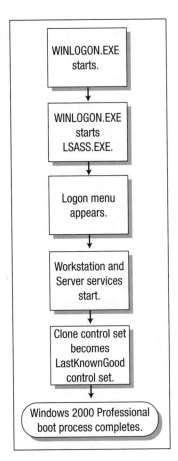

C

Figure C.5
Five tasks are completed during Logon.

Figure C.5 charts the five tasks that occur during the Logon stage.

One step in the boot process still remains. The Windows 2000 Professional boot process is completed when the Clone control set created during Kernel Initialization is written as the LastKnownGood control set.

Index

P

R

What's on the CD-ROM

What's on the CD-ROM

The *Windows 2000 Professional On Site* companion CD-ROM contains elements specifically selected to enhance the usefulness of this book, including:

- *PowerQuest PartitionMagic*—Demo software that, in its full version, can be used to create, delete, convert, and resize hard disk partitions.

- *TechRepublic White Paper: What to expect from Microsoft Windows 2000*—TechRepublic's Win2K white paper, updated January 2001, examines the new NT platform's features and the impact the new OS will have on your enterprise.

- Worksheets to help you implement numerous topics of Windows 2000 Professional. These worksheets will help you:

  - Prepare to deploy Windows 2000 Professional

  - Estimate deployment costs

  - Create a pre-installation checklist

  - Prepare for a backup

  - Prepare to create user accounts

  - Prepare to compress/uncompress files

  - A sample PDF chapter from the *Microsoft Project 2000 Black Book*. The book focuses on installing and implementing Project 2000 and includes project planning strategies.

System Requirement

Software

- Your operating system must be Windows 2000 Professional, Windows 9x, Windows NT Workstation 4, or Windows Me.

- If you wish to use the worksheets included on the CD-ROM to their fullest advantage, you'll need Microsoft Excel.

Hardware

- An Intel Pentium II processor or better is recommended.

- 32MB of RAM is recommended.

- You should ensure you have at least 100MB of empty hard disk space before installing components from the CD-ROM.

- A VGA monitor is recommended.